SECOND EDITION

JOURNEYS
of a
LIFETIME

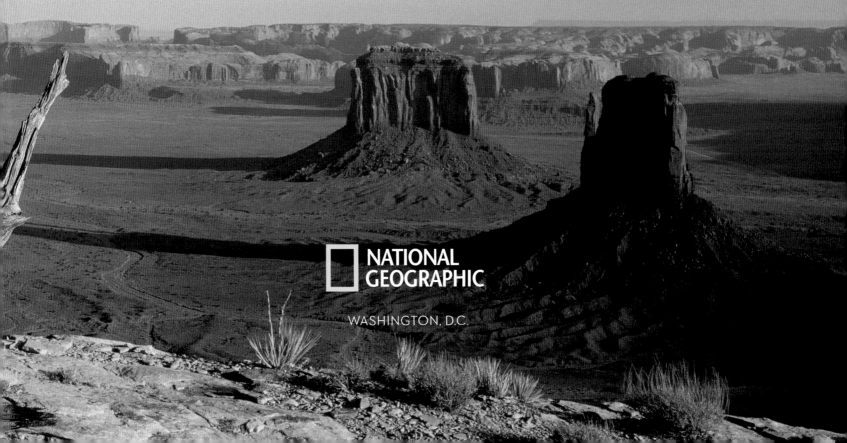

SECOND EDITION

JOURNEYS
of a
LIFETIME

500
of the World's Greatest Trips

INTRODUCTION BY GEORGE W. STONE
EDITOR-IN-CHIEF, NATIONAL GEOGRAPHIC *TRAVELER* MAGAZINE

**NATIONAL
GEOGRAPHIC**

WASHINGTON, D.C.

|CONTENTS

Previous Page: The starkly beautiful Monument Valley in the Navajo Tribal Park, U.S., was the sweeping and dramatic backdrop to countless cowboy movies. Opposite: In Chobe National Park, in Botswana, a leopard hugs a tree branch and scans the landscape for prey.

Inspiration for Exploration

Curiosity is the gift we were born with. It's the most important thing to bring on any journey, and is a quality that rewards us throughout our lives. But even the most inquisitive travelers hunger for a spark of inspiration now and again—and that's where this magical book comes in. More than just a collection of alluring places, it's a treasury of reasons to visit them now. This book is about what happens when our curiosity runs wild.

For more than a century, National Geographic has helped to bring you the world—and with this book, fully revised and updated for its tenth anniversary, we have found new ways to help you experience it. Compiled from the favorite trips of the magazine's legendary travel writers and photographers, these pages span the globe to highlight the best of the planet's most celebrated and lesser known sojourns. So whether you're looking to trek the Andes on horseback, discover the world's best cities for bike tours, cruise through Antarctica, hike the Grand Canyon, or follow in the footsteps of your favorite film heroes, this book has it all—along with expert advice for when to visit, how to get there, and secrets for making your travel dream a reality. If we're lucky, we can all pack many journeys into our single lifetime!

What I love about this book is that it's filled with new paths for pursuing enlightenment through travel. What does that even mean? For me, it's the realization that our journeys illuminate our lives by showing us the places and experiences that help connect us with the world around us. The secret, again, is curiosity, and—as luck would have it—we were all born with vast stores of it. So dream of travel, but don't stop there. Ask "What if?" and your next journey will begin.

George W. Stone
Editor-in-Chief, National Geographic Traveler

Opposite: Women celebrate the Moroccan Rose Festival
held annually at Kelaa M'Gouna in Dades Valley.

The Ultimate Journey

S uppose you could tick off every place on your bucket list in a single epic journey. Where would you go? We asked some of the world's greatest globetrotters, our authors, to come up with the ultimate journey. It starts in New York City. So many nationalities call the Big Apple home that it's a trip around the globe in its own right. In the city that never sleeps, climb up the Empire State Building. Bookend a meander through Central Park with visits to the Metropolitan Museum of Art and the American Museum of Natural History. Bike across the Brooklyn Bridge, ride the Cyclone at Coney Island, and cheer on the Bronx Bombers at Yankee Stadium.

Farther west, in California, the city by the bay sparkles even when shrouded in its celebrated summer fog. From the iconic bridges and "painted lady" Victorian mansions to the ding-a-ling cable cars and infamous Alcatraz, there isn't a more photogenic city on the entire planet. Half a century after the Summer of Love, San Francisco still exudes a counterculture vibe and a sense of creativity and adventure. Check out endearing clichés like Fisherman's Wharf, Chinatown, and Haight-Ashbury, as well as offbeat neighborhoods like Hayes Valley, Russian Hill, Dogpatch, and the multiethnic Mission District.

Continue your journey by heading south to the Peruvian city of Cusco—a name that means "navel of the world." Perched high in the Andes, Cusco was both the nexus of the Inca Empire and a Spanish colonial burg. Its eclectic culture blends Hispanic and Amerindian influences, while its architecture varies from imposing Inca monuments like Saqsaywaman citadel and cer- emonial complex to lavish baroque churches. Cusco is also the

Giraffes walk the plains of the Serengeti during a full moon in Tanzania, East Africa. The Serengeti is known for its breathtaking landscapes.

jumping-off spot for the "lost city" of Machu Picchu, hiking the Inca Trail and other Andes routes, and flights to the Peruvian Amazon and wildlife rich Manú National Park.

If San Francisco is the world's most beautiful city, then across the South Pacific, in French Polynesia, Bora Bora is certainly its most gorgeous island—a jagged volcanic landfall surrounded by a reef and tropical lagoon that shimmers a dozen different shades of blue. Scuba dive the outside of the reef, snorkel with sharks, swim with migrating humpback whales, surf the gnarly breaks, paddle across the lagoon to a *motu* (sandy islet), or pamper yourself at the world's most luxurious beach resorts.

Island hop across the Pacific to Sydney, where ferries and sailboats flit back and forth beneath two of the architectural icons of the southern hemisphere. Take in a performance at the Sydney Opera House, then climb to the top of the Harbour Bridge for a view that will literally take your breath away. Go for a dip in the sea at Bondi—or one of the 70 or so other beaches along the Sydney shore—sleep near koalas and kangaroos at Taronga Zoo, shop the posh Queen Victoria Building, and savor the city's many different flavors of ethnic cuisine and culture.

Head north into the heart of Asia. Although China's capital Beijing has evolved into a thriving modern city, it's the past that lures visitors to the Middle Kingdom. Hike a portion of the Great Wall—go early in the morning to avoid the throngs of sightseers—and try to imagine what it was like keeping the barbarians at bay. Explore the ancient *hutong* alleys on a bicycle, relish Peking duck at a gourmet eatery, sip oolong at a traditional teahouse in the Back Lakes district, and walk the statue-lined Spirit Way (Shen Dao) of the Ming dynasty.

Across the Himalaya, on the Indian subcontinent, the Taj Mahal is one of those rare places that is more astounding in person than the photos suggest. Arrive with the dawn to catch

Opposite: Victorian rowhouses or "painted ladies" line the Haight-Ashbury district of San Francisco. Above: See Shichahai Lake and the old alleys of Beijing by rickshaw.

the white marble glowing pink in the rising sun. The city of Agra, however, is more than just the Taj. Explore the massive Agra Fort—a World Heritage site in its own right—discover the ruins of a ghost city called Fatehpur Sikri, and stalk Bengal tigers with your camera at nearby Ranthambore National Park.

If wildlife is your passion, jet across the Arabian Sea to East Africa, where the Serengeti Plains of northern Tanzania are celebrated for the Great Migration—the annual exodus of millions of wildebeest, zebra, and antelope in search of fresh grazing, and the predators that trail in their wake. Serengeti wildlife is something to behold, especially on a classic tented safari. The park is surrounded by other African treasures. Commune with ancient ancestors at Olduvai Gorge, descend into massive Ngorongoro Crater, and mingle with the Masai at their wildlife conservancies in the Mara in Kenya. Follow the Nile north to the Land of the Pharaohs, then stand on the edge of the Sahara and admire the enduring grandeur of the pyramids of Giza outside Cairo. Bidding adieu to the Sphinx, visit the Tutankhamun collection at the new Grand Egyptian Museum in Giza, and then head back into Cairo for a felucca cruise along the Nile, a wander through the Khan el-Khalili bazaar (especially the stretch along El Moez Street), and a luscious Middle Eastern–Mediterranean meal at one of the city's most celebrated restaurants.

Next, hop across the Mediterranean Sea to Greece. The cradle of democracy is really two destinations—an ode to the Golden Age of Greek civilization and a modern metropolis where you can munch feta cheese and Kalamata olives in the shadow of the Parthenon, dance the night away Greek style on a beach near the Temple of Poseidon, or ogle archaeological digs

Above: With its opulent palaces, the exquisite Fatepur Sikri was once the capital of the Mughal Empire.
Previous: Bungalows suspended on stilts dot the crystal clear waters of Bora Bora, a French Polynesian island famed for its beauty.

Above: Parisian confectioner Patisserie Ladurée display their signature double-decker macarons.

integrated into the city's new metro system. As it's done for nearly 2,500 years, the Acropolis still rises above the city. In Athens, shop the chic streets of Kolonaki, attend a solemn Greek Orthodox service in Monastiraki, or bar hop with hipsters in the fashionable Gazi district.

A jump across the Adriatic lands you in the Roman Empire. Although the Eternal City may have risen and fallen centuries ago, Rome retains her regal ways by safeguarding some of the world's most iconic ruins and hosting a global storehouse of architecture and art inside the Vatican. Imagine what it must have been like to witness a spectacle at the Colosseum or a military victory parade through the Forum. Think about the genius that inspired Michelangelo while taking in the Sistine Chapel. Catch a glimpse of the colorfully dressed Pontifical Swiss Guard at St. Peter's Square. Recite a poem by Byron, Shelley, or Keats while lounging on the Spanish Steps. And don't leave without tossing three coins into the Trevi Fountain.

Then follow Julius Caesar's path to ancient Gaul for a visit to modern France. Look beyond classics like the Eiffel Tower and the Louvre as you eat freshly baked bread or croissants straight from a boulangerie, while away a day in cafés along Boulevard Saint-Germain, climb all those stairs to Sacré-Coeur to catch the view from Montmartre, or sail a vintage toy boat across the Grand Bassin in the Luxembourg Gardens.

Meanwhile, across the English Channel, the British capital is one of the best places on the planet for bird's-eye views. Peer down on the Houses of Parliament and Big Ben from the London Eye, or scope out the Tower of London and Tower Bridge from viewing decks at the top of The Shard—the tallest building in Western Europe. Come down to earth to see London icons like the British Museum, Buckingham Palace, and Covent Garden.

These sights are just a taste of the wealth of experiences to come. Turn the page, and prepare to explore a lifetime's worth of idyllic islands, soaring summits, and undiscovered paradises.

Chapter 1
ACROSS WATER

Traveling by water provides a new dimension. Rivers reach hidden places where roads can never go. The Earth's most dramatic coastlines, seen from offshore, are revealed in ways not possible from land. The world's most inspiring voyages are never simply journeys from one port to another. The sights and scenes encountered, the exotic or historic destinations, are only the beginning of the story. The vessels themselves, and the waters traveled, play an equal part in these adventures. A raft trip along Madagascar's Mangoky River brings glimpses of dancing lemurs. Canoes glide up the Orinoco into the heart of a South American jungle. Ferries in the Aegean Sea follow the trails of ancient Greece's gods and monsters. An icebreaker ventures into the Arctic fastnesses off Lapland. Airboats churn past alligators in the Florida Everglades. No continent is left unvisited. There are comfortable cruises for those desiring to drift and daydream, as well as more challenging options for adventurers eager to clamber up a mainmast or paddle a canoe past villages unaltered for a thousand years.

Traditional longtail boats sit at anchor in the turquoise waters of the Andaman Sea, off Thailand's western coast. You can take a six-day junk cruise through the sea, visiting some of its 3,500 islands.

WASHINGTON | ALASKA

Seattle to Alaska

Explore a world of fjords, humpback whales, and ancient glaciers on this cruise through North America's coastal wilderness.

The ship glides past mountains rising up to 15,000 feet (4,575 meters) above sea level, their snowcapped peaks reflected in the mirror-calm waters of a fjord. Bald eagles soar overhead, and waterfalls cascade down mountainsides. The cruise starts in either Seattle or Vancouver, and heads north through the 1,000-mile (1,600 kilometer) Inside Passage—a network of sea channels between the mainland of British Columbia and the panhandle region of southeastern Alaska and their outlying islands. On deck, you'll be absorbed in the passing drama of the coastline. Near Ketchikan, at the panhandle's southern end, wisps of cloud cling to 3,000-foot (915 meter) cliffs, rising from the steely-dark sea in Misty Fjords. On either side of the Passage, Tongass National Forest, a temperate rain forest of ancient conifers and broadleaf trees fed by the region's moisture-rich climate, forms one of the world's rarest ecosystems. Farther north, you sail into Glacier Bay, where 16 glaciers reach the sea—there is a thunderous roar as they calve, sending thousand-year-old, house-sized blocks of ice plunging into the bay. The ship also puts into small coastal towns, tucked around harbors at the feet of mountains, each revealing a diversity of influences: totem poles of the Tsimshian, Tlingit, and Haida Indians; the reds, oranges, and greens of Scandinavian-style buildings; relics of the Klondike gold rush; and the domes of a Russian Orthodox cathedral.

WHEN TO GO Ships tend to be less crowded in May and September, the beginning and end of the cruise season. The weather in early September is often pleasantly mild.

HOW LONG Cruises last from 7 to 14 days, but choose your itinerary carefully. Longer trips may follow the Inside Passage outbound, inbound, or both. Shorter cruises sometimes bypass much of the Inside Passage to spend more time in remote northern Alaska.

PLANNING Book a year ahead for the best trip selection. Small cruise ships carrying 50–100 passengers provide a more intimate, nature-based experience.

INSIDE INFORMATION Pack for weather ranging from warm and sunny to cold and rainy. Include a warm hat and jacket, rain gear, sunglasses, and good binoculars.

WEBSITES travelalaska.com, alaskatravel.com, cruisenorway.com

HIGHLIGHTS

▥ A hike through old-growth rain forest on the **Queen Charlotte Islands** may give you a glimpse of a rare white **Kermode (or Spirit) bear**.

▥ **Ketchikan** – meaning "Thundering Wings of an Eagle" in the Tlingit language – has the world's largest collection of **totem poles**.

▥ Watch for the great, shaggy **grizzly bears** fishing in Frederick Sound. **Eagles, ospreys,** and **hawks** glide aloft; orca and humpback **whales** breach and dive as they feed in the nutrient-rich waters.

▥ Take a **helicopter ride** to walk on the **Mendenhall Glacier** outside Juneau, Alaska's capital.

▥ Ride across **Glacier Bay** in an inflatable dinghy for an up-close encounter with seals, whales, and calving glaciers.

▥ The Russian influence is prominent in **Sitka**, facing the Pacific and dominated by **St. Michael the Archangel (Orthodox) Cathedral, Totem Square**, the **Russian Cemetery**, and the **Sitka History** and **Sheldon Jackson museums**.

▥ The **Trail of '98 Museum** and **Gold Rush Cemetery** in **Skagway** take you back to the Klondike days.

Opposite: Blocks of ice, calved from glaciers reaching the sea, jostle one another in an Alaskan bay. Above left: An old coastal steamer is moored at Britannia Beach, British Columbia, against a dramatic mountain backdrop. Above right: A Native American wood carving from Gunakadet Park in Juneau.

The French influence is clear in the Hotel Château Frontenac on Quebec City's St. Lawrence waterfront.

The St. Lawrence

This captivating voyage through southeastern Canada
features pristine river wilderness and historic cities.

From the time European colonists first arrived in North America, the St. Lawrence River has been one of the great routes into the heart of the continent. From Quebec City to Montreal, the forested grandeur of the scenery is the draw on this small-ship cruise along the historic waterway. You watch blue herons flap past, making for nests on the Berthier-Sorel islands, while Lake Saint-Pierre is a magnet for migrating ducks and geese. Montreal is a mesmerizing contrast—a chance to visit chic shops and nightclubs. Heading west, you enter the canals and locks of the St. Lawrence Seaway, opened in 1959, which allows oceangoing ships to sail from the Atlantic to the Great Lakes. The spectacle of the small ship negotiating the massive locks is one of the trip's highlights. Before disembarking in Kingston on Lake Ontario, you pass through the summer playground of the Thousand Islands, where motorboats speed between islands, some home to villages, others scarcely large enough for a single house to perch on top of them.

WHEN TO GO From mid-May to mid-October. Fabulous fall colors peak in early October.

HOW LONG Six-night, seven-day cruises ply both ways between Kingston and Quebec City.

PLANNING All of the onshore tours and attractions are included in the cruise price. Expect calm water, on-ship entertainment, good food, and interesting shore excursions.

INSIDE INFORMATION This is a relaxed and informal small-ship cruise. Bring sunhats, sunglasses, a light jacket, and comfortable walking shoes, as well as binoculars.

WEBSITE stlawrencerivercruise.com

HIGHLIGHTS

▓ **Vieux Québec** – Old Quebec City – is a UNESCO World Heritage site and one of the most historic and beautiful cities in North America. Give yourself a day at the start or finish of your trip to explore its cobbled streets.

▓ **Montreal**, possibly Canada's hippest city, is a showplace for French sophistication both in the modern downtown and on the historic waterfront, where some buildings date to the 17th century.

▓ Step back in time at **Upper Canada Village**, Morrisburg, where one of Canada's largest and most elaborate living history sites re-creates life in a rural riverside village of the 1860s.

▓ Ornate, century-old mansions dot the wooded shores of the glacier-carved **Thousand Islands** – there are actually more than 1,800 of them. Particularly impressive is the fairy-tale, 120-room, medieval-style **Boldt Castle** on Heart Island.

CANADA

The Trent-Severn Waterway

A favorite with boaters and nature lovers,
this journey takes you into the Canadian wilderness.

From Trenton on Lake Ontario to the pristine shores of Lake Huron's Georgian Bay, this 240-mile (386 kilometer) network of canals, lakes, and rivers forms an easily navigated path through the intimate landscapes north of Toronto. Charming villages with a European flavor, farmlands, rocky gorges, and sapphire-clear, forest-lined lakes are just a few of the constantly changing tableaus that have made this a popular water tour. The pace of the journey varies from strenuous in the easternmost section between Trenton and Frankford—six locks and a height difference of 115 feet (35 meters) to negotiate in just 6 miles (10 kilometers)—to relaxed on the maze of waterways that make up the Kawartha Lakes. These are perfect for swimming, sunbathing, and cooking lakeside meals of freshly caught fish. Keep an eye out for white-tail deer and black bears foraging for food in the surrounding forests. The canals are narrow, so there are no big cruise ships. Most people bring their own boats, or rent one. The choices range from canoes and kayaks, for those who enjoy wilderness camping, to 50-foot (15 meter) houseboats offering voyagers the luxuries of a fine hotel.

WHEN TO GO Late May through October. Late June has long, warm days. September offers warm, sunny days and cool nights. Fall colors run from late September to mid-October, which is also the best fishing season.

HOW LONG It takes about seven days to complete the Trent-Severn under power, longer for paddlers. Most houseboaters do leisurely four- to seven-day loops between Peterborough and Lake Simcoe.

PLANNING Houseboats are simple to operate and come fully equipped with all the comforts of home. Boaters must pay modest fees for lock transit.

INSIDE INFORMATION Houseboat rental operators offer full instructions. Casual clothing is the order of the day. Bring hats, sunglasses, sunblock, and comfortable shoes for shore excursions.

WEBSITES trentsevern.com, pc.gc.ca

HIGHLIGHTS

▥ Listen out for the haunting **cry of a loon** as you watch sunlit morning mist rise from the still surface of a wilderness lake.

▥ **Peterborough** has the world's **largest lift lock**, completed in 1904. The entire waterway, with all its **canals and locks**, is an incredible feat of 19th-century engineering.

▥ Visit **towns steeped in charm**, including historic **Lakefield**.

▥ Explore the stores and restaurants of **Bobcaygeon** and **Fenelon Falls**.

▥ Hook a **5-lb (2.2 kg) bass** in the Trent-Severn's crystal-pure waters.

A tranquil scene at the Peterborough Lift Lock, the world's highest hydraulic lift lock, raising boats 65 feet (19.8 meters).

Frontier Country

Savor the flavor of bygone days as you tour America's historic heart by barge along the Cumberland and Ohio rivers.

Steeped in history—the area was once inhabited by the Cherokee, Chickasaw, and Shawnee tribes, and was later home to French fur traders and the early pioneers pushing west—and rich in marvelous views, this cruise takes you back into America's past. Beginning in Nashville, Tennessee, America's country music capital, you'll travel along the Cumberland and Ohio rivers, through rich agricultural land that attracted many of the continent's earliest settlers, to Cincinnati, Ohio, enjoying the gentle pace of life on the two rivers. While still on the Cumberland River, you'll pass through a series of historic locks that were created by the Tennessee Valley Authority during the Great Depression, and navigate Lake Barkley in the Land Between the Lakes. Soon afterward you'll join the Ohio River, and pass through Paducah, Kentucky, with its railroad museum, River Heritage Museum, and National Quilt Museum. For the next couple of days, you'll glide along the Ohio River to Louisville, Kentucky, home of the Kentucky Derby. Most cruises take you by bus to tour Churchill Downs, where you can visit the Kentucky Derby Museum, walk the track, and see the graves of famous American thoroughbreds. After a stop at Aurora, Indiana, and another day's barging, the cruise culminates in Cincinnati, known in steamboat days as the Queen City of the West, and once one of the busiest ports on the Ohio River.

WHEN TO GO April to November. The Kentucky Derby is in the first week of May, so race fans may want to time their trip to coincide with a day at Churchill Downs.

HOW LONG Cruises last eight days and take you from Nashville to Cincinnati.

PLANNING Some cruises are available from Cincinnati to Nashville. Other destinations are also available.

INSIDE INFORMATION Take binoculars to watch the river and wildlife from the Sun Deck.

WEBSITE americancruiselines.com

HIGHLIGHTS

▓ The **music scene** in **Nashville** gets your trip off to a swinging start—be sure to visit the Grand Ole Opry.

▓ In **Paducah** explore its 19th-century downtown area with its many **antique shops**. Also visit the wonderful **National Quilt Museum**.

▓ At Aurora, IN, visit **Hillforest**, a National Historic Landmark, overlooking the Ohio River. Home of the industrialist Thomas Gaff from 1855 to 1891, the house includes nautical architectural features and period furnishings.

▓ Relax on the **Sun Deck** and watch the river glide by.

Excited spectators cheer on horses and riders at Churchill Downs. The twin spires of the 19th-century grandstand are the course's most famous landmark.

Historic homes and gardens line the shore in Charleston, South Carolina.

SOUTH CAROLINA | GEORGIA | FLORIDA |

Charleston and the Lowcountry Cruise

Antebellum mansions, unspoiled beaches, and tree-shaded waterways are hallmarks of this trip.

This ravishing realm of sea islands, gracious antebellum towns, and wildlife-filled salt marshes is known as the Lowcountry—one of the United States' most mysterious and compelling regions. The ship is small—more a large motor yacht than a cruise liner—and the scale of things intimate as you head south from historic Charleston, hugging the shoreline along the blue highway of the Atlantic Intracoastal Waterway. The ship puts into Beaufort, South Carolina, and Savannah, Georgia, where the 19th-century mansions of rice and cotton barons line narrow lanes shaded by moss-draped oaks. Beyond, you sail past vast salt marshes where egrets and herons wade, and myriad waterways trace sinuous curves through stands of golden cordgrass. Here and there, you glimpse an antebellum plantation house surrounded by its gardens. Farther south, you reach Georgia's wild and beautiful Sea Islands, with long pristine beaches. They were once a summer retreat for the rich and, on Jekyll Island, you can tour the lavish seaside "cottages" of families like the Vanderbilts, Morgans, and Pulitzers.

WHEN TO GO Most cruises depart in April, a beautiful time of year, when the exquisite gardens of Charleston and Savannah are in bloom.

HOW LONG 250 miles (402 km) on an eight-day, seven-night cruise between Charleston, SC, and Jacksonville, FL.

PLANNING Historic Charleston is one of the most popular destinations in the southeast, and if you have an extra day or two in your schedule, include plans to explore more of the elegant historic district and savor the gracious lifestyle.

INSIDE INFORMATION April weather offers warm days, cool breezes, and low humidity. Wear comfortable walking shoes and have good binoculars onboard for bird-watching, especially in the Sea Islands.

WEBSITE americancruiselines.com

HIGHLIGHTS

▪ Shop at the old **Charleston Market**, where Gullah women – descendents of freed slaves – sell intricately woven **sweetgrass baskets** and other crafts.

▪ The romantic charm of **Beaufort**, SC, makes it a favorite with movie directors – scenes from *The Big Chill* and *Forrest Gump* were shot here. Get a cone at **Southern Sweets Ice Cream Parlor**, and enjoy it on the porch swings that line the waterfront.

▪ Stroll along the cobblestone streets of old **Savannah**, GA, past 18th- and 19th-century mansions.

▪ Sample the bounty of **shrimp**, **crabs**, and **oysters** harvested in local waters.

Top 10
City Boat Trips

Mingle with the locals and enjoy picture-postcard views of some of the world's great cities by ferry.

❶ VANCOUVER FERRIES, CANADA

State-of-the-art ferries cross sparkling waters between Vancouver and the surrounding islands, passing dense deciduous forests and snowy peaks, glimpsed distantly across the water. Ferries run more frequently in summer.

PLANNING The company runs promotions for customers wanting to stop at ten destinations, so check the website before you go to take advantage of the savings. bcferries.com

❷ STATEN ISLAND FERRY, NEW YORK CITY

Speed past the Statue of Liberty and Ellis Island as the mighty tower blocks of Manhattan cast long shadows across the surface of New York harbor. Five miles (8 km) and 25 minutes later, you reach Staten Island. Get off to explore New York's least known borough or stay on the ferry and return to Manhattan. Best of all, the trip is free!

PLANNING No booking necessary – the ferries depart from Whitehall Terminal in Manhattan and St. George Terminal on Staten Island every half hour. The ferry is free for foot passengers. siferry.com

❸ SAN FRANCISCO TO SAUSALITO FERRY, CALIFORNIA

On the 30-minute ferry ride, you'll see splendid views of Golden Gate Bridge, Alcatraz prison, Angel Island, and the San Francisco skyline. Be sure to go on a clear day: San Francisco's famous fog often obscures the views.

PLANNING Ferries leave from behind the San Francisco Ferry Building at the foot of Market Street. You can even take your bike. goldengateferry.org

❹ NEW ORLEANS TO ALGIERS FERRY, LOUISIANA

The stately Algiers ferry carries passengers across the Mississippi River between the old neighborhood of Algiers Point and the rest of New Orleans.

PLANNING The ferry leaves seven days a week and runs every quarter hour, so no booking is necessary. Cash only, exact change required. norta.com

❺ STAR FERRY, HONG KONG, CHINA

Running between Hong Kong island and the Kowloon mainland, the famous Star Ferry takes only ten minutes, but delivers a spectacular view of the city skyline, especially later in the day when the sun is setting.

PLANNING No booking required. Ferries leave about every ten minutes, depending on the time of day. starferry.com.hk

A nighttime trip on the Star Ferry is worth it for the view alone. The ten-minute journey is one of the best ways of savoring the light-jeweled splendor of Hong Kong's fabled skyline.

❻ BRISBANE CITYCAT, AUSTRALIA

The sleek, modern CityCats of Brisbane seem almost to hover above the surface of the water. Take an exhilarating ride along the Brisbane River, past Story Bridge and South Bank Parklands. CityCats are fast—for a more sedate experience and a chance to admire the city at leisure, go for a cruise on an open-air City Ferry.

PLANNING Tickets are sold by zone, enabling you to use all modes of public transportation within a zone. brisbane.qld.gov.au, translink.com.au

❼ BOSPHORUS FERRY, ISTANBUL, TURKEY

The delicate minarets and ornate architecture of Istanbul are spread out before you from the deck of a Bosphorus ferry in this city that sits on the cusp of two continents. Sip tea in the open air as the ferry carries you past the most splendid sights in the city—from Ottoman palaces to the Bosphorus Bridge.

PLANNING June to August can be hot and humid, while November to January can be very cold. Women should dress modestly. en.sehirhatlari.istanbul/en

❽ VENICE VAPORETTO, ITALY

Although gondolas may be romantic, true Venetians speed around the city in vaporettos, or water buses. You can get in the mood of the city straight from the airport. A vaporetto will take you into the city with stops at Murano and the Lido, Venice's beach, before dropping you off right in St. Mark's Square. Other routes head to different parts of the city. Take a ferry trip to one of the city's islands or the Lido, for a glimpse of a less touristy Venice.

PLANNING Traveling without a ticket can result in a hefty fine. If you can't buy a ticket on shore, be sure to buy one from the conductor when you board. Tourist travel cards and passes are available. actv.avmspa.it/en

❾ NAPLES TO CAPRI FERRY, ITALY

The Bay of Naples boasts some of the most attractive coastline in the world. Take a boat ride from Naples to Capri over the azure sea and explore the famous Blue Grotto, where the cavern is naturally illuminated with blue light. Time your trip so that you can get to Capri for lunch; many restaurants have great views of Naples, which you can enjoy along with your Spaghetti Vongole and a glass of the local white wine made from grapes grown in Etna's rich volcanic soil.

PLANNING Depart from the Port of Molo Beverello in Naples. The trip takes around 80 minutes. capri.net

❿ MERSEY FERRY, LIVERPOOL, ENGLAND

The famous red-and-black ferries of Liverpool take an hour to cross the great Mersey River. Dating back to the 12th century, this is the oldest ferry service in Europe. As well as the standard ferry service, there are also tours of the Merseyside area and themed cruises for special occasions. The Beatles cruise celebrates the city's links with the Fab Four, who all lived in the city.

PLANNING Standard cruises depart every 20 minutes from Seacombe Ferry Terminal and Pier Head. merseyferries.co.uk

Paddle steamers were once the lifeblood of trade and passenger transport along the Mississippi and its tributaries.

Mississippi River Paddle Steamer

Experience a bygone age aboard a classic steamboat and immerse yourself in the rich culture and history of the Deep South.

Hurricanes such as Katrina in 2005 have altered the cultural and physical profile of New Orleans and its environs, but the lower Mississippi River and its legendary maritime traffic keep on rollin'. Traveling upriver from New Orleans to Memphis, you experience the living history of America's largest river, aboard one of the signature relics of a bygone age—a stern-wheeler steamship, updated with such modern comforts as large staterooms and fine food. The pace is leisurely, giving you plenty of time to savor live Dixieland jazz bands and the passing vistas of riverside plantation mansions and their gardens—one of the grandest of them, Oak Alley, is a stop along the way. Other ports of call include Natchez and Vicksburg, Mississippi, mingling the antebellum grace of tree-lined streets and the lavish town houses of 19th-century cotton magnates with the still living echoes of Elvis and the great bluesmen, from Muddy Waters to B. B. King.

WHEN TO GO Cruises depart all year round.

HOW LONG New Orleans to Memphis is a seven-night trip. Four- to eight-night round-trip cruises are also available.

PLANNING Book well in advance. Other trips are also available, ranging far and wide across the river system of the Mississippi basin—as far north as St. Paul, MN, and as far east as Cincinnati and Pittsburgh on the Ohio River.

INSIDE INFORMATION Dress is casual. Staff expect to be tipped—tip a lump sum at the end of the cruise.

WEBSITE americanqueensteamboatcompany.com

HIGHLIGHTS

▥ Get up before dawn at least one morning to watch the **sunrise** over the river.

▥ Enjoy the steamer's **Victorian-style furnishings** and its nightly musical entertainments, which cover a range of traditional genres, from **ragtime** to **bluegrass**.

▥ An avenue of ancient oak trees leads up to **Oak Alley**, among Louisiana's finest surviving plantation houses. It was built in the Greek Revival style in the 1830s for Jacques Telesphore Roman, a member of one of the state's wealthiest families.

▥ Before the Civil War, **Natchez** had more millionaires per capita than any other U.S. city. Their legacy survives in its constellation of stately **mansions**, famed for their **lavish interiors**.

▥ **Vicksburg's National Military Park** commemorates the Siege of Vicksburg in 1863, one of the key battles of the Civil War.

ACROSS WATER

BY ROAD | BY RAIL | ON FOOT | IN SEARCH OF CULTURE | IN GOURMET HEAVEN | INTO THE ACTION | UP AND AWAY | IN THEIR FOOTSTEPS

FLORIDA

Airboat in the Everglades

Ride on a jet of wind through the saw grass to meet the biggest alligators—an essential experience of Florida's Everglades.

NORTH AMERICA

Light airboats, powered by huge caged fans mounted on the stern, whip you across the Everglades. They are the best introduction to this vast subtropical wetland—a 40-mile (64 kilometer) wide "river" of saw grass, punctuated with cypress swamps and mangrove forests, which flows lethargically southward from Lake Okeechobee for more than 100 miles (160 kilometers). Egrets and herons clatter into the sky as the boat's pilot navigates through an ever changing labyrinth of channels—no place for outboard motors, whose propellers become jammed with reeds and mud. Soon, you are in the remote backcountry, where you encounter the Everglades' most famous inhabitants—alligators—which get bigger and more fearsome-seeming the farther you venture. If the airboat ride has whetted your appetite, you may want to penetrate the wetland's even more secret places, set apart in Everglades National Park, where only nonmotorized boats are allowed on most lakes. Here, you may be lucky enough to glimpse a rare Florida panther or one of the endearing, cumbersome-looking manatees—huge aquatic mammals that frequent shallow waters, grazing on mangrove leaves and algae.

WHEN TO GO Winter (December to April) has mild and pleasant weather, but can sometimes be cold. June to October is the rainy season – and also the season for mosquitoes and hurricanes.

HOW LONG Tours can last just 20 minutes, but to see a full range of landscape and wildlife you need at least two hours for a 40-mile (64 km) round-trip.

PLANNING There are numerous airboat operators, and several points of departure. Boats vary in size. Some take just one or two passengers (best for high-thrills tours), while larger boats take up to 24 (best for more gentle scenic tours). You can rent canoes in the national park at Flamingo and Gulf Coast.

INSIDE INFORMATION Many airboat operators provide earmuffs to combat the engine noise. In summer, bring protection against mosquitoes.

WEBSITES cypressairboats.com, airboatusa.com, nps.gov/ever

HIGHLIGHTS

▪ The wildlife includes a multitude of bird species – **anhingas**, **cranes**, **storks**, **roseate spoonbills** – as well as **turtles**, lustrous **dragonflies**, Florida **black bears**, mangrove **fox squirrels**, and Everglades **minks**.

▪ **Canoeing trails** take you through areas such as **Nine Mile Pond** and **Hells Bay**, perfect for bird-watching.

▪ The **Ah-Tah-Thi-Ki Museum** on the Big Cypress Indian Reservation is dedicated to the culture and history of the Everglades' Seminole Indians.

▪ **Campsites** that can only be reached by boat allow you to savor the solitude of the wilderness overnight.

Saw grass spreads out on either side as an airboat takes visitors through the Everglades.

ACROSS WATER

BY ROAD

BY RAIL

ON FOOT

IN SEARCH OF CULTURE

IN GOURMET HEAVEN

INTO THE ACTION

UP AND AWAY

IN THEIR FOOTSTEPS

| CARIBBEAN |

Eastern Caribbean Cruise

A cruise through the storied waters of the Caribbean offers luxury, shopping, and outdoor fun.

Cerulean, azure, turquoise, and sapphire are the colors of the Eastern Caribbean, and they are as intoxicating as the arc of emerald islands found there: St. Martin, Antigua, Puerto Rico, Virgin Gorda, as well as countless smaller isles waiting to be discovered. Renowned for their pristine strands of white sand, palm trees swaying in gentle sea breezes, coral reefs teeming with riotous rainbows of tropical fish, and lively towns alive with calypso music, the legendary islands of the Caribbean are an earthly paradise in the tropics. The best way to explore this watery wonderland is aboard a cruise ship, and there is a bewildering array of packages to fit every lifestyle and budget. Most ships offer lavish onboard entertainment in between port calls, ranging from golf lessons to karaoke; but it is the shore excursions that make the Caribbean the world's number one cruise destination. On St. Martin, you can indulge in some duty-free shopping as well as eat at one of the many superb French restaurants on the northern side of the island. These islands have something for everyone—idyllic beaches, water sports, and rum cocktails existing alongside a rich history of trading, piracy, and colonialism. To make the most of your trip, consider booking a place on a high-tech sailing ship, which can offer the experience of big-ship luxuries with small-ship intimacy—and, of course, the romance of sailing the azure seas.

WHEN TO GO Many cruises are available all year round. The peak season months (and the highest prices) are from December to April.

HOW LONG Most cruises average about seven days, but longer cruises of 10 to 14 days are available if you want to visit more islands.

PLANNING If your schedule is flexible, many cruise lines offer last-minute bargains. November travel is also often a bargain.

INSIDE INFORMATION Casual clothing is the order of the day, though some ships require semiformal dress for dinners. The tropical sun is strong—bring hats, sunglasses, and sunblock.

WEBSITES windstarcruises.com, carnival.com

| HIGHLIGHTS

▦ Snorkel through a wonderland of **living coral** around Virgin Gorda and St. Martin. The easily accessible reefs offer a kaleidoscope of fabulous hues: bright yellow-and-black damselfish, pink anemones, orange clownfish, and gently waving fans of red coral.

▦ **Shop till you drop** in seaside towns that date to the days of Christopher Columbus. Top stops include St. Thomas' Charlotte Amalie, tiny Cruz Bay on St. John, and the duty-free stores of Philipsburg on St. Martin.

▦ Take a **hike inland** to escape from the tourist trails. These once-volcanic islands feature trails through the high hills that offer views of fabulous seascapes, crystalline bays and coves, and luxuriant tropical landscapes.

▦ Visit lush **botanical gardens** filled with richly scented tropical flowers, where brightly colored parrots flit from tree to tree and hummingbirds hover like floating gemstones among the brilliant blossoms.

Opposite: On the island sanctuary of St. John, lush rain forest encroaches on secluded beaches of fine white sand, with great snorkeling close to shore. Above left: Pink allamandas blossom on Guadeloupe. Above right: A cruise ship approaches Virgin Gorda.

A rowboat lies moored on the shore of Ometepe Island on Lake Nicaragua. Concepción volcano looms in the background.

NICARAGUA

Lake Nicaragua

Explore the tropical wonders of Nicaragua's Sweet Sea, one of the largest lakes in the world.

This vast, tropical, freshwater lake, bordered by volcanoes and peppered with green islets, is known locally as the Sweet Sea. It lies about 10 miles (16 kilometers) from the Pacific Coast and is connected to the Caribbean by the San Juan River. It is so large—3,190 square miles (8,262 square kilometers)—that when the Spanish conquistadors arrived, they believed they had discovered another ocean. An exploration of this shimmering expanse of water will take you around some of the 350 lush, tropical islands, including Ometepe, the largest in the lake, where twin conical volcanoes rise majestically to the sky, and where you can swim off one of the deserted sandy beaches. The Solentiname archipelago, a chain of 36 unspoiled islets, scarcely populated and shaded by huge mango trees, is home to some extraordinary wildlife, including ancient turtles and striped boas. Spot the iguanas, as they sun themselves on extended branches, and enjoy the absolute silence, broken only occasionally by the calls of birds. While visiting these islands, don't miss out on a chance to see the Solentiname artisans, who specialize in paintings of the landscape that glorify its tropical colors and traditions. They happily open up their homes and display artwork to visitors.

WHEN TO GO Visit during the first half of the dry season, from December to February, when days are usually sunny and dry and the land is still lush from the rains.

HOW LONG You need two to three nights to see the lake's highlights. Boat trips between islands rarely take longer than two hours.

PLANNING If you like to shop it is a good idea to take an empty cloth bag with you, so you can take home some of the beautifully crafted hammocks from the city of Masaya, as well as traditional carved pottery, sold very cheaply in the smaller villages around the lake.

INSIDE INFORMATION Stay on the islands to get a real feel for the region. There are good, cheap hotels and hostels on Ometepe Island and basic accommodation on Mancarrón in the Solentiname archipelago.

WEBSITE nica-adventures.com, vacationsnicaragua.com

HIGHLIGHTS

▥ Climb **Maderas Volcano** (4,573 ft/ 1,394 m), on Ometepe, through thick, tropical jungle. At the top there is a mysterious cold lagoon and fantastic views to the Pacific Ocean.

▥ Take a *panga* (small motorized canoe) through the jungle canals of **Los Guatuzos Wildlife Refuge** on the Solentiname peninsula, home to 380 bird species. At night, a flashlight reveals hundreds of pairs of eyes glinting on the water's surface. These are caiman, crocodile-like reptiles.

▥ Lake Nicaragua offers excellent **sportfishing**, with an abundance of swordfish and giant tarpon. Go with a local guide for the best experience.

NORTH AMERICA

| VENEZUELA |

The Orinoco River Cruise

Go on an expedition by canoe and venture into the colossal wetland and steamy jungle of the Orinoco Delta.

SOUTH AMERICA

Journey along one of the Orinoco River's tributaries and into the delta for an intimate exploration of one of the largest and most remote wetland areas on Earth—an area accessible only by motorboat or dugout canoe. An extraordinary diversity of flora and fauna inhabits this sprawling, intricate labyrinth of waterways, which weave their way through dense jungle, mangrove swamps, and lagoons, and out into the Atlantic Ocean. During your voyage you'll glimpse flashes of colorful birdlife: macaws, toucans, parrots, spoonbills, and jabiru storks. Families of capuchin and howler monkeys hurl themselves in graceful arcs from tree to tree along the riverbank, while bottle-necked river dolphins, piranhas, and anacondas glide beneath the surface of the waters. You will also come into close contact with the Warao (canoe people), native to the region. These skilled fishermen and hunters live in *palafitos* (wooden houses built on sticks over the river). You can learn about their lifestyle, meet their craftsmen, and even sample a local Warao delicacy: the yellow grub that lives in the Mareche tree.

WHEN TO GO In the rainy season – May to December – you can expect short afternoon showers and higher water levels. January to late March/April tends to be dry, and you are likely to see more land mammals (capybaras, foxes, anteaters) and less of the aquatic variety. Trips run throughout the year.

HOW LONG Trips vary from one to three nights, depending on how deep into the jungle you go and the time of year in which you choose to travel (trips in the dry season are shorter).

PLANNING The standard of accommodation varies, depending on who organizes your trip. Nights can be spent either in hammocks beneath shelters in traditional Warao villages, or in comfortable private cabins, with bathroom, running water, and electricity.

INSIDE INFORMATION It can get cool at night, particularly during the dry season, so take a light fleece jacket. Mosquitoes are a problem; wear light trousers and long-sleeved shirts for dawn and dusk – and bring repellent as well.

WEBSITES ospreyvenezuela.com

HIGHLIGHTS

▥ Visit a **Warao village** and try the local sticky bread. It is made from the pulp of the Mareche tree, known to the Warao as "the tree of life," which is also used for making hammocks and houses.

▥ Float into a **still lagoon**, where the waters are black with tannins and carpeted with a floating mass of water hyacinths.

▥ Wake at dawn and **hear the jungle stir** with the roar of the howler monkey, the chatter of the capuchin, and the myriad birds warming up for their deafening morning chorus.

A flock of wood storks alights on a tree in the wetlands by the Orinoco River.

SOUTH AMERICA

Amazon River

Cruise along the Amazon on a classic riverboat for a truly outstanding introduction to the region's fascinating wildlife, rain forests, and people.

Gliding over the broad, muddy waters of the Amazon, it's easy to forget that this is the world's largest river. Rising in the Andes Mountains in Peru, it flows for more than 3,700 miles (6,000 kilometers) to the Atlantic. Tributaries feed in from Bolivia, Ecuador, Colombia, and Venezuela, forming a river system that drains the entire northern half of South America. Large luxury ships cruise the river throughout its course, but a traditional two-decked riverboat offers a more private, relaxed experience—and brings you closer to the rain forest's vast array of plant and animal life. Standing on deck, you'll spot friendly children waving from between the foliage, and local fishermen casting nets from the banks, or kneeling to paddle their dugout canoes. As you travel deeper into the jungle and the canopy begins to block out the sunlight, you can visit Indian tribal villages and explore the rain forest—by turns frightening, weird, and stunningly pretty—or visit calm lagoons adorned with giant water lilies. Onboard, listen to the echoing calls of monkeys and exotic birds while fishing for piranhas, and, in the evening, wrap up warm and head out in a canoe through the dusky twilight in search of sluggish alligators, sliding half-submerged through the water. When darkness has fallen, the boat slips silently downstream, where the blackness of the river is occasionally lit by a lantern or cooking fire, and you can quietly absorb the rich sounds of jungle life.

WHEN TO GO Peak flood season in April and May is the best time for bird-watching and seeing primates because of the abundance of fruit. In the low-water season (July–February), some places may become inaccessible, but you'll see animals come to the dry riverbanks for a drink.

HOW LONG The majority of organized cruises last for eight days, exploring the lower reaches of the river.

PLANNING Mosquito repellent and light, cotton, long-sleeved shirts and trousers are essential. Take clear plastic bags to protect electronic items, such as cameras, from the high humidity. Pack light—many cruise boats have luggage restrictions.

INSIDE INFORMATION Fast shutter speed and flash are a must if you're an avid photographer—it can be surprisingly dark beneath the rain-forest canopy.

WEBSITES rainforestcruises.com, amazonadventures.com

HIGHLIGHTS

▧ The **amazing wildlife** is best seen in the early morning or the evening—pink river dolphins, caimans, alligators, parrots, and parakeets are all visible from the water, while on an inland jungle trip you might see monkeys, iguanas, and butterflies.

▧ Break the monotony of the wide flatness of the river with a few trips ashore—most cruises will organize visits to **native Indian villages** and treks into the jungle.

▧ A **canoe trip** up one of the river's tributaries is a must. You will be swallowed up by the canopy and get opportunities to see plant life and wildlife and to fish.

▧ Catch, cook, and eat **red-bellied piranha fish** with cane fishing rods—just as the people of the Amazon have done for centuries.

Opposite: In Quebrada Pichana in the Peruvian Upper Amazon, local Indians sell food from their canoes. Above left: A macaw perches on a branch at Manaus in northwest Brazil. Above right: Large waterlilies float on the Yanayacu River, a tributary of the Upper Amazon in Peru.

Ferry Over Lake Titicaca

A three-day journey by boat through the islands of the world's highest navigable lake.

SOUTH
AMERICA

Every morning a flotilla of motor launches leaves the port of Puno on the Peruvian side of Lake Titicaca. First winding through the reed-choked channels of the Gulf of Puno, they putter out into the clear blue waters of the world's highest navigable lake—a landscape that looks almost Mediterranean—past fleets of small sailboats setting out for a day's fishing. As you start the voyage, you'll see the *islas flotantes* (floating islands), home to the indigenous Uros people, who have lived on the islands since the time of the Inca. These huge rafts are constructed from reeds, cropped from the vast beds that grow around the shores of the shallow, almost landlocked Gulf of Puno. The islands constantly rot away from the bottom up, so new reeds are always being added. Ringed by arid plains and treeless peaks, Lake Titicaca is a true inland sea, lying high in the Andes, 12,500 feet (3,810 meters) above sea level, and fed by the winter rains and summer icemelt of the Andean peaks. Dotted around the lake are natural islands with terraced fields separated by dry stone walls and cactus hedges, and small villages of sturdy stone houses. A few even have sandy beaches for those brave enough to swim in the lake's chilly waters.

WHEN TO GO May to October.

HOW LONG A selection of options, from one- to four-day trips.

PLANNING Come prepared for extremes of temperature, with fierce sunshine during the day and temperatures close to 32°F (0°C) at night: sunblock and a warm fleece jacket are essential. Also bring a flashlight – not all homes have electricity and few have indoor plumbing.

INSIDE INFORMATION Taquile has the widest choice of places to stay and eat, with rooms in around 70 homes and two small hostels and more than 20 simple restaurants. Very basic food and bottled water are available on Amantani, so bring canned food to share or as gifts (if staying as a paying guest) with island families. Do not bring candy for island children.

WEBSITES peru.info/en-us, peru-explorer.com

HIGHLIGHTS

▥ Spend some time exploring **Puno**, the main port on the Peruvian side of the lake. This lively and cosmopolitan small town has colorful markets and a main street lined with restaurants serving typical Peruvian dishes, such as alpaca steaks and roast guinea pig, as well as fish from the lake.

▥ Each island has its own culture, typified by **colorful costumes** – with sashes, shawls, and hats woven from wool and dyed in elaborate patterns.

▥ Stay overnight on the natural islands of **Taquile** or **Amantani**. Both islands offer basic accommodation in islanders' homes or simple guesthouses.

A fisherman stands in his traditional totoro reed boat on Lake Titicaca, drifting past a huge expanse of swaying reeds.

Above the town of Wushan, a Chinese pavilion affords splendid views over the Yangtze River and the mouth of the Wu Gorge, the second of the three great gorges.

CHINA

Yangtze River–The Three Gorges

Take China's greatest river journey through the winding Three Gorges, past ancient sites and modern engineering marvels.

The Yangtze River flows for 3,964 miles (6,380 kilometers) across China from its source in the Qinghai-Tibetan Plateau to its mouth on the East China Sea, just north of Shanghai. Although the river is no longer the great commercial highway it once was, a variety of passenger ships still travel along its most famous section, where it rushes through the winding and constricted Three Gorges. Here, forbidding cliffs throw cruise ship, coal barge, and fishing vessel alike into shadow, and the yellowing sails of traditional sampan boats can be seen bobbing next to the smart white hulls of hi-tech modern tourist vessels. In addition to assorted side trips up tributaries and to temples—which have been relocated to save them from flooding—there is also the attraction of visiting the world's most colossal dam, a great wall of steel and concrete, 594 feet (181 meters) high and nearly 1.5 miles (2.4 kilometers) across.

WHEN TO GO Early fall is best. Your trip may coincide with the Harvest Moon Festival, when families reunite and gather outside to see and celebrate the brightest moon of the year.

HOW LONG Trips begin or end with a one-hour bus journey to or from Yichang. Three or four nights are needed on cruise ships to reach Chongqing, or around 12 hours by hydrofoil (Sandouping–Wanxian), which includes bus links to Yichang and Chongqing.

PLANNING Save up to 60 percent by booking at the docks in Yichang or Chongqing instead of making advance bookings through agents or websites. Or pay even less by joining the Chinese on a Sputnik-era Russian hydrofoil.

INSIDE INFORMATION Top-notch cruise ship food is often bland, and cheap Chinese ferry or hydrofoil food inedible. Pack snacks, including bottled water if on cheaper boats.

WEBSITES victoriacruises.com, wendywutours.co.uk

HIGHLIGHTS

▪ The imposing **Three Gorges Dam** at Sandouping, just upstream from Yichang, holds back a 410-mile (660 km) reservoir and generates as much electricity as 15 nuclear power plants.

▪ Gaze upward while passing through the Three Gorges, **Qutang, Wu,** and **Xiling**, which force the abundant river traffic to zigzag between steep cliffs.

▪ Enjoy the spectacular views along the river from the red wooden pagoda of the **Shibaozhai** (Stone Treasure Fortress) **Temple**, 175 miles (280 km) from Chongqing.

ASIA

A fisherman lights his lantern in preparation for an evening of cormorant fishing.

CHINA

The Li River

This half-day cruise presents an idyllic China as you pass by scenery that inspired countless scroll paintings.

Between bustling Guilin and the village of Yangshuo, in the northeastern part of Guangxi province, the skyline is punctuated by sharp, green-trimmed peaks of karst limestone, jostling each other for space on the banks of the Li Jiang, or Li River. Rising like crooked teeth above the water, the stark shapes of these mountains have given rise to a host of names—such as Elephant Trunk Hill, where a gigantic limestone "elephant" dips its trunk into the current to drink, or Mural Hill, on which a multicolored rock face forms a dazzling natural mural. Others are named after immortal gods or mundane household objects. The river itself snakes lazily past huge sprays of skyrocketing bamboo shoots and peasant children riding on docile water buffalo. Onboard one of the many tourist barges, you'll enjoy a traditional Chinese meal as a banquet of scenery slides past the windows. This short stretch of river has provided inspiration for generations of painters and poets. At night in Yangshuo cormorant fishermen take visitors out on the river to watch their trained birds dive below the surface for fish, a technique that the villagers of Guangxi have practiced for centuries on the shallow waters of the Li River.

WHEN TO GO Spring and fall provide the most comfortable temperatures. Summer is wet and steamy.

HOW LONG Depending on water levels, there may be a 15-mile (24 km) bus journey to a dock outside Guilin, taking 30 minutes, then four to five hours on the river for 52 miles (84 km).

PLANNING No advanced booking is necessary; you can buy tickets at the dock. A hot pot–style meal is usually included in the price.

INSIDE INFORMATION Foreigners are usually charged double and herded onto tourist vessels, but the determined traveler can still sometimes get onto Chinese boats by using local agents charging proper local prices – at the cost of an English-speaking tour guide.

WEBSITE travelchinaguide.com

HIGHLIGHTS

■ The collection of peaks reflected in the water between **Yangdi** and **Xingping** represents one of China's most famous landscapes, appearing on both ancient scroll paintings and modern banknotes.

■ The **cormorant fishermen's lanterns** bob over the evening river, as the birds dart down into pools of light and return with wriggling mouthfuls for their masters.

■ Enjoy **quiet Yangshuo** after the last bar closes, with views from hotel rooftops of spiny moonlit peaks.

ASIA

ACROSS WATER

BY ROAD | BY RAIL | ON FOOT | IN SEARCH OF CULTURE | IN GOURMET HEAVEN | INTO THE ACTION | UP AND AWAY | IN THEIR FOOTSTEPS

| LAOS |

The Mekong River

Take a slow boat along the great Mekong River and gaze out at the misty riverbanks of Laos.

From high up in the mountains of Tibet, the vast Mekong River winds its way for almost 2,500 miles (4,025 kilometers) through seven countries—but it is at its most beautiful sliding through the dark green, misty hills of Laos. Reject the roaring, high-powered "fast boats" and opt for a brightly colored wooden "slow boat." Once you've got used to the puttering engine bolted to the back of the vessel, you can spend hours gazing out at the rolling forested hills and paddy fields and allow your mind to wander. However, be prepared to make friends—the cramped and uncomfortable seating enforces a sense of camaraderie. The occasional pit stop in local villages lets you buy food and drink and stretch your legs. For the more energetic traveler, there are some fascinating sites to visit on the way. In particular, stop off to explore the Buddhist shrine in the caves of Pak Ou. Set in a towering gray-green cliff face, the limestone caverns contain hundreds of Buddha statues of all shapes and sizes, which stare impassively out of the darkness. Journey's end is at Louangphrabang, which holds UNESCO World Heritage site status for its elegant blend of French colonial and traditional Lao architecture.

WHEN TO GO During the cool, dry season between December and February.

HOW LONG Various options are available, ranging from two-day to week-long trips. Alternatively, you can don a life jacket and crash helmet and tour the Mekong in a few hours on a "fast boat."

PLANNING Wait until you arrive before paying for a ticket, and buy directly at the jetty for the best price.

INSIDE INFORMATION Take a small cushion – seats can be hard and uncomfortable. The "slow boats" have toilets onboard, but make sure you bring a supply of toilet paper with you. You might also find a set of earplugs useful for blocking out the monotonous sound of the engine.

WEBSITE visit-laos.com

ASIA

| HIGHLIGHTS

▓ The small Lao **fishing villages** on the riverbanks provide a seemingly inexhaustible supply of happy, waving children.

▓ **Let time slip** slowly by with nothing to do but admire the views.

▓ Explore the **Royal Palace Museum** in Louangphrabang, where the history of the Lao monarchy is enshrined in a building typically influenced by both French and Lao architecture.

▓ At Louangphrabang, arrange for a local to drive you in a "tuk-tuk" (auto rickshaw) to the **Kuang Si waterfall**, about 15 miles (24 km) away.

On the Mekong River, a slow boat passes the Pak Ou caves, surrounded by the verdant forest of Luang Prabang.

| INDIA

Kerala Backwaters

Voyage past fishermen and pearl divers in the jade green backwaters of Kerala—a vast labyrinth of channels, islands, and lagoons in southern India.

Seemingly endless narrow channels meander into large lagoons—where the ocean is sometimes only a stone's throw away—from the lush interior of Kerala province: "God's own country," according to its thriving tourist industry. Sandbars form a natural dam, cutting Kerala off from the sea, and the waters stretch back for more than 600 miles (960 kilometers), opening India to traders, missionaries, and invaders from East and West. Small villages of pearl divers and coconut workers line the banks of the backwaters, with bales of coarse, brown coir (the fiber of coconuts) piled beside the jetties or weighing down tiny vessels. The calm waters form a highway for fast-moving "snake boats" (gondola-like craft driven by powerful outboard motors), heavy-laden, square-rigged rice barges, and tiny reed rafts with patchwork sails, used by the pearl fishers who dive for oysters in the shallow waters. Many of the villagers are Christian—said to be the descendants of those converted by St. Thomas almost 2,000 years ago—and small whitewashed churches stand on many of the islands that dot the backwaters, shaded by tall coconut palms. Visitors can experience the tranquil atmosphere in air-conditioned comfort aboard a converted *kettuvallam*. These hand-built barges, up to 80 feet (25 meters) long, are traditionally made by lashing together jackwood planks with coir rope, and are furnished with elegant wickerwork.

WHEN TO GO Daily departures, November to February. Avoid monsoon season (March to October).

HOW LONG Various options are available: six to eight hours for the trip between Kollam (Quilon) and Alappuzha (Alleppey); two to three hours from Alappuzha to Kottayam; two to three days for a longer cruise between Kochi (Cochin) and Kollam in a converted rice barge, sleeping on board.

PLANNING The nearest international airport is Kochi, which also has some of India's most stylish hotels. The backwaters are a perfect breeding ground for mosquitoes, so malaria tablets are essential.

INSIDE INFORMATION Go for a modern kettuvallam for the most luxurious experience. Most of these boats are equipped with onboard full bathrooms, kitchens, large double-bedded cabins, and a crew of three or four, including a cook.

WEBSITES keralatourism.org, lakeslagoons.com

ASIA

| HIGHLIGHTS

▪ At sunset in Kochi (Cochin), the skeletal wooden gantries of **Chinese fishing nets** cast eerie spider's leg silhouettes against the purple sky. These ancient devices are built to a design brought from the East more than 500 years ago.

▪ Suck up the translucent milk from green **tender coconuts** through a straw, once the top has been hacked off with a machete.

▪ Delicious **Indian food** is served aboard the kettuvallams, cooked by your own personal chef. Make sure you taste the local tiger prawns.

▪ Look out for the Kerala **snake boat races**, which take place throughout the region at all times of year. These events are usually accompanied by a colorful festival and give you a chance to see master oarsmen in action.

Opposite: A man paddles a sailboat in the Kerala backwaters near Ayiramthengu. Above left: Near Trivandrum, Kerala, a woman carries a basket full of green coconuts. Above right: A dancer wears bright orange face paint for a special performance in honor of the goddess Theyyam.

The Sepik River

Take a slow river cruise into the heart of a lost world and discover the ancient tribes of Papua New Guinea.

An early morning mist clings to the river as it snakes lazily through lush green forests and grassland. Silhouetted against the rising sun, a fisherman paddles his low dugout canoe across the muddy brown waters. Crocodiles bask on the bank, while overhead a harpy eagle glides on the air currents. Papua New Guinea's 700-mile (1,127 kilometer) Sepik River forms one of the world's great river systems, rising in the country's Central Range, then meandering in giant loops across the northern lowlands. It is also one of the planet's least spoiled rivers, still untrammeled by dams and free of industrial pollution. Traveling either in a small cruise boat or motorized canoes, you make your way between riverside villages where tribal elders, adorned with brightly colored ocher face paints, welcome you with traditional dances and music. The local people speak more than 300 different languages in an area a little larger than California, reflecting an astonishing cultural richness. You encounter evidence of their artistic skills on every side—in the gabled "spirit houses," which form the ritual center of village life; in fearsome wooden hunting masks, carved by local craftsmen; even in the scarring on men's backs, made during the initiation rites that mark their entry into adulthood and designed to imitate the tooth marks of a crocodile.

WHEN TO GO Papua New Guinea is hot and humid all year round. Avoid the monsoon season from December to March.

HOW LONG A four-day, three-night trip, sleeping on board a cruise boat, is a standard choice.

PLANNING Get your kina (the local currency) before leaving home – airport foreign exchange counters sometimes run out. Take small denomination notes if you're planning to buy local artworks.

INSIDE INFORMATION Don't barter – this is considered rude. You can leave a gift of, say, pens or other supplies with the village school if you wish.

WEBSITE pngtours.com

HIGHLIGHTS

▪ Each village has its own distinctive **tradition of craftsmanship**, and the finest pieces – wood-carved masks, stools, pillars, and more – are stored in the **"spirit house"** (*haus tambaran*). In some villages you may be charged to enter.

▪ Make a detour to visit **Chambri Lakes**, where during the rainy season parts of the banks break off and become **floating islands**. The local **artists and craftsmen** are considered some of the most skilled.

▪ Papua New Guinea has 38 species of **birds of paradise.** Look and listen out for these colorful creatures in the dense forests that line the riverbank.

A wood-carver at work with an adze on the shore of Wagu Lake, one of a number of beautiful lakes in the Sepik region.

ACROSS WATER

BY ROAD · BY RAIL · ON FOOT · IN SEARCH OF CULTURE · IN GOURMET HEAVEN · INTO THE ACTION · UP AND AWAY · IN THEIR FOOTSTEPS

Red gum forests line these banks of the Murray River.

AUSTRALIA

The Great Murray River Rune

Drift through the heart of southeast Australia on the Murray River, a waterway of outstanding natural beauty.

At sunset, tall silvery red gum trees cast long shadows across the golden surface of the Murray River. This leisurely cruise takes you through the sunbaked landscapes of South Australia, as the river winds its way across the continent to Lake Alexandrina and the Indian Ocean. By day, the boat glides past scenery that ranges from sheer limestone cliffs to fragrant, golden-green citrus fruit orchards. In the evening, you disembark to spend the night in one of a succession of comfortable hotels. Along the way, you will see some of the most beautiful wildlife Australia has to offer—from stately pink-beaked Australian pelicans cruising slowly downstream, to majestic wedge-tailed eagles circling the blue skies above. You may also see an excited angler landing a Murray cod, one of the world's largest freshwater fish, which regularly grows to more than 3 feet (1 meter) in length. Stopover points include riverside towns such as Morgan, whose restored wharfs recall its Victorian heyday as a busy riverport, when paddle steamers carried goods and passengers along the Murray River and its tributaries. Other excursions take you to huge sheep and cattle stations, on wine-tasting trips to vineyards, and to ancient Aboriginal sites.

WHEN TO GO All year round.

HOW LONG Renmark to Goolwa is five days and four nights.

PLANNING Cruise prices include all meals and accommodation.

INSIDE INFORMATION The Murray River has a Mediterranean climate – average temperatures range from 61°F (16°C) in July to 90°F (32°C) in January – so pack light clothing even in winter.

WEBSITE spiritaustraliacruises.com.au

HIGHLIGHTS

▧ **Orchards and vineyards** surround the town of Berri, southwest of Renmark. At the **Berri Estates** winery, the largest in the country, you can sample a selection of their Merlot and Shiraz vintages.

▧ **Waikerie** (meaning "anything that flies" in a local Aboriginal language) is the best place to see waterfowl, such as ibis, herons, and the Australian pelican.

▧ The 100-ft (30 m) **Yellow Cliffs** at **Big Bend** on Swan Reach are the highest on the Murray River, thought to be around 20 million years old.

The rising sun creates a dramatic play of light and shadow on the mountainsides in Milford Sound, adding to the majesty of the scene.

NEW ZEALAND
Cruising Milford Sound

Enter a magical world of icy mountains, bottomless fiords, and breathtaking vistas as you relax in your boat.

Cruising the waters of Milford Sound (Piopiotahi in Maori), it's the immensity of nature that hits you … and the raw power of the processes of glaciation that carved out this and the rest of New Zealand's Fiordland during the Ice Age. During a two-hour trip, the boat passes cliffs that rise to heights of 3,900 feet (1,189 meters), while far above, patches of lush rain forest cling to the rock face. Surrounding you is a combined land and seascape of lustrous blues and greens, capped by the snowy summits of the mountains, notably the 5,558-foot (1,694 meter) Mitre Peak—in fact, five peaks close together, giving it an episcopal shape. It's a trip not even rain can spoil—the precipitation creates sparkling temporary waterfalls to add to the permanent torrents gushing down the mountainsides. And if you enjoyed Milford Sound, there is plenty more to explore in the 4,680-square-mile (12,120 square kilometers) Fiordland National Park. Doubtful Sound farther south is harder to get to, but well worth the effort—it is larger than Milford Sound, with three distinct "arms" and several spectacular waterfalls. The scenery here is more expansive and serene. Inland, meanwhile, lie the limpid blue waters of the Norwest Lakes, where scenes from *The Lord of the Rings* films were shot.

WHEN TO GO All year, but during New Zealand's rainy winter months (June to August), you'll see fewer tourists and more waterfalls.

HOW LONG The average cruise time is around two hours, but if you include the time it takes to get to Milford Sound from Te Anau, the nearest town with accommodation, the trip takes a whole day.

PLANNING Book well in advance. Also, remember that this is one of the wettest places on Earth, so take waterproof gear and an umbrella. You will also need insect repellent to ward off biting sand flies.

INSIDE INFORMATION To avoid hordes of other tourists, take the first boat of the day, or book a canoe trip toward the end of the day and watch dusk fall.

WEBSITE cruisemilfordnz.com

HIGHLIGHTS

▒ The journey from **Te Anau** is one of the world's **finest alpine drives**, especially when you emerge from the **Homer Tunnel** to see the sound stretching out before you.

▒ **Bottlenose dolphins** gambol beside your boat. **Fur seals** bask at Seal Point, and, if you're lucky, you'll glimpse the rare **fiordland crested penguin.**

▒ **Stirling Falls** drop 479 ft (146 m) and are at their most spectacular after heavy rain.

▒ Take a **scenic flight** over the sound, or book an **overnight cruise**, allowing you to enjoy its beauty after everyone else has left.

AUSTRALIA AND OCEANIA

FINLAND

Sampo Arctic Icebreaker

An unforgettable journey takes you through the winter wonderland of Lapland's icy waters.

EUROPE

This is a journey into the icy heart of winter. The *Sampo* is a former working icebreaker, now operating from the Finnish port of Kemi near the northern end of the Gulf of Bothnia—the 450-mile (724 kilometer) offshoot of the Baltic Sea that separates Sweden and Finland. For five months each winter, the *Sampo* takes visitors on cruises into the gulf's fearsomely cold, inky-dark waters and through thick pack ice—floating lumps of ice that have been compacted into a solid mass. This presents no obstacle to the sturdy, 246-foot (75 meter) ship, which can maintain a steady 8 knots as it crunches its way through ice up to 20 inches (50 centimeters) thick. Be prepared, however, for a few sharp jolts when it hits thicker patches, smashes through them, and then continues on its way. Most cruises only last an afternoon, but in that time you experience a blindingly beautiful world of sea, ice, and snow, rarely disturbed by any other human presence. You can even disembark onto the pack ice and take a dip in the sea—protected from the cold in a watertight thermal suit. Other possibilities include a spin across the ice in a snowmobile or a ride with a dogsled team to visit a traditional community of the Sami (Lapp) people, the region's indigenous inhabitants.

WHEN TO GO December to April.

HOW LONG Standard trips last four hours, but overnight voyages are also available.

PLANNING The ship can only take 150 travelers, so make sure you book this popular journey well in advance.

INSIDE INFORMATION Sampo Tours provides all the equipment you need for activities such as ice swimming. But bring plenty of warm clothing, including waterproof jackets, hats, and gloves; you will need them for walking the deck. You will also need sunglasses – the sunlight reflected off the ice and snow is dazzlingly bright.

WEBSITE visitkemi.fi/en/sampo

HIGHLIGHTS

■ **Tours of the ship** include visits to the **engine room**, housing the 8,800-horsepower machinery that drives the vessel, and the **bridge**, where you can stand with the officers on duty.

■ Wood and brass fittings adorn the Arctic Restaurant, Icebreaker Bar, and Captain's Saloon, where you can retreat from the cold on deck to sample **traditional Sami food**, including **reindeer**.

■ As the short winter day comes to an end and night falls, you may witness the spectacular multicolored rays of the **aurora borealis** – or northern lights – as they light up the sky.

Passengers gather on the foredeck of the *Sampo* to watch the prow cleaving through shining white ice.

ACROSS WATER

BY ROAD | BY RAIL | ON FOOT | IN SEARCH OF CULTURE | IN GOURMET HEAVEN | INTO THE ACTION | UP AND AWAY | IN THEIR FOOTSTEPS

| ANTARCTICA |

Cruising to Antarctica

A once-in-a-lifetime journey to a
pristine paradise, Earth's last great frontier.

The icebergs floating past the ship, some of them as large as ships themselves, create weirdly surreal shapes against the blue sky. A few have fur seals catching a ride on top of them. Someone cries out "Whales!" and soon everyone is on deck to catch a glimpse of the spouts of mist these giant mammals shoot into the air as they breathe out, or the flicks of their tail flukes as they vanish underwater. As you glide past rocky shores, snow-clad peaks rise inland, and here and there you can spot the icy blue sheen of glaciers. Elsewhere, the cliffs of an ice shelf rise sheer from extraordinary, luminescent aquamarine waters. On shore trips, sturdy rubber Zodiac boats zoom you across the water to land where you may be able to walk among colonies of penguins—irresistible birds, guaranteed to make you smile. The Antarctic Peninsula, the huge spit of land jutting north from the rest of the continent toward South America, is the focus for most cruises. They are not trips that can be done on the cheap, and conditions on board the ice-reinforced vessels are comfortable, even luxurious, with observation lounges, libraries, and sometimes even gyms. But for the true experience of these waters and the vast, untouched continent of Antarctica, you have to wrap up and go on deck, where you feel the frosty grip of the air on your face and hear the sounds of ice creaking, birds crying, and the polar wind soughing in the rigging.

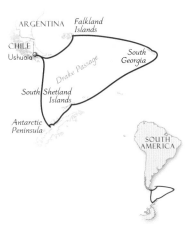

WHEN TO GO December to February are peak times, when coastal temperatures are moderate, averaging 23° to 41°F (−5° to 5°C).

HOW LONG Cruises range from 8 to 29 days. Longer journeys may include South Georgia and the Falkland Islands, and visits to emperor penguins on Snow Hill Island in the Weddell Sea.

PLANNING Ship choices include small ice-cutters with 50–100 passengers, expedition cruisers carrying 100–200 passengers, or cruise ships with up to 600 passengers. Smaller ships make more landings. Larger ships are more stable in waters that can be rough.

INSIDE INFORMATION On any cruise, bring medication for seasickness ... just in case. No need to bring heavy jackets. Most ships provide insulated jackets for passengers.

WEBSITES polarcruises.com, peregrineadventures.com, pelagic.co.uk

| HIGHLIGHTS

▨ You are likely to see **humpback and minke whales**, and orcas, or killer whales (in fact, a kind of dolphin).

▨ On the Antarctic Peninsula, **Port Lockroy** has a large colony of **gentoo penguins**, as does **Paradise Harbor**, where they live in a scenic setting ringed by ice cliffs. **Half Moon Island**, a rocky volcanic retreat, is home to **chinstrap penguins.**

▨ Visit in mid-January to see adult penguins caring for their **fat, fluffy chicks** in nests made of pebbles. Although you should stay at a safe distance from **nesting penguins**, many birds seem unfazed by company and waddle up close, as if posing for the clicking cameras.

▨ Every ship carries **expert scientists**, who will enrich the voyage with talks about the intrepid early explorers to Antarctica and its unique geology and wildlife.

Opposite: An inflatable Zodiac boat carries travelers toward the Antarctic Peninsula. Above left: Chinstrap penguins line up on top of an iceberg near Elephant Island, one of the South Shetland Islands off Antarctica's northernmost tip. The birds are named for the band of black feathers below their chins. Above right: An orca "spyhops" through the pack ice.

Fjords of Norway

This day-long journey, combining rail and boat, travels through Norway's most spectacular fjord landscape.

EUROPE

The Norwegian fjords—deep, plunging, U-shaped valleys carved out of rock by the movement of glaciers—were formed some 3 million years ago. All along Norway's western coastline, hundreds of these winding, often narrow waterways forge paths from the Norwegian Sea into the mainland. The most stunning journey is along the Sognefjord, "the king of fjords," the longest in the country, at 127 miles (204 kilometers), and its deepest, at 4,294 feet (1,309 meters). Your small cruise boat chugs through the calm surface ripples in the shadow of soaring cliffs and pine forest so thick that it blots out all light within. Waterfalls cascade down vertical rock faces, and picture-postcard villages perch on the water's edge, with distinctive red wooden houses and white church towers. Blessed with brilliant sunshine in summer, and lashed by fierce rain in winter, the elemental beauty—and sheer size—of the fjords is a humbling experience. To reach the coast, take a train to Myrdal on the Oslo-Bergen line, then get on the Flåm railway, an engineering feat of open tunnels cutting through otherwise impassable cliff faces. This hour-long trip is one of the world's best for views of waterfalls and sheer drops from the track as it clings precariously to the mountainsides.

WHEN TO GO The summer months – May to September – are the tourist high season and are often sunny; the long, dark winters, on the other hand, offer a stormy, atmospheric experience.

HOW LONG Trips vary in length depending on the tour operator. Allow one to three days if you intend to visit Bergen and ride the Flåm railway.

PLANNING All seating on both the boat and the train is standard class. There is a chance to stop for lunch or refreshment in the town of Flåm, and snacks are available on the boat.

INSIDE INFORMATION Even the Norwegian summers are chilly, so bring a warm jacket or fleece so you can stay out on the open deck and enjoy the best views. Bring a pair of binoculars if you're hoping to spot some seals.

WEBSITES norwaynutshell.com, visitnorway.com

HIGHLIGHTS

Bergen, Norway's second city, is a beautifully preserved town of medieval timber houses, particularly along Bryggen Harbor, which is now a UNESCO World Heritage site.

Naeroyfjord, the narrowest of the fjords, is home to one of the most beautiful natural landscapes in northern Europe. Blue waters contrast with green pine trees, while snow-capped mountains loom overhead.

If you're lucky, you might see **seals basking** on the banks of the water.

For the energetic, the tiny village of Flåm (a name that means "small place between steep mountains") provides a perfect base for **kayaking** in the waters of the fjords.

Near Flåm, the Stegastein viewpoint gives a jaw-dropping panorama of Aurlandsfjord and the surrounding mountains.

Boats lie moored alongside one of the 64 islands that make up the municipality of Vaxholm.

SWEDEN

Stockholm Archipelago

Cruise through the thousands of islands and waterways that surround Scandinavia's most beautiful capital city.

There are some 24,000 islands in the Baltic Sea that make up the Stockholm Archipelago (Skärgården in Swedish), from Arholma in the north to the southernmost outpost, Landsort. Touring these waterways by cruise boat is one of the most idyllic trips in Europe, and evokes a time when men went to sea for six months of the year, while women tended the land. You can explore islands just an hour's journey from Stockholm, or travel to the south, where the archipelago meets the open sea. The attractions are both natural and man-made, and seemingly dovetail into each other as you glide along. You pass long sandy beaches and dense woodlands filled with mushrooms and wildflowers, the coastline dotted with characteristic red wooden summerhouses; the vegetation is lusher in the more protected inner archipelago. You can pause at secluded fishing spots to try your luck at catching salmon, or possibly glimpse a seal or two basking on the shore. Along the way, you slip past decorative merchants' houses, historic palaces, and castles—and, of course, at the heart of it all lies the stylish island city of Stockholm.

WHEN TO GO Steamboat cruises run from May to September.

HOW LONG Allow one to five days.

PLANNING The Båtluffarkortet is a five-day pass that allows for island hopping in the archipelago, available from tourist centers in Stockholm. All accommodation is standard class. Some day trips include a lunch stop in the fare.

INSIDE INFORMATION Waterproof clothing, insect repellent, and bottled water are essentials. There are basic campsites on the islands of Finnhamn, Grinda, Ränö, Nåttarö, and Utö. Fishing with rods is free from either the waterside or from rowboats. Fall is longer and warmer in the archipelago than on the mainland, and there are more hours of sunshine.

WEBSITE www.waxholmsbolaget.se/visitor

HIGHLIGHTS

▓ Cruise back to the 19th century on a **traditional steamboat.**

▓ Explore 17th-century **Vaxholm**, the archipelago's largest town (apart from Stockholm itself), with its citadel and antique wooden villas.

▓ Admire the **summerhouses** of the wealthy, with their turrets and gables, on the inner archipelago leading into Stockholm.

▓ **Swim and relax** on the vast sandy beaches from which the island of Sandhamn gets its name.

EUROPE

Waterways of the Tsars

Experience the grandeur of Imperial Russia as you cruise along the waterways of St. Petersburg.

EUROPE

A crisp, chilly morning. Your boat emerges from the narrow corridor of the Moika Canal into the broad Neva River, and Peter the Great's monumental city unfolds before you. Between bridges adorned with lions, griffins, and charioteers, the skyline is dominated by gigantic palaces and churches. To the left are the baroque columns of the Winter Palace, once the main residence of the tsars. Across the river, the gleaming white, neoclassical splendor of the old Stock Exchange catches the eye, and, to its right, the soaring, gilded spire of the Peter and Paul Cathedral, rising from the island Peter and Paul Fortress, pierces the sky. The extensive system of granite-lined waterways links over one hundred islands, and St. Petersburg has been called the Venice of the North, but, in truth, the Russian city dwarfs its Italian counterpart. In summer, the midnight sun bathes the whole city in soft twilight—the famous white nights. Also known as Peter's Window on the West, St. Petersburg was renamed Leningrad after the fall of the tsars, and regained its original name only after the breakup of the U.S.S.R. in 1991. Far more than Moscow, the city retains the mystery and grandeur of pre-Soviet, feudal Russia, when the all-powerful tsars held court in the city.

WHEN TO GO Go in May to July to experience the white nights. The phenomenon is usually at its peak during the last week of June.

HOW LONG The cruise itself lasts a few hours, but allow at least two days if you intend to visit the Hermitage museum and the Peter and Paul Fortress.

PLANNING Cut through tedious Russian bureaucracy by booking through a travel agent.

INSIDE INFORMATION Do not drink the local water if you don't want an upset stomach. Bottled water is easily available. There are mosquitoes in St. Petersburg, so pack insect repellent. If you are visiting during the white nights, you might find sleep masks useful to block out the light and help you sleep at night.

WEBSITES visitrussia.org.uk, saint-petersburg.com/river-trips

HIGHLIGHTS

▒ Visit the Winter Palace, which is now part of the **Hermitage**, one of the largest and most impressive museums in the world.

▒ See the **Bronze Horseman** – the statue of Peter the Great that stands in front of St. Isaac's Cathedral.

▒ Explore the **Peter and Paul Fortress**, formerly a political prison whose denizens included Trotsky and Dostoyevsky. In its grounds stands the Peter and Paul Cathedral, where Peter the Great, Catherine the Great, and other tsars are buried.

▒ See the **Stock Exchange** (now the Naval Museum) with two red granite beacons, decorated (Roman style) with the prows of captured ships.

At dusk on the banks of the dark Neva River, the splendid facade of the Winter Palace turns gold in the evening light.

Pfalz Castle stands on an island in the middle of the Rhine.

| GERMANY |

Rhine River Cruise

This romantic river trip passes fairy-tale castles perched high above steep valleys, deep green forests, and medieval villages.

This evocative voyage from Mainz to Koblenz has been a favorite with travelers since the 19th century. Imbued with the spirit of German Romanticism, the Rhine River has inspired fairy tales, fables, poetry, and paintings, while its mythical underwater maidens and their magic gold inspired Wagner's *Ring* opera cycle. The stretch from Bingen, just west of Mainz, to Koblenz runs through a steep and narrow gorge, and has more castles than any other river in the world; they tell the story of medieval princes, knights, and barons keen to secure their power bases, who accrued wealth by extorting tolls from river traffic. Below these cliff-top fortresses sit villages of half-timbered houses, like Bacharach, that owe their existence to the world-famous Riesling grape, grown in vineyards along the sheer but sheltering hillsides. Try regional fare at any point: fresh venison, veal, and handcrafted cheeses—with wine, naturally.

WHEN TO GO April to October.

HOW LONG The trip takes seven hours one way, but many travelers use the "hop-on, hop-off" facility to sightsee and only do part of the journey.

PLANNING Get a Rhine pass before boarding a boat in Mainz. This will entitle you to all-day boat-hopping, allowing you to disembark whenever you want and to stay for as long or as short a time as you want. Not all castles can be visited. Purchase a guide in advance to give you details of history, location, and opening times.

INSIDE INFORMATION Take a cushion, as most boats only have hard chairs on the viewing decks. Almost every little village on the Rhine holds its own wine festival, most on Saturdays, in August or September. Many of these wines are not sold outside the region.

WEBSITE k-d.com/en

HIGHLIGHTS

▓ Stop at **Rüdesheim**, which has the oldest castle on the river, dating from the 9th century, and a large number of wine taverns.

▓ Visit the island castle of **Pfalz**, which perches in the middle of the river near Kaub.

▓ Combine history and luxury with an overnight stay at **Schönburg Castle** in the walled town of Oberwesel.

▓ Look out for the **Lorelei rock**, a steep cliff at the narrowest point in the river, where, according to mythology, a singing siren lured sailors to their deaths.

▓ Catch the **Rhine in Flames festival**, a series of firework extravaganzas celebrating the river held at St. Goar and other places in July and August.

▓ Also look out for **Katz** (cat) and **Maus** (mouse) castles, on the right bank, opposite the partly ruined **Rheinfels** castle.

Top 10 Canal Trips

Often built to transport goods during the industrial revolution, these peaceful waterways are now mainly used for recreation.

❶ THE PANAMA CANAL, PANAMA

Joining the Atlantic and Pacific Oceans, this 50-mile (80 kilometer) engineering marvel is used by thousands of ships large and small each year. On partial or complete transits of the canal (a complete transit takes a day), you can sail beside giant cargo ships and the little tugs that guide them from one sea to another through three sets of double locks.

PLANNING The dry season is from November to the end of April. canalandbaytours.com

❷ NEW YORK STATE CANALS, NEW YORK

These canals—built in the mid-19th century—comprise 524 miles (843 kilometers) of waterways and towpaths between Albany and Buffalo, New York. The Erie Canal travels through Rochester, where you can tour Susan B. Anthony's home. You can rent a boat and sail it yourself, or hire a crew.

PLANNING The canals are open from May to early November. canals.ny.gov

❸ BALTIC SEA CANAL, RUSSIA

The White Sea—an extension of the Arctic off northwestern Russia—is connected to St. Petersburg, on the Baltic, by a 140-mile (225 kilometer) canal system. It was constructed in the 1930s by prisoners, working mainly with spades and picks. You'll pass traditional villages and old wooden chapels.

PLANNING This trip has to be organized by a tour operator. nordictravel.ru

❹ COPENHAGEN, DENMARK

Travel around Denmark's capital city on the hop-on, hop-off water buses that ply its many canals. Some of the routes give great views of the Little Mermaid statue. The boats are open in summer, glass-roofed in winter, and run year-round.

PLANNING Buy a two-day transfer ticket for unlimited travel along the city's canals. visitcopenhagen.com

❺ AMSTERDAM, THE NETHERLANDS

Low bridges, arching trees, and historic narrow houses line Amsterdam's many canals. Take a sightseeing or dinner cruise; or, better yet, stay in a houseboat hotel and make the canals your base. Alternatively, you can pedal along the canals yourself; Canal Bike rents pedal boats, which you can rent at one mooring and drop off at another.

PLANNING Book via blueboat.nl, stromma.nl/amsterdam

During the industrial revolution, brightly painted narrow boats carried goods all across England's canal network. Now they are perfect for an easygoing vacation through beautiful scenery.

❻ THE BLACK SEA CANAL, ROMANIA

The 40-mile (64 kilometer) Black Sea canal, completed in 1984, goes from Ruse, on the Bulgarian section of the Danube River, to Constanta, a popular Romanian resort on the Black Sea. The canal is part of the wildlife-rich Danube Delta area, the second largest river delta area in Europe, home to pelicans, herons, egrets, and up to 300 other species of bird.

PLANNING This trip can form part of a longer cruise along the Danube. romaniatourism.com, romania.travel

❼ GÖTA CANAL, SWEDEN

The canal connects a series of lakes, allowing boats to travel almost all the way across Sweden from Lake Vänern, near Gothenberg, to the Baltic. Along the way are 58 locks; be sure to come on deck to watch the crew open them and maneuver the ship through. Dozens of different boats ply the canals, and you can cruise for a few hours or a whole week. For a more active canal experience, rent a canoe or kayak and paddle along the canal.

PLANNING Visit in midsummer for nearly 24-hour daylight and temperatures as warm as southern Europe. vastsverige.com/en

❽ WATERWAYS OF BRANDENBURG, GERMANY

Between Berlin and the Baltic, explore a network of lakes and canals that takes you past castles and quaint towns. Along the way you'll see herons standing silently in the shallows and catch glimpses of irridescent turquoise kingfishers darting along the surface of the water. On lazy summer afternoons fishermen line the banks; in the evening, sample their catch in the local restaurants where carp and other freshwater fish are a specialty.

PLANNING Not heavily touristed, so English is not widely spoken. cruisegermany.com

❾ ENGLISH CHANNEL-MEDITERRANEAN, FRANCE

France's 5,000-mile (8,050 kilometer) network of canals can take you from north to south, or anywhere in between, exploring towns and villages on the way. To the south, the Canal du Midi passes through a land of vineyards and walled cities, many in easy reach of the canal. Tie up outside a small town, and go ashore to sample local food and wine. Many restaurants feature regional specialties. Most towns have weekly markets through which you can browse and stock up on provisions.

PLANNING Rental companies give lessons before letting you loose on the canals in your floating home. leboat.co.uk

❿ SHROPSHIRE UNION CANAL, ENGLAND

The northern half of the Shropshire Union Canal in England's West Midlands meanders through gently rolling landscape. South of Nantwich it travels in a nearly straight line through hills and across valleys via deep cuttings and magnificent bridges. The canal is a monument to the early days of the industrial revolution; the brightly painted narrow boats also seem to come from another era. Boats go at walking speed so that their wakes don't erode the banks.

PLANNING England's weather is best from May to October. canalrivertrust.org.uk, ukcanalboating.com

Danube River Cruise

A scenic journey along a storied river includes visits to two of Europe's most beautiful cities—Vienna and Budapest.

From the Black Forest to the Black Sea, the blue Danube cuts east through the heart of Europe, through empty countryside, tiny villages, and bustling cities, past sun-touched vineyards, wooded hills, angular church spires, and lone hilltop castles that have stood for centuries. What makes this trip, however, is the string of grand old cities along the banks of the river—and the great pleasure of being able to walk directly off the boat and into entirely different surroundings of cobbled streets, top-notch shops, and fabulously ornate architecture. Even the short cruises make stops in two great European cities: Vienna (Wien)—a cultural treasure-house—and Budapest—the Queen of the Danube. While in Budapest, pay a visit to Váci utca, the pedestrian shopping street that captures the spirit of the city by combining up-to-the-minute shops with perfectly preserved 18th-century buildings. Some cruises also take in Bratislava, the historic capital of Slovakia, and two Austrian villages, Dürnstein, with ruins of the 12th-century castle where King Richard the Lionheart was imprisoned, and Melk, with a grand baroque Benedictine abbey. An excursion in Esztergom gives the chance to visit Hungary's largest basilica and its dazzling treasury.

WHEN TO GO Most cruises sail from April through October; a few travel in December during the Christmas holiday period.

HOW LONG Cruises range from 7 to 14 days for round-trips between Passau (Germany) and Budapest. Many offer optional city stays and extensions to nearby cities, such as Prague and Munich.

PLANNING Pack layers and rain gear; Central European weather is notoriously changeable. Comfortable walking shoes are also a must for city exploring.

INSIDE INFORMATION When calculating your cruise costs, don't forget about tips. They will add around $10–12 per day to your costs.

WEBSITES cruisingholidays.co.uk, vikingrivercruises.com

| HIGHLIGHTS

■ Ships dock just a five-minute walk away from the famous **1890 Budapest Central Market**, which overflows with picture-perfect produce, sausages, and the city's best selection of handcrafted souvenirs.

■ Evening excursions to Europe's premier **opera and concert halls** in Vienna are memorable experiences for classical music lovers.

■ **Viennese pastries** are delicious, especially Sacher torte, a cake with a layer of apricot jam and covered with a thick chocolate coating. One place to try them is Demel Konditorei, Kohlmarkt 14, which has an old-world interior and amazing marzipan creations in the windows.

The sun sets on the parliament building in Budapest. Margitsziget, a small island lying in the middle of the Danube between Buda and Pest, can be seen in the distance.

Flags flutter on the docks at Menaggio, a small town on the shore of Lake Como.

| ITALY |

The Italian Lakes

Calm blue waters, snowcapped mountains, and grand villas highlight this delightful journey along the Italian-Swiss border.

Known as the Italian lake district, these three lakes—Como, Lugano, and Maggiore—have attracted tourists since the days of the Grand Tour, when they became playgrounds for wealthy Europeans during the 17th and 18th centuries. Towns and villages hug the shoreline, their delicately colored, terra-cotta-roofed houses reflected in the sparkling water. Some areas, such as Bellagio on Lake Como, boast impossibly elegant villas, shrouded by rhododendrons and azaleas, built by affluent Italians over the centuries—a tradition lasting from the time of the Roman Empire, when the region first became popular for a summer sojourn. All year round, passenger boats and car ferries share the waters with wading ducks and swans. Breathing in the crisp, alpine air on deck and looking out across a shimmering expanse of blue water, with snowcapped mountains rising in the distance, the noisy bustle of nearby Milan seems a million miles away. Back on dry land the terrain is ideal for cycle tours along the banks or hiking in the vales and mountains surrounding the lakes. Less energetic travelers can take a peaceful stroll through the villages.

WHEN TO GO Although the weather is best in spring and summer, fall can be mild and is less crowded with tourists. In winter the snowy caps on the mountains provide an alternative attraction.

HOW LONG You can spend as much or as little time as you like on the water. The length of the trip depends on which lake and which route you choose.

PLANNING The major towns of Como and Bellagio have numerous dockside boat companies offering to take visitors on either ferries or hydrofoils for tours of the lakes; tickets can be bought just before boarding. There is a vast choice of accommodation in and around all the lakes.

INSIDE INFORMATION If taking a trip with landings in both Italy and Switzerland, note that the former's currency is the euro and the latter's is the Swiss franc—however, euros are generally accepted.

WEBSITE lakecomo.is

| HIGHLIGHTS

▪ Visit the **classical villas and gardens** that were home to the Dukes of Lombardy. Make sure you include a trip to Villa Carlotta outside Tremezzo, where you can see the sculptor Canova's masterpiece, "Cupid and Psyche."

▪ Pay a short visit to **Switzerland** by boat on Lake Maggiore or Lake Lugano (remember your passport!).

▪ Explore the medieval old town of **Como**, with its narrow streets and the peaceful Basilica di San Fedele.

▪ Venture to the mountains for **hiking and horse riding**, and, during the winter, **skiing**.

Top 10 Small Cruises

With their shallow draft and shorter length, small cruise ships can anchor at exotic ports, bays, and beaches off-limits to larger vessels.

❶ CANADIAN ARCTIC

Voyages through the warren of waterways in northern Canada follow the seafaring trail of the Vikings, and track the 19th- and 20th-century maritime expeditions of famous captains searching for the elusive Northwest Passage. The season generally runs June to September, when weather and sea ice make the cruise too treacherous.

PLANNING With more than a quarter century of experience in polar waters, Quark Expeditions offers several Canadian Arctic itineraries. quarkexpeditions.com

❷ BAHAMAS

With more than 700 islands scattered across an area larger than California, the Bahamas offers plenty of scope for small-ship cruising, including voyages on the tall ship Liberty Clipper. Sailing from Nassau, the 24-passenger, gaff-rigged schooner visits Eleuthera and the Exumas, with opportunities for kayak tours, snorkeling, and shore excursions, before returning to the capital.

PLANNING Week-long voyages on the Liberty Clipper take place November through May. Bring your boat shoes for the heightened grip. libertyfleet.com

❸ CUBA

The thaw in relations between Havana and Washington opened up a whole new world of cruising in the Caribbean. In addition to adding Havana and other Cuban ports to region-wide itineraries, there's also the possibility of circumnavigating the huge island with stops at historic cities and UNESCO World Heritage sites, such as Santiago, Trinidad, and Cienfuegos, among others.

PLANNING Zegrahm Expeditions circumnavigates Cuba on 56-passenger sailing ship *Le Ponant.* zegrahm.com

❹ GALÁPAGOS ISLANDS, ECUADOR

Land-based visits are possible in the archipelago that Charles Darwin immortalized. But the best way to discover the Galápagos and its incredible wildlife is a live-aboard ship that calls on at least half a dozen islands. More than a hundred vessels offer trips ranging from a few days to several weeks, with the sea lions, blue-footed boobies, and other rare animals unafraid of human presence.

PLANNING With more than 50 years experience in the Galápagos, Lindblad offers several small cruise options. expeditions.com

Sailing ships provide a relaxing way to cruise the islands of the Caribbean and explore their history, as well as their secluded bays and beaches.

❺ FRENCH POLYNESIA

Since 1954, five iterations of the M/V *Aranui* have carried passengers and cargo between Tahiti and the scattered islands of French Polynesia. Nowadays, the two-week voyage includes stops in the Tuamotu and Marqueses islands, as well as Tahuata, Ua Huka and Bora Bora.

PLANNING Launched in 2015, the 254-passenger *Aranui 5* now plies the inter-island route. aranui.com

❻ MELANESIA

Spangled with unspoiled coral reefs, WWII battlefields, and more than 1,300 distinct cultures, the tropical islands of the southwestern Pacific offer one of the planet's most diverse landscapes. Small-ship cruises through the region call on ports in New Guinea, the Solomon Islands, and Vanuatu.

PLANNING New Zealand–based Heritage Expeditions cruises Melanesia in the 50-passenger *Spirit of Enderby*. heritage-expeditions.com

❼ KIMBERLEY COAST, AUSTRALIA

Down Under's remote and rugged Kimberley Coast— which spans a mostly uninhabited arc between Broome and Darwin — can be reached only by helicopter or small ship. Among its many quirky wonders are reverse waterfalls, disappearing islands, and oceanic whirlpools.

PLANNING The *Coral Discoverer* and *Coral Expeditions I* ply the Kimberley Coast between March and October. coralexpeditions.com

❽ NUSA TENGGARA, INDONESIA

Stretching between Bali and Timor, the exotic eastern isles of Indonesia offer a montage of human culture and natural wonders as the landscape gradually transitions from Asia to Pacific. Ikat weaving, Komodo dragons, active volcanoes, and Sumba's horseback warriors spangle one of the globe's most eclectic archipelagos.

PLANNING Silolana sails the islands in modern versions of wooden Bugis schooners. silolona.com

❾ STRAIT OF MALACCA, SOUTHEAST ASIA

Although it's been one of the world's busiest trade routes for millennia, the Strait of Malacca is relatively new to modern small-ship cruising. But the route is strewn with natural and cultural gems, from the pristine reefs of the Similan Islands and the karst landscapes of Phang Nga Bay to Malacca's Peranakan culture and Langkawi's laidback beaches.

PLANNING Star Clippers stages week-long cruises between Phuket and Singapore in March–April and October–December. starclippers.com

❿ NORWEGIAN FJORDS

Established in 1893 as a passenger, cargo, and mail service for secluded Norwegian coastal communities, the historic Hurtigruten line still plies the scenic fjords between Bergen and Kirkenes, and allows ample opportunity to see the Midnight Sun in summer and the Northern Lights in winter. Ships of old have been replaced by modern vessels with all the expected amenities.

PLANNING Hurtigruten also cruises the iceberg- and wildlife-filled waters around Spitsbergen in the summer. hurtigruten.us

Gleaming white motorboats bob at anchor in the marina at Baska Voda, near Makarska on the Dalmatian coast.

CROATIA

The Dalmatian Coast

Sprinkled with some of the prettiest islands in the Adriatic, the Dalmatian coast is pure magic.

From the Zadar archipelago in the north to Dubrovnik and the Elaphite Islands at the southern tip, the countless islets and shallows of the Dalmatian coast retain an untouched feel that sets them apart from Europe's most popular island-hopping routes. The scenery is characterized by jagged mountains for much of the way and a meandering, often deeply indented coastline, where uniform red-and-white villages nestle in pine groves and flawless white pebble beaches shine with reflected sunlight. Croatia claims over 1,000 islands altogether, and those along its Dalmatian coast take an amazing variety of shapes and sizes: some long and thin, others perfectly circular; some mere rocks bristling out of a turquoise sea, others lush, inhabited islands dotted with quiet resorts and marinas. The assorted collection of sailboats bobbing up and down in almost every port along the coast will whet your appetite for an ocean adventure; this trip is a sailor's dream, with fine breezes to bear you from islet to islet. On the islands themselves, you can continue to enjoy the sea with kayaking, snorkeling, and windsurfing. Be sure to spend some time in Dubrovnik, the Pearl of the Adriatic—stroll its high city walls for splendid views over city and sea alike.

WHEN TO GO May to September, but avoid August if you don't like crowds.

HOW LONG The Croatian coast stretches for about 1,250 miles (2,000 km), with numerous attractions on the Dalmatian strip. Be selective if time is limited, and consider the popular one-way sailing route from Split to Dubrovnik.

PLANNING You can catch the ferries that ply between the islands or sail your own yacht or charter, with skipper if needed. If sailing, the Kornati Islands are considered best for beginners.

INSIDE INFORMATION A number of documents are required to sail through Croatian waters, including, in most cases, an official "vignette" that must be displayed at all times.

WEBSITES croatia.hr, croatiatraveller.com, www.jadrolinija.hr

HIGHLIGHTS

▥ Listen to the sounds of the **sea organ of Zadar**, a gigantic pipe organ played by the movements of the sea.

▥ See **Brac**, famous for its stone (used in the White House in Washington, D.C.) and the Golden Cape, a haven for sun worshipers and windsurfers.

▥ On **Hvar**, the island of lavender and pine-covered hills, explore the quaint town of Jelsa, with Venetian-style buildings mirrored in the harbor and fishing nets drying along the lanes.

▥ Visit **Vis**, an island known for its scenery, quality wines, and diving sites, and **Mljet**, an island popular for its national park.

TURKEY

Turkey's Turquoise Coast

Dotted with the ruins of many civilizations, Turkey's southwest coast offers a unique combination of leisure and history.

Rugged mountains overlook the aptly named waters of the Turquoise Coast, range after range receding into the far distance, hinting at the huge hinterlands of Asia Minor. This is the Lycian peninsula, in the southwest of Turkey, its shoreline and interior dotted with the relics of civilizations spanning more than 4,000 years— from the ancient Hittites to the city-states of Greece, from the Roman, Byzantine, and Ottoman empires to the piratical crusading knights of the Order of St. John. Two-masted, ketch-rigged *gulets*—built in the shipyards of Bodrum and Marmaris, and typically around 49–82 feet (15–25 meters) in length—have plied these waters for centuries, and many have been converted into luxury cruising vessels. Most travel from Fethiye eastward along the coast to Kekova, calling at small yacht ports, anchoring overnight in isolated coves, or venturing into Greek waters to visit the lonely island of Kastellórizo, with its pastel-colored houses and barren hillsides. Onboard, you won't have to lift a finger—the crew is constantly on hand to serve drinks and meals, or even to join you in a game or two of backgammon.

WHEN TO GO June to October for the best sunshine.

HOW LONG One-week round-trip.

PLANNING Charter flights depart from most European airports to Dalaman. You can join a cruise organized by an all-inclusive tour operator. Alternatively, groups of up to ten people can charter an entire gulet for themselves.

INSIDE INFORMATION Most gulets have a crew of four, including a skipper, deckhand, engineer, and cook, and have comfortable cabins with full bathrooms. It is sometimes easier to get to Turkey via nearby Greek islands, such as Rhodes and Kos, using cheap holiday charter flights and local ferry connections to Turkish ports, including Marmaris (from Rhodes) and Bodrum (from Kos).

WEBSITES bluecruise.org, journeyanatolia.com, cachet-travel.co.uk

HIGHLIGHTS

▓ Look out for the silvery flicker of the **flying fish** that leap from the water by the side of your boat.

▓ The Lycian coastline is blessed with some very well-preserved **classical sites**. On many gulets, crew members will take you on a guided tour; the ancient Lycian city of Xanthus is a particular highlight.

▓ Off the north coast of Kekova you can **snorkel** over sunken ruins of the Hellenistic city of Apollonia, inundated by an earthquake centuries ago.

▓ Enjoy the superb Turkish **breakfasts** onboard – with coffee, yogurt, honey, and much more offered.

The gulet is a modern version of the ancient cargo ships that worked along the coast of southwest Turkey.

ACROSS WATER

BY ROAD | BY RAIL | ON FOOT | IN SEARCH OF CULTURE | IN GOURMET HEAVEN | INTO THE ACTION | UP AND AWAY | IN THEIR FOOTSTEPS

Greek Island-Hopping

Terraced hillsides, olive groves, whitewashed villages overlooked by windmills, and blue-domed churches—these are the scenes that give the Cyclades their unfailing delight.

The graceful columns of a ruined temple stand out against a brilliant blue sky. White houses sparkle on rocky hillsides, while on the shoreline a sandy beach faces out across the azure waters of the Aegean. Variety, and almost complete flexibility as you hop from island to island, are among the delights of a journey through the Cyclades, scattered over the southern Aegean from Andros in the north to volcanic Santoríni in the south. Every day, dozens of ferries ply between them and the mainland, allowing you the freedom to base yourself on one island and explore its neighbors, or to keep moving on. Each island—and there are some 220 of them, although many are uninhabited specks—has its own distinct character, so you can pick according to your mood. If it's nightlife you're after, Mykonos will probably suit you. But if you tire of beaches, bars, and clubs, Delos lies within sight, a short ferry-ride away. In Greek mythology, it was the birthplace of the god Apollo and his twin sister, the huntress Artemis. Among many ancient remains, you can visit the Terrace of the Lions, an avenue of marble lions, built before 600 B.C. and dedicated to Apollo, or marvel at the mosaics in the House of the Dolphins. On Folegandros, farther south, a labyrinthine village of white houses perches giddily above steep sea cliffs, while the vast, sea-filled crater of Santorini (Thira)—the product of a volcanic cataclysm more than 6,000 years ago— has some of the most stunning views and sunsets in all of Greece.

WHEN TO GO From early June to mid-October, but avoid the mid-August Asomatos holiday week.

HOW LONG Allow two to four hours between islands, depending on whether you use conventional ferries, fast catamarans, or even faster hydrofoils.

PLANNING Ticket agencies line each island harbor. You can buy last-minute tickets at the pier an hour or so before departure, but it is best to buy at least a day in advance. Guesthouse representatives meet every ferry, advertising rooms to rent. For stylish or luxurious accommodation, book ahead.

INSIDE INFORMATION Accommodation on the ferries ranges from Pullman-style reclining seats to first-class cabins with bunks. On longer journeys, take your own bottled water and snacks or a picnic lunch.

WEBSITES gtp.gr, gadventures.co.uk

HIGHLIGHTS

▥ The **ferry rides** are part of the pleasure of the trip. For the best views, travel by **conventional ferry**. Hydrofoils get there faster, but have only airport-style, interior seats.

▥ Explore **Tínos**, where donkey tracks crisscross the peaceful hills, and goats, butterflies, and lizards are your only companions. The island's **Church of Panagia Evangelistria** is a place of pilgrimage, famous for its icon of the Virgin Mary, reputed to have miracle-working powers.

▥ **Swim, snorkel, and sunbathe** on the big (but often crowded) beaches of **Mykonos** or in tiny coves on **Tínos** or **Folegandros.**

▥ Hotels, bars, and tourist shops crowd the shoreline of **Naxos**, the largest of the islands. Inland, you will find **fruit and olive groves** surrounding **ancient villages**, with the peak of **Mount Zas**, the highest point in the Cyclades, rising above.

▥ On **Santoríni**, rent a **donkey** to take you to the rim of the 900-ft (275 m) crater. Or you can take the **cable car** – faster and more comfortable than the donkey ride.

Opposite: A bell tower in the cliff-top village of Oía on Santoríni glows in the soft light of dawn, while hundreds of feet below a schooner glides over the tranquil waters of the Aegean. Above left: Donkeys are still used as beasts of burden on steep hillsides. Above right: The gateway to the unfinished Temple of Apollo on Naxos frames the sea.

Greater kudu, about to drink, look up at the merest hint of danger.

Into the Okavango

Gliding through the wetlands in a dugout canoe offers an entirely different take on Africa's bounteous inland delta.

Virtually no roads cross the world's largest inland delta. But for thousands of years, local inhabitants have hunted, gathered, and explored the Okavango wetlands of northern Botswana in wooden dugout canoes called *mokoros.* Punted along in the same manner as Venetian gondolas, the tiny boats (which normally seat no more than two or three passengers) are a slow and serene means of moving through one of Africa's most important wildlife habitats. The vast swamps are home to thousands of crocodiles and hippos, a good number of elephants and predators, as well as specialized wetlands creatures like the water-adapted lechwe antelope. Birdlife is also profuse, with more than 400 species. Rather than disturb the animals with an outboard engine, mokoros allow for a covert approach, at times so close it's exhilarating. Gliding through the warren of waterways in a dugout also allows for plenty of time to study the local flora, a mosaic of marshlands, small salt pans, open savannah, and small palm-studded islands. Most of the safari camps in and around the Okavango offer mokoro day trips, or for a longer safari—including overnight camping journeys in the heart of the wetlands—try the operators in the town of Maun.

WHEN TO GO The winter dry season between June and August brings the mildest weather to the Okavango, as well as high water to expedite mokoro safaris.

HOW LONG Stay at least ten days to explore the vast delta by air, land, and water, camping out or staying at luxury wilderness camps or lodges.

PLANNING Old Bridge Tours & Safaris in Maun offers self-catered and fully catered mokoro safaris into the Okavango lasting from one to four days. Trips include a local poler/guide to propel your boat through the swamps.

INSIDE INFORMATION In addition to wildlife, mokoros are used for visiting ethnic groups in the Okavango, including the Bugakhwe and Lanikwhe Bushmen (San) people.

WEBSITES botswanatourism.co.bw, africansafaribotswana.com, okavangobudgetsafaris.com

HIGHLIGHTS

■ Camp beneath the stars on **Chief's Island**, a former royal hunting ground in the middle of the delta.

■ Photograph the "big five" in **Moremi Game Reserve**, a national park that protects much of the Okavango.

■ Hop a scenic flight from **Maun** for a bird's-eye view of the vast wetlands that you will soon be canoeing through.

■ Ogle the ancient artwork of **the Tsodilo Hills**, a World Heritage site on the western edge of the Okavango that preserves more than 4,500 ancient rock paintings.

MALAWI

Steamship Cruise on Lake Malawi

A journey across Lake Malawi on the vintage steamer Ilala *channels a bygone age of African travel.*

Humphrey Bogart and Katharine Hepburn may not be along for the ride, but a cruise across Lake Malawi on the MV *Ilala* is a throwback to the romantic era when steamboats were the primary means of traveling the great lakes of Africa. Built in Scotland just after World War II, the vessel was taken apart, shipped around the Cape of Good Hope, and then transported by train and truck from the Indian Ocean coast to the British protectorate of Nyasaland, where it was reassembled and launched in 1951. It's been a Lake Malawi fixture ever since. Nowadays, the diesel-powered vessel makes weekly cargo/passenger runs from its home port of Monkey Bay to sleepy Chilumba in the far north with stops at a dozen towns and villages along the western (Malawi) shore. It also calls on the secluded Chizumulu Island and historic Likoma Island, where David Livingston's missionary society established an Anglican outpost in 1880. The route also passes within sight of Liuli (formerly Sphinx Haven) on the Tanzanian shore, where a British gunboat and German armed steamer clashed in the first naval engagement of World War I. Recently retrofitted and upgraded, the *Ilala* features four classes of service from sleeping on the open deck to cozy little cabins.

WHEN TO GO Between May and August – the cooler part of the dry season.

HOW LONG With a scheduled departure time of 8 a.m. every Wednesday morning, the round-trip journey from Monkey Bay takes five full days to complete.

PLANNING Monkey Bay is a short commuter flight or a three-hour drive from Lilongwe International Airport in Malawi's capital. A bar and restaurant on the top deck serves modest African-style meals and local beer. At each port of call, seafaring hawkers provide an alternative to onboard food and drink.

INSIDE INFORMATION The Owner's Cabin offers the most comfortable accommodation once aboard.

WEBSITE malawitourism.com

HIGHLIGHTS

▦ Catch the Lake of the Stars **music festival** in late September, staged on the lakeshore in different towns along the *Ilala* route.

▦ Dive into the sun, sand, and inland sea of **Cape Maclear** in Lake Malawi National Park, a World Heritage site near Monkey Bay.

▦ Admire the unexpected immensity of **St. Peter's Cathedral** (1903) on Likoma and then swim at one of the island's beaches.

▦ Spot wildlife while hiking, biking, or **horseback riding** in Nyika National Park near Chilumba.

The MV *Ilala* ferries both people and cargo in a leisurely route across the lake, stopping in both Mozambique and Malawi.

The Lower Zambezi River

Paddle down one of Africa's legendary rivers, and see some of the world's most extraordinary wildlife along the way.

British explorer David Livingstone, the first westerner to paddle down the Zambezi River, said of the journey that "scenes so lovely must have been gazed upon by angels in their flight." Little has changed since then—modern-day explorers can venture out on the Lower Zambezi in a two-man Canadian canoe and find themselves mere feet away from towering elephants, hippos dipping lazily through the water, and zebra grazing on the banks. The river winds its way past two great swathes of national parkland—the Mana Pools World Heritage site to the south and Lower Zambezi National Park to the north—so you can look forward to seeing an array of wildlife: baboons, impala, and, if you're lucky, lions and leopards. Such close proximity to the animals means that the thrill of danger is never far away, but seasoned river guides provide protection and expert knowledge—warding off crocodiles and hippos by banging the side of the boat with their paddles, or guiding the canoes into the shallows when necessary. From your boat you'll enjoy views across sweeping, open plains and golden grasses, and, in the evening, watch the legendary African sunset from your comfortable riverside encampment.

WHEN TO GO Bird-watchers should go in the summer months – December to April – for the greatest range of birds. May to August provides cooler, drier weather.

HOW LONG The majority of safaris depart from Kariba and travel downstream, lasting from three to ten days. It's a good idea to plan for some time to unwind in Kariba after the safari.

PLANNING Most canoe safari companies offer two types of trip: the more expensive "backed-up" option, which includes comfortable campsites with pre-erected tents, proper beds, and electric lighting; and the cheaper "participatory" option, where travelers are expected to help out, pitch their own tents, and cook their own dinners.

INSIDE INFORMATION Take a waterproof container for your camera and any other valuables. Most trips require no previous canoeing experience, but it's best to check before booking.

WEBSITE riverhorsesafaris.com

HIGHLIGHTS

▥ Nudge your canoe past large **pods of hippos**, their broad backs slick and glistening with water.

▥ Take a lunchtime **siesta** for a break from paddling. Lie under a tree and relax in the shade.

▥ Fish for the aggressive **tiger fish**, and cook and eat your catch at the end of the day.

▥ Visit **Lower Zambezi National Park**, where you can see big game animals such as lions and elephants in their natural habitat.

▥ If you have time, consider taking a **houseboat out on Lake Kariba** for a luxury counterpoint to canoeing.

A safari by canoe along the Zambezi allows all the time in the world to gaze and be gazed upon.

Giant baobab trees dot the landscape on either side of the Mangoky River.

ACROSS WATER

BY ROAD · BY RAIL · ON FOOT · IN SEARCH OF CULTURE · IN GOURMET HEAVEN · INTO THE ACTION · UP AND AWAY · IN THEIR FOOTSTEPS

| MADAGASCAR |

The Mangoky River

A peaceful journey in a raft on the remote Mangoky River will take you past the matchless landscape of western Madagascar.

Madagascar is the land of *mora-mora* ("slowly-slowly"), and the leisurely pace of your inflatable raft as it drifts downstream perfectly encapsulates the laid-back Malagasy approach to life. More than 80 percent of the flora and fauna is unique to the island, and the still, green Mangoky River in the southwest carries you through some of the most exceptional scenery that you will ever see. In places, the riverbanks are lined with stunted baobab trees, their spindly branches reaching up like fingers toward the clear skies, forming the largest baobab forest in the world. Elsewhere, you'll be paddling silently past dense forest or the rough scrub of spiny deserts. Keep your eyes peeled for lemurs, the curious, monkey-like primates that scamper through the undergrowth and hurl themselves in elegant arcs from branch to branch. Look out for the sprightly ring-tailed and red-fronted varieties, as well as the extremely rare Verreaux's sifaka, whose wise black face is framed with tufts of snow white fur. Buzzards, peregrine falcons, and herons nest along the river. Nighttime brings further delights: camping out on one of the many glorious sandy beaches that are strewn along the riverbank—and waking the next morning to the trilled calls of the lemurs.

WHEN TO GO Go during the Madagascan winter (May to October) for warm and dry weather. The rest of the year can be uncomfortably hot.

HOW LONG Trips are usually around a week long.

PLANNING Package trips to the southwest often include a period of calm-water rafting on the Mangoky. Alternatively, arrange your own trip with a local boatman, camping out on the banks at night.

INSIDE INFORMATION The waterborne disease bilharzia is present throughout Madagascar, so be wary of taking a dip, and make sure that the water you use for bathing is safe.

WEBSITE remoterivers.com

| HIGHLIGHTS

▦ Watch out for unique species of **waterfowl** and **rare orchids** along the riverbank, as well as the **lemurs**, in this nature-lover's paradise.

▦ **Camp out** on the empty beaches, light a fire to cook your meal, and gaze up into the brilliant, starry night sky.

▦ If you are lucky, you might catch sight of a **crocodile**, although poaching in recent times has vastly reduced their numbers.

▦ Take advantage of encounters with **Malagasy villagers** — all unfailingly polite, friendly, and welcoming.

MADAGASCAR

Bevoay · Bereroho

Mangoky

AFRICA

Chapter 2

BY ROAD

The world's greatest overland journeys are like a series of endlessly unfolding stories. Some roads are passages from nature's own narratives—climbing mountain ranges carved by ice and fire, crossing multicolored deserts or wildernesses sheltering the planet's rarest wildlife. Others tell tales of human lives—unfolding the mysterious remnants of long-vanished peoples, historic battlegrounds, ancient trade routes, imposing palaces, and soaring cathedrals. The itineraries here span the globe and come in every shape and size. Some, such as the Vermont fall foliage tour, are short and easy drives you can do in a weekend. Others, longer and more demanding, offer great adventure. The Grand Trunk Road is a 1,190-mile (1,920 kilometer), four-week journey from border to coast of India. Between these extremes are routes that offer varying degrees of challenge. Some are cultural icons. The corniches of the French Riviera have starred in countless movie car chases. And US Route 66, in both literature and music, is the highway to the heart of the American dream.

"Get your kicks on Route 66" run the words of a popular song from the 1940s. John Steinbeck evoked the great Chicago-to-Los Angeles highway in *The Grapes of Wrath*, his classic novel about Dust Bowl farmers seeking a new life in the west.

The Fall in Vermont

This panoramic mountain drive through Vermont's astonishing fall colors reveals a tapestry of brilliant hues.

A scenic loop of about 140 miles (225 kilometers) starting in Burlington takes you through the full splendor of the fall in Vermont, where on crisp, clear days, blue skies make a vivid background to the red, yellow, and orange leaves. Connoisseurs of seasonal foliage know that this display is unmatched, and the annual show brings visitors from around the world. Two factors account for the color. Hardwood trees that produce the most vivid hues are abundant, especially the bright red sugar maples that yield Vermont's famous maple syrup. And the mountain slopes that traverse the state provide a sweeping canvas for the spectacle. While the main Burlington-to-Stowe route offers many appealing stops, don't be limited by it; make your own discoveries on quiet leafy byways. Stop at country stores to stock up on two Vermont specialties, cheddar cheese and maple syrup, and at cider mills serving up this seasonal drink. Many small towns celebrate the fall with festivals featuring local crafts and homemade foods. Stowe, with its quaint green-and-white-steepled church, is particularly historic—large parts of the town are on the National Register of Historic Places. Before leaving Stowe, take the ski lift for a last lingering view of the fall color.

WHEN TO GO Early to mid-October is usually when the colors are at their fullest.

HOW LONG Three days will allow for a good sampling of the towns and vistas.

PLANNING The first two weekends of October are the busiest of the year, so book as early as possible. You need to reserve rooms at the smaller country inns months ahead. Reservations are generally much easier to come by midweek rather than on weekends. The less formal ski mountain lodges are best bets for last-minute bookings; most ski areas have their own reservation services to help.

INSIDE INFORMATION Different areas peak at different times. The foliage forecaster on the Vermont Vacation website gives details.

WEBSITES vermontvacation.com, foliage-vermont.com, visit-vermont.com

HIGHLIGHTS

▪ **Shelburne** offers two attractions: the superb folk art and Americana collections at the **Shelburne Museum**, and the beautiful rolling landscape of **Shelburne Farms**, a 1,645-acre (665 ha) working farm.

▪ **Middlebury**, a pretty college town, is home to the **Vermont State Crafts Center** at Frog Hollow, featuring work by some of the state's best artisans.

▪ **Brandon Gap**, a dramatic up-and-down route across the **Green Mountains**, shows off the color blanketing the mountainsides. There is a lookout at the highest elevation, 2,170 ft (660 m). Hikers will find excellent trails along the gap.

This white barn is nearly hidden by the red, orange, and gold foliage of the maples.

The Straits of Mackinac separate Lakes Michigan and Huron. Here, yellow clapboard houses face the water on Mackinac Island.

ACROSS WATER

BY ROAD

BY RAIL

ON FOOT

IN SEARCH OF CULTURE

IN GOURMET HEAVEN

INTO THE ACTION

UP AND AWAY

IN THEIR FOOTSTEPS

| MICHIGAN | WISCONSIN |

Lake Michigan Shoreline

The magnificent Lake Michigan shoreline lures with big cities, quaint villages, giant sand dunes, and vistas as wide as an ocean.

A clockwise drive around Lake Michigan is a sampling of the best of America. The lake feels like an inland sea—118 miles (190 kilometers) wide and 307 miles (494 kilometers) long—with Wisconsin spreading out to its west and Michigan to the north and east. On the eastern shore, miles of white sand invite you to relax, while towering dunes are fun to climb … and then slide down. Near Empire, Michigan, is Sleeping Bear Dunes National Lakeshore, where white-capped waves crash onto the shore and you can strike out along a 7.5-mile (12 kilometer) scenic drive—you can also leave your car and follow a hiking trail. As you round the bend of the lake's southern end, you reach the sprawling cities of Chicago and Milwaukee. Pleasant harbors stud the western, Wisconsin shore, ranging from fishing villages to refined towns. Door County is dubbed the "Cape Cod of the Midwest" for its lighthouses and waterside resorts. A 75-mile (120 kilometer) peninsula, separating the main body of Lake Michigan from Green Bay, it has two moods—calm on the sheltered Green Bay shore, wild along Lake Michigan. Finally, in the north, you reach the wilderness of Michigan's Upper Peninsula.

WHEN TO GO Spring blossoms, summer beaches, and fall colors make this a prime destination nine months of the year.

HOW LONG A complete loop of the lake covers 1,160 miles (1,867 km); one week is a minimum to enjoy the many sights. If time is short, either side of the lake is rewarding on its own.

PLANNING Some of the choicest inns are found in the town of Union Pier and Saugatuck, MI, and in Egg Harbor and Fish Creek in Wisconsin's Door County. Avoid the Green Bay area during a home football game weekend, as hotel prices are greatly escalated.

INSIDE INFORMATION To shorten the trip, take the ferry between Ludington and Manitowoc. The four-hour crossing on the SS *Badger* runs from mid-May to mid-October. The ferry takes bikes, cars, and RVs, as well as foot passengers.

WEBSITES travelwisconsin.com, experiencegr.com

HIGHLIGHTS

▥ The **world's largest weather vane** stands 48 ft (15 m) tall in the city of Montague, MI.

▥ Saugatuck, MI, is both an artists' colony and a beach destination known for its **dune-schooners**, buggies giving rides through the high dunes.

▥ **Mackinac Bridge** stretches for 5 miles (8 km) across the Straits of Mackinac between Lake Michigan and Lake Huron. It is one of the **longest suspension bridges** ever built and provides spectacular views.

▥ Door County, WI, blooms with **more than a million daffodils** each May during its Festival of Blossoms.

As the sun rises at Cape Hatteras, fishermen cast their lines out to sea.

NORTH CAROLINA

Route 12 in the Outer Banks

Wild seascapes and the footprints of pirates lure visitors to the sunshine and charm of North Carolina's Outer Banks.

This 80-mile (129 kilometer) beach drive runs along a meeting place of land and ocean, of human activity and wilderness. The Outer Banks of North Carolina are a chain of narrow barrier islands that curve out into the Atlantic and back again like a protecting arm. Slender but enduring, they have withstood thousands of years of onslaught by wind and wave. Long stretches of beach and dunes, fringed with wetlands and woodlands, the Outer Banks are a magnet for windsurfers and beachcombers. Their blue-green water may be dotted with fishermen, snorkelers, and sailboats, or buffeted by an approaching gale, the beaches empty except for scampering sandpipers. Now and again, storms expose an old wreck, testament to the treachery of these waters. Today, fishermen still keep a constant eye on the changing weather and current systems. But it was also here that the first white settlers found landfall and Blackbeard the Pirate cast anchor. Symbols of human endurance dot the islands: historic lighthouses and seaside villages like Ocracoke, where shrimp boats sit at weathered docks awaiting the next tide. Here, too, as migrating geese or seabirds screech overhead, you can relive the moment when the first engine-powered human flight took off, over a century ago.

WHEN TO GO Early March through mid-October; the least chance of rain is in May and June.

HOW LONG The 80-mile (129 km) drive can be done in three hours, but to make the most of it, you should plan on a full day.

PLANNING The drive begins in the north as you enter the Outer Banks over Wright Memorial Bridge and ends in Ocracoke, with a ferry trip to the mainland. Be sure to make a ferry reservation in advance. Camping and lodging are available on the Outer Banks for longer stays.

INSIDE INFORMATION On warm, sunny days this route can be crowded with cyclists and beachgoers, so allow extra time for delays.

WEBSITES outerbanks.org, ocracoke-nc.com

HIGHLIGHTS

■ The Wright brothers first took flight at **Kill Devil Hills**. Today, modern-day aviators launch themselves skyward in colorful hang gliders from the dunes of Jockey's Ridge State Park.

■ The **North Carolina Aquarium** on Roanoke Island, just south of Kill Devil Hills, captures in microcosm the region's underwater world, from mountain streams to the offshore marine realm.

■ **Cape Hatteras Lighthouse** is the tallest brick lighthouse on the American coast. A climb of 268 steps to the top brings you sweeping vistas of Cape Hatteras National Seashore.

Miami to Key West on Highway 1

Take a dreamlike drive down Florida's Overseas Highway from the neon-chic of Miami's South Beach to lush, tropical Key West.

Pure, ethereal beauty is the hallmark of the legendary Overseas Highway. The route begins in the sun-and-sand playground of Miami, with its ultratrendy, art-deco South Beach. Hopscotching from island to island along the causeway brings moments when land is not visible ahead or behind, and you have the delightfully surreal sense of driving across the surface of the limitless, radiant Caribbean sea. Then the road arrives at yet another in the chain of emerald green keys—a name derived from *cayos*, the Spanish for "small islands"—decked with tropical palms, hibiscus, and bougainvillea. Along the way, you'll discover fine sand beaches and a wonderful collection of state parks that conserve portions of the keys' fragile and beautiful wildlife environments. At journey's end is Key West, the fun-and-funky, self-proclaimed capital of the "Conch Republic," where artists have renovated old key houses as B&Bs and the independent spirit of "Papa" Hemingway still infuses the island's culture. Join in the nightly sunset celebrations at Mallory Square—the sword swallowers, chainsaw jugglers, and other buskers are quintessentially Key West.

WHEN TO GO All year, but there is the risk of hurricanes between August and October.

HOW LONG Allow at least four days to see the highlights of this 168-mile (270 km) journey, but stay a week if you can.

PLANNING Make reservations well in advance to secure the best accommodations, and in Key West choose lodging with a parking space.

INSIDE INFORMATION Mile markers are posted along the road so you always know just where you are and how far you are from Key West.

WEBSITES fla-keys.com, keywest.com, floridastateparks.org

HIGHLIGHTS

▨ Have breakfast in a **sidewalk café** along Ocean Drive and watch the endless parade of beautiful people skating and cycling along the bike path of Miami's South Beach.

▨ Tour the elegant mansion and gardens of **Vizcaya**, the 1920s Miami home of International Harvester heir James Deering.

▨ **Snorkel** among the coral reefs and wrecks at Key West. Then head for delicious seafood at one of the many restaurants.

The causeway of Highway 1 links the Florida Keys like the thread of an emerald necklace.

Top 10
City Bike Tours

Cycling is an enthralling way to experience your surroundings. Navigate the hidden depths of these cities alone or in a group tour.

❶ BIKE & BAGELS, MONTREAL, CANADA

Montreal is a city of bikes and neighborhoods, with more than 400 miles (644 km) of bike paths connecting Old Montreal with various ethnic and lifestyle enclaves. Ça Roule Montréal's guided neighborhood bike tour includes the Gay Village, the Plateau, Mile End, and the Latin Quarter, with a stop along the way for cream cheese, lox, and bagels. There are also tours geared toward families of up to two parents and two children, and a Vista-Architecture tour, which explores green spaces in the area and shows off Montreal's stunning panoramic views.

PLANNING Montreal's Bixi bike-sharing system includes more than 5,000 bikes at 450 stations. caroulemontreal.com/en

❷ BREWERIES BY BIKE, PORTLAND, OREGON

Stop at three trendy microbreweries on this relaxing cycle through the East Side "Brewery Blocks" of the city that invented craft beer in the 1980s and is now home to over 60 breweries in total. Guided by a local suds expert, the tours run rain or shine and the brews to sample change with the seasons. Bikers must be at least 21 years of age, and don't forget to take home your free pint glass at the end.

PLANNING Portland's popular Waterfront Loop bike path unfolds 11 miles (18 km) along the Willamette River. portlandbicycletours.com

❸ LA CICLOVIA, BOGOTÁ, COLOMBIA

On Sundays and holidays, motor vehicles are banned from 7 a.m. to 2 p.m. on major streets in central Bogotá and cyclists, rollerbladers, skateboarders, and pedestrians take over the thoroughfares. A much-loved tradition since 1976, La Ciclovia is easy to bike on your own or join a guided tour to see the best of the city.

PLANNING The Vuelta a Colombia, one of the globe's premier bike races, takes place in August. biketoursandrentalsbogota.com

❹ IMPERIAL HUTONG BIKE TOUR, BEIJING, CHINA

Beijing's old alleys (*hutongs*)—some of them 700 years old—provide an insight into both the past and contemporary daily life in the Chinese capital. This cycle down the cobblestone lanes of the city's ancient warren includes a spin around the Shichahai Lakes, the Imperial Palace, and Tiananmen Square, and sheds light on local civilian life from past to present.

PLANNING Bicycle Kingdom also organizes guided mountain biking rides through the Fragrant Hills on Beijing's west side. bikebeijing.com

Mornings on Boat Quay in Singapore are perfect for a peaceful bike ride, but come nightfall, the area changes character as locals and visitors hit the streets to eat and drink at trendy restaurants and bars.

❺ BIKES & BITES TOUR, SINGAPORE

Eat and drink your way across the Lion City on this full-day gastronomical ride that includes a traditional *kopi tiam* coffee shop, lunch in Little India, and several exotic spice and food shops. The city's flat terrain makes for easing cycling.

PLANNING DIY bikers can cycle between Singapore's various green spaces via the bike paths of the Park Connector Network. letsgobikesingapore.com

❻ EARLY MORNING BIKE TOUR, MUMBAI, INDIA

With streets largely devoid of traffic and the tropical air cool and fresh, early morning is the best time to explore Mumbai on a bike. Marine Drive along the Indian Ocean, the city's Victorian train station, and the fishermen of Sassoon Dock are some of the sights along the way.

PLANNING The tour is run by a nonprofit organization, with 80% of proceeds going to community projects. realitytoursandtravel.com

❼ FROM DUSK TILL DAWN BIKE TOUR, MOSCOW, RUSSIA

Literally staged in the middle of the night (1–5:30 a.m.), this insomniac cycle around the Russian capital avoids the crowds and cars while whizzing past the Kremlin, Red Square, the old KGB headquarters, the Sparrow Hills, Novodevichy Convent, and more. Depending on your mood, it includes optional stops at a vodka bar and all-night bookshop.

PLANNING Given the harsh winters, most Moscow bike tours run only from April through October. moscowbiketours.com

❽ DANISH DESIGN BY BIKE, COPENHAGEN, DENMARK

In a city where more than one-third of all journeys are by bike, this tour combines the two traditional Danish passions: cycling and design. The route includes more than a dozen independent shops that produce everything from furniture and chocolates to ceramics, glassware, and jewelry.

PLANNING The I Bike CPH app for cell phones includes voice navigation instructions and very detailed maps. visitcopenhagen.com/copenhagen/sightseeing/bike-tours

❾ BERLIN WALL BIKE TOUR, GERMANY

Checkpoint Charlie, the Berlin Wall Memorial Museum, and the infamous Mauerpark "Death Strip" of what the communists called the "Anti-Fascist Protection Rampart" (aka the Berlin Wall) are some of the stops on this 9.5-mile (15 km) cycle through the heart of the German capital.

PLANNING Just outside of Berlin, Potsdam offers the half-day Alter Fritz bike route through several centuries of Prussian history. berlinonbike.de/en

❿ SUNSET BIKE TOUR, SEVILLE, SPAIN

Riverside promenades, wide paseos, and broad plazas make the Andalusian city a perfect place for cycling, especially at sunset when the city's waterways glimmer like molten silver. With around 125 miles (200 km) of dedicated bike paths, Seville is considered Spain's most cycle-friendly city.

PLANNING Sevici municipal bike rental offers 2,500 bikes at 250 stations for just over €1 per hour. sevillabiketour.com

The Golden Highway

Sample some real hidden delights as you travel
this quirky route through the heart of the Midwest.

Once a coast-to-coast route between the Atlantic and the Pacific, Route 40 was the first transportation link from the East to California. On this stretch through Missouri, Kansas, and Colorado, Route 40 has been mostly replaced by I-70. Pull off the interstate to explore tranquil state parks or discover quirky and sometimes downright odd attractions, such as Leila's Hair Museum in Independence, Missouri. In Kansas, visit sites that range from Mushroom Rock State Park outside Brookville with its 25-foot (7.6 meter) high mushroom-shaped rocks, to an 80-foot (24 meter) tall easel bearing a giant copy of Van Gogh's "Sunflowers" in Goodland, to the Fort Wallace Museum in Wallace, which gives an insight into life at an army post. In Glenwood Springs, Colorado, enjoy a gondola ride that gives sweeping views of the Rocky Mountains before exploring Glenwood Caverns. The section of I-70 at Glenwood Canyon was opened in 1992—the last part of this cross-country highway to be completed. Finish your trip in Fruita, Colorado, where fossil remains of more than 30 dinosaur species have been discovered. At Dinosaur Journey, you'll see many of these prehistoric bones on display, alongside robotic reconstructions. Nearby, you can take guided hikes past quarries where dinosaur remains are still being discovered.

WHEN TO GO Spring or fall are more pleasant than the intense heat of summer or the bitter chill of winter. However, skiers, snowboarders, and ice fishermen will find winter the best time to go.

HOW LONG Doing the drive in a week allows plenty of time for sightseeing stops.

PLANNING If you are making the trip in winter, check ahead for snowstorm warnings. Ski resorts Vail and Aspen are both easily accessible from I-70 just west of Denver.

INSIDE INFORMATION Kansas City is world famous for barbecue and has more than 100 barbecue restaurants that range from tiny shacks to fancy (and expensive) eateries.

WEBSITES route40.net, visitmo.com, travelks.com, roadsideamerica.com

HIGHLIGHTS

■ Churchill coined the phrase "Iron Curtain" when making a speech at Westminster College in Fulton, MO, in 1946. Today, the college has a **Winston Churchill Memorial and Library**, and a rebuilt London church, designed by Sir Christopher Wren in 1677. It incorporates 700 tons (710 tonnes) of stones from the original, destroyed in World War II.

■ Kansas may or may not be **tornado capital of the world**, but you might catch sight of a twister on your drive.

Huge fields of corn and wheat – the crops that brought wealth to the Midwest – spread out on either side of the highway.

ACROSS WATER

BY ROAD

BY RAIL

ON FOOT

IN SEARCH OF CULTURE

IN GOURMET HEAVEN

INTO THE ACTION

UP AND AWAY

IN THEIR FOOTSTEPS

The trail twists and turns down the sides of the Columbia River Gorge in Oregon.

| MISSOURI | KANSAS | NEBRASKA | WYOMING | IDAHO | OREGON |

The Oregon Trail

Follow the Conestoga wagons across prairies and mountain passes to re-create the pioneers' trek from Missouri to the Oregon Territory.

Emigrants seeking farmland in Oregon and gold in California started traveling America's east-west overland route in 1843. From Missouri this dogged human trickle crept, on foot and in wagon trains, over the uncharted expanses of Kansas, Nebraska, Wyoming, and Idaho, to Oregon. They followed the Platte River to its source in the Rockies, crossed the mountains via South Pass in southwest Wyoming, then trailed the Snake and Columbia Rivers—a 2,000-mile (3,220 kilometer) journey across prairie and desert, along gorges and over ridges. Following the route today you experience the history that shaped America, and relive the wonder of first seeing that beautiful landscape—the 470-foot (143 meter) Chimney Rock near Bridgeport, Nebraska; the Craters of the Moon near Arco and Shoshone Falls near Twin Falls, Idaho; and the most welcome sight of all to the settlers: the lush Grande Ronde valley, gateway to Oregon.

WHEN TO GO Spring is the best time to see the West, when it is at its greenest, freshest, and prettiest.

HOW LONG Aiming for about 300 miles (483 km) a day allows stops at interesting points along the way, and means the 2,000-mile (3,220 km) journey takes about a week.

PLANNING The National Park Service has identified the official route and it has been designated a National Historic Trail. No road precisely follows the path, but each of the six states along the way distributes a free guide to the highways and back roads most closely approximating it.

INSIDE INFORMATION West of central Nebraska, towns with lodging facilities are often many miles apart, so make reservations in advance for a summer trip.

WEBSITES nps.gov/oreg, oregontrail101.com

| HIGHLIGHTS

▥ **Courthouse Rock** and **Jail Rock** near Bridgeport, NE, were among the first landmarks for the original pioneers. These huge stones rear out of the prairie, towering above the grasses and dwarfing humans.

▥ The giant red rock of **Scotts Bluff** juts above the Great Plains in western Nebraska "like a splendid old fort," in the words of one emigrant. You can also see original wagon ruts there.

▥ Many pioneers carved their names in **Independence Rock** near Casper, WY. If they were on schedule, they should have reached the rock by the fourth of July.

▥ Southern Idaho's **Lava Hot Springs** make a relaxing stop. The natural hot spring pools are set among grottoes and surrounded by mountain peaks. You can float in the water and stare up at the sky.

The San Juan Skyway

An unforgettable Rocky Mountain adventure offers sky-high peaks,
Butch Cassidy's hometown, and the haunting ruins of Mesa Verde.

The San Juan Skyway serves up America's preeminent Rocky Mountain scenic drive—a tour starting in the chic Western streets of Durango and looping through the high-country mining towns of Silverton, Ouray, and Telluride. Fortunes in silver and gold have been made in these hills. In fact, the road between Ouray and Silverton is called the Million Dollar Highway for the value of the low-grade gold ore said to have been used to pave it. Today, the riches here are for all to enjoy—views of 14,000-foot (4,267 meter) peaks, sparkling mountain streams, alpine meadows smothered in wildflowers, and forests, such as San Juan National Forest. Telluride, outlaw Butch Cassidy's home, has a Wild West flavor, but is also an outdoor recreation and cultural center, with superb skiing, fine galleries, and film and jazz festivals. From Telluride, the road descends through the stunning landscapes of the Colorado Plateau, to the 1,000-year-old cliff ruins of Mesa Verde National Park, where the ancestors of the modern Pueblo people once lived. You can explore these sites, still sacred to their descendants, on ranger-guided tours. The cliff dwellers grew crops on the mesa's top, but lived in stone-walled homes below its rim, sheltered by the overhanging cliffs.

WHEN TO GO The road is open year-round, but is most traveled in July and August.

HOW LONG You can do the 233-mile (375 km) drive in one day, but allow three days for sightseeing in the major towns and exploring Mesa Verde National Park.

PLANNING Check on road conditions in winter; four-wheel-drive is recommended from November to April, when snowfalls can be heavy. Be prepared for afternoon thunderstorms in the summer. Although Mesa Verde National Park is open year-round, some ruins are closed in winter.

INSIDE INFORMATION Fall is the most spectacular season, when the aspens turn color and blanket the mountains in shades of gold and amber.

WEBSITES durango.org, nps.gov/meve, codot.gov/travel/scenic-byways

HIGHLIGHTS

▨ Walk down Silverton's infamous **Blair Street**, with its Western facades, and picture those Wild West days of gamblers, miners, gunslingers, and dance-hall girls.

▨ Ride a **mine tram** deep into the Old Hundred Gold Mine at Silverton to learn how the precious ore was mined.

▨ Revel in steamy luxury at the **hot springs** outside Ouray.

▨ Enjoy **Rocky Mountain views** from the gondola that links Telluride with the ski resort of Mountain Village.

▨ Climb the **long ladders** into Mesa Verde's Balcony House to see how the ancient Pueblo people once lived.

In fall, the aspens of San Juan National Forest turn yellow and gold, while snow coats the peaks of the Sneffels Range beyond.

ACROSS WATER

BY ROAD

BY RAIL

ON FOOT

IN SEARCH OF CULTURE

IN GOURMET HEAVEN

INTO THE ACTION

UP AND AWAY

IN THEIR FOOTSTEPS

Red rock spires, called hoodoos, loom through low-lying clouds above the snow-dusted slopes and pine forests of Bryce Canyon.

UTAH

Route 12 From Bryce Canyon to Capitol Reef

Journey through Utah's canyonlands past eerie rock formations, breathtaking mountain ridges, pine forests, and mountain meadows.

In southern Utah, Route 12 curves, rises, and falls through a multicolored high-desert world of spiky rock formations, canyons, cliffs, creeks, and secret green valleys. Start in Panguitch and head for Bryce Canyon, whose vast natural amphitheaters are filled with towering pink, orange, and red stone spires. Then cross the captivating canyons of Grand Staircase-Escalante National Monument, climbing along the Hogsback, where the shoulderless ribbon of road traces a knife-edge ridge, with sheer drop-offs on both sides. Heartrate back under control, you arrive in the green oasis of Boulder, which until the 1950s still received its mail by mule team. Beyond are the alpine forests and meadows of Boulder Mountain and the green canyons of Capitol Reef National Park. In Cathedral Valley, sandstone monoliths, rising up to 500 feet (150 meters) above the valley floor, seem like the work of some great architect of nature and have been named accordingly— Temple of the Sun, Temple of the Moon, and the Walls of Jericho.

WHEN TO GO The best weather is in the spring and fall when the national parks are less crowded, but most visitors travel in the summer. The road is open all year, with occasional closures for thunderstorms or snowstorms.

HOW LONG You can cover the 140 miles (225 km) in about five hours, but you'll need four days to allow ample time to explore the national parks and other attractions.

PLANNING The national parks get very busy in summer. Make camping or lodging reservations well ahead of time for the best selection.

INSIDE INFORMATION Obtain current weather and road condition information at visitutah.com, allow extra time, and carry plenty of drinking water. Fill up with gas when it is available.

WEBSITES utah.com/scenic-drive, brycecanyoncountry.com, nps.gov/brca

HIGHLIGHTS

▥ Hike through narrow **"slot" canyons** and below towering red rock hoodoos (rock spires) on the 1.3-mile (2.1 km) Navajo Trail in Bryce Canyon.

▥ In Calf Creek Recreation Area, east of Escalante, a 5.8-mile (9.3 km) hike leads to **falls** where the **Calf Creek** tumbles 135 ft (40 m) into a crystalline pool.

▥ Wander through the ancient **ruins** of a long-vanished people at Anasazi State Park in Boulder.

▥ Take a 4x4 along the **Burr Trail**, heading east from Boulder through Capitol Reef National Park.

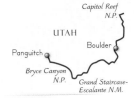

ACROSS WATER

BY ROAD

BY RAIL

ON FOOT

IN SEARCH OF CULTURE

IN GOURMET HEAVEN

INTO THE ACTION

UP AND AWAY

IN THEIR FOOTSTEPS

| CANADA |

The Icefields Parkway

Travel back into the ice age along this majestic Canadian road, skirting wild tundra, ice-capped peaks, glacial lakes, and the massive Columbia Icefields.

Linking Jasper and Banff National Parks in Canada's Rocky Mountains, the Icefields Parkway curves around mountains and climbs high passes as it crosses one of the most exceptional landscapes in North America. Giving you close-up views of the kind of scenery normally inaccessible by road, the parkway runs along the Continental Divide, the backbone of the Rocky Mountains, close to the border of Alberta and British Columbia. Craggy, ice-clad peaks, many rising to more than 11,000 feet (3,350 meters) above sea level, tower above crystalline lakes, subalpine meadows splashed with wildflowers, and treeless tundra, speckled with patches of snow even in midsummer. The road passes along the fringe of the 30-square mile (78 square kilometer) Columbia Icefields, the largest subpolar glacial area in North America. This remnant of the last great ice age feeds eight major glaciers including the Athabasca, Dome, and Stutfield Glaciers, and is the source of three of the continent's major river systems—the Athabasca, North Saskatchewan, and Columbia rivers. The names along the way give a hint of the sights to be seen—Vermilion Lakes, Crowfoot Glacier, Weeping Wall.

WHEN TO GO The Icefields Parkway is open year round. In winter, expect temporary closures (as much as three days) after heavy snowfalls. The Columbia Icefield Centre, 65 miles (105 km) from Jasper, is open from mid-April to mid-October.

HOW LONG Allow at least five hours for the 142-mile (230 km) trip, but the region is better explored over three days by staying in lodges or campsites along the way.

PLANNING Reserve accommodation or a campsite several months in advance, especially for July and August. In winter, be sure to carry blankets, flashlights, and a shovel in your car. If you're not traveling in your own vehicle, you can take a tour bus.

INSIDE INFORMATION If you intend to cover the parkway in a single day, set off as early as possible because you are most likely to spot wildlife at dawn and dusk. Avoid wandering unescorted far from the road, because of the risk of falling into a deep crevice. You can also take one of the regular tours of the Columbia Icefields in all-terrain vehicles. The 2-mile (3 km) round-trip takes you to the middle of the glacier, where you can explore on foot.

WEBSITES www.icefieldsparkway.ca, travelalberta.com, banffjaspercollection.com/attractions/glacier-adventure

HIGHLIGHTS

▪ The trip gives you an exceptional chance to see **mountain wildlife** in its natural environment. Watch out for bighorn sheep, mountain goats, elk, moose, caribou, and bears.

▪ A 90-minute ride in a giant six-wheeled **Ice Explorer** (available from mid-April to mid-October) takes you into the very heart of the Columbia Icefields.

▪ At **Stutfield Glacier Viewpoint** you will be awed by the sight of the icefield spilling dramatically over a cliff.

▪ The pristine mountain setting provides a magical backdrop for **white-water rafting** in summer and **cross-country skiing** in winter.

▪ The color of **Peyto Lake**, set far below the parkway in a deep glacial valley, is astonishing – a vivid robin's egg blue.

Opposite: The mountains of Jasper National Park provide an impressive setting for painted First Nations totem poles, brought here from their original home on Canada's Pacific coast. Above left: In Banff National Park, the waters of Bow Lake reflect crags rising above them. Above right: Elk are just some of the wildlife you can see.

Route 66 Through Arizona

Star in your own road movie on nostalgia-rich Route 66.

Running from Chicago to Los Angeles, Route 66 was America's primary east-west highway for much of the 20th century and won fame in a song recorded by Bob Dylan among others. Migrant farmers of the Depression era dubbed it the "mother road" and followed it west to California. By the 1950s and '60s it was the "main street of America" as the first generation of modern tourists took to the highways seeking fun and adventure. Today, the longest remaining stretch of the original Route 66 in Arizona is a celebration of nostalgia and a rich seam for those wanting to discover a more innocent time. The main streets of Holbrook, Flagstaff, and Williams still feature classic Route 66–style motels and diners. Beyond Williams, the original two-lane blacktop veers off today's I-40 and leads through tiny towns like Peach Springs and Hackberry, many lying on old wagon trails and railroad routes. Up in the Black Mountains sits the gold-mining town of Oatman, once the scene of many frenzied gunfights, and the last stop before pioneers braced themselves for crossing the California desert.

WHEN TO GO Route 66 is drivable all year, but late spring and early fall offer the best combination of comfortable temperatures and open attractions.

HOW LONG The Arizona stretch of Route 66, from Holbrook to Oatman, is 367 miles (590 km) long. Allow three to five days for leisurely exploration.

PLANNING Portions of Route 66 are in remote areas of the desert so take accurate maps, extra water, sunblock, sunglasses, and hats. Plan for stretches where gas is not easily available, such as between Williams and Kingman.

INSIDE INFORMATION Old Route 66 does not appear on current road maps, so check the maps at historic66.com/arizona. In eastern Arizona you'll travel along I-40, stopping to sample remnants of the original road in Holbrook, Flagstaff, and Williams. Take Old Route 66 from Seligman to Oatman.

WEBSITE 66funrun.com

HIGHLIGHTS

▦ Take a **walk underground** at Grand Canyon Caverns near Peach Springs, one of Route 66's oldest and most-visited attractions.

▦ Route 66 is not about high culture, so go ahead and enjoy the slightly cheesy **Old West gunfights** staged in Oatman. Also visit the galleries and fine shops owned by area artisans.

▦ Join the millions who have used Route 66 as the jumping-off place for a side trip to the south rim of the **Grand Canyon**, north of Williams, or stunning **Havasu Canyon**, north of Peach Springs.

Spend a night in a teepee at the Wigwam Motel in Holbrook. These concrete teepees are one of the finest remaining examples of Route 66's roadside architecture.

ACROSS WATER

BY ROAD

BY RAIL

ON FOOT

IN SEARCH OF CULTURE

IN GOURMET HEAVEN

INTO THE ACTION

UP AND AWAY

IN THEIR FOOTSTEPS

Bixby Creek Bridge, built in 1932, spans a rocky canyon along Highway 1.

CALIFORNIA

Pacific Coast Highway 1 Through Big Sur

Savor the sweeping Pacific vistas and hairpin bends of the highway that literally clings to America's western edge.

If there is a single road that embodies California's heady spirit, it is Highway 1 through Big Sur—the region early Spanish colonists called the *país grande del sur* ("big country of the south"). This route begins at Hearst Castle, just north of San Simeon, then follows the mountainous coastline north through the art colony of Carmel to end at historic Monterey. From the 1930s' "Cannery Row"–era of John Steinbeck through the "California Dreamin'" days of the 1960s and into the present, images of this serpentine highway winding high above the surf-carved seascapes of Big Sur have inspired adventurers to take to the road. Join them, and along the way you'll find wilderness parks that offer the peace of redwood groves and refreshing streams, and countless places to pause and enjoy magnificent views of the shoreline. Brown pelicans and other seabirds wheel overhead, and you may catch sight of migrating gray whales. Just north of San Simeon, elephant seals gather year-round at Point Piedras Blancas, and flocks of monarch butterflies from Canada overwinter in Pacific Grove, near Monterey.

WHEN TO GO Spring, summer, and fall are the best seasons. June, July, and August are the busiest months. In summer, mornings can be foggy.

HOW LONG The drive—95 miles (153 km) one-way—can easily take a full day with plenty of leisurely stops.

PLANNING Camping and lodging options are varied and plentiful; many are either nestled in the woods or offer stunning ocean vistas. Gas stations are scarce, so fill up in Morro Bay, south of San Simeon.

INSIDE INFORMATION The views are best driving north, on the land side of the narrow, curvy road—that way you steer clear of the occasionally steep drop-offs on the ocean side. Watch out for rainstorms, which can cause landslides. Strong currents and cold water make swimming dangerous.

WEBSITES carmelchamber.org, seemonterey.com/regions/big-sur

HIGHLIGHTS

▪ Enjoy a picnic at the Ragged Point overlook, 15 miles (24 km) north of San Simeon. This **panoramic view** has been called "the most breathtaking coastal vista in America."

▪ Take a hike around **Julia Pfeiffer Burns State Park**, 37 miles (60 km) south of Carmel. A trail leads to a cove where a waterfall drops 80 ft (24 m) to the sea; or follow longer trails into the surrounding mountains.

▪ Stroll the **beach** at Carmel. Pretend you're not trying to spot movie stars as you explore the art galleries, or enjoy a glass of wine at the Hog's Breath Inn, once owned by Clint Eastwood.

Mountain crags loom above a small farmer's house and plot of land near Puerto Harberton in Tierra del Fuego.

The Pan American Highway

Stretching from Alaska to Tierra del Fuego, the Pan American Highway was created to link the countries of the Americas.

This network of interlinking roads runs through 15 countries along the length of North and South America. Although you can travel the entire route, most people sample portions—such as its southernmost stretch on Tierra del Fuego. Shared between Chile and Argentina, Tierra del Fuego is South America's ultimate frontier, and the drive from Chilean Punta Espora, in the island's far north, to Argentine Ushuaia, in the south, lets you experience its isolation and drama. The windswept north is a vast, undulating grassland dotted with sheep, while jagged, snow-topped peaks, glaciers, tundra, lakes, and beech forests cram the damp south. Ushuaia, the highway's terminus, is also a gateway to Antarctica, 750 miles (1,207 kilometers) due south.

WHEN TO GO The summer months of December through February have the best weather. Winters in Tierra del Fuego are harsh, and roads can be treacherous.

HOW LONG It takes a full day to travel by bus or car between Punta Espora and Ushuaia.

PLANNING If renting a car, be sure that the rental agency provides documents allowing the vehicle to cross the Chilean-Argentine border. High-factor sunblock is essential.

INSIDE INFORMATION If you are lucky enough to see the early morning mists that rise on the coastal waters, looking like drifts of smoke, you will see why the first explorers named this the "land of fire."

WEBSITES enjoy-patagonia.org, visitchile.com

HIGHLIGHTS

■ Anglers will enjoy fishing for **giant brown trout** in the waters around Río Grande, half way down the island.

■ **Ushuaia** is the world's southernmost city. Once a penal colony, its buildings are made of brightly colored zinc. You can take a tour on a green-painted, double-decker bus.

■ The evocatively named **Tren del Fin del Mundo** (End of the World Train) runs west from Ushuaia to **Parque Nacional de Tierra del Fuego**, where you can watch sea lions and fur and elephant seals playing in the surf.

■ You can have a meal or stay a night at Estancia Harberton, an **historic sheep farm** overlooking Puerto Harberton that dates from 1886.

■ In summer a boat trip from Estancia Harberton takes you to **Martillo Island** in the Beagle Channel, home to Magellanic penguins. Around you, petrels, black-browed albatrosses, cormorants, and steamer ducks sail through the skies or skim the waves.

BOLIVIA | CHILE

Crossing the Andes From Bolivia to Chile

Intrepid drivers on the world's highest road reap rewards of volcanic hot springs, shimmery salt flats, and flamingos on a rose red lake.

SOUTH AMERICA

Freezing cold, bumpy, and uncomfortable, this guided trip across the Andes none-theless has the magic of being the world's highest road journey. Leaving the bleak, windswept town of Uyuni in Bolivia, you are soon squinting across the white expanse of huge salt flats (*salares* in Spanish)—the salt-caked beds of dried-up lakes—framed by the deep blue sky of the Andean altiplano (high plateau). These are the world's highest and largest salt flats, scattered with cacti-covered islands and pyramidal salt mounds. Against a backdrop of snow-capped peaks, your journey takes you through copper-colored sands and past high-altitude desert scenery peppered with surreal-looking rock formations. Perfect conical volcanoes rise above crimson and emerald lakes that change color as the sun moves across the sky, and steaming geysers spurt out of the icy earth. In Laguna Colorada, pink flamingos blend into the windswept water. Then, as you cross the Andean ridge into Chile, the adobe oasis of San Pedro de Atacama greets you in a desert landscape with volcanoes and thermal pools.

WHEN TO GO 4x4 vehicles leave Uyuni daily throughout the year. June to September are the coldest months, but the chill brings clear blue skies.

HOW LONG Roads—when there are any—are in very bad condition, so the 170-mile (274 km) trip usually takes four days and three nights, spent by the Salar de Uyuni, Laguna Colorada, and Laguna Verde.

PLANNING You need to prebook your place in the 4x4. Temperatures become extremely low at night, sometimes to −13°F (−25°C), so pack warm, windproof clothing and a warm sleeping bag.

INSIDE INFORMATION You will not be allowed to take any organic produce (including wooden or leather goods) across the Chilean border. They are very strict!

WEBSITES lastfrontiers.com, www.lata.travel

HIGHLIGHTS

▓ In the wet season, **the salt flats** submerged beneath a skin of water perfectly reflect the Andean sky.

▓ At **Laguna Colorada**, as the temperature drops at sunset and the icy wind whips up, the lake turns a deep red that contrasts with the snow white salt deposits in the water.

▓ In the **Salvador Dalí desert**, between Laguna Colorada and Laguna Verde, folds in the sand, jutting rocks, and shadows turn the landscape into a 3-D surrealist masterpiece.

▓ After a night of subzero temperatures, warm yourself in the hot **springs of Challviri**. You can boil your breakfast eggs in them.

Cactuses fringe Bolivia's largest salt flat, the Salar de Uyuni, with a lone 4x4 crossing its astonishing snow white surface.

Exhibits at Nara's Kofukuji National Treasure Museum include this fearsome wooden face.

JAPAN

The Takenouchi Highway

Japan's oldest highway passes gardens and flowery slopes en route from Osaka's buzzing modernity to Nara, the ancient capital.

The Takenouchi Highway conjures up the entire shifting panorama of Japan's history. Modern buildings nestle alongside traditional houses and ancient gardens. Meticulously manicured schoolgirls gossiping on cell phones overtake old ladies bent double from a lifetime of tilling rice. The highway winds through the outskirts of Osaka, Japan's vibrant second city, to Nara, the original capital created by the first divine emperor, Jimmu. Prince Taishi in the Asuka Era (circa A.D. 600) built the highway, the oldest in Japan. Korean and Chinese influences helped to shape ancient Japan, and this highway acted as a conduit for all kinds of imports, including Buddhism, Ramen noodles, and chopsticks. All arrived through the port of Osaka and were transported on to the imperial capital. Along the way, you can visit wooden houses and temples, and climb to the top of Mount Nijo, site of the burial mound of the tragic poet-prince Otsu-no-Miko, forced to commit suicide after a court intrigue in A.D. 686.

WHEN TO GO Spring and fall are the best seasons. It is possible to travel at any time, but conditions are freezing in winter and humid in summer. Most sights are open on weekends and closed on weekdays, so it's always best to check ahead.

HOW LONG The route is 33 miles (53 km) long, and you can visit most of the major sights in a day.

PLANNING Check for sightseeing tours and the possibility of hiring an English-speaking guide for the day.

INSIDE INFORMATION Plan your trip to coincide with the Dakenobori (Mountain-climbing) Festival on April 23 and join Japanese hikers as they climb Mount Nijo.

WEBSITES osaka-info.jp/en, japan-guide.com/e/e2165.html

| HIGHLIGHTS

▥ Get a taste of the **sumo tradition** at the Kehaya-za Sumo Museum in the outskirts of Nara. It has a life-size *dohyo* (sumo ring) and displays of artifacts. There is also a sumo tournament in Osaka, held in March.

▥ Enjoy the **spring flowers** covering the slopes of the mountains along the highway.

▥ Visit **Mount Nijo**, considered sacred by locals as a gateway to heaven. Wait to see the sunset between the twin peaks of the mountain – it is said to be one of Japan's finest.

▥ **Nara**'s seven Buddhist temples include the **Todai-ji** – said to be the world's largest wooden building – which houses a giant 50-ft (15 m) high statue of the Buddha. The city is a UNESCO World Heritage site.

ASIA

| INDIA |

From Delhi to Agra

The Taj Mahal, wonder of the world and shrine to undying love, provides the climax to a journey through India's throbbing heart.

India, its myriad sensations and abrupt contrasts of poverty and beauty—this is what you encounter at close range on the road from Delhi to Agra. Leaving behind the spice-filled, noise-riven air of Delhi, you wind south through farmland dotted with mud huts and farmers plowing with oxen. Vivid snapshots flash into view: women washing clothes, men eating from steaming bowls at roadside stalls. You pass a number of dilapidated stores, collapsing but still in business. Then, suddenly, a gleaming mosque or garlanded Hindu statue appears, tenderly cared for. And all along the way, cows, oxen, and water buffalo wander across the road, or stand stock-still in the middle as the traffic veers around them. Anything that can be ridden or driven is on the highway: camels, tractors, old bicycles, patched-up cars, trucks lurching under impossible loads. Sometimes, they topple over completely, leaving their driver sitting, stranded, on the roadside. Jewels from India's Mogul past adorn this road, from the Red Fort above Delhi, to the deserted city of Fatehpur Sikri along the way, and at its end, the shimmering Taj Mahal, a monument to human skill as well as an emperor's love. Visit it at sunrise to watch the white marble change color with the light.

WHEN TO GO September to March to avoid the hot summer and rainy monsoon months (July–August).

HOW LONG The 126-mile (203 km) drive takes four hours but, to see all the sights, spend two days.

PLANNING Take a tour, or hire a chauffeur-guide and enjoy a ride in one of India's classic white Ambassador cars. Driving yourself in India is not advisable – the roads are bad and the traffic is worse. The Taj Mahal is closed to non-Hindus on Fridays.

INSIDE INFORMATION Dress respectfully. Women should not wear shorts or short skirts, and should cover the tops of their arms. If these guidelines are ignored, entry to sites may be refused or you will be given a garment to cover yourself. Drink only bottled water, and avoid eating from street stalls.

WEBSITES delhitourism.gov.in, incredibleindia.org

HIGHLIGHTS

■ **The Gandhi Memorial** in Delhi is a moving and tranquil spot, dedicated to India's spiritual leader, who is still considered the father of the nation.

■ **India Gate** in Delhi was originally erected to honor Indian soldiers killed fighting for the Allies during World War I. It has become a symbol of the city and of independence.

■ The ruined fort city of **Fatehpur Sikri** is a collection of palaces and pavilions in red sandstone and a prime example of Islamic architecture.

■ The Mogul emperors built the **Agra Fort Complex**, embellishing it with marble, gemstones, and pretty landscaped gardens.

The light of the setting sun bathes in pink the tomb of the 16th-century Mogul emperor Humayun in Delhi.

ACROSS WATER

BY ROAD

BY RAIL

ON FOOT

IN SEARCH OF CULTURE

IN GOURMET HEAVEN

INTO THE ACTION

UP AND AWAY

IN THEIR FOOTSTEPS

| PAKISTAN | INDIA |

The Grand Trunk Road

A life-enhancing expedition from the border of Pakistan to the Indian metropolis of Kolkata embraces the glories of Mogul architecture and Hinduism's holy places.

Built by imperial decree in the 15th century, the Grand Trunk Road carves its way from the North-West Frontier, across the border between Pakistan and India and down the Ganges to meet the sea at Kolkata (Calcutta) on the Bay of Bengal. The writer Rudyard Kipling called the road the "great river of life," a name that still rings true. Your journey begins at Amritsar in India, scene of a notorious massacre of Indian nationalists by British troops in 1919, before moving on to Delhi, the capital of two great Indian empires, the Mogul and the British. Farther along lies mystic Varanasi, one of the holiest places of Hinduism, and finally Kolkata, among India's most overwhelming cities. Along the way you will see a cavalcade of vehicles and people: oxcarts, barefoot pilgrims, the occasional elephant, gaudily painted buses, Ashok trucks piloted by turbaned Punjabis, rickety Ambassador taxis, and the air-conditioned Toyotas of politicians and officials. Sacred cows, goats, poultry, and pedestrians somehow manage to avoid being flattened by vehicles vying for position and swerving around potholes, while the constant pall of dust is enhanced by a rich transfusion of diesel fumes. The constant movement has also given rise to culinary delights, such as a North Indian street-food of crisp-fried pastry and chickpeas, and the magnificent vegetarian dishes of Varanasi. At its busiest, the Grand Trunk Road seems like a continent in motion.

WHEN TO GO November to January, when daytime temperatures in India are bearable and it can be crisp and cool at night.

HOW LONG The road extends for 1,190 miles (1,920 km). Allow up to two weeks between Amritsar and Delhi, and at least two weeks between Delhi and Kolkata.

PLANNING The best way to travel the Grand Trunk Road is with a private car (preferably 4x4 and air-conditioned) and driver. Several adventure tour companies offer escorted tours on the most popular section, between Delhi and Varanasi.

INSIDE INFORMATION Dust is always a problem, so take a face mask or a scarf thin enough for you to breathe through.

WEBSITES tourism.gov.pk, visitindia.com

| HIGHLIGHTS

▥ **Amritsar**'s Harimandir Sahib **(Golden Temple)** rises resplendent above its lake. Sikhism's most holy place, it throngs with pilgrims, especially for the great festival of Vaisakhi on April 13 or 14.

▥ Mogul emperor Shah Jahan built **Delhi**'s great **Red Fort** in 1639. Covering 120 acres (49 ha), at one time the fort supported a population of 3,000. The building is a superb example of Mughal architecture.

▥ **Varanasi**, believed to be the world's second-oldest continuously inhabited city (after Jerusalem), also buzzes with humanity. Millions visit the holy city each year to bathe in the Ganges, a purifying act.

▥ Just about everything is on offer in **Kolkata**'s colorful bazaars – gold, silver, jewelry, ceramics, textiles, not to mention the beautiful and rare flowers at the **Howrah Phool Bazaar**, on the east side of the city.

Opposite: The riverbank in Varanasi is a scene of vivid color as pilgrims from all over India bathe themselves in the waters of the Ganges. Above left: The canary yellow of taxis and motor rickshaws adds to the tapestry of color in city streets. Above right: Richly brocaded textiles are sold in markets in Pakistan's North-West Frontier.

By the roadside, you may spot bearded dragons, lizards which can grow to be 22 in (56 cm) long.

AUSTRALIA

The Tanami Track

In one of the planet's loneliest expanses, see rare wildlife, stunning landscapes, and the brilliant artworks of the Warlpiri Aborigines.

Despite its name, the Tanami Track is a highway—albeit a well-maintained dirt one—crossing one of the most isolated and arid areas on Earth, the Tanami Desert. Like many of the outback trails, it originated as a cattle-droving route, linking Alice Springs in the Northern Territory with Halls Creek in Western Australia. North of Alice Springs, the route along the slopes of the MacDonnell Ranges brings mountain views dotted with striking rock forms and ribboned by dry riverbeds. Beyond that, the red sand plains open out, tufted with herbs and spinifex grass, relieved occasionally by hills, ridges, ocher rocks, and pockets of woodland, all laid out under the blue dome of the Australian sky. Along the way, you can visit the Warlpiri Aboriginal communities of Yuendumu and Balgo (Wirrimanu), centers of art and culture where you will find artists working in both traditional and innovative media. Remote cattle stations and thriving gold mines are the only other signs of human activity.

WHEN TO GO April to October is the best time to travel, as Sturt Creek at the end of the route can become flooded in the wet season.

HOW LONG The journey is more than 625 miles (1,005 km) long, and takes two days – expect to camp overnight. You have to take it slow – the dirt roads mean that you can't drive too fast.

PLANNING You can join a 4x4 tour, or rent a 4x4 in Alice Springs. Before you leave home, get a pass from the Central Land Council to visit the Tanami Desert Wildlife Sanctuary. Yuendumu and the Aboriginal lands will also require a pass if you want to stop and explore. If you're planning to stop at Balgo, call in advance and the artists will organize this for you.

INSIDE INFORMATION In addition to camping equipment, carry enough drinking water to last for two trips. Water from all dams and bores along the way is undrinkable. Bring adequate fuel supplies – refueling points are few and far between. The Aboriginal lands around Yuendumu are alcohol-free.

WEBSITES australia.com/en-gb, warlu.com, balgoart.org.au

HIGHLIGHTS

◼ At the **Granites Gold Mine,** northwest of Alice Springs, savor the atmosphere of the old workings and original 1930s buildings.

◼ Newhaven Reserve – 650,000 acres (263,045 ha) of **dunes, salt lakes, and clay pans** – lies 226 miles (364 km) northwest of Alice Springs. It is home to many bird species – look out for rare night parrots.

◼ Yuendumu and Balgo are both worth a short detour for their arts centers: the **Warlukurlangu Artists' Aboriginal Corporation** in Yuendumu, and the **Warlayirti Art and Cultural Centres** in Balgo.

AUSTRALIA

The Blue Mountains

*Savor spectacular vistas, rare plants, and exotic wildlife among the
hazy blue peaks shimmering far above Sydney's hustle and bustle.*

Dizzying gorges, cliffs, creeks, and waterfalls sculpt the rugged, forest-covered
tablelands of Blue Mountains National Park, a World Heritage area of protected
wilderness. The range's name derives from the blue haze caused by its countless
eucalyptus trees, which load the air with fine, blue-tinged droplets of eucalyptus oil.
The best way to approach the park is along the Bells Line of Road—an early stock route
leading from Richmond, northwest of Sydney, through rolling hills and orchards and
into the mountains. The road becomes steep and winding as it climbs to Mount Tomah,
where the cool climate, rich soil, and high rainfall create ideal conditions for an important botanical garden. Here, the forest comprises an understory of tree ferns and vines,
pierced occasionally by massive eucalypts. The road then follows a narrow ridge along
the Grose Valley to the highest point, Mount Victoria, 3,490 feet (1,064 meters) above sea
level. Beyond lie the scenic centers of Blackheath and Katoomba, the latter perched on
a cliff above the Jamison Valley. You leave the mountains through Glenbrook on the
lower slopes, where you can also swim in a waterhole, see Aboriginal art at Red Hands
Cave, and go bushwalking.

WHEN TO GO In summer, the mountains offer cool relief from the sticky heat of Sydney; in winter it is
chillier, but there are fewer tourists.

HOW LONG About 60 miles (97 km) from Richmond, depending on detours. Allow a day to explore.

PLANNIN Get to the park early to watch the sun rise and avoid the crowds. Take your own water; local
water is unsafe, even if boiled. It is also possible to camp near Glenbrook.

INSIDE INFORMATION Wildflower enthusiasts should visit in September, when waratahs, gymea lilies,
and other native beauties are in bloom in the lower mountains. Visit Blackheath for its Rhododendron
Festival in November. If you go bushwalking, allow enough "turn-around time" before the park closes.

WEBSITES bluemountainsgazette.com.au, australianexplorer.com, uk.sydney.com

HIGHLIGHTS

▥ There are fine forest walks in the
Cathedral of Ferns, where the road
turns off to Mount Wilson between
Richmond and Mount Victoria.

▥ At Blackheath, you can explore the
Grose Valley and see the **waterfall at
Govetts Leap.**

▥ **Katoomba** has superb views from
Echo Point to the Three Sisters,
pinnacles of rock that are one of the
park's landmarks. You can go down
into Jamison Valley by foot or rail.

▥ Cascades plunge down three
levels of cliff at **Wentworth Falls,**
below Katoomba.

According to Aboriginal legend, the Three Sisters were, indeed, three sisters turned to rock by a magician after falling in love with three brothers from a rival nation.

ACROSS WATERS

BY ROAD

BY RAIL

ON FOOT

IN SEARCH OF CULTURE

IN GOURMET HEAVEN

INTO THE ACTION

UP AND AWAY

IN THEIR FOOTSTEPS

NEW ZEALAND

The West Coast Road

Remote, yet easily accessible, the west coast of New Zealand's South Island offers a unique, unspoiled landscape, and a wide range of outdoor pursuits.

The cloud-piercing peaks of the Southern Alps rise dramatically to the east as the road runs down the South Island's west coast from the secluded haven of Karamea to Jackson Bay. Between the mountains, which form a natural barrier to the rest of the island, and the Tasman Sea only a narrow strip of land is habitable, and just 31,000 people live there. The area's low population and isolation protects the temperate rain forest—a primal ecosystem of giant fir trees, palms, and ferns—that covers much of the coastal plain and mountains. From the outset, the drive brings together exceptional ocean vistas with Alpine scenery watered by fast-flowing rivers and waterfalls. You can stop off here and there for a walk in beech forest, a dip in a natural thermal pool, a boat trip on a forest-fringed lake, or some gemstone hunting or gold panning. The final third of the route is known as Glacier Country; here two of the mountain glaciers (Fox and Franz Josef) have plowed through the rain forest to just above sea level. Farther on, the Haast Pass creates a stunning change of scene: a river valley bordered by lowland forest and alive with native species, including parakeets, bellbirds, and kiwis. After this, wend back to the coast at peaceful and remote Jackson Bay. If you are in search of activity, the west coast is an adventure and outdoor paradise. If your taste is for serenity, simply watch the waves pound the jagged rock formations.

WHEN TO GO The peak tourist season runs from late October to late April (spring to fall), which is also the west coast's rainiest period. Winter weather on the west coast is generally very settled, with crisp mornings, blue skies, and snow on the mountaintops, giving the region a fresh feel.

HOW LONG Winding roads make for slow progress along the 375-mile (604 km) route. Allow at least three days, if driving yourself. If using the buses that connect the coastal settlements, allow at least four.

PLANNING This is a popular destination for visitors from other parts of New Zealand and, unless pre-booked long in advance, accommodation is hard to come by.

INSIDE INFORMATION In recent years artists and craftspeople have been attracted to the west coast, with local roadside galleries showcasing their work. Alternatively, follow the signs, often through remote valleys or alongside otherwise hidden coves, to their workshops.

WEBSITES westcoast.co.nz, nzsouth.co.nz, newzealand.com

HIGHLIGHTS

▦ View the breeding colony of **New Zealand fur seals** (*kekeno*) at Cape Foulwind, near Westport.

▦ Take a helicopter flight into the mountains, followed by **white-water rafting** down one of the wild rivers leading back to the coast.

▦ Relish the quietude of remote fishing villages, such as **Jackson Bay**, and the wildness of the ocean beating out rock formations along the coast.

▦ Enjoy great opportunities for **adventure sports**, from kayaking and surfing to mountain biking, caving, and climbing.

▦ Clamber along the **ice tunnels** and arches of Franz Josef Glacier, and see the shimmering reflections of Aoraki (Mount Cook) and Mount Tasman in nearby Lake Matheson.

Opposite: At Jackson Bay there are stunning views across the bay to Mount Aspiring and the snowy peaks of the Southern Alps. Above left: Road signs alert you to the presence of kiwis, the flightless birds that have become an emblem for New Zealand. Above right: Hikers admire an ice cave in Fox Glacier.

More plentiful than wood, turf was often used for roofing in Iceland — as in these old farmhouses at the Skagafjördur Heritage Museum at Glaumbær in northern Iceland.

ICELAND

Iceland's Ring Road

Encounter bubbling geysers and gushing waterfalls while circling this eerie land of northern lights and volcanic fire.

Restive volcanoes, glaciers, geysers, and waterfalls are forever carving, scoring, and pluming a landscape evocative of the ancient sagas of Iceland's Viking past. Known as the Ring Road because it circles the entire island, Highway 1 snakes past towering cliffs overlooking the Atlantic as it leaves Reykjavik heading north. After that, it follows a hairpin course around fjords, where dolphins plunge through icy waters, and skirts fields of petrified lava, tundra forests, and volcanic craters. Turn off the route and more discoveries unfold: steaming pools and sulfur cauldrons glowing purple and yellow; valleys of wildflowers; puffins and Arctic terns roosting along seacliffs; and streams and cascades, including Europe's largest waterfall, the Gullfoss—Golden Falls—where the White River (Hvítá), fed by a combination of rainwater and meltwater from glaciers, crashes 105 feet (32 meters) into a canyon. Elsewhere, sheep graze on carpets of velvety green grass around red-roofed farmhouses, set against snow-capped mountains. Or you can take a dip into Iceland's history in villages that re-create the life of the Vikings and people at other periods in the island's past. At Eiríksstadir in the east, visit the home of Eric the Red, the explorer and hero of one of the sagas.

WHEN TO GO May to September. In winter, daylight hours are short, although you do get the chance to see the aurora borealis (northern lights) in the night sky.

HOW LONG You need at least a week to take in all the sights along the full 900-mile (1,448 km) route.

PLANNING Icelandic weather is always unpredictable, so take waterproof clothing even in summer.

INSIDE INFORMATION Highway 1 is Iceland's only major road that is fully paved for most of its length. Conditions are generally good, but there are unpaved stretches in the east, and wet weather can make parts hazardous. For up-to-the-minute information on road conditions, go to: road.is.

WEBSITES inspiredbyiceland.com, visitreykjavik.is

HIGHLIGHTS

▥ Explore the capital, **Reykjavik**, and savor its nightlife—one of the most vibrant and sophisticated in Europe.

▥ View the spectacular **glacial landscape** around Jökulsárlón in the south, where Europe's largest glacier, Vatnajökull, breaks off in great turquoise chunks into the lagoon.

▥ Visit **Lake Mývatn** in the north—a haven for birdlife, with the largest breeding duck population in Europe.

▥ Take **whale-watching trips** from fishing villages, such as Húsavík.

ACROSS WATER

BY ROAD

BY RAIL

ON FOOT

IN SEARCH OF CULTURE

IN GOURMET HEAVEN

INTO THE ACTION

UP AND AWAY

IN THEIR FOOTSTEPS

SCOTLAND

Through the Highlands of Scotland

Follow in the footsteps of Bonnie Prince Charlie on a journey of high romance among Scotland's mountain-ringed lochs and dreamy glens.

Craggy mountains stretch into the distance, Highland cattle graze in serene glens, and ever changing skies frame romantic vistas of lochs with the ruins of ancient castles rising from their shores. The route crosses the wildest, most atmospheric landscape in Britain, redolent of the stirring history of the Highlands. Near Inverness are 14th-century Cawdor Castle (where Shakespeare, inaccurately, set Macbeth's murder of King Duncan) and the field of Culloden, where the Jacobite troops of Bonnie Prince Charlie met their final defeat. From there, the road runs south down the Great Glen (Glen Mor), a 60-mile (100 kilometer) fissure carved out by glaciers in the last ice age. It passes along the shores of Loch Ness (where you can either ignore or relish the kitsch souvenirs of the "monster" industry) and Loch Lochy. At Fort William, you make a detour to Ben Nevis, at 4,406 feet (1,344 meters) Britain's highest peak, and then head north and west once more through one of Scotland's most haunting regions, dominated by the peaks known as the Five Sisters of Kintail. Finally, you cross the bridge to Skye, the largest island of the Inner Hebrides, where a landscape of rugged beauty awaits you.

WHEN TO GO April to September.

HOW LONG Allow at least a day for the 174-mile (280 km) journey.

PLANNING Western Scotland is notoriously wet, so take waterproof clothing. Midges (biting gnats) are also a serious pest, and insect repellent is a must.

INSIDE INFORMATION If visiting in summer you are likely to come across Highland Gatherings. The Glenurquhart Highland Gathering and Games is held on the last Saturday of August on the banks of Loch Ness, with bagpipers, Scottish dancing, and sports including tossing the caber.

WEBSITES visitscotland.com, scotland.org.uk

HIGHLIGHTS

▊ Visit **Culloden**, scene of the last major battle in mainland Britain, in 1746. You can walk the battlefield with its poignant memorials and clan graves, and visit an exhibition of Jacobite memorabilia.

▊ Hike up **Ben Nevis** for views across the deeply fretted west coast. The tourist route, starting in Glen Nevis, takes six hours to the top and back.

▊ Linger on **Skye**, with its sculpted mountain peaks, fishing villages, and resident otter population.

▊ If you claim Scottish ancestry, visit a **kiltmaker** to buy garments in the tartan of your clan.

Clouds seep into a heather-clad valley, with the blue peaks of Ben Nevis and the Mamore Mountains rising beyond.

Green mountains rise above a lonely road, with a single farmhouse nestling at their feet.

IRELAND

Connemara's Sky Road

Scoured by Atlantic waves, the wild Connemara Peninsula beckons travelers with moors and mountains, cliffs, and sandy beaches.

The Connemara Peninsula, jutting from Ireland's west coast into the Atlantic, packs much of the country's wildness into its small space—including bogs, moorland, hills, loughs, streams, and woodland. This short loop around one of its westernmost tips adds the drama of sea, cliffs, and white-sand beaches. It starts and finishes in the market town of Clifden, set above its harbor, with traditional Irish pubs, a reputation for gourmet restaurants, and an arts festival in September. From there, the ribbon-like road climbs toward the west, opening up views of the cliff-lined coast, the offshore islands of Inishturk and Turbot, and the endless ocean, dotted with boats and porpoises leaping in the surf. On the landward side stand isolated farms—including Kingstown Farm, where Connemara ponies are bred—backed by the peaks of the Twelve Bens. You have all the time in the world on this leisurely half-day trip, so park the car, get out, and explore one of the walking trails or an old drovers' road.

WHEN TO GO All year round, but best from spring to fall. Many tourist sights in Ireland have restricted opening hours or are closed during the low season, so check ahead.

HOW LONG You can do the 7-mile (11 km) trip in an hour, but give yourself at least a morning to savor the views and stop to stretch your legs.

PLANNING Many car rental companies operate in Ireland, but it is best to book in advance to ensure availability and take advantage of cheaper rates.

INSIDE INFORMATION Irish bed-and-breakfasts are a great way to meet local people. Your host is likely to make homemade soda bread for breakfast.

WEBSITES discoverireland.ie, connemara.ie

■ You will almost certainly see **gray seals** along the coast and wild Connemara ponies on the moorland.

■ **Clifden Castle** is a ruined 19th-century Gothic mansion overlooking the sea. Its builder was local landowner John D'Arcy, who also founded the town of Clifden.

■ Clifden is a good place to sample **traditional music** and enjoy the local *craic,* or conversation, especially during the Pony Show in August or the Arts Festival in September.

■ **Derrygimlagh** bog outside Clifden is where **Alcock and Brown** crash-landed after completing the first transatlantic flight in 1919.

■ A **memorial** south of Clifden marks the site of a **wireless station** established by the half-Irish radio pioneer, Guglielmo Marconi, in 1907. From there, the first commercial radio service was transmitted across the Atlantic to Newfoundland.

EUROPE

ACROSS WATER

BY ROAD

BY RAIL

ON FOOT

IN SEARCH OF CULTURE

IN GOURMET HEAVEN

INTO THE ACTION

UP AND AWAY

IN THEIR FOOTSTEPS

| GERMANY |

The Romantic Road of Bavaria

With castle-crowned mountains and glorious churches and palaces, this route explores the heartland of German fairy tales, music, and art.

Lakes, medieval castles, fairy-tale palaces, and onion-domed churches, all overlooked by thickly forested mountains—this is Germany's deep south. The Romantic Road runs from the banks of the Main River and the lush vineyards of Franconia through a string of historic cities to the Bavarian Alps. It crosses one of Germany's most traditional regions, with a calendar of colorful events, all calling for local costume, music, and, of course, beer. Architectural gems stud the route, starting with Würzburg in the north, famous for its Romanesque churches and its baroque and rococo mansions. Augsburg was the base of the Fuggers, medieval merchant-princes who introduced the styles of the Italian Renaissance into Germany. Continuing south, Friedberg and Landsberg, the jewels of the Lech Valley, are set among gently rolling hills. The grand finale is the medieval Alpine town of Füssen, set in countryside that shelters more than 60 castles and palaces. Most famous of these is graceful Neuschwanstein, the 19th-century confection built by "mad" King Ludwig II of Bavaria.

WHEN TO GO Any time of the year. In spring and summer, the landscape is lushly green with flowering meadows and orchards; in fall, mellow colors splash the countryside, and, in winter, snow lends it magic.

HOW LONG Allow a week for relaxed enjoyment of the 210-mile (338 km) journey.

PLANNING You can drive yourself, but there are other options. From April to October, the Deutsche Touring Company runs regular Europabuses along the route, allowing you to get on and off wherever you like. You can also take to two wheels – the Romantic Road Tourist Association has a cycle route that avoids steep hills and main roads.

INSIDE INFORMATION Accommodation of all types is plentiful. Local tourist offices can help you on arrival.

WEBSITE romantischestrasse.de

| HIGHLIGHTS

▥ The **Residenz** (Palace) of the Prince-Bishops of **Würzburg** is one of Europe's finest 18th-century buildings, with superb frescoes by Tiepolo.

▥ It is worth making a side trip to Munich's **Oktoberfest**, a celebration of Bavarian beer, food, and brass-band music held during the 16 days leading up to the first Sunday in October.

▥ At **Neuschwanstein**, King Ludwig set out to recreate "the authentic style of the old German knights' castles" – as he told the composer Wagner. But he made sure it included modern comforts, including central heating and flushing toilets.

The Singers's Hall in Neuschwanstein is decorated with colorful murals depicting the saga of the Holy Grail.

Top 10 Ancient Highways

Follow in the footsteps of ancient traders, empire builders, and nomadic peoples on the highways they created across the world.

❶ THE OLD NORTH TRAIL, NORTH AMERICA

The Blackfeet Indians traveled along the Old North Trail, which originally stretched nearly 2,000 miles (3,220 km) from Canada to Mexico, running along the "backbone of the world" that later Americans called the Rockies. It took the Blackfeet four years to go from end to end on trips to trade, make sacred journeys, or find a wife. You can visit fragments still visible in Glacier National Park in Montana.

PLANNING Blackfeet Historic Tours covers the Old North Trail, and there is an Old Trail Museum at Choteau, MT. centralmontana.com/specialinterest/historictrails/oldnorthtrail

❷ QHAPAQ ÑAN, COLOMBIA TO ARGENTINA

The Royal Road of the Inca reached its height in the 15th century A.D., stretching 4,000 miles (6,400 km) through Colombia, Ecuador, Peru, Bolivia, Chile, and Argentina. Enabling control of the Inca Empire and facilitating travel along the total network of nearly 20,000 miles (30,000 km) of connecting roads, the famous Inca Trail, linking Cusco to Machu Picchu in Peru, is but one small part.

PLANNING The UNESCO World Heritage listing includes detailed maps and descriptions. Although walking is possible, it will take the average walker approximately nine months. qhapaq-nan.com

❸ THE NAKASENDO WAY, JAPAN

This narrow, 17th-century highway linking Kyoto and Edo (modern Tokyo) was built along the route of an older trail. Running for 310 miles (500 km) along the shores of Lake Biwa, across mountain ranges and down onto the Kanto plain around Edo, it was meant for horses and pedestrians— the Japanese did not use carts. Parts of the tranquil route have been preserved and restored, which means that you have to walk them, as most of its original travelers did.

PLANNING The most popular stretch is the 5-mile (8 km) portion between the historic towns of Tsumago and Magome. If possible, go in March/April – the cherry blossom season. web-japan.org

❹ THE YUEN TSUEN ANCIENT TRAIL, HONG KONG, CHINA

For centuries, people traveled along this rugged footpath between Yuen Long and Tsuen Wan in what is now Hong Kong's New Territories. Today, both ends of the trail are embedded in a thoroughly urban sprawl of malls and traffic jams, but the middle remains a delicious haven of peace.

PLANNING The 5-mile (8 km) central portion has been preserved as a hiking trail. But be warned: it's hilly. discoverhongkong.com

The King's Highway winds through the baked hills of modern Jordan. Frankincense and spices were among the many goods traded along this great artery of the ancient Middle East.

❺ THE KHMER HIGHWAY, CAMBODIA/THAILAND

This ancient 140-mile (225 km) highway ran between Angkor, Cambodia, and Phimai, Thailand, and was sacred to the Cambodian empire's "god-kings," who traveled the highway visiting temples and performing religious ceremonies involving fire, water, and *linga* (stone phallic sculptures). Most of it is now overgrown with jungle, but you can still visit many of the temples and drive along a section near Phimai.

PLANNING January is dry and cool and a good time to visit, but Angkor is also stunning in the lush rainy season from June to October. tourismcambodia.com

❻ THE OLD GREAT NORTH ROAD, AUSTRALIA

Famous as a masterpiece of 19th-century engineering, the road is also infamous for the use of forced convict laborers, some of them in leg irons, to build it. It started in Sydney and ended at Newcastle in the Hunter Valley of New South Wales. Some sections follow ancient Aboriginal tracks.

PLANNING A 27-mile (43 km) hiking and biking trail starts at Wisemans Ferry. It's a two- or three-day walk or a one-day bike ride, but there are other more bite-sized routes. australia.com/en-gb

❼ THE KING'S HIGHWAY, JORDAN

This was one of the great trade routes of the Middle East during biblical times, running from Egypt to Syria. In Jordan, the route passes Biblical towns, Roman sites, crusader castles, and glorious Petra, as well as Mount Nebo where Moses is said to have seen the Promised Land.

PLANNING The road started in Heliopolis (modern Ain Shams, a suburb of Cairo), but regional political instability means that nowadays the section in Jordan is the safest sector to explore. atlastours.net

❽ THE VIA EGNATIA, ALBANIA TO TURKEY

The Romans, Greeks, Byzantines, Crusaders, Venetians, Ottomans, and Austrians have all used this astonishing road across the mountains of the Balkan peninsula. Roman proconsul Gnaeus Egnatius built it in the 1st century B.C. to link the Adriatic with the Aegean Sea and the Bosporus.

PLANNING The route starts in Durrës, Albania (known as Dyrrachium by the Romans), and ends in Istanbul, Turkey (Roman Byzantium). viaegnatiafoundation.eu

❾ THE AMBER ROAD, RUSSIA TO ITALY

From ancient times, amber—"the gold of the north"— was traded along this route linking the Baltic with the Adriatic. Today, it makes an intriguing trail to follow from St. Petersburg across eastern and central Europe to Venice.

PLANNING The route runs from St. Petersburg through Riga, Latvia; Vilnius, Lithuania; Gdansk and Wrocław, Poland; Szombathely, Hungary; and Ptuj, Slovenia to Venice. www.lithuania.travel/en-gb

❿ THE VIA AUGUSTA, SPAIN

Follow the road named after the Emperor Augustus, from Cádiz in Andalusia north through the modern-day Coll de Panissars in Catalonia to the Pyrenees. There it joined the Via Domitia, and went on to Rome, where all roads meet.

PLANNING The modern N340-A7 follows much of the route. eyeonspain.com/blogs/bestofspain/11954/tour-spain-along-the-roman -roads.aspx

An umbrella pine frames a view of Monaco from the Moyenne Corniche.

The Riviera Corniches

Impossibly glamorous, photogenic as a movie star, and thrilling to drive, three coast roads symbolize the romance of the French Riviera.

Everyone knows the coast between Nice and Menton. Even if you've never been there, its lavender-scented cliffs, hilltop villages, and views of the Mediterranean have been hardwired into you by countless films and paintings. Three corniches (coast roads)—themselves familiar from many a movie car chase—allow you to explore these fabled scenes for yourself: the Grande Corniche, the highest, built under Napoleon; the Moyenne Corniche; and the Corniche Inférieure, hugging the coast. To combine the best of all three, follow the Moyenne Corniche east from Nice as it twists past Monaco and below the castle of Roquebrune, before merging with the Corniche Inférieure at Cap-Martin. Return along the Grande Corniche for the most spectacular stretch of all three roads, the 11 miles (18 km) from La Turbie to Nice. Or take the longer route along the Corniche Inférieure for stops in Monaco and Beaulieu-sur-Mer.

WHEN TO GO All year, but the corniches are prettiest and least crowded in April and May. They are very congested in July and August.

HOW LONG Each corniche is about 20 miles (32 km) long. Allow two hours for the Moyenne Corniche, and one hour for the Grande Corniche; plan for a whole day with stops for lunch and sightseeing.

PLANNING If you don't have your own car, you can rent one in Nice or Menton, allowing you to stop wherever you want. Alternatively, buses operate regularly on all three corniches.

INSIDE INFORMATION The Corniche Inférieure running east between Cap-Martin and Menton is fairly humdrum. Skip it by turning off onto the Grande Corniche, about 1 mile (1.6 km) east of Cap-Martin.

WEBSITES cote.azur.fr, provenceweb.fr

HIGHLIGHTS

▨ The medieval **village of Eze** (a bus trip northeast of Nice) is a labyrinth of narrow lanes wrapped around a rocky pinnacle high above the Mediterranean. It is crammed with restaurants, art and antique shops, and cafés.

▨ A curious landmark is the **Trophée des Alpes**, a 115-ft (35 m) high stone plinth, near La Turbie on the Grande Corniche. It was built in 6 B.C. to support a colossal statue of the Emperor Augustus, now long gone.

▨ A **fortress-like crag** above Monaco gives you an eagle's-eye view of the ministate and its harbor crammed with sleek yachts and motor cruisers.

▨ A walk along the coastal path on **Cap-Martin** gets you out of the car and brings you up close to the Riviera shoreline of white rocks and pines.

EUROPE

PORTUGAL

From Lisbon to Porto

Explore western Europe's last truly undiscovered corner on a tour of Portugal's unique medieval architecture and varied landscapes.

Linking Porto in northern Portugal with Lisbon, one of Europe's most attractive and relaxed capitals, this route takes you along the continent's Atlantic-washed western rim through one of its least-spoiled coastal areas. It runs south through a diverse region of salt pans, flatlands, pine forests, wooded hills, and vine-clad valleys. And you can turn off the highway to the coast to enjoy a stunning landscape of white-sand beaches, lagoons, and cliffs. From Porto, standing in a commanding position at the mouth of the Douro River, you can visit Vila Nova de Gaia, heart of the port wine industry, served by terraced vineyards lining the slopes inland along the Douro Valley. The region also has some of Portugal's most imposing architecture, from the churches, convents, and university buildings of stately Coimbra, a former capital, to medieval castles perched above villages and towns, such as in Leiria. Figueria da Foz is a charming seaside resort, where you can enjoy delicious meals of freshly caught sardines. Farther south on the alluvial plain watered by the Tejo (Tagus) River, vineyards, wheatfields, and market gardens flourish, and you'll glimpse black fighting bulls and fine horses at pasture. Along the way look out for villages where traditional handicrafts, including weaving and pottery, are still practiced—all part of a quiet, deeply rural way of life.

WHEN TO GO Any time of year.

HOW LONG You can drive the 198-mile (320 km) journey in half a day, but allow at least three days to take in the cities, towns, and other sights along the way.

PLANNING Take insect repellent in summer and waterproof clothing in winter.

INSIDE INFORMATION *Pousadas* are accommodations set in architecturally important and often historic buildings, such as castles and mansions, and make an extra-special stay en route.

WEBSITES visitportugal.com/en, pousadasofportugal.com

HIGHLIGHTS

■ Wander the streets of **medieval Porto**, from which both the country and the fortified wine take their name. Its wonderfully preserved architecture has earned it UNESCO World Heritage site status.

■ Try to visit the ancient **university city of Coimbra** when the students are there. They still wear their traditional black gowns.

■ Stop off in the beautiful coastal town of **Aveiro**, with its canals, fishing boats, and whitewashed houses.

■ Explore the alleyways of **Lisbon**'s Alfama district, the port area of Belém, and listen to the nation's folk music in one of its many fado houses.

Gustave Eiffel designed Porto's Maria Pia Bridge, opened in 1877, across a gorge in the Douro. The modern road bridge crosses the river beyond.

ACROSS WATER

BY ROAD

BY RAIL

ON FOOT

IN SEARCH OF CULTURE

IN GOURMET HEAVEN

INTO THE ACTION

UP AND AWAY

IN THEIR FOOTSTEPS

| ITALY |

The Dolomites

*Majestic mountainscapes and bizarre rock
formations abound on this spectacular Italian route.*

Vertiginous cliffs tower overhead, their splintered spires and crags reflected in deep green lakes. Cows graze in lush Alpine meadows, carpeted in spring and early summer with Alpine poppies, edelweiss, and rhododendron, and edged by dense, dark forests. The Great Dolomite Road, from Bolzano to Italy's most popular ski resort, Cortina d'Ampezzo, takes you through the heart of this fantastical southern spur of the Alps which juts into northeastern Italy. The nature of the rock, called dolomitic limestone, gives the region its magic—over thousands of years, erosion has carved it into sawtooth ridges, pinnacles, and plunging gorges. It changes color with the light, from battleship gray to glowing pink in the setting sun. The present-day route (SS241 and SS48) was begun in 1891 and took 14 years to reach Cortina—a marvel of engineering linking valley, village, lake, and mountain. Heading southeast from the old town of Bolzano you enter a deep canyon, then climb via the lovely Fassa Valley to the road's highest point, the Pordoi Pass (7,345 feet/2,239 meters above sea level). From here the road weaves northeast down to Cortina in a series of steep curves and S-bends. Set in a wide valley, Cortina hosted the Winter Olympics of 1956, and remains a glossy jet-set haunt. Vary your return journey as you wish; side trips from Canazei to Ortisei or the Sella Pass bring their own delights, as will any detour you care to make.

EUROPE

WHEN TO GO Late May to mid-October. Many of the passes are closed at other times. In July and August there is a lot of traffic, but the weather is at its best. The wildflowers in early summer and the foliage in fall are further attractions.

HOW LONG Allow a day for the 68-mile (109 km) one-way journey; for a circuit, allow two or three days.

PLANNING From Verona, it's an easy two-hour drive up to Bolzano. Another convenient airport is Venice-Treviso; Milan and Munich are also fairly well situated. Canazei, Arabba, and Cortina are good places to stop for the night en route.

INSIDE INFORMATION Like all mountain roads, those in the Dolomites require full concentration – they can be narrow, with hairpin bends. Speed limits on roads outside urban areas are 55 mph (89 km/h). Pull off at suitable places along the way to take in the views.

WEBSITES dolomiti.org/en, enit.it/en, italiantourism.com

HIGHLIGHTS

▓ Take the **cable car** from Bolzano for the views up to the Renòn, a region of lower, wooded mountains dotted with pretty villages.

▓ Pause to soak up the panorama from the **Sella Pass**, with a vista of the Dolomites' highest peak, Marmolada, rising to 10,970 ft (3,344 m) above sea level.

▓ Flirt with vertigo by taking the cable car at **Malga Ciapela**, which ascends to 10,650 ft (3,246 m), close to the summit of Marmolada.

▓ Watch the **beautiful people** in Cortina d'Ampezzo, one of the most glamorous resorts in the Alps.

▓ Marvel at the mummified remains of prehistoric celebrity **Ötzi the Iceman** at Bolzano's Museo Archeologico dell'Alto Adige. His frozen, 5,000-year-old body was found in a glacier near the border with Austria in 1991.

Opposite: This is Italy, but the architecture and landscape around Castelrotto are unmistakeably Alpine. Beyond the church tower, wisps of cloud veil the crags of the Dolomites. Above left: In addition to fine views, the region offers fine food, as displayed in a shop in Cortina. Above right: Jagged peaks stretch to the horizon beyond a ruin in Cortina.

Historic Spain

A journey through the heart of Spain offers timeless cities, succulent regional dishes, and the luminous skies that inspired El Greco.

Segovia, dwarfed by the soaring arches of its Roman aqueduct; Ávila, walled city of saints; Salamanca, seat of one of Europe's most ancient universities; Cáceres and Trujillo, enriched by the gold of the conquered Americas; Toledo, home of the painter El Greco—the list evokes all that makes Spain one of the most fascinating countries in Europe. This round-trip from Madrid climbs northwest from the capital over the softly silhouetted mountains of the Sierra de Guadarrama before descending through pine forests to Segovia. Continuing west through Ávila and Salamanca, it then turns south through a wild and remote region where small towns and villages seem like sets for a costume drama. It emerges onto the plains of Extremadura, from where many of the conquistadors set forth for the New World, and then returned to build magnificent palaces and endow richly adorned churches and convents in Cáceres, Trujillo, and other towns. The final lap takes you back toward Madrid, passing through Guadalupe—shrine of Our Lady of Guadalupe and since medieval times one of Spain's holiest pilgrimage sites—and Toledo, among the country's most historic cities, set above the Tagus River and dominated by the profiles of its great cathedral and *alcázar* (castle).

WHEN TO GO Any time of year, but in spring and early summer there are fewer tourists and wonderful wildflowers, and snow still caps the mountains.

HOW LONG Allow up to a week for this 535-mile (861 km) round–trip.

PLANNING The route is well endowed with paradors – state-run hotels often sited in castles, palaces, former monasteries, and other historic buildings. Try to stay in at least one of these – it is well worth the relative expense – but make sure to book in advance.

INSIDE INFORMATION Virtually every city and region in Spain has its own special dish – suckling pig in Segovia, for example. Be sure to ask what a place's specialty is, and then sample it.

WEBSITES spain.info, www.parador.es/en

HIGHLIGHTS

▥ The **Valley of the Fallen**, on the way to Segovia, is a bizarre and controversial memorial to the dead of Spain's Civil War. The late dictator Francisco Franco is buried there.

▥ **Salamanca** is an architectural gem, with two adjoining cathedrals and a Plaza Mayor (main square) regarded as one of the finest in Spain. Sit in a café there and watch people stroll by.

▥ Peru's conqueror, Francisco Pizarro, came from **Trujillo**. There is a superb statue of him, armed and mounted, in the impressive Plaza Mayor.

▥ Muslims, Jews, and Christians all left their mark on **Toledo**. Don't miss El Greco's house and museum.

A Roman bridge spans the Tormes River leading visitors into Salamanca – the Old Cathedral is to the right.

ACROSS WATER

BY ROAD

BY RAIL

ON FOOT

IN SEARCH OF CULTURE

IN GOURMET HEAVEN

INTO THE ACTION

UP AND AWAY

IN THEIR FOOTSTEPS

Against a background of cloudless blue sky, the white-limed houses of Casares reflect the sunlight with almost blinding brilliance.

| SPAIN |

White Villages in Andalusia

Roam the hills and villages of southern Andalusia to seek out treasures from prehistoric cave paintings to Moorish remains.

It is said that there's a special light in Andalusia, and nowhere is this more apparent than in the region's *pueblos blancos* (white villages), set high on hilltops or nestled in valleys against a rocky backdrop. Berber hill farmers from North Africa built many of the pueblos—places such as Grazalema—when the Arabs still ruled in Spain. They were constructed as fortresses, designed to resist Christian claims on Al-Andalus. Moorish influences continue to saturate the local art and architecture, and each limed village, no matter how tiny or remote, has its own story. Olvera, for example, was on the line of defences separating the Arab kingdom of Granada from Christian territory to the north and west; Benaoján dates back even further, lying near the site of important prehistoric settlements; and Arcos de la Frontera, with its steep, winding streets, nooks, and archways, is a shining example of Arab design. This trip, from Antequera west to Jerez de la Frontera, takes in the pick of the villages and the Andalusian landscape. As you travel from one jewel to the next, you meander along mountain roads, beside rivers, down narrow valleys and gorges, and through fir and oak forests. Eagles wheel overhead, and in pastures beside the road you will see fighting bulls grazing.

WHEN TO GO From March to June, and September to November. Avoid the heat of high summer.

HOW LONG The 230-mile (370 km) journey along frequently winding roads can be done in two days, but aim for three or more to make the trip more relaxed.

PLANNING In late fall, take warm clothing as the nights can be cold, though the sun still gets hot in the daytime. Carry water and sunblock.

INSIDE INFORMATION The siesta still exists in small communities, so don't expect much action from 2 to 5 p.m. Go to Tourist Information in the larger towns and check for local fiestas – if you attend one deliberately, it's a great experience, but if your car gets stuck in a long procession, it can be a nightmare.

WEBSITES spain.info, andalucia.com

| HIGHLIGHTS

▥ Caves and dolmens near **Antequera** bear witness to the region's ancient Iberian inhabitants.

▥ The nature reserve of **El Peñón de Zaframagón**, near Olvera, has a large population of tawny vultures.

▥ A dramatic gorge carves through **Ronda**, also the headquarters of Spanish bullfighting.

▥ **Cueva de la Pileta**, near Benaoján, has some fine prehistoric cave art.

▥ **Arcos de la Frontera** perches on top of a limestone cliff, with superb views across the Guadalete Valley.

The fort at Nakhl stands amid its oasis, with the rocky slopes of the Jabal Akhdar Mountains rising behind.

| OMAN |

The Forts of Oman

A desert circuit via 4x4 takes in spectacular fortresses, timeless mud-brick villages, and challenging mountain passes.

Around a thousand castles, watchtowers, and forts of mud and stone dot Oman, testimony to its strategic importance at the mouth of the Persian Gulf. Head southwest along the highway from the capital, Masqaṭ (Muscat), and you'll witness these wonders of improvised architecture, clinging to ridges, melting into the landscape among mud villages, date plantations, and rugged mountains. The Ya'ariba dynasty, who expelled the Portuguese in 1650, and their successors, the Al Bu Saids, built most of the forts. Your first stop is the ancient capital of Nizwá, famous for its 17th-century fort flanked by a huge circular tower. Nearby are Bahlās and Jabrīn, both of which combine fortress and palace all in one. Enjoy the eerie moonscape around you, then test your nerves as you leave the highway, cross the mountains, and snake down to the Batinah plain below. You'll reach the strongholds of Ar Rustāq and Ḥazm, before returning to the highway and a string of coastal defences. Finally, you'll visit Nakhl at the edge of the Jabal Akhdar Mountains, as you head back to Masqaṭ.

WHEN TO GO November to March, though it can be cold in the mountains. Avoid the heat of summer.

HOW LONG Allow a minimum of four days for this 470-mile (756 km) trip, including two nights in Nizwá, your base for visiting Bahlās and Jabrīn, and one on the coast in As Suwayq, which makes a good place to stay the night before visiting Nakhl.

PLANNING Conditions on the highway are good, but to go off-route you need a 4x4.

INSIDE INFORMATION Signs are in English, drivers cautious, and traffic regulations strictly enforced, including fines for driving a dirty vehicle. The road has little traffic and gas stations are spaced out, so fill up when you can, carry plenty of water, and be prepared in case of breakdown.

WEBSITES omantourism.gov.om, mark-oman.com

HIGHLIGHTS

▥ Stop for lunch in **Sayq** on the way to Nizwá for superb mountain vistas.

▥ Bargain for pottery and silver in **Nizwá**'s souk and relish the 360° views from the city's castle.

▥ Take a side trip from Nizwá to **Wadi Ghul**, Oman's "Grand Canyon" in the shadow of the country's highest peak, the 9,840-ft (3,000 m) Jabal Shams.

▥ Patrol the 7-mile (11 km) walls of **Bahlās**, a UNESCO World Heritage site, recently restored.

▥ Picnic in the shade of date palms by the **hot springs of Nakhl** oasis. Watch children play and women wash clothes in the pools of warm water.

▥ Go **wadi bashing** – taking your 4x4 through a dry river bed.

▥ Enjoy the fragrance of **frankincense** and the bubbling of hookah pipes after dinner.

AFRICA

From Cairo to the Cape

It is the stuff of dreams—traveling the length of Africa on a journey encompassing wildlife, waterfalls, deserts, and huge cultural diversity.

Taxis ply the busy streets of Cairo, Egypt, accompanied by a cacophony of horns, while men dressed in galabaias (long robes) sit drinking coffee and share *shisha* (water) pipes. From there fly to Nairobi, Kenya, as travel by road through strife-torn Sudan and Ethiopia is dangerous. In Tanzania, the road fringes game parks, where the barking of zebras can be heard on the warm afternoon breeze. They kick up dust waiting their turn to visit the river in the valley below your safari camp, while at night elephants tramp through, searching for acacia seedpods, and at dawn drink from a nearby water hole. On Lake Malawi in the Great Rift Valley, fish eagles snatch their prey from crystal clear waters. At dusk the lake mirrors the deep colors of the sunset and the chorus of birds gives way to the night opera of insects. A misty spray rising from the Zambezi Gorge cloaks Victoria Falls—locally known as Mosi-a-tunya (Smoke that Thunders). The bush and scattered trees change to rocky scrub and a sea of dunes in the Namib Desert, where the occasional gemsbok or oryx searches out meager water holes. In the final stretch, you may spot whales and dolphins along the Cape coast, with Table Mountain rising above your destination—Cape Town, South Africa.

WHEN TO GO October to April.

HOW LONG 5,500 miles (8,850 km) in total; 3,510 miles (5,649 km) by road from Nairobi to Cape Town. You need at least six weeks to take advantage of stopovers along the way.

PLANNING Advance booking is recommended for most hotels and activities to be sure of getting a place. Check out visa requirements for the various countries on the route; many also require proof of a yellow fever vaccination.

INSIDE INFORMATION Daily flights connect Cairo and Nairobi. From Nairobi, you can continue your journey overland. April is the best month for microlight flights over Victoria Falls.

WEBSITES africa.com, tourism-africa.co.za, africatravelresource.com

HIGHLIGHTS

▦ Watch game from the comfort of your tent in a safari lodge in **Tarangire National Park** in Tanzania. The park is famous for its elephants, which can be seen in herds of more than 200.

▦ Kayak in **Lake Malawi National Park**, a UNESCO World Heritage site, and stay on **Mumbo Island**.

▦ Take a flight in a **microlight** plane over **Victoria Falls**.

▦ Watch the animals at the **Namutoni** water hole in **Etosha Pan**, **Namibia**. It is floodlit for night viewing.

The majestic view of Table Mountain, with Cape Town tucked around its feet, provides a dramatic finale for this astonishing adventure across an entire continent.

Touring Morocco

A journey along age-old trade routes brings a taste of ancient cultures, exotic markets, and imposing mountain and desert scenery.

The bustle of cities contrasts with the tranquility of the desert. Stopping at towns along the way, you hear the muezzin's call to prayer, echoing around a maze of narrow streets, rising above the voices of haggling traders in the souk (market). Jostling crowds disperse in the heat of midday; street cafés fill up, and the scent of spices infuses the air. This enchanting journey starts in Ceuta, a North African city that is officially part of Spain—12 miles (19 km) away across the Strait of Gibraltar. It ends in the tiny Moroccan fishing port of Tarfaya on the border with Western Sahara. In central Morocco, Marrakech comes into view in the foothills of the Atlas Mountains, its ocher adobe buildings introducing an African feel, unlike the more Mediterranean north. Kasbahs, high-walled Berber palace-fortresses, blend with the landscape. Then the terrain changes—you pass from high mountain passes to desert toward the end of your journey. Huge skies dominate the landscape and, as the road follows the coastline, the desert appears to dissolve into the Atlantic. Along the way, you'll hear Moroccan Chaabi folk songs on roadside café radios and become used to the sight of camels, goats, and sheep wandering into the road.

WHEN TO GO September to March. These are cooler months in Morocco.

HOW LONG 1,100 miles (1,770 km). Don't rush this journey—allow at least two weeks.

PLANNING Make sure you have a visa, if needed. Check travel conditions, including possible political unrest. Take advice and prepare carefully if planning to drive yourself; avoid driving after dark. Road signs are in French and Arabic.

INSIDE INFORMATION If going by bus, remember that timetables in the Western sense don't always exist—for example, buses often don't leave until they're full.

WEBSITES muchmorocco.com, morocco.com

HIGHLIGHTS

▓ In Morocco, Fès's walled medieval city – **Fes el-Bali (Old Fès)** – is a labyrinth of alleyways and covered markets. Try to find the henna souk.

▓ Winding roads lead through the High Atlas Mountains of southern Morocco to **Todra Gorge**, the highest in the country, and the **Dadès Valley**, the "valley of a thousand Kasbahs."

▓ The kasbahs of the fortified village of **Aït Benhaddou** rise sharply out of the desert landscape of southern Morocco. Visit the Hassan II Mosque.

In the Dades River valley, a man gathers dried rose petals for the Moroccan Festival of Roses.

ACROSS WATER

BY ROAD

BY RAIL

ON FOOT

IN SEARCH OF CULTURE

IN GOURMET HEAVEN

INTO THE ACTION

UP AND AWAY

IN THEIR FOOTSTEPS

Glorious displays of fiery-blossomed aloes, indigenous to the Cape, spike the mountainsides above the Garden Route.

SOUTH AFRICA

The Garden Route

A beautiful and popular drive that boasts white beaches, rugged cliffs, ancient forests, and mountain scenery along the way.

For early Dutch settlers trekking east from Cape Town, this fertile stretch of the Western Cape coast, bathed by the waters of the Indian Ocean and nurtured by a benign Mediterranean climate, seemed like the biblical Garden of Eden. The name has stuck, and the region is now one of South Africa's most deservedly popular tourist destinations. Running from Mossel Bay to the town of Storms River, the Garden Route passes by hidden coves and endless beaches that link up with a varying pattern of lakes, rivers, and wetlands. Inland, it leads into great forests and nature reserves overlooked by the Outeniqua and Tsitsikamma mountains. The town of George offers a taste of sophistication and is an excellent base for exploring. Farther on, immerse yourself in tranquil, untouched nature at Wilderness and Knysna, where the sea floods the lagoon at the river's mouth. Here, at the heart of the route, you enter the Knysna forest, the largest native forest in South Africa, with ancient species such as the giant yellowwood, white alder, and Cape chestnut, as well as ferns and wildflowers. Take a detour to visit Tsitsikamma National Park—the Storms River has forged a steep canyon through the cliffs where it crashes into the ocean. Few journeys end more dramatically.

WHEN TO GO November to February, the Southern Hemisphere summer. In December, however, the area is packed with South Africans on vacation.

HOW LONG You could drive the 230-mile (370 km) journey in one day, but most people stop off for a day or two in a couple of places.

PLANNING Book accommodation well in advance. Numbers are limited for some of the best hiking trails so, again, book in advance.

INSIDE INFORMATION Make sure to sample the local fish delicacy, *snoek*, a relative of the mackerel. If you can get past the bones – which are numerous – the flavor of snoek grilled on a *braai* (barbecue) is delicious.

WEBSITES gardenroute.co.za, gardenroute.com, southafrica-travel.net

HIGHLIGHTS

▦ Take a hike through **Wilderness National Park**, one of the area's most peaceful and wildlife-rich areas.

▦ Watch out for **whales and dolphins**. You can see these magnificent creatures from several points along the Garden Route.

▦ Visit **Tsitsikamma National Park**, which shelters Africa's largest marine reserve. It also embraces lush forest with plentiful birdlife.

▦ Take advantage of the abundant opportunities for **hiking** and just about every kind of **adventure and water sport**.

Chapter 3

BY RAIL

Luxurious or spartan, relaxing or adventurous, the world's greatest rail journeys have one thing in common—an aura of glamour. To step onto any of these trains is to enter a world of dreams, to star in a vintage Hollywood romance, to cross ravishing landscapes, to glimpse the dramas of daily life unfolding alongside the tracks. Some of these journeys, such as the Venice Simplon-Orient-Express or the Trans-Siberian Railroad between Moscow and Beijing, are world famous. Others are well-kept secrets. Apart from Antarctica, every continent has its share of rail adventures, from South Africa's safari trains to a route into northern Sweden in search of Arctic wildlife and the midnight sun. There are journeys back in time: perfectly preserved steam locomotives rattling through gold-mining country in the Southern Rockies or a trip across a relic of World War II—the bridge over the River Kwai. Others are entirely of today, such as the high-speed dazzle of Japan's bullet trains or the high-altitude Qingzang Railway, which climbs from China into Tibet.

The Jacobite steam train service operates in the West Highlands of Scotland, traveling through some of the country's wildest scenery, past moorland, lochs, and glens, and along the beautiful west coast.

The mountain goat is a native inhabitant of the Rockies, where it lives on steep slopes above the timberline.

CANADA

The Rocky Mountaineer

Follow the route of a pioneering and dramatic railroad through the Canadian Rockies from Vancouver to Banff.

The train plunges into the spiraling tunnels through Cathedral Mountain; the soaring pine trees and rocky gradients out the window are replaced by pitch blackness. Minutes later, you emerge amid scenery that has been deeply etched by ancient glaciers. This is just part of the impressive route of the *Rocky Mountaineer*—a train that travels only in daylight, through tunnels, along ledges, and over high trestle bridges. Departing from Vancouver, the train climbs into the Canadian Rockies through the Fraser Canyon, way above the roaring rapids at Hell's Gate. Passengers with vertigo are advised not to look out the windows. After a night in Kamloops, the really steep climbing begins via the Connaught Tunnel and then to Kicking Horse Pass, 5,000 feet (1,524 meters) above sea level. High above, golden eagles overlook your journey, while sheer rock faces, snowy peaks, and evergreen forests quicken the pulse.

WHEN TO GO The First Passage to the West route runs from early April to mid-October. Go during April or October if you are hoping to see snowy scenes.

HOW LONG Two days from Vancouver to Banff or Calgary, with an overnight stop at a hotel in Kamloops. The journey can be made westbound as well.

PLANNING Choose between the sumptuous GoldLeaf with its bi-level dome coach (a photographer's dream), the SilverLeaf class with a single-level observation dome, or the more basic RedLeaf service.

INSIDE INFORMATION For upgraded hotel accommodation, book the Deluxe GoldLeaf service.

WEBSITES canadiantrainvacations.com, rockymountaineer.com

| HIGHLIGHTS

▦ Marvel at the stunning scenery, such as the sheer-sided, 1,980-ft (604 m) deep **Fraser Canyon**, and **Hell's Gate**, where the Fraser River surges through the gorge below.

▦ Meet the friendly blue-shirted volunteer cowboys of the **Kamloops Mounted Patrol**, who ride out to meet the *Rocky Mountaineer* as it pulls into their town.

▦ Look out for the abundant **wildlife** after leaving Kamloops on the second morning. You may see elk, bears, ospreys, and timber wolves. If three passengers see an animal, it counts as an official sighting.

▦ Enjoy the outstanding **service** onboard, which keeps passengers supplied with high-quality food and drink. Treats can include everything from chocolate cookies to local liqueurs.

COLORADO | UTAH

The California Zephyr

Journey into the authentic Wild West on this route through the heart of the Rockies.

This is a voyage into the real Wild West—high mountain ledges, dusty red ocher rocks, and yellow-gold grasslands. Between Denver, Colorado, and Salt Lake City, Utah, the *California Zephyr* runs on the tracks of the now-defunct Denver & Rio Grande Western Railroad, whose motto was: "Through the Rockies, not around them." From Denver, the *Zephyr* wiggles steeply upward into the eastern mountains through 28 tunnels. Sheltered from fierce winds by lines of old freight cars, passengers enjoy sweeping views across vast, high plains. The continental divide is crossed in darkness, halfway through the 6-mile (9.5 kilometer) long Moffat Tunnel, before the train descends to Tabernash and traces the snaking Colorado River through vertiginous canyons to Glenwood Springs, and on to the Utah stateline. At the edge of the Moab Desert, the train climbs to the bleak scrubland of Soldier Summit, Utah, before descending once more toward Salt Lake City. There is hardly a sign of human activity—aside from the odd kayaker splashing along the Colorado River—so it is easy to imagine yourself back in the era of the pioneering settlers of the 19th century.

WHEN TO GO In summer, the journey has contrasts of snowy summits, green riverside meadows, rocky deserts, and tumbling rivers. In winter, the route transforms into a fairy-tale land of ice and snow. Trains run daily.

HOW LONG The overall journey from Denver to Salt Lake City takes approximately 15 hours.

PLANNING The *California Zephyr* is operated by Amtrak. Trains 5 and 6 (from east to west) operate between Chicago's Union Station and Oakland Train Terminal via Omaha, Denver, Salt Lake City, the Donner Pass, and Sacramento. Buses are available from Oakland Train Terminal to San Francisco.

INSIDE INFORMATION Find a seat in the sightseer coach as soon as you can, as it can fill up very quickly. Sit on the left-hand side for the best views (or on the right-hand side if you are traveling east).

WEBSITE amtrak.com

HIGHLIGHTS

▓ Between Granby and Glenwood Springs, CO, gaze through the ceiling windows at the rugged tops of **Gore Canyon**. The Zephyr follows the canyon for about 20 miles (32 km).

▓ At **Glenwood Springs**, home to volcanic springs and resting place of the gunfighter "Doc" Holliday, **white-water rafters** greet the train as they ride the Colorado rapids.

▓ Before reaching Soldier Summit, UT, look out for the **Castle Gate** rock formation.

▓ To your right, beyond Soldier Summit and shortly before Provo, UT, you can see the roofs of the town of **Thistle**, buried by a landslide in 1983.

Amtrak's *California Zephyr* snakes through the fall-colored valleys of Tolland, Colorado.

NEW MEXICO | COLORADO |

The Cumbres & Toltec Scenic Railroad

Get the authentic flavor of the Old West on a steam train trip through spectacular mountain scenery.

A lonesome whistle echoes through the 600-foot (183 meter) deep Toltec Gorge. Hugging the mountainside, the narrow-gauge locomotives of the Cumbres & Toltec Scenic Railroad move with a symphony of hissing steam and rattling cars, while the engine belches out black smoke and explosive exhaust blasts. You cross high, spindly trestle bridges spanning rocky gullies, cut through swaths of green and yellow grassland, and descend through wide valleys by sparkling streams. Standing in the open observation car, you will be transported back to the age of gold bonanzas and fabled heroes and villains. The Denver & Rio Grande Western Railroad built the line (America's highest and longest narrow-gauge railroad) in the 1880s to carry gold over the Southern Rockies from the mining towns of the San Juan Mountains to Alamosa, Colorado. Today, the trains run for 64 miles (103 kilometers) on a section of the original route: across the Conejos Mountains from Chama, New Mexico, to Antonito, Colorado. The 10,015-foot (3,053 meter) altitude at Cumbres Summit, the cliffside views at Windy Point and Toltec Gorge, and the trestle bridges at Lobato and Cascade make your heart leap into your mouth, while the gentle swaying of the period-piece parlor cars captures a time when sheriffs and outlaws, such as Bat Masterson and Soapy Smith, traveled the route.

WHEN TO GO Trains run from late May through mid-October, departing seven days a week.

HOW LONG This is not a high-speed experience. The full journey between Chama and Antonito, plus the return to your departure point by coach, takes most of a day.

PLANNING Accommodation is limited in Chama and Antonito, but Alamosa, near the latter, has more facilities and camping. Wheelchair access is available on every train. Trains stop at Osier, CO, for lunch, which is included in the fare.

INSIDE INFORMATION Trains carry one or two open observation cars, which are subject to cacophonous demonstrations of steam's power on the steep gradients and the occasional shower of cinders. A sun hat and sunglasses – to protect against the cinders – are musts, but the inconvenience is more than compensated by the far superior viewing position.

WEBSITE cumbrestoltec.com

HIGHLIGHTS

▥ Most of the buildings and equipment on the C&TSRR date back to the turn of the 20th century, or even earlier. Rail enthusiasts will want to explore **Chama Yard**, which houses a vast collection of antique narrow-gauge train equipment.

▥ Eastbound from Chama en route to Cumbres Summit, via one of the steepest grades in the U.S., admire the **views over Chama**, 2,000 ft (610 m) below. Next comes the horseshoe Tanglefoot Curve, the wastes of Los Pinos, and the great chasm of the **Toltec Gorge**.

▥ Crossing **Cascade Trestle**, at 100 ft (30 m) the highest bridge on the line, passengers feel as if the ground has been taken away, leaving nothing but empty space on either side of the train.

▥ To the east of Osier, look out for the **Garfield monument**, erected to commemorate President Garfield's assassination in 1881.

▥ As the train descends to Antonito, the 3-ft (0.9 m) gauge line negotiates **amazing curves** at Big Horn, Whiplash, and Lava Tank.

Opposite: A Cumbres & Toltec Scenic Railroad train negotiates Cumbres Pass on a late fall day. The west slope is an unusually steep four percent grade. Above left: Water is taken onboard to power the steam engine. Above right: Cattle are driven across the tracks at a convenient point.

National Parks of the West

*This luxury train ride links some of the
best-known national parks in the western U.S.*

A gleaming, quarter-mile-long ribbon of black and red, the *Great Western Limited*, with its complement of fully restored and modernized Pullman-style railcars, is a model of 1940s luxury. You can happily spend all day sitting in the upper level of the dome car for superb 360° views through the curved glass viewing windows. A little later, sink into a soft armchair in the sumptuous lounge coach, and sip cocktails while the glorious vistas roll by. In addition to the luxurious environment onboard, the tour of the national parks of the West prides itself on providing passengers with a kaleidoscopic vision of the finest and most varied scenery in the U.S. Included on the four-state itinerary are Glacier National Park, a cruise on Lake MacDonald, the Snake River, and Yellowstone National Park in Wyoming, the dry lake, desert, and intermountain basin country of Utah and Nevada, and a full day visit to Yosemite National Park, with an overnight stay at the Yosemite View Lodge along the rushing Merced River. Leisure, cultural, and historical interests can be enjoyed in Whitefish, Montana; Jackson Hole, Wyoming; Old Sacramento; and, at journey's end, San Francisco, California. There you are treated to a two-night stay in a hotel on the iconic Fisherman's Wharf, from which you can tour the city at your leisure.

WHEN TO GO The National Parks of the West tours depart in the spring and summer, but exact dates vary each year. Check the website for details.

HOW LONG The tour takes about nine days; a few nights are spent in luxury hotels, and the rest onboard the train.

PLANNING Tours within the national parks are organized by Uncommon Journeys. Book online or by telephone, and be prepared for the added expense of tips (around $15 per day).

INSIDE INFORMATION Dress is casual. Take walking boots for the parks.

WEBSITE uncommonjourneys.com

HIGHLIGHTS

▓ Onboard, you'll be pampered by the **uniformed staff** and have access to experts on the local scenery.

▓ In **Yellowstone National Park** see geysers, hot springs, bison, bald eagles, bears, and elk. The landscape was sculpted by thermal springs and volcanic activity.

▓ Use your binoculars to spot climbers clinging to El Capitan and the Half-Dome in **Yosemite National Park**.

Yellowstone National Park is famous for its strangely colored volcanic springs and pools.

El Chepe winds through the Copper Canyon near Divisadero.

MEXICO

El Chepe

This journey takes you through Copper Canyon,
deep in Mexico's Sierra Madre Mountains.

From the dazzling Sea of Cortez in the Pacific to the lofty heights of the Sierra Madre Mountains, the Chihuahua al Pacifico railway (El Chepe for short) crosses 39 vertiginous bridges and passes through 88 tunnels, surrounded by vertical rocks and copper-colored walls. The railroad was built to ferry gold prospectors into the rich Sierra Madre Mountains and took almost a century to complete. Nowadays, the attraction is the route itself, through the largely unexplored and unspoiled expanses of the mighty Copper Canyon. Four times the area of the Grand Canyon, this epic landscape comprises a vast network of lush gullies, arid gorges, and waterfalls—all visible from the large viewing windows of El Chepe. The region is home to the Tarahumara Indians, the second-largest indigenous group in Mexico, who maintain a traditional way of life in tiny villages scattered through the canyon. During stops, you can watch the children play beside the tracks, while women sit weaving or offer wood carvings, dolls, and straw baskets for sale. When you reach Chihuahua, take time to visit the baroque Cathedral of St. Francis of Assisi in the Plaza de la Constitución.

WHEN TO GO El Chepe runs all year. The scenery changes dramatically in the dry season (March to July), turning the otherwise lush, verdant landscape arid and copper-tinged.

HOW LONG The 572-mile (921 km) journey takes 16 hours.

PLANNING The tourist train (*Primera Express*) leaves from Los Mochis at 6 a.m. and reaches Chihuahua at 10 p.m. Travelers on a budget can take the *Clase Económica* train (Economic Class, half the price), which leaves at 7 a.m. and arrives at 11 p.m. You can also do the journey the other way round: trains leave and arrive at the same times.

INSIDE INFORMATION Consider starting your journey at El Fuerte rather than Los Mochis. That way you can explore the town, and you won't miss the most spectacular part of the trip – between Temoris and Bahuichivo. Get a seat on the south side of the train for the best views.

WEBSITE chepe.com.mx/index-eng.jsp

HIGHLIGHTS

▪ Lovely, colonial-style hotels line the cobbled streets of **El Fuerte**'s historic downtown area. The town was a trading center for silver and gold miners from the nearby mountains.

▪ Enjoy the sweeping views over the canyon as the train negotiates the **ascent between El Fuerte and Creel**, rising 6,560 ft (2,000 m) through a series of sharp switchbacks.

▪ In **Chihuahua**, visit the National Museum of the Revolution in the former home of the revolutionary leader **Pancho Villa**. Exhibits include the bullet-ridden Dodge in which Villa was assassinated in 1923.

The Chiva Express

Enjoy fantastic views of the Andes and the coastal lowlands of Ecuador along this historic route.

Since the El Niño floods of the 1980s, the unreliable and rickety Ecuadorian train that once ran from Quito to Guayaquil has been replaced by the Chiva Express. A riot of primary colors, the Chiva Express is really a bus, garishly decorated and specially adapted to run on train tracks. Sitting on the roof in the thin, chilly air, strapped in with a seat belt and gripping tightly to the steel railings, you'll enjoy a cross-country rollercoaster ride from the Andes Mountains to the tropical lowlands. The journey begins at the foot of the volcano Chimborazo in Riobamba, a bustling town with cobbled streets, colonial plazas, and a vibrant Saturday market. From there, the Chiva Express descends south along the 100-year-old track through a variety of climate zones. The cold Andean air rapidly gives way to the mysterious stillness and hanging mist of the cloud forest, soon to be replaced by the tropical air of the hot coastal jungle, forcing you to whip off more layers of clothing the farther you travel. The landscape is similarly varied, as distant snowcapped volcanoes are replaced by rolling hillsides and fields of purple lupins, which in turn give way to the lush tropical vegetation of banana plantations and palms as you reach Guayaquil near the coast.

WHEN TO GO The Ecuadorian climate varies very little throughout the year, so go at any time.

HOW LONG The journey from Riobamba to Guayaquil takes about eight hours and covers approximately 160 miles (257 km).

PLANNING Make sure you check the schedule, as it changes frequently. Seats on the Chiva are not numbered, so arrive early to secure your place.

INSIDE INFORMATION It is a good idea to wear layers as you will be experiencing several changes of climate zone on the route. Be prepared for rain and take something soft to sit on.

WEBSITES metropolitantouring.com, ecuador.com/blog/chiva-express

HIGHLIGHTS

▧ At the **Devil's Nose**, an imposing granite mountain, the train ascends the almost perpendicular rock face with a hair-raising section of zigzagging switchbacks.

▧ Drink the local alchoholic beverage **canelazo**, a kind of hot toddy made from firewater, *naranjilla* fruit, cinnamon, and sugar.

▧ The Chiva Express itself, with its exuberant paintwork and the chance to **sit on the roof**, is one of the major attractions of this trip.

The colorful, one-coach Chiva Express, actually a bus on rails, travels through spectacular Andean scenery.

A herder drives her flock of llamas across the altiplano near Lake Titicaca.

| PERU |

The Spirit of the Water

Travel through the Andes to Lake Titicaca,
the highest navigable lake in the world.

Departing from Cusco, the old capital of the Inca empire, the *Andean Explorer* embarks on a gentle climb through lush green fields, following the meandering path of the Huatanay River, past eucalyptus groves, plunging gorges, and small local settlements with adobe rooftops and colonial churches, while the dark Andes rise beyond. Outside your carriage window you can watch life go by: a tiny boy herds massive oxen with a slim switch, a woman leads an alpaca adorned with colored wreaths, farmers toil in the cornfields. After nearly 160 miles (257 kilometers) the gentle grasslands give way to the altiplano, a bleak high-altitude plain stretching into the far distance, where vicuña and alpaca graze, circled by snow-draped Andean peaks. The route allows a unique glimpse of the remote rural communities of Andean Peru. In the bustling town of Juliaca, market sellers hastily shift their stalls off the line to allow the train to pass before they set up again behind it. From the back of the train, you can watch waving children running along the tracks, trying to keep pace with you. On arrival in Puno you are greeted by the azure waters of Lake Titicaca, the world's highest navigable lake.

WHEN TO GO The service runs throughout the year, departing every Tuesday morning. The skies are clearer and the service more reliable in the dry season from late May to September.

HOW LONG The train takes approximately 11 hours to travel 175 miles (282 km).

PLANNING Four different cabin types are available, each with its own bathroom and shower: the Deluxe Double Bed Cabin, Junior Double Bed Cabin, Twin Bed Cabin, or Bunk Bed Cabin. The journey offers a three-course meal and access to the open-air "bar car."

INSIDE INFORMATION Bring some medicine for altitude sickness as the stop at La Raya Pass is a long way above sea level. You might also have trouble breathing. If you don't mind skipping dessert, grab a space in the lounge car right after eating, before it gets too crowded.

WEBSITES belmond.com, perurail.com

HIGHLIGHTS

▓ At 14,176 ft (4,321 m), the stop at **La Raya Pass** is the highest point on the journey. The train makes a 20-minute stop so that you can enjoy the air of shimmering stillness hanging over the silent station. Here, too, local artisans lay out their wares – sweaters and shawls made from soft alpaca wool.

▓ At Raqchi, look out for the ruins of the **Temple of Viracocha**, the creator god, on the left-hand side of the train – one of the biggest buildings the Inca ever built.

▓ The 11 a.m. **Pisco Sour** – Peru's favorite cocktail – is served on board.

Top 10 Steam Train Trips

Enjoy the drama of steam travel through some of the world's most rugged landscapes.

❶ AUSTIN & TEXAS CENTRAL RAILROAD, TEXAS

This line operates two round-trip services allowing you to view the Texas landscape from the comfort of refurbished 1920s cars. The *River City Flyer* runs from Austin, alongside the Colorado River and through the cotton fields of the Blackland Prairies to Littig, before returning. The *Hill Country Flyer* runs through ranches and rolling hills on its route from Cedar Park to Burnet.

PLANNING Trains operate throughout the year. Reservations are advisable. austinsteamtrain.org

❷ MOUNT RAINIER SCENIC RAILROAD, WASHINGTON

Enjoy a round-trip on the southern slopes of 14,410-ft (4,392 m) Mount Rainier. The trains climb through farmland and forests, and over trestles and creeks to Mineral Lake for a 15-minute stopover before returning. En route, the engine often rouses Roosevelt elk, bears, eagles, and other wildlife.

PLANNING Trains depart two or three times a day from Elbe, southeast of Tacoma. Reservations are not usually necessary. mtrainierrailroad.com

❸ THE CENTRAL RAILWAY, PERU

The section of line from Lima to La Oroya in the Andes includes the world's steepest railway climb. It reaches the highest point—15,693 ft (4,783 m)—in 90 miles (145 km). The line teeters on the edge of defiles, tiptoes over high trestles, tunnels through rock, and gains height through successions of switchbacks, where in places four levels of track lie directly above one another. The Ferrocarril Centro Andino (FCCA) has retained one of its "Andes"-class steam locomotives for tourist excursions on a seasonal basis.

PLANNING FCCA operates seasonal weekend tourist trains and steam excursions. It is best to book through an experienced operator. ferrocarrilcentral.com.pe/en_index_.php

❹ THE PUFFING BILLY RAILWAY, AUSTRALIA

This 30-mile (48 km) round trip runs along a narrow-gauge line from Belgrave north of Melbourne through the southern foothills of the Dandenong Ranges. The air is thick with birdsong and the scent of eucalyptus as the train ascends through Menzies Creek, Emerald, Lakeside, and Cockatoo to the pretty town of Gembrook, where you stop awhile before the return journey to Belgrave.

PLANNING Trains run every day except Christmas Day. puffingbilly.com.au

The *Puffing Billy* chugs across Trestle Bridge on its winding journey through Belgrave. This railway line originally opened in 1900 to serve local farmers and timber communities.

❺ THE NILGIRI MOUNTAIN RAILWAY, INDIA

Such is its attraction, this railway through the Nilgiri range in southern India has been declared a UNESCO World Heritage site. The line climbs for 28 miles (45 km) from Mettuppalaiyam to Ootacamund (Udhagamandalam), 7,440 ft (2,268 m) above sea level. It is so steep in one section that trains are propelled uphill on a steam-powered rack-and-adhesion system.

PLANNING The journey takes five hours. It can be very hot, and there is only one departure each way per day. irctctourism.com/tourpackages/railtour/vacation-special-coonoor-day-tour.html

❻ THE CHILDREN'S RAILWAY, BUDAPEST, HUNGARY

The railway was built in the Soviet era to train children aged 10 to 14 for work on the Hungarian State Railway. All operations carried out by the children accord with the practices of the national railway; adults drive the trains. Steam engines are used on the weekend. The line runs past many of Budapest's tourist attractions and through forests, where you may see deer, long-eared owls, and wild boar.

PLANNING Trains run throughout the year from 9 a.m. to 5 p.m. in winter (7 p.m. in summer). www.gyermekvasut.hu/english_eng

❼ THE HARZER SCHMALSPURBAHNEN, GERMANY

This meter-gauge line from Wernigerode to Nordhausen has a steam branch from Drei Annen Hohne that climbs steeply to the 3,747-ft (1,142 m) summit of the Brocken Mountain. Trains struggle up the steep, twisting, forested countryside of Harz National Park. They run all year round despite a harsh winter climate.

PLANNING There is a train service from Wernigerode to Brocken station, which connects to the national network. Booking in summer is strongly recommended. nationalpark-harz.de/en/start

❽ *THE JACOBITE*, SCOTLAND

The train takes its name from the area's association with Bonnie Prince Charlie and the Jacobite Rebellion of 1745. Starting from Fort William, it crosses the Great Glen, skirts Loch Eil, then traverses the magnificent curving Glenfinnan viaduct. A fabulous panorama of the Inner Hebrides opens out on the final descent to Mallaig on the west coast.

PLANNING Reservations are essential in high summer. www.westcoastrailways.co.uk

❾ THE FFESTINIOG RAILWAY, WALES

Built to transport slate from the Moelwyn Mountains to the quays at Porthmadog, the Ffestiniog still has some of its earliest engines hard at work. Beginning in Porthmadog, the line climbs 700 ft (213 m) to Blaenau Ffestiniog deep in the Moelwyn Mountains. Here you can take a trip hundreds of feet underground into the vast old slate mines.

PLANNING festrail.co.uk

❿ THE ISLE OF MAN VICTORIAN STEAM RAILWAY, U.K.

This 3-ft (0.9 m) gauge railway runs from the Isle of Man's capital Douglas to Port Erin, climbing steep gradients and offering superb sea views. All its locomotives but one date from a design of 1874, and the carriages from the 1880s.

PLANNING The railway runs Easter to October. www.iomguide.com

The Shinkansen

*Race between Japan's ancient and modern capitals on
the futuristic, high-speed, high-frequency bullet train.*

Since 1964, Japan's major cities have been linked by an ultrahigh-speed service, the Shinkansen super express. In little more than two hours, these sleek bullet trains travel the 320 miles (515 kilometers) between Kyoto, the former imperial capital and spiritual heart of Japan, and Tokyo, known as Edo under Shogunate rule in the 17th and 18th centuries. Called the Tokaido line after an ancient highway that linked the two cities during feudal times, the service combines speeds of up to 170 miles (274 kilometers) per hour with quiet comfort and an unfolding pageant of scenery. Leaving Kyoto's sprawl of ancient Zen temples, Shinto shrines, and modern suburbs, the train skirts Lake Biwa, paddy fields, and woodlands as it tears across the Nobi Plain. Beyond Nagoya is Fuji-Hakone-Izu National Park and more intensive agriculture, with the ever present backdrop provided by the 12,000-foot (3,658 meter) snowcapped cone of Mount Fuji. Soon after Yokohama, the Shinkansen enters Tokyo's suburbs and arrives at the main or new Shinagawa station. If the train is so much as a minute behind schedule, you'll receive a polite apology from the driver.

WHEN TO GO March and April, when the cherry blossoms are out and the weather is not too hot. The Shinkansen runs every day, all year round.

HOW LONG The Nozomi train from Kyoto to Tokyo takes 2.25 hours; the Hikari takes 2.75 hours.

PLANNING There are three types of train on the Tokaido route: the Nozomi stops only at major stations (the Japan Rail Pass is not valid on this type of train); the Hikari makes additional stops at intermediate stations; the Kodama is an "all stations" service. There is a choice between "ordinary" and premium "green" class.

INSIDE INFORMATION The term "bullet train" is not used on signs in English; look for "Shinkansen."

WEBSITES us.jnto.go.jp, japanrailpass.net

HIGHLIGHTS

▥ At sunset, admire the reflections of the sky in **Lake Biwa**, the largest freshwater lake in Japan, northeast of Kyoto.

▥ The delicate white and pink cherry blossoms of Japan's **sakura trees** can be spotted from the train's windows.

▥ **Fuji-Hakone-Izu National Park** has mountains, hot springs, volcanic landscapes, and caldera lakes.

The Shinkansen passes over the hustle and bustle of Yurakucho station on the route between Kyoto and Tokyo.

A farmhand tends to the rice crop. Rice is grown intensively, and about three-quarters of all farmland is given over to it.

VIETNAM

The Reunification Express

Travel the length of the country on a route
that combines ancient culture and modern life.

Vietnam has been described as "two rice baskets joined by a long, thin pole"—an apt analogy for this long, thin land. The "rice baskets," Hanoi and Ho Chi Minh City, are located at opposite ends of the country and are opposites in other ways, too: the former exudes a faded, leafy charm, the latter is brash, noisy, and upbeat. A week spent on the Reunification Express, a 1,000-mile (1,600 kilometer) rail odyssey linking the two cities, takes you through virtually the entire length of the country, past lush tropical landscapes colored by iridescent paddy fields and wallowing buffalo, crumbling imperial cities, and the golden beaches of resorts on the South China Sea. If you tire of gazing out of the window, life onboard the train is a world in itself, and the Vietnamese are engaging company. The steady rhythm of the rails is punctuated by occasional stops at bustling stations, where you can purchase succulent tropical fruit, drinks, and snacks from the jostling vendors outside your window. You can stop at the ancient imperial capital of Hue, halfway along the route, to relax, explore the museum of Cham sculpture, and try the delicious local food.

WHEN TO GO Go in October through December – the driest months. Trains run several times daily.

HOW LONG Trains take around 30 hours straight through, but breaking the journey at Hue and Da Nang is recommended. From Da Nang, you can make trips to My Son and Hoi An. If you are doing this, allow a full week from Hanoi to Saigon. The total distance is 1,070 miles (1,722 km).

PLANNING If you plan to break your journey, you will need to buy separate tickets for each stage. It is easiest and quickest to buy tickets online at the website below. If you have plenty of time and patience to wait in line, you can buy tickets for about half the price at your starting point.

INSIDE INFORMATION The soft-sleeper class is worth the slightly higher price if you are averse to sleeping in cramped conditions. Both soft- and hard-sleeper cars are air-conditioned. Make sure you catch the SE1 or SE3 train. SE5 passes much of the best scenery at nighttime and arrives at Hue at 3 a.m.

WEBSITE vietnamtourism.com

HIGHLIGHTS

▦ Explore **Hue's Forbidden Purple City**, a UNESCO World Heritage site on the Perfume River. You can also visit the **imperial tombs** nearby.

▦ From Da Nang take a trip to the magical 14th-century ruins of the Cham civilization at **My Son**, deep in the Vietnamese jungle.

▦ Visit the cave-riddled **Marble Mountains** near Da Nang. The beautiful coastal scenery around the city can be appreciated from the comfort of the train.

▦ Absorb centuries of history in the perfectly preserved town of **Hoi An**, near Da Nang, an important port in the 15th century.

| CHINA | TIBET |

The Qingzang Railway

Travel across the roof of the world on the highest railroad line ever built.

The 710-mile (1,143 km) Qinghai-Tibet or Qingzang Railway links China's western province of Qinghai with Tibet in a phenomenal feat of engineering that many international experts considered impossible prior to the railway's completion in 2006. This remarkable route crosses the nigh-impassable Kunlun Mountains, deep ravines, and mile upon mile of harsh, icy terrain, using a specially designed, high-altitude train complete with oxygen supplies and tinted windows to protect against ultraviolet rays. As the train leaves from the Chinese outpost of Golmud, it begins to climb steeply through foothill country, past glistening white glaciers. From there, the train moves onto a barren, unpopulated plateau of permafrost rising to over 15,000 feet (4,572 meters). Inside, the pristine white dining car and bar give the train's interior the look of a space shuttle while, in each carriage, a scrolling LCD display keeps passengers updated with information about the altitude and the temperature outside. Many passengers need the oxygen provided to stave off the effects of altitude sickness. The train passes little more than the occasional antelope or yak on its final climb to 16,640 feet (5,072 meters) at Tanggula Pass, where the skies take on the startlingly deep blue of high altitudes. The train descends over the gracefully symmetrical Liuwa three-span, bowstring-arch bridge into Lhasa's new seven-platform station. A bus link covers the final 20 miles (32 kilometers) to the center of the Tibetan capital.

WHEN TO GO The service runs all year, though in winter it is bitterly cold. In summer the whole trip can be made in daylight. Check the schedule of departure times from Golmud.

HOW LONG The overall journey from Beijing to Lhasa takes two days, and begins with a rail trip from Beijing to Golmud. Golmud to Lhasa on the Qingzang Railway takes 11 hours.

PLANNING Take the T27 train from Beijing West station. Due to the extreme altitude, individuals with heart disease or high blood pressure are not allowed to travel on the Qingzang Railway; all passengers must complete a Health Registration Card to confirm that they are safe to travel. There are two classes: hard- and soft-sleepers. There is also an additional charge for forward-facing seats.

INSIDE INFORMATION Make sure you get a window seat, as those in the aisle give a very restricted view out of the train. As in an airplane, be careful if you are drinking – the high altitude increases the effects of alcohol.

WEBSITE chinatibettrain.com

HIGHLIGHTS

▧ Enjoy the vivid contrast between the **shining glaciers** and the barren brown glacial rock debris on the initial climb from Golmud.

▧ On the plateau, you can see the **vent pipes** alongside the track and **sun canopies** that protect the permafrost trackbed foundation from the warming rays and prevent the track from moving.

▧ The **high-altitude diesel locomotives** were built in the U.S., while the Canadian-designed coaches are pressure-sealed and have an oxygen supply at every seat.

▧ Glancing out at the harsh and forbidding landscape, you cannot help but wonder at the **astonishing engineering** that went into the construction of the track, which includes 283 viaducts – the longest is more than 7 miles (11 km) long.

▧ On arrival in Lhasa, do not miss the Dalai Lama's **Potala Palace** perched high above the city, and the 7th-century **Johkang Temple** – rare traces of tradition in an increasingly modernized Tibet.

Opposite: A monk looks out from the Drepung Buddhist monastery, outside Lhasa. This was Tibet's largest and most influential monastery and still attracts visitors and pilgrims from all over the world. Above: A Qingzang train races across the almost deserted high Tibetan plateau.

The famous bridge over the River Kwai, built during World War II, is still crossed by passenger trains.

THAILAND

Bangkok-Kanchanaburi-Nam Tok Line

The journey passes through beautiful jungle but also evokes memories of the horrors of war.

This journey through Thailand's beautiful scenery is also a chilling reminder of war. The route from Bangkok to Nam Tok runs partly along the infamous Burma-Thailand Railway (the "death railway") and across the bridge at the River Kwai, both built by the Japanese during World War II, using Allied prisoners-of-war and conscripted local labor, at the cost of thousands of lives. Leaving Bangkok's Thonburi Station, the wooden carriages clatter through lush jungle on the route west. A few miles beyond Kanchanaburi, you cross the Kwai bridge, immortalized in a book by Pierre Boulle and the 1957 film. Today, you see painted speedboats from the bridge—dots of red, blue, and yellow moored beside the bank or scudding along the muddy surface. Beyond the Kwai, the line runs along the Wampo Viaduct, a ribbon of steel bestriding the green hillside, supported by concrete blocks and wooden struts. The track into Myanmar (Burma) has been lifted, so the journey terminates at Nam Tok.

WHEN TO GO October through February is the best time, when it is cool and not too rainy. Go in late November if you are hoping to enjoy the River Kwai Festival. Trains run all year with two departures a day from Bangkok: trains 257 and 259. An additional service runs from Kanchanaburi to Nam Tok.

HOW LONG The full journey from Bangkok to Nam Tok takes 4.75 hours.

PLANNING It is worth breaking your journey for a night at Kanchanaburi and the Kwai bridge. Trains are third class only, but clean and comfortable, and cost about 100 baht ($3) from Bangkok to Kanchanaburi. On the weekend it's possible to book a second-class place on a tourist train.

INSIDE INFORMATION Reservations are not required, but a window seat is recommended as it can be very hot. Sitting on the "river" side of the train (the left-hand side) gives better views north of the Kwai Bridge.

WEBSITES thailandbytrain.com, seat61.com

HIGHLIGHTS

▒ Wander through the **floating market** in Bangkok, where women offer food for sale from their canoes.

▒ At **Kanchanaburi**, visit the war memorials, or explore the Thai and Chinese temples, hot springs, and national and war museums.

▒ If you are in Thailand in the last week of November, head to Kanchanaburi for the **River Kwai Bridge Festival**, which includes a vast sound and light display at the bridge itself.

▒ After crossing the Wampo Viaduct, look out for **cliffside views** of the river and shaky looking trestles.

SINGAPORE | MALAYSIA | THAILAND

Eastern & Oriental Express

The only direct train between Singapore and Bangkok is an Oriental palace on wheels.

The Eastern & Oriental Express offers the ultimate experience in opulent, modern rail travel. Inaugurated in 1993, it is the first and only service to connect Singapore and Bangkok, a journey of some 1,260 miles (2,030 kilometers). The overall design evokes a more leisurely, pampered era: there are several onboard restaurants, a piano bar, and a small library, while afternoon tea can be served in your stateroom. The cars have specially enlarged windows to give panoramic views, and are decorated with Eastern motifs and materials, the walls covered in wooden marquetry veneer, and the bar and restaurants gleaming with Chinese and Thai lacquer, carvings, and engraved mirrors. From orderly Singapore, the train trundles over a causeway to the Malaysian mainland. In some places, rows of palms stretch away into the distance; in others, disorderly jungle closes in on the train. A sidetrip to Pinang's historic George Town, with lunch at the E&O Hotel, and a boat ride down Thailand's River Kwai are included in the price of the trip. The final stretch into Bangkok is a gentle ride through the Thai countryside, with views of rivers, paddy fields, and water buffalo.

WHEN TO GO The train runs about 20 times a year, with departures most frequent in February, March, September, and December.

HOW LONG Three days and two nights, beginning on Wednesdays from Singapore or Sundays from Bangkok. The train can also be boarded at intermediate stations. Longer trips are also available.

PLANNING Booking well in advance is strongly recommended. Once on board, all needs are taken care of. Discounts of 25 percent may be available on some departures from October to December, and complimentary hotel nights in Singapore and Bangkok are sometimes offered on summer departures.

INSIDE INFORMATION Daytime wear is smart casual, but be prepared to dress for dinner.

WEBSITE belmond.com/trains/asia/eastern-and-oriental-express

HIGHLIGHTS

▥ Watch from the open deck of the **teak observation car** at the rear, cocktail in hand, as the single-track line disappears into a jungle that seems about to swallow it up.

▥ Enjoy **dinner** while the sun sets beyond the dining cars' specially broadened windows.

▥ Explore the ornate **Buddhist temples** and **colonial architecture** that distinguish George Town, the capital of Pinang.

Watch the world go by from the exquisite luxury of the Eastern & Oriental's dining car.

| INDIA |

The Palace on Wheels

Step back into the world of India's maharajas as you luxuriate in their opulent lifestyles both onboard and off.

Rajasthan in northern India was once home to the wealthiest and most extravagant maharajas (royal princes) and their sumptuous *havelis* (palaces). Their pavilions, temples, and hilltop *mahals* (forts) provide a rich architectural heritage that draws visitors from around the world. The maharajas lost power after Indian independence in 1947, but the intricate and elaborate details with which they decorated their palaces and railway cars have been preserved with loving attention. On board this renovated train you can experience the royal indulgence of the Raj era, as turbaned waiters in silk tunics bring you Earl Grey tea in palatial saloons decked out with polished wood and elegant tapestries. Starting from New Delhi, the train calls at Jaipur, surrounded by hilltop forts and known as the Pink City after its ancient, pink-hued houses. Next is Jaisalmer, dominated by an imposing yellow sandstone fort. This is followed by a day in Jodhpur, and another visiting the tiger reserve at Ranthambhor, and the ancient Chittaurgarh Fort. As the train pulls into Udaipur, you are greeted by dancers, musicians, even garlanded elephants, before sightseeing and eating lunch in one of the splendid former palaces of the Raj. The train visits Agra before returning to New Delhi. It might be easy to get carried away with such royal treatment, but all this luxury can't shield you from the real essence of any trip to India: the hubbub of streets crammed with rickshaws, sacred cows, camels, and the ever present aroma of spices.

WHEN TO GO September to April.

HOW LONG The round-trip lasts seven days (Wednesday to Tuesday).

PLANNING There are three classes of cabin: single beds, double beds, or *couchette*-style beds. All are air-conditioned with private facilities. You should book at least eight to ten months in advance.

INSIDE INFORMATION Lightweight clothes, insect repellent, and bottled water are essential. Respectful clothing, particularly for women, is also a must – don't wear shorts, short skirts, or sleeveless tops. The same route can be done easily and more cheaply on standard state railways, although facilities on board most Indian trains are basic.

WEBSITE palace-on-wheel.com

| HIGHLIGHTS

▦ Sample the **bustle of Delhi's main train station** for a traditional Indian welcome before setting off on your magical journey.

▦ Dine on **delectable curries** served in one of the train's opulent restaurants, and then retire to your sleeping car, where your own *khidmatgar* (butler) can cater to all of your needs.

▦ **Ride an elephant** up the steep path to the Amber Fort in Jaipur.

▦ Enjoy a **traditional British tea** of cucumber sandwiches in the Lake Palace Hotel in Udaipur, and imagine yourself as the guest of a maharaja.

▦ Delight in the **bird-watching** at Bharatpur, between Udaipur and Agra.

▦ Spend an unforgettable afternoon in the tranquil setting of the **Taj Mahal**, the great declaration of love built in Agra by the emperor Shah Jahan as a mausoleum for his wife.

Opposite: Jaipur's Palace of the Winds (Hawa Mahal) was built in 1799 from local sandstone. The women of the court would sit behind the screened lattice windows to enjoy the cooling winds and watch processions go by. Above: Jagmandir Island Palace on Lake Pichola in Udaipur was built as a royal pleasure palace.

Darjiling Toy Train

Travel in style from the paddy fields of northern Bengal to the misty tea gardens of the Himalayan foothills.

Most of India's main rail routes are dominated by freight-hauling locomotives and modern, high-speed passenger trains running between the country's megacities. The narrow, 2-foot-gauge (0.6 meter) Darjiling Railway, zigzagging from the rice bowl of Bihar to the misty, tea-growing highlands, is the antithesis of the modern lines. Completed in 1881, the toy train was the brainchild of Franklin Prestage, the agent of the East Bengal State Railway. Worthy of a museum, its tiny locomotive labors from low-lying Shiliguri into the hills, providing a leisurely way to see the scenery of Bengal. Puffing uphill at not much more than jogging pace (it covers 51 miles/82 kilometers in eight hours), the train hits its zenith at Ghoom railway station before trundling the last 4 miles (6 kilometers) down to Darjiling, which lies at an altitude of 6,811 feet (2,076 meters). One can only marvel at the determination of the engineers and workers who blasted the line out of these obdurate, jungle-clad hills. Along the way, the scenery changes from green-gold paddy fields to mist-shrouded slopes, while the line passes tea plantations and villages where women and children, dressed in the vivid colors and silver jewelry of the Bhutia and Lencha hill people, wave as you pass. Arriving in Darjiling, the clouds part to reveal the faraway Himalaya.

WHEN TO GO November to February.

HOW LONG Minimum two days with one night in Darjiling; the trip takes about eight hours each way.

PLANNING The toy train leaves on alternate days. Schedules vary, and advance booking is essential. New Jalpaiguri, the connecting station for the toy train, has rail connections to Kolkata (Calcutta) and Delhi.

INSIDE INFORMATION Pack mineral water or soft drinks and preorder a picnic lunch from your hotel (the train has no dining car), and take a sweater or fleece and a waterproof jacket – Darjiling can be cool and wet at any time.

WEBSITES darjeeling-tourism.com, irctctourism.com

ASIA

HIGHLIGHTS

▪ When ordering a **packed lunch** from your hotel, take the delicious Indian vegetarian option (usually a combination of spicy dal, potatoes, and other curried vegetables, with a generous portion of sticky rice).

▪ Darjiling has a large community of **Tibetans** exiled from their homeland following the Chinese occupation, so look for groups of saffron- or maroon-garbed monks as well as villagers in Tibetan costume.

▪ Darjiling's most **striking panorama** is the view north to the peak of Kanchenjunga, which seems to loom impossibly close on the horizon, though it is in fact almost 100 miles (160 km) away.

The train, pulled by a tiny engine, climbs into the Darjiling hills via a series of giant loops.

Indian Pacific streaks across the outback near Broken Hill.

AUSTRALIA

Indian Pacific

Take the straightest way to gold's riches and dog's despair.

Take a slice coast to coast across Australia, and experience the haunting isolation and cloudless skies of the outback. Only possible as a through run since 1970, this spectacular 2,704-mile (4,352 kilometer) journey travels through three different time zones and rolls across some of the most singular and deserted terrain on Earth. The train leaves Perth in the twilight heading east toward the nostalgic gold-rush regions of Coolgardie and Kalgoorlie. Then it heads out into a red desert wilderness, the Nullarbor Plain, where the tracks shoot ahead into the far distance. Utterly treeless and once nick-named "dog's despair," this area is so deserted and flat that the track has no curves for almost 290 miles (467 kilometers)—a world record. The train stops at the tiny town of Cook (said to have a population of two) to allow travelers to appreciate this arid landscape firsthand. Eventually, civilization reappears as the train heads alongside the Spencer Gulf into Port Pirie and Adelaide, before climbing through more mountainous country to Broken Hill and over the Darling River into a much greener world. The train then crosses the eucalyptus forests of the Blue Mountains on twisting grades, before descending into cosmopolitan Sydney.

WHEN TO GO *Indian Pacific* runs twice weekly all year in both directions between Perth and Sydney.

HOW LONG The journey is 2,704 miles (4,352 km) and takes 69 hours (three nights).

PLANNING Advance booking is essential. The Gold Kangaroo Service offers twin or single sleeper cabins with shower and bathroom, with meals included. The cheaper Red Kangaroo service offers twin sleeper cabins or day-night recliner seats with shared showers and bathrooms. Light meals are extra. Parties of six to ten can book one of the luxurious self-contained private carriages.

INSIDE INFORMATION Travelers with a car can take it along—cars can be loaded onto a flat wagon and attached to the train at extra cost.

WEBSITE greatsouthernrail.com.au

HIGHLIGHTS

▥ Relax in **Perth**, a stylish city with a Mediterranean climate and excellent parks and beaches.

▥ Spot **kangaroos** lolloping through the outback on either side of the track and, if you are lucky, the superb wedge-tailed eagle.

▥ Take in a tour of the old **mining** and **ghost town** areas in Kalgoorlie and Coolgardie.

▥ Stretch your legs in **Cook**, an atmospheric, nearly deserted settlement in the dusty heart of the Nullarbor Plain.

The TranzAlpine crosses the Bealey River in Arthur's Pass National Park, below the Southern Alps.

NEW ZEALAND

The TranzAlpine

New Zealand's most dramatic railway line scales the sheer
Southern Alps to connect the South Island's east and west coasts.

The TranzAlpine departs from quiet, orderly Christchurch—a city bounded by the Pacific Ocean to the east, volcanic hills to the south, and the Waimakariri River to the north—and crosses the mainland to Greymouth on the western shore. This extended rollercoaster ride, complete with breezy, open-air observation car and running commentary by tour guides, cruises through the tidy, green farmlands of the Canterbury Plains, dotted with grazing sheep. Once you have crossed the Waimakariri River gorges on towering viaducts, the scenery instantly turns wild, and the train passes through multiple tunnels as it makes straight for the snowcapped peaks of the Southern Alps. The track climbs steeply and sinuously up to Arthur's Pass, the highest point on the journey and the border between Canterbury and Westland. There may well be a blizzard raging outside as the train enters the long, steeply descending Otira tunnel, yet it emerges unexpectedly into a region of silent lakes and beech forests at the base of the mountains before finally snaking into the sleepy port of Greymouth. From seashore to farmland, mountains, forests, and back to seashore, it is the variety of landscape that makes this journey truly special.

WHEN TO GO Go in December through February for the New Zealand summer. Trains leave Christchurch daily at 8.15 a.m. year-round.

HOW LONG The trip takes around 4.5 hours. Take a day trip with a quick lunch in Greymouth or break the journey in either direction at Lake Brunner Lodge, alighting at Jacksons (a request stop).

PLANNING Seven-day rail passes covering all of the South Island, or both islands, are bargain-priced, and optionally include the interisland ferry. Hot drinks and snacks are available on board the train.

INSIDE INFORMATION Keas, a type of large parrot, have a knack for stealing snacks and souvenirs. Those taking a stroll on the platform need to beware.

WEBSITES greatjourneysofnz.co.nz/tranzalpine, lakebrunner.co.nz

HIGHLIGHTS

▓ The sheer-sided **Waimakariri River gorges** that once provided a route for gold and jade prospectors, today play host to jet-boaters, fishermen, and kayakers. Fifteen tunnels and four viaducts are required to cross the river.

▓ At 3,018 ft (920 m), wintry **Arthur's Pass** is often snow-laden while the coasts remain balmy; it is nevertheless home to a species of parrot called the "kea."

▓ Arthur's Pass is a good base for **long and short hikes** through alpine scenery to views of dramatic ravines and threadlike waterfalls.

| RUSSIA |

The Bolshoi Express

Ride Russia in style on the Grand Express
between St. Petersburg and Moscow.

Get a taste of Russian extravagance aboard the *Bolshoi (Grand) Express.* Both the cities it connects and the route itself have an unbroken and rich tradition of opulence. When it began operating in 1851, only the affluent were allowed on board—social upheaval was feared if the masses were allowed to travel by railway. After the revolution, communist grandees used the *Bolshoi Express* to travel in a style comparable to the tsars they had ousted. Russia's first post-Soviet luxury train, this hotel on wheels is so sumptuous that its service starts at First Class, rising to Premium, Grand, and Grand de Luxe, each of which includes spacious compartments decorated in red, white, and gold, with air-conditioning, TV, DVD players, and Internet access. The Grand travels only at night, but the train itself is worth the journey. If, however, you want to see the countryside, go from May to July, when the Russian White Nights provide gentle twilight all night, and you can see the endless forests of the Russian hinterland cut by rivers and interspersed with lakes, bogs, and swamps. Keep your eye out for bears, which you can watch from the safety of the warm interior. On the *Bolshoi* in summer, it's easy to find yourself staying up all night.

WHEN TO GO May to July for the White Nights.

HOW LONG The trip lasts one night (nine hours), but allow at least a week if you want to explore Moscow and St. Petersburg.

PLANNING The *Grand* travels in both directions. All carriages sleep two, although a carriage can be reserved for one if you are prepared to pay the price of a double. Trains depart from Leningrad Station in Moscow and Moscow Station in St. Petersburg.

INSIDE INFORMATION Toiletries, a bathrobe, and slippers are included in the ticket. If you intend to sleep, it's worth setting your alarm so that you don't miss the beautiful sunrise.

WEBSITE grandexpress.ru/en

HIGHLIGHTS

▥ Marvel at the grand scale of the rail terminals in Moscow and St. Petersburg. Built in the mid-19th century by the same architect, these **Italianate stations** reflect the conservative taste of Tsar Nicholas I. The railway was his pet project.

▥ Take a tour of the **Kremlin** in Moscow. Visit the Armory with its fabulous collection of gold, silver, jewelry, Fabergé eggs, carriages, and imperial thrones.

▥ Enjoy more Fabergé jewelry in **St. Petersburg's Hermitage** museum, along with the Russian crown jewels and a superb collection of paintings from Michelangelo to Matisse.

The Russian State History Museum and the equestrian statue of Marshal Zhukov on Moscow's Red Square.

RUSSIA | MONGOLIA | CHINA

Trans-Siberian Railroad

This legendary route crosses Siberia and northern Mongolia on its way to the Chinese capital.

The sun beats down on the Mongolian plains. Racing through the sweeping grassy steppes, you catch sight of a cluster of round, beige yurts—the tent homes of nomads. A group of their camels stand nearby. The day before, you were in the gentle hills and rustic rural villages of Siberia, and tomorrow, you'll pass through wooded mountains and see the Great Wall of China. This is the Trans-Siberian Railroad, Moscow-Beijing route via Mongolia, the famous week-long train ride from the ancient capital of Russia to the ancient capital of China. You'll travel via the Russian hinterlands of Siberia, the wilderness of Mongolia, and the wastes of the Gobi, following in the footsteps of Ghengis Khan's Golden Horde. Completed in 1956, this is the newest and the most exciting of the Trans-Siberian railroad lines, a network that crosses eight time zones. The first four days are spent crossing the empty wastes of Siberia, taking in birch forests, the occasional onion dome of a Russian Orthodox church, and the crystal clear waters of Lake Baikal. On the fifth day you'll awake in entirely different surroundings, in the arid, dusty plains of Mongolia, where you may be able to spot camels, ponies, and eagles. During the night, the train reaches the Mongolian-Chinese border, where it stops for several hours to be adapted for the narrower Chinese gauge. The next day it travels alongside the Great Wall before finally reaching Beijing.

WHEN TO GO Go in late September for fall color, warm days, and crisply cold nights. Go in winter (December to January) if you want to see snow.

HOW LONG From Moscow to Beijing without stopovers takes six days. It is possible to make the journey in sections, in order to visit the main places of interest along the way.

PLANNING Traveling with friends or family may be preferred, as carriages sleep two to four people. A confirmed sleeping-birth reservation for each section of the trip, for the correct day, is essential.

INSIDE INFORMATION The official time on the train is Moscow time. As the train goes through eight time zones, the gap between the official time, which is used for stops, and local time gradually widens. In winter, it can be so cold outside that hands can freeze to the metal handrails between the carriages.

WEBSITE transib.net

HIGHLIGHTS

▧ Sandwich your trip with stays in **Moscow** and **Beijing**, both of which offer a feast of history and culture. In particular, visit the spiritual centers of these great cities: Red Square in Moscow and Tiananmen Square in Beijing.

▧ Get a window seat as the train loops around **Lake Baikal** – the deepest and oldest lake in the world – and enjoy great views over the water.

▧ Dine on **cuisine** from all three countries: in Mongolia the Russian restaurant car is switched for one serving Mongolian food; another switch is made in China so that passengers can sample Cantonese cuisine.

Opposite: In Tov, a girl wears traditional Mongolian dress during Naadam, a summer festival with ancient roots. Above: Horses of the Buryat people, from the eastern shore of Lake Baikal, race across the frozen ground.

The verdant greens of summer clothe steep hills as the *Flåmsbana* rushes along beside a river.

NORWAY

The Bergen Railway

This stunning journey between Norway's two main cities crosses a landscape of glaciers, mountains, and fjords.

Prepare for an exhilarating ride when you travel the Bergen Railway between Oslo and Bergen. As the train climbs through the mountains, clinging to cliff edges and rattling through tunnels, it offers breathtaking vistas of snowcapped peaks, tumbling waterfalls, glistening glaciers, and tranquil fjords. With 300 bridges and 182 tunnels, the line runs all through the year, even in winter. Traveling from Oslo, you begin the climb into the mountains at Gol. West of Gol, the train rolls into Ustaoset, a popular ski area in winter which is dominated by the Hallingskarvet mountain ridge. When you reach Finse, you'll be at the highest point on the journey, at an altitude of 4,000 feet (1,219 meters). The stretch after Finse is very exposed to the elements, and part of it is enclosed in a tunnel to protect it from heavy snow and strong winds in winter. Next, you'll descend toward the western fjords and Bergen. Oslo and Bergen offer first-rate museums and atmospheric harbor areas. En route you can stop off to enjoy skiing in winter, hiking in summer, and boat trips on the fjords. From Myrdal, you can make a detour on the Flåm railway, which travels down through the mountains, in and out of spiraling tunnels, to the town of Flåm.

WHEN TO GO Despite being subject to heavy snow and high winds in winter, the line is open all year. There are more departures each day in summer.

HOW LONG 310 miles (499 km). The journey takes six to seven hours, excluding stopovers. The detour to Flåm is 12 miles (19 km) each way.

PLANNING Ustaoset has around 700 traditional redwood holiday cabins for rent, providing a superb break in the mountain landscape.

INSIDE INFORMATION Even in summer, take an extra layer as the weather is changeable.

WEBSITES visitnorway.com, visitflam.com

HIGHLIGHTS

▦ Visit Oslo's **Viking Ship Museum** and the **Kon-Tiki Museum**, where you can see the explorer Thor Heyerdahl's original rafts.

▦ In winter, stay at Geilo or Voss for **skiing** and **snowboarding**.

▦ Take the **Flåm railway**, one of the steepest normal-gauge lines in the world, with spectacular views of the **Kjosfossen waterfall**.

▦ In **Bergen**, don't miss the harborfront **fish market** or the **funicular** ride up Mount Floyen, with superb views over the city.

The Inland Railway

*Travel northward from central Sweden
to the land of the midnight sun.*

Sweden's Inlandsbanan, or Inland Railway, runs through one of Europe's last great wilderness areas. Starting at Mora in central Sweden, and traveling gently along at 30 miles (48 kilometers) per hour, you enjoy the rolling panorama of forests, small settlements, lakes, rivers, mountains, and upland plateau. Östersund is on the shore of Sweden's fifth-largest lake—Storsjön—in the Swedish Lake District. The stretch of line between Östersund and Arvidsjaur is the best for spotting wildlife. You may be able to see elk, roe deer, golden eagles, and, more rarely, lynx and brown bears. The landscape becomes more open as the line passes northward into Lapland. Beyond Arvidsjaur you cross the Arctic Circle, where the train stops for a brief ceremony and certificates are presented to the passengers to mark the occasion. After that, you'll soon reach Jokkmokk, where the Sami people have grazed their herds of reindeer for many centuries. In high summer the sun never sets here. North of Jokkmokk, you'll enter the Laponia World Heritage area, where the Sami people have lived since the last ice age, in a landscape abounding in mountains, clear rivers, lakes, and marshlands. The Inland Railway terminates in the resort iron-mining town of Gällivare, where, in summer, 24-hour daylight proves a delight for wakeful sightseers.

WHEN TO GO Summer. Trains depart once a day in each direction.

HOW LONG Two days from Mora to Gällivare, plus breaks to view attractions en route. Tours are available starting in Stockholm and take six or eight days.

PLANNING Tickets for independent travel usually cover each journey section, unless you purchase an Inland Railway Card which gives 14 days of unlimited travel. Reservations in high summer are desirable but not essential. Refreshments are available at stops only, but can be preordered.

INSIDE INFORMATION Insect repellent is essential in summer as the area is plagued with mosquitoes.

WEBSITE inlandsbanan.se/en

HIGHLIGHTS

▥ Visit the **Silver Museum** in Arjeplog, which has a large collection of silver and Sami artifacts. You can get there from Arvidsjaur or Slagnäs.

▥ Take the **steam trains** that run between Arvidsjaur and Slagnäs on Fridays and Saturdays in July and the first week of August.

▥ Visit the **Ajtte Museum** in Jokkmokk, which has displays on the life and hunting history of the indigenous Sami people.

▥ In **Gällivare**, summer visitors can take a bus to the summit of Dundret to see the midnight sun and a far-reaching view that takes in more than 9 percent of Sweden's total land area.

Zorn House in Mora was built by the 19th-century Swedish painter Anders Zorn and exemplifies the folk tradition of the area.

Top 10 Metro & Subway Lines

Some of the globe's most intriguing train rides occur underground—in the metro and subway lines that run within major urban areas.

❶ IRT LEXINGTON AVENUE LINE, NEW YORK CITY

This fabled route beneath the Big Apple runs down Manhattan Island via the Upper East Side, Grand Central Station, Little Italy, Wall Street, and other landmarks. The line passes through several closed "ghost stations" including City Hall with its Romanesque Revival architecture.

PLANNING The full journey between Harlem and Battery Park takes approximately 30 minutes. mta.info/nyct

❷ CHIYODA LINE, TOKYO

Snaking across the middle of the Japanese capital, the "green" line of the Tokyo Metro calls on many of the city's most celebrated places, from Yoyogi and Ueno parks to the Imperial Palace, the funky Harajuku neighborhood, and nightlife crazy Roppongi.

PLANNING Although once notorious for Japanese-only signage, the Tokyo Metro is now signposted in English to assist foreign visitors. tokyometro.jp

❸ TAMSUI LINE, TAIPEI

Stretching both under and over ground, this MRT route across Taiwan's capital is celebrated for its shopping malls, art galleries, and eye-catching architecture. Jiantan Station is shaped like a giant, futuristic dragon-boat.

PLANNING Taipei's MRT bundles its 24-, 48-, and 72-hour passes with discount coupons to local cultural and entertainment attractions. english.metro.taipei

❹ LINE 1, ALMATY

KGP Metropolitan in the Kazakhstan capital features stations blending dramatic Soviet-era and post-independence design and architecture. Stations are decorated with stained glass, mosaic floors, and elaborate chandeliers.

PLANNING Single rides on the Almaty Metro are 80 tenge (approximately US$0.25). urbanrail.net/as/kz/almaty/almaty.htm

❺ KOLTSEVAYA LINE, MOSCOW

Constructed in the 1950s during the height of the Cold War, stations of the Russian capital's Circle Line are renowned for their iconic Stalinist architecture. Komsomolskaya Station features a lavishly decorated baroque vaulted ceiling while Taganskaya boasts ceramic panels with Red Army motifs.

PLANNING Get into a Moscow Metro mood by reading *Metro 2033*, a post-apocalyptic novel by Russian author Dmitry A. Glukhovsky. mosmetro.ru/metrotour/en

The vibrant geometric ceiling of Kungsträdgården station in Stockholm's Tunnelbana was painted in 1977 by Swedish artist Ulrik Samuelson. Find it near the Arsenalsgatan exit.

⑥ BLUE LINE, STOCKHOLM

Larger-than-life sculptures, rock formations, mosaics, paintings, art installations and engravings adorn 90 of the 100 stations of Stockholm's Tunnelbana (T-bana) subway system, causing it to be dubbed "the world's longest art gallery." The Blue Line has some of the finest work; among the more dramatic stops are T-Centralen, Rådhuset, and Kungsträdgården stations.

PLANNING SL Travelcards for the T-bana range from 24 hours to seven days. sl.se/en

⑦ DOCKLANDS LIGHT RAILWAY (DLR), LONDON

This futuristic aboveground extension of the London Underground gives passengers an aerial view of the skyscrapers, yacht havens, and waterfront parklands that populate the revitalized Canary Wharf and Docklands area. Opened in 1987, the DLR includes 45 stations and serves several other London transport icons: the *Cutty Sark* clipper ship (get off at Cutty Sark for Maritime Greenwich) and the Emirates cable car (reach it from Royal Victoria station). The *Cutty Sark* can also be reached by a Victorian foot tunnel under the Thames (get off at Island Gardens).

PLANNING The DLR operates Mon-Sat 5:30 a.m. to 12:30 a.m., and Sunday 7 a.m. to 11:30 p.m. tfl.gov.uk/dlr/route/dlr

⑧ LINE 1, PARIS

This very first Métro line includes stations for many Parisian landmarks, from La Défense and the Arc de Triomphe to the Louvre and Bastille. Created for the 1900 Universal Exposition in Paris, a number of stations boast original art nouveau entrances designed by Hector Guimard. Louvre station features replica museum pieces and a direct connection to the museum entrance.

PLANNING Purchase metro tickets online at the official Paris Tourism website. en.parisinfo.com

⑨ LINE 1, NAPLES

Nicknamed "Il Metrò dell'Arte" for its permanent and temporary displays, 11 of the stations on this underground line in the Italian coastal city feature vibrant art and stunning architecture. The mesmerizing star-spangled ceiling of Toledo Station is the most renowned, but the flamboyant pop art of Università and the classical sculptures of Museo are just as brilliant.

PLANNING A three-day Tutta la regione Campania ArtCard includes admission to 80 tourist sights and all public transportation in the Naples region. campaniartecard.it

⑩ LINE 3, ATHENS

Built for the 2000 Summer Olympics, the "blue" line of the Athens Attiko Metro features several stations with permanent archaeological exhibits stocked with some of the 50,000 artifacts found during the metro's construction. Among the treasures are an ancient cemetery and baths at Syntagma, everyday objects from ancient Greece at Aigaleo, and the remains of a 5th-century B.C. bridge at Elaionas.

PLANNING A trip from start to finish takes around 40 minutes. carris.pt/en/home

Inverness to Kyle of Lochalsh

*Britain's most dramatic rail journey
links Scotland's east and west coasts.*

From the capital of the Scottish Highlands to the Kyle of Lochalsh, the journey traverses rolling moorland, haunted glens, and heather-covered mountains through the castle-dotted heartland of the Highland clans. Leaving Inverness, you will cross the River Ness and follow the south shore of the Beauly Firth. At the firth's western end the line turns north through the flat moorland of Easter Ross. After the market town of Dingwall, the line swings west and into increasingly dramatic scenery, overlooked by summits such as 1,153-foot (351 m) Cnoc nah Iohlaire and Sgurr a' Mhuilinn, then crosses the Drumalbain watershed, Glen Carron, and the thick, ancient woodland of Achnashellach Forest, where with luck you may glimpse herds of deer. From here, it's not far to the waters of Lochcarron, Loch Kishorn, and the rugged Atlantic coastline. Plockton village, standing on a sheltered bay afloat with yachts and studded with tiny islands, is postcard-pretty. The last stretch of line, along the coast from Duirinish to Erbusaig Bay and Kyle of Lochalsh, is perhaps the prettiest of all—you'll see the small islands of Raasay, Scalpay, Longay, and Pabbay silhouetted on the western horizon.

WHEN TO GO Any time, but preferably June to September. July and August are the busiest months.

HOW LONG Four hours.

PLANNING Up to three departures daily on the Inverness–Kyle of Lochalsh/Thurso/Wick line in high season. Connections at Inverness to Edinburgh, Perth, Glasgow, and Aberdeen. Bus connections at Kyle of Lochalsh for Skye (via road bridge) and ferries to the Western Isles.

INSIDE INFORMATION Winter landscapes can be spectacular, but the north of Scotland gets little more than six hours of daylight in midwinter and cold, wet weather can be expected.

WEBSITES visitscotland.com/destinations-maps/highlands, greatrail.com/trains/kyle-line

HIGHLIGHTS

▓ Explore **Inverness**, Scotland's newest city. Although a castle stood here as early as the 12th century, the Capital of the Highlands really came into its own only in the 18th and 19th centuries, and it did not gain city status until the 21st.

▓ Spot seals and dolphins in the **Beauly Firth**, as these waters shelter large populations of both.

▓ Look for the **stone towers** of Redcastle on the firth's northern shore, and to its north Kilcoy Castle – centuries-old keeps of the Clan Mackenzie – and, after crossing the Beauly River, the 800-year-old Beauly Priory.

The distinctive-looking and hardy Highland cattle, found throughout western Scotland, are one of Britain's oldest breeds.

The Orient Express travels through typical Alpine scenery.

| ENGLAND | FRANCE | SWITZERLAND | AUSTRIA | ITALY |

Venice Simplon-Orient-Express

The Venice Simplon-Orient-Express is possibly both the most luxurious and most famous train journey in the world.

With luxury carriages, fine food, and first-rate service, you can easily imagine you are on the European Grand Tour. Leaving London in superbly restored Pullman cars, enjoy lunch as you travel through Kent, the Garden of England, to the English Channel. After traveling into France through the Channel Tunnel, you board the splendidly restored, blue-and-gold, 1920s wagon-lits for the journey to Venice. Dinner is served on the way to Paris. The train travels across France, and next morning you wake up surrounded by mountains and lakes. Crossing into Austria, you can watch spectacular views of high Alpine pastures and rocky peaks glide past as you eat breakfast. At Innsbruck, the train turns south and hugs the mountainsides as it climbs a sharply ascending track up to the Brenner Pass, which tops 4,000 feet (1,219 meters) above sea level. Tea is served as you descend through the Dolomites to Verona, Italy. You approach Venice across the causeway from the mainland as evening falls, arriving at Santa Lucia Station on the Grand Canal.

WHEN TO GO The Venice Simplon-Orient-Express runs from March to November. The London to Venice service departs on Thursdays and Sundays; Venice to London departs on Wednesdays and Saturdays.

HOW LONG Two days and one night.

PLANNING You cannot be overdressed on the Orient Express – smart casual during the day and either cocktail or full evening wear for dinner – but remember cabin luggage space is limited to two light cases. Additional baggage can be accommodated in the baggage car.

INSIDE INFORMATION The restoration of the train is true to the period, so there are sinks in each cabin but no showers. The compartments convert to sleeping accommodation. The whole train is nonsmoking.

WEBSITES orient-express.com, belmond.com/luxury-trains

| HIGHLIGHTS

▥ **Dress for dinner** in black tie or evening dress.

▥ The scenery through the **Arlberg Mountains** and along the Inn Valley approaching Innsbruck, Austria, is especially magnificent.

▥ The **Brenner Pass** is the only transalpine rail route that does not include a major tunnel.

▥ The ragged **Dolomites** contrast sharply with the Alps. Their irregular shapes resemble walls, towers, or even ruined castles. And they change color, from yellow, to gray, to pink, to deep sienna, with the time of day.

The Glacier Express

Travel in comfort past high Alpine passes, glaciers, and pretty villages in one of the world's most dramatic mountain regions.

Often called "the world's slowest express train," the Glacier Express averages 22 miles (35 kilometers) per hour, slow enough for you to savor the thrilling and constantly changing panorama of snowcapped peaks, dense forests, rushing rivers, Alpine meadows, and mountain villages near Switzerland's southern borders with France and Italy. After leaving the chic ski resort of St. Moritz, the train begins its climb into the mountains, with views of glaciers, larch-filled valleys, and tiny villages huddling on the mountainsides, punctuated by sudden plunges into darkness as you enter tunnels cut through the mountains. Near Fusilier, you'll have the unforgettable sensation of traveling through air as you emerge from a tunnel onto a lofty viaduct overlooking the Landwasser Gorge. After passing through the medieval town of Chur, the train climbs more steeply until it reaches the 6,670-foot (2,033 meter) Oberalp Pass, the highest point on the journey—and the highest mountain pass in the Swiss Alps. After a looping, switchback ride down to Andermatt, the route follows the Rhône Valley, with good views of the Aletsch Glacier, to Brig. The train then starts climbing again, past some of the highest vineyards in Europe, around the town of Visp. As evening approaches, you will finally spot the famous jagged outline of the Matterhorn looming 14,692 feet (4,478 meters) above sea level over Zermatt.

WHEN TO GO Skiers prefer winter, hikers summer, but from frozen white to lush green, the scenery is spectacular year-round.

HOW LONG The train ride takes 7.5 hours. Zermatt and St. Moritz each deserve a minimum of one additional day.

PLANNING Reservations are essential. Tickets and reservations are available at any Swiss railway station or directly from the Glacier Express. Plan well ahead during high seasons. Also book ahead for the dining car.

INSIDE INFORMATION There isn't much difference between regular second- and first-class seats; the luxury choice is first-class panorama cars with windows in the roof for towering mountain vistas.

WEBSITES glacierexpress.ch, raileurope.com

HIGHLIGHTS

▥ Glacier Express scenery is non-stop, but special highlights include the climb over the **Oberalp Pass**; crossing the **Rhine Gorge**, known as the Swiss Grand Canyon; and the Aletsch Glacier descending to the Rhône Valley.

▥ **Chur** is full of old town houses, quiet courtyards, and cobbled alleys. The city is dominated by a large 12th-century cathedral.

▥ The village of Disentis (between Andermatt and Chur) boasts a lovely **8th-century abbey**.

▥ Enjoy a meal in the **vintage dining cars**, which have wood paneling, brass fixtures, and tilted wine glasses to prevent them from spilling on steep climbs and descents.

▥ The onion-domed towers of Brig's **Stockalper Castle** can be seen from all over the city. This Italianate palace was built by a wealthy merchant in the 17th century.

▥ As you approach Zermatt, watch out for your breathtaking first view of the mighty, steep-sided **Matterhorn**.

Opposite: Summer or winter, the distinctive, towering outline of the Matterhorn dominates the view around Zermatt. Above left: In spring, the meadows are full of Alpine flowers. Above right: Even in deepest winter, trains chug up the narrow rail track near Zermatt.

The Jungfraujoch Railway

This is a journey of contrasts, as you emerge from the heart of the mountains into a wonderland of snow-covered glaciers and peaks.

EUROPE

The towering, knife-edged mountain masses of the Eiger, Mönch, and Jungfrau, each rising over 12,000 feet (3,658 meters), dominate the Bernese Oberland ("highland") in central Switzerland. This is the dramatic setting for Europe's highest mountain railway, the Jungfraubahnen. The railway starts from Kleine Scheidegg, at the base of the 6,000-foot (1,829 meter), near-vertical north face of the Eiger. The train climbs across open terrain to the Eigergletscher (Eiger Glacier) station, where you can visit the polar dog kennels. It then enters the 6-mile (10 kilometer) Eiger Tunnel and ascends through the inside of the mountain. Along the way, the train stops for a few minutes at the Eigerwand (North Wall) and Eismeer (Sea of Ice) stations, and you can enjoy spectacular views from huge observation windows. It then continues to the Jungfraujoch plateau, at 10,700 feet (3,261 meters) above sea level, just below the Jungfrau summit. Emerging from the station into the observation hall and onto the terrace, you are in the middle of a magical landscape of ice and snow. All around you is the Aletsch Glacier, which begins here and is the longest in the Alps. On a clear day you can see the Vosges Mountains of France and Germany's Black Forest.

WHEN TO GO Trains run all year, but winter conditions on the summit can be severe. Good weather is essential, so watch the local forecasts.

HOW LONG The single journey takes about an hour.

PLANNING Kleine Scheidegg station can be reached from either Wengen or Grindelwald.

INSIDE INFORMATION Fares on the railway are very expensive, although off-peak and rail-pass rates are available. Discounts on early morning trains are considerable.

WEBSITES jungfrau.ch/en-gb, myswitzerland.com/en-gb

HIGHLIGHTS

▦ From the Eigerwand station, enjoy views of the north face of the **Eiger and the Grindelwald Valley** as far as Interlaken. From Eismeer, wonder at a landscape of **permanent rock and ice**.

▦ Explore the **Ice Palace**, a series of permanent ice caves at the top of the Jungfraujoch containing sparkling carved ice sculptures, and the **High Alpine Research Exhibition**.

▦ In summer (June to September), you can snowboard, ski, or go on a **husky-hauled sled ride** on the glacier at the summit.

The Eiger, with its forbidding north face here cast in deep shadow, and its neighbors the Jungfrau and Mönch, dominate the Alpine skyline.

The Konya skyline is dominated by the turquoise tiles of the top of the Mevlana Rumi.

TURKEY

The Taurus Express

From Istanbul, travel an ancient route through the wild Taurus Mountains and along the coast of the eastern Mediterranean.

The Toros Ekspresi, or Taurus Express, originally linked Istanbul with Damascus, Syria, and Baghdad, Iraq. It now goes as far as Adana, Turkey. Leaving Istanbul, the train runs beside the Sea of Marmara to the port of Izmit. Turning south, it then climbs onto the Anatolian plateau that makes up much of central Turkey. As you approach Afyon, look for the ruined fortress on top of a rock pinnacle. Coming into Konya, you'll see the turquoise roof of the mausoleum of Mevlana Rumi among the minarets. Then the route climbs through the Taurus Mountains. A single-track section passes through deep gorges and over viaducts, with stunning views of valleys and mountain streams below. The line reaches a height of 4,812 feet (1,467 meters), then descends to Adana, following the coastal plain past orange plantations. Once in Adana, try the world-famous kebabs, a delicacy made from lamb and aromatic sumac.

WHEN TO GO The Taurus Express runs three times a week in both directions throughout the year. If you like cold temperatures and snow scenes, travel in winter. Summer can be extremely hot and humid.

HOW LONG The 708-mile (1,139 km) journey between Istanbul and Adana takes about 24 hours.

PLANNING Reservations are essential for all but basic fares. Through tickets do not allow for a break in the journey. Once a week, an extra sleeping car goes on to Aleppo in Syria, with connections to Damascus; passengers must purchase sleeping-car accommodation to Aleppo.

INSIDE INFORMATION Bring your own food and water, as there's no restaurant car. During Ramadan, restaurants in centers like Konya may be closed from sunup to sundown, and alcohol is often not available.

WEBSITES turkeytravelplanner.com, tcdd.gov.tr

HIGHLIGHTS

▓ The Teutonic fortress-style **Haydarpasa Station** in Istanbul was donated by Kaiser Wilhelm II of Germany in 1908.

▓ The stunning scenery is constantly changing, from the vast skyline of the **Anatolian plateau**, and the rugged and wild **Taurus Mountains**, to the lush, Mediterranean **Adana Plain**.

▓ Afyon is dominated by the **Black Fortress of Opium**, so-called because opium poppies were grown in the area in the past. The town is also renowned for its **Turkish delight**, made with rich local heavy cream.

▓ In Konya, you can visit the mausoleum of the Sufi poet, **Mevlana Rumi**, who founded the **Whirling Dervish Sect**. Members of the sect lived in a monastery, which has since been turned into a museum.

| SOUTH AFRICA |

Wildlife Safari

*Experience dramatic landscape and a chance to see the
"big five" when you take a luxury train safari in traditional style.*

For those who love luxurious, old-style trains, rugged landscapes, and wild animals, a train safari between Durban and Pretoria in South Africa is a chance not to be missed. The refurbished, vintage wooden coaches are an attraction in themselves, and for the last part of the trip the train is hauled by a steam engine. This is a chance to experience a safari as in days gone by, with opportunities to spot all of the big five species—lion, leopard, elephant, black rhinoceros, and buffalo. Leaving Durban in the morning, you can watch the wild lush hills of KwaZulu-Natal roll by—often dotted with villages consisting of traditional round huts—followed by the flatter plains of Swaziland. The open Observation Car offers great views. Early on day two, you can enjoy the first game drive in the privately owned Mkhaya Game Reserve. Getting up before it's properly light, and traveling in open Land Rovers, you have a great chance of seeing the animals before they see you. A few hours farther north, there's a late-afternoon game drive in world-famous Kruger National Park, followed by a traditional Boma dinner. The Boma—a courtyard where food is cooked simply on a barbecue—is surrounded by flaming bonfires to scare away the animals. Next morning, as you enjoy breakfast, the train makes a dramatic ascent through the heart-stopping Drakensberg escarpment before delivering you to Pretoria in the afternoon.

WHEN TO GO The trip takes place around once a week from January to April and October to November. The dry winter season is a good time to see game as the grass is low, there are no leaves on the trees, and animals visit the water holes regularly.

HOW LONG Three days, two nights.

PLANNING The journey can also be made from Pretoria to Durban, with a slightly different itinerary; the game drives take place in Mkhaya and Hluhluwe reserves. Make sure you pack correctly for game drives: beige, brown, or green clothing that you can layer for warmth on cold mornings.

INSIDE INFORMATION Rovos Rail trains operate an all-you-can-eat-and-drink policy.

WEBSITE rovos.com

▌ HIGHLIGHTS

▪ The **Mkhaya Game Reserve**, which is privately owned, is a refuge for endangered species. It has a good network of game-viewing roads, and is one of the best places in South Africa to spot black rhino and a host of other wildlife.

▪ The **train suites**, with beautiful wood paneling and other Edwardian features, are among the most luxurious in the world.

▪ **Kruger National Park**, a huge conservation area the size of Israel, is home to a vast range of animals and birds as well as the big five.

▪ The ascent of the **Drakensberg escarpment** from Waterland Onder to Belfast (6,434 ft/1,961 m) provides spectacular views.

Opposite: An elephant roams South Africa's Kruger National Park, where the elephant population has increased rapidly in recent years. Above left: The sun picks out the dramatic escarpment of the Drakensberg Mountains. Above right: The game reserves of Swaziland are among the best places to see the endangered black rhino.

Chapter 4

ON FOOT

A journey on foot is the purest and simplest of pleasures. Walking offers perfect freedom—no tickets, no timetables, no limits apart from those geography or your own desire dictates. Every walk in this chapter begins with a single step. An amble around New York's Greenwich Village becomes a journey into the lives of famous artists and writers. A few hours browsing through Istanbul's Grand Bazaar becomes a treasure hunt through time and space—as well as a lesson in the art of bargaining. At the other end of the spectrum are demanding wilderness treks, taking days or weeks to accomplish. Peru's Inca Trail literally rises above the clouds on its way to the Lost Citadel of the Inca Empire. In between lies a world of inviting hikes, from the Great Wall of China to California's John Muir Trail. Even in the most populous places lie wonders reachable only on foot, such as the miles of catacombs beneath Rome or the High Line above Manhattan. No other form of travel brings you so close to nature, including human nature. And no other form is so kind to the planet— nor so satisfying to body, mind, and soul.

In Morocco, a hiker traces a route through the High Atlas Mountains using a makeshift stone bridge. This mountain range runs for over 620 miles (1,000 km) and is known to the locals as Idraren Draren, or "mountain of mountains."

At St. Luke's Place west of 7th Avenue in the West Village, the genteel town houses are covered in lush vines.

Greenwich Village

The leafy, twisty streets of this one-time country village
have long been a magnet for artists, writers, and the chic.

Breaking with Manhattan's high-rise, grid pattern, Greenwich Village (often referred to simply as "the Village") was once a Bohemian haven for artists, writers, actors, and the gay community. Today, it is more mainstream, but a stroll of its tree-lined streets and alleys still reveals a wealth of historic buildings, hidden mews, and courtyards. Start your walk in Washington Square. On the north side is a row of Greek Revival town houses where writers Henry James, Edith Wharton, and John Dos Passos, and artist Edward Hopper lived. From the Washington Memorial Arch opposite, a group of artists led by Marcel Duchamp proclaimed the "state of New Bohemia" in 1916. A few blocks northwest nestles Patchin Place, once home of playwright Eugene O'Neill. At Sheridan Square, heart of the Village, a web of seven streets converges. Here, you can browse antiques emporiums and bookshops, check out off-Broadway theater, pick up Italian goodies on Bedford Street, then eat at Chumley's, a former speakeasy.

WHEN TO GO Any time, but summer can be very hot. Fall's sunny, crisp days are ideal.

HOW LONG It can take an hour or an entire afternoon, depending on how long you linger at the sights and cafés along the way.

PLANNING The most convenient routes for getting to Greenwich Village are the #1, #2, or #3 Fifth Avenue buses or the West 4th Street/Washington Square station on the A, B, C, D, E, or F subway lines.

INSIDE INFORMATION Enjoy people-watching in Washington Square Park, with its shady benches and street performers. The Village is famed for its jazz venues – check out Blue Note, 55 Bar, Smalls, or Garage.

WEBSITES nycgo.com, nyc-architecture.com

HIGHLIGHTS

▓ Many writers and artists occupied the converted stables and carriage houses in **MacDougal Alley**, a quiet cobblestone mews off Washington Square. Sculptor Gertrude Vanderbilt Whitney opened the first Whitney Museum behind her studio there.

▓ The **Jefferson Market Courthouse** is a grand Victorian Gothic building, now part of the New York Public Library. Its lovingly tended garden offers a peaceful stopover.

▓ **New York's narrowest house**, just 9.5 ft (2.9 m) wide, is at 75 1/2 Bedford Street. Built in 1873, it has been home to the actors John Barrymore and Cary Grant.

▓ The novelist Theodore Dreiser began *An American Tragedy* in one of the 1850s Italianate houses lining **St. Luke's Place**.

NORTH
AMERICA

WASHINGTON, D.C.

The National Mall

Lined with stately museums and monuments, the National Mall is the heart of ceremonial Washington and a perfect place to stroll.

Elms flank the green lawns of the National Mall, bracketed at one end by the slim obelisk of the Washington Monument and at the other by the dome of the U.S. Capitol. A stroll along this 2-mile (3.2 kilometer) axis offers a wealth of fascinating things to do and see. Outside the National Museum of Natural History sits a 2.5 billion-year-old boulder from Michigan, a taste of the million or so exhibits within. Farther on rises the famous central office of the Smithsonian Institution, a red sandstone "castle" in Romanesque and Gothic styles. Next comes the National Gallery of Art with its adjoining Sculpture Garden, offering a green and relaxing art tour, and a little farther on is the National Museum of the American Indian. Climbing up to the observatory of the Washington Monument rewards you with a superb view of the city. Continue into the parkland around the Tidal Basin, and you find thousands of cherry trees—a vision of pink blossoms in spring. Martin Luther King made his "I Have a Dream" speech from the Lincoln Memorial in 1963. Nearby, the Korean War Memorial comprises 19 lifelike sculptures of American soldiers. Seemingly on the move, their appearance is especially haunting in the falling shadows of dusk.

WHEN TO GO Spring is prime time, particularly late March to early April – the cherry blossom season. If possible, avoid summer, when the weather is hot and muggy, and the city crowded with tourists.

HOW LONG Three days is a minimum for sampling the Mall and its many sights and museums.

PLANNING Reserve accommodation well in advance for the cherry blossom season.

INSIDE INFORMATION Washington's metro is quick, clean, and economical, the best way to get around the city. Take the metro to Smithsonian station. You cannot tour the U.S. Capitol on your own, but guided tours are free. From mid-November through mid-March the skating rink in the National Gallery of Art Sculpture Garden is open. Skate in the open air while listening to music and viewing the sculptures.

WEBSITES washington.org, thedistrict.com, nps.gov/nama

NORTH AMERICA

HIGHLIGHTS

▓ The **National Gallery of Art** offers an outstanding survey of painting, decorative arts, and sculpture.

▓ The **Smithsonian Institution**'s 11 museums on the Mall include the National Museum of African American History and Culture, and the National Air and Space Museum.

▓ The **Lincoln Memorial**, with its huge marble figure of the president who preserved the Union, is one of the nation's best-loved shrines. Enjoy the view all the way to the Capitol.

▓ The **Vietnam Veterans Memorial** is a moving tribute, its low black marble walls inscribed with the names of the 58,318 Americans lost in the conflict.

Clad in bronze-colored panels, the National Museum of African American History and Culture gleams in the sunlight.

Great Smoky Mountains

Wildlife riches await you in Great Smoky Mountains National Park, whose forests shelter one of Earth's most diverse ecosystems.

NORTH
AMERICA

A wispy, smokelike fog, the result of rainwater evaporating from trees, overhangs the Great Smoky Mountains, giving them their name. Rising at the southern end of the Appalachian range, the mountains boast one of the world's most diverse ecosystems—more than 100 native tree species, 1,500 kinds of flowering plants, and bountiful wildlife. And with more than 800 miles (1,287 kilometers) of hiking trails, the opportunities to explore are almost endless. For an introduction, try the Porter's Creek Trail, starting near Greenbrier in the north of the park. In spring, wildflowers blossom profusely along the first part of the trail. Then you wind uphill, through a forest with hemlocks, magnolias, and rhododendron. A crooked bridge, made from two split tree trunks, crosses a creek, overlooked by trilliums and other flowers—a perfect place to stop for a picnic. The tree cover now changes to huge buckeye trees and tulip poplars. Just after the trail levels, a side path leads to Fern Branch Falls, where the creek slides over boulders into a fern-filled valley. Continuing high above the stream, the trail ends at a campsite, where most people turn back, but experienced hikers can follow an off-trail route to Charlies Bunion, a rocky promontory with superb views across the park.

WHEN TO GO Any time of year. The wildflowers are at their peak in April and May, and the fall foliage is spectacular in October. In summer, the park tends to be hot, hazy, and crowded.

HOW LONG The Porter's Creek Trail is 3.7 miles (6 km) one way. Other trails include the 5.8-mile (9.3 km) Big Creek Trail and some "overnighters," such as the 18.4-mile (29.6 km) Mount Sterling Loop.

PLANNING This is the most heavily visited national park in the U.S., so you'll feel closer to nature out of season. If you can't avoid the peak seasons, consider exploring its less crowded North Carolina side.

INSIDE INFORMATION The weather in the Smokies is very changeable, especially at the higher elevations in the winter and spring. Make sure to carry rain gear and a warm shirt.

WEBSITES nps.gov/grsm, adventuresingoodcompany.com

HIGHLIGHTS

▓ In spring, you can see **more than 30 wildflower species**, including yellow trillium, ladyslippers, jack in the pulpit, lavender, dwarf crested iris, wild ginger, and purple-crested phacelia.

▓ Twenty-six families lived in **Greenbrier Cove** until the 1930s, when the creation of the national park forced them to leave. Passing stone walls, chimneys, foundations—even a reconstructed barn—it is easy to imagine that the trickling of the creek is the laughter of children raised here.

▓ A visit to the **Museum of the Cherokee Indian** just outside the park in Cherokee, NC, gives a fascinating insight into the lives of the region's indigenous inhabitants.

The characteristic blue haze veils the soft, forested outlines of the Great Smoky Mountains.

Fall leaves and patches of brilliant sky create a glorious kaleidoscope of color, reflected in the still waters of a Vermont pond.

ACROSS WATERS

BY ROAD

BY RAIL

ON FOOT

IN SEARCH OF CULTURE

IN GOURMET HEAVEN

INTO THE ACTION

UP AND AWAY

IN THEIR FOOTSTEPS

| VERMONT |

On the Appalachian Trail Through Vermont

This glorious snippet gives you a weekend glimpse of the entire Appalachian Trail—and may whet your appetite for more.

The hike north over Vermont's Glastenbury Mountain is just a fragment of the 2,174-mile (3,499 kilometer) Appalachian Trail, running between Georgia and Maine. But within this fragment—where primeval wilderness beckons just beyond white-clapboard villages—lies the entire trail in miniature. You pick it up east of Bennington at William D. MacArthur Memorial Bridge. Briefly following a rocky rivulet, you begin an ascent into deep beech woods, where you may see a black bear foraging for berries. Crossing Hell Hollow Brook on a wood puncheon (walkway), you climb 1,300 feet (396 meters) to find yourself in damp, spruce-bound woods. Mountains and forest, home to warblers and thrushes, surround you as the trail climbs yet again to the wooded summit of Glastenbury (3,748 feet/1,142 meters). An overnight stop in the Goddard shelter brings an early morning reward. Climb to the fire tower, and you'll see what Vermont really means—green mountains, lying rumpled in all directions: Haystack, Taconic, Berkshire, Equinox. A gentle descent to the next road crossing brings this trek to a close—but not your peaceful thoughts garnered along the way.

WHEN TO GO June through September. Early summer offers wildflowers in abundance, fall the spectacular colors of the forest.

HOW LONG You need two days for the 22 miles (35 km) of the Glastenbury Mountain section of the trail. To cover the entire Appalachian Trail from Springer Mountain, GA, to Mount Katahdin, ME, most people take six months in all, usually doing it in stages of a week or so at a time.

PLANNING A backpack, sleeping bag, tent, boots, and waterproof clothing are musts for all hikers. Take insect repellent to keep the flies at bay in summer.

INSIDE INFORMATION For staying overnight, lean-tos are located along the trail, available on a first-come, first-served basis. The fire towers provide the highest possible standpoints above the trees; you can even watch birds floating on the thermals from them.

WEBSITES appalachiantrail.org, greenmountainclub.org

HIGHLIGHTS

▪ You will see **spectacular wildlife**, including black bear, lynx, bobcat, pine marten, deer, beaver, ruffed grouse, and high-altitude songbirds.

▪ Around Manchester, VT, you can canoe or fly-fish on trout-rich **Battenkill River**.

▪ Manchester also has **The American Museum of Fly Fishing**, with the fishing tackle of famous anglers, from Andrew Carnegie to Ernest Hemingway, and the **Orvis Company**, America's oldest mail-order vendor.

▪ In southern Vermont there are farmers markets in **Brattleboro**, and in September you can pick your own apples in orchards in **Putney**.

NORTH AMERICA

Top 10 Long-Distance Trails

Don your hiking boots, take out your map, and follow these trails through areas of outstanding natural beauty.

❶ THE WIND RIVER MOUNTAINS, WYOMING

The mountains climb over 13,123 ft (4,000 m) into the skies southwest of Dubois in Wyoming. Native American tribes hunted here, and their rock drawings and paintings are visible from the trails. In late September, moose chase each other through snow willows, and the hillsides are ablaze with orange and yellow cottonwood. In total, there are more than 155 miles (249 km) of trails.

PLANNING Shoshone and Bridger-Teton National Forests cover large parts of the mountains. You don't need permits to walk in them, but you must register. The best time to go is between June and September. windriver.org

❷ THE MILFORD TRACK, NEW ZEALAND

Described by hiking aficionados as the finest walk in the world, the track—from Glade Wharf on the northern shores of Lake Te Anau to Sandfly Point near Milford Sound on the west coast of the South Island—takes four days. The track starts by meandering through the beech-tree forests of the Clinton Valley, and climbs to the Mackinnon Pass through subalpine tussock and alpine herbs. From there the track descends into the more diverse forest of the Arthur Valley with its ferns, mosses, and lichens.

PLANNING It is essential to make a reservation for this walk between October and May, with places limited to 90 people a day – 40 Independent and 50 Guided. Lodges are run by the Department of Conservation. milfordtrack.net, doc.govt.nz/milfordtrack

❸ CONCORDIA TREK, PAKISTAN

Situated on the border of Pakistan and China, Concordia is a remote and isolated place. Huge glaciers spilling from the mountains of K2, Broad Peak, and Gasherbrum meet here and melt to form tributaries of the Indus River. It is a 14-day trek from Askole to K2 base camp. At the end of the trip, refresh your tired body in the hot springs in the Braldu Gorge near Askole.

PLANNING The trek is best done with an organized group. concordiaexpeditions.com

❹ THE PINDOS TRAVERSE, GREECE

The mountains of the Pindos stretch 180 miles (290 km) from the Gulf of Corinth to the border of Albania. The highest of these mountains are over 6,562 ft (2,000 m), and even on the sunniest days the air is cool. In springtime the wildflowers are among the loveliest and rarest in Europe.

PLANNING It is best to go between May and October. sherpaexpeditions.com

The mighty Karakoram range in northern Pakistan is the spectacular backdrop for the Concordia Trek. The area is the most heavily glaciated in the world outside the polar regions.

❺ HAUTE ROUTE, CORSICA, FRANCE

This 124-mile (200 km) trail crosses the spine of mountains that run the length of the island, from Conca in the southeast to Calenzana in the northwest. The walk will take you through high mountains and pine forests frequently punctuated by clear streams and pools. There is the occasional snowfield to cross early in the summer.

PLANNING The best time to go is between June and September. corsica.forhikers.com

❻ HAUTE ROUTE, FRANCE/SWITZERLAND

The Haute Route, from Chamonix in France to Zermatt in Switzerland, is a demanding two-week trek through some of Europe's highest peaks, linking Mont Blanc with the Matterhorn. The paths are not heavily used, and there is a superb variety of Alpine flowers. Wildlife includes ibex and chamois as well as the marmot with its shrill alarm call.

PLANNING The best time to go is between late June and early September. The route is well serviced by mountain huts. exodus.co.uk

❼ PYRENEAN HAUTE ROUTE, FRANCE/ANDORRA/SPAIN

For the purist, the Pyrenean Haute Route starts on the shores of the Mediterranean and finishes 44 days later on the shores of the Atlantic Ocean. However, most people tend to walk the middle section, taking about 24 days from Lescun in France to El Serrat in Andorra. This route often crosses the tops of Pyrenese mountains at over 9,842 ft (3,000 m).

PLANNING The best time to go is between late June and September. mountainbug.com/trekking-holidays/hrp-hautes-route-pyrenees

❽ THE SOUTHERN UPLAND WAY, SCOTLAND

Scotland's longest trek stretches 211 miles (340 km) west to east from the old fishing village of Portpatrick to the dramatic North Sea cliffs of Cockburnspath. The trail is varied, sometimes plunging deep into dense fir forest, at other times crossing high moorland.

PLANNING The best time to go is between late May and September. southernuplandway.gov.uk

❾ THE PENNINE WAY, ENGLAND/SCOTLAND

The Pennines, a range of high moorland hills, form the backbone of England. The Pennine Way is a long-distance footpath running the length of these hills from Edale in Derbyshire to Kirk Yetholm in Scotland.

PLANNING This 250-mile (402 km) trek is the toughest in England and is often done in stages rather than all at once. thepennineway.co.uk

❿ SOUTH WEST COASTAL PATH, ENGLAND

The longest National Trail in the U.K. stretches 630 miles (1,014 km) from Minehead in Somerset, west along the Bristol Channel, through north Devon, around Cornwall, then east to Poole Harbour in Dorset. The path is rich in archaeological history, from the dinosaurs of the Jurassic Coast (Dorset) to the tin mines of Cornwall.

PLANNING The whole walk takes about eight weeks; it can easily be split into weekend, one-week, or two-week sections. southwestcoastpath.org.uk

The Colorado Trail

A long-haul trek through the Colorado Rockies takes you through flower-filled mountain meadows and past stunning snow-clad peaks.

A bighorn sheep stares down at you from a rocky pinnacle, then suddenly a flock of them are careering down the almost sheer valleyside, across the trail ahead of you, and scrambling surefootedly up the other slope. The path passes along gorges, winds through forests of pine and aspen, crosses tumbling rock-filled mountain streams, and then emerges above the timberline, taking you into high mountain tundra, carpeted in spring with a spectacular tapestry of wildflowers—blue sky pilot, purple moss campion, yellow cinquefoil, rose paintbrush, and many others. This is high-altitude hiking—most of the Colorado Trail is above 10,000 feet (3,048 meters) and many stretches are above 12,000 feet (3,658 meters). The superlatives continue: the 479-mile (771 kilometer) trail crosses eight major mountain ranges, seven national forests, and six wilderness areas. The northeastern half—from the trailhead at Waterton Canyon, southwest of Denver, to Monarch Pass—is easier, but the southwestern half through the San Juan Mountains is more dramatic. Here you climb to the trail's highest point, the 13,334-foot (4,064 meter) Coney Summit and on through the Weminuche Wilderness, before descending to the southern trailhead at Junction Creek, Durango.

WHEN TO GO Summer is best. Snow can lie here until the end of May and into early June. In July and August you'll avoid blizzards.

HOW LONG 479 miles (771 km), divided into 28 segments of 11–31 miles (18–50 km). Allow 40 days for the entire trail, but you can hike each segment on its own.

PLANNING Make sure to acclimatize well beforehand to avoid high-altitude problems. The Colorado Trail Foundation's Official Guidebook provides useful information.

INSIDE INFORMATION Carry waterproof clothes for summer storms, and plan your days to avoid being exposed to thunderstorms on high ridges in the afternoon.

WEBSITES coloradotrail.org, coloradotrailhiking.com, wildernesstravel.com

HIGHLIGHTS

▓ At **Cottonwood Hot Springs**, you can pause for a while and take the weight off your feet. Soak in the spa's thermal pools, or have a massage.

▓ The **Weminuche Wilderness** is 763 sq miles (1,976 sq km) of some of the most spectacular scenery along the trail. It includes the Animas River Canyon and breathtaking views of the Needle and Grenadier ranges.

▓ Historic **Durango**, built as a railroad town in the 1880s, is a place to linger. Explore its atmospheric Victorian downtown area with mountains rising all around. And take a steam-powered ride on the Durango & Silverton Narrow Gauge Railroad to the old mining town of **Silverton**.

In fall, the aspen forests that cover the Colorado mountainsides become a wondrous sea of yellow and gold.

Buckskin Gulch's strangely contorted red-rock cliffs glow in sunlight filtering down from far above.

UTAH   ARIZONA

Paria Canyon

This extraordinary journey through a crack in the Earth's surface is widely recognized as one of the world's best canyon walks.

Thousands of years of river water wearing away at faults in the rock have created this wondrous twisting "slot" canyon, running across the border between Utah and Arizona. As you enter it from White House, Utah, you vanish into a fantastical world, where sunlight seeping down from above creates unusual plays of light and dark on its high, sculpted red-rock walls. In places, the cliffs are only a few yards apart and rise up to 1,000 feet (305 meters) on either side. At—and often around—your feet, the Paria River ("muddy water" in the Paiute language) flows fast over sand and boulders. From time to time, you pass a tree sprouting from the rock with a mini Garden of Eden of greenery and wildflowers spreading out around it. As night falls, you find a ledge to camp on, and the next day it starts all over again. It seems strange to reenter the "real" world at Lee's Ferry, where the Paria flows into the Colorado River.

WHEN TO GO All year, but late April–May and October are best.

HOW LONG 38 miles (61 km). Allow four days and three nights. Add an extra day for Buckskin Gulch.

PLANNING Only 20 hikers can start the trail each day. Ten permits can be booked in advance, and ten are allocated by lottery 24 hours beforehand. Check with the Arizona Bureau of Land Management (BLM). You may spend up to 40 percent of your time in knee-deep water, so take proper water-hiking boots.

INSIDE INFORMATION Check the location of natural springs with the Paria Information Station when you pick up your hiking permit. The Paria is muddy and difficult to filter. There is also the risk of flash floods, but the Information Station will warn you.

WEBSITES blm.gov, besthike.com, americansouthwest.net

HIGHLIGHTS

▥ **Buckskin Gulch**, which joins Paria Canyon about halfway through the trail, is even narrower – less than 10 ft (3 m) for most of its length – and more spectacular. Marvel at the swirling shapes of its waterworn cliffs.

▥ A side trip up Wrather Canyon brings you to **Wrather Arch**, rarely visited but the world's sixth-largest natural span – 246 ft (75 m) across.

▥ **Pictographs** on the cliffs bear witness to Native American travelers who passed this way long before you.

▥ **Pronghorn antelope, coyotes, cottontails**, and **ground squirrels** roam the canyon, while fish, including the flannelmouth sucker and speckled dace, dart through the water.

▥ While in the region, visit the **Wave**, a multihued "chute" scoured into a sandstone mountainside in the Coyote Buttes, west of Paria Canyon.

NORTH AMERICA

CALIFORNIA

The John Muir Trail

*The raw, untouched majesty of California's Sierra Nevada is the
setting for this classic long-distance hike, culminating on Mount Whitney.*

Named for the 19th-century pioneer of the modern conservation movement—and forming part of the mammoth 2,650-mile (4,265 kilometer) Canada-to-Mexico Pacific Crest Trail—the John Muir Trail cuts a glorious course through California's Sierra Nevada, weaving past limpid mountain lakes, across flower-carpeted meadows, through deep-carved canyons, and over dizzying passes. Starting at Happy Isles in Yosemite Valley, the 211-mile (340 kilometer) path crosses three national parks—Yosemite, Kings Canyon, and Sequoia. From Happy Isles, you climb steadily for 9 miles (14.5 kilometers), and from then on you feel like you're walking across the roof of the world, rarely anything less than 8,000 feet (2,438 meters) above sea level. Donohue, Muir, Mather, Pinchot, Glen, and Forester Passes all take you above 11,000 feet (3,353 meters)—opening up stupendous views of the Sierra's high peaks. A golden eagle soars through the sky above, while marmots scurry among the rocks around you. Then you dip down into forests, where blue grouse flutter through the undergrowth. Finally, you reach the trail's crowning point, the 14,495-foot (4,418 meter) summit of Mount Whitney, the highest peak in the U.S. outside Alaska. You can spend the night in a cabin there—it will be very cold, with blustering winds, but you'll see stars glittering in the crystal clear heavens as you've almost certainly never seen them sparkle before.

WHEN TO GO July to September. Much of the trail is snowbound for the rest of the year.

HOW LONG Allow up to three weeks to hike the entire trail. If you want to do an abbreviated version, there are various points at which you can join or leave the trail.

PLANNING You will need Wilderness Permits allowing you to camp along the trail and for any entry into the Mount Whitney zone. Also, this is mostly uninhabited terrain, so plan your food supplies carefully. For the southern half of the trail you will have to carry your supplies with you.

INSIDE INFORMATION Take it easy at first to acclimatize to the altitude. There are campsites at regular intervals. Make sure to protect your food supplies from black bears, which regularly raid campers' unguarded stores; some campsites have "bear boxes" you can use.

WEBSITES pcta.org, yosemiteconservancy.org, fs.fed.us

HIGHLIGHTS

▥ Anglers love fishing for trout in the pristine waters of Lyell River as it flows through **Lyell Canyon.**

▥ **Thousand Island Lake** may not have a thousand islands, but camping on its shores, overlooked by Banner Peak and the summits of the Ritter Range, is unforgettable.

▥ The symmetrical "posts" of the **Devil's Postpile** are huge basaltic columns – formed by cooling lava thousands of years ago – scattered in stacks over 800 acres (324 ha).

▥ A ferry across Edison Lake takes you to the **Vermilion Valley Resort,** a little under halfway through the trail. Take a break here, before heading on for the tougher southern sector.

▥ A scree-filled lunar landscape leads up to **Forester Pass,** at 13,200 ft (4,023 m) the highest on the trail, with intoxicating views of its surrounding peaks.

▥ Although not on the trail, the granite monolith of **Yosemite's Half Dome** is only a short detour from its start. A strenuous climb to the summit – 4,737 ft (1,444 m) above the valley floor – brings views over Yosemite.

Opposite: Backpackers hike alongside the mirror-like Rae Lakes in Kings Canyon National Park, high in the Sierra Nevada toward the end of the trail. Above left: Early summer is the time to see rampant displays of wildflowers. Above right: The forested slopes and tranquil river and lakes of Lyell Canyon offer a peaceful place to pause en route.

The McKinley River flows through open taiga grassland, with the snowy heights of North America's highest peak, Denali, rising beyond.

On the McKinley Bar Trail to McGonagall Pass

Tread carefully across a mile-wide river to experience the haunting grandeur of the taiga landscape in Alaska's Denali National Park.

You wind through a moist taiga forest of spruce and willow, and then you face an unusual challenge—crossing the mile-wide (1.6 kilometer) McKinley River without a bridge. There are two things you need to do. First, at this and the other river crossings along the way, you must make a noise—it alerts grizzly bears, which may be fishing or frolicking on the gravel bar, to get out of your way. Second, grab a length of driftwood. You will need to use it as a staff as you pick your way across the river, boulder to boulder, avoiding a dunking in its milky-blue glacial meltwater. Denali National Park spreads out around North America's highest peak, Denali, meaning the "high one" in the Athabascan language. Climbing the 20,320-foot (6,194 meter) peak is for mountaineers, but the McKinley Bar Trail, starting at Wonder Lake in the park's center, takes you to McGonagall Pass near its base. Crossing rivers, creeks, and forests, and camping at night, you reach the pass, where you should spend a full day before returning. That way you can enjoy the splendor of both sunrise and sunset—garish pink and orange—at the feet of the High One.

WHEN TO GO June through early September.

HOW LONG Allow five to six days for the 38-mile (61 km) trail, and add a couple of days, based at the campground at Wonder Lake, to tour the rest of the park.

PLANNING Practice fording rivers with a full pack. You will also need a backcountry permit and bear-proof containers, both of which you can get at the Denali National Park Visitor Center.

INSIDE INFORMATION Bring mosquito netting. Wear bells on your pack or boots to help avoid unwelcome encounters with grizzly bears.

WEBSITES nps.gov/dena, reservedenali.com, themilepost.com

▓ Take a **bus tour** of the park to experience the full range of its extraordinary mossy green **taiga** and rocky **tundra** landscapes.

▓ Feast your eyes on the **wildlife**: grizzly bears, Dall sheep, timber wolves, moose, arctic foxes, caribou, ptarmigans, and a plethora of waterfowl, including goldeneye ducks and loons, at Wonder Lake and on the McKinley River.

▓ Watch the park's **sled dogs** being put through summer training at their kennels. They pull ATVs (all-terrain vehicles) in order to condition themselves for winter patrolling.

NORTH AMERICA

HAWAI'I

The Kalalau Trail

A challenging hike on the third-largest island in Hawai'i brings sheer precipices, switchback climbs, and a night on a beach under the stars.

NORTH AMERICA

Be prepared for highs and lows on this walk along cliffs and through rain forest on the Garden Isle of Kaua'i in Hawai'i. The Kalalau Trail is just 11 miles (18 kilometers) long, but in that space you zigzag into and out of five steep-sided valleys—your spirits sinking with fatigue, then soaring in exhilaration in step with them. Persevere for the sake of the breathtaking views of the Pacific surf smashing against the cliffs beneath your feet, sending up giant columns of spray. Inland, waterfalls leap down valley sides (like the wild goats you will also see), and forest-clad mountains are an ever present backdrop. The trail, the only land route into Nā Pali Coast State Park, divides into three sections. The first, from Ke'e Beach to Hanakapi'ai Beach, is easiest, with superb vistas along the coast. The next, to Hanakoa Valley, starts with an 800-foot (244 meter) switchback out of Hanakapi'ai Valley. Vertigo adds drama to the final stretch, where in places the red-dirt path narrows to a mere ledge in the sides of plunging cliffs. Awaiting you at the end of your hike is Kalalau Beach, where a waterfall tumbles down a rockface and the 3,000-foot (914 meter) cliffs of the Kalalau Valley rise behind. Pitch your tent and fall asleep to the sound of waves washing the shore.

WHEN TO GO All year, but in winter (October to May) the weather is less predictable and the beaches are often partly washed away.

HOW LONG Allow two days at least – a day to get to Kalalau Beach and a day to get back.

PLANNING You need a permit to go beyond Hanakapi'ai, even if you are not planning to go the whole way to Kalalau and camp. If camping, you need a camping permit. Numbers are strictly limited, so book well in advance with the Hawaiian State Parks authority (camping.ehawaii.gov).

INSIDE INFORMATION The beaches are beautiful, and the sea looks tempting. But don't swim unless you are familiar with local conditions. People have drowned due to unpredictable surf and rip currents.

WEBSITE kalalautrail.com

HIGHLIGHTS

▓ Short side trails lead up both the **Hanakapi'ai** and **Hanakoa valleys** to **waterfalls**. People like to take refreshing natural showers under them, but beware of falling rocks.

▓ **Coffee** plants grow wild on former agricultural terraces in the **Hanakoa Valley**. Native Hawaiians – long since departed from the region – carved the terraces into the valley sides.

▓ **Guavas**, **Java plums**, and **mangoes** grow on terraces in the Kalalau Valley. You can pick and eat them in season as you follow a 2-mile (3.2 km) trail up the valley to **two beautiful pools**, perfect for swimming.

Lush vegetation frames Hanakapi'ai Beach, a strand of perfect white sand, lapped by Pacific waves.

COLOMBIA

Cartagena Street Art Tour

The narrow streets of the city's coolest neighborhood, the barrio of Getsemaní, are alive with colorful paintings and murals.

Hip and happening, Getsemaní, where dazzlingly colorful urban art covers the crumbling stucco walls, is just a stone's throw from the historic city center. Street artists have come here from all over the world to join locals in creating an alfresco art gallery. On Calle de la Sierpe, the epicenter of the street art scene, you'll see "Pedro Romero Vive Aqui," a street art portrait gallery created by residents in response to the omission of this local hero from the country's national portrait gallery. Romero, a Cuban laborer and Cartagena legend, fought to liberate the city from Spanish rule in 1811 at the head of a militia made up of men and women from all walks of life. You can see his statue outside the church in Plaza de la Santisima Trinidad. While you are in the plaza, look for "La India Catalina," a beautiful Indian woman with a jaguar tattoo and a vivid aquamarine eyemask, by Irish artist Fin DAC. In nearby streets, artists have also immortalized Benkos Bioho, the 17th-century slave liberator and leader of the maroons, and boxing great Kid Pambele. The subjects of the murals range from political protest over neighborhood gentrification to indigenous land rights and racism, but also include paintings of locals, tropical scenes, and fruit sellers. As you meander through this colorful barrio to a soundtrack of Latin beats and Caribbean melodies, note the connection between the art and the community that inspired it. The barrio is indeed gentrifying and changing but you'll still see old men playing dominoes, families relaxing in homemade rocking chairs, and barefoot kids showing off impressive soccer skills.

WHEN TO GO All year, but expect short and sharp showers during the rainy season months from June to November.

HOW LONG Three hours to thoroughly cover all the streets.

PLANNING Bring your camera, bottled water, and sun protection. Getting lost as you wander the maze of narrow streets is half the fun.

INSIDE INFORMATION For an added bonus, time your tour for a Sunday during baseball season to enjoy the spectacle of the hotly contested games played in the middle of the street.

WEBSITES cartagenaconnections.com, facebook.com/vertigograffiti, tucultura.co

SOUTH AMERICA

HIGHLIGHTS

▥ Look out for handwritten signs propped up in windows advertising **bolis** for sale. These delicious homemade fruit popsicles are the perfect antidote to Cartagena's summer heat.

▥ Get a jolt of java at **Café del Mural** on Calle de San Juan. This coffee laboratory serves only Colombian coffee, a rarity in Colombia where most of the local crop is exported.

▥ See if you can find all six of the whimsical paintings of round little yellow figures scattered throughout the neighborhood by Madagascan artist **Jaceticot**.

▥ The **"Prisma Afro"** painted by Vertigo Graffiti on the side of Hotel Stil, just outside **Getsemaní**, is the tallest graffiti in Colombia.

Opposite: The grackle, a symbol of Cartagena known locally as Maria Mulata, is immortalized here in a mural by artist Yurika mdc. The brightly painted walls, doors, and fruit seller are typical of this vibrant neighborhood.
Above: Children play soccer in Plaza de la Santisima Trinidad in Getsemaní.

Top 10 Urban Walks

Some of the most diverse trails are not found in the wilderness but in big cities, on paths that reveal a new side to urban areas.

❶ HIGH LINE, NEW YORK CITY, NEW YORK

This repurposed viaduct draws more than five million people each year. The narrow green space, enlivened with wild-flower meadows and waving grasses, stretches 1.5 miles (2.4 km) between Gansevoort Street in the West Village and West 34th Street in Chelsea. Stop and relax at viewing platforms, doze on wooden benches dotted throughout, or come to watch the sun set over the Hudson River.

PLANNING The High Line hosts a year-round slate of guided tours, performances, and other events. thehighline.org

❷ STONE MOUNTAIN TRAIL, ATLANTA, GEORGIA

Stretching 19 miles (31 km) between Centennial Park in downtown Atlanta and Stone Mountain Park on the eastern periphery of the city, Stone Mountain Trail unfolds as a medley of modern and bygone Georgia. Highlights include the childhood home of Martin Luther King, Jr., the Carter center, and downtown Decatur. The trail walk concludes in front of Stone Mountain with its giant bas-reliefs of Stonewall Jackson, Jefferson Davis, and Robert E. Lee.

PLANNING Another (steep) one-mile (1.6 km) trail leads up Stone Mountain. pathfoundation.org/trails/stone-mountain

❸ PEDRA DA GÁVEA, RIO DE JANEIRO, BRAZIL

Rio's most spectacular view isn't from Sugar Loaf or Corcovado, but from the summit of Pedra da Gávea, a monolithic granite peak that rises 2,769 ft (844 m) nearly straight up from the ocean. Trails on this mountain have been accessible to the public since they were opened by local land farmers in the early 19th century. Starting from seaside Joá, the round-trip hike takes around seven hours.

PLANNING Rio Hiking offers guided walks to the top of Pedra da Gávea and other Rio peaks. riohiking.com.br

❹ SENDERO DE LAS GRANDES TRAVESÍAS, SANTIAGO, CHILE

True to its name, the "Grand Traverse" takes hikers around 6 miles (10 km) across the top of Cerro San Cristóbal, a massive mountain that rises above central Santiago. Among the variety of sideshows along the way are the national zoo, botanical garden, two municipal swimming pools, and plenty of excellent vistas.

PLANNING Get a head start on the elevation by hopping the vintage 1925 funicular to the summit. chile.travel/en

Following the path of Jesus' final walk through Jerusalem brings you closer to the myriad faces of the city itself, as you observe citizens, the faithful, and tourists on a walk through the Old City.

❺ COAST TO COAST TRAIL, AUCKLAND, NEW ZEALAND

America's Cup racing yachts, World War I relics, ancient Maori sites, and extinct volcanoes are among the many treasures along this 9-mile (15 km) route across the Auckland Isthmus from Viaduct Harbour to Onehunga.

PLANNING The Coast to Coast is part of Te Araroa Long Pathway, an 1,860-mile (3,000 km) trail all the way across New Zealand. aucklandnz.com

❻ MANLY TO SPIT BRIDGE COASTAL WALK, SYDNEY, AUSTRALIA

Starting from the Manly ferry pier, this 6-mile (10 km) trail winds around the north shore of Sydney Harbour through natural bush, parkland, and beaches. The route traverses Sydney Harbour National Park via landmarks like Dobroyd Head, Grotto Point Lighthouse, and the Clontarf Reserve.

PLANNING Sydney Harbour National Park features many other scenic urban trails. nationalparks.nsw.gov.au

❼ MACLEHOSE TRAIL, HONG KONG

Hike across the backs of the fabled "nine dragon" peaks on this 62-mile (100 km) trail that meanders across the Kowloon Peninsula between Pak Tam Chung and Tuen Mun. With views of the city on one side and the countryside on the other, the trail offers a vertiginous glimpse of Hong Kong's split personality.

PLANNING The MacLehose splits into ten stages, ideal for day hikes. hiking.gov.hk/eng/index.htm

❽ VIA DOLOROSA, JERUSALEM, ISRAEL

This zigzag "Way of Sorrows" through Jerusalem's Old City follows the traditional path that Jesus took from his condemnation by Pontius Pilate to his death on the cross and burial in the stone tomb of his resurrection. Nowadays, the narrow cobblestone path is flanked by souvenir shops, cafés, and the 14 Stations of the Cross.

PLANNING Travel Jerusalem offers a free phone/tablet app with 15 audio walking tours including the Via Dolorosa. itraveljerusalem.com

❾ RUNDUMADUM, VIENNA, AUSTRIA

The "All the Way Around"—*rundumadum*—trail literally circles Vienna. The 74-mile (120 km) route crosses the Danube twice and meanders through the Vienna woods, farmland, and suburban villages as it circumnavigates the capital. The trail is divided into 24 stages, each of which can be easily hiked in a couple of hours.

PLANNING Another great Vienna walk is the 3-mile (4.5 km) Hauptalle through Prater Park. wien.info/en

❿ PLATTEKLIP GORGE, CAPE TOWN, SOUTH AFRICA

Starting from the top of Table Mountain, this rugged 2-mile (3.2 km) path plunges off the north face and downward through a narrow ravine to Tafelberg Road in central Cape Town. Conversely, those with energy can hike this steep trail to the summit and ride the cable car back down.

PLANNING The five-day Hoerikwaggo Trail stretches between Table Mountain and Cape Point with overnights in tented camps. sanparks.org/parks/table_mountain

| PERU |

The Inca Trail

A hike along an ancient Inca way takes you above the clouds into a magical realm, where the remains of an astonishing civilization cling to the sides of soaring mountains.

The air gets thin more than 8,000 feet (2,438 meters) above sea level, and as the ancient stone-paved trail climbs higher and higher, every step seems to leave you gasping for breath. But the rewards are immediate and immeasurable. Clouds drift by, above, below, alongside you, and monumental Inca remains cling to the mountainsides, looking more like giant sculptures than the surviving terraces and buildings of a vanished civilization. The Inca Trail is a minute fragment of an astonishing engineering feat—a 14,000-mile (22,531 kilometer) network of roads that once crisscrossed the entire mountain, rain forest, and desert terrains of the Inca Empire, stretching from Ecuador in the north as far south as Argentina and Chile. Your hike starts at Chillca in the Urubamba Valley. Passing the terraces and ruins of the Inca village of Llaqtapata, you start the inexorable climb, reaching the highest point at Warmiwañusca (Dead Woman's Pass)—13,779 feet (4,200 meters) above sea level—usually on day three of the walk. Mist often shrouds the pass but, if it clears, you find yourself gazing out over a vista of plunging ravines and snow-clad Andean peaks as you rest from the ascent. The presence of the Inca, who clearly reveled in the beauty of their aerial home, is never far away, especially in the climax of the journey: your entry through the Intipunku (Sun Gate) into the Inca's Lost Citadel, Machu Picchu—preferably at dawn, as the first shafts of sunlight break over the surrounding peaks.

WHEN TO GO All year, but the weather is drier from May to October.

HOW LONG 28 miles (45 km). The so-called "classic" Inca Trail takes five days, including the journey from Cusco to the start of the trail and the journey back again.

PLANNING There are strict quotas for the number of people allowed on the trail at any one time, so you need to book well in advance, especially for the high season from June to August. You must go as part of a group with guides and porters.

INSIDE INFORMATION Spend two or three days in Cusco before setting out on the trail. You need that time to acclimatize to the altitude.

WEBSITES peru.info/en-us, andeantravelweb.com

SOUTH AMERICA

HIGHLIGHTS

▓ The landscape changes dramatically as you climb through different climate and vegetation zones – from the dry, cactus-studded **Urubamba Valley** to the high open grasslands of the **Andean puna**, and finally humid **cloud forest**, where tree ferns grow along with more than 250 species of orchid.

▓ The sound of falling water is the ever present backdrop to the Inca remains at **Huinay Huayna** (Wiñay Wayna), which you reach on the fourth day of the hike. These include layers of spectacular terracing, ceremonial baths, and the twin Temples of the Rainbow and the Waterfall.

▓ **Huayna Picchu**, the craggy outcrop that rises above Machu Picchu to the north, offers the best views of the ruined city. Be sure to climb it.

▓ **Andean condors** soar majestically through the sky. If you are lucky you may also glimpse one of the rare and endangered spectacled bears.

Opposite: A veil of cloud shrouds Huayna Picchu, while beneath it spread the ruins of Machu Picchu, the forgotten city American archaeologist Hiram Bingham rediscovered in 1911. Above: Andean peoples love bright colors, as in these containers for sale at Aguas Calientes, the railhead beneath Machu Picchu, and in the adornments of their llamas.

Mountaineers climb a peak above Shackleton Gap. Beyond stretches Murray Snowfield.

SOUTH GEORGIA

The Shackleton Crossing

An astonishing trek across the snow and ice on a dot in the Southern Ocean follows the route Shackleton took to rescue his crewmates.

You are treading in the steps of heroes on this hike across a glacier-covered mountain massif soaring out of the icy depths of the Southern (Antarctic) Ocean. British explorer Ernest Shackleton crossed South Georgia in 1916 to get help for the stranded crew of his ship, which had become trapped in pack ice and sunk. It took him and two companions 36 hours in almost unendurable conditions to cross from King Haakon Bay in the west to a whaling station at Stromness in the east. Today, you can re-create that journey with experienced guides. From King Haakon Bay, you climb to Shackleton Gap, then cross the 5-mile (8 kilometer) wide Murray Snowfield to Trident Ridge. Furious winds batter you as you crest the ridge, and ahead lies the vast Crean Glacier. Crossing this and the Fortuna Glacier, you reach a mountain gap with views of your next goal—Fortuna Bay far below. Elephant and fur seals congregate around the bay, along with penguins. The last section runs along the coast to Stromness.

WHEN TO GO January and February. The weather is harsh in the summer and extremely cold in winter.

HOW LONG 24 miles (39 km). If the weather is good, the crossing takes three days and two nights.

PLANNING You need previous experience in extreme weather camping and traveling across glaciers. Take a good expedition sleeping bag and a strong tent that can withstand the battering of high winds. Your tour operator will give you a list of other equipment you need and may rent it to you.

INSIDE INFORMATION Not for the fainthearted! There is the possibility that you will be stormbound in your tents – or that the crossing will be canceled at the last minute because of bad weather.

WEBSITES iaato.org, jagged-globe.co.uk, exploradus.com

HIGHLIGHTS

▦ The **birdlife** is incredible. In Fortuna Bay, as well as seals, you will see skuas and thousands of king and macaroni **penguins**. Other birds include the South Georgia pipit and South Georgia pintail duck, and out to sea you will spot albatrosses, petrels, and Antarctic prions.

▦ The pinnacles of **Trident Ridge** beckon you across the Murray Snowfield, rising more than 4,000 ft (1,219 m) above sea level.

▦ **Crean Glacier** – named after Tom Crean, one of Shackleton's two companions – is a huge plain of ice and snow, crisscrossed with crevasses and dotted with nunataks (the peaks of icebound mountains jutting above the surface of the glacier).

▦ The small **graveyard** at **Stromness** bears witness to the harsh lives of whalers who died while working at the station there.

SOUTH AMERICA

ARGENTINA

The FitzRoy Massif

Trek across glaciers, past glittering lakes, and through forests on this majestic hike among mountain peaks in Argentine Patagonia.

Patagonia's Los Glaciares National Park is 2,300 square miles (5,957 square kilometers) of Andean peaks, *lenga* (southern beech) forest, rivers, and glaciers—the glaciers forming part of the Hielo Sur, the world's largest ice field outside Antarctica and Greenland. This hike takes you to the north of the park, an area dominated by the twin peaks—Mount FitzRoy and Cerro Torre—of the FitzRoy Massif. You cross icy, rushing creeks, traverse valleys, and circuit lakes. At other times, you walk through airy lenga forest, where you see and hear squawking parakeets and Patagonian woodpeckers; the puma prowling the forest may see you, but you will be lucky if you see it. Setting out from the village of El Chaltén, you start gently, climbing northwest to Laguna Capri. Beyond that lies a steep ascent to the huge, turquoise Laguna de los Tres, bringing the first close-up views of the FitzRoy Massif, shrouded in cloud or swept by wind-driven snow. Returning to Laguna Capri, you turn south to Laguna Torre, where icebergs, calved from a glacier on its western side, jostle the shore, driven there by the wind. Crowning the trek, before your return to El Chaltén, is a hike across the Torre Glacier. The blinding surface stretches to the skyline. You can see the curve of the horizon, and you feel like you're looking at the edge of the world.

WHEN TO GO November to late February, summer in the Southern Hemisphere.

HOW LONG Three nights and four days. You camp two nights at Laguna Capri and one at the foot of Cerro Torre.

PLANNING This is not a trip you should take on your own. Check out the various tour operators offering guided treks through the FitzRoy Massif. Usually you fly to El Calafate, then take a bus to El Chaltén.

INSIDE INFORMATION Good-quality all-weather gear is essential. It can get bitterly cold at night and winds can reach up to 100 mph (160 km/h). Take plenty of layers.

WEBSITES losglaciares.com/en/index.html, amazonadventures.com, fitzroyexpediciones.com.ar

SOUTH AMERICA

HIGHLIGHTS

▦ Get up early one morning at Laguna Capri and watch the rising sun bathe **Mount FitzRoy** in pink and orange. Or wait for sunset, when smoky clouds collect on top of the massif, lit up in an explosion of fiery color.

▦ Relish the view from Laguna Torre up to **Cerro Torre**, a colossal granite needle jutting 10,260 ft (3,127 m) into the sky. It presents a serious challenge to climbers, but can be appreciated just as well from below.

▦ Visit the **Perito Moreno Glacier** while in the park. You can cross its towering spikes of mauve and electric blue on a wooden walkway and watch chunks of ice breaking off and crashing into Lago Argentino below.

The snowy heights of Mount FitzRoy are reflected in a blue mountain lake. The 11,073-ft (3,375 m) peak is named after the captain of Charles Darwin's ship, HMS *Beagle*.

| CHILE |

The Torres del Paine

The glaciers of the Patagonian ice cap inch their way across the landscape, while snowcapped peaks tower skyward, on this awe-inspiring hike through Chile's far south.

The high-flying condor, eagle, and buzzard were made for the terrain of Chile's Torres del Paine National Park, a place where the scale of glaciers and mountains dwarfs any human presence and challenges the habits of everyday life. The park is named for its three "blue towers"—*paine* (pronounced "pine-ay") means "blue" in the local Tehuelche language—whose sharply chiseled granite peaks pierce the stormy Patagonian sky. They are the first day's goal on this W-shaped trek. Setting out from the park's eastern side, you climb an alpine valley forested with beech, scramble over moraine, your hands grasping at boulders for leverage, very likely with a strong wind at your back … and there they stand, rising a sheer 330 feet (101 meters) from the base of the glaciers. More valley hikes and mountain views await you in the days that follow. Crossing the verdant Valle del Francés, farther west, brings into focus the jagged shapes of the Cuernos (Horns) del Paine, whose names fit them perfectly: Hoja (Blade), Espada (Sword), Catedral (Cathedral), and Aleta de Tiburón (Shark Fin). At sunrise a crimson light floods them, and their shadows turn purple. At Lago Grey, even farther west, you feel the presence of the huge Patagonian ice field, whose offshoot, the 38-mile (61 kilometer) long Glaciar Grey, deposits blue-veined icebergs in the water. You can get even closer to the landscape by kayaking across a lagoon, climbing an ice cliff, riding horseback over moorland, or simply contemplating the view from a rocky outcrop.

WHEN TO GO The weather in Torres del Paine is notoriously unpredictable, but from November to February you will have a better chance of seeing clear skies.

HOW LONG About 60 miles (97 km). The hike lasts four days, walking for six to eight hours each day.

PLANNING To get to Torres del Paine, you fly from Santiago to Punta Arenas, then go by road. Layering and wind- and waterproof clothing are essential; temperatures can drop as low as 32°F (0°C), even in summer, and winds over 60 mph (97 km/h) are common.

INSIDE INFORMATION An extension of the trail, around the top end of the "W," allows you to do a complete circuit, in which case do it counterclockwise to avoid the strong headwinds.

WEBSITES torresdelpaine.com/en, welcomepatagonia.com

SOUTH AMERICA

HIGHLIGHTS

▥ You won't forget your first glimpse of the glistening **Patagonian ice cap** from a window seat on the flight from Santiago to Punta Arenas.

▥ The black tips of the **"Horns"** contrast with the bright snow and the pale granite of their base. These peaks are the most beautiful in the park, and their reflection shimmers in the turquoise waters of Lake Nordenskjöld.

▥ At Lago Grey your guide may offer you a **pisco sour** (a strong local drink made from Chilean brandy, lime juice, sugar, and ice), using crushed ice from one of the floating icebergs!

▥ As you hike to the tongue of the immense **Glaciar Grey**, 4 miles (6.4 km) wide and 200 ft (61 m) high, you will hear bewildering thunder-like crashes, as huge chunks of ice calve into the lake below.

Opposite: The rising sun composes a symphony of rich pinks and purples in the skies above the Cuernos del Paine, mirrored in the lake waters beneath. Above left: A yellow-painted corrugated iron hut provides an overnight refuge for hikers. Above right: Guanacos, relatives of the llama, prized for their wool, graze against a backdrop of rocky peaks.

Climbing Mount Fuji

Watch the dawn rise in splendor from the summit of Japan's most famous landmark, the perfect volcanic cone of Mount Fuji.

ASIA

Sacred and snow-capped, Fuji-san—rising 12,388 feet (3,776 meters) above sea level—is a dormant volcano, its image immortalized by the printmaker Hokusai in "Thirty-Six Views of Mount Fuji." The most popular starting point is Kawaguchiko 5th Station, more than halfway up the mountain, where tourists and locals congregate, creating a sense of camaraderie as they get ready for the nighttime trek to watch the dawning of the day. The trail winds upward, with long sections of steep steps that take a toll on calf muscles. As you climb, the forest known as Aokigahara (Sea of Trees) falls away and you enter a moonscape of rocks and shrubs. Look up and you will see a pristine night sky dusted with the Milky Way. The temperature drops quickly, and the rest stops and huts become more frequent. Welcoming futons are laid out, fires glow invitingly, and hot food and drinks are served. At the summit you find other climbers huddling in groups to stay warm and watch the sky slowly filling with light. Now clouds come into view way below, hovering over the hills that melt into the sea in the distance. A pinpoint of sun pierces the horizon, pauses, then explodes with light, and bathes the vast panorama of metropolitan Tokyo in its morning glow.

WHEN TO GO July and August, when the summit is usually snow-free. Avoid the Obon festival in honor of ancestral spirits in August, when numbers swell so much that you have to wait in line in places.

HOW LONG The climb takes about six to seven hours. The journey down can take up to four hours.

PLANNING Buses run from Shinjuku station in central Tokyo to Kawaguchiko 5th station; aim to get there at 9 p.m. Wear warm, waterproof clothes, as the summit is cold and it often rains. Take gloves for sections where you have to use your hands scrambling over stony terrain.

INSIDE INFORMATION Food and drinks are expensive at the summit, so bring your own. Altitude sickness can start over 8,000 ft (2,438 m); take it slowly and drink lots of water.

WEBSITES jnto.go.jp, japan-guide.com

HIGHLIGHTS

▥ Peer down from the summit at the **torchlit procession** of climbers wending their way upward – they look like a line of flaming ants.

▥ Stay on **after sunrise**. Walk around the crater and step on what is officially Fuji's highest point at the weather station.

▥ Send your friends a postcard from the **Mount Fuji post office**, the country's highest, or buy a certificate proving that you made it to the top.

▥ Explore the serene **Fuji Five Lakes region** at the foot of the mountain. It provides the most evocative close-up views of Mount Fuji, its image reflected in the lakes' waters.

Cherry blossoms and Mount Fuji – the view across Lake Kawaguchi, one of the Fuji Five Lakes, emcompasses both classic images of Japan.

The sheer scale of the world's most famous wall is matched only by the beauty of the landscapes that surround it.

CHINA

The Great Wall of China

The Great Wall leaps from hilltop to hilltop across northern China's most rugged terrain, challenging trekkers to keep up.

Built more than 2,000 years ago to keep out invaders from the north, the Great Wall runs like a monumental backbone across China. For long stretches it sprawls in extravagant decay, battered by time, weather, and neglect. The Jinshanling to Simatai section, northeast of Beijing—rocky underfoot and largely unchanged since the 16th-century Ming period—offers a glorious trek above rolling, forested country. East of Simatai the wall is 200 years older and even more dilapidated and dramatic, climbing steep ridges and plunging into valleys. This section is challenging even for experienced hikers, and from the 12th tower you may have to take the adjacent path. An almost perpendicular climb, the Stairway to Heaven leads to the 15th, or Fairy, Tower, with finely sculpted stonework. A sliver of ridge, the Sky Bridge, links this to the highest point, Watching Beijing Tower. Beyond here the walkway is so narrow that access is forbidden, and after such a heady experience it is time to return to Earth.

WHEN TO GO Spring and fall. Summer is hot and wet; snow and ice make conditions dangerous in winter.

HOW LONG Jinshanling-Simatai section: 7 miles (11.3 km), three hours; section east of Simatai: 3 miles (5 km), two to three hours. Allow two hours by road from Beijing to Jinshanling.

PLANNING Parts of the route can be treacherous underfoot, so go with a guide or someone who has been before. Take sunscreen, bottled water, a picnic, and pocket money for any purchases.

INSIDE INFORMATION Be sure to haggle over the prices of everything you can buy at the wall. At Simatai be prepared for a second entrance fee and a small fee to cross the chain bridge over the reservoir.

WEBSITES travelchinaguide.com, worldexpeditions.com, wildwall.com

HIGHLIGHTS

▓ Ancient **watchtowers**, which once housed troops and sent signals along the route, make perfect **standpoints** over an infinite landscape of peaks and valleys. You can picnic inside them, enjoying a sentry's view north toward Mongolia.

▓ At **Jinshanling**, the wall soars along high ridges and is visible for miles in either direction. A 1.8-mile (2.9 km) section here has been restored and is illuminated by colored light at night.

▓ The reward for climbing the **Tian Qiao** (Stairway to Heaven) is a dizzying view across the Miyun reservoir and over to Beijing.

▓ For a luxury experience of another part of the wall, mixing the ancient with the ultramodern, check out **Commune by the Great Wall Kempinski** hotel in Badaling. It won't be cheap, but the hotel itself is an architectural experience and offers superb mountain views of the wall.

ASIA
Beijing

MALAYSIA

The Headhunters' Trail

*Today, the trail is peaceful as it meanders through lush rain forest and across creeks,
but once fierce headhunting warriors used it, intent on raiding villages in a neighboring valley.*

Three mountain ranges cross Gunung Mulu National Park in Sarawak, one of two Malaysian states on Borneo. They form part of an astonishing limestone landscape, where rocky pinnacles rise like spires from the surrounding rain forest and caves honeycomb the ground beneath—including the world's largest cavern, the Sarawak Chamber, big enough for 47 jumbo jets to fit inside. Hiking trails cross the park, leading to caves and waterfalls, and to the limestone pinnacles of the Gunung Api range. The Headhunters' Trail is a route once taken by warriors of the Kayan people living along the Baram River. After paddling up the Melinau—part of the Baram river system—to the Melinau Gorge, they dragged their canoes overland to the Terikan River. From there they made their way down into the Limbang Valley, where they attacked its inhabitants, bringing back their foes' heads as trophies. The trail follows their route between the Melinau and Terikan. First, you travel by boat up the Melinau to the settlement of Kuala Berar, then you hike to a clearing called Camp 5, near the 2,000-foot (610 meter) cliffs of the Melinau Gorge. After that, you wind through forest to Kuala Terikan on the Terikan, where a boat will take you to spend the night in a traditional longhouse of the Iban people (related to the Kayan). You can continue downriver to Nanga Medamit, from where a hike leads to the town of Limbang.

ASIA

WHEN TO GO All year.

HOW LONG 7 miles (11.3 km) between Camp 5 and Kuala Terikan. Allow three days if you are heading on to Limbang, and five days if you include treks to the Gunung Api pinnacles and the park's caves.

PLANNING You have to take your own food supplies, cooking utensils, and sufficient water for overnight stays in jungle base camps. You need good walking boots and a sleeping bag (or blanket), as it can get cold at night. Take waterproof clothes as the climate is warm, but very wet. The trails are guided.

INSIDE INFORMATION Don't miss the opportunity for an Iban meal. Meat, fish, vegetables, and rice are cooked in bamboo stems, giving them a unique flavor. Seasonings include saffron, wild ginger, and galangal, which looks a bit like gingerroot, but has a more citrus-like taste.

WEBSITES mulupark.com, mmadventure.com

HIGHLIGHTS

▦ An overnight stay in a **traditional longhouse** – called a *rumah panjai* in the local Iban language – is an extraordinary experience. Whole villages live in these buildings, raised off the ground on stilts, with a public area down one side and families' living quarters down the other.

▦ There are 15 types of rain forest in Gunung Mulu National Park, resulting in astonishing **biodiversity**, including more than 170 species of **orchid**, 110 species of **palm tree**, and 10 species of carnivorous **pitcher plants**.

▦ The park's **birdlife** includes wrinkled hornbills, Storm's storks, and two exotic pheasants: Bulwer's pheasant and the crested fireback pheasant, whose males have a shimmering plummage of blues, yellows, and reds.

▦ One of the park's trails leads to Deer Cave, where at sunset you can watch **three million bats** pour out of its entrance in a seemingly endless stream as they head off for a night's foraging for insects.

Opposite: Hikers along the Headhunters' Trail prepare to climb the rocky entrance to the Deer Cave and explore the extensive cave systems within. Above left: Iban men sit in a longhouse making their traditional costume. Above right: The limestone spires of the Gunung Api pinnacles soar skyward through the forest canopy.

Around Chiang Mai

Trek through northern Thailand's lush green hills and experience the smiling, always colorful hospitality of its tribal villages.

ASIA

You're breathless as you reach the top of a steep path winding through the jungle, but with endorphins flooding your veins, you're happy. You're especially delighted when, a short while later, you spy stepped terraces of young rice plants and trees laden with mangoes. You've arrived at a village of the Lahu tribe. The villagers bring tea and supper, and you go early to bed. This is northern Thailand, close to the border with Myanmar (Burma), and there are many different routes you can take to reach the hill villages. Usually, you work your way westward from Chiang Dao to Pai to Mae Hong Son (taking to road transport in places to help move you along the trail). All the time you are passing through the villages of different tribes. One belongs to the Akha tribe, where smiling girls wear ornate headdresses piled high on their heads. You sit cross-legged in a rickety thatched hut and sip bitter tea from a smooth bamboo cup. Too soon, it's time to leave, but there's not far to go. The path leads downhill, flanked by banana trees, and you arrive at the lodge where you'll stay the night. This time your hosts are the Lisu tribe, who entertain you with cold drinks and dancing. And the next morning it will all begin again—different tribes, different colorful costumes and ways of life, but always waterfalls, toffee-colored rivers, and green hills.

WHEN TO GO The best time to go is after the rainy season, from October through February. The months from March through May are hot and dry.

HOW LONG Most trips last two or three days, though longer journeys and day trips can also be arranged.

PLANNING This is not a journey to do on your own. Local tour operators with local guides are best; they will provide all necessary equipment, food, and drink.

INSIDE INFORMATION Each itinerary differs, but this is a hilly area and some of the walking sections of the treks can be rigorous. Be sure to take good walking boots.

WEBSITES tourismthailand.org, chiangmai-chiangrai.com

HIGHLIGHTS

▓ It is well worth taking the time to chat to the **tribal elders**. Your guide will be happy to translate, and these old men are fascinating characters who'll love to drink tea with you and to talk about their lives and yours.

▓ The tribal people are known for their **hospitality**. Despite their smiles, their lives have not usually been easy. Many came here to escape persecution in Myanmar.

▓ Keep your eyes peeled for snakes, especially the **king cobras** that live in these hills—a beautiful sight so long as you don't get too close!

▓ Many treks incorporate **elephant riding**, rafting, and mountain-biking.

Brilliant color is the keynote in the costumes of these Lisu women from Chiang Rai in full traditional dress.

Porters like this one will carry your bags for you in towering loads while wearing no more than flip-flops on their feet.

NEPAL

The Annapurna Circuit

The giant peaks of the great Annapurna massif are the sublime backdrop to this hike through Nepal's Himalaya.

Prayer flags flutter on walls of sacred stones. Snow-clad peaks soar above green paddy fields and rhododendron forests, pink-bloomed in spring. As you ascend at the start of this circuit around the Annapurna massif you encounter diverse scenery and medieval-style villages, with hay and timber stacked on roofs. From the lush Marsyangdi Valley you enter the Manangbhot Gorge, crossing suspension bridges to the far side of the river, where spruce and juniper forests take over. The ascent from Manang to the 17,800-foot (5,425 meter) Thorong La Pass leads through high pastures where yak graze, and at the top the sight of Annapurna and her sister peaks—nine of them above 23,000 feet (7,010 meters)—awaits you. Descending westward through Kali Gandaki, you may see a mule caravan carrying salt and barley. Gradually, pine forests return, then rice terraces, orange groves, and poinsettias appear. A dip in the hot springs of Tatopani energizes you for the final stage to the bazaar town of Birethanti.

WHEN TO GO There are two trekking seasons, April–May and October–November. Rhododendrons bloom in spring, but skies are clearest in fall, giving superb views of the peaks.

HOW LONG The 150-mile (241 km) circuit divides into 19–21 trekking days. Allow 24 days for the whole trip.

PLANNING From Kathmandu you will go by road to Besisahar, where the trek starts. Although there are still visible signs of the 2015 earthquakes, much has been rebuilt, and the circuit is now running as before.

INSIDE INFORMATION Crossing the Thorong La involves climbing 3,000 ft (914 m) and descending an exhausting 5,000 ft (1,524 m) in one day. Start well before dawn to avoid the high winds that sweep the pass.

WEBSITES mountainkingdoms.com, worldexpeditions.com

HIGHLIGHTS

▥ You will spend a day in the high village of **Manang**, acclimatizing to the altitude. Visit the nearby monastery of **Braga** or the tiny hermitage perched above the village.

▥ After Thorong La, **Muktinath** is a major pilgrimage center, holy to both Buddhists and Hindus. A sacred flame lit by natural gas burns above a bubbling spring in a grove of poplars.

▥ The **Kali Gandaki Canyon** is the world's deepest gorge, between towering Dhaulagiri and Annapurna.

▥ Near the end of the trek, there are superb views from **Poon Hill** above the village of **Ghorepani**, especially at sunrise or sunset. You can see Annapurna and Machhapuchhare, the sacred fishtail mountain.

▥ **Kathmandu** is a maze of twisting alleyways, ancient shrines, and busy markets, many rebuilt after the tragedy of the 2015 earthquake. Don't miss the Buddhist temple of **Swayambunath** and the Hindu shrine of **Pashupatinath.**

Top 10 Underground Walks

Take a journey below ground to discover a fascinating subterranean world of natural and man-made wonders.

❶ UNDERGROUND CITY, MONTREAL, CANADA

Take one of the 120 entrances into the largest man-made underground network in the world. About 500,000 people a day use its 20 miles (32 km) of shopping malls, hotels, banks, offices, museums, and universities; there are also metro and train stations, a bus terminal, and an ice-hockey arena.

PLANNING Don't forget your credit card. mtl.org/en

❷ MAMMOTH CAVE NATIONAL PARK, KENTUCKY

Place-names such as Grand Avenue and Frozen Niagara give a notion of what's in the world's longest cave system. The oldest part was formed 10 million years ago, 9.5 million years before *Homo sapiens* made an appearance.

PLANNING 31 miles (50 km) from Bowling Green, Kentucky, with good transportation links. nps.gov/maca

❸ AKTUN CHEN ECO PARK CAVES, YUCATÁN, MEXICO

Walk by subterranean rivers (locally called cenotes) and peer through deep, crystal clear water to the white floors of natural wells. Peace reigns in this surreal world of spectacular stalactites, stalagmites, fossils, and fruit bats lying beneath untouched rain forest. Explore by foot or in the water.

PLANNING Tours or car rental from Cancún. Take insect repellent. aktun-chen.com

❹ CU CHI TUNNELS, VIETNAM

Crawl through a small trapdoor into narrow, stifling tunnels and enter an "underground village" with kitchen, dormitory, meeting room, and hospital. During the Vietnam War (1954–75) thousands of Viet Cong were based in the 125-mile (200 km) network of tunnels. The "village" was never captured despite being bombed many times.

PLANNING Guided tour, from any travel agent in Ho Chi Minh City. thesinhtourist.vn

❺ HANNAN'S NORTH MINE, KALGOORLIE, AUSTRALIA

Descend 100 ft (30.5 m) in a cage elevator to tunnels excavated during Australia's 19th-century gold rush. If you're feeling lucky, try your hand at panning for gold. Kalgoorlie still produces 10 percent of the world's gold.

PLANNING Find more information at hannansnorth.com.au

There are over 335 miles (539 km) of mapped and explored passages at Mammoth Cave in Kentucky. Many of the most famous parts of the cave – such as Fat Man's Misery – can be seen on lighted tours.

❻ WIELICZKA SALT MINE, KRAKÓW, POLAND

It all started when salt was the medieval equivalent of today's oil. Nine centuries of mining have produced miles of subterranean passages and gigantic caverns to a depth of 440 ft (134 m). More than one million people a year visit the UNESCO-listed site, which features lakes, chapels, and statues sculpted from salt, the world's largest mining museum, a sanatorium for those suffering from asthma and allergies, and concert halls with peerless acoustics.

PLANNING Train from Kraków central (Glowny) station (6 miles/9.7 km). 400 steps to negotiate and a 1-mile (1.6 km) walk. Use the elevator for a small fee. Disabled tours available. krakow-info.com/wielicz.htm

❼ BERLIN NUCLEAR BUNKER, GERMANY

Take a few minutes to adjust to the dim light of this 1971 radiation-proof Cold War bunker. Feel the cold creep into your bones in the deathly silence. Tiers of narrow bunk beds for 3,562 people take up most of the space. The bunker could operate for 14 days, after which you would be cast out into the radiation-saturated debris of Berlin after a nuclear attack. It's a spine-chilling experience.

PLANNING Guided tours only from the Story of Berlin Museum, Kurfürstendamm 207–8. Metro: Kurfürstendamm. story-of-berlin.de

❽ THE PARIS SEWERS, FRANCE

Every day 42 million cu ft (1.2 million cu m) of wastewater gush through this 1,300-mile (2,092 km) system. See 457 ft (139 m) of sewer at work (with attractions including a manual flusher trolley that keeps detritus on the move) and learn about waste disposal through the ages. The smell is only a tad tangy and postcards are available, according to one guide, from a "sewer-venir store."

PLANNING Free guided tour. Enter between Quai d'Orsay and the Seine. Metro: Alma-Marceau. en.parisinfo.com/paris-museum-monument/71499/musee-des-egouts-de-paris

❾ THE CATACOMBS, ROME, ITALY

Walk the galleries, chambers, and churches of the necropolises abandoned in the Middle Ages for centuries beneath the Eternal City. Imagine it in the early centuries of Christianity, when Rome was a dangerous place for believers and the caverns were lit by a myriad of flickering oil lamps. Don't miss the graffiti—thousands of prayers written by anyone from popes to plumbers.

PLANNING Bus 218 from Piazza di Porta San Giovanni to Fosse Ardeatine. catacombe.roma.it

❿ THE GREAT PYRAMID, GIZA, EGYPT

Descend 330 ft (101 m) through a 3.5-ft (1 m) wide passage into the heart of the only wonder of the ancient world that survives to this day. Inside the awesome inner sanctum is a sarcophagus, built of granite from Aswan, 625 miles (1,006 km) away. About 5,000 years old and 30 times larger in area than the Empire State Building, the Great Pyramid has been the subject of centuries of speculation about its origins, construction, and purpose.

PLANNING Car rental and tours available from any travel agent in Cairo (12 miles/19 km). Air-conditioned bus (355/357) from Cairo (Egyptian Museum) to Giza. egypt.travel

The colorful interior of the Rangjung Woesel Choeling Monastery in Eastern Bhutan.

The Rigsum Gompa Trek

A trek into a "lost" valley in Bhutan takes you on an enchanted tour through a land where age-old ways of life carry on into the present.

Eastern Bhutan is a place of precipitous slopes where rivers tumble through gorges and villages nestle in the shadow of holy rocks. Tilling the land, weaving, turning wood, every task is an act of worship for the villagers following the teachings of Guru Rinpoche, who introduced Buddhism into the area in the 8th century. North of Trashigang, you reach the lost valley of Trashiyangtse, start of this circular trek. Meandering through paddy fields and forests, you follow the course of the Womanang River, before crossing the hills to Rigsum Gompa, the Temple of the Three Gods. You descend through the Bumdeling wildlife sanctuary, then walk along the Kolong Chu River, heading for the shrine of Chorten Kora. Bears live in the forest, but you're more likely to meet a wandering cow or boy monks on their way to a *puja* (a series of Buddhist rituals). Little disturbs the peace but the sound of waterfalls and rustling bamboo.

WHEN TO GO Fall (from mid-October) for the best weather, early spring for blooming rhododendrons.

HOW LONG 28 miles (45 km). The trek takes three days; travel is slow due to the mountainous terrain. Allow four days for the drive from Bhutan's capital, Thimphu, more if you want to sightsee on the way.

PLANNING Bring binoculars. If you take photographs, double the amount of memory you think you need. Be prepared for changes to your schedule.

INSIDE INFORMATION Anyone reasonably fit can cope with this trek, but you will climb to around 8,200 ft (2,499 m), so pace yourself to acclimatize to the altitude and drink plenty of fluids. When entering a temple, remove your shoes and allow time for your guide's devotions.

WEBSITES kingdomofbhutan.com, bluepoppybhutan.com

HIGHLIGHTS

▓ You'll never forget your first view of the lost valley of **Trashiyangtse**, its rice terraces, and its *dzong* (fortress) perched on a hilltop.

▓ The **people you encounter** are one of the trail's delights—an old man fingering prayer beads, a teacher inviting you into a school. They cover their mouths as they speak to avoid polluting the air you breathe and are delighted to pose for the camera.

▓ On the first night, you will camp by the river, a **holy site** which an enthusiastic lama will tell you about in the morning.

▓ From Rigsum Gompa you watch the **sun rise** over a panorama of mountains and valleys, while monks prepare bowls of fresh water in a temple dedicated to compassion, power, and knowledge.

▓ Rare **black neck cranes** from Tibet overwinter on sandy river islands in the Bumdeling Wildlife Sanctuary.

ASIA

Everest Base Camp

Climbing the world's highest peak may be beyond your reach, but on this trek to its base you can imagine yourself up there on its heights.

ASIA

You pass Sherpa villages and monasteries, cross rivers, and wind around hillsides on this rugged trek up the Khumbu Valley to the foot of Everest, where its permanent Base Camp stands below the Khumbu Icefall. The Sherpa name for this region is Solu Khumbu, and your gateway to it is the busy, ancient trading post of Namche Bazar. Here, Tibetan traders, who once bartered salt for cloth and other commodities from Kathmandu, now deal in trekking and mountaineering gear. Setting out from Namche, you soon get your first glimpse of Everest hiding behind the great wall of her sister mountain, Nuptse. The slow ascent continues, sometimes dipping by rivers and through rhododendron forests, but always making for the goal: Kala Pattar, the 18,000-foot (5,486 meter) peak that offers the clearest views of Everest, better than from Base Camp itself. The air here is thin, and breathing is labored, but the final push across moraine (rocky terrain) and up to the peak is worth all the effort. The highest mountain on Earth stands before you. Your gaze sweeps from the Khumbu Icefall to the glacial valley of Western Cwm and up to the South Col, where the long west ridge stretches out to Everest's summit—the lure of many a mountaineer and Sherpa.

WHEN TO GO Any time between October and May, although it's very cold in December and January. The clearest views are usually from mid-October to the end of November. The busiest time is October.

HOW LONG 19 miles (30.6 km) one-way, from Namche Bazar to Kala Pattar. It takes about eight days, allowing for altitude acclimatization, breaks, and detours.

PLANNING Take a really good sleeping bag. Days are often warm, but it gets cold at night. You need high-factor sunblock and lip balm; the UV is fierce at high altitude.

INSIDE INFORMATION Enjoy the teahouses offering all kinds of food from Nepalese *dahl bhat* (lentils and rice) to pizza – they were quickly rebuilt after the 2015 earthquake, as were the excellent lodges.

WEBSITES welcomenepal.com, explore.co.uk

| HIGHLIGHTS

▩ One of the first villages you pass through is **Khumjung**, north of Namche, where you can see a so-called **yeti skull** in the monastery.

▩ An imposing monastery stands at the entrance to the village of **Thyangboche**. You can join in the twice-daily prayers and meditation.

▩ **Ama Dablam** comes spectacularly into view at Thyangboche. The Sherpa people call this beautiful mountain the "necklace of Chomolungma," the Tibetan name for Everest.

▩ Above the village of Dingboche you have **superb views** of the stars of the Himalayan range, including Ama Dablam, Makalu, Lhotse, and Everest.

Yaks still carry supplies to and from Everest Base Camp. The trek's destination, Kala Pattar, rises from the sides of the higher Pumori, just visible in the background.

Lake Issyk-Kul

A blue lake rimmed by snowcapped peaks and views across the wild steppe—all these are yours on a cross-border trail in Central Asia.

ASIA

The towering summits of the Tien Shan—Mountains of Heaven in Chinese—dominate the eastern part of the small Central Asian republic of Kyrgyzstan. And cradled in their midst is the ethereal lake of Issyk-Kul (Ysyk-Köl), its blue waters surrounded by the range's jagged, snowy peaks. Many superb hikes lead out from its shores, taking you across herb-filled meadows, through juniper forests, and along broad green mountain valleys where you encounter Kyrgyz nomads with herds of sheep and goats. From the town of Karakol, you can head south along the red sandstone canyon of the Jeti-Ögüz Valley, on to Lake Ala Kul—famous for its rapid changes from green to blue to violet—then along the Altyn-Arashan Valley. A glorious medium-range trail takes you north from Balbay at the lake's eastern end into the neighboring republic of Kazakhstan. You climb steeply at first to the 10,745-foot (3,275 meter) Sary-Bulak Pass in the Kungei Alatau range. Pause here to enjoy the breathtaking views—south to Issyk-Kul and north across the Kazakh steppe. Next, the three beautiful Kolsai lakes beckon you across the border into Kazakhstan, before winding downhill to Saty, from where you make your way by road to Almaty, Kazakhstan's largest city.

WHEN TO GO July to September for higher altitudes. Late May and June are wonderful below about 9,840 ft (2,999 m).

HOW LONG 40 miles (64 km) from Balbay to Saty. Allow four to five days.

PLANNING The trekking industry is in its infancy in Kyrgyzstan and facilities are basic. Join an organized tour (preferably one using a local guide), or arrange your own guide after arriving in Kyrgyzstan. Visas are required for Kyrgyzstan and Kazakhstan.

INSIDE INFORMATION There are few settlements in the mountains, so bring plenty of food and fluids. Anyone you do meet may offer you a drink of *kumuz*. Try it—it's fermented mare's milk.

WEBSITES dostuck.com.kg, turkestan.biz, geoex.com

HIGHLIGHTS

▓ You can swim in **Issyk-Kul**'s warm, **mineral-rich waters**, reputed to be therapeutic. There are also hot springs in the Altyn-Arashan Valley.

▓ **Wildlife** you may see includes wild sheep, brown bears, wolves, lynx, piping hares, and even snow leopards.

▓ Issyk-Kul's waters are blue, but the **Kolsai lakes** are green, set among alpine meadows and forests in the foothills of the Kungei Alatau range. They are known for good trout fishing.

▓ While you are in the region, spend a night in a **yurt** – a portable home made of felt – under a colorfully woven traditional **Kyrgyz rug**. There are some yurt guest-camps.

Thermal activity helps to keep Lake Issyk-Kul's waters warm enough to swim in; beyond lie the snowy summits of the Tien Shan.

Eucalyptus trees line the Murray River, where its deep blue waters flow round a bend.

ACROSS WATER

BY ROAD

BY RAIL

ON FOOT

IN SEARCH OF CULTURE

IN GOURMET HEAVEN

INTO THE ACTION

UP AND AWAY

IN THEIR FOOTSTEPS

| AUSTRALIA |

Murray Valley Trail

A hike through South Australia's Murray River Valley reveals the region's diversity—vineyards, old settlers' homes, and a rich wildlife.

The Murray River is Australia's greatest watercourse—together with the Darling River it drains the country's entire wheat and sheep belt. A tourist route follows the river from its source among New South Wales's Snowy Mountains to its mouth in South Australia, connecting scenic drives with boat trips and bushwalks along the way. For a good hiking trail, start at Murray Bridge, South Australia. You head north through the town's historic waterfront, then leave the river as you turn into the Rocky Gully Gorge. It is now a gentle climb into the foothills of the Mount Lofty Ranges. From Mount Beevor, you have stunning views north to the vineyards of the Barossa Valley, east over the wandering course of the Murray, and south to Lake Alexandrina, a lagoon near the river's mouth. You can finish at Tungkillo or continue another 16 miles (26 kilometers) to Springton, a gateway to the vineyards.

WHEN TO GO March to November. Other months are dry, and the trail is often closed to prevent bushfires.

HOW LONG Allow three days for the 50 miles (80 km) to Tungkillo. Add another day if heading for Springton – a total distance of 66 miles (106 km).

PLANNING You will need boots, as a few sections are steep. Take prepared food – stoves are not allowed – and enough water. A water filter will allow you to collect water en route if needed. Camping is not permitted on the trail so you must organize accommodation before you start.

INSIDE INFORMATION Stock up with last-minute supplies at the Monarto Zoo shop and café a little way past Rocky Gully.

WEBSITES australia.com, lavenderfederationtrail.org.au

| HIGHLIGHTS

▥ If the river water is low, look out for the wrecks of **sunken paddle steamers** near the start of the trail at Sturt Reserve, Murray Bridge.

▥ The **Rocky Gully Reserve** on the northern outskirts of Murray Bridge is a wetland area, and has been attracting bird-watchers for a long time. The Aboriginal name for the area is Moop-poltha-wong, meaning "a haven for birds."

▥ Among the mallee (eucalyptus shrubs) in the Mount Lofty foothills you are likely to see **gray kangaroos** and **goannas** (large monitor lizards). If you are lucky you might also spot **echidnas** and **pygmy possums**.

▥ If you make it to Springton, take a look at the home of its first inhabitant in the 1850s. German immigrant Friedrich Herbig lived in a **hollowed-out red gum tree**, which still stands on the main street.

AUSTRALIA AND OCEANIA

The electric brilliance of the Emerald Lakes comes almost as a shock amid the grays of the surrounding volcanic landscape.

The Tongariro Crossing

The volcanic splendor of steaming peaks is the keynote of this North Island trek—along with shimmering lakes and colorful wildflowers.

Set in the heart of New Zealand's North Island, Tongariro National Park is home to three active volcanoes: Ngauruhoe, Ruapehu, and Tongariro. It owes its existence to Te Heuheu, Chief of the Ngati Tuwharetoa Maori nation, who gifted the land to the New Zealand government in 1887 to protect it from farmers and loggers. The area is a paradise for hikers. From the Mangatepopo Valley, the trail climbs bare volcanic rock in steep zigzags to the rim of South Crater. To the south the towering mass of Ngauruhoe looms, its top venting steam and smoke in a steady stream. After crossing the flat expanse of South Crater, another steep climb leads along an exposed ridge to the Red Crater, where a hot upward draft reminds you that you are walking on a very active volcano. But views across the Oturere Valley, Rangipo Desert, Kaimanawa Ranges, and the Emerald Lakes soon dispel any misgivings about the climb. Ahead of you lies the azure waters of Blue Lake, steaming in the cool mountain air. The descent to the Ketetahi parking lot is long, but there are several distractions—hot springs near the Ketetahi hut, a profusion of wildflowers, and splendid views north to Lake Taupo.

WHEN TO GO Any time between mid-November and March. Some people do the walk in winter, but at that season it becomes a serious mountaineering experience.

HOW LONG 11 miles (17.7 km) from Mangatepopo Valley to the Ketetahi parking lot: a nine-hour walk.

PLANNING Base yourself in National Park Village, near the base of Ruapehu, at the intersection of the SH4 and SH47 highways. The park headquarters on the slopes of Ruapehu is a mine of information.

INSIDE INFORMATION Beware the rapidly changing weather in mountainous regions. Waterproof clothes are essential, and take a sweater or an extra layer. Transportation to and from the start and end of the walk is readily available, usually provided by the hostels, hotels, and campsites around the park.

WEBSITE tongarirocrossing.org.nz

HIGHLIGHTS

▪ The steep-sided cone of **Ngauruhoe** is ever present to the south. It was Mount Doom in Peter Jackson's *Lord of the Rings* movies.

▪ On a clear day from the summit of **Tongariro**, you can see **Taranaki**, another active volcano, 75 miles (121 km) to the west.

▪ Smoking and steaming, **Red Crater** assaults the senses, filling the air with sulfur smells.

▪ If you are lucky, you may spot one of the rare white-breasted **North Island robins.**

AUSTRALIA AND OCEANIA

NEW ZEALAND

The Grand Traverse

Green is the color of this South Island trail, as you follow a jade river,
cross beech forests, and listen to water cascading over falls.

The Grand Traverse is a five-day walk through The Divide, a range at the south end of New Zealand's South Island, where the rain forests of Fiordland give way to the snowcapped peaks and deciduous forests of the Southern Alps. Starting at the Greenstone parking lot, west of Lake Wakatipu, the trail follows the valley of the Greenstone River, so-called because its water is the color of jade—highly valued by the Maoris for tools, weapons, and ornaments. The valley narrows to a gorge, at the top of which Greenstone Lodge nestles under Tooth Peak. After crossing The Divide, you reach Lake Howden's cold waters. The trail then climbs, leveling out above a mottled green mosaic of beech trees reaching down into the Hollyford Valley. Only the screech of keas (mountain parrots) disturbs the silence, their red wing feathers flashing as they glide on the breeze. At the Earland Falls, rest and enjoy the cooling spray. Above Mackenzie Lodge you cross the Hollyford Face with streams and bushes of mountain flax. The 4,190-foot (1,277 meter) high Harris Saddle is the next landmark, where on a clear day you can see Lake Harris. Already you hear water tumbling down the Routeburn Falls below, and beyond them lies your destination, the Routeburn Shelter.

WHEN TO GO Any time between mid-November and March, with the clearest views during February and March. For the flowers, go in November.

HOW LONG 45 miles (72 km). Most people take five days.

PLANNING You must book in advance as local lodges have limited capacity and camping is restricted. Take your own cooking pan and food, and a lightweight sleeping bag. Mattresses are provided.

INSIDE INFORMATION Base yourself in Te Anau, on the eastern edge of Lake Te Anau. The Department of Conservation office here is very helpful, and it's an easy place to arrange transportation for getting to and from the start and finish of your trek, as most transportation companies have an office here.

WEBSITE ultimatehikes.co.nz

AUSTRALIA AND OCEANIA

HIGHLIGHTS

▦ **Lake Howden**, with a lodge on its southern shore, is an ideal place for lunch and a swim. But beware – the water is very cold. From the lodge you can see down into the Hollyford Valley over the beech-tree canopy.

▦ At the **Harris Saddle**, climb **Conical Hill** for a glorious panorama of the Darran Mountains. The Saddle has two shelters, where you can huddle if caught in a blizzard or storm.

▦ Birds you will see include **keas** (mischievous mountain parrots with a penchant for stealing bootlaces and getting into backpacks), **paradise ducks** on the flats of the Rees and Dart rivers, **bellbirds**, and **tuis** filling the forest with their songs.

The path follows a rocky course above the Hollyford Valley, with snow-dusted peaks rising on the valley's other side.

Top 10 Bridges

Serving as vantage points, links from A to B, or as landmarks in their own right, these bridges, ancient and modern, help to define a place.

❶ BROOKLYN BRIDGE, NEW YORK CITY

Cross this majestic symbol of emergent 19th-century America and feel the dynamic pulse of a great city. The bridge, which crosses the East River connecting the boroughs of Brooklyn and Manhattan, was the largest suspension bridge in the world when it was completed in 1883.

PLANNING Get on at the entrance near City Hall in Manhattan or at the entrance next to the Federal Court in Brooklyn. nyc.gov

❷ PUENTE DE LA MUJER, BUENOS AIRES, ARGENTINA

The streets of Buenos Aires' Puerto Madero neighborhood are all named after women, but this connection is the only thing that's traditional about the stunning cantilever Woman's Bridge, completed in 2001, crossing a disused dock. Its designer, the Spanish architect, Santiago Calatrava, is said to have modeled the bridge on a couple dancing a tango.

PLANNING Take subway (Subte) Line A to Plaza de Mayo or Line B to LN Alem. galinsky.com

❸ Q'ESWACHAKA BRIDGE, APURIMAC RIVER, PERU

Those with the nerve to cross this seemingly fragile reed bridge, 13,000 ft (3,962 m) above the churning river, will get a unique glimpse of a vanishing culture as well as a spectacular view of the Apurimac Canyon.

PLANNING Tour recommended. perurail.com/blog/qeswachaka-the-last-inca-suspension-bridge

❹ DAGU BRIDGE, TIANJIN, CHINA

Stop on the curving pedestrian paths of the Dagu Bridge in China's third city and enjoy a composite view of the old and new. This elegant bridge, built to withstand floods and earthquakes, symbolizes the sun, moon, and stars accompanying the dancing dragon of the Hai River.

PLANNING Visa essential. Transportation links are good – 75 miles (121 km) from Beijing. travelchinaguide.com

❺ SPEAN PRAPTOS, KÂMPÓNG KDEI, CAMBODIA

This exotic 12th-century bridge deep in the tropical jungle is the largest on a network of roads built by the Khmer god-kings, creators of Angkor Wat. This feat of engineering is 280 ft (85 m) long with 21 arches and four original massive stone snake guardians flanking the entrances.

PLANNING Visa essential. The bridge is off the tourist track, 43 miles (69 km) down Route 6 from Siem Reap (near Angkor) to Phimai. You'll need to hire a car and driver and be prepared for a bumpy ride on bad roads. tourismcambodia.com

The incomparable Sydney Harbour Bridge is one of Australia's most famous landmarks. The walkways over the bridge offer panoramic views of the harbor, city, and surrounding areas.

❻ SYDNEY HARBOUR BRIDGE, SYDNEY, AUSTRALIA

The dramatic panorama of the bridge teamed with the concentric shells of the Opera House is an iconic image of Australia. Opened in 1932, the "coat hanger" is still the world's tallest steel arch bridge with the apex standing 440 ft (134 m) above the water.

PLANNING The southeast pylon includes a lookout with an exhibition on the bridge's history. The entrance is from Cumberland Street, close to the Shangri-la Hotel. BridgeClimb organizes spectacular guided climbs to the top of the bridge. bridgeclimb.com

❼ CHARLES BRIDGE, PRAGUE, CZECHIA

Walk though the chunky Gothic portals onto this lovely medieval bridge with baroque statuary. Those wanting to return some day are told to touch the shiny plaque of the Czech martyr, St. John of Nepomuk. The bridge, which is the main pedestrian route linking the Old Town with Mêla Strana, affords fairy-tale views of the city, dominated by the magnificent Prague Castle.

PLANNING Metro: Staromestska (line A). If you want the bridge all to yourself, and it's well worth it, go late or early in the day. myczechrepublic.com

❽ PONTE VECCHIO, FLORENCE, ITALY

Feel the confidence and unbounded energy of the early Renaissance. Built in 1345, the "Old Bridge" spanning the Arno River has been feted in art and opera and is famous for its shops, its lovers, and its gold—the bridge has been occupied by jewelers since the 16th century. Built by Giorgio Vasari in 1565, the Corridoio Vasariano runs along the top of the bridge linking the Uffizi Gallery with the Palazzo Pitti on the other side of the Arno.

PLANNING Guided tours of the Corridoio Vasariano must be prearranged at the Uffizi Gallery. The tours take around three hours. tours-italy.com

❾ CLIFTON SUSPENSION BRIDGE, BRISTOL, ENGLAND

Effortlessly combining elegance with utility and strength, this bridge is a classic. Designed in the early 19th century by the brilliant engineer Isambard Kingdom Brunel, it spans the beautiful wooded Avon Gorge. Though made for horse vehicles and pedestrians, it carries 12,000 motor vehicles across it every day. Essential for lovers of Victoriana.

PLANNING Guided tours available for groups by arrangement. clifton-suspension-bridge.org.uk

❿ CARRICK-A-REDE ROPE BRIDGE, NORTHERN IRELAND

Breathe in the refreshing Atlantic Ocean in an area of rugged natural beauty, famous for its plant- and birdlife. The exhilarating walk across the swaying rope bridge, suspended 80 ft (24 m) above the rocks, connects the mainland to the offshore island fishing grounds. There's been some form of bridge here for 300 years, but be careful; this heady walk is not for the fainthearted.

PLANNING Open daily (weather permitting) from March to the end of October. Guided tours available. Maximum of eight people on the bridge at any one time. nationaltrust.org.uk/carrick-a-rede

The Kungsleden

This is the King's Trail, a 275-mile (443 kilometer) hike through a quiet wilderness at the roof of the world in Swedish Lapland.

Starting at a mountain station in Abisko National Park in the far north of Sweden, the historic King's Trail runs through four national parks and a nature reserve in Swedish Lapland, Western Europe's last true wilderness. The region lies 100 miles (160 kilometers) above the Arctic Circle and is a land of forests, birch-covered mountains, sweeping bogland, ravines, glaciers, and powerful rivers plunging into pristine lakes. The trail offers views and side trips to linger over. As you follow the Abisko River along its deeply scored, 66-foot (20 meter) canyon, you can stop to take a drink, so pure is the water. Look out for the delicate flora—rare orchids, purple saxifrage, and moss campion. Sturdy suspension bridges take you across fast rivers. Ecozone changes are abrupt and dramatic, occurring in just a few hundred feet. Ascending above the refuge at Abisko-jaure, you move beyond the timberline into sheer Arctic wilderness, where the main signs of activity are herds of reindeer tended by Sami. These are northern Scandinavia's indigenous people, and they live as they have done for more than 10,000 years. Traverse the pass at Tjäktja and before you lies Tjäktjavagge, a long, low, and suddenly lush valley, a world of vibrant green among these barren slopes.

WHEN TO GO June to mid-September.

HOW LONG Allow a month or so for the entire 275 miles (443 km), or a week for the northernmost section—the 50 miles (80 km) from Abisko Mountain Station to Kebnekaise Mountain Station.

PLANNING Fly Stockholm to Kiruna, then take a bus or train to Abisko Tourist Station. Wilderness huts along the way, mostly located a day's walk from each other, offer washing and cooking facilities, and even saunas. The larger stations also have restaurants and shops. There are no camping restrictions.

INSIDE INFORMATION You can hike in either direction, but it's best to travel from north to south and keep the sun warming your face. Take mosquito repellent in the earlier part of summer.

WEBSITE swedishtouristassociation.com

HIGHLIGHTS

■ **Mount Nuolja**, rising west of Abisko at the start of the trail, is the perfect place to watch the midnight sun from late May to mid-July. A chairlift will take you up.

■ Around **Alesjaure** in June you might see the Sami mark their reindeer calves by cutting patterns into their ears with knives.

■ **Tjäktjavagge** is the most majestic valley in Lapland, more than 30 miles (48 km) long and swathed in seasonal shades of green or amber like a giant, textured tapestry.

Clumps of purple saxifrage stud the Arctic landscape with patches of vivid color.

The harvest has been reaped, and the hay stacked up in tall ricks propped up with sticks. It will be used to feed livestock during the long, cold mountain winter.

ROMANIA

The Carpathian Mountains

Glaciers, caves, gorges, forests, and a rich wildlife—explore all these in Transylvania's Carpathians ... and then, of course, there's Dracula.

The first shafts of sunlight play on mists swirling around the mountain slopes, turning the leaves golden and throwing into relief blue-green ranks of fir trees. Is that a castle high up on a ridge—now a blur, now sharply defined as the early morning haze shifts—or just a rocky outcrop? These are the Carpathians, a 621-mile (1,000 kilometer) arc around Transylvania in central Romania, giving the country a charismatic landscape to match its haunting, legendary past. For this is the land of Dracula, an historic figure turned literary antihero, lord of the undead. Here, the Apuseni Range, home to bears, wolves, chamois, wild cats, and eagles, is now a national park, where you can choose from a range of marked trails. South of Cluj take the hike that leads through the sheer Turda Gorges, perforated with caves where early humans once lived, and carved with natural towers and arcades. The gorges' microclimate supports 1,000 plant species and is a haven for rare butterflies and birds. Other trails take you through forests; over terrains of sculpted Jurassic limestone, seamed by rivers above and below ground; and into wondrous caves, hiding underground glaciers, where the sunlight seeping in creates rainbows in the water vapor evaporating off them.

WHEN TO GO May to October. According to folk myth, vampires tend to appear just before and after the tourist season: on St. George's Eve (April 22), on Halloween, and on St. Andrew's Eve (November 29).

HOW LONG Most of the trails are day walks. Allow at least a week to enjoy a few of them.

PLANNING Buses run from Cluj to Turda and other villages from where you can start hiking. You can camp or stay in the huts dotted around the Apuseni; not all provide meals. Some tour operators offer walking holidays with guides, which can be tailored to groups or individuals.

INSIDE INFORMATION The area around Cluj is famed as a haven of authentic Magyar (Hungarian-speaking) culture, and here you will find people selling handicrafts by the road, including their vivid embroidery.

WEBSITES romaniatourism.com, visit-transylvania.us, responsibletravel.com

HIGHLIGHTS

▥ The **Padis Plateau** is a dramatic karst (limestone) tableland northwest of Sighisoara. In the depths of its Scarisoara Ice Cave lurks the largest underground glacier in Europe.

▥ You can also visit the plateau's 4,920-ft (1,500 m) long **Bear Cave** and an underground stream complex called the **Citadels of Ponor**.

▥ **Sighisoara** itself is worth exploring. As well as being an almost intact medieval city, it was the birthplace of **Vlad Tepes** (Vlad the Impaler) – aka Dracula, Son of the Devil. Although a ruthless leader, he is respected in Romania for defeating the Turks.

EUROPE

Moors rise above the verdant valley-floor meadows of Swaledale, crisscrossed with drystone walls.

ENGLAND

Wainwright's Coast to Coast Walk

Hillwalker Alfred Wainwright devised this trail, taking you from one side of England to the other through wild, majestic countryside.

From the town of St. Bees, set on red cliffs on England's northwest coast, this trail leads through the glorious scenery of three national parks—the Lake District, Yorkshire Dales, and North York Moors—to Robin Hood's Bay on the northeast coast. It is named after Alfred Wainwright, the legendary hillwalker whose brainchild it was. You reach the highest point and toughest climb in the Lake District: the 2,635-foot (803 meter) Kidsty Pike, part of the High Street massif, along which Roman soldiers marched to an outpost of Hadrian's Wall in the north. The descent from Kidsty Pike is steep but, below, the tranquil lake of Haweswater beckons. Ahead are the lush Yorkshire Dales where the pretty valley of Swaledale abounds with drystone walls and brown-faced, curly-horned sheep. The heather-covered plateau of the North York Moors brings you finally to Robin Hood's Bay—famous not for any connection with the fabled outlaw, but for its magnificent sweep of cliff and beach along the North Sea.

WHEN TO GO Any time of the year, though spring and summer are best for covering the miles in daylight.

HOW LONG 190 miles (306 km). Most people take about 14 days.

PLANNING In summer, book accommodations well in advance. You can backpack the entire route; campsites and camping barns are frequent.

INSIDE INFORMATION Most of the route is well marked, but some stretches are remote and the path crosses open moorland prone to mist and rain. Even in summer, conditions on the fells and hills can change dramatically in a few minutes. Take appropriate warm- and wet-weather clothing.

WEBSITES coast2coast.co.uk, sherpaexpeditions.com

HIGHLIGHTS

Ennerdale, the westernmost lake in Lake District National Park, is also the most remote, with no vehicle access. Even in high season it is a place of peace and quiet.

Near the shore of **Haweswater** is a bird hide where you may be lucky enough to catch a glimpse of England's only nesting **golden eagles**. Look back from here to enjoy the ruggedness of the Lakeland mountains you have just crossed.

A walk along grassy riverbanks takes you to **Shap Abbey**, 3.7 miles (6 km) east of Haweswater, where you can still enjoy the solitude sought there by monks in the late 12th century.

Disused lead mines at Swinner Gill, Gunnerside, and Hard Level in the Yorkshire Dales are a step back into the region's industrial history.

IRELAND

The Dingle Way

Take a walk along cliffs and beaches, past ancient Celtic remains,
and through quaint country villages in the wild southwest of Ireland.

The Dingle Way circles Ireland's westernmost peninsula, a region of wild seacliffs and steep hills, of farmland dotted with villages, and surf-pounded Atlantic beaches. You start in Tralee, from where the trail goes clockwise around the peninsula, much of it following boreens—small country roads. From Tralee, you pass through Blennerville, then climb the slopes of Slieve Mish, with views of Tralee Bay beyond. Crossing the saddle of the Corrin Mountain, you enter a region of woods and low hills before reaching the peninsula's south coast east of Anascaul. West of the town of Dingle, there are long, sandy beaches for you to explore before you loop around the peninsula's western tip and cross the slopes of Mount Eagle. The lonely Blasket Islands stand out on the horizon, and tumbledown stone *clochains*—ancient beehive huts—scatter the hillsides. The traverse of the 3,127-foot (953 meter) Brandon Mountain is the path's highest point, with sweeping views of the peninsula's north coast and Brandon Bay. You should attempt this part of the walk only in good weather as there are steep sea cliffs and vertical drops to be carefully avoided. After this, the going is easier but still spectacular, and for 7 miles (11.3 kilometers) you walk along Ireland's longest beach, between Fermoyle and Castlegregory, before the last stretch back to Tralee.

WHEN TO GO May to September.

HOW LONG 111 miles (179 km). Allow eight to ten days – comprising eight stages of 10.5–18 miles (17–29 km), each taking six to nine hours.

PLANNING Be prepared for wet and windy weather at any time of year. Good walking footwear, warm clothing, and a waterproof outer layer are essential.

INSIDE INFORMATION The trail passes through numerous villages and small towns, none of them more than a few hours apart. Accommodation is plentiful, but reserve in advance to be sure of a place to stay.

WEBSITES dingleway.com, irishways.com

HIGHLIGHTS

▪ **Ancient relics** include prehistoric menhirs, stones inscribed in the Gaelic Ogham script, and beehive huts built by Christian hermits.

▪ The ruin of the 15th-century **Minard Castle** is a picturesque landmark, set on a lonely beach after Anascaul.

▪ **Ventry Harbour**, west of Dingle, is a good place for a swim in summer.

▪ The early medieval **Oratory of St. Gallarus**, near Ballydavid, is one of Ireland's oldest Christian sites.

▪ Other delights include the first cool pint of Guinness in a **village pub** after a long day's walking, or a **ceilidh** – an evening of music and dancing.

Celtic hermits in the early Middle Ages found peace for prayer and contemplation in these drystone *clochains*, or beehive huts.

Top 10
Shopping Streets

Take a stroll downtown and savor the sights and sounds, colors, and flavors of some of the most exciting slices of street life.

❶ HELL'S KITCHEN FLEA MARKET, NEW YORK CITY

Once the refuge of poor Irish immigrants, this west Manhattan neighborhood now draws crowds to its bustling weekend markets. Antiques, collectibles, memorabilia, junk—all the flotsam and jetsam of the past is here. Mingle with designers, artists, celebrities, and actors. Afterward, head for one of the area's many ethnic restaurants.

PLANNING $9 will get you a cab from Hell's Kitchen Flea Market on 39th Street and the Antiques Garage/West 25th Street Market. annexmarkets.com/hells-kitchen-flea-market

❷ PLAZA DORREGO, BUENOS AIRES, ARGENTINA

On Sundays visitors flock to the antique stalls of the Feria de San Pedro Telmo in Plaza Dorrego. The cobblestone streets around the square come alive with tango musicians and dancers, buskers, and puppeteers. Enjoy local food and watch the activities from one of the sidewalk cafés.

PLANNING Sundays, from 9 or 10 a.m., until late afternoon. The nonprofit Cicerones (cicerones.org.ar) offers a free local-guide service. buenostours.com/plaza-dorrego

❸ TEMPLE STREET NIGHT MARKET, HONG KONG, CHINA

Soak up the atmosphere of Hong Kong after dusk with a stroll down Temple Street in Kowloon. Hundreds of stalls sell everything from arts and crafts to bargain clothes, watches, and electrical goods. Tempting aromas waft from the many food stalls and sidewalk restaurants.

PLANNING The market is open from 4 p.m. to 11 p.m. discoverhongkong.com

❹ PATPONG NIGHT MARKET, BANGKOK, THAILAND

This pedestrian precinct, awash with bars, sex shows, and massage parlors, is transformed into a busy market after sunset. If you want the latest imitation Gucci, Levi's, Nike, or Rolex, then this is the place for you.

PLANNING Train to Sala Daeng. Beware of pickpockets. bangkok.com

❺ CHANDNI CHOWK, DELHI, INDIA

Plunge into the vitality of Asia's largest wholesale market. The air is pungent and elephants vie with scooters as you forge through the crowds to sniff spices, search for saris, cruise for curios, and go with the frenetic flow.

PLANNING Take water and plenty of loose change. delhitourism.gov.in/delhitourism/shopping/chandni_chowk.jsp

Immortalized in the 1999 movie *Notting Hill*, this area of west London is one of the capital's trendiest. Portobello Road buzzes on Saturdays, when bargain hunters head for the antiques market.

⑥ GRAND BAZAAR, ISTANBUL, TURKEY

Enter the handsome Nuruosmaniye Gate (the Light of the Ottomans) to explore this endless warren of passages with mosques, banks, eateries, and more than 4,000 shops. Turkey's largest covered market offers traditional goods including carpets, jewelry, glazed tiles and pottery, precious metals, and objects made from fabulous materials, such as alabaster and meerschaum (a high-quality hard white clay). Be prepared to bargain for the best prices.

PLANNING Zeytinburnu-Kabatas-Besiktas tram to Carsikapi. Closed on Sunday. Watch your wallet. mygrandbazaar.net

⑦ NAVIGLI ANTIQUE MARKET, MILAN, ITALY

Nestled among canals built to convey stone for building the cathedral, the once poor area of Navigli is now a fashionable neighborhood with a lively nightlife. Wander beside the lazy waterways among cafés, art galleries, and craft shops in low buildings with thick wooden doors. You'll almost certainly see an artist at work in a brightly colored courtyard. Large crowds flock to the monthly Sunday market with more than 400 stands selling antiques, bric-a-brac, and collectibles. Local shops, bars, restaurants, and several art galleries stay open throughout market day.

PLANNING Between Naviglio Grande and Naviglio Pavese canals. Metro: Porta Genova. Tram 3 to Corso di Porta Ticinese. Market last Sunday of the month, except July. navigliogrande.mi.it

⑧ DAPPERMARKT, AMSTERDAM, THE NETHERLANDS

Venture off the tourist track to the "true people's market," situated right in the middle of Amsterdam's multicultural area. Peruse an incredible diversity of clothes, food, and exotic goods at great prices in more than 250 stalls put up and taken down every day.

PLANNING Eerste van Swindenstraat: trams 9 and 14. dappermarkt.nl

⑨ LES PUCES, PARIS, FRANCE

Arguably Europe's largest flea market, Les Puces ("the fleas") stretches on and on. Expensive antiques, jewelry, and upscale goods are indoors, but outside you can rifle for hours among the secondhand clothes, worn-out toys, obsolete electrical goods, vinyl records, and saucy belle-epoque postcards. If you can imagine it, it's probably on sale here—somewhere!

PLANNING Metro: Porte de Clignancourt. Watch your wallet. Don't hang around after dark. parispuces.com

⑩ PORTOBELLO ROAD, LONDON, ENGLAND

On Saturdays, crowds pour into the world's longest street market, stretching for 1.5 miles (2.4 km) and selling an eclectic mix of antiques, secondhand clothes, bric-a-brac, handicrafts, and New Age paraphernalia. A host of cafés, bars, arcades, galleries, and food stalls adds to the vibrant and cosmopolitan atmosphere. Europe's biggest street party, the Notting Hill Carnival, erupts in August when the area becomes a riot of color, music, and dance.

PLANNING Underground: Ladbroke Grove (antiques) or Notting Hill Gate (everything else). portobelloroad.co.uk

The red spire of a Tyrolean village church contrasts with the emerald green of the surrounding countryside.

The Tyrol

Leave your skis behind and head for the Tyrol between spring and fall for glorious hikes through postcard-perfect Alpine scenery.

The Austrian Tyrol is best known for its skiing, but this beautiful Alpine region is also fabulous walking country. The area doesn't have many long-distance trails, so base yourself in one or two places and take daily walks. The ancient city of Kufstein in the lower Inn Valley is one perfect base. Setting out from there you zigzag up into the 6,560-foot (1,999 meter) Wilder Kaiser massif on a hike to the Walchsee, a mountain lake. After you reach the top, you descend again through pastures and forests with dramatic views of the peaks of Zahmer Kaiser, Naunspitze, and Pyramidenspitze before reaching the lake and a nature reserve. Other walks go to the Kitzbüheler Horn, southeast of Kufstein, or the pretty mountain village of Söll, a popular ski resort.

WHEN TO GO Spring to fall. Wildflowers are wonderful in spring and early summer; July and August can be very busy. In fall the scenery is a glorious symphony of rich yellows and golden browns.

HOW LONG All the walks are day hikes.

PLANNING Do some preparatory exercise before leaving home, as these routes can be quite demanding. Always take a waterproof jacket, sunscreen, a bottle of water (or thermos of tea, depending on the weather), and broken-in walking boots that protect your ankles.

INSIDE INFORMATION Check out the local weather forecast before setting out on a long walk; conditions can change quickly. Most Austrians under 50 years old speak good English.

WEBSITES tyrol.com, tannheimertal.com

HIGHLIGHTS

▥ Another exhilarating walk along the **Wilder Kaiser** massif takes you from Scheffau to St. Johann, with superb views to the peaks of the Kitzbüheler Horn and Hohe Salve to the south.

▥ You can take a cable car from **Brixen** to **Söll** over the **Hohe Salve**, then spend a night in Söll, and walk back to Kufstein through Alpine valley scenery so perfect it could come straight from a postcard.

▥ The **Tannheimer Valley** is another glorious base for walking – a largely undiscovered corner of the western Tyrol with two lakes, five unspoiled villages, and the opportunity to enjoy local cooking at one of the *gasthofs*.

▥ There are more splendid walks across the border in the Italian autonomous state of **South Tyrol**. While there, visit the medieval Tyrol Castle, regarded as emblematic of the whole region.

EUROPE

FRANCE | SWITZERLAND | ITALY

Tour du Mont Blanc

A circuit around the Mont Blanc massif takes you through three countries, six mountain passes, and countless flower-filled meadows.

The Tour du Mont Blanc in the Alps is a classic, long-established trail that links seven valleys encircling the massif of western Europe's highest peak—Mont Blanc, towering 15,770 feet (4,807 meters) above sea level. Along the way, you pass through three countries—France, Switzerland, and Italy—each with its own architecture, language, and culture ... and its own views of Mont Blanc. The French resort of Chamonix is the starting point. Working clockwise from there, you cross into Switzerland over the Col de Balme, the first of six high passes en route, and head for the lakeside village of Champex. The Grand Col Ferret—at 8,465 feet (2,580 meters) the highest point on the trek—takes you into Italy's beautiful Valle d'Aosta, before reentering France across the Col de Seigne. Good pathways, following ancient pack-animal routes, make the hike relatively easygoing as you pass through conifer forests and Alpine meadows studded with pink azaleas, purple cranesbill, and deep-blue gentian. Above you loom towering rock needles, glaciers cut with turquoise crevasses, and the great peaks of the western Alps. The only sounds are the muted clang of cowbells, the rippling tinkle of waterfalls, and the whistles of marmots among the rocks.

WHEN TO GO Late June to September.

HOW LONG About 100 miles (160 km). It takes 10–11 days, walking five to eight hours a day, with overnight stays in refuges, valley hotels, or campsites.

PLANNING Take standard mountain-hiking gear, including a compass. Although the usual way to do the tour is counterclockwise, taking it clockwise helps to avoid crowds, especially in August.

INSIDE INFORMATION You can split the long stretch between Courmayeur in Italy and Les Chapieux in France—19 miles (30.5 km) including a high pass—by staying at the Rifugio Elisabetta, or reduce it by bussing the leg through the Italian Val Veni.

WEBSITES sherpaexpeditions.com, alpineexploratory.com

HIGHLIGHTS

▦ Hike up to the **Fenêtre d'Arpette** between Trient and Champex. You climb through a notch (the *fenêtre*, or window) past the Trient Glacier.

▦ Experience the thrill of **climbing Mont Blanc**; it's not difficult, though you may get a high-altitude headache. Hire a guide from Chamonix or Courmayeur in Italy.

▦ Ride the **cable car** from Chamonix up the Aiguille du Midi for a glorious panorama of the Mont Blanc ice fields and the Matterhorn beyond.

▦ Take the railway from Chamonix to Montenvers for a grandstand view of the **Mer de Glace** (Sea of Ice), Europe's longest glacier.

Above 6,500 ft (1,981 m), you may glimpse an Alpine ibex, a mountain goat, leaping nimbly across the slopes.

| ITALY |

The Cinque Terre

Walk the Blue Path linking the five villages of Cinque Terre like five jewels on a necklace, while below you the sparkling azure waters of the Ligurian Sea stretch to the horizon.

A shore-hugging path, the Sentiero Azzurro (Blue Path), runs between the fabled Cinque Terre: five villages—Riomaggiore, Manarola, Corniglia, Vernazza, and Monterosso al Mare—perched dramatically between two promontories on the rocky shoreline of northwestern Italy's Ligurian coast. Combining the quaintness of traditional fishing communities with Italian elegance, the villages' pastel-colored houses, jostling each other for space on the steep slopes above the Ligurian surf, are almost guaranteed to bring a smile to your face and zest to your spirit. Narrow streets and alleys (called *carugi*) run at unexpected angles, affording sudden glimpses of the sea. Clothes flutter in the breeze on washing lines above you, and varnished wooden boats nestle in parking spaces where cars should be. Between the villages, you pass through olive and lemon groves and shady chestnut woods, while the region's characteristic stepped terraces of vineyards climb the hillsides above. Each village has a distinct character. You start in the southeast at Riomaggiore, the prettiest of the villages, and follow the Via dell'Amore (Lovers' Way) to Manarola, the oldest. Hewn into the rockface of the cliffs in the 1920s, this is the easiest stretch of the trail and, in the opinion of many, the most romantic. The next stage finishes with a clamber up 368 steps into Corniglia, which lies farther inland and is more rural than the other villages. A steep climb leads from Corniglia to Vernazza, quiet and full of fishermen, and beyond that lies your finishing point, Monterosso al Mare, bustling and full of visitors.

WHEN TO GO March through May.

HOW LONG 7 miles (11.3 km). Allow a day to include wandering around the villages.

PLANNING A bottle of water and sun protection are essentials. Only attempt the steep uphill path from Corniglia to Vernazza if you are feeling fit. It should take 1.5–2 hours to climb.

INSIDE INFORMATION The villagers take a siesta and shut up shop between 1 and 4 p.m., so this is a good time to be walking rather than in a village. If you don't want to walk the whole way or are running out of time, there is a railway line linking all the villages.

WEBSITES cinqueterre-travel.com, cinqueterreonline.com

EUROPE

HIGHLIGHTS

■ The **Belforte tower** in **Vernazza** stands on a headland jutting into the Ligurian Sea. It was built as a watchtower and called Belforte ("loud cry") from the shouts of the watchmen. You can climb it and enjoy stupendous views over the harbor and along the coast.

■ Each village has a **sanctuary** (shrine) to the Virgin Mary perched among olive and lemon groves on the hillside above it. If you're lucky you'll catch one of the annual festivals held at the shrines, involving processions, fireworks, and other celebrations.

■ **Anchovies** are a local specialty, and the region produces two **wines**: a dry white called Cinque Terre and a dessert wine called Sciacchetrà. And don't forget, Liguria is the birthplace of **pesto sauce** – the climate is perfect for basil. The locals mix the basil with cheese, garlic, pine nuts, and olive oil.

■ If the Sentiero Azzurro has whetted your appetite for more, try all or part of the more arduous **Alta Via** (High Road), running 25 miles (40 km) from Portovenere to Levanto.

Opposite: Vines partly hide Manarola, its colorful houses tightly packed on a high headland above the Ligurian Sea. Above left: Your walk will give you an appetite for the delicious local food, some of it laid out in front of this delicatessen in Riomaggiore. Above right: Poppies line the path near Vernazza.

The Dolomites High Routes

Hike through this dramatic limestone landscape in the Italian Alps, and in the evenings feast on polenta followed by grappa.

Rock pinnacles rear high above Alpine pastures. Shady forests, tangy with the scent of pine, give way to upland meadows bright with lilies and gentian. You find a marine fossil on a mountaintop. It could only be the Dolomites, a wonderland of jagged peaks in the eastern Alps. This limestone massif in northern Italy is a magnet for climbers and skiers. But hikers, too, can sample its rugged beauty thanks to eight long-distance trails, the *alte vie* ("high routes"), with steel cables and ladders to help you on tricky stretches—the famous *vie ferrate*, "iron ways." Originally constructed by Austrian and Italian Alpine troops during World War I, these have been extended to allow hikers to explore the wilderness. The Alta Via 1 (AV1) is the easiest, most popular route, taking you on a north-south traverse from Lago di Bràies, close to Austria, to Belluno in the Veneto, and crossing the Dolomites' most famous peaks on the way. At night you stay in *rifugi*, atmospheric refuges where you'll find a warm welcome and traditional mountain fare, including freshly cooked polenta. At dawn and dusk the rock spires and towers turn salmon pink, like fairy-tale castles. At night the sky is thick with stars as you swap hiking tales over a glass of grappa, the local spirit.

WHEN TO GO Late June to late September.

HOW LONG The AV1 is 80 miles (129 km) long, divided into ten stages. Allow 15 days for the whole trip.

PLANNING Come prepared for all kinds of weather even in summer, including snow, hail, rain, and fierce sun. Space is tight in the rifugi, so you will need to book in advance with the Club Alpino Italiano. No extra gear is needed for the easiest vie ferrate. On more advanced routes, you'll need a helmet and a special harness, with built-in brake and carabiners, to clip onto the steel cables.

INSIDE INFORMATION Refuge guardians offer invaluable advice about the local vie ferrate and your onward route. They also offer emergency shelter to anyone caught in a storm.

WEBSITE dolomiti.org/en

HIGHLIGHTS

▓ **Monte Lagazuoi**, high point of the AV1, has glorious sunset views over the entire range. You can reach the top-notch refuge here by cable car. Nearby are relics of the **White War** of 1915–18, so-called because of the high, snowbound conditions. They include galleries, caverns, and a staircase hidden inside the mountain.

▓ The Dolomites are a **plant-spotter's paradise**. Among many species you may see are vanilla orchids, purple irises, and yellow globeflowers.

▓ If you walk the AV1 in July, don't miss the **Sunday lunchtime concert** at the Pramperet refuge. A choir hikes up from the valley below to perform arias in a natural rock amphitheater.

Craggy peaks, thick forests, and, in the foreground, lush green Alpine meadows – this is the glorious landscape you pass through on the *alte vie* of the Dolomites.

Your rambles take you past hilltop towns and villages that rise above terraced slopes where vines, olives, and fruit trees grow.

ITALY

Walking in Umbria

The spirit of St. Francis of Assisi hovers over this delightful Italian region, offering tempting hikes through ravishing countryside.

Tuscany and Umbria are like sisters—except that landlocked Umbria remains more or less undiscovered by tourists and hikers. Despite sharing with Tuscany the classic Italian landscape of rolling hills, distant cypress trees, and crumbling Etruscan and medieval hill towns, Umbria retains a primal, wilder quality. Here, the rocks are jagged, the hills are steep, and the routes are rough and stony—this is walking country. For a region that takes you into an unspoiled natural world, it is fitting to start in the birthplace of St. Francis: Assisi, sprawled across the hills, where white stone towers reach toward the blue skyline. Departing the city, there is a variety of tempting routes through the countryside. One takes you east to the misty heights of Monte Subasio (4,230 feet/1,289 meters), begging to be climbed and offering 360° views for miles around. Its upper reaches are home to wildcats, goshawks, and buzzards. Or you can head south into green valleys dotted with aromatic olive groves and ancient holm oak forests. To the north, you can follow the course of the Chiascio River, bordered with sprinkles of delicate wildflowers and sun-touched fields. Rocky paths wind in every direction; the joy of this area is setting out for a long, lazy day of rambling, without any idea of where you might end up—or what you might see.

WHEN TO GO March to August. Spring leading into early summer brings glorious sunshine and sunsets.

HOW LONG You need at least a week to explore the countryside fully. You have a huge selection of walks of varying lengths to choose from.

PLANNING Either book a hotel in Assisi and use it as your base, or move on from town to town—places such as Spello, Spoleto, Ravegna, Montefalco, Todi, and Orvieto. Some travel companies offer all-inclusive walking holidays, which provide accommodation.

INSIDE INFORMATION Avoid renting a car if possible. Notorious Italian driving is compounded by the steep gradients and sharp curves of local roads.

WEBSITES umbriatourism.it/en, assisionline.com

HIGHLIGHTS

▥ Feast on Umbrian **wild boar ham** after a long day's walking; it is hearty, substantial, and delicious. If you have the budget, indulge in Umbrian **truffles**, one of the world's most highly prized gourmet foods.

▥ Keep a lookout for **wolves** and **wild boar**. To see one of these noble creatures is a rare treat.

▥ Gaze up into the Umbrian **night sky**, full of stars and untainted by any city lights for miles around.

▥ Don't miss the huge medieval **Basilica of San Francesco** in Assisi or its ancient **Roman temple** of the goddess Minerva.

EUROPE

Top 10 City Walls

History is embedded in the bricks and mortar of these old city walls, built to protect and withstand attack.

❶ CARTAGENA, COLOMBIA

Picturesque shady plazas and cobbled streets basking in the Caribbean sun have changed little in five centuries since Cartagena was the treasure city of the Spanish Main. Peek into courtyards from the walls. Don't miss the Castillo de San Felipe, built to protect shipments of gold from pirates. The Church of San Pedro Claver contains the glass coffin of the Slave of Slaves, the first saint of the New World.

PLANNING A knowledge of Spanish is useful. cartagenaconnections.com

❷ XI'AN, CHINA

Look down on 3,000 years of history as you hike or bike the ramparts. Covering 8.5 miles (13.7 km) the wall, enlarged at the start of the Ming dynasty (1368–1644), once guarded the start of the Silk Road from China to Asia Minor. Don't miss the nearby terra-cotta army of Emperor Qin Shi Huang.

PLANNING cnto.org/iconic/the-great-wall-tourism-belt

❸ FATEPHUR SIKRI, INDIA

For a brief period in the second half of the 16th century, the red walls of the Deserted City protected the exquisite capital of the Mogul Empire. All the trappings of Mogul power—palaces, mosque, stables, harems (for Christian and Hindu wives), and an elephant hitching post—are here.

PLANNING Hire a car and driver in Agra (home of the Taj Mahal). Visit in the early morning or late afternoon. mapsofindia.com/agra/places-of-interest.html

❹ BAKU, AZERBAIJAN

Here you can view the crossroads of Europe and Asia from crenellated 12th-century Arab ramparts. The old town of Baku boasts a picturesque maze of cobbled alleys, a palace (with the shah's mosque, a reservoir, a bathhouse, and mausoleums), caravansaries (inns), and the Maiden Tower.

PLANNING More information is available at advantour.com

❺ ISTANBUL, TURKEY

Built during the reign of Byzantine emperor Theodosius II, in A.D. 447, the walls remained unbreached until 1453, when Sultan Mehmet II won the siege that changed the city of Constantinople to Istanbul.

PLANNING While the total length is 4 miles (6.5 km), the walk could take up to two days, as you wind around traffic and construction projects. istanbulwalks.com/tur/walk-on-the-city-walls

Saunter peacefully along the beautifully preserved white stone of Dubrovnik's city walls. Hear the gentle ebb and flow of the ocean as you admire the view from the walls' ancient towers and forts.

❻ JERUSALEM, ISRAEL

A walk along the ancient wall encircling the old city is a must for any visitor. From this vantage point, the venerable domes, towers, and steeples mingle with everyday slices of life—sheets on washing lines, kids playing football, pensioners tending lemons, a Jewish wedding, and an Arab vendor. And rising above it all is the magnificent golden dome that crowns the Dome of the Rock, the Muslim shrine built in the 7th century A.D. The wall, which hasn't changed since Süleyman the Magnificent rebuilt it in 1536, is open for 2.5 miles (4 km).

PLANNING Enter by the Jaffa or Damascus Gates. jerusalem-insiders-guide.com/ramparts-walk.html

❼ DUBROVNIK, CROATIA

Take in the sun-drenched red roofs and the radiant blue of the Adriatic Sea from the huge bastions of Dubrovnik's mile-long (1.6 km) walls, built so well that they have never been breached, despite numerous sieges during the Middle Ages. Jewels of the old town include the beautiful Baroque Church of St. Ignatius and the Franciscan Monastery. The beautiful white pebble beach has a great view of the wall. The town's popular summer festival features music, theater, and dance.

PLANNING Tickets at the Pile Gate. dubrovnik-travel-experience.com/dubrovnik-city-walls-walk.html

❽ LUCCA, ITALY

This quintessential Tuscan town is the only one in Italy to be entirely surrounded by a wall. See palaces, towers, churches, and charming gardens; peer into the hidden crevices of old-world Tuscany against a panorama of vineyards, villas, and mountains. Walk or cycle around this 3-mile (4.8 km) Renaissance wall complete with trees and a restaurant. The view from the Guinigi Tower, which has an ancient oak tree on top, is worth the 130-ft (40 m) climb.

PLANNING Bicycle rental available. welcometuscany.it

❾ ÁVILA, SPAIN

The medieval obsession with security often manifested itself as intimidation, and this formidable wall, emblematic of the city, proves it—its awesome 1.5 miles (2.4 km) bristle with battlements, towers, and gates. Ávila was important in the clash between the Spanish Christians and the Muslim Moors; the wall contains elements of both architectural styles and is now proudly maintained by the descendants of both.

PLANNING A day trip from Madrid. Open April to October. world-guides.com/europe/spain/castilla-y-leon/avila

❿ GREAT ZIMBABWE, ZIMBABWE

If only these walls could talk! Undulating in the wooded African savanna against stark hills, the stone walls have no mortar, rise to 32 ft (9.8 m), and are up to 17 ft (5 m) thick. This ancient stone structure is the largest of its kind in sub-Saharan Africa. In its heyday in the 14th and 15th centuries, Great Zimbabwe was the capital of a vast Shona empire with trade networks stretching as far as China. Archaeologists have studied the site but mystery still shrouds the ruins.

PLANNING Bus services from Harare and Bulawayo. Nearby Lake Mutirikwe is a popular water-sports resort. zimbabwetourism.net

Trees have managed to take root in the gorge's cliffs. It's easy to feel dwarfed by the dramatic splendor of the scene.

CRETE

Samaria Gorge

This extraordinary slice cut into the mountains of western Crete is a haven for wildlife, with fragrant air and crystalline streams.

Descending from the high Omalos plateau in western Crete's Lefkà Óri (White Mountains) to the island's warm southern coast, Samaria is one of Europe's longest and deepest gorges. Its head appears suddenly, almost like a trapdoor opening in the earth, at Xyloskalo, named after the rough staircase local people made for climbing it. The vertiginous track descends almost 3,300 feet (1,006 meters) through pine and cypress forest. Shortly before you reach the bottom, you see the small church of Agios Nikolaos. From there the path flattens out, but the scenery remains spectacular, the air scented with herbs. After the abandoned village of Samaria, the ravine becomes steadily narrower, culminating in a sliver of a chasm known as the Iron Gates. The final stretch to the coast is over easy terrain, but your legs will be tired and there is little shade. Just rewards await you in the attractive village of Agia Roumeli.

WHEN TO GO The gorge is open from early May to late October only, and closed in wet weather. May is the ideal month – not too hot, with fewer people and an abundance of wildflowers.

HOW LONG The walk from Omalos village to the coast is 12.5 miles (20 km). Allow five to seven hours, including stops and a lunch break.

PLANNING Stay overnight in Omalos, then start at dawn to avoid the crowds. Consider taking an organized trip with a local specialist. Take food as none is available en route.

INSIDE INFORMATION You can replenish your water supply from the springs in the ravine, so don't carry more than one bottle. Wear walking boots with ankle support, as the trail is very rocky in places. Walking through the heat of a July or August afternoon is not recommended.

WEBSITES great-adventures.com, west-crete.com, explorecrete.com

HIGHLIGHTS

▨ You may see a **mountain goat** or, if very lucky, a **Cretan ibex**. Birdlife in Samaria Gorge includes spectacular birds of prey, such as the rare **lammergeier**.

▨ The church of **Ágios Nikólaos** (St. Nicholas) stands among cypress trees. If you sense something even more ancient here, it may be because a sanctuary dedicated to the god Apollo is believed to lie beneath it.

▨ The deserted village of **Samaria** is a good place to pause. You can still visit its ancient Byzantine church of Óssia María (St. Mary), from which both the village and the gorge get their names.

▨ At the **Iron Gates** at the gorge's southern end, the walls of the ravine are a mere 11 ft (3.4 m) apart but soar skyward to 100 times that height.

▨ At the end of the trek, **Agía Rouméli** greets you with appealing taverns and restaurants and a pebbly beach. Take a dip in the clear, warm Libyan Sea.

EUROPE

| MOROCCO |

High Atlas Mountains

Berber villagers greet you with traditional hospitality as you trek to Toubkal, the highest peak in the High Atlas Mountains.

Castle-like kasbahs perch on rocky crags. A river threads a green ribbon through a dry landscape. Flat-roofed villages blend into stony slopes and are home to Berbers—herders and farmers who grow wheat, barley, and corn on the terraced mountainsides. Mules carry your baggage as you trek through this spectacular scenery, and your day starts soon after dawn as the muleteers call "*Yalla!*" ("Let's go!"). At night frogs burble from streams choked with scented oleander. The High Atlas Mountains are a world apart from modern life, arcing for hundreds of miles across central Morocco. Snowbound in winter, they rise to Jebel Toubkal, North Africa's highest peak, 13,670 feet (4,167 meters) above sea level. This is the goal of the most popular treks. From the rose-colored city of Marrakech you go by road to the Mizane Valley, where your hike begins. At first, the going is relatively easy—allowing you to acclimatize to the altitude—as you make your way in a loop through the valleys around the base of Toubkal, trekking from village to village, to be welcomed by excited children, toasted almonds, and tangy, refreshing mint tea. The four-hour ascent of Toubkal is tougher, with steep slopes to scrabble up, but the summit greets you with an exhilarating panorama of the snow-dusted peaks of the western High Atlas.

WHEN TO GO April to September. Winter treks are also possible, but you'll need an ice axe and crampons.

HOW LONG 50 miles (80 km), including a loop through Berber villages and then the ascent of Jebel Toubkal. Allow up to two weeks.

PLANNING Bring light, durable hiking gear including stout boots, sunscreen, and sun hat, with a lightweight sleeping bag for summer trekking. Water-purifying tablets are essential, and a headlight is useful.

INSIDE INFORMATION Guides, mules, and advice (but not extensive stores) are available in the villages of Imlil, Aroumd, and Tacheddirt near Toubkal.

WEBSITE explore.co.uk

AFRICA

| HIGHLIGHTS

▨ Allow time to enjoy **Marrakech**, where donkey carts weave among motorized traffic, and at night snake charmers, acrobats, and storytellers perform in the torchlit main square, the Jemaa el-Fna.

▨ Take a break in the shade of almond and walnut trees around **Aroumd**. It's almost impossible to tell where one mud-brick house ends and the next begins in this village overlooking terraced fields of barley, corn, and vegetables in the Mizane Valley.

▨ Have a dip in the milky-turquoise waters of **Lac d'Ifni**, southeast of Toubkal, surrounded by towering scree-covered mountain slopes. It is the only sizeable lake in the Atlas.

In the Dades Valley, the kasbahs of Ait Ouglif are dwarfed only by the rolling peaks of the High Atlas Mountains.

| PORTUGAL |

The Levadas of Madeira

Built as irrigation channels, Madeira's levadas *and the paths alongside them make perfect hiking trails for exploring the stunningly varied scenery of this paradise island.*

Madeira's incredible network of watercourses runs through tunnels, over aqueducts, and across a land some have described as paradise, carrying rainwater from the mountain heights to the island's terraced sugarcane plantations and vineyards. The earliest *levadas* (from the Portuguese *levar*, "to carry") date from the 15th century, when the first Portuguese settlers arrived on the island. The narrow canals now stretch for more than 1,240 miles (1,996 kilometers), ranging from brooks beside wide paths planted with aromatic plants to precipitous channels hewn centuries ago into mountainsides by workers suspended in wicker baskets. They offer you an astonishing array of walking experiences, reflecting the island's range of climates—which made it necessary to build them in the first place. For a spectacular introduction, try the Levada da Serra de São Jorge in a remote area in the northeast. Starting at Queimadas, 2,950 feet (899 meters) high above the coastal town of Santana, you head west through emerald green scenery with staggering views of villages in valleys far below. The route passes a waterfall and runs through some short tunnels before arriving at Caldeirão Verde (Green Cauldron), where another waterfall tumbles majestically down 1,000 feet (305 meters) into a pool. If you're feeling fit and aren't prone to vertigo, you can carry on to Caldeirão do Inferno (Hell's Cauldron), where yet more falls plunge down huge cliffs and tumultuous waters crash through narrow gorges.

WHEN TO GO All year. Summer is generally less rainy; winter is pleasantly warm.

HOW LONG 8 miles (13 km) from Queimadas to Caldeirão Verde and back again – allow four to five hours. Give yourself four to five days to enjoy a good sampling of the other levadas.

PLANNING Some of the older levadas can be quite demanding and steep; you must be reasonably fit to walk them. Also, arrange to be dropped off and picked up by car (or by one of Madeira's remarkably cheap taxis), because most levadas are long and will take up to ten hours if you do them both ways.

INSIDE INFORMATION Madeiran laws make material damage and personal injury the responsibility of the individual, so be careful in the country and don't walk alone. Guided tours are available.

WEBSITES visitmadeira.pt, madeira-levada-walks.com

HIGHLIGHTS

▇ One of the best-known levadas starts at **Ribeira Frio**, north of Madeira's capital, Funchal. It's a long walk at 7.5 miles (12 km) one way to **Portela**, but well worth the effort as the views of Porto da Cruz and Eagle Rock are exceptional.

▇ Ancient trees and rock formations line the 8-mile (13 km) path from **Pico do Arieiro** to **Achada do Teixeira** in the western half of Madeira. You pass by **Pico Ruivo**, at 5,380 ft (1,640 m) the highest point on the island.

▇ A shorter walk from Pico do Arieiro passes through the Santa Luzia Valley, Levada do Barreiro, and Pico Alto and finishes at **Poça da Neve**.

▇ The **Levada das 25 Fontes** leads from Rabaçal to a lake at the foot of a cliff, with 25 natural springs cascading into it.

Opposite: Sylvan beauty marks the scene where an old stone aqueduct carries the Levada das 25 Fontes across a valley. The walkways alongside the levadas were built as maintenance paths. Above left: Brilliant wildflowers line the levadas in spring. Above right: Pico Ruivo rises above the path from Pico do Arieiro to Achada do Teixeira.

Climbing Kilimanjaro

The ascent of Africa's highest peak takes you on an extraordinary journey from hot savanna grassland to icy glaciers at its summit.

AFRICA

Montane forest and moorland give way to high-altitude desert as you climb Africa's highest mountain, Kilimanjaro, before you catch sight of the blue-streaked glaciers at its summit. You start your trek at the gates of Kilimanjaro National Park, where the aroma of *ugali* (maize porridge) cooking on wood fires follows you, along with the sound of women chattering and children playing. Soon the rain forest greets you, the air dank and misty, its canopy laced with moss-coated vines. Vervet monkeys call ahead to announce your approach but fall silent in curiosity when you take a rest. On the second day, the forest pathway opens into moorland scattered with towers of giant lobelia and groundsel, and the trail begins to climb. Higher up, a rocky alpine desert like a lunar landscape leads to the "saddle" between Kibo and Mawenzi peaks— Kilimanjaro is one mountain, but it has three volcanic summits: Kibo, Mawenzi, and Shira. You begin the final lap by night, zigzagging up Kibo on a path of stony scree. Taking it slowly, you meet the final challenge, and just as dawn tinges the snow cap with shades of pink, you set foot on Africa's highest point, Uhuru—on the rim of Kibo's crater, 19,336 feet (5,894 meters) above sea level.

WHEN TO GO January, February, or September

HOW LONG About 30 miles (48 km) one-way. Allow five days to climb and descend the mountain.

PLANNING There are several routes up Kilimanjaro. The Marangu Route is the most popular, with huts to sleep in and an emergency evacuation procedure. Various companies organize climbs with guides and porters. Before setting out, spend at least a week above 5,000 ft (1,524 m) to acclimatize to the altitude.

INSIDE INFORMATION Take it slowly, even if you feel you could go a lot faster, and drink plenty of water (6–8 pints/3–4 liters a day). Bring a small tripod for taking photos at the summit; you may be too cold to hold your camera steady.

WEBSITES climbingkilimanjaro.com, responsibletravel.com

HIGHLIGHTS

▪ The rain forest is rich in **wildlife**, including colobus and blue monkeys and a myriad of exotic birds, from hornbills to turacos with crimson wing feathers. Leopards prowl the forest, but you will be lucky if you see one.

▪ A detour takes you to the rim of **Maundi Crater** just above the timberline. From there, you will get your first impressive view of Kibo— on a clear day its glaciers shimmer in the sun.

▪ Standing on Uhuru Peak you have an incomparable sense of exhilaration. You are on the **roof of Africa**, and the views sweep from the glaciers and ice cliffs around you to the hot plains far below.

A tall and stately giraffe pauses in its search for food on the open plain, with snow-capped Kilimanjaro rising beyond.

Reds, browns, and blues prevail in the Drakensberg's dramatic sandstone landscape, capped with angular basaltic peaks.

SOUTH AFRICA

The Drakensberg

Southern Africa's highest mountain range is a hiker's paradise, offering every kind of trail from strolls to serious mountaineering.

Streams and waterfalls tumble down the sides of towering mountains and deep valleys, interspersed with sandstone cliffs and lofty buttresses. Stretching from South Africa's Eastern Cape northeast through Lesotho and into KwaZulu-Natal, this is the Drakensberg (Dragon's Mountain in Afrikaans). For hikers, its centerpiece is the Cathedral range on the borders of Lesotho and KwaZulu-Natal: the freestanding summits of Cathedral Peak, the Bell, the Inner and Outer Horns, and the Chessmen marching away from its escarpment edge. Numerous paths crisscross this dramatic landscape, catering to every kind of walker, from ambles taking you to caves etched with ancient San (Bushman) paintings to chain ladders leading to the range's highest peaks. For the day hiker, the trail to World's View in Giant's Castle Game Reserve culminates in a 360° panorama. If you want a steeper incline, hike to Mont-aux-Sources and the 3,120-foot (951 meter) high Tugela Falls. In the Monk's Cowl area, spend a night behind a waterfall, camping in Zulu Cave, and carry on to explore Didima Gorge. The Grand Traverse is the ultimate challenge for experienced mountain hikers—a 12- to 16-day trek along the Drakensberg's entire eastern escarpment.

WHEN TO GO Year-round. Winter (May–August) has the most stable weather, with warm sunny days and cold clear nights. Summer (September–April) is less predictable with rain and sudden thunderstorms.

HOW LONG Allow at least three full days to get a sampling of what's offered.

PLANNING Most overnight hikers sleep in caves, many with room for up to 12 people; they have to be prebooked. Take a tent as well – if the weather turns bad, you may not find your cave or be forced to camp early. Bring a good-quality sleeping bag – it gets cold at night, even in summer.

INSIDE INFORMATION Carry plenty of water and fill up in streams or rivers. Before setting out, fill in the mountain rescue register (available at KZN Wildlife offices) and remember to sign back in on your return.

WEBSITES kznwildlife.com, bergfree.co.za

HIGHLIGHTS

▥ Listen for the barking of **rock baboons**, and look for different kinds of antelope: bushbuck, oribi, mountain reedbuck, tiny duiker, and eland. At night you may be lucky and spot anteaters and porcupines. Bearded **vultures** and **eagles** soar overhead and nest on high rocky outcrops.

▥ Relish carpets of **wildflowers** in spring and coverings of waist-high pink, white, and red blossoms in the fall. Gullies are dotted with **cycads** and **proteas**.

▥ Brave the icy mountain water and **bathe** in one of the **crystal clear pools** hidden in the sandstone bedrock.

AFRICA

Chapter 5

IN SEARCH OF CULTURE

The journeys in this chapter are truly voyages into the human mind and heart. Each one celebrates the imagination in all its exuberant diversity. Some of the destinations are world-famous wonders, others are hidden gems. Some hark back to the beginning of recorded time, others are the handiwork of men and women still among us. Together they encompass sacred spaces, hotbeds of artistic talent, haunted ruins of ancient cultures, lovingly preserved fragments of lost worlds, and revolutionary experiments in design. Be inspired by the light and color of Normandy as you explore favorite haunts of the French Impressionists. If you enjoy the performing arts, you can join a discerning audience to watch the stylized performances of Japanese Kabuki. A trip up the Nile River will take you to several of the haunting monuments of ancient Egypt. Or you can immerse yourself in the vibrant cultural life of South Africa's Zulu communities. Lovers of the fine arts, history, and culture in all its forms will find a wealth of possibilities that span the globe.

With the head of a pharaoh and the body of a lion, the Sphinx has guarded the pyramids of Giza, in Egypt, for at least 4,500 years. Carved out of a limestone plateau overlooking the Nile, its origins and significance are still disputed.

Colonial Virginia

*Explore two centuries of English settlement
along southern Virginia's coast.*

NORTH
AMERICA

One of the largest living-history museums in America, Colonial Williamsburg's tree-shaded lanes are lined with carefully restored 18th-century buildings staffed by reenactors in period costume. On arriving, you are transported back to a day in 1776, and the fire of rebellion is sweeping through the colonies. Everyday activities fill the streets and shops, while special programs present colonial citizens and political leaders debating controversial issues of the day, including slavery, the rights of colonial women, and the criminality of rebellion. Williamsburg is just one of three sites that make up Virginia's Colonial Historical Triangle. At Historic Jamestowne, you can walk among the ruins of the first successful English settlement (built in 1607), and watch ongoing archeological excavations. At nearby Jamestown Settlement, re-enactors inhabit a Jamestown-like fort, a Powhatan native village, and replicas of the three small ships that brought the settlers to the new world. A leisurely drive leads to Yorktown, where the British commander, Gen. Charles Cornwallis, surrendered to Gen. George Washington in 1781, ending the American Revolution. The town's center has a large historic district, while nearby is Yorktown Historic Battlefield.

WHEN TO GO This popular year-round destination (closed on Christmas Day and New Year's Day) can be very crowded during school holidays, making spring and fall the most pleasant times to visit. Although cooler, December offers a month of special Christmas events, including carolers and candlelit concerts.

HOW LONG Allow at least a full day and evening in Williamsburg, and another day or two to explore Jamestown and Yorktown.

PLANNING Ask for a two-, three-, or four-day accommodation package that includes admission to the popular attractions throughout your stay.

INSIDE INFORMATION All the best sites require walking, so wear comfortable shoes and dress in layers.

WEBSITES gowilliamsburg.com, virginiaisforlovers.com

HIGHLIGHTS

■ At Williamsburg, enjoy a lively discussion with **Thomas Jefferson**, as portrayed by actor and historian Bill Barker, who has made an accurate portrayal of Jefferson his life's work.

■ Attend one of the 18th-century **evening programs** at Williamsburg, such as a walking tour by lantern light, a concert, or a play.

■ At Historic Jamestowne, watch **glassmakers** produce beautifully crafted everyday items in primitive outdoor furnaces.

■ Tour Jamestown Settlement's **museum**, where an outstanding selection of artifacts offers a compelling view of early colonial life.

A wheelwright in 18th-century costume uses traditional techniques to make carriage wheels at Colonial Williamsburg.

The Moore-Dugal residence was Frank Lloyd Wright's first independent commission in Oak Park.

ILLINOIS

Frank Lloyd Wright in Oak Park

See the largest collection of Frank Lloyd Wright homes in the world by bicycle.

Many people are surprised to discover that the quiet, unassuming suburb of Oak Park, just west of Chicago, is one of the most popular destinations for lovers of innovative architecture. It was here in the last decade of the 19th century that celebrated American architect Frank Lloyd Wright got his start, and it was here that he introduced his radical Prairie Style architecture. This new style featured long, low buildings with gently sloping roofs, multilevel terraces, and the cantilevered overhangs that became one of his trademarks. A relatively short bicycle tour of the area will lead you past a dozen or more Wright residences. Extend your explorations and you can take in as many as 27 houses designed by Wright, not to mention another 60 buildings of architectural significance. Further treats are Wright's own home and studio, where he first tried out new concepts, and the nearby Unity Temple with its high windows and near-perfect acoustics, which he once described as "my little jewel."

WHEN TO GO May to September are the best months for a bicycle tour. Each May, the Preservation Trust offers a one-day architecture and history tour, the Wright Plus Housewalk, which features the interiors of significant privately owned Wright homes.

HOW LONG There are about 80 buildings of architectural note in Oak Park and the adjacent suburbs of River Forest. Allow at least one day.

PLANNING You can rent a bicycle at a Divvy bike station, near the visitor center, where you can purchase a map showing the locations of all the architecturally significant buildings.

INSIDE INFORMATION The May tour of Wright homes fills up quickly, so reserve places well in advance. If taking this tour, allow another day for exploring the rest of Oak Park.

WEBSITE flwright.org/wrightplus

HIGHLIGHTS

▪ The guided tour of the **Wright Home and Studio** provides valuable insights into Wright's ambitions and his development as an architect. The house also contains excellent examples of his furniture.

▪ The **Frank W. Thomas House**, the first Prairie Style house in Oak Park.

▪ The exterior of the **Arthur B. Heurtley House** has brickwork that varies in texture and color, linking the house to its surroundings.

▪ **Unity Temple** was Wright's first public building and has a bold Cubist interior.

NORTH AMERICA

| PENNSYLVANIA |

Amish Country

Tour the byways of rural Pennsylvania
and discover the Amish heartland.

They're not hard to spot, driving sleek, black, horse-drawn carriages past the neatly tended farms, gold and green meadows, and covered bridges of Pennsylvania's tranquil Lancaster County, home to one of the best-known communities of Amish people in the country. Lancaster's Amish live the rural life of a century ago. Electricity and autos are avoided; at night, farms are lit by candles and oil lanterns; and phones exist only in public places. Most traditional are the Old Order Amish, who use no modern conveniences. Slightly more modern are the New Order Amish (some power machinery allowed), and the even more lenient Mennonites (who allow group-owned autos). Touring the backroads, it's not uncommon to see Old Order Amish working their fields with draft horses or gathering at a farm for Sunday services. Although small, Lancaster County has enough backroads and byways to keep even seasoned road-trippers happy for a long weekend of touring. With so many roads to choose from, most people just pick one and go. Along the way, you'll find plenty of distractions. The Amish have built a burgeoning industry selling their finely crafted quilts and furniture at shops and roadside stands. And museums like the Lancaster Cultural History Museum or the Landis Valley Museum offer a thorough and intriguing look at Amish culture and history.

WHEN TO GO Spring offers lush green countryside and the best access to Amish auctions on Saturdays.

HOW LONG A weekend allows enough time to drive down country lanes, attend an auction, visit attractions, and enjoy a family-style dinner.

PLANNING Stop in at the Pennsylvania Dutch Visitor Center in Lancaster and pick up a detailed map so you can explore without getting lost. If you prefer to follow a route, start in the village of Bird-in-Hand and follow Route 340 east through Intercourse to Route 82. Head north to Route 23, and follow it southwest to Leola. Turn southwest on 772 to rejoin Route 340 in Intercourse.

INSIDE INFORMATION Drive down country lanes rather than main roads, visit some of the covered bridges, and sample local foods such as shoofly pie.

WEBSITES discoverlancaster.com, strasburgrailroad.com

NORTH
AMERICA

HIGHLIGHTS

▥ Take a ride in an Amish **horse-drawn buggy** and watch the rural landscape flow slowly by.

▥ Spend a night on a **working farm**, with simple, clean accommodation, lantern light, no telephones, and a chance to watch or participate in traditional farm activities.

▥ Take part in a springtime Amish **mud sale**, a farm auction which can draw hundreds of Amish and non-Amish bidders from all over the region. It's the perfect place to buy quality antiques, quilts, or your own horse-drawn carriage.

▥ Take a tour through Amish country aboard the 19th-century **Strasburg steam train**.

▥ **Picnic** in a sunny meadow, enjoying the fresh country breezes laden with birdsong and the occasional heady farmland scents of manure and fresh-mown hay.

Opposite: The Amish wear plain styles of clothing and have a strong tradition of hospitality and community spirit. They prefer a farming lifestyle, believing that they can best maintain their way of life in a rural environment.
Above: An Amish farmer uses a pair of mules to pull a wagon bringing in the crops.

The ruined temples of Tikal are half hidden in the jungle. The top of Temple IV's roof comb can be seen to the right of the foreground temple.

Maya Temples

Discover the monumental archeological sites of the ancient Maya in a diverse journey rich in wildlife and tropical flora.

As you clamber carefully up stone steps barely a foot deep, cut into the near-vertical wall of Tikal's Temple IV, looking down is not recommended. Edging to the top, you are surrounded by the tops of other roof combs emerging from the thick jungle canopy. The Maya civilization dominated Mesoamerica for hundreds of years, and its city-centered empires were characterized by extraordinary, monumental architecture. Built from quarried limestone, the cities comprised palaces, plazas, temples, observatories, and ball courts. Begin in Mexico's flat, arid Yucatán Peninsula with the ruins of Uxmal and Chichén Itzá, and continue past Cancún to Tulum, which enjoys a spectacular coastal location overlooking the turquoise waters of the Caribbean. From here, travel on to Lamanai, on the New River Lagoon deep in the Belize jungle. And finally, cross the Guatemalan border to reach the monumental site at Tikal. Building began here in 600 B.C., and it remained an important religious and political center for 1,500 years. At the height of its power, it had 100,000 inhabitants. Shrouded in dense rain forest and teeming with wildlife, its massive temple structures are among the most impressive archeological ruins on the continent.

WHEN TO GO The climate is subtropical and the dry season is December to April. During the wet season there are short, heavy showers, often in the afternoon. Avoid the hurricane season (August to October).

HOW LONG You will need two to three weeks to take in the major Maya sites.

PLANNING You can use Cancún or Mérida as a base for the Mexican sites, Orange Walk for Lamanai in Belize, and Flores for Tikal in Guatemala.

INSIDE INFORMATION Good, English-speaking, local guides can be found within many of the sites. Official guides will be able to produce identification. Take some shoes with grip because humidity and frequent rain showers can make the steps up to some of the temples very slippery.

WEBSITES mayasites.com, sacred-destinations.com/mexico

HIGHLIGHTS

Chichén Itzá has one of the best preserved **ball courts** of any Maya site.

Tulum's El Castillo is perched on top of cliffs overlooking the Caribbean. You can also go **snorkeling** off Belize's barrier reef.

Temple IV at **Tikal**, Guatemala, is the tallest of all the Maya temples.

Watch **dawn break** over the rain forest from the top of Tikal's Temple IV. Listen to the sounds of the jungle as monkeys and birds begin their morning chorus.

| MEXICO |

Mexico's Colonial Cities

The extravagant colonial architecture of New Spain will surprise you on this tour of Mexico's central highlands.

North of Mexico City lies the country's colonial heartland. While the Spanish conquistadors mined the hills in the region for silver and gold to send back to the Spanish crown, they established a series of beautiful cities packed with grand cathedrals, baroque palaces, palm-fringed plazas, and winding, cobbled streets. These colonial centers exude architectural extravagance and European pomposity, yet the warm, bright hues of the houses and the characteristic exuberance of the people make them uniquely Mexican. Begin in Morelia, which is a four-hour drive west of Mexico City. It contains a number of mansions and churches, many of which were constructed in a pink-colored stone and have intricate facades. Not far from here, the quiet, highland village of Pátzcuaro has a stunning central plaza and a mixture of indigenous and colonial buildings. Built on a hillside, Guanajuato is perhaps the most beautiful of the "silver cities." Nearby is the fascinating old town of San Miguel de Allende, which, with its mansions and cobbled streets, has a cosmopolitan air and a rich cultural life. The journey ends in Zacatecas, which represented the northern frontier of Spain's empire in the New World.

WHEN TO GO The central highlands are temperate and generally mild and dry, with rains most likely between June and September.

HOW LONG Road travel is increasingly easy in this part of Mexico, and ten days is sufficient to visit the highlights of this colonial region.

PLANNING Try to coincide with Semana Santa (Easter Week). Festivities are loud, brash, and fun. Hotels are booked up early.

INSIDE INFORMATION Visit the indigenous villages of the Huichol and Cora in the Sierra Madre for a glimpse of a very different way of life.

WEBSITE visitmexico.com/en

| HIGHLIGHTS

Guanajuato has excellent examples of baroque colonial architecture, such as the Basilica Senora de Guanajuato, the Templo de San Diego, and the Alhóndiga de Granaditas.

The **facade of Zacatecas Cathedral** is a fine example of the extravagant Spanish baroque style of architectural ornament known as churrigueresque.

The **cable car** from Cerro de la Bufa to Cerro del Grillo provides a splendid view over Zacatecas.

The Parroquia, or parish church, of St. Michael the Archangel in San Miguel de Allende was built in the 17th century.

Top 10 New Museums

A wave of new museums around the world showcase art, human and natural history, and the wonders of modern architecture.

❶ NATIONAL MUSEUM OF AFRICAN AMERICAN HISTORY AND CULTURE, WASHINGTON, D.C.

Slavery and segregation, civil rights and soul music are among the themes explored at a museum that has been in the works for more than a hundred years. Ghanaian-British architect David Adjaye and his firm won a competition between some of the world's top designers to create the stunning modern structure.

PLANNING Free-of-charge timed passes are required for admission, available in advance online. A limited number of walk-up passes are available from 1 p.m. on weekdays. nmaahc.si.edu

❷ BLOCH BUILDING, NELSON-ATKINS MUSEUM, MISSOURI

Comprising five frosted glass "lenses" that telescope into the museum's sculpture garden, the futuristic Bloch Building houses the contemporary, African, and Impressionist collections of the acclaimed Nelson-Atkins Museum in Kansas City. Such was the contrast to the Beaux Arts–style main building, that many locals detested the Bloch when it opened in 2007. Now it's one of KC's favorite structures.

PLANNING The Bloch is best viewed at night, when it resembles a cluster of giant ice cubes. nelson-atkins.org

❸ PIERRE LASSONDE PAVILION, CANADA

"Quietly stunning" is how one architecture critic describes the fourth and latest addition to the Musée National des Beaux-Arts in Quebec City (MNBAQ). Essentially three giant glass boxes stacked atop one another, the new wing (unveiled in 2016) features majestic staircases that connect galleries where natural light illuminates intriguing pieces of Canadian contemporary art.

PLANNING Tempéra Québécor, the museum's new gourmet restaurant, is located in the pavilion lobby. mnbaq.org/en

❹ NATIONAL MUSEUM OF AUSTRALIA

Perched on a peninsula jutting into Lake Burley Griffin in Canberra, the NMA is eclectic both inside and out. The playful architecture, said to represent a huge jigsaw puzzle, reflects down under's diverse cultural heritage. Inside, a wide-ranging collection embraces everything from cricket and Holden motorcars to Aboriginal artifacts, kitschy kangaroo figurines, and the extinct Tasmanian tiger.

PLANNING Moored on the lakeshore, the 1878 paddle steamer *Enterprise* is also part of the collection. nma.gov.au

The angular Porsche Museum near Stuttgart in Germany is as streamlined as the cars it celebrates. The avant-garde exhibition hall seems to float in midair; inside you can admire iconic Porsches.

❺ LANYANG MUSEUM, TAIWAN

Wedged between the mountains and the sea on Taiwan's rugged east coast, the collection revolves around the region's natural history, agricultural heritage, and seafaring. Fashioned largely from gray stone and blue glass, the museum building, with its steeply slanted walls, is inspired by the region's striking geological formations.

PLANNING The museum is a 45-minute drive from downtown Taipei via National Highway 5. www.lym.gov.tw/eng/index_en.asp

❻ LOUVRE ABU DHABI, UNITED ARAB EMIRATES

Set beneath a massive "Rain of Light" dome on Saadiyat Island, this Middle Eastern branch of the celebrated French collection is one of the most expensive museum projects ever undertaken. Many years in the planning, the museum has a collection that ranges through all periods and artistic media, and includes just about every corner of the globe.

PLANNING Saadiyat is also the venue for the new Guggenheim Abu Dhabi and Zayed National Museum of the UAE. louvreabudhabi.ae

❼ M/S MARITIME MUSEUM OF DENMARK

Hamlet would have no doubt appreciated the irony inherent in this seafaring collection in the shadow of Kronborg Castle in Helsingør. The ultramodern museum lies underground, built in the remains of an ancient dry dock. Glass-and-aluminum bridges lead visitors through exhibits on sailors, ships, and warfare, and an amazing gallery of models.

PLANNING Visitors of any age can decorate their skin with temporary sailor-style tattoos at stands around the museum. mfs.dk/en

❽ PORSCHE MUSEUM, GERMANY

Motorheads from around the globe relish this shrine to sleek, fast automobiles near Stuttgart. Christened in 2009, the radically angular building showcases more than 80 vehicles from the Porsche past, as well as high-tech exhibits like the Porsche Touchwall interactive archive.

PLANNING Museum visits can be combined with a tour of the adjacent Porsche factory. porsche.com/museum/en

❾ THE SWITCH HOUSE, ENGLAND

This angular 2016 addition to London's Tate Modern soars ten stories above the nearby River Thames, offering stunning panoramic views of the city center. But the most intriguing aspect of the museum is belowground: the conversion of two giant oil storage tanks (that once fueled the power plant) into a permanent space for performance and live art.

PLANNING A viewing gallery on the top floor of Switch House provides a sky-high view of central London. tate.org.uk/visit/tate-modern

❿ GUGGENHEIM BILBAO, SPAIN

Frank Gehry's masterpiece of modern architecture in many ways overshadows the works by Warhol, Koons, and other contemporary masters that lie inside. Reflected in the adjacent Nervión River, the titanium, glass, and limestone structure opened the floodgates of modern museum development when it debuted in 1997.

PLANNING "Art After Dark" at the museum mixes artwork and DJs in a unique nightclub setting. guggenheim-bilbao.eus/en

A kabuki actor in sumptuous costume and wig commands the stage.

JAPAN

Japanese Kabuki Theater

Mesmerizing stories of samurai derring-do, thwarted love, and bloody betrayal from Japan's golden age are played out on stage.

From the stalls of Tokyo's Ginza Kabuki-za theater, the stage is so broad that to see one side and then the other requires turning the head through as many degrees as an umpire at a tennis match. The eerie squeal of *shakuhachi*, or traditional bamboo flutes, subdues the audience, but as the first actor enters, shouting breaks out from all corners of the hall. Calling out the actor's guild name is a sign of approval. The English audio guide not only immerses the listener in the details of the complicated and often racy plots, but also in all the cultural niceties, such as when and how to applaud. The stars of Kabuki become household names, especially the *onnagata*, the men who play the women's roles. The snowy-necked maiden with the complicated coiffure, tripping delicately across a stage design as exquisite as an 18th-century woodblock print, is male, as are all kabuki actors, and quite possibly middle-aged as well.

WHEN TO GO There are performances throughout the year. Matinees typically start at 11 a.m. and evening performances at 4.30 p.m.

HOW LONG It's rare for complete works to be performed; usually, three acts from different plays are performed, sometimes punctuated with kabuki dance. Total running time is usually around four hours, including two or three intermissions.

PLANNING Advance booking is essential. Tickets can be ordered by telephone or at the box office and credit cards are accepted.

INSIDE INFORMATION Dress should be smart. Rent an audio guide in English from the lobby. A limited number of fourth-floor and standing tickets for a single act are available.

WEBSITE japan-guide.com/e/e2090.html

HIGHLIGHTS

▥ Characters make dramatic **entrances** and **exits** along the *hanamichi*, a narrow extension of the stage that passes through the audience.

▥ *Kabuki no mie* is a ritualized stance accompanied by a grotesque, cross-eyed grimace. When done well, it brings wild applause from the crowd.

▥ The musical accompaniment consists of the haunting, plangent notes of the **shamisen**, a three-string lute, and the hair-raising wails of the **shakuhachi** flutes.

▥ Male and female characters alike have **sumptuous costumes** and **elaborate hairstyles**.

ASIA

JAPAN

Ancient Kyoto

*Explore a world of exquisite temples and
shogun castles that date back to feudal times.*

Wander the streets of Kyoto, once Japan's feudal capital, and around every corner you'll find reminders of its past. Neon-lit convenience stores nestle next to classical tearooms, and groups of Japanese businessmen shout into their cell phones while one of the few remaining geisha walk past, wearing an exquisite kimono worth millions of yen. On a hillside above the city, the Kiyomizu-dera (or "pure water temple"), dating from the 8th century, stands in woodland, surrounded by numerous smaller shrines. According to legend, to drink from the three waterfalls at the temple confers long life and good luck. In northwestern Kyoto is the Kinkaku-ji Temple (Golden Pavilion). Although the original was burned down by a disturbed young monk in 1950, the rebuilt temple is just as impressive. The Sanjusangen-do Temple in eastern Kyoto is Japan's longest wooden building and houses 1,001 statues of the 1,000-armed Kannon, the Buddhist goddess of mercy. In central Kyoto, visit Nijo Castle, built by Ieyasu, the first Tokugawa Shogun, and try to walk silently across the nightingale floors. These wooden floors were designed to "sing," no matter how gently they were stepped upon, to alert residents to attacks from even the most light-footed intruder.

WHEN TO GO Although Kyoto can be visited at any time of year, summer is so hot that touring the city on foot can be very unpleasant. Kyoto looks its best in fall, or during the very short, but rightly famed, cherry blossom season in April.

HOW LONG Allow at least a week to see Kyoto's main attractions.

PLANNING Local tour operators can organize walking tours in English.

INSIDE INFORMATION If you are in Kyoto during the cherry blossom season, join the Japanese in one of the parks, or along the Kamo River, for *hanami* (flower viewing). Take a picnic, and relax under the cherry trees for the quintessential Japanese experience.

WEBSITE www.pref.kyoto.jp/en/index.html

ASIA

HIGHLIGHTS

▥ If you visit Kiyomizu-dera, don't miss the **Jishu Shrine**. If you can walk between the two love stones with your eyes closed, you will be lucky in love.

▥ When you visit the **Nanzen-ji Temple** in eastern Kyoto, take the short walk through the forest to the **Oku-no-in shrine** by a waterfall in a shady glen. Intrepid pilgrims can sometimes be seen praying under the waterfall.

Kyoto's Kinkaku-ji Temple, or Golden Pavilion, is reflected in the Kyo-ki Pond.

Temples of Thailand

*The 30,000 Buddhist temples scattered across
the country will delight the eye and the senses.*

The first rays of the sun light up the Temple of Dawn in Bangkok, mirroring it in the cool waters of the Chao Phraya River, while Buddhist monks shuffle along the banks clutching alms bowls under their saffron robes. The scene is repeated across the country as devout Thais prepare daily offerings for the monks and the spirits of the land. Theravada Buddhism reached the country in the 13th century, during the Golden Age of the Sukhothai Kingdom. Today around 95 percent of Thais are Buddhist, and men, royalty included, traditionally join the monkhood for a week or more at least once in their lives, to earn merits for their families. Thailand's temples are influenced by neighboring cultures yet remain unmistakably Thai: stepped roofs and dazzling tiles, images of the Buddha, mythical creatures, lotus, gold leaf, incense, and flickering oil lamps. Each one is an intriguing maze of courtyards, cloisters, and halls filled with the chanting of monks and the ringing of bells and gongs. You can consult your horoscope and, on holy days, visit the temple fair. Begin by exploring the gleaming "wats" (temples) of Bangkok, then head into the central plains for the ancient sites of Ayutthaya and Sukhotai, and continue north to Chiang Mai and Mae Hong Son for its exquisite, Burmese-style pagodas. Any festival will enhance your experience.

WHEN TO GO Temperatures remain high from November to February, but humidity drops. This is also a good time for festivals.

HOW LONG 574 miles (924 km) from Bangkok to Mae Hong Son. Allow three weeks for in-depth sightseeing.

PLANNING Combine rail, road, and air travel according to your time availability. You can visit Ayutthaya on a day trip from Bangkok, returning by river cruise. Local agents or tour operators will have information.

INSIDE INFORMATION Dress modestly. Don't sit with your feet pointing to a Buddha image; don't make physical contact with a monk (place offerings in bowl); and don't take pictures of the Emerald Buddha.

WEBSITE insider-journeys.com

HIGHLIGHTS

▓ **Wat Po,** the oldest and largest temple in Bangkok, houses a 150-ft (46 m) long Reclining Buddha.

▓ **Wat Phra Kaeo**, Bangkok, is home to the small but highly revered Emerald Buddha.

▓ The Golden Buddha in **Wat Traimit**, Bangkok, is five tons of solid gold.

▓ At 410 ft (125 m), the **Phra Pathom Chedi**, west of Bangkok, is said to be the tallest in the world. A *chedi* is a shrine containing relics of the Buddha.

▓ The gilded **chedi** of **Doi Suthep**, near Chiang Mai, stands at the top of 290 steps guarded by carved seven-headed mythical snakes.

Offerings of flowers are laid on the hand of a Buddha at a temple in Sukhotai.

One of the world's most treasured monuments, the matchless Taj Mahal gleams in the sunshine.

INDIA

India's Golden Triangle

Take a step back in time to the world of India's maharajas, who adorned their domains with breathtaking palaces and forts.

India is a vast and diverse country, and several visits are usually needed to take in its glorious complexities and landscapes. But a visit to the relatively small area known as the Golden Triangle, encompassing the northern cities of Delhi, Jaipur, and Agra, provides a wonderful introduction to the exotic romanticism of this intriguing nation. As the capital, New Delhi offers up all the contrasts of India in one fell swoop, from the elegance of Connaught Circus, still reminiscent of the Raj, to the eternal bustle of Chandni Chowk, filled with the heady aroma of spices and busy shops selling traditional tiffin-carriers, saris, rugs, and more. Jaipur, with its pink-hued Palace of the Winds and spectacular Amber Fort, rendered all the more impressive when entered on the back of an elephant, clearly demonstrate the splendor with which the royal maharajas of old filled their lives. And in Agra is one of the world's most famous man-made sights, the marble Taj Mahal. This enduring symbol of love and romance was built between 1632 and 1648 by the Mogul emperor Shah Jahan as a memorial to his beloved wife, Mumtaz Mahal. Between the cities, you can absorb the atmosphere and rural landscape of northern India, where the fields are still worked by turban-wearing farmhands.

WHEN TO GO Year-round, but the best times are October to April.

HOW LONG Approximately 155 miles (249 km). Most organized tours last around five or six days.

PLANNING You can travel between the cities by bus, train, car, or taxi. The tourist office in Delhi can arrange for a private driver, so you can take in the sights from a traditional white Ambassador car. The Taj Mahal is closed to non-Muslims on Fridays.

INSIDE INFORMATION Drink only bottled water, and avoid unbottled beverages or drinks with ice. Insect repellent is a must, and antimalarial medication is advised.

WEBSITE goldentriangletourindia.com

HIGHLIGHTS

▥ Visit the open-fronted cafés of Delhi's **Chandni Chowk** to snack on traditional dosas and Indian sweets.

▥ Take a heart-stopping **rickshaw ride** through the streets of Jaipur, where you'll share the roads with cars, buses, camels, and elephants.

▥ At **Jantar Mantar** in Jaipur, marvel at the scientific knowledge of an 18th-century maharaja through the instruments in his observatory.

▥ Despite the crowds, the gardens of the **Taj Mahal** remain a wonderfully peaceful place for contemplation in a setting given over to romance.

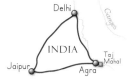

The Treasury at Petra is several stories high. Its beautifully decorated facade was carved out of the sandstone cliff.

JORDAN

Treasures of Jordan

Follow a 5,000-year-old route to visit ancient
Petra and the wonders of the Jordanian desert.

Starting in Amman, drive south down the King's Highway, once traveled by Moses and the Israelites, but now a paved two-lane route. Stop at Madaba, a city whose buildings were filled with Byzantine mosaics, now displayed in the museum. From here, you can make a short detour to Mount Nebo, to the monastery at the reputed site of Moses's tomb. The ruins of a great crusader fortress, now only a shell with immense arched halls (once living quarters, stables, and fighting galleries), dominates Al Karak, the scourge of caravans en route to Egypt and Mecca. Finally, you come to Petra, called the "rose-red city half as old as time," hidden in the mountains. Its origins are obscure, but it bears the stamp of Assyria, Egypt, Greece, and Rome. In the 4th century B.C., the city was occupied by the Nabataeans, who controlled the caravan routes of the spice trade that stretched as far as China. Sales of frankincense and myrrh, cloves, and cinnamon to the lucrative markets of Europe made the city wealthy. Petra continued to flourish until an earthquake in the 7th century crippled the ingeniously planned water supply. It was completely abandoned following the 12th-century Muslim conquest of the Middle East.

WHEN TO GO Any time of year.

HOW LONG Amman to Al 'Aqabah is 163 miles (262 km). Allow at least one week to see the sites.

PLANNING Hire a car in Amman. The King's Highway has well-developed tourist services. There are hotels in Madaba (30 miles/48 km from Amman), Al Karak (77 miles/124 km from Amman), and Petra (163 miles/262 km from Amman).

INSIDE INFORMATION Petra looks its most romantic in the early morning and late afternoon, when the sunlight catches and intensifies the rose red color of the rock facades. You can hire a guide at the gate.

WEBSITES atlastours.net/jordan, onthegotours.com

HIGHLIGHTS

■ In the Basilica of St. George at Madaba, see the 6th-century **mosaic map** of Palestine and the Nile Delta.

■ From the top of Mount Nebo you can enjoy a **dazzling view** across the Jordan Valley and the Dead Sea to Jerusalem and Bethlehem.

■ Be stunned by your first sight of the **Treasury** (El Khazneh) at Petra as you emerge from the entrance gorge. This sumptuous, 131-ft (40 m) tall building is the most famous here. No one knows its original purpose – except that it was not a treasury. It may have been a royal tomb, or a temple.

DENMARK | SWEDEN | NORWAY

The Viking Legacy

Tour the lands of Norse seafarers and warriors on long summer days, and experience Viking life.

The Vikings were bands of fearsome raiders whose remarkable shipbuilding and seafaring skills enabled them to cross previously uncharted waters and settle all over northern Europe. Between the 8th and 11th centuries, they occupied northern Britain and France, Iceland, and even parts of North America, but it is in their Scandinavian homeland that their legacy is strongest. Begin your tour at Ribe, which is Denmark's oldest town. Ribe Viking Center recreates a full Viking village, including a marketplace and agricultural activities, on an 8th-century site. Ålborg, in northern Jutland (Jylland), was first settled by the Vikings 1,300 years ago. It has a museum of Viking culture and several large grave sites. In Oslo, Norway's capital, you can visit the Viking Ship Museum and the Historical Museum, where you can learn about Vikings as farmers, warriors, and traders. Finally, Birka, on an island near Stockholm, is Sweden's oldest city. Founded in the 8th century, it became an important trading center for the whole of northern Europe. The excavated remains of the town, together with models and reconstructions in the museum, reveal the daily life and traditions of Viking culture.

WHEN TO GO All year, but the best times are between May and September.

HOW LONG There is no official Viking trail, but to take in the sights described above allow at least a week. There are air, rail, and ferry links between the cities.

PLANNING Esbjerg is the nearest airport for visiting Ribe. Scandinavia, and Norway in particular, is the most expensive region in Europe, so budget accordingly.

INSIDE INFORMATION Scandinavia is plagued by gnats in summer so wear a good insect repellent.

WEBSITES visitdenmark.com, visitsweden.com, visitnorway.com

HIGHLIGHTS

▪ The Ribe Viking Center has unparalleled exhibits dedicated to **Viking culture**.

▪ Ålborg has several impressive Viking **grave sites**.

▪ The Viking Ship Museum in Oslo displays three wooden **Viking ships**, complete with carved dragon heads, excavated from the waters of Oslofjord.

▪ Birka, Sweden, offers visits to ongoing **archaeological digs**.

The Viking site at Lindholm Hoje near Ålborg in northern Denmark has more than 700 graves.

England's Gardens

The masterworks of England's greatest garden designers cluster together in the south. Come in June and smell the roses.

The garden culture of southern England is a lovingly preserved tradition. Traveling through London's suburbs past a patchwork of green fields in Surrey, Sussex, and Kent, this region is a horticultural treasure trove, from the striking landscaping of stately homes to the personal creations of legendary green thumbs such as Vita Sackville-West and Christopher Lloyd. In spring and summer these stunning and peaceful locations, filled with a profusion of color and perfume, capture the true essence of this "green and pleasant land." On the western outskirts of London are Hampton Court Palace, Henry VIII's favorite home, the Royal Botanical Gardens at Kew, and the Savill Gardens in Windsor Great Park. The Royal Horticultural Society runs Wisley Garden, near Woking in Surrey, which offers 200 acres (81 hectares) of beautiful gardens, together with an excellent nursery and advice on growing plants. Polesden Lacey, also in Surrey, has summer and winter displays. Sheffield Park in East Sussex has a 100-acre (40.5 hectare) garden landscaped by Lancelot "Capability" Brown in the 18th century. At Ticehurst is romantic Pashley Manor; near Rye, Great Dixter has extensive cottage gardens designed by Christopher Lloyd. The gardens at Sissinghurst Castle, at Cranbrook in Kent, were the life's work of Vita Sackville-West, and the National Trust still carefully tends her glorious plantings. Hever Castle, near Edenbridge, was the childhood home of Anne Boleyn. The gardens, which were laid out between 1904 and 1908, include an Italian garden, a rose garden, and a Tudor garden.

WHEN TO GO April to September.

HOW LONG Organized garden tours usually allow a week to see all the gardens in the area, but you could cover the highlights in three days.

PLANNING While the gardens are beautiful throughout spring and summer, if you visit in May, you can add the annual Chelsea Flower Show in London to the tour.

INSIDE INFORMATION Tickets to the Chelsea Flower Show sell out fast, so book in advance online at rhs.org.uk.

WEBSITE britishtours.com

HIGHLIGHTS

▓ Allow time to get lost in Hampton Court's **maze**.

▓ Enjoy the quiet seclusion of Polesden Lacey's **walled rose garden** at Great Bookham, near Dorking.

▓ Sheffield Park, near Uckfield, is home to the **National Collection of Ghent Azaleas**. It also has superb **fall color**.

▓ The gardens at Sissinghurst are designed as ten distinct "rooms," the most famous of which is the **White Garden**.

▓ Hever Castle's **Italian garden** combines statuary from Roman to Renaissance times with displays of shrubs and herbaceous plants.

Opposite: The gardens at Sissinghurst are laid out as a series of rooms around the surviving parts of an Elizabethan mansion. Above left: Poppies and other wildflowers provide a wonderful display of color in early summer. Above right: The garden at Polesden Lacey provides wonderful views of the North Downs.

Dutch Masters Tour

Marvel at the work of Rembrandt, Frans Hals, Vermeer, and other painters from the Netherlands' Golden Age.

EUROPE

The Netherlands is a tiny country, about the same size as the state of Maine, yet in the 17th century it controlled an empire that circled the world, producing a Golden Age in commerce, science, and the arts. Many Dutch artists stand out in this glorious era, but the greatest was Rembrandt van Rijn. Beginning in Amsterdam, where Rembrandt found fortune as a young man, you can visit his home, now the Rembrandt House Museum. The rooms have been restored, and many of his drawings and etchings are on display. Traveling west through the countryside to Haarlem, you can see the huge skies and flat landscape that fascinated artists, such as Jacob van Ruisdael and Aelbert Cuyp. Haarlem has the Frans Hals Museum in the almshouse where the portraitist spent his last years; his later, more somber work can be seen here, along with good examples of the Haarlem School. Next head south, past swathes of bulb fields—a reminder of the importance of flowers in Dutch life and art. In The Hague, the Mauritshuis has Jan Vermeer's "View of Delft." Vermeer's paintings are few, but their serene quality and pearly light are unique even in Dutch art. The tree-lined canals and gabled houses of nearby Delft conjure up the still world of this enigmatic artist.

WHEN TO GO Year-round. The Mauritshuis is closed on Mondays.

HOW LONG Amsterdam to Delft is 40 miles (64 km). Allow five days to take in the sights and to stop off along the way. If cycling, allow longer.

PLANNING You can reach all the sights by train or bus. The Netherlands is very bicycle-friendly, so cycling is a great option, too, both between and within cities. Driving around the country is also easy.

INSIDE INFORMATION It's worth getting a Museumkaart (Museum Annual Card). This will give you access to 400 sights nationwide for a reasonable one-time payment.

WEBSITES cycletours.com, traveleditions.co.uk, holland.com

HIGHLIGHTS

▨ The **Rijksmuseum** in Amsterdam has a superb collection, including Rembrandt's "The Night Watch," Vermeer's "Woman Reading a Letter," and Hals's "The Merry Drinker."

▨ A **boat trip** is the best way to view Amsterdam's canals, lined with merchants' houses.

▨ Relax over a beer in one of Amsterdam's **"brown cafés,"** where the tiled floors and wood paneling echo many a painted interior.

▨ The **Mauritshuis** collection includes Rembrandt's "Anatomy Lesson of Dr. Nicolaes Tulp," Gerard ter Borch's "Hunting for Lice," and Vermeer's "Girl with a Pearl Earring."

Holland's gabled houses and windmills are reminiscent of scenes from Dutch Old Master paintings.

The Thiepval Memorial is inscribed with the names of the missing from the Battle of the Somme.

| FRANCE |

The Battle of the Somme

Tour the sites of desperate battles that were fought in this tranquil countryside, which is now dotted with cemeteries and memorials.

It is hard to imagine the fertile plains of northern Picardy—today ablaze with the gold of wheat and barley—transformed into a sea of mud, the trees blasted, and the wide horizons obscured by sickening green and orange smoke. But here it was that, from July 1 to November 18, 1916, the Battle of the Somme was fought. During this desperate British offensive against the German lines, more than half a million lives were lost, though only a few acres of land were gained. Arrive at Albert along the old Roman road from Bapaume, and you have driven the 8 miles (13 kilometers) that the British advanced during the entire battle. From here you can make a tour of the sites, each with its own story. At the northern end of the Front Line, near Serre, the first attack was launched from Jacob's Ladder trench and the Sunken Lane, and a massive mine detonated at Hawthorn Ridge. Farther south, Montauban marks one of the few military successes of the first day. But the gigantic Lochnagar Crater, made by a 60,000-pound (27 tonne) mine, is a reminder of the prolonged and deadly fight to gain La Boisselle. Walking through Delville Wood, where South African troops fought for five days, you can try to reconstruct the bitter battle that took place among the trees.

WHEN TO GO The best time to visit is between March and October, when longer days and better weather prevail. After plowing, the old trench-system lines become apparent.

HOW LONG A minimum of three days.

PLANNING Organized tours with an experienced guide are the best way to see the battlefields. The Albert tourist office has local guides, and it is possible to rent bicycles on a daily basis. Tours are also organized through War Research Society Battlefield Tours. If you wish to visit a particular grave or memorial, contact the Commonwealth War Graves Commission.

INSIDE INFORMATION Wartime shells, grenades, and bullets still lie in the fields. Never touch them as they may still be live.

WEBSITES cwgc.org, battlefieldtours.co.uk

HIGHLIGHTS

▥ The **Musée des Abris** In Albert, set in the town's old air-raid shelters, has displays of artifacts and maps.

▥ The **Thiepval Memorial to the Missing** is the largest war memorial in the world. It commemorates some 73,000 young men who have no known grave.

▥ The **Caterpillar Valley Memorial** commemorates 1,330 men of the New Zealand Division killed on the Somme.

▥ British and German **trench systems** have been preserved at Newfoundland Park Beaumont-Hamel. There is also a memorial to the Canadian troops who died here.

EUROPE

Top 10 Vanishing Places

Climate change, poaching, and deforestation pose a threat to much of the world's land and its living creatures. See them while you can.

❶ THE EVERGLADES, FLORIDA

The Seminole people, an indigenous tribe of the Everglades, named the area Okeechobee, or "river of grass," in reference to its vast saw grass marshes. Dredging and surrounding urban developments have halved the Everglades in size since the early 20th century, and continue to pose a threat to many of its species. Despite this, boating, biking and hiking are the three best ways to catch a glimpse of the area's manatees, Florida panthers, and American crocodiles.

PLANNING Get the full-on Everglade experience by paddling the Wilderness Waterway, a 99-mile aquatic trail that takes 7–10 days to paddle while camping along the way. nps.gov/ever

❷ GLACIER NATIONAL PARK, MONTANA

Climate change has reduced the number of glaceries in this beloved Rocky Mountain park to just 25; these form part of a truly spectacular rock-and-water landscape carved by glacial action over thousands of years. Visitors can drive Going-to-the-Sun Road over the crest of the Rockies or hike the Continental Divide Trail to Canada's Waterton Lakes, all while marveling at the park's vibrant wildlife.

PLANNING Although it has shrunk by around 40 percent since the 1960s, Grinnell remains the park's most accessible glacier, reached via an 5.3-mile (8.5 km) trail from Many Glacier. nps.gov/glac

❸ AMAZON BASIN, SOUTH AMERICA

Divided between eight nations, the vast Amazon Basin is threatened by deforestation, yet still sprawls across 40 percent of South America. Take a river journey to explore the main river and its many tributaries. To experience both the majesty of the trees and the amazing array of wildlife that dwell beneath the forest canopy, hiking is the best option.

PLANNING Cusco-based Inkanatura organizes photo safaris to Manu National Park in the wildlife-rich Peruvian Amazon. inkanatura.com

❹ GALÁPAGOS ISLANDS, ECUADOR

This remote volcanic archipelago is famous for inspiring Charles Darwin's theory of natural selection. Take a lava rock trail hike alongside blue-footed boobies and marine iguanas. Conservation efforts protect the islands' wildlife from illegal hunting, which threaten many native species, including the giant tortoise, sea cucumbers, and 30 species of shark.

PLANNING Natural Habitat maintains an online resource guide to the islands that monitors environmental threats. aboutgalapagos.nathab.com

Of all the lemur species of Madagascar, the eastern lesser bamboo lemur is one of the few whose habitat is slowly expanding. Since they eat young bamboo shoots, they thrive when virgin forest is cut down.

❺ GREAT BARRIER REEF, AUSTRALIA

Despite coral bleaching caused by climate change, the Great Barrier Reef remains one of the globe's natural wonders and an underwater paradise. Comprising nearly 3,000 separate reefs and over 900 tropical islands, the Great Barrier Reef stretches as far as the distance between Boston and Miami.

PLANNING The most pristine section of the Great Barrier Reef is the southern sector between Mackay and Fraser Island. queensland.com

❻ SUMATRA RAIN FOREST, INDONESIA

Tigers, rhinos, orangutans, and elephants are among the iconic creatures that inhabit this giant Indonesian island, yet all face possible extinction due to the expanding oil palm industry. See them in the wild at Kerinci Seblat, Gunung Leuser, and Bukit Barisan Selatan national parks.

PLANNING To explore all three parks in a single trip, take the 1,200-mile (1,960 km) road trip along the western branch of the Trans-Sumatra Highway. indonesia.travel

❼ KATHMANDU VALLEY, NEPAL

Teeming with palaces, stupas, and temples, Nepal's cultural heartland is threatened by urban development. Lying in the literal shadow of the Himalaya, there are breathtaking views of Mount Everest from vantage points around the valley. Seek refuge from urbanization in Changu Narayan's ancient temples.

PLANNING A number of local travel companies offer guided tours of the valley's World Heritage sites including Kathmandu's Durbar Square and Swayambhunath stupa. nepaltourism.net

❽ THE MALDIVES, INDIAN OCEAN

Around 80 percent of the Maldives' islands are no more than 3 ft (1 m) above sea level and—while climate change may one day submerge them—the Maldives archipelago is celebrated for its pristine beaches, posh over-the-water bungalows, and romantic electric blue shorelines.

PLANNING Base yourself at a single private island resort or make landfalls on several atolls during a charter cruise aboard the *Four Seasons Explorer*. fourseasons.com/maldivesfse

❾ DEAD SEA, ISRAEL AND JORDAN

Although shrinking due to its waters being diverted for urban usage, this salt lake is still a geological, historical, and biblical wonder. Upscale waterfront resorts near Sweimeh offer swimming, mud baths, and lakefront dining.

PLANNING Photojournalist Noam Bedein leads boat trips of geological wonders on the Israeli side of the Dead Sea. deadseastory.com

❿ LEMUR RESERVES, MADAGASCAR

Ranomafana, Kirindy, and Andasibe-Mantadia national parks are three of the most critical habitats for the island's 32 lemur species, all threatened by slash-and-burn agriculture. Reachable only by air, Anjajavy private nature reserve in northwest Madagascar safeguards seven lemur species and over 1,800 species of plant across its 1,853 acres (750 ha).

PLANNING Visitors are welcome at Centre ValBio, a conservation center on the edge of Ranomafana where Dr. Patricia Wright and her team carry out vital research to save and protect lemurs. stonybrook.edu/commcms/centre-valbio

Impressionist France

Walking across the Japanese bridge in Monet's water garden,
you'll feel as if you are stepping into an Impressionist painting.

The Impressionists acquired their name from a painting by Claude Monet. It is called "Impression, Sunrise," and shows a hazy scene of Le Havre on the Normandy coast. Monet grew up here and painted in the open air with the older artist Eugène Boudin, so discovering his vocation for capturing light and atmosphere. Starting in Le Havre, you can visit the beaches of Deauville and Trouville and the fishing village of Honfleur, then follow the "Alabaster Coast" east to Dieppe, taking in the cliffs at Étretat and Fécamp. At various times these places attracted Monet's fellow Impressionists: Pissarro, Manet, Degas, Renoir, and Berthe Morisot. The trail then leads inland to Rouen, where Monet produced an epic series of the cathedral facade. Farther upriver, on the east bank of the Seine, lies Giverny, Monet's home for the second half of his life. Here, you can visit the garden that he so lovingly created and which inspired his water-lily series. Arriving in Paris, you are reminded of the Impressionists' love of urban subjects. The city was being modernized at the time, so today it looks much as they painted it—imagine people in 19th-century dress and horse-drawn carriages rattling by, and you have stepped into Renoir's "Pont Neuf" or Degas's "Place de la Concorde."

WHEN TO GO March to November, when Monet's house and garden and the Musée des Impressionnismes in Giverny are open. Spring and early summer show the flowers at their best.

HOW LONG The journey from Honfleur via Le Havre and the coast to Dieppe and then Paris is about 200 miles (322 km). Allow three days minimum; five for a relaxed tour.

PLANNING The independent traveler can easily follow the route along the Seine Valley by rail or car. For Giverny by rail from Rouen or Paris, get off at Vernon. In Normandy, the administrative district, or département, of Seine-Maritime arranges excellent Impressionist-themed itineraries along the coast.

INSIDE INFORMATION For a really authentic stopover in Giverny, stay at Le Bon Maréchal, a café/bed-and-breakfast with just three rooms, where Monet and his friends used to meet and talk.

WEBSITES francetourism.com, lehavretourisme.com, giverny.org, www.marmottan.fr

HIGHLIGHTS

▦ Wander the Normandy cliffs and watch the changing **northern light**.

▦ In Monet's house at Giverny, the colorful rooms are hung with his collection of **Japanese prints**.

▦ The **Musée des Impressionnismes** in Giverny displays American painters from 1750 to the present, including Mary Cassatt, Winslow Homer, and James McNeill Whistler.

▦ Visit the **Bois de Boulogne**, a park west of Paris, painted by Renoir and Morisot.

▦ The **Musée Marmottan** has the world's largest collection of works by Monet, and many by Morisot, Renoir, Pissarro, and their contemporaries.

One of Monet's best-known subjects – his water garden at Giverny – has been lovingly preserved.

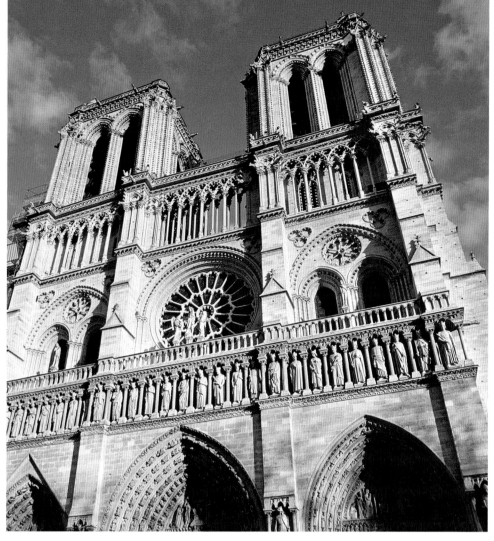

The sublime west front of Notre Dame in Paris incorporates several levels topped by two towers.

HIGHLIGHTS

▥ The nave in Amiens is supported by 126 slender pillars inside, and by a double row of **flying buttresses** outside. The **oak choir stalls** are carved with over 4,000 biblical, mythical, and real-life figures.

▥ In Reims, see the great **rose window** at sunset. The window in the last chapel at the rear of the cathedral, showing the Crucifixion and the sacrifice of Isaac, is by **Marc Chagall**.

▥ In Chartres, don't miss the **West Rose Window** showing the Last Judgment; the **Tree of Jesse**, illustrating Christ's genealogy; and the **Blue Virgin Window**.

▥ **Sainte-Chapelle**, in Paris, was described as a gateway to heaven for its beautiful proportions and exquisite stained glass.

FRANCE

Cathedrals of France

Built centuries ago in carved stone and richly colored stained glass, these Gothic masterpieces are still awe-inspiring.

This circular route around northern France takes in the region's resplendent Gothic cathedrals. With towering naves supported by flying buttresses, rib vaults, pointed arches, and rose windows—features that grew in popularity in the mid-12th century—each is a work of art. Beginning with Amiens, the largest, you ponder the feats of engineering and craftsmanship needed to create and embellish these towering buildings. Traveling via Laon to Reims brings you to the cathedral of angels, Notre-Dame de Reims, where the kings of France were crowned. At Strasbourg, France's tallest cathedral is distinguished by a single tower and pink sandstone carved as finely as lace. Heading west to Chartres, the greatest of all Gothic cathedrals comes into view across the plains. Its glorious stained glass covers 28,000 square feet (2,601 square meters). Notre Dame, in Paris, is a symbol of France and filled with history. Rouen, a masterpiece of delicate stone carving inside and out, completes the tour.

WHEN TO GO Year-round.

HOW LONG About 860 miles (1,384 km) using the most direct, intercity routes. Allow at least eight days.

PLANNING A France Rail Pass gives four days a month of unlimited travel. For groups of two or more, a France Saver Pass is even cheaper. A France Rail 'n Drive pass combines two days of rail travel with vouchers for two days of car rental.

INSIDE INFORMATION The stained-glass windows were created to teach stories and lessons from the Bible, and a good guide to religious and medieval symbolism will help you to "read" them.

WEBSITES tripsavvy.com/france-4139036, sacred-destinations.com, raileurope.com

ROMANIA

The Painted Monasteries of Moldavia

Be transported back in time by the brilliant blues of the frescoes,
the beauty of the countryside, and the chanting of the monks.

Their exterior walls alive with scenes of bibilical and historical events, the painted monasteries of Bucovina in northeastern Romania resemble the pages of illuminated manuscripts enlarged in scope and form. There are some 15 monasteries in the region, but most people visit Voronet, Humor, Moldovita, and Sucevita. They are drawn by the exquisite artistry of the frescoes that coat both exterior and interior walls in a vivid riot of imagery, although the buildings themselves are beautiful as well, and are surrounded by an unspoiled rural landscape. Voronet is perhaps the most spectacular of all; thanks to the quality of its frescoes, it is often called the Sistine Chapel of the East. Sucevita has a superb setting and is dramatically fortified, Moldovita is more isolated, smaller and quieter, while atmospheric Humor has a spectacular interior. These UNESCO World Heritage–listed ecclesiastical treasures mostly date from the 16th century and were built partly to cement Moldavia's expansion into the area and partly to rally the people—the images were intended to inspire the illiterate Orthodox Christian population facing conquest by the ever expansive Ottoman Turks. Today, the monasteries are fully functioning Orthodox churches, with several daily masses and an important role in the community. They also attract many pilgrims, most notably at Easter and on feast days.

WHEN TO GO Any time between April and October.

HOW LONG To get the most out of the area, stay for at least three days.

PLANNING This part of Romania is poorly served by public transportation and, if you are not on a guided tour, a car is the only practical way to see all the monasteries. If you are traveling independently, stay in Gura Humorului, very close to Voronet and Humor, or, if you want more comfort, in Suceava – the largest town in the area. Week-long walking tours are also available.

INSIDE INFORMATION The monasteries have nominal opening hours, often 8 a.m.–8 p.m. with mass at least four times a day, but you are unlikely to be refused entry at any time. All have admission charges. Dress respectfully – no shorts, and women are expected to cover their heads.

WEBSITES beyondtheforest.com, romanianmonasteries.org

EUROPE

HIGHLIGHTS

▓ Admire the vivid colors and artistry of **Voronet's frescoes**, notably the "Last Judgment." The dominant blue in the frescoes is due to the use of **lapis lazuli**.

▓ Wonder at **Sucevita's exterior frescoes**, especially the "Ladder to Paradise," They are protected from the elements by massive eaves.

▓ Sucevita also has a **museum** containing a fine collection of ecclesiastical silverware, books, and illuminated manuscripts.

▓ Moldovita's brilliant **Tree of Jesse**, has been described as "a parchment dipped in blue."

▓ Hike through the **glorious landscape** of beech woods and hills between the Humor and Sucevita, or Sucevita and Moldovita, monasteries.

▓ Visit one of the monasteries on a **feast day**, when pilgrims and local residents gather for a celebration.

Opposite: The exterior frescoes of the 16th-century monastery church at Humor glow with brilliant blues and red-browns. Above left: The monastery complex at Humor includes a defensive tower. Above right: The fresh colors and fine detail of the frescoes can be seen in this detail from the "Last Judgment" at Voronet.

Vienna is filled with tributes to the music of Johann Strauss, including this statue in the city park.

CZECHIA   AUSTRIA   HUNGARY

Musical Journey to Central Europe

Walk in the footsteps of great composers, explore their homes, and hear their music played by the world's finest orchestras.

Visit the heart of Europe, where the masters of European classical music lived. Here, you can glimpse the cultures that inspired them and hear their works in some of the most stunning concert halls and opera houses in the world. Starting in the city of Prague, in Czechia, seek out the Dvořák Museum, the composer's home until his death in 1901, where evening concerts are held with musicians in period costume. Then move on to Vienna, the Austrian capital, where Beethoven was taught by Haydn, and the waltz king Johann Strauss gave the world the "Blue Danube." Strauss, Haydn, Mozart, Schubert, and Beethoven all lived here, and you can visit museums dedicated to each of them. Mozart's birthplace, Salzburg, is three hours from Vienna. The highlight of the year is the Salzburg Festival, beginning in late July, where the world's most prominent musicians gather to perform in the theaters and opera house. Finally, in Budapest, Hungary, visit the Academy of Music, whose Grand Hall is the premier concert hall in the city and seats 1,200.

WHEN TO GO Any time.

HOW LONG Two to three weeks.

PLANNING This is a journey to make by road as rail connections are patchy. Buy a Eurolines bus pass. Eurolines can also arrange accommodation and car rental.

INSIDE INFORMATION Avoid wearing jeans when you attend a concert.

WEBSITES praguecitytourism.cz, wien.info, salzburg.info, budapestinfo.hu

HIGHLIGHTS

▥ In Prague, hear an **afternoon concert** at the 18th-century Bertramka Villa, where Mozart completed *Don Giovanni*.

▥ In Vienna, the highlight of the calendar is the **New Year's Concert** of the Vienna Philharmonic Orchestra. If you want to waltz, **Carnival** (November–February) is the time to go, as balls are held every weekend.

▥ In Budapest, you can attend a performance at the **Opera House**, where Liszt and Mahler conducted (the season is September–June), or the Art Nouveau **Liszt Academy of Music** (closed July and August).

ITALY | GREECE

Venetian Legacy

*This journey combines beautiful Venetian architecture
and the sun-soaked islands of Greece and Cyprus.*

From the 12th to 18th centuries, the Venetians controlled a large trading empire—including parts of Greece—from their city-state of canals and lagoons. When they were finally driven out, they left behind a rich architectural legacy of mansions, civic buildings, fortresses, and arsenals. Begin in Venice, where the Doge's Palace and the palaces of wealthy merchants along the Grand Canal attest to the affluence and power of the city at that time. Then cross to Corfu (Kérkira) and follow the Venetian trail down the coast of Greece to Cyprus. Corfu was occupied by Venice for 400 years, and the mansions and town hall in the labrynthine old area of Corfu town are strongly influenced by the Venetian style. The nearby islands of Kefaloniá and Zákinthos also have extensive Venetian ruins. Náfplio on the Peloponnisos was the Venetian capital on mainland Greece, and here you can explore the harbor fortifications and wander the old part of the town. Crete was another important Venetian base: in Chania, you can walk around the old Venetian harbor wall to the lighthouse and discover some stylish bars and restaurants on the way; while the fortress at Réthimno was one of the largest the Venetians built. The journey ends on Cyprus, where the Venetians fortified several towns in order to defend the island against regular raids by the Ottoman Turks.

WHEN TO GO Year-round.

HOW LONG The full distance from Venice to northern Cyprus is 1,310 miles (2,108 km) and requires at least a week.

PLANNING To make this journey, you may need to charter a private yacht, although several places can also be reached by Greece's efficient ferry service.

INSIDE INFORMATION The best way to enter northern Cyprus (claimed by Turkey) is by land, via southern Cyprus. Dock there, and cross the border on foot or by car.

WEBSITES enit.it/en, ferries.gr/booking

HIGHLIGHTS

▌ The **Doge's Palace** in Venice, built of pink marble in intricate Gothic style, is one of the city's most spectacular and important buildings.

▌ **Palamidi** in Náfplio is the largest Venetian fortress on the Greek mainland and still dominates the town from its cliff-top position.

▌ **Iráklio** in Crete is still home to a Venetian arsenal and bastions that illustrate the empire's one-time dominance in the region.

▌ Both Famagusta (Ammochostos) and Kyrenia (Keryneia) in northern Cyprus reveal lingering **Venetian influences**, with the remains of fortresses and city walls.

The ruined fortress of Palamidi in Náfplio provides an excellent view of the harbor and the fortified island of Bourtzi, which was also part of the Venetians' defences.

The Basilica Palladiana in Vicenza is one of the architect's masterpieces. He worked on it for most of his life.

Palladio's Italy

A master of symmetry and harmonious proportion, Palladio created architectural gems that can still be visited today.

A generous sprinkling of rural villas, created by the 16th-century Renaissance architect Andrea Palladio, graces the lush Veneto, its rolling hills and vineyards framed by the Dolomites. This area was ruled by the republic of Venice, whose population needed a local food source. The Venetians built villas from which estates could be run, and Palladio set the gold standard for their design: classical and symmetrical, utilizing the forms of ancient Greek and Roman architecture. Begin at Vicenza, Palladio's birthplace just west of Venice, which he transformed into a fine Renaissance city. The road running south, then east, via the Monti Berici is dotted with his creations, such as the Villa Pisani at Bagnolo, set on the Guà River. A separate route from Vicenza leads north to the most famous Palladio gem of all, the Villa Barbaro at Maser. Contemplate this, and the nearby Villa Emo at Fanzolo, and you can see the inspiration for the design of the U.S. Capitol.

WHEN TO GO May to September, to be sure of entry to the main sights. Spring and early summer are the best times to avoid intense Veneto heat and see the countryside and gardens at their best.

HOW LONG Vicenza to Villa Foscari is about 80 miles (129 km). Allow a day for winding roads and relaxed viewing. Vicenza to Villa Barbaro is about 30 miles (48 km); allow at least half a day.

PLANNING The villas do not follow a uniform timetable, and some open only from May to September or October. If you stay over, you can complete the experience by staying in a villa in the countryside.

INSIDE INFORMATION In summer visit Villa Foscari by boat from the Brenta Riviera, the original route between Padua (Padova) and Venice. This watery thoroughfare is flanked by grand residential villas.

WEBSITES boglewood.com/palladio, whc.unesco.org/en/list/712, tours-italy.com

HIGHLIGHTS

▥ The **Villa Rotonda** is within walking distance of Vicenza. It is Palladio's most influential design, with a temple portico on each side and a central dome inspired by the Pantheon in Rome.

▥ Interiors of **Villa Foscari** (also known as La Malcontenta), on the Brenta Riviera near Venice, have **frescoes** by Palladio's contemporaries, Giambattista Zelotti and Battista Franco.

▥ The Villa Barbaro has ravishing illusionistic frescoes by **Paolo Veronese**. The villa is a perfect example of Palladio's philosophy of **balance**: the central dwelling area is fronted by Ionic columns, and the farm buildings extend symmetrically on either side with a series of arches ending in dovecotes.

EUROPE

ITALY

Renaissance Italy

Take a few days, or weeks, to savor Tuscany,
the heart of the Italian Renaissance.

The Renaissance began in Tuscany, and to walk around the center of Florence is, quite simply, to take a peek at the rebirth of the West. The city flourished during the 14th century, and its wealthy residents funded the building of elegant piazzas, churches decorated with fresco cycles, and palaces that now house fine collections of Renaissance art. At its center is the Duomo, the cathedral dedicated to the Madonna of Florence. Its exquisitely crafted dome was designed by Filippo Brunelleschi, who was one of the founders of the Renaissance style. In the Uffizi Gallery, considered by many people to be the greatest art museum in the world, you can see paintings by Giotto, Botticelli, Leonardo da Vinci, Raphael, Michelangelo, and countless other Renaissance artists. Then tear yourself away and travel south to Siena through the classic Tuscan landscape of rolling hills and hilltop towns and villages, still looking much as it did in the paintings of Piero della Francesca. Siena flourished during the Renaissance, though its central square, the graceful Piazza del Campo, dates from the 12th century. From Siena, travel to Rome, where you can see masterpieces of the High Rennaissance by its defining artists—Michelangelo, Raphael, and Da Vinci.

WHEN TO GO Spring and fall have the most comfortable temperatures.

HOW LONG This trip can be made in three days, with one day in each city, but better yet, take a week or two, to allow time to wander the streets, piazzas, galleries, and gardens of each city, and to explore the Tuscan countryside.

PLANNING Tickets for trains and buses can be bought at the time of travel. Car rental is best arranged before arriving in Italy.

INSIDE INFORMATION Book entrance to major sights a day in advance, as lines to get in on the day can be very long.

WEBSITES enit.it/en, italiantourism.com, tuscanytours.com

HIGHLIGHTS

▥ In Florence, explore some of the lesser known museums and churches, such as the private collection of the Medici family in the **Pitti Palace** and Fra Angelico's frescoes in the **Convent of San Marco**.

▥ From the top of the Campanile, enjoy **fabulous views** of Florence.

▥ In Siena's **Palazzo Pubblico**, you can find the **early Renaissance mural**, "Good Government," by Ambrogio Lorenzetti.

▥ In the Vatican Museum, wonder at Michelangelo's frescoes in the **Sistine Chapel**, and Raphael's in the **Raphael Room**. And don't miss Michelangelo's "Pietà" in St. Peter's Basilica.

While the circular structure of Florence reflects its Roman-era origins as a garrison settlement, much of its current-day architecture dates to the Renaissance.

Top 10 Journeys Into the Past

These unique destinations allow you to step back in time and experience a way of life far removed from the 21st century.

❶ PLYMOUTH SETTLEMENT, MASSACHUSETTS

Tread the creaky planks of the *Mayflower*, a reproduction of the ship that set sail from Plymouth, England, in 1620, and walk around the streets of timber-framed houses in the 1627 Pilgrim Village. Visit a Native American house made of reed panels, with its furs, open fire, and woven mats. Hear why the pilgrims left England and what the native peoples thought about their arrival in their own words.

PLANNING Tours on foot (by tin lantern at night), bus, or train. seeplymouth.com

❷ GAIMÁN, CHUBUT TERRITORY, PATAGONIA, ARGENTINA

In 1865 a group of Welsh settlers who wanted to escape English domination carved out Y Wladfa (the Homeland) on the inhospitable pampas at the foot of the Andes. Today, Gaimán feels as if it was plucked from the Welsh hills and put down carefully in South America. Walk the idyllic quiet streets, past parks and chapels, eat homemade pastries in one of the teahouses, and then head off to see a penguin colony.

PLANNING Pick up a sightseeing tour or rent a car in Trelew. Gaimán is 11 miles (18 km) away. patagonia-argentina.com/en

❸ CORDILLERA URUBAMBA MOUNTAINS, PERU

Leave the 14th-century Inca trail and hike up into the snow-capped mountains north of Cusco, to villages where the people still herd alpaca and llama, farm the Andean slopes, and weave superb, brightly colored textiles. Return to the trail via Puma town (Pumamarca) through a series of grand agricultural terraces to visit the impressive ruins of Ollan-taytambo, a village where Inca streets are still in use.

PLANNING Guided tour recommended. You will need to be fit. inkanatura.com

❹ KIRIWINA ISLAND, PAPUA NEW GUINEA

Hear the calls of birds of paradise on the edge of an orchid-strewn rain forest beside a turquoise sea. Watch island villagers as they fish, garden, cook yam, build huts, and carve rosewood and ebony—just as they have done for centuries. Join in the storytelling, sing and dance on the beach, and then sleep on a woven mat in a hut without electricity.

PLANNING Kiriwina is the largest of the Trobriand Islands. The airport is a 15-minute drive from Losuia. Organized tour recommended. www.em.com.pg

The Sami people of Lapland still follow their reindeer-herding tradition. A woman in traditional costume and carrying a cast antler attends a roundup.

❺ GORKHI-TERELJ NATIONAL PARK, MONGOLIA

Visit a Mongolian family living in a *ger*, and stay in one of these traditional huts. Walk for miles through untamed landscape and spot brown bear and some of the 250 species of bird found in the park. For a longer trek, go 50 miles (80 km) upstream from Gorkhi-Terelj to Khagiin Khar Nuur, a 66-ft (20 m) deep glacial lake.

PLANNING About 50 miles (80 km) from the capital Ulaanbaatar. Guided tour recommended. Ideal for trekking or horse/camel riding. visitmongolia.com

❻ SAUTOSJOHKKA, SWEDEN

Travel by snowmobile across a frozen lake into a dazzling white forest to the soft sound of husky paws on snow to meet the Sami, the indigenous people of Lapland. Sit by the open fire of a Sami tent and eat smoked reindeer with cranberry jam and homebaked bread. All this can be done using the astonishing Ice Hotel, built anew every winter from ice bricks and complete with sauna, as a base.

PLANNING Organized tour only. icehotel.com

❼ LAKE PEIPSI, ESTONIA

The serenity of the sandy shores, thick reeds, and sandstone cliffs hasn't changed since the Russian Old Believers arrived in the late 17th century, fleeing religious persecution. Church services are still conducted in sonorous Old Church Slavonic in little wooden churches with onion domes. The Museum of the Old Believers (in the schoolhouse at Kolkja) has beautiful embroidered costumes and pink caftan shrouds.

PLANNING Arrange a museum visit at the tourist office at Tartu 22 miles (35 km) away. Public transportation is possible, but car rental is best. visitestonia.com/en/where-to-go/south-estonia/peipsi-area

❽ ETHNOGRAPHIC OPEN-AIR MUSEUM, RIGA, LATVIA

Experience the tough, self-sufficient life of 19th-century Latvian peasants. Stroll in the tall forest by the lake, and visit wooden farmhouses, windmills, fishermen's cottages, churches, and kitchen gardens. Watch craftsmen at work and enjoy traditional hospitality at the tavern.

PLANNING 8 miles (13 km) from Riga. Book guided tours in advance. English-language plan essential. brivdabasmuzejs.lv/en

❾ GRŪTAS PARK, DRUSKININKAI, LITHUANIA

Opened in 2001, this superbly landscaped park is the last resting place of a collection of Soviet-era statues, including those of Lenin, Stalin, and famous Lithuanian communists. Watched over by guard towers and surrounded by barbed wire, the statues resemble prisoners in the Soviet gulag camps.

PLANNING 75 miles (121 km) from Vilnius. Hire a car or take bus No. 2 from the bus station. grutoparkas.lt/en_us

❿ SINAI DESERT, EGYPT

Take a safari to the heart of the spectacular Sinai Desert and spend time with the Bedouin. Learn how to survive in the mountainous terrain, ride camels, sleep in Bedouin tents, and bake flat bread on open fires.

PLANNING Strictly organized tours allow you to explore the area by foot. bedouin-safari-dahab.com

Romanesque Churches

The village churches of the Vall de Boí are proof of the cultural interchange that took place across the Pyrenees in medieval times.

EUROPE

The hidden Vall de Boí in the Spanish Pyrenees is a magical place of high pastures, clear streams, and tiny villages, hemmed in by the peaks of the Parc Nacional d'Aigües Tortes. Yet it is the valley's ancient villages of Boí, Taull, Erill la Vall, Barruera, Durro, Cardet, and Coll—some little more than a huddle of stoutly built houses of native gray stone—that make it special, for each includes at least one remarkable church. Dating from the 11th and 12th centuries, the churches form a unique treasury of Romanesque architecture. This style spread through Europe along the major pilgrimage routes and was characterized by thick walls, round arches, square towers, and barrel vaulting. While the tall towers and slate roofs of the churches are distinctive, some also have strikingly colorful interiors, decorated with murals of biblical scenes. Perhaps the most stunning is Sant Climent de Taull, with its three naves separated by columns, and its six-tier bell tower adorned with blind arcades and pilasters. Barruera and Durro are good bases for exploring the Vall de Boí—or find a house or apartment in another of the ancient, tiny villages.

WHEN TO GO Any time of year, although May to September is best (heavy snow is possible between December and March).

HOW LONG Allow three to seven days to explore all the churches and the surrounding countryside.

PLANNING The nearest main town is Veilha. Public transportation is limited. The route linking the villages is no more than 12 miles (19 km) long from start to finish, so energetic walkers can cover the valley on foot.

INSIDE INFORMATION Some hotels rent out bicycles.

WEBSITE aralleida.cat/en

The churches are among the purest surviving examples of the Romanesque style. The pristine setting adds to the delight of a visit.

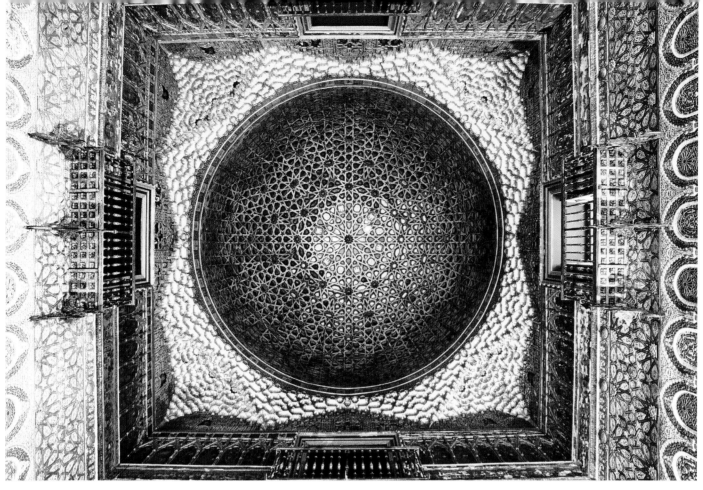

The rich decoration in the interior of the Alcázar in Sevilla includes this stunning gilded wooden dome.

SPAIN

Moorish Spain

Explore the wonderful intricacies of Islamic architecture and design in the heart of southern Spain.

From the 8th century, the Moors from North Africa ruled southern Spain, which they called Al-Andalus and we now call Andalusia. They irrigated the dry plains and planted new crops: pomegranates, oranges, lemons, apricots, saffron, sugar, and rice. For some 400 years the region was the most civilized and prosperous in Europe. From the hilltop town of Ronda, famous for its precipitous gorge, you can trace a semi-circle via Sevilla and Córdoba to Granada that takes in the most important Moorish sights. In Sevilla, the narrow winding streets, low white houses with balconies, and fountain-cooled courtyards are classic features of Arab design. Córdoba was the Moorish capital for 250 years. With 70 libraries, it was a beacon of scholarship in science, medicine, philosophy, and music, and its mosque, Mezquita—now the cathedral—was famed as Europe's largest and most beautiful holy building. As Andalusia was reconquered by the Catholic monarchy, Granada became the capital of the surviving Moorish kingdom. Today the Albaicín, or Arab quarter, thrives, its maze of alleyways lined with bakeries, grocery stores, and cafés. Wind up here, at the Mirador (viewpoint) de San Nicolas, to see the Alhambra against a backdrop of the Sierra Nevada.

WHEN TO GO Year-round.

HOW LONG About 150 miles (241 km). Allow three or four days to make the most of the cities.

PLANNING Wear lightweight clothes and comfortable shoes, and make sure you pack long-sleeved clothing to wear to religious sites.

INSIDE INFORMATION In summer, long lines are inevitable at the major sights. You can book tickets in advance at tourist offices or, for the Alhambra, at ticketmaster.es. Your visit will entail a walk of about 3 miles (5 km), so plan your tour with the help of a guidebook.

WEBSITES andalucia.org, alcazarsevilla.org, alhambradegranada.org/en

HIGHLIGHTS

▓ Sevilla's **Alcázar** is richly adorned with stucco arches, and the gardens are filled with refreshing fountains and citrus groves.

▓ Córdoba's cathedral, **Mezquita**, has a forest of double-tiered arches and a superb mihrab (prayer niche).

▓ Granada's **Alhambra** is a complex of Moorish palaces surrounded by pools and gardens. The Alcazaba, the oldest part of the fortress, offers spectacular views from its summit.

▓ Granada's **Albaicín** district is full of Moroccan tearooms, where you can enjoy a cup of mint tea.

Classical Greece

*The glory that was Greece awaits you in Athens
and its surrounding sites.*

Above the dusty sidewalks and chaotic traffic of narrow Athenian streets rises the Acropolis, the hill on which stands the serene Parthenon, temple to Athena—a monument to timelessness amid the transitory bustle of Greece's capital. In the contrast between this precise marble construction and the rough, rocky mound on which it stands, you are struck by what seems like an attempt to conquer nature itself. The next morning, board a bus and bounce along the coast road, crossing the sheer escarpments of the Corinth Canal and following the shoreline to the great theater of Epidavros. Row upon row of stone steps are hewn into the hillside, leading down to the distant stage. Beyond are olive trees, the rocky coast, and the shimmering sea. A short journey brings you to Mycenae, with its imposing Lion Gate and the tomb of Agamemnon, before you race through the late afternoon heat, between the steep hills of the Peloponnisos, to arrive at Olympia in the twilight. The following day, explore the sandy tracks and temples at this birthplace of the Olympic Games, before heading north and crossing back onto the Greek mainland and a short ride east to the final destination, Delphi, where a priestess once delivered the oracles of the sun god Apollo.

WHEN TO GO In the summer months for the Epidavros festival, held in conjunction with the Hellenic festival when international artists perform in the ancient Greek theaters. Your visit will be cooler and less crowded if you avoid July and August.

HOW LONG Three days will allow enough time to take in the top sites. Add a few more days for a more leisurely experience and to ensure that you have time in Athens to visit museums and the Acropolis.

PLANNING Many travel companies offer deals that include all these sites. If you travel independently, however, you will have more control over the amount of time you spend at each site.

INSIDE INFORMATION Take sun protection and bottled water everywhere you go.

WEBSITES visitgreece.gr/en, culture.gr, greekfestival.gr/en

HIGHLIGHTS

■ Climb the well-worn path up the Acropolis to the **Parthenon.**

■ **Stand in the orchestra** (the stage area) at Epidavros and declaim to the vast auditorium. The carefully engineered acoustics enabled every audience member to hear clearly, even at the very back.

■ If you are visiting in the summer, do not miss the **Epidavros festival,** which features a selection of ancient Greek plays performed in the original language.

■ In the museum at **Delphi** is the great **Naxian Sphinx,** a stone statue of the monster that the hero Oedipus outwitted to save the city of Thebes.

The Parthenon in Athens is unsurpassed as an example of the beauty, serenity, and romanticism of the architecture of ancient Greece.

As the Mediterranean Sea laps against the southern coast of Malta, remnants of the ancient temple complex of Mnajdra bask in the midday heat.

| MALTA |

Megalithic Earth Goddess Temples

Erected more than 5,000 years ago, Malta's megalithic shrines preserve some of the world's oldest architecture.

Although legend holds that giants built the megalithic temples of Malta and Gozo islands, it was ancient islanders who erected the Ġgantija (Giants' Tower) and other shrines that comprise this World Heritage site in the Mediterranean Sea. The discovery of the Sleeping Lady and the Venus of Malta leads modern researchers to believe that an earth goddess was among the major deities worshipped at these shrines. Constructed during the 4th and 3rd millennium B.C., the six temples—Ġgantija, Tarxien, Ħaġar Qim, Mnajdra, Skorba, and Ta' Ħaġrat—are among the world's oldest freestanding structures, as well as an expression of how an advanced culture developed in Malta centuries before mainland Europe or the Middle East. A supreme statement of Neolithic architecture, the twin Ġgantija temples on Gozo were built several hundred years before Stonehenge of sturdy coralline limestone. The other five sites are scattered around Malta island, and with their trademark spirals and decorative stonework, the four Tarxien temples are especially handsome, with fascinating examples of prehistoric art.

WHEN TO GO Avoid the dry, hot summers to make the most of exploring the Maltese countryside.

HOW LONG At least a week to take in all six temples and Malta's other historic and natural attractions.

PLANNING With good roads and light traffic outside of Valletta, it's easy enough to self-drive around Malta. Reaching Ġgantija requires a 20-minute ride on the ferry between Malta and Gozo islands. Several local operators offer guided temple tours. However, Gozo is normally done as a separate all-day tour.

INSIDE INFORMATION Before touring the temples, visit the National Museum of Archeology in Valletta to see the Sleeping Lady, Venus of Malta, and other artifacts gathered from the temple sites.

WEBSITES visitmalta.com/en, heritagemalta.org

HIGHLIGHTS

▥ Explore the new Interpretive Center at Ġgantija for insights in **Neolithic life** on Malta and Gozo.

▥ An **elevated walkway** at Tarxien provides the best views of the spirals, farm animals, and other stone reliefs that adorn the temples.

▥ Perched above Malta's south coast, Ħaġar Qim and Mnajdra are easily combined with a visit to the nearby **Blue Grotto**.

▥ Check into a **farmstay** or B&B in Xaghra village near the Ġgantija archeological park for a taste of Gozo rural life.

EUROPE

Rock Churches of Cappadocia

Concealed in the strange landscape of central Turkey are hundreds of rock-hewn and beautifully decorated Byzantine churches.

Cappadocia in central Turkey is famous for its extraordinary rock formations and its natural beauty. It was also an important center of early Christianity, and hidden away in quiet valleys are hundreds of churches hewn out of the local volcanic rock. The best-known group of churches are in the Göreme Open Air Museum, and include the Apple, Snake, Dark, and Sandal churches. Clamber up a rickety ladder to a dark entrance in the rocks, step inside, and your gaze is met by the faces of saints decorating walls, arches, and pillars carved by local Christians some 700–1,300 years ago. The lower sections of some columns have been worn away so they hang from the ceilings, and domes hover unsupported. Some of the churches are decorated with simple geometric patterns; others have frescoes of the lives of Jesus and the saints. Just northeast of Göreme is the Zelve Valley, which was home to one of the largest communities in the area. Houses, dovecotes, and churches can all be seen carved out of the richly colored rock. South of Göreme is the Soganli Valley, which has 150 churches with frescoes dating from the 9th to 13th centuries. The 10-mile (16 km) long Ihlara Valley, to the southwest of Göreme, forms an extraordinary cleft in the ground. It is a beautiful green canyon lined with ancient concealed Byzantine churches and rock dwellings.

WHEN TO GO Spring and fall: mid-April–early June and September–October are the best times to avoid the intense summer heat and crowds. If there's snow in winter, the place glistens magically and captivates all the more.

HOW LONG Allow at least three days to see the main highlights or a week to explore the area in detail.

PLANNING The best way to see the area is by renting a car, although bus and minibus services operate from the local towns. The area is well supplied with hotels and pensions, including some built into the rock cones, with cave-style rooms. Organized tours are also available.

INSIDE INFORMATION If driving, buy a road map in advance, as detailed maps are difficult to find outside Istanbul. Visit the sites early in the morning to avoid crowds. If you use a tour operator, make sure they do not take you on endless tours of carpet and pottery shops.

WEBSITES middleearthtravel.com, great-adventures.com

HIGHLIGHTS

▦ In the Göreme Open Air Museum, the 11th-century **Dark Church** has brilliant paintings. **Buckle Church** is the largest church in the valley.

▦ Pasabag, near the Zelve Valley, has some of the most striking rock formations known as **rock cones**.

▦ Explore the underground city of **Derinkuyu**, south of Göreme, which provided refuge for the local population possibly from Hittite times to the rise of the Turks. Complete with dormitories, dining areas, storerooms, chapels, wells, and air shafts, it could shelter several thousand people for months at a time.

▦ Take a day's **hike** through the beautiful Ihlara Valley.

▦ A **balloon ride** provides stunning views of the area, with changing light and shadows on the rock formations.

Opposite: Geometric patterns mark the entrance to one of the many rock churches in the Göreme Valley.
Above left: The churches are hidden away in the strange landscape of rock cones. Above right: The paintings in many of the churches are well preserved due to the darkness of the interiors.

The death mask of Tutankhamun, made from beaten gold and precious stones, is one of Cairo's many treasures.

EGYPT

Ancient Egypt

See the treasures of ancient Egypt in Cairo, and visit the cities and temples of this once-thriving civilization.

Dusty, busy, bustling Cairo is home to the Museum of Egyptian Antiquities, the longtime treasure-house of the ancient Egyptian civilization. And, on some days, looking west toward the city's desert fringes, you can see the pyramids of Giza through the haze—4,500 years old and never ceasing to amaze with their vastness. Close by is Saqqara, the vast necropolis of the ancient capital of Memphis, with its step pyramid and painted tombs. The other capital of ancient Egypt was Thebes (Luxor), 310 miles (499 km) to the south. Luxor's temple was completed by Pharaoh Ramses II and is connected by a processional way to the vast Temple of Karnak. On the western shore of the Nile is the Valley of the Kings, where royal tombs lie buried among the Theban hills. You can begin a Nile cruise at Luxor, visiting a string of ancient temples at the water's edge on a journey south to Isna, Idfu, Kôm Ombo, and Aswân. From Aswân, you can take a trip to the Temple of Ramses at Abu Simbel.

WHEN TO GO Any time of year. The peak time for Nile cruises is December to February. In the hottest part of summer (June to August), temperatures can exceed 104°F (40°C).

HOW LONG The distance from Cairo to Aswân is 560 miles (901 km), and it is an additional 174 miles (280 km) to Abu Simbel. A trip lasting 14–17 days is ideal, but you could cover the ground in a week.

PLANNING The principal sites are in two locations: in and around Cairo and in the south around Luxor. You can travel between the two by air, rail, road, or river.

INSIDE INFORMATION For a touch of historic grandeur, stay at the Mena House Oberoi, a former hunting lodge, by the pyramids; or at the Sofitel Old Cataract Hotel, Aswân, built in Moorish style in the 1890s.

WEBSITES egypt.travel, touregypt.net, audleytravel.com

HIGHLIGHTS

▥ The Museum of Egyptian Antiquities in Cairo was for decades home to the **Treasures of Tutankhamun**. Today it feeds the visitor's imagination with everyday objects that made ancient Egypt a living, thriving civilization, while its treasures now reside at the Grand Egyptian Museum in Giza.

▥ The **pyramids of Giza** are the sole survivors of the Seven Wonders of the Ancient World.

▥ The **Great Hypostyle Hall** in the Temple of Amun, Karnak, consists of a tightly packed forest of 134 hieroglyph-covered columns.

▥ The temple at **Abu Simbel** is fronted by four colossal statues of Ramses II. It was raised to the present site in the 1960s to save it from the flooding of Lake Nasser when the Aswân High Dam was built.

Zulu Culture Tour

*Discover the distinctive history and lifestyle
of one of southern Africa's most colorful nations.*

Beginning in Durban, visit the Killie Campbell Africana Museum for an introduction to Zulu culture before you head off to the historical sites and present-day villages in the surrounding area. Outside Durban, perched on a hill overlooking the Mhlathuze River, is the living museum of Shakaland at Eshowe. Here you can find out about the Zulu way of life, social system, dancing, and artisan skills. Then move on to eMakhosini, or the Valley of the Kings, between Eshowe and Ulundi. This is the birthplace of Shaka Zulu—warrior king and founder of the Zulu nation—and the burial site of seven Zulu kings. The KwaZulu Cultural Museum houses an outstanding collection of historical and cultural artifacts. While in Eshowe, take a minibus taxi to King Dinuzulu Township, where you can walk through the streets and chat with shopkeepers and passersby to find out about the modern, urban Zulu way of life. To become fully absorbed in contemporary rural culture, and to appreciate the hospitality of the Zulu people, visit a village in the Valley of a Thousand Hills to the northwest of Durban, where you may be invited to stay with a Zulu family.

WHEN TO GO Year-round. If you want to go to the Zulu Royal Reed Dance, you need to be there in early September, and in mid-September for King Shaka Day.

HOW LONG At least five days to learn about the Zulu culture, visit historical sites, and experience contemporary Zulu life (make sure you allow time to be an overnight guest in a village or township).

PLANNING You can visit the established Zulu cultural sites on your own by car (car rental in Durban is easily found), but it is best to visit the villages with a local guide to get the most out of the visit and to help in translation; Zululand Eco-Adventures can organize this for you.

INSIDE INFORMATION Along Route T4 in the Valley of a Thousand Hills, stop at Isithumba Village opposite the Indunakazi Store, where visitors are warmly welcomed.

WEBSITES sa-venues.com, zulu.org.za

HIGHLIGHTS

▌ In early September, the **Royal Reed Dance** (Umkhosi woMhlanga) at the KwaNyokeni Palace in Nongoma, near Eshowe, is a colorful procession of Zulu maidens accompanied by singing and dancing.

▌ Visit Dumazulu village, in the north of KwaZulu-Natal province, to experience the **traditional way of life**.

▌ **King Shaka Day** is a vibrant celebration held in mid-September showcasing the living connection between present and past kings.

▌ Visit a **Sangoma**, or **divine healer**, for the "scattering of the bones" to read your past and future.

Zulu dancers in tribal dress perform at Dumazulu Village in the heart of Zululand.

AUSTRALIA

Arnhem Land Cultural Safari

The world's oldest living culture thrives in the northernmost region of Australia's Northern Territory—this is the true outback.

Arnhem Land is one of the last unspoiled areas of Aboriginal culture and society in Australia. About 20,000 indigenous people inhabit the region, representing a number of different tribes and language groups, and tourism is restricted to enable environmental conservation and traditional ways of life to continue. The best way to get there is to drive or fly from Darwin, Cairns, or Jabiru to Mount Borradaile. The area around Borradaile has some of the most impressive examples of Aboriginal rock art. Dating as far back as 40,000 years, the paintings depict scenes from everyday life and the Dreamtime—the time of the creation of all things, according to the Aboriginal belief system, when the land, plants, and animals were given their present form. Mount Borradaile is also in the heart of an intricate ecosystem of subtropical savanna and home to abundant wildlife, such as saltwater crocodiles, wallabies, and turtles, and plantlife unique to the area. Farther north is the glorious Cobourg Peninsula and Garig Gunak Barlu National Park, with its secluded mangrove swamps and white beaches, rich in marine and birdlife. The clear waters of the Arafura Sea are excellent for snorkeling and diving. From here you can head farther into East Arnhem Land, one of the last remaining great wilderness areas in Australia, or travel south to Oenpelli, a settlement known for its distinctive Aboriginal bark paintings and rock art at Injalak Hill.

WHEN TO GO Arnhem Land has a tropical climate, and is best visited during the dry season (May to October), when temperatures range from 59° to 80°F (15° to 27°C). Driving is not recommended during the wet season (November to April) as the roads become impassable.

HOW LONG One week.

PLANNING The area can be reached from Darwin. Licensed tour operators can take you on an organized itinerary. All tourists must have written permission to enter Arnhem Land, as it is owned by the indigenous population. This can be organized by your tour operator or by applying directly to the Northern Land Council (nlc.org.au).

INSIDE INFORMATION Driving conditions in the area can be difficult, even in the dry season, and is only recommended for people experienced in this type of terrain.

WEBSITE northernterritory.com

HIGHLIGHTS

▓ At Mount Borradaile, wonder at the 18-ft (5.5 m) long **Rainbow Serpent,** an important symbol in Aboriginal culture since the Dreamtime.

▓ **Sit by a campfire** under the Southern Cross and listen to stories of the Dreamtime. This is also the perfect time to enjoy some bush tucker, especially the tasty witchetty grubs!

▓ **Fish** for barramundi and **swim** in billabongs and creeks—check with your guide about crocodiles first.

▓ Watch an authentic **corroboree** (sacred ceremony), a central part of the Aboriginal connection with the land and their ancestors.

▓ Visit **Aboriginal art** and **craft** centers, and take some original works home with you.

▓ Photograph your **first crocodile** in Cooper Creek, near Mount Borradaile.

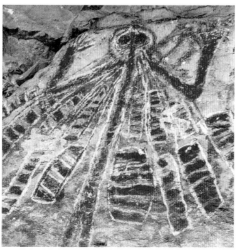

Opposite: This painting of a white kangaroo at KarbenadjarInglawe is done in the traditional x-ray style, with internal bones and organs visible. Above left: Pandanus leaves are used for weaving colorful baskets. Above right: The wealth of rock art, such as this at Injalak Hill, provides inspiration for artists working today.

Chapter 6

IN GOURMET HEAVEN

For those who appreciate the pleasures of the table, there are no happier reasons to travel than the chance to explore the world's great culinary traditions, to sample new dishes and exotic flavors at source, or to visit the vineyards, distilleries, and breweries where grapes and grains are turned—by ancient alchemy and modern skills—into legendary wines, whiskey, and beers. Pleasing as they are to the senses, these are also voyages of intellectual discovery. Every kitchen and every cuisine tells a story about landscape, climate, history, and culture. On the menu you will find tours of the world's great wine regions and pilgrimages to legendary shrines of haute cuisine. But be prepared for more down-to-earth adventures: a trip to the spectacular food counters of Japanese department stores, a bowl of cilantro-scented noodle soup in a lively Vietnamese street market, spicy Cajun sausage at a food festival in Louisiana, and face-to-face encounters with the farmers, fishermen, bakers, and cooks who transform nature's bounty into a thousand gustatory delights.

A wonderful array of fruit is laid out on a market stall to tempt passing customers. Enjoyment of the flavors and textures of natural ingredients are at the heart of all the great cuisines of the world.

New York Deli Tour

Enjoy pastrami or corned beef on rye with a dill pickle and other deli treats. Then walk off the calories exploring Manhattan.

A large Jewish population is responsible for some of New York's best-known food specialties, all available for sampling in the city's legendary delicatessens. A deli tour easily can be combined with sightseeing. Savor a breakfast of bagels and lox, or other smoked fish, at Barney Greengrass, "The Sturgeon King," on the Upper West Side, then visit the American Museum of Natural History. In midtown, have blintzes (crepes filled with sweetened cottage cheese, sautéed, and served with sour cream or apple sauce) or a mile-high pastrami on rye with a dill pickle at the 2nd Ave Deli. Shopping at Macy's? Fortify yourself with a bowl of matzo ball soup at Ben's Kosher Deli, home of the Matzo Ball Eating Contest. The old Jewish Lower East Side is fast gentrifying, but Katz's Delicatessen is still going strong on Houston Street, along with several traditional take-out delis. The Lower East Side is home to more than just delis. Other sources of traditional Jewish food are Yonha Schimmel's Knish Bakery on Houston Street (knishes are made from soft dough filled with onion-flavored mashed potato) and Russ & Daughters, begun in 1900. Combine the lox and cream cheese at Russ & Daughters' branch at the Jewish Museum on the Upper East Side with a visit to the museum.

WHEN TO GO Any season is eating season in New York.

HOW LONG You could take one day – or several.

PLANNING Two Upper West Side hotel choices: The Lucerne, 201 West 79th Street, 212-875-1000, thelucernehotel.com; The Excelsior, 45 West 81st Street, 212-362-9200, excelsiorhotelny.com. The Gatsby Hotel is near all the noshing on the Lower East Side, 135 E. Houston St., between First and Second Aves., 212-358-8844, gatsbyhotelnyc.com.

INSIDE INFORMATION At the 2nd Ave Deli, one sandwich easily feeds two. Regulars split the sandwich to leave room for the trademark cheesecake.

WEBSITES nycgo.com, thejewishmuseum.org

NORTH AMERICA

HIGHLIGHTS

■ The orgasm scene in *When Harry Met Sally* was shot in **Katz's Delicatessen**, a landmark founded in 1888.

■ Sample a classic kosher dill pickle at **Pickle Guys** before visiting the Lower East Side Tenement Museum.

■ Kosher dietary laws forbid selling or eating meat and dairy products together. Appetizing stores, which sell fish and dairy products, sprang up around the city in the late 19th century, but today only **Russ & Daughters** remains. The pickled herring in cream sauce is a must.

Katz's Delicatessen has fed generations of New Yorkers. Each week, it serves 5,000 lb (2,273 kg) of corned beef, 2,000 lb (909 kg) of salami, and 12,000 hot dogs.

Racks of oak barrels hold the maturing bourbon whiskey.

HIGHLIGHTS

▓ Join 50,000 other whiskey connoisseurs for the five-day **Kentucky Bourbon Festival** held in the third week of September in Bardstown, where bourbon's been a local tradition since 1776.

▓ Bardstown, known as the Bourbon Capital of the World, is also home to the **Oscar Getz Museum of Whiskey History**, where Abraham Lincoln's liquor license is displayed.

▓ **Gourmet souvenirs** include bourbon-flavored whole bean coffee, chocolates, and cherries (for garnishing your Manhattan, of course) sold at Maker's Mark Distillery.

▓ **Buffalo Trace** has an impressive history. Operations continued during Prohibition because it was producing a "medicinal whiskey." Tours of its distillery are available.

KENTUCKY

Bourbon Trail

Traveling through the rolling countryside of Kentucky,
you can sample the delights of America's native whiskey.

As you drive past thoroughbred horse farms in Kentucky's bluegrass country, the air is filled with the caramel and vanilla scents of aging bourbon. What is it about this landscape that, in the late 1700s, gave rise to the first generation of bourbon distillers, and that keeps it at the forefront of world bourbon production? They say the secret is in the water. This part of Kentucky, southeast of Louisville, rests on a limestone shelf that filters out iron, resulting in the pure springwater that is an essential ingredient in a fine bourbon whiskey. The Kentucky Bourbon Trail is a self-guided driving tour of ten distilleries: Angel's Envy, Four Roses, Heaven Hill, Jim Beam, Maker's Mark, Bulleit Fronteir, Evan Williams, Woodford Reserve, Town Branch, and Wild Turkey. Guides detail the craft of bourbon making—from cooking and mashing to fermentation, distillation, and maturation in oak—and the tastings afterward let you try America's "Native Spirit."

NORTH AMERICA

WHEN TO GO Fall foliage and a warming bourbon make a nice pairing. Avoid Sundays, when a few of the distilleries are closed.

HOW LONG The distance between the Kentucky Bourbon Trail distilleries is short enough that you can visit them in a day. But you should linger, taking in the tours, films, and tastings over at least two days.

PLANNING A downloadable brochure and map of the Kentucky Bourbon Trail is available from the Kentucky Distillers' Association website, which gives opening times and booking arrangements.

INSIDE INFORMATION While Buffalo Trace, a National Historic Landmark, is not on the "official" trail, it's worth a visit.

WEBSITES kybourbontrail.com, kentuckytourism.com, buffalotrace.com

Boils are social events where crawfish are cooked in spices with potatoes, onions, and corn.

LOUISIANA

Cajun Cooking in Louisiana

Dance to the beat of a zydeco band and discover the soul of Cajun cooking in the heart of Acadiana.

Folks frequently mention New Orleans when talking Cajun cooking, but they're about a hundred miles off the mark. While the Big Easy's sophisticated Caribbean-Creole culinary roots are flavored with Cajun influences, you'd best head west for the genuine article. Cajun cooking was born in the region of Louisiana known as Acadiana, where the French colonists of Nova Scotia were forcibly relocated in 1755 after refusing to pledge allegiance to the British Crown. Left to wade ashore on the coast of present-day Louisiana, the Acadian people (today's Cajuns) turned adversity into industry as they blazed a path of food, and joie de vivre, that you can follow today. If you base yourself in Lafayette, Acadiana's de facto capital, you can make sorties to Breaux Bridge, Avery Island, Opelousas, Carencro, Mansura, Basile, and other Cajun towns. Cajuns love to celebrate, and towns throughout Acadiana hold festivals devoted to the foods of Cajun Louisiana, from rice at Crowley, to *boudin* (a sausage made from onions, pork, and rice) at Carencro, to *cochon de lait* (roast suckling pig) at Mansura.

WHEN TO GO Any time of year, but the heat and humidity of late summer can be energy-sapping. If you brave the crowds in the weeks before Lent (Mardi Gras), pack a sense of patient humor with your mask.

HOW LONG Allow at least three full days to make day trips from Lafayette to outlying Cajun towns.

PLANNING The best flights arrive in New Orleans. Book a rental car for the three-hour drive west to Lafayette. From there, most of the towns mentioned are less than 1.5 hours' drive.

INSIDE INFORMATION Leave space in your schedule to discover that special *tasso* (intensely smoky-spicy cured ham used to flavor sauces) in a little roadside charcuterie during your travels.

WEBSITES louisianatravel.com/festivals, lafayettetravel.com/things-to-do/food-tours

HIGHLIGHTS

▦ Spot **herons**, **egrets**, and maybe an **alligator** or two in roadside bayous as you venture between Cajun towns.

▦ Enjoy the **patois** of the locals as they "save the groceries" and "pass a good time."

▦ Listen to a Cajun **reed accordian** and **fiddle music** while you unravel the mysteries of **crawfish peeling**.

▦ Test your **capsaicin tolerance** at the mothership of the hot-sauce phenomenon, McIlhenny's Tabasco bottling plant on Avery Island.

NORTH AMERICA

CALIFORNIA

Napa Valley Wine

Combine California sunshine and a year-round pageant of color with visits to wineries and fine restaurants.

NORTH AMERICA

The predawn darkness is shattered by a strong light that follows calloused hands feeling for plump clusters of grapes concealed in the foliage. In the harvest season, known locally as Crush, floodlights illuminate vineyards throughout the region, from the Carneros Plain above San Pablo Bay in the south to Mount St. Helena in Calistoga to the north. It's a race against time as winemakers hurry to harvest grapes matured by the last blast of summer heat, at the precise moment of ripeness, in the safe, cool hours before sunrise. At this time of year, Napa Valley reveals the mysteries of winemaking. As you peer over the railing of a tasting-room deck at a mountain winery such as Sterling, resist the panoramic views around you, and look down as gondolas overflowing with Cabernet or Pinot Noir grapes trundle in for crushing. Juice flies as skins split open to create the indigo must of infant wine. Every season is a joy in Napa. In winter, when the bones of old vines are laid bare and tasting rooms are empty, you can have a real conversation about what's in the glass. With spring comes budbreak, when the vineyards are bright with yellow flowers, and barrel tastings abound to test young wine. And in summer, when the valley heats up, you can take refuge in cool wine caves hidden in the hillsides.

WHEN TO GO Tasting rooms, restaurants, and attractions are open all year. The valley reaches a crescendo of excitement and color during Crush, from late August to early November.

HOW LONG Allow at least three days to avoid palate fatigue, and go midweek for smaller crowds.

PLANNING Many of the better and boutique wineries hold tastings and tours by appointment only. Michelin-rated restaurants such as The French Laundry require reservations two months in advance.

INSIDE INFORMATION To escape the heavy traffic, take one of the crossroads heading east in Yountville, Oakville, Rutherford, or Zinfandel in St. Helena. Within a few miles you'll reach the valley's lush east flank and the Silverado Trail, home to some of the most distinguished wineries.

WEBSITE napavalley.com

HIGHLIGHTS

▪ Napa Valley bubbles with **thermal springs**. Between wine tastings, slip into a mineral pool in one of Calistoga's resorts, or ease into a mud bath of local volcanic ash.

▪ Visit the 19th-century wineries, such as **Inglenook**, owned by Francis Ford Coppola, and **Beringer**, which has a Victorian mansion set among grounds shaded by the awe-inspiring California redwoods.

▪ From a ridge above Calistoga, reached along the Palisades Trail, you get the full sweep of more than **40,000 acres (16,187 ha) of vineyards** in fall regalia, while spotting red-tailed hawks and peregrine falcons.

Sun-soaked vineyards stretch into the distance at a winery in Calistoga, Napa County.

Top 10 Food Pilgrimages

Some eating places and their signature dishes are worth crossing the world for. Here are a few such gastronomic pilgrimage sites.

❶ PETER LUGER STEAK HOUSE, BROOKLYN, NEW YORK

Since 1887 steak-loving New Yorkers have crossed the bridge into Brooklyn for what many believe is the finest prime beef the nation can provide. Rigorously selected, perfectly marbled short loin of beef is dry-aged on the premises, broiled simply, and served in generous portions, usually for two hungry diners to share. The atmosphere is strictly no frills, but the prices reflect the quality of the beef.

PLANNING Peter Luger's does not accept credit cards. peterluger.com

❷ THE FRENCH LAUNDRY, YOUNTVILLE, CALIFORNIA

Chef Thomas Keller's restaurant earns a place in virtually every "top ten" restaurant list in the U.S. He is passionate about the seasonality and sourcing of his ingredients. Rather than a single signature dish, The French Laundry is famous for its nine-course tasting menus, which change daily. Expect playful surprises like the "Oysters and Pearls," a savory custard of pearl tapioca garnished with caviar and oysters.

PLANNING Expect to spend three to four hours at the table to give each dish the attention it deserves. thomaskeller.com/tfl

❸ ANTOINE'S, NEW ORLEANS, LOUISIANA

This grande dame of American restaurants has been run by the same family since it opened in 1840, hosting local and international gourmets, U.S. presidents, foreign royalty, and Hollywood stars. Antoine's most celebrated specialty is Oysters Rockefeller, invented here in 1899 and named—because of its intensely rich, luxurious sauce—after the wealthiest American of the day. The precise recipe, despite many attempts to reproduce it, remains a secret.

PLANNING Antoine's dress code requires male guests to wear a jacket at dinner. antoines.com

❹ BEIJING DADONG KAOYA DIAN ("BEIJING ROAST DUCK") RESTAURANT, BEIJING, CHINA

Versions of Peking Duck—that sublime combination of crisp roast skin, juicy duck meat, and pungent condiments, all wrapped in a pancake—turn up in supermarket freezers worldwide. But at the Beijing Dadong Kaoya Dian, you can enjoy this Chinese classic at its best—just choose your ingredients, roll them up in a pancake, and enjoy. The menu also offers a wide range of other dishes.

PLANNING Reservations always essential. Ask your hotel to book. Address: Tuanjie Hu Beikou, Building 3. Phone: 010/6582-2892

Caviar with crustacean jelly and cauliflower cream, like all of Joel Robuchon's signature dishes, is meticulously crafted and gorgeously presented.

❺ 49 BAT DAN STREET, HANOI, VIETNAM

Vietnamese are passionate about their national dish, pho—a rich meat broth packed with noodles, meat or poultry, scallions, ginger, fresh herbs, and spices. The citizens of Hanoi claim theirs is the best pho of all. Small cafés and sidewalk vendors are the usual sources. Locals and foreigners alike agree that the stall at 49 Bat Dan Street offers some of the most delicious pho in town.

PLANNING This is spur-of-the-moment dining. When you see a stall that's busy serving a long line of hungry customers, consider it worth the wait.

❻ HOTEL SACHER, VIENNA, AUSTRIA

The world's most famous chocolate cake, the Sacher torte, is to patisserie what Strauss waltzes are to music—an embodiment of the delights of café society in 19th-century Vienna. Devised by Franz Sacher in 1832, the torte holds a ribbon of apricot jam between chocolate layers and is accompanied by a generous helping of whipped cream.

PLANNING This is a luxury hotel, so even if visiting the café you'll feel more comfortable if not too casually dressed. sacher.com/en

❼ HARRY'S BAR, VENICE, ITALY

In Venice, the peak of self-indulgence is a Bellini cocktail, of fresh white peach juice and sparkling Prosecco, imbibed where the drink was first devised. The cocktail was named in honor of the 15th-century Venetian artist Giovanni Bellini. Harry's Bar itself is a cultural icon, appearing in Ernest Hemingway's novel, *Across the River and Into the Trees*.

PLANNING Meal prices are very high, so limit yourself to a drink at the bar unless on an unlimited budget. cipriani.com

❽ L'ATELIER DE JOËL ROBUCHON, PARIS, FRANCE

Robuchon has been hailed as the most influential French chef of his generation, with a focus on simplicity and natural flavors. His food is by no means austere. Truffles and caviar abound, but they are likely to be paired with such partners as cauliflower or his ethereally rich mashed potatoes.

PLANNING L'Atelier has two restaurants in Paris, one in Saint-Germain, the other off the Champs Elysées. joel-robuchon.com/en/restaurants-paris.php

❾ THE FAT DUCK, BRAY, BERKSHIRE, ENGLAND

Heston Blumenthal's take on Britain's beloved "chips"—french-fried potatoes—has become the stuff of culinary legend. It involves three days of preparation—smoking hay and the application of adventurous kitchen technology—to achieve a state of dry, crisp perfection.

PLANNING The restaurant can accommodate a maximum of only six diners per table. thefatduck.co.uk

❿ EL CELLER DE CAN ROCA, GIRONA, SPAIN

Heir to El Bulli, which closed in 2011, El Celler de Can Roca is run by three brothers who act as chef, sommelier, and pâtissier. The molecular gastronomy is meticulous—an oyster cooked for five minutes at exactly 85°C (105°F)—but the resulting flavors are worth the celebration, and the journey.

PLANNING Located 60 miles (96.5 km) north of Barcelona, a visit to the unpretentious restaurant can easily be tied into a weekend – as long as you factor in the year-long waiting list. cellercanroca.com

Blue Mountain Coffee

One of the world's finest coffees is grown in the hauntingly beautiful setting of Jamaica's high, lush Blue Mountains.

The full-bodied smoothness of its flavor has earned Blue Mountain coffee the reputation of "best coffee in the world." Jamaica's Blue Mountains, rising to more than 7,000 feet (2,134 meters) above the island's capital, Kingston, are indeed blue, being shrouded most of the time in mist. And this is one of the coffee's secrets— protected by the mist, the berries ripen slowly, developing their flavor to the full. From Kingston, head north into the mountains to The Cooperage, a hamlet where barrels were made for transporting the beans, and on through Guava Ridge to Mavis Bank. Here you can visit the Jablum factory and watch the process of berry selection (which includes floating them in a tank of water, allowing defective berries to float to the top), drying, and roasting. Return to Guava Ridge and head north along a rugged mountain road through Content Gap and Silver Hill to Section, all coffee-growing communities. Turn west to Hardwar Gap, a pass across the high backbone of the mountains, and drive on to Newcastle. Below Newcastle, visit the Cold Spring Estate, where you can see 18th-century coffee-making installations, including floating ponds and barbecues for roasting the beans. Then wind down the mountainside, with spectacular views on all sides, to Kingston.

WHEN TO GO December to April are the best months, avoiding the heat of summer, the wet months of April and November, and the hurricane season in August and September.

HOW LONG About 40 miles (64 km). The roads are winding and often in poor condition, so allow at least a day; two would be better.

PLANNING In view of the poor roads, you should rent a four-wheel drive vehicle. You need to book in advance to visit David Twyman's Old Tavern Estate.

INSIDE INFORMATION Most Blue Mountain coffee is grown by small farmers, who are often more than happy to show you around their farms.

WEBSITE visitjamaica.com

HIGHLIGHTS

■ At Mavis Bank, soak up the **majestic views** of the Yallahs River Valley and Blue Mountain Peak, the island's highest point (7,402 ft/ 2,256 m above sea level).

■ Between Content Gap and Silver Hill, stop off in Clydesdale, a Jamaican Forestry Department nursery. A 2.5-mile (4 km) walk takes you to the beautiful, though now somewhat neglected, **Cinchona Botanical Garden**.

■ At Section, visit the **Old Tavern Coffee Estate**, belonging to the Twyman family, headed by its patriarch David, the Blue Mountains' only single-estate coffee producer.

Blue Mountain coffee berries get their distinctive flavor from the area's volcanic soil.

March and April are the main harvest months in Chile's Central Valley.

HIGHLIGHTS

▥ Absorb the vastness of **Santiago** as it slips from urban chaos into the agrarian solitude of the vineyards.

▥ Enjoy a tour and tasting at **Concha y Toro** in Pirque, one of the largest and oldest wineries on the valley floor.

▥ Compare the **contrasting styles** of the lean and chiseled mountain wines grown near the Andes and the broader styles with prominent fruit flavors from the fertile valley floor.

▥ Visit **Almaviva**, the vineyard that is part-owned by the Rothschild family and combines Bordelais know-how with Chilean management.

CHILE

Central Valley Wine

Chile's fertile central plain, fed for centuries by meltwater from the Andes, nurtures fruit that is full of character.

The Andes are visible from every vineyard in Chile's Central Valley, which lies between mountains to the east and the Pacific to the west, with the Atacama—the driest desert on Earth—to the north. This unique local climate ensures dry growing conditions free of disease, while the rivers that run through the fertile plain provide water to ripen the fruit. To the south of Santiago, the Maipó River flows west from the Andes foothills across the Central Valley. The fertile Maipó Valley floor is one of the oldest and most important winemaking areas in Chile, while newer vineyards have been established in the upper valley, or Maipó Alto. Cabernet Sauvignon, Chardonnay, and the indigenous Carmenere variety all flourish here. The finest wines predominate in the higher vineyards of the Maipó Alto. These include Antiyal, Chile's first "garage winery," which produces small quantities using biodynamic techniques. Just five minutes away is Perez Cruz, another well-designed modern winery. Throughout the lower Maipó, large wineries boast fine restaurants and an artillery of the latest winemaking equipment.

SOUTH AMERICA

WHEN TO GO April–May (fall) and September–October (spring) are best for visiting the wineries.

HOW LONG Three days is sufficient to see the highlights of the lower and upper Maipó Valley.

PLANNING The Maipó Valley is about 50 miles (80 km) south of Santiago. Base yourself in Santiago and rent a car to explore the area. It is wise to contact the wineries in advance to check on opening times and the availability of wines.

INSIDE INFORMATION If you want to try Chile's most avant-garde wines, head west for the cooler Casablanca area between Santiago and Valparaíso. Here, vineyards such as Matetic and Casa Marin in the San Antonio Valley are producing new styles of Sauvignons and Pinot Noirs.

WEBSITES chile.travel/en, upscapetravel.com

At Bodegas Weinert in Mendoza, wine is aged in large, 100-year-old, French oak barrels.

ARGENTINA

Malbec in Mendoza

Tour vineyards that produce the finest examples of
Malbec wines in the clear, sunny air of the Andes foothills.

Mendoza's warm, sunny days, cool nights, and mineral-laden snowmelt add complexity and mystique to what could be just another lush, fruit-juicy wine. Heading south from the broad avenues of old-world Mendoza, in western Argentina, you can visit most of the wineries producing world-renowned Malbec, including Catena Zapata, Achaval-Ferrer, Paul Hobbs Vina Cobos, Dominio del Plata, Bodega Norton, and Bodegas Salentein. The picturesque 100 miles (160 kilometers) or so to Valle de Uco is a tasting lesson in itself, as the northern areas just outside Mendoza produce a more strapping, structured Malbec, while farther south the higher elevations offer more elegance and floral characteristics. The vertiginous cliffs and gaping crevices of the regal, glacier-draped Andes provide a constant backdrop to your travels up and down the Mendoza foothills, radiating broad swaths of colored light and shadow throughout the day. Make time to visit Maipú's Museo del Vino San Felipe. It is devoted to the history of winemaking in the region and has one of the most extensive collections of equipment and artifacts in the world. At the end of each day spent rambling the vineyards, Mendoza will seduce you with its European charm, homemade gelatos, and world-class cuisine.

WHEN TO GO Argentine fall (March–April) is best. Spring (September–October) is also a good time. The annual Fiesta Nacional de la Vendimia, or grape harvest, takes place during the first weekend of March.

HOW LONG Allow at least two to five days to visit the vineyards.

PLANNING Many of the wineries take visitors by appointment only, so contact them a week or so in advance. Also, most are closed on Saturdays and Sundays. For the Vendimia Festival, hotel reservations should be made six months in advance.

INSIDE INFORMATION Once you are off the main highways it is easy to become lost as there are no road signs and maps are not much help, so book a driver and car.

WEBSITE argentinawinetourism.com

HIGHLIGHTS

■ Relax at the end of the day with an empanada or two and a bottle of a fine, inky Malbec on the patio of Mendoza's Park Hyatt, overlooking the **Plaza Independencia.**

■ Explore the Sunday **antique fair** in the main square of Chacras de Coria, 20 minutes south of Mendoza, and sip a fragrant, high-altitude Chardonnay at an outdoor café.

■ Enjoy **wonderful cuisine** at Restaurant 1884 and Francesco Barberà Ristorante, in Mendoza, and at the Familia Zuccardi winery.

SOUTH AMERICA

| VIETNAM |

Vietnamese Cuisine

*Take a gourmet trip down the length of Vietnam
to enjoy a perfect combination of cuisine and culture.*

A sprinkling of fresh cilantro wilts as it hits a steaming bowl of pho, Vietnam's ubiquitous noodle soup. Thick black coffee dribbles from a small steel strainer into a white demitasse below. A quiver of fresh baguettes vibrates in a basket on the back of a scooter. Throughout Vietnam, the flavors are fresh, light, and lively, and a food-lover's tour is one of the best ways into the local culture. Tasty treats include *cha ca* (a fried fish dish) in Hanoi, *banh beo* (rice-flour pancakes topped wih shrimp, scallions, and fish sauce) in Hue, and *banh mi* (a baguette sandwich) at a sidewalk restaurant in Ho Chi Minh City (Saigon). Many Vietnamese dishes reflect colonial influences—a dash of Chinese, a touch of Cambodian, and a little French. To this are added local ingredients, such as fresh herbs and seasonings—cilantro, basil, green onions, beansprouts, and *nuoc nam* (fish sauce). Vietnamese cooking classes start in the local markets, among bowls of mandarin oranges, stacks of coconuts, and dried shrimp piled into conical heaps that echo the straw hats of the merchants hunched nearby. Don't worry about disturbing the merchants; they're almost always eager to chat and bargain with visitors, even if the only shared language is a nod of the head and a handful of dong, the local currency.

WHEN TO GO The best time to travel is generally November to April, when it's dry throughout most of the country. June to August tends to be hot and humid all over Vietnam, with intermittent, sometimes heavy, showers.

HOW LONG 10 to 14 days is ideal for dipping deep into Vietnam's culinary regions.

PLANNING Travel with a well-connected tour operator for the best local culinary experiences and to gain access to unique places off Vietnam's main tourist routes.

INSIDE INFORMATION Eating at street stalls is a great way to taste local flavors, but be careful of raw foods.

WEBSITES artisansofleisure.com, vietnam-guide.com

HIGHLIGHTS

▦ Dine in a restored French **colonial-era villa** in Hanoi, where candlelight and ceiling fans create the romantic atmosphere of a classic film.

▦ Navigate the chaos of local markets with a **celebrity chef**, then learn her secrets to crafting tasty regional dishes in her own kitchen.

▦ Prepare a **vegetarian lunch** alongside Buddhist nuns in Hanoi, then dine together, and learn about their unique lifestyle.

▦ Feast on **imperial-style cuisine** in the former home of a royal princess in Hue, on the central coast.

A local vendor sells steamed buns from a riverboat.

| THAILAND |

Thailand Cuisine Tour

*Take a gourmet journey through the exotic
and complex cuisine of this ancient land.*

The streets of Bangkok sizzle. Marinades drip from pieces of roasting chicken and pork onto food vendors' grills. The noise and the aromas from the street kitchens—on sidewalks and lining small streets—waft through the air, enticing passersby to try a plate of noodles, deep-fried bananas, curries with coconut milk, or even a breakfast of porridge rice with a poached egg. Locals drive off, balancing meals on motorbikes that carry two, three, sometimes even four people through the busy streets. Influenced by the cuisines of China, Europe, and India, food also has a spiritual dimension in Thailand. In the Buddhist religion, an offering of a plate of eggs symbolizes rebirth or achievement, while lotus blossoms indicate purity. At the *wat* (Buddhist temple) at the Grand Palace in Bangkok, you might see chicken, sticky rice, shrimp paste, fruit, a green vegetable, and water presented in six small white bowls. In Chiang Mai you can visit the local markets, tour a noodle-making factory, and enjoy exquisite traditional meals. Take an excursion by road to Tha Ton on the Kok River. Outdoor tables in small towns are loaded with strange, hairy, or spiky fruits that sellers in sarongs slice, peel, or hack open to reveal a bright, juicy, tangy, or sweet prize, while fresh coconut milk in its shell quenches the thirst.

WHEN TO GO For a cooler, relatively dry visit, the best time to travel most anywhere in Thailand is between November and March. Bangkok is hot in April and wet in October. When most of Thailand is simmering in the heat between April and June, the south offers some respite.

HOW LONG For a true taste of Thailand, allow nine days to two weeks.

PLANNING Find tour companies that provide Thai tour guides who know their foods and spices and can explain unusual flavors during your travels. Or find cooking schools individually, city by city.

INSIDE INFORMATION Follow the locals to the street stalls where they buy their meals and snacks for more authentic and exotic choices.

WEBSITES artisansofleisure.com, gourmetontour.com, bangkok.com/thai-cooking-class, thaicookery school.com

HIGHLIGHTS

▪ Wander through a lively Bangkok market, searching for the best galangal root, basil, kaffir limes, and cilantro leaves in preparation for a **Thai cooking class**.

▪ Arrive early at the **Damnoen Saduak Floating Market**, southwest of Bangkok, and hop on a longtail boat to watch sellers paddling their boats in the *klongs*, or canals, as they barter with other traders for fresh tropical fruits, vegetables, and flowers.

▪ Revel in the traditional flavors presented at a meal at **Old Chiang Mai Cultural Center**, and watch performances of the 12-sword dance, the candle dance, and the fingernail dance.

▪ On the porch of a bamboo hut in a **Lahu tribe village**, dine on a meal cooked fresh in a cooking hut next door while local village children sneak up close to see what you're up to.

Opposite: Vendors' boats jostle for position at the Damnoen Saduak Floating Market near Bangkok. Above left: The exotic rambutan, a hairy, red, lychee-like fruit, is common in Thailand. Above right: Red chili peppers and Thai basil are two of the country's signature flavors.

JAPAN

Search for Sushi

Sample some of Tokyo's multitude of sushi restaurants for the ultimate in sushi heaven.

ASIA

tart your morning at Tsukiji, the world's largest fish market. The stalls start selling at 7 a.m., and the market is at its busiest between 8 and 10. From the frozen tuna to the sea urchin roe (*uni*), much of the produce is headed for the sushi shops. In the market itself, stand in line at Sushi Dai or Daiwa Sushi for the freshest sushi in the world. If you don't have time to wait, find one of the more casual restaurants in the outer part of the market serving *donburi*—large bowls of rice topped with tuna, salmon, salmon roe (*ikura*), crab, and sea urchin roe. From the market, walk down Harumi-dori to Ginza. Here, in the Mitsukoshi or Matsuya *depachika*, you can see the different styles of sushi. Assorted fish and vegetables scattered on rice are known as *chirashizushi*; squares of pressed rice, topped with vinegared or cooked fish, are *oshizushi*; and sushi rolls are called *makizushi*. Follow with the ultimate dinner at Kyubey Sushi in Ginza. Marvel as the fish is sliced gently and precisely in one long stroke. Sticky, vinegared rice is carefully molded into a bite-sized piece, topped with a dab of wasabi and carefully draped with a piece of fish. Pick up the sushi, lightly dip the fish side in the soy sauce, and experience the explosion of flavor in your mouth.

WHEN TO GO Any time of year.

HOW LONG One day, or sample a little at a time over several days.

PLANNING Tsukiji market can be reached on the Hibiya Line or the Oedo Line. Traditional sushi restaurants can be very expensive, so ask for advice first. If you are visiting one, you may want to take a translator, as they do not usually have English-version menus. In *kaiten-zushi* restaurants, where plates of sushi circle the eating area on a conveyor belt, prices are more reasonable.

INSIDE INFORMATION Eat a piece of pickled ginger between different types of sushi—it will clean the palate and enhance the flavors. Tea or beer, rather than sake, is usually served with sushi.

WEBSITES boutiquejapan.com/food, tsukiji-market.or.jp/tukiji_e.htm

HIGHLIGHTS

▥ Take a guided tour of the **ultraclean Tsukiji fish market**. Although tons of fish pass through every day, it doesn't smell of fish at all.

▥ **Conger eel** (*anago*) lightly grilled and brushed with sweet soy sauce, creamy **sea urchin roe** (*uni*), and **bonito** (*katsuo*) garnished with ginger and chives are all divine.

Eating sushi in one of Tokyo's thousands of sushi restaurants is one of the unmissable highlights of a visit to the city.

Gift boxes of exquisite confectionery are a popular item in Tokyo's depachika.

| JAPAN |

Depachika Shopping in Tokyo

For the ultimate food-shopping experience, tour the depachika, or food basements, of Tokyo's department stores.

Walking into the basement of Takashimaya department store in Tokyo's Nihon-bashi district, you are hit by sensory overload. From vendors touting their goods, to mouthwatering aromas wafting through the air, to the sight of offerings at the multitude of stalls, the experience is overwhelming. Most of Tokyo's large department stores have a food basement, or *depachika*, packed with stalls selling all kinds of delicacies and gourmet items—food gifts, dishes from famous restaurants, specialties from all over Japan, and treats from overseas. Start off in the bakeries, where you can find authentic French croissants and baguettes. Meat departments have row after row of marbled *wagyu* (Japanese-style beef), cut paper thin for shabu-shabu (thinly sliced meat and vegetables served with dipping sauces). Imahan, a restaurant famous for its sukiyaki, has a counter in Takashimaya's meat section, where you can sample meat that melts in your mouth. The prepared foods sections tempt with grilled yakitori chicken, delicately fried tempura, and colorful bento lunch boxes. For dessert, don't miss the exquisite *wagashi* (Japanese confectionery) at the Toraya stall, which reflects the seasons with motifs of cherry blossoms in spring and autumnal maple leaves in fall.

WHEN TO GO Any time of year.

HOW LONG A few hours, or link visits to different depachika with other sightseeing.

PLANNING Most major department stores in Tokyo have depachika, and many can be accessed from major train stations. Among the best are Isetan in Shinjuku, Daimuru at Tokyo station, Mitsukoshi in Ginza, and Takashimaya in Nihonbashi. If you want to avoid the crowds, visit during the week rather than on weekends, and avoid public holidays. Closing time is usually around 8 p.m.

INSIDE INFORMATION If you are a chocaholic, visit Tokyo during the first two weeks in February, leading up to Valentine's Day, when a huge array of samples will be on offer in the depachika.

WEBSITE www.jnto.go.jp/eng/attractions/dining/depachika

| HIGHLIGHTS

■ The Takashimaya and Isetan department stores have rooftop gardens, where you can eat an **impromptu picnic**.

■ The ultimate **chocolate shop** is Jean-Paul Hevin in Isetan. The chocolates are displayed as if they were precious jewels.

■ Sit at the counter of a fruit stand and enjoy a slice of the juiciest – and most expensive – **melon** you are ever likely to encounter.

■ In Takashimaya, visit Peck from Milan, which imports **Italian cheeses and cured meats**.

■ The buttery **cigar wafers** at the Yoku Moku stand are addictive and make elegant hostess gifts.

ASIA

| KOREA |

Seoul Food Tour

*South Korea's capital buzzes with lively markets
and hidden eateries packed day and night with local foodies.*

Korean cuisine is about more than just the food—it's a very social experience, as friends gather around charcoal barbecue pits eager to sample bubbling stews, fermented kimchis, and fresh vegetables. During a night out, you might taste spicy *sundubu-jjigae* (tofu stew), *galbijjin* (slowly marinated and braised beef ribs), or *dakgangjeong* (crispy fried chicken). Do like the Koreans and visit a few different places over the course of the evening to try a variety of food, drink, and activities. In Seoul, locals head to Jongno 3ga, Hongik University, Dongdaemun, or Gangnam Station for food and fun. The night starts with Korean BBQ. Take a bite of crisp pork belly topped with fermented bean paste, veggies, and raw onion. Then knock back a shot of *soju*—a sharp, vodka-like drink. The next course could be *haemal pajeon* (savory onion and seafood pancakes) washed down with *makgeolli* (milky rice beer). Next, get physical with an activity—visit a karaoke bar and belt out your favorite song or hit a few balls at a batting cage. Then it's time for another snack—drop by a traditional market like Gwangjang to nosh on Korean favorites such as *hotteok* (sweet pancakes) or *kkwabaegi* (twisted donuts). End the evening with a relaxing bath and a sweat at a Korean sauna. Everything stays open into the small hours, so expect to sleep late the next day.

WHEN TO GO March to May and September to November. Avoid the hot, humid summers and brutally cold winters.

HOW LONG 5 hours for your night out, but you'll need longer to get to know Seoul.

PLANNING For fine dining in Seoul, book a visit to Mingles, a Michelin-starred restaurant in the Cheongdam-dong district. Reserve your table as soon as you book your flights – reservations are hard to get. Plan your trip for October and take a day trip to Jeonji (just two hours away by train) for the *bibimbap* festival, which celebrates a Korean classic – mixed rice with meats and assorted vegetables.

INSIDE INFORMATION Choose a restaurant that specializes in one dish, such as Goryeo Samgyetang, a well-loved spot famous for its slow-cooked *samgyteang* (ginseng chicken soup).

WEBSITES seouleats.com, afatgirlsfoodguide.com, zenkimchi.com

HIGHLIGHTS

■ **Hongik Art University** district has great street food, shopping, and buskers. There are also many cafés, including some where you can nap, and others where you can pet dogs, cats, or even meerkats.

■ The 123-story **Lotte World Tower** with its impressive food courts has the best night views of the city. The elevator ride takes you to the top in just one minute.

■ Love highly marbled, top grade beef? Head to **Majangdong Beef Market,** pick out your meat, and take it to a nearby restaurant where they will cook it for you.

■ Join November's **kimchi-making festival** as hundreds of people turn tens of thousands of heads of cabbage into kimchi for the poor. It's free to join in.

■ For the brave eater, enjoy a platter of fermented skate at **Noryangjin Fish Market**.

Opposite: From its opening in 1905, the stalls of Dongdaemun market have been a mecca for food and shopping, but you can also get your fortune told. Above left: Fiery *Kimchi chiggae* (kimchi stew) is one of the best-loved dishes in South Korea. Above right: Korean BBQ is a feast that's made to share.

| INDIA |

India Cuisine Tour

Goa's special mix of Indian and western influences is evident in its cultural traditions, its architecture, and especially its cuisine.

A slow-moving rhythm is palpable in this tropical paradise, where you can lounge on sun-drenched beaches or nurse a cold *feni* cocktail in a picturesque corner of Old Goa, the former Portuguese capital in India. Whether you are touring Goa's current capital, Panaji, and lunching on spicy prawn *balchão*, or strolling past old, colonial-style churches in Old Goa, a 6-mile (10 kilometer) taxi ride from Panaji, you are in touch with Goa's diverse past. It is one of the few places in India where beef and pork can be found on the menu. Slowly simmered dishes, such as pork vindaloo (or *vindalho*), are ceremoniously spiced for the Catholic community's festive occasions. Differences in seasonings define the approach of the various traditions: a dash of vinegar is the Christian cook's touch to bring out flavor, while the Hindu choice is a scoop of tamarind and kokum (a sour, sharp-flavored, deep red fruit). Fresh fish and seafood are turned into a lemon-marinated fish curry simmered with mango, or into *ambot tik*, a hot and sour fish dish. Peppers inform but do not dominate Goan marinades and curries. Coconut is a key ingredient, used to enrich and soften stronger elements. When it comes to sweets, the egg-rich, layered crêpe specialty, *bebinca*, is given a twist of nutmeg and cooked for several hours over a low, charcoal fire, in the natural rhythm of the Goan kitchen.

WHEN TO GO October to March is best, with April and May very hot. Avoid the monsoon season, from June to September.

HOW LONG About ten days.

PLANNING Early December is a time of pilgrimages and festivals, so reserve a hotel room well in advance. Hotels are also heavily booked over the Christmas period, and prices can double. Self-drive rental cars are unusual. Chauffeur-driven private cars or taxis are the usual way of getting about.

INSIDE INFORMATION Although some of the beaches of northern Goa have evolved from thatched huts to high-rise hotels and condos, quiet spots can be found. Bambolin Beach is good for a quiet picnic. Candolim Beach, although popular with foreign tourists, is not crowded.

WEBSITES goa-tourism.com, goacentral.com

ASIA

HIGHLIGHTS

▮ The Friday **bazaar** draws crowds in Mapusa, a north Goa commercial hub.

▮ The **Bondla Wildlife Sanctuary** is the easiest to reach of Goa's wildlife parks. In addition to elephant rides and wildlife, there is a botanical garden displaying Goa's numerous native herbs and spices.

▮ A sharp, fiery **spicy paste** known as *rechad masala* is a Goan specialty. It is used in curries and to marinade meat and fish.

▮ A highly alcoholic drink called *feni*, available in versions distilled from either coconut sap or cashew nuts, is mixed with fruit juice for delicious **cocktail coolers**.

Opposite: A farmhand sits in front of a mountain of chili peppers, a key ingredient in Goan cuisine. Above left: A fruit stall adds to the colorful street scene in Panaji. Above right: A market trader's stall overflows with vegetables in prime condition. They are used in a vegetable stew called *khatkhate*.

Sri Lanka Tea Estates

*Enjoy a leisurely journey around Sri Lanka's tea plantations—
set in spectacular mountain scenery—and relax over a cup of tea.*

Gazing at the endless plantations rolling across the hills, one can hardly believe tea came to Sri Lanka by a "happy accident" when disease killed the coffee crops in the late 1860s and planters turned to tea. Tea is grown across the southern half of the country, where different brews are produced depending on altitude. Galle in the southwest specializes in Orange Pekoe, while most tea grown at Ratnapura is used in blends. From Ratnapura, the road climbs into the central mountains, where old plantation houses and tea factories sit like white dots in a sea of green. Dimbula province yields its best brew in winter; the tea of Uva province achieves its mellow flavor in the summer wind; Kandy, the ancient capital, is famous for temples, palaces, and tea. But the queen of Ceylon teas comes from Nuwara Eliya: it is golden and bright, yet delicately scented. With its flower gardens and quaint dwellings, this cool resort is a delightful base for exploring the tea highlands. You can ramble or drive along the trails in the early mornings and watch the women plucking "two leaves and a bud." Waterfalls tumble in the distance, and the smell of roasting leaves hovers in the air.

WHEN TO GO The finest tea is produced in the dry season (summer in the east, winter in the west).

HOW LONG A week in the highlands; add four or five days if you include Galle and Ratnapura.

PLANNING Conservative dress is appreciated, so pack accordingly. You need warm clothes for Nuwara Eliya, where at 6,200 ft (1,890 m), nights are cool. On the rest of the island, cotton is best. The Kandy Perahera Festival takes place in August. If you plan to visit at this time, book your hotel well in advance. Be aware of political tensions on the island, and check the latest security advice before traveling.

INSIDE INFORMATION Unless you have booked a tour, the best way to travel is to hire a car and driver from a reputable local agent, but agree on the price beforehand. Sri Lankans are relaxed and courteous; aim to be likewise. Gifts are traditionally given and received with both hands.

WEBSITE resplendentceylon.com/teatrails

HIGHLIGHTS

■ Visit a **tea factory** to discover the secrets of processing and grading, before enjoying a fresh brew packed with health-giving properties.

■ Enjoy **dawn in the highlands** as veils of mist drift across the plantations and the first sunbirds flit through the air.

■ **Picnic** by a waterfall, looking across lush estates toward the sacred Adam's Peak (Sri Pada) in the distance, where pilgrims gather in the winter months.

■ Spend the night in a luxurious **converted tea factory**; your room might be an old drying loft complete with original machinery.

Women pick tea leaves on a plantation high in the Sri Lankan hills.

Central Otago's vineyards are set in some of New Zealand's most spectacular scenery.

NEW ZEALAND

Central Otago Wine Trail

This exciting young wine-producing region in the heart of New Zealand's South Island is famous for its Pinot Noir.

State Highway 6 follows the narrow corridor of the Kawarau Gorge east from Queenstown, in the deep south of New Zealand's South Island. Rapids foam in deep ravines, and tawny mountains of schist tower above. It is hard to believe that anything could grow in this barren vastness. Then you see the vines—neat rows on precious pockets of gravel, soaking up the sun on the southern slopes. Chard Farm, Gibbston Valley, and Peregrine wineries produce some of the cleanest flavors in the country. Grapes have been replanted here only since the 1980s, 100 years after the first planting, but already Central Otago's distinctive, dark Pinot Noir has achieved international recognition. The region is split by the rugged terrain into at least four subregions. Of these, the Gibbston region is closest to Queenstown (a 25-minute drive), but all are within easy reach. Most northerly is Wanaka, where, beneath snowcapped peaks, the vines of Rippon Vineyard run down to Lake Wanaka. To the east, vineyards sweep down the silty slopes of the former gold-mining center of Cromwell, now home to the region's greatest concentration of wineries. Nearby is Bannockburn, and to the south is Alexandra, location of actor Sam Neill's Two Paddocks vineyard.

WHEN TO GO October to May – the spring, summer, and fall months – from budburst to harvest time. Most vineyards are closed to the public in winter.

HOW LONG Three to four days based in Queenstown allows time for wine touring, dining, lake cruising, and adventure activities. Then spend a night at Lake Wanaka to visit Rippon Vineyard and Winery.

PLANNING The range of guided tours include traveling by luxury Jaguar limousine, by jetboat, and even flitting between tastings by helicopter.

INSIDE INFORMATION There is a wide range of accommodation, but the best tends to be snapped up early, so book well ahead. Some wineries are open by appointment only.

WEBSITES queenstownnz.co.nz, queenstownwinetrail.co.nz

HIGHLIGHTS

▪ Visit the **Gibbston Valley** winery's cavernous cellar carved into solid schist. You can sample wines and produce from the cheese factory.

▪ Walk across the Kawarau Bridge, the birthplace of **bungee jumping**, and watch the jumpers, even if you don't take the plunge yourself.

▪ Cruise the clear, deep-blue waters of Queenstown's **Lake Wakatipu**. Or take the heart-thumping **jetboat ride** up the fast-moving Shotover River.

▪ Travel the **Central Rail Trail** from Middlemarch to Clyde near Alexandra on foot, bicycle, or horseback.

The Sydney Opera House provides a stunning backdrop for a waterside eatery.

AUSTRALIA

Eat Your Way Around Sydney

From harborside to hilltop, Sydney's mix of cultures and unbeatable ingredients has created a vibrant restaurant scene.

Australia is a cultural and culinary melting pot. The fusion of cuisines from Europe and Asia has produced a distinctive style that, combined with a cornucopia of fresh produce, makes for seriously good eating—and Sydney, the country's biggest city, now has some of the best fish, meat, and vegetables available anywhere. The diversity of seafood at the Sydney Fish Market is impressive and includes farmed barramundi and salmon; mountains of prawns, mussels, octopus, and plump oysters from the New South Wales coast; and fish from Tasmania, South Australia, and even from the crystal waters off New Zealand. Dine in the city first, exploring the eastern, Circular Quay, and Opera House areas, then move on to stylish beachside restaurants with lovely views. Later, head for the hills and the vineyards. The Blue Mountains are only a couple of hours' drive away. After a day or two there, move on to the Hunter Valley, New South Wales' oldest winegrowing area. Some of the region's best restaurants are located close to the tasting rooms and cellar doors of the region's many wineries.

WHEN TO GO Spring or summer, including the Christmas summer season and Sydney's January Festival, or late summer–early autumn (late February–early April), are both good times.

HOW LONG Allow at least a week if you want to try out a representative sample of the area's best restaurants and see the major tourist locations.

PLANNING Allow exploration time when driving between Sydney, the Blue Mountains, and the Hunter Valley as the roads offer scenic stops.

INSIDE INFORMATION Bring-your-own (BYO) wine is possible at many Sydney restaurants, particularly at less expensive eateries, though a fee may be charged for uncorking the wine. Check with the restaurant.

WEBSITES visitnsw.com, eater.com/sydney

HIGHLIGHTS

■ At **Quay**, on West Circular Quay, the food matches the great setting in the heart of the harborside action.

■ **Regatta Restaurant**, in Rose Bay, offers diners some of the best seafood in Sydney and views across Rose Bay to the leafy North Shore.

■ At **Solitary**, near Leura in the Blue Mountains, the views of Mount Solitary and the Jamieson Valley are likely to inspire a walk after your meal.

■ **Circa 1876**, on the Pepper Tree Vineyard in Hunter Valley, uses French, Italian, and Asian influences to inspire stylish dishes using local produce.

AUSTRALIA AND OCEANIA

AUSTRALIA

Margaret River Wine Region

Sun, sea, and wine are the main ingredients on this tour of Australia's most southwesterly corner.

Gazing out over the blue waters of the Indian Ocean, it's hard to believe you're so close to Western Australia's premium wine region—stretching from Cape Leeuwin in the south to Cape Naturaliste in the north. Head inland, and within minutes the windswept coastal vegetation gives way to lush farmland and forest—and thousands of neat rows of vines. The wineries are spread out around the small townships, and tasting rooms (the Australian term is "cellar doors") pop up everywhere (there are around 80). Much of the land is flat, but gentle hills create microclimates that favor one grape variety over another. A large range of wines is produced, from the cooler southern areas close to Cape Leeuwin up to the warmer vineyards between Cowaramup, Yallingup, and Carbunup. A trip that moves from Augusta through the central Margaret River area to the newer areas is a good option, particularly if you're heading back to Perth afterward. At some of the older wineries, such as Voyager Estate, Vasse Felix, Cape Mentelle, Leeuwin Estate, Xanadu, Cullen, and Pierro, you'll find spacious tasting rooms in luxurious settings, often with elegant restaurants overlooking lakes or waterways. The atmosphere in cafés and wineries is laid-back, a mix of surfing chic and relaxed wine aficionado.

WHEN TO GO Late summer or early fall (late February or mid-March) after schools are back in session. Musical events and festivals are also held around this time. Alternatively, in November the Margaret River Wine Region Festival brings together all the region's culinary and winemaking delights.

HOW LONG Allow at least one or two days visiting wineries and another two to three for highlights of the area. A minimum of four to five days.

PLANNING All types of accommodation are available in the area. Take a guided tasting tour (customize your tour if you can afford it) so that you don't drink and drive and can do justice to the wines.

INSIDE INFORMATION Most wineries offer tours a 10–15 percent discount on cellar-door sales.

WEBSITES margaretriver.com, westernaustralia.com

| HIGHLIGHTS

▓ Cape Leeuwin is the place where **two oceans meet**, the Southern and the Indian. You can look out past the lighthouse to see waves rolling in from two directions and crashing into each other on the rocks.

▓ The region's abundant **wildlife** includes rich birdlife, kangaroos, and wallabies. The **whale-watching** season is from May to September. You can see **dolphins** between June and August and often at other times.

▓ Enjoy wonderful views and an intense tasting experience in the **Howard Park tasting room**, where you can try a dry riesling, followed by an herby Chardonnay, a bright Cabernet Sauvignon, and a spicy Shiraz.

Although the Margaret River region produces only 3 percent of Australia's grapes, it commands 20 percent of the country's premium wine market.

The Baltic Gourmet

*The sharp tang of fresh dill and the soothing balm of
sour cream enliven the hearty cuisine of the Baltic states.*

Tuck into cuisine that has been influenced by Poles, Swedes, Germans, and Russians (all have ruled the Baltic roost), but with quirky local twists. The basic fare of the region is meat, fish, root vegetables, sour cream, and dill, and regional differences are subtle and legion. Vegetarians can feast on sweet and savory pancakes, weight watchers can nibble on vegetable salads dressed with sour cream or vinaigrette, and everyone can enjoy forest berry dessert. Begin in Vilnius, Lithuania, whose Old Town has a rich mix of Gothic, Baroque, and Renaissance architecture. Pork and potato dishes, pancakes, and dumplings are among local specialties, as is *sakotis*, an elaborate, multilayered cake. Then move on to Riga, Latvia, on the Baltic coast, and enjoy its open-air beer gardens, cafés, and pastry shops, set among wonderful Art Nouveau architecture. Beet soup, fish, and kebabs are often on the menu. You can sample the best of Estonia's cooking in Tartu, the country's cultural center and home to a famous university. Here you can sample pickled herring, pork and sauerkraut, and fried black bread with sour cream. Beer is the preferred drink of Balts, but these former provinces supplied Mother Russia with more than 10 percent of its vodka, and all have venerable distilleries.

WHEN TO GO Avoid winter unless you like snow and ice.

HOW LONG Two weeks.

PLANNING The rail system is not well-developed, but Eurolines runs an excellent bus service between Vilnius, Riga, and Tartu. There is no airport at Tartu, but there are frequent buses, which take about 2.5 hours to get to Tallinn airport.

INSIDE INFORMATION Very large portions are served in restaurants, and bread, including the distinctive Baltic rye, is served with everything, everywhere.

WEBSITES inyourpocket.com, baltichotelsonline.com, eurolines.com

HIGHLIGHTS

■ In Vilnius, visit **Sturmu Svyturys** for traditionally prepared dishes such as smoked lamprey.

■ Riga's Centraltirgus (Central Market) is a labyrinth of stalls serving delicacies such as **caraway cheese** (*Jâñu siers*).

■ Soak up the atmosphere in **Gunpowder Cellar** (Püssirohukelder), a high-vaulted cellar built by Catherine the Great of Russia for storing gunpowder and now a beer restaurant in Tartu. Try Püssirohu Punane, the delicious red house beer.

A vendor arranges her baked goods in Riga market, which is widely considered to be one of the best food markets in the region.

A view from the pier at Bruichladdich, where one of Islay's coastal distilleries is based.

| SCOTLAND |

Scotland's Whiskey Trails

Make a pilgrimage through the Highlands and to the Inner Hebrides to visit some of the sources of the "Water of Life."

Scotland's hundreds of superb malt whiskeys derive their distinctive and varied characters from the magnificent landscapes where they are born: the sea-scoured land and peat bogs of Islay and Jura or the heathery moorlands and hidden glens of the Highlands. A journey to the venerable distilleries where they are made is a journey into the soul of the amber spirit itself. Malt whiskey is produced in several areas of Scotland, but two are particularly rewarding destinations for those who love both fine whiskey and intensely romantic open spaces. The Speyside region in the northeast of the country, and the small islands of Islay and Jura that lie off the west coast, are home to high concentrations of important distilleries and are famous for two classic—and contrasting—styles of malt: Speyside malts are the sweetest whiskeys, with rich, fruity flavors; Islay and Jura malts tend to be dry and peaty, with very distinctive flavors. The two regions can be visited separately or combined in a leisurely exploration of one of the most beautiful small countries in the world.

WHEN TO GO Scottish weather, always changeable, is generally at its best between April and September.

HOW LONG Allow at least two to three days for each area. To combine both trails, break the journey with a one- to two-day stopover in Edinburgh, Scotland's historic capital, or in lively Glasgow, less than three hours' drive from the Islay ferry.

PLANNING Some distillery tours require advance booking. You can travel to Speyside by road or rail from Glasgow or Edinburgh. You can reach Islay by air from Glasgow, or by car ferry from Kennacraig on the Kintyre peninsula. Jura can be reached by ferry from Islay.

INSIDE INFORMATION Scottish drunk-driving laws are strictly enforced, so to enjoy a distillery's samples with a clear conscience, make sure there is always one nondrinking driver in your party.

WEBSITES maltwhiskytrail.com, islayjura.com

HIGHLIGHTS

▪ Marvel at the **huge copper stills** on a tour of the Glen Grant Distillery at Rothes, Speyside, and enjoy a dram at the end of the tour.

▪ Sip a fine **local malt** in a Speyside inn in the golden light of a long summer evening, watching the shadows lengthen over the granite Grampian Mountains.

▪ Explore the **small, friendly distilleries** lining Islay's rocky shores, overlooking ruined castles and colonies of seals and seabirds.

Taking beer seriously, these three sample the wares at the spring Temple of Hops and Beer Festival in Žatec, in the north of Czechia.

CZECHIA

A Taste of Czech Lager

A visit to the homeland of beer makes for a relaxing trip and gives you the chance to try lots of local lagers while visiting historic cities.

There's a Czech proverb, "Where there's beer, there's cheer!", that sums up more than a millennium of brewing, quaffing, and purveying its delectable liquor. Lager beer of Czechia (originally known as Bohemia) is among the world's best because conditions are ideal for hop-growing and traditional brewing methods are used. Savor it in the country of its birth, and you'll gain fascinating insights into its history. For example, the 10th-century Bohemian king, Wenceslas, executed anyone caught smuggling hop cuttings out of the country. Early on people made beer at home, just for their own consumption; one of the oldest microbreweries, U Fleků in Prague, has been going strong since 1499. Base yourself in the capital, and sample the nation's favorite drink—it's even sold in breakfast cafés—then visit outlying centers. In Žatec to the northwest the best hops are grown, and its beer festival includes tasting sessions and dancing competitions. The biggest festival is at Plzeň(Pilsen), where in 1842 the world's first light golden lager was produced: Pilsner Urquell. Its taste is due to the low-sulfite, low-carbonate water and cannot be replicated elsewhere. Every year the production of the first batch is greeted with tastings, tours, food, music, and fireworks.

WHEN TO GO Anytime, but beer festivals take place from August through early October.

HOW LONG One week.

PLANNING Check into the growing number of beer tours available and the timing of festivals. Plzeň is one hour on frequent buses from the Zličín metro station on Line B (yellow), or from the main bus station at Florenč.

INSIDE INFORMATION In Plzeň, the Brewery Museum is in a medieval malt house and there are tours by guides in period costume, who have a wide-ranging knowledge of brewing from earliest times.

WEBSITES myczechrepublic.com, mesto-zatec.cz, prazdroj.cz

HIGHLIGHTS

■ The **Strahov Monastic Brewery** in Prague is a hostelry with a 600-year history of brewing. Try Svaty (Saint) Norbert, flame-colored *svetle* (pale), and *tmave* (dark) beer.

■ At the Kozel Brewery in Velké Popovice, just outside Prague, see how **caramel ale with dark foam** is distilled from the water of forest springs, hops, and barley. Sample the brews, and eat in the restaurant.

■ At the Pilsner Urquell Brewery, **taste the legend!** Drink the unfiltered, unpasteurized "benchmark" beer (kept for quality control) from one of the old barrels.

EUROPE

BELGIUM

Trappist Monastery Beers

Sample the delicious, world-class beers that are produced in the quiet, contemplative setting of Belgium's Trappist monasteries.

Six of Belgium's Trappist monasteries—Saint Sixtus of Westvleteren, near Ieper (Ypres); Our Lady of Scourmont, Chimay; Our Lady of Orval, near the village of Florenville; Our Lady of Saint-Remy, Rochefort; Saint Benedict, Achel; and Our Lady of the Sacred Heart, Westmalle—are authorized to use the Authentic Trappist Product label. To carry this badge of honor, the entire production process must be carried out, or supervised, by Trappist monks inside a Trappist monastery. Within these limits, there is considerable variety—in all, the six monasteries brew some 20 different beers. Founded in the 11th century, Orval is the oldest brewery, so 1,000 years of tradition go into your drink. Only the best natural ingredients are used, and the beers are brewed using traditional, nonmechanized processes. The breweries are not open to the public, but each abbey's beers can be sampled in the abbey shop or in local cafés, and all but Westvleteren's are widely distributed in Belgium. All profits go to the maintenance and charitable work of the religious communities.

WHEN TO GO Any time of year. To witness the process firsthand, Orval brewery opens its doors to the public for two days a year; check the monastery's website for dates and booking arrangements.

HOW LONG Two or three days.

PLANNING Rent a car in Antwerpen (Antwerp) for a round-trip of approximately 450–500 miles (725–800 km). Most of the monasteries are not open to the public except for their churches.

INSIDE INFORMATION Private buyers and retailers can purchase supplies of Westvleteren beer only at the abbey. It is produced in limited quantities and must be reserved in advance. See the monastery's website for details.

WEBSITES belgium-tourism.be, orval.be, sintsixtus.be, trappistes-rochefort.com

HIGHLIGHTS

▥ Sample Westvleteren's rich, malty, and **very rare Abbott** beer in the Café In De Vrede next to the monastery.

▥ Taste Chimay's classic **Blue beer** with a piece of the abbey's **beer-flavored cheese**.

▥ Tour Orval's medieval **abbey ruins** and **museum**, then taste the beer, dubbed the **"Queen of Trappists."** The abbey's beer and cheese can be bought in the shop.

▥ Try **Rochefort's dark, sweet beers,** which are available in three strengths: 6, 8, and 10.

Set in tranquil countryside, Our Lady of Orval brews one of the best-known Trappist beers.

Wine Route Through Hungary

Wander the intensely rural northeast of the country to find some of the world's most ancient golden wines made in traditional ways.

The highways out of Budapest in summer take you through vast fields of buttery sunflowers spreading to the horizon. Your goal is Tokaj-Hegyalja, a pastoral wine region beneath the Carpathian Mountains known for a singular amber wine that Voltaire said, "weaves the golden threads of the mind." In controlled production since the 17th century, Tokaj is one of the oldest demarcated wines in the world. The signature Tokaj is the Aszú, made from the local Furmint and Harslevelu grapes that hang late on the vine, until the fall mists off the Bodrog River cause *botrytis*, the noble rot that gives the wine its intense sweetness. And you feel Old World Europe here as you plunge into musty wine caves—ancient warrens dug into the hillsides—where wooden tasting bars are set among the oak casks. The region extends from the town of Tokaj in the south to Sárospatak in the northeast. From either place, you are in easy reach of the wineries around towns such as Màd, Tarcal, and Tolcsva, which also has a small museum. Along the way, as you pass through villages of low, red-roofed buildings, you'll find yourself slowing down for a man struggling with a load of hay or driving a donkey cart, or pausing to watch an elderly woman with a water bucket returning from the well to her cottage—which has a satellite dish on the roof.

EUROPE

WHEN TO GO In April and May the weather is pleasant and the hills are splashed with wildflowers. During harvest in October and early November, you can watch the grapes being handpicked into baskets, sometimes amid a light snowfall.

HOW LONG Tokaj is about three hours' drive east from Budapest. Tokaj and Sárospatak are about 25 miles (40 km) apart along the main N37 road. Allow around five days to explore the towns and villages, taste the wines, and take in some nature hikes.

PLANNING Tasting is readily available at many wineries: you pay a flat fee or per glass. Most wineries require you to book at least 24 hours in advance for a tour.

INSIDE INFORMATION In Hungary, you are not permitted to have any alcohol at all in your bloodstream while driving, so be prepared to appoint a driver. Some hotels may help with this, but it can be expensive.

WEBSITES tokaji.com, gotohungary.com/wines

HIGHLIGHTS

▪ If you are lucky, you may have a chance to try the very rare and expensive **Essencia**, the liquid gold drippings from grapes pressing down on each other in the bin.

▪ Visit Tokaj's **museum**, which houses exhibits of regional religious art and of winegrowing and winemaking.

▪ The area has unrestricted **vineyard walking** and **hiking** up hillsides forested with oak, hornbeam, and beech.

▪ Visit **the 19th-century wine house** in Disznoko, near Mád, where you can dine, then taste the dessert wine in the cellar.

▪ Don't miss the opportunity to try one of the wines made by **István Szepsy**, one of the best-known Tokaj winemakers.

Opposite: Tokaj wine is matured in the bottles in labyrinthine cellars. The mold that develops on the cellar walls and on the bottles allows the wine to age indefinitely. A long aging process gives the wine its rich, sweet character.
Above: Tokaj-Hegyalja is the only winemaking region in the world that is a World Heritage site.

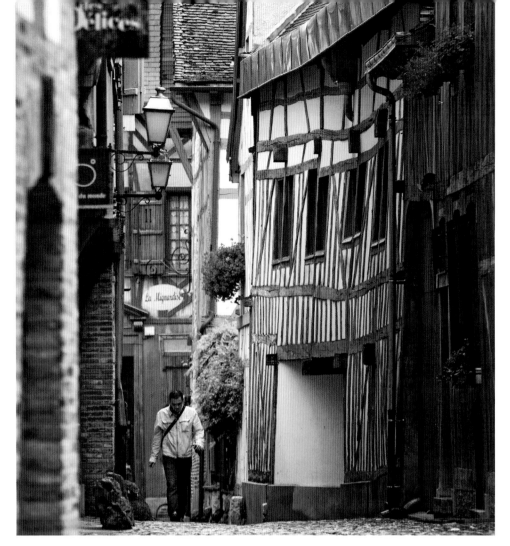

The Rue des Chats in the historic center of Troyes looks like something out of a fairy tale.

Champagne Tour

A sparkling tour through the vineyards of
Champagne gives cause for celebration at every turn.

Julius Caesar trained his troops in the Champagne region, and later Romans defeated Attila the Hun there. Today, neatly trimmed vineyards fill the area, growing the white-skinned Chardonnay and black-skinned Pinot Noir and Pinot Meunier grapes used to make the sparkling wines for which Champagne is now famous. Beneath the chalky soil between Reims, the regional capital, and Épernay, the Romans also carved miles of tunnels, providing the ideal environment for aging fine champagne. Many of the major houses are based in Reims and Épernay, most of them offering tours and tastings. After sampling these, ramble south toward the Côte des Blancs, between Épernay and Sézanne, home to many small wine-producers. Some make *blanc de blancs* champagnes, using only Chardonnay grapes. Chardonnay and Pinot go into the wines from around Vertus; and from Troyes, you can reach the Aube vineyards around Bar-sur-Seine and Bar-sur-Aube, another bastion of small winemakers.

WHEN TO GO The best time is in May and June.

HOW LONG The distance from Paris to Reims or Épernay, by car or train, is short enough for a weekend, but plan on a week for exploring the whole region, its medieval villages, and small wineries.

PLANNING You can explore the area independently by car, or join a tour. Wine sampling, or dégustation, in the major houses is usually included in the price of a cellar tour. Call about a visit in advance.

INSIDE INFORMATION Mailly-Champagne holds a village fête each May. Its regional wine cooperative is a good place to shop.

WEBSITES champagne.fr/en, en.ot-epernay.com

HIGHLIGHTS

▦ In Épernay, visit de Castellane for a tour of the **champagne-making process** and a tasting. You can then clamber up the 216-ft (66 m) high tower and enjoy a good view of the town and the Marne Valley.

▦ Stop in the village of Cuis, south of Épernay, for a **wonderful view** of the vine-covered plains of Champagne.

▦ Book a visit to the family winery of **Launois Père & Fils** at Le-Mesnil-sur-Oger on the Côte des Blancs. The tour includes a small museum, housing a collection of antique winemaking equipment, and a tasting.

▦ Explore the unspoiled **medieval center** of Troyes. It also has fine Renaissance buildings.

| FRANCE |

Cheeses of Normandy

To the French, bread, cheese, and wine are known as the holy trinity of the table—where better to enjoy them than Normandy!

The villages tucked into Normandy's lush, green valleys set—and jealously guard—the standards for the legendary cheeses that bear their names. These include luscious Camembert, spicy Livarot, creamy Pont l'Eveque—a type that dates back to the 13th century—and Neufchâtel from Bray, which is available in a variety of shapes, including square, round, and cylindrical. This is a journey into a region of picturesque villages, black-and-white, half-timbered farmhouses, and ancient churches. Normandy wears its gastronomic laurels with pride. In Camembert, for instance, an exhibition center honors the local product with a facade that resembles the cheese's characteristic round, wooden box. Not far away is a statue of Marie Harel, who, according to local tradition, perfected the recipe in 1791, during the turbulent years of the French Revolution. Visitors to these lush valleys often remark that the sleek, black-and-white Normandy cows grazing in pastures fringed by apple trees seem to carry themselves with a degree of self-conscious dignity not commonly seen in dairy herds elsewhere, as if aware of their importance in the gastronomic scheme of things.

WHEN TO GO May, June, and September are best. If possible, avoid July and August, when the roads are very crowded (July 14 is France's biggest national holiday).

HOW LONG Two to three days by car, or longer, to allow ample time to explore nearby historic towns.

PLANNING Caen and Lisieux are close enough to the cheesemaking villages to provide useful locations for an overnight stay. Rouen, although a little farther from Camembert, is rich in cultural and culinary attractions and would also make a fascinating base. All are within easy reach of Paris by car or train.

INSIDE INFORMATION Do what the locals do and balance the richness of Normandy's cheese-, cream-, and butter-based cuisine by enjoying a *trou normande* – a small glass of calvados – as a digestif between courses or at the end of a meal.

WEBSITES en.normandie-tourisme.fr, normandie-degustation-terroir.fr/fromages-normandie

| HIGHLIGHTS

▨ Visit one of the many **open-air markets** to gather the ingredients for the world's finest picnic: rustic breads, a selection of Normandy cheeses, local pâtés, and fresh fruit (especially in apple season).

▨ Sample unique **farmhouse cheeses** in the places where they are made.

▨ Quaff the delicious (but potent) **apple ciders** made on local farms and often sold right at the cider press.

▨ Discover other rich local **dairy delicacies**, such as *confiture de lait*, a milk preserve with a salty-sweet flavor, Normandy's answer to the more widely known *dulce de leche*.

The village of Camembert, surrounded by idyllic Normandy farmland, has given its name to one of the world's most famous cheeses.

Top 10
Vineyard Stays

Vineyard resorts make wine tastings into country getaways, blending gourmet cuisine, spa treatments, and outdoor recreation.

❶ KENWOOD INN & SPA, SONOMA VALLEY, CALIFORNIA

Famous Sonoma county has almost 60,000 acres (24,000 ha) of vineyards and more than 400 individual wineries for the energetic oenophile. After a day of sipping wine, floating in hot-air balloons, and browsing the shops around Sonoma's historic town square, Kenwood's guests can relax at a spa that features treatments like the Vinoperfect Facial, Honey Wine Wrap, and Crushed Cabernet Scrub.

PLANNING The valley is also home to the historic (1895) Sonoma Mission Inn & Spa. kenwoodinn.com

❷ VIÑA VIK, MILLAHUE, CHILE

Chile's first destination winery, Viña Vik is the brainchild of Scandinavian billionaire Alexander Vik and his wife, Carrie, who wanted to combine fine wine, gourmet food, and modern art at one location. The 22 guest rooms, all of them strikingly different, were designed by leading Latin American, European, and Asian artists.

PLANNING Viña Vik offers horseback trips to Lapostolle, another user-friendly winery on the other side of the Coastal Range. vikchile.com

❸ THE LOUISE, BAROSSA VALLEY, AUSTRALIA

The German vintners who pioneered South Australia's Barossa Valley never imagined anything like this— a culinary resort set amid some of the region's most famous names in wine. This outback adventure includes private wine tastings and vineyard experiences at nearby wineries as well as cooking classes and the chance to have a bush breakfast with kangaroos.

PLANNING Founded in 1851, nearby Seppeltsfield Estate is renowned for its fortified wines. thelouise.com.au

❹ ARGOS OF CAPPADOCIA, TURKEY

One of the cradles of wine, Turkey's Cappadocia region now abounds with vineyards again thanks to destination wineries like Argos. Built into the remains of a medieval monastery near Göreme, the resort features guest rooms in underground caves and ancient monks' quarters. While the grape varieties of Turkey are unfamiliar—whites Narince and Emir and reds Bogazkere, Öküzgözü, and Kalecik Karası—they produce award-winning wines that are worth the trek.

PLANNING Argos grows and produces wine from three different grapes. argosincappadocia.com

In the Sonoma Valley, California, lush vineyards bake in the afternoon sun. The steep hills of Hood Mountain Regional Park tower in the distance.

❺ LOISIUM RESORT, DANUBE VALLEY, AUSTRIA

The Kamptal wine region north of Vienna is the setting for this postmodern hideaway, designed by cutting-edge American architect Steven Holl. Dramatic design aside, the local white wines are superb, especially the Riesling, and wine features prominently in both the resort restaurant and treatments in the Aveda Spa.

PLANNING Austria's Wachau and Kremstal wine districts are nearby along the north bank of the Danube. loisium.com

❻ POGGIO AL CASONE, TUSCANY, ITALY

While the Chianti is certainly tasty—not the least because it's made with organically grown grapes—it's the small things that make this Tuscan villa resort such a special place. Like the saltwater pool, the yoga sessions amid the vineyards, the delicious pumpkin and leek soup, and the fact that it's still family owned and operated.

PLANNING A wide selection of Tuscan wines is available at the Cantina delle Colline Pisane co-op in nearby Crespina. poggioalcasone.com

❼ LES SOURCES DE CAUDALIE, BORDEAUX, FRANCE

Caudalie describes the lingering essence of wine on the palate, an apt name for a five-star vineyard resort in the heart of the Bordeaux wine country. The 72 guest rooms are divided between a rustic modern campus and the 18th-century Château Le Thil. The surrounding vineyards can be explored on foot, bike, or by horse-drawn carriage.

PLANNING The resort can arrange private limo, boat, or helicopter tours of the Bordeaux region. sources-caudalie.com/en

❽ CAN BONASTRE WINE RESORT, CATALONIA, SPAIN

With views across the vineyards to Montserrat Mountain, a gourmet eatery, pampering spa, and 13 varieties of wine produced on the property, Can Bonastre has all the fixings for an ideal Spanish wine country getaway. Top it off with the fact the resort has just 12 rooms, and if often feels like you've got the place all to yourself.

PLANNING Barcelona is less than an hour away for those who crave an urban escape. canbonastre.com/en

❾ L'AND VINEYARD RESORT, EVORA, PORTUGAL

This chic boutique in the storied Alentego region goes all in on the wine theme with its own vineyards, a Vinothérapie spa, and a wine club that lets members harvest and blend grapes into wines with their own personalized labels. The modern, minimalist design includes Sky Suites with private plunge pools and retractable ceilings that let guests literally sleep beneath the stars.

PLANNING In addition to wines, the Alentejo region produces gourmet cheese, olive oil, sausages, and smoked ham. l-and.com/landvineyards

❿ ASARA WINE ESTATE, STELLENBOSCH, SOUTH AFRICA

Hidden in the Polkadraai Hills on the western edge of Stellenbosch, Asara offers a modern take on the Cape vineyard stay. The 21st-century ambience masks the fact that the Asara farm traces its roots back to 1691. Resort activities include golf, cycling, spa treatments and, of course, wine tasting.

PLANNING Asara also boasts a tasty gin lounge. asara.co.za

Poppies in bloom add color to the vineyards of the Graves region.

FRANCE

Bordeaux Wines

Elegant reds, floral whites, and sweet Sauternes
make this tour a treat for serious vinophiles.

This tour begins on the gentle, gravelly slopes that produce the Graves wine region's first-class growths, now covered by the appellation (official name) Pessac-Léognan. Graves, which extends from Bordeaux southward along the Garonne Valley, has always been renowned for its complex reds and Sémillon and Sauvignon whites. Driving past the gates of the prestigious Château Haut-Brion and the pointed rooftops of Château Pape-Clément, both at Pessac on the outskirts of Bordeaux, one catches a glimpse of these bastions of fine wines. The route continues through a more pastoral landscape to the Château de Chantegrive at Podensac, where you can sample elegant reds and floral white wines with a hint of flint. Then turn south to Preignac, where you can taste dry whites and sweet Sauternes at Château de Malle, well-situated on the edge of Graves and Sauternes. The formal Italianate garden of this 17th-century château is an ideal setting to ponder the remarkable range of the region's wines. At the end of the season, workers handpick grapes in the last stages of *Botrytis cinerea*, the essential noble rot. It is this natural element that gives Sauternes a distinctive, silky sweetness, aided by the fall fogs that hug vineyards along the Ciron River.

WHEN TO GO March to April, or October to November during the last days of harvest in Barsac and Sauternes. Châteaux and most historic sights are open only from Easter to early November. Spring is the best time if you want to tour the area by bicycle.

HOW LONG The Graves Chais Ouvert (Open Cellars) in early November can be visited in a weekend. Otherwise, allow a week to explore the area and make tasting stops.

PLANNING You can rent a car in Bordeaux. Check châteaux websites in advance; an appointment is usually necessary to visit for tasting and purchasing wine.

INSIDE INFORMATION Bicycles can be rented in Léognan.

WEBSITES bordeaux.com/uk/Our-Terroir/Graves-and-Sauternais, activegourmetholidays.com

HIGHLIGHTS

▪ In late October, watch out for **gray cranes** migrating in waves over the Gironde, sending their burbling cries echoing across the skies.

▪ Visit **Château La Brède**, home of 18th-century philosopher, writer, and winemaker, Baron de Montesquieu, off the D108 running through the town of La Brède.

▪ Relax while you enjoy a **majestic Sauternes** made from the overripe grapes produced in the Château de Malle vineyard.

EUROPE

| ITALY |
Truffles and Mushrooms

Go in search of one of the rarest and most highly prized of all culinary delights—the white truffle.

No one with a passion for good food and wine needs an excuse to visit Italy, whatever the time of year. But those who can make time for a brief fall journey to the ancient town of Alba, in the lovely vineyard-covered Langhe hills southeast of Turin, will be able to enjoy one of the golden moments of the Italian gastronomic calendar. This is the season when wild mushrooms—porcini, chanterelles, and other richly flavored varieties—burst into life in northern Italy's fields and woodlands. It is also the time when that rare jewel among fungi—the intensely aromatic white truffle—is dug out from its hiding places among the roots of trees with the help of specially trained dogs. There are five varieties, depending on the species of tree—oak, poplar, weeping willow, linden, or vine—on whose roots it grows, and the color varies from white to gray or brown. At truffle auctions held in Alba and its environs, chefs and rich gourmets bid astronomical sums for these "white diamonds." Truffles can be hard to find if the weather is bad, and the price can double in a week. Their heady perfume fills the streets outside local restaurants, where they feature heavily on menus throughout the season.

WHEN TO GO Fall; the National Truffle Fair at Alba is held in October. Other towns, including Asti and Acqui Terme, hold truffle fairs and markets in October or November. Dishes featuring truffles and other fresh wild fungi feature on restaurant menus from late September through the winter season.

HOW LONG Three to five days for a leisurely exploration of the area by car.

PLANNING If visiting Alba during the Truffle Fair, be sure to reserve hotel accommodation well in advance.

INSIDE INFORMATION White truffles do not suit cooking. They should always be used raw and grated over food. When tinned or bottled, truffles also lose their unique flavor so are not worth buying as souvenirs.

WEBSITES italia.it/en/discover-italy/piedmont.html, lebaccanti.com

EUROPE

HIGHLIGHTS

▦ Relish the intense perfume of a dish of the buttery local pasta – *tajarin* – topped with a shower of finely shaved fragments of **raw white truffle**.

▦ Savor the succulent flavors and sensuous texture of fresh **porcini mushrooms** in a perfectly made, soul-satisfying dish of risotto.

▦ Explore the fairs and markets for **local gastronomic delights**: salami flavored with Barolo wine, chestnut honey, and cheeses such as *bruz* and Piedmontese ricotta.

A *trifolau*, or professional truffle hunter, watches as his dog digs for the precious fungus.

Slow Food of Tuscany

Forget fast food—go slow as you explore this much-loved region of Italy, tasting classic dishes made from carefully tended ingredients.

The contemporary international movement known as Slow Food—dedicated to encouraging and protecting regional culinary traditions, local produce, and environmentally sensitive food production—was founded by Italians. Although its official headquarters lie farther northwest, in Piedmont, Tuscany makes a perfect starting point for a journey into the heartland of the Slow Food philosophy. For the people of Tuscany, good honest food is a passion. They argue enthusiastically about differing versions of ancestral recipes and eagerly anticipate the arrival of seasonal delicacies. Winter brings thick soups made with beans (so beloved of Tuscans that they are known to their compatriots as "bean-eaters"), deep green *cavolo nero*, known in the U.S. as lascinato kale, and *farro*, an ancient variety of wheat. Spring and summer offer more delicate vegetables, such as baby broad beans to accompany a young, fresh Pecorino cheese. Fall sends foragers into the woods for game, porcini mushrooms, and chestnuts. Rustic sourdough breads, spit-roasted meats, and pappardelle—wide, flat noodles that are traditionally served with braised hare sauce—grace the table year-round. Tuscany's Renaissance cities and landscape make an incomparable setting for such feasts.

WHEN TO GO Every season brings its own treats, so for food-lovers there is no "bad" time of year. But many family-run restaurants and food shops close in August, while the countryside is especially lovely in spring and fall.

HOW LONG At least five days by car; more to explore the romantic cities, villages, and landscape.

PLANNING Siena, Florence, and Lucca make ideal bases for day trips in all directions; or stay in the countryside at one of the farms that welcomes guests as part of the Agriturismo program.

INSIDE INFORMATION When you stop in towns and villages, look for bulletin boards, usually outside the town hall or in the main square, advertising *sagras*. These are food festivals celebrating local specialties with large communal meals to which visitors are warmly welcomed.

WEBSITES slowfood.com, agriturismo.com

HIGHLIGHTS

▪ *Finocchiona* **salami** – taking its name from wild fennel seeds – is one of a huge array of regional cured meats, sausages, and hams. You will find platters of these at small restaurants and *osteria* (wine shops with tables).

▪ **Extra-virgin olive oils** are sold fresh from the mill. There are hundreds from small growers and large estates.

▪ Enjoy a thick, succulent slab of T-bone steak, **Bistecca alla Fiorentina**, grilled over a wood fire and sourced from rare Chianina cattle.

▪ Visit **wine estates** that produce classic Chiantis, the noble Brunello di Montalcino, and vibrant whites, such as Vernaccia di San Gimignano.

The windows of this long-established Sienese delicatessen are replete with bunches of salami and cured ham.

Catania's morning fish market is a hive of activity during the week.

ITALY

Sicilian Food and Wine

Explore the rich and diverse culinary tradition of this ancient island on a drive from Palermo to Syracuse.

In Palermo's old quarters, vendors sell fish of all shapes and sizes—and the freshest of sardines are rolled into a classic favorite, *Sarde a Beccafico*. Leaving Palermo, a drive across the island's mountainous heart is at once a journey through heart-stopping vistas and a revelation of Sicily's multilayered history. After a stop to see 15th- and 16th-century churches in the hill town of Enna, a reviving lunch on Piazza 6 Dicembre might consist of *Braciole alla Siciliana*. This variation on marinated pork chops grilled and seasoned with aromatic oregano is a favorite across inland regions. Sicilian wines run from deep, tannic Nero d'Avola and hearty Corleone reds to whites made of Catanese Bianco and Grecanico varieties. South of Mount Etna on the Ionian coast, spend a morning in Catania's fish market—the Mediterranean's largest. At last, overlooking Syracuse's historic Ortigia port, end your journey nibbling a marzipan *Frutta Martorana* and wash it down with a glass of sparkling Castelmonte Frizzante.

WHEN TO GO Avoid the summer months. In October, the sea is still warm enough for swimming along Capo Passero beaches, while grape harvests are underway in vineyards southwest of Syracuse.

HOW LONG Allow at least two weeks to enjoy the cuisine and explore the island.

PLANNING Comfortable shoes for irregular terrain are recommended, as many treasures are waiting to be found off the beaten path. Catania's fish market is open Monday through Saturday, 5 a.m. to 11 a.m.

INSIDE INFORMATION Road signs are irregular and often hidden behind branches or shrubbery. If renting a car, study maps thoroughly before starting out.

WEBSITES bestofsicily.com, thinksicily.com

HIGHLIGHTS

▥ People taking the **passeggiata**, an early evening local stroll for all ages, fill the squares and main avenues of most Sicilian towns. Observe the action from a sidewalk café table with a refreshing gelato.

▥ Central Sicily's hill towns are ideal for **picnics**, and spicy sausages, Pecorino cheese, and *grissini* bought from a local market are perfect fare.

▥ Sicilian wines are good sipping companions to **Arancine**, the round, deep-fried saffron-rice balls filled with mushrooms, cheese, minced greens, or ham.

▥ If you have time, travel west from Palermo to Trapani to explore the seaport famed for its salt flats and windmills.

ITALY | FRANCE | SPAIN

From Pesto to Paella

Marvel at the distinctive local specialties that reveal themselves on this journey along Europe's southern shores.

The sun-blessed Mediterranean coastline—from the Italian region of Liguria, along the French Riviera, through Provence, and into northeastern Spain—is a food-lover's paradise. All along this storied coastline, the hills are fragrant with wild herbs: marjoram, wild fennel, lavender, and thyme. Local markets in the ancient hill towns and atmospheric coastal cities excite the senses with a rainbow of local fruits and vegetables. Vibrant flavors and simple presentation predominate: lusciously fruity or peppery olive oils, aromatic salad leaves, tomatoes that truly taste of sunshine, the voluptuous intensity of fresh garlic, and sparkling-fresh seafood. Savor Liguria's pungent pesto sauce, a blend of pounded garlic, local olive oil, pine nuts, and the basil that grows in profusion—that bears scant resemblance to the versions found in supermarkets back home. In Provence, taste *pissaladière*, a rich, savory tart topped with caramelized onions and anchovy. Explore the countless variations on fish soups concocted from the daily catch, culminating in the celebrated, saffron-gilded bouillabaisse of Marseilles. Crossing the Spanish border, discover the cuisine of Catalonia—lobster casseroles, goose with glazed pears, fiery Romesco sauce, and the simplicity of fresh curd cheese with honey. Complete your explorations in the rice fields of Valencia, birthplace of the classic paella and a repertoire of other intriguing rice dishes.

WHEN TO GO If possible, avoid the peak tourist season of July and August, when roads, restaurants, and hotels are at their most crowded.

HOW LONG Allow at least seven to 10 days for the 750- to 800-mile (1,207–1,287 km) journey. Allow ample time to explore ancient seaports, glamorous coastal resorts, and atmospheric villages hidden in the hills.

PLANNING The Mediterranean coast draws food-lovers and sunseekers from all over Europe, so reserve hotel accommodation and tables at well-known or Michelin-starred restaurants in advance.

INSIDE INFORMATION Take a morning stroll through the local market to check out the fishermen's catch, and note what seasonal produce is at its peak. Then look out for restaurants with daily specials making the most of these wonderful ingredients.

WEBSITES deliciousitaly.com, francetourism.com, spain.info/en

HIGHLIGHTS

▪ Linger over an aperitif on a seaside terrace, marveling at the blue light of a **Mediterranean evening** and anticipating the pleasures of dinner to come.

▪ Savor **timeless, rustic Provençal** specialties at one of the town's oldest and best-loved restaurants, La Mère Besson. If it's on offer, don't miss the Grand Aïoli – chickpeas, salt cod, and an array of fresh vegetables swathed in Provence's gloriously garlicky mayonnaise-style sauce.

▪ Treat yourself to breakfast or an early lunch alongside the locals in **La Boqueria**, Barcelona's vast covered market. Perch at a counter to sample thick wedges of tortilla, the substantial Spanish omelette. Or be adventurous and ask for what your neighbor is having – maybe a savory little stew of beans and baby squid.

Opposite: At the Cours Saleya Flower Market in Nice, the best produce from the region – including seafood, fruit, and vegetables – is on sale. Early morning is the best time to visit. Above: Olive trees have been cultivated in the Mediterranean region for more than 1,000 years, and olives and olive oil are at the heart of Mediterranean cooking.

Tapas of Barcelona

Move from bar to bar sampling small plates
of local delicacies on this tapas tour.

Aromas of warm pastries, espresso coffee, and sugary *xurros* (fried pastry snacks) waft from stalls in the Boqueria food market. Enter the market from La Rambla to discover a hive of activity as stallholders spread out their wares, be it seafood, fruit, or vegetables in season. Here, too, are Bar Pinotxo and El Quim, two of Barcelona's best-known tapas bars. Open for breakfast and lunch, they serve tapas dishes made from fresh market produce. You can wash them down with Cava (the local sparkling wine), a still wine, or a beer. Exploring the central districts of Barri Gòtic (Old Town), El Born, L'Eixample, and La Ribera, you can find simple or exotic tapas dishes on offer at every turn. At Bodega La Palma, a traditional bar on Calle Palma, wines are served straight from the barrel into glasses or ceramic jugs. At Euskal Extea, a Basque cultural center and one of the city's many Basque restaurants on Placeta Montcada, tapas are served at the bar and specialties include octopus and stuffed peppers. Barcelona's medieval alleyways are crammed with bars and restaurants, and the city offers an irresistible combination of fresh, tasty foods mingled with a rich mix of art and architecture. This was the home not only of Gaudí, but also of Picasso, Miró, and Dalí.

WHEN TO GO Barcelona has much to offer all year round, but in spring (mid-March to early May) and fall (mid-September to end October), the weather is mild and the streets and cafés less crowded.

HOW LONG Allow a minimum of three days to get a feel for the different central precincts, though to make the most of the food, architecture, galleries, and museums, a week is better.

PLANNING September 24 each year is the Festa de la Mercè, held in celebration of Barcelona's patron saint.

INSIDE INFORMATION When ordering tapas, make sure you know what you will be charged for. In some cafés, if you are seated at a table, waiters deliver dishes until told to stop; this can get expensive. In bars, they may count the empty dishes in front of you or the plastic swords or wooden sticks you eat with.

WEBSITES meet.barcelona.cat/en, barcelonaturisme.com

EUROPE

HIGHLIGHTS

▥ Visit Gaudí's **Sagrada Familia cathedral** on Avinguda de Gaudí, in El Eixample. There is a fine view from the top of the towers.

▥ The **views of city and sea** from Montjuïc are impressive, and you'll discover just how many parks and squares Barcelona has. Combine this with a visit to the **Joan Miró Foundation**.

▥ **Museu Picasso** occupies five buildings on Carra Montcada in El Born.

Tapas bars offer a wide range of mouthwatering local dishes and delicacies: seafood, tortilla, vegetable dishes, and meats.

Casks of port wine are transported down the Douro River in special boats known as *rabelos*.

| PORTUGAL |

Porto and the Douro River

*Enjoy the finest products from the region where
the world's best-known fortified wine is produced.*

Tawny and ruby—the names describe the gemlike colors of port wine, a fortified wine created in the late 1600s by English merchants. Brandy was added to wine to stabilize and preserve it so that it would survive the sea voyage to England without spoiling. Today, port is made in the same way, but the method is used not to preserve the wine but to give the drink its characteristic flavor. The gateway to the port-wine region is Porto (Oporto), the city that gave the drink its name. Here, the big producers have their warehouses and the wines are shipped around the world. Built in a gorge on the mouth of the Douro River, Porto is a vibrant city whose houses climb the steep hillsides. You can taste port here, but to learn more about the wines you need to travel up the Douro to the vineyards. The most scenic way to make the trip is by train or boat to the sleepy riverside towns of Regua and Pinhão. From Regua, where the ferry stops, you can rent a car or take the train to Pinhão, in the heart of the region. Or you can stay nearby in the beautiful Pousada de Mesao Frio built high above the river in a vineyard. The 18th-century house is furnished with antiques and has an excellent restaurant and a formal garden full of roses and orange trees. From your balcony, you can watch the moon shining on the river far below.

WHEN TO GO September is the best time as you can see the harvest, but the weather is good in spring and fall.

HOW LONG Two to three days will give you time to relax, unwind, and enjoy the area and the port.

PLANNING Book well in advance if you want to stay at a *pousada*, a boutique-style hotel in a historic home or castle. They are small, so book in advance.

INSIDE INFORMATION Take the boat in one direction and the train in the other, so that you can experience both kinds of trip.

WEBSITES visitportugal.com, douroazul.com

HIGHLIGHTS

▪ Walk through the vineyards, and enjoy the **view of the river valley** spread out beneath you.

▪ Go to a **winetasting** in a *finca*, or port winery, and learn how port is made. Then take a tutored tasting to learn more about this heady wine.

▪ Take the **boat trip** between Porto and Regua with the cliffs of the Douro Valley towering over you and vineyards gliding by on both sides.

EUROPE

Coffee is an important symbol of hospitality among the Bedouin. It is flavored with cardamom pods and brewed in front of guests.

JORDAN

A Bedouin Feast

Relish cardamom coffee and lamb roasted in yogurt,
all in a setting of cinnamon-colored stone in Jordan's Wadi Rum.

Palms mark the entrance to a Bedouin camp of thatched goat-hair tents. The sheik greets you with cardamom-laced coffee, and soon two of his desert guards shovel the blistering sand off an underground oven, releasing the scent of *mansaf*: lamb slow-roasted in dried yogurt, served with rice and pine nuts. You are in Wadi Rum, a seasonal streambed (wadi) in southwest Jordan, famous for its connection with Lawrence of Arabia and the Arab Revolt during World War I—and with David Lean's classic movie of 1962, which was shot here. Lawrence called this terrain "vast, echoing, and God-like," and it is. Burnt-orange massifs rocket from the desert floor; you pass through the damp shadows of Khazali Canyon, where ancient petroglyphs dance alongside you. In the camp, you lounge on a rug and take your pick from the fare spread out before you. You use flat bread to pinch portions of hummus and baba ghanouj (eggplant and sesame paste), or slip garlic chicken from skewers. A dish of tabbouleh represents the land's strength and simplicity (the cracked wheat), as much as its defiant spark (the parsley, tomato, onion, mint, lemon). Your hosts also capture that essence—the Bedouin of Wadi Rum, where sand, scrub, and stone become an oasis each winter.

WHEN TO GO Year-round. Winter is damp, January the coolest month, and July the hottest (97ºF/36ºC).

HOW LONG Allow two days for a taster. Serious trekkers and archaeologists may prefer four to five.

PLANNING The Wadi Rum Visitor Center will arrange for you to enjoy a traditional Bedouin meal. Camping is the best way to experience the wadi. Bring your own tent and sleep under the stars, or stay in a Bedouin-style *bayt ash-sha'ar* (house of hair). The more deluxe campsites are near the village of Diseh, preferable to grimy Rum (Ramm). Camel, horseback, and jeep tours of the wadi are also available.

INSIDE INFORMATION Traditionally, the Bedouin offer three cups of coffee: one for the soul, one for the sword, and one to honor the guest. It's bad manners to ask for more.

WEBSITES visitjordan.com, wadirum.jo, captains-jo.com

HIGHLIGHTS

■ Climb Jordan's second-highest peak, **Jabal Rum** (5,741 ft/1,750 m), to see stupendous views. You have to book in advance at the Visitor Center.

■ Take a 4x4 tour of **Barrah Canyon,** where the early-morning or late-evening sun turns the rock a vivid orange. Burdah and Um Frouth are spectacular natural rock arches not to be missed.

■ Spot wildlife, such as the **Syrian wolf, striped hyena, and Nubian ibex**. In 2007, 20 Arabian oryx were reintroduced; their former presence is known from rock drawings in the wadi, and their numbers have grown to 50.

ASIA

SOUTH AFRICA

Cape Winelands

South African wines are renowned for their diversity and quality; see where they are made and you enter a garden of earthly delights.

Centered around the university city of Stellenbosch, east of Cape Town, with its oak-lined streets and historic buildings dating back to the 17th century, the Cape wine routes offer a rich diversity of scenic beauty, cultural history, and a variety of wines to tempt the palate. More than 100 estates are open to the public, allowing you to sample wines across a wide range of cultivars (grape varieties)—some even offer a picnic or complete lunch, which you can enjoy in resplendent gardens. The wine industry started here when Jan van Riebeeck, the first Dutch governor of the Cape, planted a vineyard in 1655—at the time, the Cape was being settled as a provisioning post for the Dutch East India Company. Later, between 1680 and 1690, French Huguenots (Protestants expelled from their homeland) arrived, and the industry began to flourish. Today, there are 15 different wine routes, so take care when planning a tour. You can't visit them all in a limited period of time. Use Stellenbosch as a base and follow up three or four international, award-winning wine producers over a few days, interspersing these with visits to the area's historic Dutch and Huguenot sites or drives through the beautiful Cape mountain passes and fertile valleys.

WHEN TO GO October to May – late spring to early fall. Serious vineyard hiking over a day is best done in spring or fall.

HOW LONG Allow four to five days to explore the area by car.

PLANNING Stellenbosch and the countryside around it are popular tourist attractions, so make sure that you book your accommodation and estate visits in advance. The Stellenbosch Tourist Information Centre provides maps and makes recommendations. Its staff will help you to book accommodation online.

INSIDE INFORMATION Make plenty of time to visit the Rustenberg vineyard with its farm and winery because the tranquility of the setting is exceptional.

WEBSITES stellenbosch.travel, wineroute.co.za

AFRICA

HIGHLIGHTS

▥ **The Rustenberg vineyard** near Stellenbosch has South Africa's finest cellar for Bordeaux-blend wines, mingling Cabernet Sauvignon, Cabernet Franc, and Merlot.

▥ Kanonkop Wine Estate is the closest South African equivalent to a Premier Cru vineyard. Sample the **Pinotage wines**, produced from a uniquely South African cross between the Pinot Noir and Hermitage grapes.

▥ Dating back to 1702, when Jan Meerland bought the farm, Meerendal Wine Estate is renowned especially for its **Shiraz vintages**. You can also sample Cabernet and Pinotage wines.

The serried ranks of vines around Stellenbosch, ripening under the South African sun.

Malaysian Melting Pot

*From street stalls to smart restaurants, the food of Malaysia
provides a rich and colorful culinary experience.*

Start in Singapore and journey up peninsular Malaysia, from the country's hot, flat south to its hilly, jungly north, and you'll see the influences that Chinese, Indian, and Arab traders have had on the region's cuisines during the last two thousand years. In Malacca, an ancient spice-trading port on the country's west coast, try dishes that combine Chinese and Indian ingredients with Malay cooking sensibilities, such as *popiah*, jicama-stuffed Chinese spring rolls drizzled with a typically Malay-style peanut sauce. Then travel by bus to Kuala Lumpur, Malaysia's largest city. The culinary identity of its three million residents is shaped by the three ethnic groups that call it home: the Malays, the Chinese, and the Indians. Stroll through Chinatown and enjoy excellent Hokkien and Hainanese fare. Take a trip to Kampung Baru, one of the city's Malay enclaves, and sample *nasi lemak*, Malay-style coconut rice, fragrant with ginger. Visit Brickfields district for an authentic taste of south India. Or savor the elements of all three in such uniquely Kuala-Lumpur dishes as *kare laksa*, one of Southeast Asia's—if not the world's—most delicious noodle dishes. End your travels in George Town, a city on the small Malaysian island of Penang. Street foods reach their South Asian apogee here: it seems as if every square inch of public real estate has been taken over by vendors (or hawkers, as they're called locally) offering their tempting fare.

WHEN TO GO The weather is warm all year. There are two rainy seasons, in April–May and October–November, but rainstorms do not usually last long.

HOW LONG A month is ideal, but the trip could be done in two weeks.

PLANNING You can make the entire journey by train, or mix train and bus. If you are traveling by train, change at Tampin for Malacca. You can catch the ferry to Penang at Butterworth.

INSIDE INFORMATION Food is usually eaten with the fingers of your right hand, without the help of utensils. Pick up the food in smallish, bite-sized clumps employing only your fingertips, as though gently squeezing a large strawberry. Use your thumb to slide the food away from your fingertips and into your mouth. The exception is noodle dishes, which are consumed with chopsticks by nearly everyone.

WEBSITE motour.gov.my/en

HIGHLIGHTS

▐ In Singapore, seek out **ketam lada hitam** (black pepper crab), a street-hawker specialty flavored with ginger, fresh turmeric, and black peppercorns.

▐ Nibble on a **satay stick** when it's warm and infused with the primal aroma of the fire it was cooked over. The origins of the dish are thought to be the kebabs that Arab spice merchants introduced to Java, Indonesia, in the 8th century. The Javanese embraced the Arab kebabs, developing marinades with their favorite aromatics, including cilantro, ginger, galangal, lemongrass, garlic, and shallots.

▐ Malaysia is a snacker's paradise, and street food has been raised to an art form. Visit a **hawker center**, where as many as 300 merchants offer their specialties from tiny stalls under constantly whirring ceiling fans.

Opposite: Malay fishermen use wooden boats and handmade nets and fish traps to catch the fish, squid, lobster, and shrimp that are a vital part of the Malay diet. Above: Spices are used liberally in Malay cooking. Cloves (left), which are dried flower buds, are used in savory dishes and curries, and nutmeg (right) in curries and sweet dishes.

Chapter 7

INTO THE ACTION

These journeys are perfect for people who love to be at the heart of things. Some are for the super-fit and daring, offering a chance to push yourself to the limit; others are gentler experiments. But all are voyages of discovery, because wherever they take you, and whatever activities they offer, they will help you to know yourself that little bit better. Wilderness lovers can taste the icy joys of dogsledding in Alaska. If you like to get up close with wildlife in warmer climes, ride an elephant in Nepal or take a photo safari through Botswana, where meetings with rhinos, leopards, buffalo, lions, and elephants are almost guaranteed. Skiers will enjoy a swoop off Mont Blanc, or its tropical equivalent—hang gliding over Rio de Janeiro. Another journey leads into the depths—a cave network under the Caribbean island of Puerto Rico. But not even the most robust extreme sports enthusiasts should underrate the courage needed to dance the tango in Buenos Aires, where local adepts, with flashing limbs and smoldering glances, delightedly welcome you to the dance floor to share their passion but take no prisoners.

White-water rafters are all focus as they ride the rapids on Arizona's Colorado River. Enjoy this high-adrenaline activity wherever rivers plunge through narrow gorges – try other sections of the Grand Canyon or West Virginia's New River.

Alaskan huskies are famed for their endurance in dogsled races.

ALASKA

Dogsledding in Alaska

Pulled by a team of huskies, you whisk across a snow-covered wilderness to experience the solitude of unspoiled nature.

In the dog yard, the dogs are barking—they know an outing across the snow-covered Alaskan wilderness is being prepared. The chosen few are hooked up to the line, frantic with excitement. Then you take your place on the back of the runners, release your snow hook, and the dogs fall silent as they bound toward the trail. All you hear now is the gentle creaking of the sled and the patter of paws on snow. You are mushing, traveling on a dog sled—from the Canadian French word *marcher*, to walk. Steam billows from the dogs' mouths as they settle into a rhythmic trot. To the side of the trail, spruce trees are laden with the jagged gems of hoarfrost; beyond them towers Denali, North America's highest peak, rising to 20,320 feet (6,194 meters). The prints of moose and foxes pockmark the snow, while ravens track your team overhead. Occasionally, the dogs' heads pivot to one side, and following their gaze, you spot pure-white ptarmigan or perhaps a lolloping Arctic hare. Beyond these brief encounters, you meet nobody. In this pristine wilderness, you're alone with your dogs.

WHEN TO GO Mid-November to mid-April, snow and trail conditions permitting.

HOW LONG Trips can last from an hour and a half to five days.

PLANNING Operators will provide full outer clothing and winter boots. Pack wool and fleece, not cotton, to wear underneath. Merino wool long johns are a must.

INSIDE INFORMATION Don't sweat! If you sweat, your wet clothing will make you cold later on. It's better to feel slightly cool than to risk getting sweaty.

WEBSITES dreamadreamsleddog.com, tokoshacamp.com

HIGHLIGHTS

▓ The mushing trails run through **Denali National Park**. Covering some 9,500 sq miles (24,600 sq km), the park encompasses a complete subarctic ecosystem that's home to grizzly bears, wolves, Dall sheep, and moose. Don't worry about the bears—most of them hibernate in winter.

▓ If you choose a three- or five-day tour, you'll get a chance to drive dogs along part of the 1,151-mile (1,852 km) **Iditarod Trail**—the course used for a dogsledding race held each March between Nome and Anchorage. You'll spend a night at one of its checkpoints, where you can talk to veterans of the race.

▓ Some trips overnight at **Tokosha Mountain Lodge**, set between the Tokositna River and Pirate Lake and inaccessible by road. Enjoy the solitude, the stunning mountain views, and the owners' delicious cooking, including homemade cookies and pies.

NORTH AMERICA

CANADA

Polar Bears in Canada

On this safari, the world appears in shades of white and gray and a polar bear can be behind every rock and snowdrift.

The most alarming aspect of coming across a polar bear in the wild is not its well-earned reputation as a man killer, nor the contemptuous eyes through which it peers at you, nor the ominous poise with which it moves across the Arctic landscape, but the fact that so huge an animal can camouflage itself so effectively—even when there's *no* snow. Sleeping on a rocky shore between boulders and floating ice, a bear is often impossible to spot until you are steps away. Nowhere are the white creatures more accessible than Churchill in the northern reaches of Canada's Manitoba province. The town is renowned for outsized bears—it lies astride one of their major migration routes on the western fringe of Hudson Bay. As the pack ice starts to break up with summer, the bears make their way onto dry land in search of food. You can see them foraging around the town, but they are best viewed in the wilderness, from the safety of four-wheel-drive "tundra mobiles" with huge tires and lofty suspension. After more than 20 years of interaction, the bears have lost their fear of the vehicles and often come up to the windows to press their snouts against the glass. Expect to spend a few hours each day traveling out of town in search of bears.

WHEN TO GO October and November are the best months for bear-watching. This is when the bears congregate along the bay shore waiting for the seawater to freeze over.

HOW LONG Allow at least three nights. A week is better if you really want to soak up the arctic ambience.

PLANNING Most of the better outfitters provide you with a good cold-weather jacket. But fall temperatures dip below freezing even in the middle of the day, so you should pack your own thermal underwear, gloves and inner mittens, ski hat, and waterproof, all-weather shoes.

INSIDE INFORMATION The Hudson Bay Railway provides a leisurely alternative to flying between Winnipeg and Churchill. Operated by VIA Rail Canada, the 810-mile (1,300 km) journey takes roughly 45 hours.

WEBSITES nathab.com, everythingchurchill.com, viarail.ca/en

HIGHLIGHTS

▦ You can spend the night in **mobile lodges** in the area east of Churchill. This is like a zoo in reverse – humans inside with the bears looking in.

▦ The **aurora borealis** (northern lights) appears more than 300 nights each year, making Churchill one of the best places in the world to see them.

▦ If you visit Churchill in summer, **birds** are the attraction. Rare species in **Wapusk National Park** to the south include Hudsonian godwits, ivory gulls, Caspian terns, and gyrfalcons.

▦ In July and August you can visit Prince of Wales Fort, the remains of an 18th-century **Hudson's Bay Company fur-trading post**.

A mother and two cubs take a rest in the snow in Wapusk National Park, south of Churchill.

CANADA

The Great Trail

Hike through forests, cycle along the coast of Vancouver Island, kayak on the Athabasca River...
the choices are endless on this mammoth trail crisscrossing the whole of Canada.

When Canadians look back to 2017, and the 150th anniversary of Confederation, they will remember another great feat: the completion of the Great Trail, a 15,000-mile (24,000 kilometer) network slinking east to west from St John's, Newfoundland, to Victoria, British Columbia, and northward from Edmonton, Alberta, to the Arctic Ocean. The trail touches every province, every territory, every terrain—traversing the entire, variegated landmass of Canada, offering a range of different activities, including hiking, horse-riding, cycling, skiing, snowmobiling, kayaking. You have an appetizing choice for your first bite at the trail. How about the 168-mile (270 kilometer) section on tiny Prince Edward Island? Alternatively, you can skirt Lake Ontario and, in northern Ontario, penetrate majestic boreal forest and wilderness areas. You can paddle the Athabasca River from Alberta to British Columbia, or you can cycle the Galloping Goose—a 44-mile (71 kilometer) trail from Victoria to the Sooke Hills and the abandoned mining site of Leechtown—which gives you ocean and rural vistas all along the way. Those with a fascination for history can follow the scenic Cowichan Valley Rail Trail on Vancouver Island, the Kettle Valley Railway Trail in British Columbia, or the Whitehorse Copper Trail in the Yukon. Meanwhile, in the Northwest Territories, the truly adventurous can relive—although in much more comfort and safety—the experience of Samuel Hearne, the first European to chart the Coppermine River overland to its mouth in the Arctic Ocean.

WHEN TO GO Year-round, as it is a multiuse trail, with different sections suitable for different activities.

HOW LONG The trail is perfect for everything from hour-long recreational hikes (with a bit of bird-watching thrown in) to months-long backpacking adventures.

PLANNING Contact the local tourism board before taking to the trail to make sure your sport of choice is welcome in the province you plan to visit.

INSIDE INFORMATION The trails are in daily use by locals from more than 800 nearby cities and towns. Look for the trail pavilions along the route if you need help or advice.

WEBSITES thegreattrail.ca, canadatrails.ca

HIGHLIGHTS

▓ There are plentiful **chances to spot wildlife**. The trail winds through territory inhabited by grizzly and black bears, moose, deer, cougar, and more. On Vancouver Island, watch for the endangered Vancouver Island marmot: there are just 300 left.

▓ You can hike around the clock—if you so choose—during the **never-ending daylight** of the **Yukon** in the summer. Or take a break in the territory's capital, Whitehorse, for a vaudeville review that will rip you right back to the gold-rush days.

▓ Every section of the trail has its charms, but the 27-mile (44 km) **Guysborough Nature Trail** in Nova Scotia has, perhaps, more than its fair share, including waterfalls, a suspension bridge, and, at its eastern end, views of the largest bay on the Atlantic coast, Chedabucto Bay.

Opposite: Colors are intense in the pure air of high valleys in the Canadian Rockies. Here, the greens of the valley grass and a forest of larches contrast with the brilliant blue of the near-cloudless sky above. Above: A river scene near Banff, Alberta, creates an equally striking pattern of vivid color.

A helicopter crew unloads hiking equipment which will soon be used to scale the mountainous terrain.

Heli-Hiking in British Columbia

Helicopters transport you to remote and dramatic mountain ridges, virtually inaccessible by any other means.

The shout "Everybody huddle" rings out, and one by one hikers scuttle into the helicopter. Once gear, trekking poles, and lunches are loaded, the chopper rises above the timberline in British Columbia's Adamant Range, where you've spent the night in a mountain "hut" (a luxury refuge). Today, you are heading for the so-called Waldorf Towers—a narrow passage in a W-shaped rock formation—where you land on a snowfield above a huge glacier. After unloading passengers and gear, the chopper roars away, leaving you and your guide alone in this remote region, too far from towns for hikers to buy supplies or arrange transportation—it would take days of trekking just to reach the timberline. At the end of the day the chopper will return, taking you back to your hut. Hikes are customized to your fitness and interests. Spend an afternoon looking at alpine wildflowers, or stretch your limits by climbing a snow-covered peak.

WHEN TO GO Heli-hiking is available from early July through mid-September. August is the best month as the previous season's snow is all melted and there are fewer insects.

HOW LONG Most trips are three nights, with the exception of hut to hut adventures (see below), which are six nights.

PLANNING CMH Heli-Skiing & Summer Adventures, who organize the tours, pick you up in Banff, Alberta, at the start of the tour and take you back there at the end. They provide all hiking gear, including boots.

INSIDE INFORMATION Up the adventure quotient by hiking from hut to hut or by trying some of the more challenging climbs (which must be arranged in advance). All climbs and hikes are weather dependent.

WEBSITE www.canadianmountainholidays.com

HIGHLIGHTS

▪ Have your camera ready to capture the **view from the front seat** of the chopper as it brings you seemingly within arm's reach of the towering mountain walls.

▪ Feel free to ask plenty of questions. Your hiking and mountaineering guides are experts on the **region's ecology, geology, and natural history**, as well as mountaineering safety.

▪ At day's end, a helicopter returns you to your huts – luxurious versions of traditional alpine refuges, complete with **gourmet multicourse dinners**.

▪ Allow yourself time to explore **Banff**, the quintessential mountain town of the Canadian Rockies and site of the annual Banff International Mountain Film and Books Festivals.

NORTH AMERICA

| VERMONT |

Vermont's Catamount Trail

Ski across Vermont's glorious backcountry ... and in the evenings enjoy the comforts of a good meal and a warm bed.

The woods are silent except for the swish of your skis breaking trail through virgin powder snow and the faint staccato drilling of a distant woodpecker. As you herringbone up a steep creek bank, a trio of black-capped chickadees joins you, flitting noisily from tree to tree. Your bold foray into their territory occurs as you ski inn to inn on an 8-mile (13 kilometer) stretch of Vermont's Catamount Trail, a backcountry ski route stretching 300 miles (480 kilometers) from the Canadian border in the north to the Massachusetts border in the south. Accessing the trail from Blueberry Hill Inn in Goshen, you pass through the Moosalamoo region of Green Mountain National Forest. You follow the track as it dips down a frozen streambed before veering uphill. Then, heading south, you glide through stands of pine and spruce and past stately sugar maples and beech trees stripped by winter of their leafy finery. If you take the side trail to Churchill House Inn near Brandon, you might spy a family of browsing deer, which disappear into the forest, their white tails bobbing in unison.

WHEN TO GO December to March. Check on snow conditions and trail closures before you head out.

HOW LONG Allow four to five hours for this section of the Catamount Trail. Skiing the entire trail will take a month in all; end-to-enders typically ski it in sections, a few days at a time.

PLANNING It is essential to have proper backcountry equipment including skis and clothing, along with items such as trail maps, first-aid supplies, and a ski-repair kit.

INSIDE INFORMATION In addition to country inns, overnight accommodation is available in U.S. Forest Service cabins and at ski touring centers along the trail.

WEBSITES catamounttrail.org, inntoinn.com

HIGHLIGHTS

▧ The trail provides unparalleled access to **backcountry snow and vistas** not seen from main roads.

▧ Although many animals hibernate in winter, a surprising number don't. You may encounter **moose**, **white-tailed deer**, and even **bobcats** on the trail.

▧ The night before you set out, relax in the wood-fired sauna at **Blueberry Hill Inn** or nibble on homemade cookies. The next evening, after a long day on the trail, enjoy an après-ski glass of wine by the woodstove at **The Lilac Inn**.

It's just you, the snow, and nature all around as you ski through a wilderness of white.

Dune Buggies on the Sands of Oregon

Take a rollercoaster ride up dunes and down them in a sandy terrain that changes from day to day.

NORTH AMERICA

An iridescent blue tree swallow casts a speck of shadow over sand dunes and valleys raked by time and weather. Beneath its path, coyotes and black-tailed deer rustle in tree "islands" surrounded by the undulating sand hills of Siuslaw National Forest. Winds sweep up the grains of sand, piling them into towers rivaling skyscrapers. Suddenly, the engine of your dune buggy roars. The break to catch your breath is over. Seat belt clasped? Goggles adjusted? On this one-hour joyride, your guide zooms you and fellow passengers through the dry "sea" at speeds of up to 60 miles (97 kilometers) per hour. The scenery is a beige blur. Waves of sand are smacking your body at every zig and zag. Your driver rockets toward a hill and shouts that this mother of all dunes is 40 stories high. No one except your guide knows what lies on the other side, for the fickle terrain shifts daily. The buggy crests the bluff, slows, then plummets down into a bowl-like valley. The rollercoaster plunge takes your stomach into your throat, and when you land, you wonder if you left your brain back on the top of the dune.

WHEN TO GO May through August, after the rainy season.

HOW LONG You can choose a 30-minute or one-hour guided excursion. Set aside at least two to three days to explore the dunes recreation area and the coastal fishing villages nearby.

PLANNING Call tour operators one or two weeks ahead to schedule your trip. Temperatures are mild, but you will get cold as the relentless winds whip an average of 20 to 30 miles per hour. Wear closed-toe shoes, long pants, and a parka.

INSIDE INFORMATION Ride in the morning before it gets too windy. Don't bring your good camera because sand will dive into its crevices.

WEBSITES sandland.com, hecetalighthouse.com

HIGHLIGHTS

▓ Look for the **endangered western snowy plover** that inhabits only flat sandy areas. Other native species include the wrentit, rufous hummingbird, common murre, and pigeon guillemot.

▓ Ride the elevator down to **Sea Lion Caves**, the world's largest ocean cave, home to hundreds of Stellar sea lions.

▓ Visit the interpretive center at **Heceta Head Lighthouse**, topping a 205-ft (62 m) bluff. The former lighthouse keeper's cottage is now a bed-and-breakfast, offering the rare delights of a seven-course gourmet breakfast.

With its heavy open chassis, a dune buggy is the perfect vehicle for roaring across the sands.

Rafters swirl in the rapids as the water crashes through a canyon in New River Gorge National River.

| WEST VIRGINIA |

White Water in West Virginia

If you like a thrill a second—and getting a soaking—rafting down the New and Gauley rivers is the holiday for you.

You just have time to catch your breath before, with a *whoosh*, you're dropping another 10 feet (3 meters). The front of your raft dips beneath the water, then pops up again, sending spray flying back into your face. Sandstone cliffs rise on either side of the river, confining the water as it churns through the canyon. You know that for days and weeks to come, you'll think back on this wild ride, trying to reconstruct every twist and turn of the raft as you try to guide it around boulders and through rapids. But for now, you can't do anything except be in the moment. You are in West Virginia, where the New and Gauley rivers offer some of the best white-water rafting on the East Coast, with everything from languid floats to challenging Class IV and Class V rapids. Rising in North Carolina, the New River crosses Virginia, then goes over the border into West Virginia, plowing its way through deep gorges in the Allegheny Mountains, before meeting the east-to-west-flowing Gauley at Gauley Bridge. The Gauley, meanwhile, is one of the most challenging white-water rivers anywhere in the world, notably on the 9.8-mile (16 kilometer) Upper Gauley stretch downriver from Summersville Dam. If you're planning to negotiate the Upper Gauley's narrow chutes and machine-gun rapids, you'll need supreme technical knowledge and skill.

WHEN TO GO April to October. September, when the water releases from Summersville Dam start, is considered the beginning of the wild-water season.

HOW LONG You can go for half-day, full-day, or multiday trips.

PLANNING Fayetteville, WV, is your best base for white-water adventure and outfitters. But reserve well in advance because trips get booked up and be prepared to get hooked on the thrill – the sport's popularity grows every year!

INSIDE INFORMATION Don't wear cotton because it becomes heavy when wet – and you're going to get wet.

WEBSITES raftinginfo.com, rafting.allaboutrivers.com, nps.gov/neri

| HIGHLIGHTS

▦ You'll have a wild ride on the **Gauley** in September and October. About 20 times each fall, the U.S. Army Corps of Engineers opens the floodgates of the **Summersville Dam**, releasing around 2,500 cu ft (70.8 cu m) of water per second.

▦ In a calm moment, look up and you might see a **peregrine falcon** soaring in the canyon. The National Park Service is reintroducing them to the New River's sandstone cliffs.

▦ On the third Saturday in October, hundreds of **BASE (Building, Antenna, Span, and Earth) jumpers** come to the New River Gorge Bridge to parachute 876 ft (267 m) into the gorge below.

Ride a horse alongside the Santa Fe trail for a sense of what the journey was like for early settlers.

| MISSOURI | KANSAS | NEW MEXICO |

Riding the Santa Fe Trail

The historic Santa Fe Trail passes through some of the most awe-inspiring desert scenery of the American Southwest.

Sagebrush and cacti spread out over the desert on either side of you. The horses kick up dust as they walk along the path, and it's hot, without even the promise of shade, but the stark beauty of the landscape and the sense that you are reliving history amply make up for any temporary discomfort. The Santa Fe Trail was originally a 19th-century commercial and military highway connecting Franklin, Missouri, with Santa Fe, New Mexico. After the Mexican-American War in 1846, branches of the 800-mile (1,290 kilometer) trail brought thousands of settlers through parts of Kansas, Colorado, and Oklahoma to the newly acquired territory of New Mexico—until by the 1880s, the railroad had made it obsolete. Today, motorists can travel the trail through Colorado and New Mexico on a National Scenic Byway, but if you really want to experience a bit of American frontier history, bring your horse and see it on horseback. The historic trail is too fragile to ride on so you use companion trails alongside the old route. One such companion trail crosses Cimarron National Grassland near Elkhart in southwestern Kansas, tracking the longest segment of the Santa Fe Trail on public lands.

WHEN TO GO All year round, but spring and fall are best. Summers are hot, with dry winds, and there is usually some snow in the winter.

HOW LONG Allow a week to take in different sections of the trail. The longest stretch for horseback riding, across Cimarron National Grassland, is 19 miles (31 km), an easy day's ride.

PLANNING This is a BYOH (bring your own horse) adventure as facilities for renting horses are limited. Occasionally, someone will organize a Santa Fe Trail ride along longer stretches of the trail so search the Internet from time to time to find out about these trips.

INSIDE INFORMATION Bring water for the ride. Make sure to take a hat and sunscreen. Both ends of the Cimarron companion trail have restrooms and facilities for loading and unloading horses.

WEBSITES naturalkansas.org/cimarron.htm, nps.gov/safe/planyourvisit/maps.htm

HIGHLIGHTS

▥ Wildlife along the trail includes numerous bird species – including **golden eagles, prairie chickens,** and **roadrunners** – and mammals such as coyote, porcupine, elk, and pronghorn antelope.

▥ About 15 percent of the original trail is still visible today. If you keep your eyes open you can see **wagon ruts** worn into the desert floor.

▥ **Buffalo wallows** – low areas where the huge grazing animals rolled (maybe to get rid of biting flies) and loosened the soil – are still noticeable from the trail, especially in spring when they fill with water.

Rafting Through the Grand Canyon

Experience the raw power of the Colorado, the river that carved the Grand Canyon.

At its wildest the Colorado River cuts through the bottom of the Grand Canyon with dizzying speed and fury. It seems impossible that a human could survive a trip down such a torrent—until you witness the skill of the veteran river guides who maneuver rafts, kayaks, and dories (flat-bottomed rowboats) along the 280-odd miles (450 kilometers) between Lee's Ferry and Lake Mead. The scenery is little changed since 1869, when one-armed Civil War hero Maj. John Wesley Powell led the first water-borne expedition downriver. Much of the journey is along calm water—plenty of time to kick back and enjoy the spectacular scenery—and about once a day there's time for a hike to explore prehistoric Anasazi ruins or natural wonders like the flower-filled grotto of Saddle Canyon. Fed by snowmelt from the Rockies, the Colorado isn't exactly conducive to swimming, but in spring pools form in some side canyons, perfect for a dip. Tranquil moments camped along sandy banks alternate with spurts of pure adrenaline as rafts challenge rapids like the aptly named Roaring Twenties.

WHEN TO GO Rafting trips run between April and October. Spring and fall offer the best weather; summer temperatures along the river can reach 120°F (49°C).

HOW LONG Three to five days is the minimum for overnight camping along the river. You need two weeks to make the entire journey from Lee's Ferry to Lake Mead.

PLANNING Licensed tour operators organize the river trips. All food and cooking equipment is provided, but passengers need to bring their own sleeping bags, duffle bags, day packs, and water bottles.

INSIDE INFORMATION Float trips are a good way to introduce children to the wonders of both the Grand Canyon and white-water rafting. Some trips take children as young as seven.

WEBSITES oars.com, nps.gov/grca

HIGHLIGHTS

▦ Those with a quick eye and a good pair of binoculars may catch a glimpse of canyon habitués like the **mountain lion**, **bighorn sheep**, **coyote**, **beaver**, and Grand Canyon pink **rattlesnake**.

▦ The **Havasupai Indian Reservation** is home to about 650 Native Americans, who still speak their mother tongue. Known for its towering waterfalls and turquoise pools, it offers both camping and a cozy little lodge.

▦ Spilling out from the Grand Canyon, the Colorado pours into **Lake Mead**. Created by the Hoover Dam, the lake's shores have myriad bays for fishing, waterskiing, and houseboating.

Navajo Bridge crosses the canyon high above Lee's Ferry, where many of the rafting trips begin.

ARIZONA

The Grand Canyon by Mule

Journey by mule into the hidden, mile-deep recesses of America's Grand Canyon, encountering its most secret beauties.

Any thoughts you might have that this is a lightweight "tourist trip" will vanish into the chilly morning mist as you stand outside the corral and listen to a weathered mule skinner barking out this advice: "If you have any heart trouble … go home! If you have any trouble breathing … go home! If you have any reason whatsoever to doubt your ability to make this trip … go home!" The message is clear: this classic Grand Canyon adventure is challenging. Several times a year, riders have to be evacuated by air for a variety of reasons, including heat, cold, dehydration, and altitude changes. Even so, thousands of people straddle the broad backs of sturdy mules every year to follow the 10.5-mile (17 kilometer) trail that descends almost a mile to the Colorado River and the floor of the Grand Canyon. The reason is simple: this is the best way to see the immense grandeur of the inner canyon. Each turn in the trail opens new vistas of towering spires of stone. On one side of you, a sheer rock wall rises in a hundred shades of red, brown, orange, and gray; on the other side, a yawning abyss opens up, seemingly just beneath the stirrup on the outboard side of your saddle. At the bottom, the charming, if rustic, Phantom Ranch has offered good food, a comfortable bed, and the lush green silence of the canyon floor to saddle-weary riders for 80 years. Sleep well—in the morning you saddle up for the long ride back up to the rim.

WHEN TO GO March, April, and May are the most popular months, with comfortable temperatures and the greenest flora. September through November also offer comfortable temperatures, along with fall colors.

HOW LONG Allow three nights in the Grand Canyon. The mules descend into the canyon early the first day and return late on the second day.

PLANNING You have to reserve in advance and can do so up to 13 months ahead. Follow the warnings and instructions provided when you register, and be sure to take along a camera that can be secured to your body when not in use, as you will often need both hands for mule-riding.

INSIDE INFORMATION When you arrive at Phantom Ranch you will be sore, so work out the kinks with a short walk to the wild and scenic Colorado River and gaze up at the mile-high canyon walls.

WEBSITES nps.gov/grca, grandcanyonlodges.com/things-to-do/mule-trips

NORTH AMERICA

| HIGHLIGHTS

▪ You may well glimpse a **California condor**, huge wings spread, gliding on the canyon's updrafts. These birds once teetered on the brink of extinction but are now bred in captivity and released in the canyon.

▪ The "oohs!" and "aahs!" of your fellow riders will be a constant refrain as you round another bend and yet another **panoramic view** of the canyon comes into sight. These are all the sweeter because only those who venture this far by mule or on foot get to enjoy them.

▪ You descend past seemingly endless banded layers of rock that together represent more than **2 billion years of geologic time**, about a quarter of the Earth's history.

▪ The colors of the afternoon sun glint off the rushing waters of the **Colorado River**. The river, which lies just a few hundred yards from Phantom Ranch, is still shaping the canyon today.

▪ At the end of the trip, you can rest your mule-tired body in the warm sun at Phantom Ranch, listening to birdsong and the rushing river. The hearty **steak dinner** will also do much to replenish body and soul.

Opposite: A condor's-eye view of the Grand Canyon gives a sense of the sheer majestic scale of the scenery, contrasting with the more intimate contact you will have with it on muleback. Above left: Riders make their way single file along the trail. Above right: The desert star, a relative of the daisy, blossoms in nooks in the rock.

Surfing in Hawai'i

Learn to surf on Kaua'i, Hawai'i's "Garden Isle,"
and then put what you've learned into exhilarating practice.

NORTH AMERICA

Lesson number one in the art of surfing: it usually takes a lot more energy (and time) to paddle out to the break—the line where the waves start to break—than to ride your board back into the beach. If you're prepared for that, all you need is desire—and about two hours—to learn the basics of surfing at Po'ipu Beach on the scenic south shore of Hawai'i's Kaua'i island. The retired pros who run the local surf schools teach you how to read the waves, spring into an upright position on the board, balance your body as you shoot the wave, and, most important, slam on the brakes at the end of your ride. After a week or two of practicing what you've learned on Po'ipu's 3- to 4-foot (0.9–1.2 meter) swells, you're ready for bolder stuff. Make the pilgrimage to Waikiki Beach in Honolulu on O'ahu, where Elvis once frolicked. Having outfitted yourself with board, shorts, and other gear, you drive around to O'ahu's fabled north shore, where many pro-surfers cut their teeth on the monster waves of Waimea Bay. Watching from the sand you wonder if you're ready to "hang ten"—ride at full speed with the toes of both feet hooked over the nose of the board—with the best. Taking a deep breath, you tuck your board beneath an arm and venture into the surf.

WHEN TO GO Any time of year, but the water is warmest in summer. Winter storms in the North Pacific generate the biggest surf, but you'll need a wetsuit in December or January.

HOW LONG Most introductory surf classes last a couple of hours. Beginners will need a week or two of daily surfing before they can take on the waves with confidence and panache.

PLANNING Surf schools provide everything you need: basically, a board and "leash" to wrap around one ankle. If you get hooked, there are dozens of shops where you can purchase your own board and accessories.

INSIDE INFORMATION Hoku Water Sports meets daily at Po'ipu Beach. Lessons include an hour with an instructor and an hour of individual practice to perfect what you've learned.

WEBSITE hokuwatersports.com

HIGHLIGHTS

■ **Waikiki Beach** may not have the highest waves, but it's still the archetypal Hawaiian surf experience. Diamond Head rises in the background as you "hang ten" in front of the coral-pink Royal Hawaiian resort.

■ The waves are big and the action is fast in the celebrated surf spots, **Waimea Bay** and the **Banzai Pipeline**, on O'ahu's north shore.

■ Get yourself outfitted with a genuine aloha shirt – the **classic Hawaiian print shirt** – at boutiques in Honolulu and elsewhere around the archipelago. Reyn Spooner makes some of the most sought-after shirts.

Confidence grows with practice, but it may be a while before you can ride the waves with the aplomb of this daredevil Hawaiian surfer.

You'll soon get used to ropework as you rappel down the ropes in some places and clamber up them in others.

PUERTO RICO

Caving in Puerto Rico

Be prepared to get wet, dirty, and tired on this unforgettable underground adventure into a cave system hidden in dense jungle.

The day starts at dawn as you meet your guides and head into a lush tropical forest. It's hard to believe that you are only 50 miles (80 kilometers) from Puerto Rico's bustling capital, San Juan. On the way, you stop for a crash course in rappelling (abseiling). Then you're zip-lining over the forest canopy, getting a bird's-eye view of the area as you head for Angeles Cave. There's a heart-stopping moment when you peer down and see a vast sinkhole beneath you: you'll have to go down into that to get to the cave. Hanging onto the rappelling rope, you slide down the 250 feet (76 meters)—about the height of a 25-story building—to the mouth of the cave. Wearing a hard hat with a headlight, and a life jacket, you're ready to explore an underground world where you never know what's around the next corner. There are bats, spiders, scorpions, crabs, and huge stalagmites and stalactites, the fossils of strange sea creatures that lived millions of years ago, and a fast-flowing underground river. You make your way over jagged limestone rocks, into narrow chambers, through vast caverns, and then you float on your back, feetfirst, body rafting along the Río Camuy. When you exit the labyrinthine network of caves and emerge into the daylight, you blink in the sunlight, already missing the magical underground world you've left behind.

WHEN TO GO Year-round.

HOW LONG A full day, starting at 5:45 a.m.

PLANNING You will need to book a place on a guided tour. Touring the caves is strenuous so you need to be physically fit and over 15 years old.

INSIDE INFORMATION Wear old sneakers or hiking boots – they will get very wet and muddy. Wear light trousers or shorts, not jeans, which soak up water and become heavy. If this trip sounds too tough, you have an easier option: a trolley tour of the caves in the nearby Río Camuy Caves Park.

WEBSITE aventurastierraadentro.net

HIGHLIGHTS

▪ At the base of the sinkhole, you plunge into the bracing waters of an **underground pool** in order to enter the cave.

▪ As you **float on your back** from one cave chamber to the next along an underground river, the only light is from your headlight, the only sound, rushing water.

▪ You eat your lunch in a **candlelit cavern**, where the flickering flames make the snacks you've brought along taste like a gourmet meal.

NORTH AMERICA

You can scarcely believe the wonder of it all as you paddle through crystal clear waters of dazzling turquoise.

Sea Kayaking off Baja

Paddle around a deserted Pacific island in the wildlife-rich waters off Mexico's western coast.

Rounding a rocky peninsula on the shimmering waters of the Gulf of California (Sea of Cortez), you catch sight of the white sands of a deserted bay where you will make camp for the night. With each smooth paddle stroke, details emerge from the shore: cacti, a craggy path leading up into the hills, waves breaking on the coral beach. This week-long expedition takes you around Isla Espíritu Santo, off the coast of Mexico's Baja California peninsula. Your mornings are spent kayaking clockwise around the island, passing offshore islets, a rugged shoreline, and a series of headlands and deep bays. The west coast of the island has a succession of idyllic, deserted beaches, while towering, jagged cliffs dominate the eastern side. In the afternoons you are free to explore the island trails or to snorkel in the crystal clear bays, and having set up camp along the shore, there is nothing better than a margarita as you watch the sunset.

WHEN TO GO Avoid the summer months, which tend to be too hot. From October to early December, the water is very warm and perfect for snorkeling.

HOW LONG The trip lasts seven full days, with three to four hours' kayaking each morning.

PLANNING The tour starts in La Paz, capital of Baja California Sur, from where a motor skiff takes you to Isla Espíritu Santo. Camping equipment and food are provided and carried in the skiff to each new bay, along with any personal belongings you don't need while paddling.

INSIDE INFORMATION You must be adequately protected from the sun and well hydrated since you are constantly exposed to the hot sun and its reflection on water. Sunscreen, water, and a camera can be carried in small dry bags attached to elastic straps aboard each kayak.

WEBSITES kayactivities.com, discoverbajacalifornia.com

HIGHLIGHTS

▥ The gulf is home to **31 species of marine mammals**, several types of turtle, and 500 species of fish, while Isla Espiritu Santo has animals found nowhere else on Earth, including the **blacktailed jackrabbit** and a species of tiny **ground squirrel**.

▥ As you reach the northern tip of the island, you come across a raucous **sea lion colony**. Snorkeling with these graceful mammals and their playful pups is exhilarating.

▥ While you are paddling in shallow waters, **manta rays** sometimes accompany you, leaping out of the water and gliding alongside the kayak.

▥ Toilet stops have never been so scenic: at each campsite, a portable lavatory is placed on a discreet bluff with **fantastic views** over the ocean!

NORTH AMERICA

| BELIZE |

The Belize Barrier Reef

*Enter a colorful underwater world in this
diver's paradise in the western Caribbean.*

For any diver, Belize's barrier reef—the longest in the Northern Hemisphere—is an unforgettable plunge. The reef is shorter than Australia's Great Barrier Reef, but its complex ecosystem is just as colorful, with more than 500 fish species and 65 kinds of coral. Inshore, between the reef and the coast, lie shallow lagoons and wetlands where pelicans plunge and manatees bask, and more than 450 tropical islets, called cays, where frigate birds and red-footed boobies nest. The best place to base yourself is San Pedro on Ambergris Cay—the largest island at the northern end of the reef. For many visitors, the most memorable dive is into the eerie, turquoise waters of the Blue Hole, a huge, circular gap in the center of the Lighthouse Reef system, less than 50 miles (80 kilometers) southeast of San Pedro. Belize's shallower waters include places with even richer marine life—such as the magnificent Half Moon Cay Wall or the fish-filled site aptly nicknamed the Aquarium off Long Cay, where you often encounter wild dolphins. Try to fit in a shallow-water night dive, revealing yet more denizens of this breathtaking underwater world—bright green octopus, nocturnal lobsters and shrimp, and huge parrot fish that could have been painted by Picasso.

WHEN TO GO November to June. Between July and October wind and rain may impair diving conditions.

HOW LONG Allow at least a week.

PLANNING Fly to Belize City on the mainland, then catch a connecting flight in a light aircraft to San Pedro on Ambergris Cay. You can reach other islands by boat from either Belize City or San Pedro. You don't have to take your own diving equipment; you can rent it in Ambergris Cay.

INSIDE INFORMATION The depths of the Blue Lagoon are far beyond the reach of even skilled divers, and good underwater skills and self-discipline are called for even at shallower depths, with a real risk of nitrogen narcosis – a state similar to alcohol intoxication.

WEBSITES ambergriscaye.com, reefandrainforest.co.uk

NORTH
AMERICA

| HIGHLIGHTS

▦ On **Ambergris Cay** you can watch sharks, rays, and turtles penned in an underwater corral below the deck of **Sharks Bar**. You can see a cavalcade of reef denizens while snorkeling from the island's jetties.

▦ Loggerhead, green, and hawksbill **turtles** lay their eggs on sandy beaches and you often see them in shallower waters. You may spot a **manatee** lazing on the surface at sunset.

▦ Some of the islands in the three offshore coral atolls – **Glover Reef**, the **Turneffe Islands**, and **Lighthouse Cay** – are inhabited, but most are left to seabirds and hermit crabs. Sharks and barracuda patrol the deeper waters here.

Color and variety are everywhere as you dive through the blue Caribbean waters, including multihued fish and delicately filigreed fan corals.

Top 10 Jetboat Adventures

One of several adrenaline sports pioneered in New Zealand, jetboating combines speed, amazing scenery, and outdoor adventure.

❶ MONTREAL, CANADA

The St. Lawrence River seems fairly mild-mannered until you run Lachine Rapids near Montreal in a jetboat. The bygone French voyageurs and First Nations people used to portage their canoes around this maelstrom of whirlpools, rocks, and waves rather than face its liquid fury head-on.

PLANNING Local outfitters also organize white-water rafting down the Lachine. jetboatingmontreal.com, raftingmontreal.com

❷ NIAGARA FALLS, NEW YORK

It's not quite as hairy as tumbling over the celebrated cascades in a wooden barrel, but jetboat rides on the Niagara River downstream from the falls are certainly white knuckle. Speeding along at 50 mph (80 km/h), the open-top boats take on the Devil's Hole and the Whirlpool.

PLANNING The historic Maid of the Mist (founded in 1846) makes a much more tranquil pass beneath the falls. whirlpooljet.com

❸ MIAMI, FLORIDA

Based at Sea Island Marina, Jetboat Miami offers half-hour "adrenalin junky" trips around Biscayne Bay in a speedy little craft called the Orange Twister. Cue the old theme song from *Miami Vice*, because this is as close as it gets to taking part in a scene from that classic 1980s television show.

PLANNING Jetboat Miami also offers Jet Skis, banana boat rides, and flyboard jetpacks. jetboatmiami.com

❹ TALKEETNA, ALASKA

Flowing down from snowcapped Denali, the Susitna River offers ideal conditions for jetboats based in the historic waterfront town of Talkeetna. In this area there is also a chance of spotting wildlife—moose, grizzly bears, wolves, and even caribou—as you zip through the Alaskan wilderness.

PLANNING Jetboats also operate on the Talkeetna and Chulitna rivers south of Denali. mahaysriverboat.com

❺ CANCUN, MEXICO

The popular resort on the Maya Riviera offers mini-jetboat adventures. Organized into guided multi-boat caravans, the little speedsters carry two or three people on self-piloted tours of the Nichupte Lagoon and the Mesoamerican Barrier Reef, second largest in the world after the Great Barrier.

PLANNING Farther down the Maya Riviera, the Adrenalina jetboat is based at Xcaret theme park. jungletourcancun.com

There's no time to think as the jetboat driver plunges you through the grandeur of New Zealand's Shotover River Canyons, with their steep walls and lush vegetation.

❻ IGUAZU FALLS, ARGENTINA/BRAZIL

Even the most powerful "rain forest shower" in a five-star hotel bathroom doesn't come close to matching the soaking you get during a jetboat ride beneath Iguazu Falls—the largest waterfalls system in the world. Starting from San Martin Island on the Argentine side, the sturdy little boats make their way along the Iguazu River to the thunderous Tres Mosqueteros (Three Musketeers), Garganta del Diablo, and Salto San Martin.

PLANNING Jetboat trips are also launched from the Brazilian shore. iguazujungle.com/eng, macucosafari.com.br

❼ QUEENSTOWN, NEW ZEALAND

The birthplace of modern jetboat adventures features fast-paced trips through the Shotover River (which earns its name for its fast-flowing and numerous rapids) and its narrow canyons. Launched in 1965, the swift boats have carried more than three million people including Queen Elizabeth II during a visit in 1990. Queenstown's other jetboat experience is the Dart River Wilderness Jet, traveling through Mount Aspiring National Park.

PLANNING The drivers execute 360° spins that leave you exhilarated and more than a little bit wet. If you want to stay dry, aim for the middle of the boat! shotoverjet.com, dartriver.co.nz

❽ SYDNEY, AUSTRALIA

"Thunder boats" whisk passengers on a lightning-fast ride across Sydney Harbour starting from Circular Quay. The voyage includes a pass beneath the Harbour Bridge, a quick peek at the Opera House, and a spray of open ocean as the boat passes through the Sydney Heads into the Tasman Sea. There are also family and group discounts available.

PLANNING Queensland's Gold Coast is the other place to catch jetboats down under, leaving the urban environment for a wilder view. thunderjetboat.com.au, paradisejetboating.com.au

❾ DUBAI, UNITED ARAB EMIRATES

Operated in original Hamilton speedboats from New Zealand, the bright red Sharkjet offers a whole new perspective on Dubai's incredible skyline during 45-minute jaunts in the Persian Gulf. The 460-horsepower engines rev up plenty of power for 360° spins and sudden "duck tail" stops that surprise you and leave you breathless.

PLANNING Across the gulf in Qatar, Blue Marine offers new-wave aqua adventures on fly boards and hover boards. bluemarine-me.com

❿ VICTORIA FALLS, ZAMBIA

Batoka Gorge on the Zambezi River is the setting for Africa's most extreme boat ride. The adventure starts with an eight-minute cable-car ride down into the gorge below Victoria Falls, and continues with a series of spins, twists and 360° donuts between rapids 23 and 27 on the Zambezi. The 700-horsepower jetboat is a force to be reckoned with. It can reach speeds of more than 60 mph (100 km/h) and can actually go airborne for short stretches of time.

PLANNING Cape Town is southern Africa's other jetboat hot spot, offering views of whales, African penguins, and Cape Fur seals. jetextremezambia.com, waterfrontadv.co.za

Tango in Buenos Aires

It's more than just a dance ... the tango, born in the poor neighborhoods of Buenos Aires, is the very soul of Argentina.

SOUTH AMERICA

t's well after midnight in Buenos Aires when tango fanatics start arriving at the city's *milongas* (tango salons). More than a dance, tango is an obsession for both *porteños* (the city's residents) and those who have journeyed to its home. Tourists at large tango palaces witness the history of love in three minutes while dining on Argentine beef; in smaller basement haunts, the same local patrons have reserved some tables for 30 years. If you've come here to learn the tango or improve your technique, you can choose from a range of tango-related services—at the top end of the scale, suites at the Abasto Plaza have dance floors for private lessons. The ritual starts with a look—couples choose one another by the intensity of their gaze. Dancing counterclockwise around the floor, they simulate attraction and attack, their legs chasing each other and slicing the air like knives. The story of tango goes back to the 19th century, when *candombe* rhythms brought to South America by African slaves mingled with other immigrant musical styles in poor tenement courtyards. As with the blues, tango was about the difficulties of working people, but it soon caught on worldwide—by 1913 London's smart Waldorf Hotel was holding tango teas. Tango went underground during the military junta but resurfaced in the mid-1980s as an inescapable feature of Argentine life.

WHEN TO GO The weather is best in fall (March–May) and spring (September–November). September offers low-season discounts.

HOW LONG Buenos Aires has enough to keep you busy for at least six days.

PLANNING Take tango lessons before leaving to feel at ease with the basic steps and to develop stamina.

INSIDE INFORMATION *Porteños* dress in high fashion for work and café-lounging so pack accordingly. Take a nap in the evening before a late dinner and dancing that might last until dawn. Consult listings in the magazines *B.A. Tango* or *El Tangauta* and pick up a tango map.

WEBSITES turismo.gov.ar, borellotravel.com, narrativetangotours.com

HIGHLIGHTS

▥ Watch for the *viborita* step (**"the little snake"**), in which the man places his right leg between his partner's legs and displaces first her left and then her right leg using a back-and-forth slithering motion.

▥ Take a break from dance halls among jacaranda and other blooms. The **Palermo quarter** offers restorative walks in the Botanical Gardens, a rose garden, a lake with beautifully landscaped promenades, and Palermo Woods.

▥ Find antique silver and statuary, or a Victrola phonograph or record, at the Sunday flea market in **San Telmo's Plaza Dorrego** amid dancers showing off their tango steps in the streets.

Come to Buenos Aires and learn the secrets of one of the world's most passionate dances.

A jabiru stork stands on top of its nest high above the Brazilian Pantanal.

HIGHLIGHTS

▥ When horse-riding at dusk you will probably come across a family of **capybara** – the world's largest rodent. With their flat snouts and doglike bodies, these unusual creatures look like giant guinea pigs and can reach a weight of 176 lb (80 kg).

▥ The 3-ft (1 m) long **hyacinth macaw** is the world's largest parrot. This is now an endangered species – macaw eggs are poached and sold for thousands of dollars – but it is still commonly seen in the region.

▥ The **giant anteater** has an unmistakable figure. Its long, delicate snout, shaggy coat, and loping gait often catch your eye when you are out walking.

▥ You are sometimes joined at breakfast in your lodge by peckish **toucans**, which come to pluck berries with their perfect, fragile beaks as the sun comes up.

BRAZIL | BOLIVIA | PARAGUAY

Wildlife in the Pantanal

Discover the wildlife riches of the largest wetland on Earth, the Pantanal, covering huge areas of Brazil, Bolivia, and Paraguay.

SOUTH AMERICA

At dusk, you make out the stooping figure of a giant jabiru stork, nearly 5 feet (1.5 meters) tall, as it picks its way down to the water's edge. When the northern reaches of the Paraguay River burst and flood the fields, the Pantanal becomes a giant water garden, where you can make boat trips to see (and hear) swarms of aquatic birds feast on fish and mollusks. Or you can climb on horseback to higher ground, the refuge of many land mammals. Sunset bathes the watery scene in gold and pink, and a rainbow often appears. At all times the 81,000 square miles (210,000 square kilometers) of the Pantanal are a treasure-house of wildlife. In the dry season, pools of stranded fish make rich pickings for wood ibis. You may come across bush dog, marsh deer, tapir, skunk, or clouds of butterflies dancing in the air. Nighttime excursions are a particular treat, when—who knows?—you may catch the luminous eyes of a spotted cougar.

WHEN TO GO You can see astonishing wildlife throughout the year. In the dry season (April–September), the emphasis is more on walking tours and jeep safaris. During the wet season (October–March), some areas with interesting wildlife are accessible only by boat or light aircraft.

HOW LONG Four days is enough to see the best of the Pantanal wildlife.

PLANNING Accommodation varies from the very basic (hammocks strung up on porches) to comfortable cabins in working cattle ranches. For the more basic lodges, pack a sleeping bag and mosquito repellent.

INSIDE INFORMATION You need a good guide from a reputable agency or lodge – rather than striking a deal with the many people touting for business at the airports and bus stations.

WEBSITES pantanal.org, caiman.com.br/en

Built in 1893, Valparaíso's Ascensor Artillería takes you on a bone-shaking ride up the steep slopes from the harbor.

Following Che Through South America

Bring the Motorcycle Diaries *to life by taking to the open road yourself, crossing pampas, mountains, and hot dry desert.*

Tracing "Che" Guevara's *Motorcycle Diaries* route from Argentina into Chile, then north into Peru, is likely to be both a pilgrimage and an adventure. You do it because you admire the spirit of the man, but the journey will also test your endurance, not to mention your means of transportation. Che and his friend Alberto Granado traveled on an old 500cc Norton motorcycle, ironically named La Poderosa (The Powerful One). But to handle these challenging roads, you'll be safer with an all-terrain motorcycle and a good GPS. Extreme conditions are the norm as you rise and fall across steep slopes, past rivers of crystalline water. Adrenalin rush is a constant. You cross the Andes, then roar north through the Atacama Desert, before heading back up the mountains to the ancient Inca capital of Cusco and beyond to Machu Picchu.

WHEN TO GO Starting in January allows you to explore Patagonia in the Southern Hemisphere summer and then reach the Atacama in the cooler fall.

HOW LONG Roughly 5,000 miles (8,050 km). Allow at least a month for the full trip.

PLANNING You can rent all-terrain motorcycles from Renta Moto in Buenos Aires. For information about places along the route, check out the online bulletin board of the South American Explorers Club.

INSIDE INFORMATION Che and Alberto carried on into Colombia and Venezuela, but without their motorcycle, which was unsuitable for the terrain. So finish your journey in Machu Picchu – a sublime end point.

WEBSITES rentamoto.com.ar, lapoderosatours.com/en

HIGHLIGHTS

▓ **San Carlos de Bariloche** lies on the shores of Nahuel Huapí Lake in the Argentine skirts of the Andes. The city is a gateway to Argentine **Patagonia** to the south. You might want to make a detour into this region of lakes and glaciers, leading eventually to the southernmost point on Earth outside Antarctica.

▓ The Chilean port of **Valparaíso** ascends sharply from the harbor to its residential neighborhoods; 15 rickety, funicular-like outdoor elevators help pedestrians travel quite literally up and down its streets. Visit the former home of poet and Nobel laureate Pablo Neruda (Che's favorite poet): La Sebastiana at 692 Ferrari.

▓ In Peru, the mountain **El Salkantay** looms over **Machu Picchu**. Since ancient times, local people have venerated it as a divine protector. It's also home to the *sachacabra*, a tiny deer only 15.8 in (40 cm) high.

| BOLIVIA

The Death Highway by Bike

Complacency can be deadly on the world's most dangerous road— a twisting, plummeting descent through the Bolivian Andes.

A biting wind claws at your skin, while around you llamas scratch the brick-hard earth. You are 15,420 feet (4,700 meters) high among the peaks of the Cordillera Real, a granite range striding across the Bolivian Altiplano (High Plain). Under the gaze of a statue of Christ, you and your fellow oxygen-starved mountain bikers mutter prayers and check your brakes. For those making the descent of Bolivia's Carretera de la Muerte (Highway of Death)—part of a route linking the capital La Paz with the subtropical north—preparation may be life-preserving. Hewn into cliffs by prisoners-of-war during the 1930s Chaco War between Bolivia and Paraguay, the road plunges 11,155 feet (3,400 meters) in 38 miles (61 kilometers) from the mountain pass of La Cumbre to the town of Coroico. The tortuous 15-mile (24 kilometer) stretch leading to the village of Yolosa, southwest of Coroico, will strike fear into the most hardened biker. Here, after the initial rocket-like descent from La Cumbre, asphalt gives way to mud and rock. Accentuating the sense of peril is the sound of horns—buses climbing fog-enveloped hairpin bends—and the sight of roadside crosses where fatal accidents occurred. Every bone-jarring rock and rut invokes fear and excitement, and long before emerging into Coroico, you know oblivion is just one misjudged corner away.

WHEN TO GO March to October; La Paz receives its highest rainfall between November and February.

HOW LONG Five to six hours.

PLANNING A number of La Paz–based outfitters run day trips down the Carretera de la Muerte. Allow yourself a few days to acclimatize to the altitude before attempting the expedition.

INSIDE INFORMATION Take some clean clothes to change into at the end of the ride – the outfitter's support vehicle will carry them for you. Then, having survived the trip, enjoy your lunch in Coroico before the bus journey back to La Paz.

WEBSITES gravitybolivia.com, travel-tracks.com

| **HIGHLIGHTS**

▦ You will see plenty of **llamas**, and in stops along the way you may spot **wild dogs** and **rare birds**, including the rufous-bellied seed-snipe.

▦ Your guide may stop to scatter sweets by the roadside. This **offering to Pachamama** (Mother Earth) is to ensure your safe passage.

▦ The brightly woven **ponchos** and **bowler-like hats** – *sombreros de cholita* – of Bolivian women are particularly eye-catching.

▦ The snow-covered, serrated crest of the **Cerro Mururata** (19,255 ft/5,869 m) is one of countless Andean peaks you will spy along the way.

The world's most dangerous road snakes along hillsides with sheer drops to the valley below during the dramatic descent from a high Andes pass into the Bolivian jungle.

The warm air blows in your face and beneath you spreads one of the world's most glorious urban landscapes.

Rio Hang Gliding

For breathtaking views over Brazil's iconic city
of Rio de Janeiro, nothing tops hang gliding.

Taking the run-up along a ramp for your glide is a leap of faith, but as the ground disappears from beneath your feet and the view over Rio de Janeiro opens out in front of you, you soon forget your fears and enjoy this extraordinary, exhilarating journey. After a short briefing, you and your pilot launch yourselves from Pedra Bonita in Tijuca National Park, the world's largest urban rain forest, a short drive southwest of the city's center. Rio has one of the most spectacular locations of any city on Earth, crammed between the glistening waters of the Atlantic to the east and steep mountains clad in dense Atlantic rain forest to the west. As you soar down toward the beach at São Conrado, its iconic sights are laid out before you: Sugar Loaf Mountain; the granite peak of Corcovado ("hunchback" in Portuguese), crowned with the Christ the Redeemer statue; the wide, white sands of Copacabana and Ipanema beaches; the small forested islands that litter Guanabara Bay and Rio's sister city of Niterói on the far side of the bay. Tandem rides require no experience; your guide will take care of the hard work, leaving you free to relish the spellbinding view spread out below you.

WHEN TO GO Departures take place seven days a week throughout the year. It doesn't have to be sunny, as long as there are no low clouds or rain coming down from the mountains.

HOW LONG A straight glide will take 12 minutes, but if conditions are right, you can soar above the city for up to half an hour.

PLANNING Take an extra layer of clothing – it can be cool at takeoff because of the altitude. Comfortable shoes are also important for the run-up and landing.

INSIDE INFORMATION If you have a few days in Rio, it is a good idea to contact your hang gliding guide immediately. He or she will be able to identify the best day to fly, which will not necessarily be the sunniest or the best day for the beach.

WEBSITES riohanggliding.com, rioturismoradical.com.br

HIGHLIGHTS

▪ The **moment of takeoff** is a unique sensation, and as you gently lift and turn in the tropical air, the feeling of freedom and weightlessness is both exhilarating and serene.

▪ Surveying the geography of this **astounding city** from the air gives you some idea of how special Rio is. Its residential districts, divided by **jagged granite peaks**, can be identified by the length and shape of their beaches.

▪ Long after your feet have made contact with the soft sand of **São Conrado beach**, your heart will still be hammering with excitement.

SOUTH AMERICA

| ARGENTINA | CHILE | PERU | ECUADOR |

Horse Treks in the Andes

*Take to life in the saddle on a high-altitude ride
through the majestic scenery of the Andes.*

SOUTH AMERICA

The horses walk along a trail cut into the mountainside. On scree-covered slopes, tiny alpine plants cling to life, and occasionally a black-and-white Andean condor with a 10-foot (3 meter) wingspan glides over the valley. Everything looks and feels different from horseback; you seem to be part of the natural world around you. Up ahead, muleteers guide the mules carrying tents, stoves, pans, and food—in the evening you'll dine by a lake. The Andes are the world's longest mountain range, stretching 4,500 miles (7,240 kilometers) from Venezuela to Tierra del Fuego, with the Western Hemisphere's highest peak, Aconcagua, 22,835 feet (6,960 meters) above sea level. So the opportunities for horse trekking are almost limitless, with dozens of outfitters offering their services, chiefly in Argentina, Chile, Peru, and Ecuador. One trek crosses high grasslands in the Ecuadorean Andes, with snowcapped volcanic peaks rising on either side—some active and puffing out smoke. Another follows an old smugglers' route from Chile through the Patagonian Andes into Argentina, passing stunning mountain lakes along the way. Others bring you into contact with indigenous cultures, almost unchanged for hundreds of years. The choice is yours.

WHEN TO GO It varies. In the northern Andes, such as the highlands of Ecuador, you can ride year-round; in the south – Chile and Argentina – ideal riding weather lasts from January to June.

HOW LONG You can book rides as short as a day or as long as two weeks.

PLANNING Some of these rides take you into high altitudes so give yourself time to acclimatize. Many outfitters say you don't need previous riding experience, but it's never a good idea to go without having some idea of how you're likely to feel after a day in the saddle.

INSIDE INFORMATION Bring strong sunscreen, a broad-brimmed hat to shade your head, and a bandana to protect your neck. No matter what the time of year, the sun's rays are strong at high altitudes.

WEBSITES rideandes.com, equitours.com/horseback-riding/ride-across-the-andes

HIGHLIGHTS

▥ Riding through the Andes is a **feast for the eyes** – look for pristine lakes, alpine meadows, and glorious wildflowers. Don't forget to look up at night; the stars will seem much more intense in the clear mountain air.

▥ You cover a lot of ground on a horse, and if you're lucky, you'll see a **range of wildlife**, including llamas, alpacas, cougars, hawks, eagles, chinchillas, and Andean condors.

▥ Not only will the muleteers and guides set up camp and cook **delicious meals** for you while in the mountains, many of the outfitters send along **musicians** to provide dinnertime entertainment.

Riders follow a trail through the Chilean Andes. Chile's capital, Santiago, is the base for many horse treks.

Australian Cattle Drive

Days on horseback, nights round the campfire ... following an old droving route brings you the sensations and camaraderie of life in the Outback.

Thousands of stars shine in the vast, blue-black sky, the Southern Cross identifiable by its even brighter splashes of light. After a day in the saddle, you settle down in your campsite, the gentle sounds of 500 cattle as the constant background accompaniment. There'll be no more whip-cracking or shouts of "C'mon, move yourself!" until tomorrow. Beyond the camp lies the silence of dunes and gibber plain (stony desert). You are on South Australia's Oodnadatta Track, a historic cattle-droving route from Oodnadatta deep in the Outback across the Tirari Desert to the old railhead at Marree, some 250 miles (400 kilometers) southeast of Oodnadatta. The drovers you are traveling with look a bit like the Outback itself—lean and rugged. They crack bullwhips and ride with practiced ease. In them, the spirit of the Outback is still alive—a certain resourcefulness with a store of knowledge and humor. For you, it is a chance to experience the harsh beauty of central Australia, one of the most remote locations on Earth. Just being in the clean air, gazing over the vast plains and deserts seems to soothe a fractious mind. Blue tents, blue skies—and the occasional touch of blue language—transport you to another world. This is "droving for softies"—although you start early and the days are long, you don't ride for more than around 8.7 miles (14 kilometers) in a day. Moreover, the tents are comfortable and a well-stocked bar travels with you.

WHEN TO GO Currently the cattle drives are held every other year, early May through the end of June.

HOW LONG The drive is split up into sections of four nights and five days. Tourists can join for any one of the sections. Allow a few extra days for South Australia's capital, Adelaide, as the city has a lot to offer.

PLANNING Book well ahead to secure a place – only 70 people are allowed on each trip. Also, drought means that some trips have had to be cut back. Follow guidelines on clothing and personal safety (everyone has to wear a riding helmet). Take along strong insect repellent.

INSIDE INFORMATION A sing-along around the campfire can be a great way to unwind and get to know your fellow riders and drovers. If you play a (portable) instrument take it along. And you will develop a thirst on these rides, so make sure you have cash or credit cards with you – the bar accepts both.

WEBSITES harryredford.com.au, australia.com/en-gb

HIGHLIGHTS

▦ Some trips take you through the world's largest working cattle station, **Anna Creek**, which spreads out across more than 11,620 sq miles (30,100 km²) – an area almost the size of Maryland.

▦ Lake Eyre is the **world's largest salt-pan lake**, extending over 463,320 sq miles (1.2 million km²). Because the lake has no outflow, water evaporates, leaving vast, eerie white deposits of salt. Usually it is empty, but every five years or so it floods and blooms with wildflowers and birdlife before the water evaporates. Take a scenic flight over the area if the lake is full.

▦ **Marree Man** is a mysterious man-made artwork, 37 miles (60 km) west of Marree. Best seen from the air, it is 2.5 miles (4 km) long and depicts a man with a stick or boomerang.

▦ You'll get more than one chance to meet an Aboriginal elder and explore traditional **Aboriginal culture** including bush tucker, dreamtime stories, art, and crafts. The Arabunna people, traditional owners of the Lake Eyre region, are one such community.

Opposite: Stockmen and cattle on the move are silhouetted against a blaze of early morning light ... this is the romance of the Outback. Above left: Filling the billy, or traditional water pot, is an essential task after the campfire has been lit for the night. Above right: Cattle wait patiently for mustering at a station along the way.

Elephant Safari

A gentle giant carries you through the grassland and jungle of Royal Chitwan National Park in the southern Terai plains of Nepal.

ASIA

Chitwan is defined by the Narayani and Rapti rivers and consists of wetlands, hills, and tropical and subtropical forest—home to numerous animal species, several of which are endangered and enjoy vital protection here. Walking along beside an elephant, you'll be able to get close to this abundant wildlife. If you are lucky, you might encounter the Indian one-horned rhinoceros. These armor-plated creatures, though large and impressive, are generally quiet in the presence of elephants. Though at the command of the mahout (handler), your elephant guide saunters freely through his habitat, allowing you to stroll beside him and even feed him straight from your hand. Within a couple of minutes you are entering grasslands dotted with deer, and here the mahout may slow the elephant to a halt so that you can fully appreciate the wildlife. As you continue your adventure, you and your elephant guide expertly navigate the forest, padding across muddy slopes, passing through streams, and climbing verdant banks. Every animal you see in its habitat brings a fresh thrill, whether a strutting peacock with shimmering blue tail, wild boar rooting around, diminutive deer, smooth-coated otters splashing in a creek, or a gharial crocodile.

WHEN TO GO October through May; mornings can be quite cold in December and January.

HOW LONG To get the most out of Chitwan, stay for three nights. An elephant ride lasts two to three hours.

PLANNING Chitwan is 110 miles (175 km) southwest of Kathmandu. The nearest town is Bhaktapur, which has a small airport. Bring binoculars, walking boots, mosquito repellent, and warm clothes if visiting late November–February. There is a range of accommodation within the park. Chitwan Jungle Lodge and the famous Tiger Tops Jungle Lodge are comfortable and can arrange safaris.

INSIDE INFORMATION The bond between elephant and handler is close and may last many years. Some tours offer you the chance to join in with bathing, feeding, and training these massive creatures.

WEBSITES welcomenepal.com, tigertops.com, chitvan.com

HIGHLIGHTS

▪ Being perched some 10 ft (3 m) up gives a **fantastic panorama** over the tall, aptly named elephant grass.

▪ The **dazzling array of wildlife** includes sloth bears, striped hyenas, various species of antelope, deer, and monkey, as well as a small number of Bengal tigers and leopards.

▪ Float down the **Narayani River** in a dugout canoe looking out for long-snouted gharial crocodiles, which can grow up to 18 ft (6 m), and exotic birds of the park's 450 or so species.

▪ Complete the elephant experience with a visit to the **Elephant Breeding Center**, which cares for mothers and their babies.

In Royal Chitwan National Park, Nepal, two one-horned rhinoceros cross the river to graze.

Spying a female tiger cooling herself and her cubs in a pool in Ranthambore National Park is a magical experience.

INDIA

Tiger Safari

The majestic Bengal tiger is now rare and elusive. The best place to see it is in Ranthambore National Park in eastern Rajasthan.

There may be as few as 20 tigers in Ranthambore, but as the area is compact (152 square miles, 394 square kilometers) and the animals are less reclusive and less nocturnal than in most reserves, they are relatively easy to spot. Picturesquely set around the ruined fort from which it takes its name, the park was once the hunting preserve of the maharajas of Jaipur. There is a high density of wildlife inhabiting a varied landscape of dense forest, rocky outcrops, crisscrossing streams, and areas of grassland. On a safari you may see deer species, such as sambar and chital, as well as jackals and striped hyenas. You may also come across a sloth bear, cobra, and possibly a leopard. But the main goal is never forgotten: the guide often stops the jeep to check for footprints or listen for telltale signs, such as the warning bark of a chital. The magical moment when you finally set eyes on the regal tiger repays all the effort spent on its trail.

WHEN TO GO In March–May before the monsoon season, when vegetation cover is at a minimum and the animals are more active in seeking water – but it can be extremely hot. Winter (December–February) is almost as good and much less hot. Ranthambore is closed June–October.

HOW LONG For a reasonable chance of seeing a tiger, stay on the reserve for at least two days.

PLANNING There is a range of accommodation within the park. Warm clothes are needed between late November and February.

INSIDE INFORMATION The code for wildlife-watching is to keep quiet and not to wear bright colors or perfume. The park has well-placed viewing points.

WEBSITES ranthamborenationalpark.com, india-wildlife-tours.com

HIGHLIGHTS

▓ The walk up to **Ranthambore Fort** brings magnificent views on a level with the circling eagles and vultures. Even on the way here the big cats can be seen.

▓ **Three lakes** are among the park's major features. Padam Talao is the largest, overlooked by a hunting lodge, where animals gather to drink at dawn and dusk. In Raj Bagh Talao, swamp deer favor the water vegetation. Birdlife is prolific in the smallest lake, Malik Talao, and you may see Indian marsh crocodiles.

▓ The **Raj Bagh Ruins**, the crumbling remnants of a palace near Raj Bagh Talao, may even be graced by a reclining tiger.

▓ The **raw beauty** of the landscape is best appreciated through the misty dawn or in the golden light of late afternoon, when tours take place.

ASIA

| SCOTLAND |

Golfing in Scotland

With more than 500 courses, Scotland is indeed a golfer's paradise. But of them all, only a handful are true legends, attracting golf pilgrims from all over the world.

St. Andrews, with its rolling, windswept links fringed by dunes and the long, sandy, seal-haunted beaches of the North Sea, is the true home of the game. Founded in 1754, the Royal and Ancient Golf Club organizes the Open Championship and is the ultimate arbitrator of the rules of the game. The Auld Grey Toun lives and breathes golf, and waiting lists to tee off on its Old Course—which has hosted the Open more times than any course in Britain—can be months or years long. The reward, for those prepared to wait, is one of the most challenging courses in the golfing world, with sloping, bumpy double greens and bunkers that have earned names like Hell and Coffins from golfers unlucky enough to hit a ball into their treacherous sands. Still on the east coast, and only about 30 miles (48 kilometers) north of St. Andrews, on the north shore of the Firth of Tay, is Carnoustie, where it is usually easier to get a round. As with St. Andrews, here you always have to take into account the North Sea wind. For golfers with nongolfing partners, cultured Edinburgh offers the best of both worlds. Muirfield, just outside the city center, home of the Honourable Company of Edinburgh Golfers, is, if anything, even more exclusive than St. Andrews; while the venerable course at Musselburgh is also nearby. On the west coast in Ayrshire, Turnberry and Royal Troon have almost equal status with St. Andrews.

WHEN TO GO Spring (April–early June) or fall (September–October). Golf is played year-round, but winter is wet, cold, and windy with as few as seven daylight hours, and the summer high season is crowded.

HOW LONG Scotland is a small country (the drive from St. Andrews to Turnberry takes two hours). With planning, it could be possible to play most of the favorite courses in a week.

PLANNING Booking accommodation well in advance is essential all year round. The easiest and often most affordable way to arrange a golf tour is to go through a specialist company.

INSIDE INFORMATION Even in summer the weather is uncertain, with crosswinds blowing in from the coast, but for true golfers this makes Scotland a unique and perennial challenge. On St. Andrews Old Course, each hole offers a memorable experience, but the first, eleventh, fourteenth, and seventeenth holes are considered the finest. The last, or Road Hole, is one of the most awe-inspiring in golf.

WEBSITES visitscotland.com, golfing-scotland.com

HIGHLIGHTS

▦ The beautiful parkland course of **Charleton**, with views of the Firth of Forth, offers a variety of wide fairways and unexpected hazards to tempt players of all levels.

▦ On the promontory of Fife Ness, **Crail Balcomie Links** was established in 1895. Small but appealing, it attracts the world's top players when the Open is in progress at nearby St. Andrews.

▦ Troon's deceptively short signature hole, nicknamed the **Postage Stamp**, has been known to make grown men weep with frustration; while Turnberry has its place in Open legend as the venue for the nail-biting "Duel in the Sun" between Jack Nicklaus and Tom Watson in 1977, won by the latter.

▦ The **rocky Fife coastline** has sweeping cliffs, bays, and sandy beaches, and you can explore it via the coastal path. In summer look for basking sharks and dolphins, while offshore islands are home to thousands of seabirds. The tiny fishing villages, too, with their stone harbors – Crail, St. Monans, and Pittenweem – are well worth visiting.

Opposite: Scotland's many courses, like this one on the Isle of Arran, are integrated with its rugged and bracing landscape and offer both an unparalleled sporting challenge and stunning views from the links. Above: The Old Course at St. Andrews is overlooked by the headquarters of the Royal and Ancient Golf Club.

Through Ireland in a Horse-drawn Caravan

This placid form of transportation is a fitting way to explore the fair isle, allowing you to pause by lake, stream, or wooded valley.

Take a bag of books, a fishing rod perhaps, and prepare to explore the wooded beauty of Ireland's Wicklow Mountains—with history at every turn. A caravan with beds for four, a table, sink, and small stove is a cozy shelter, and the operator provides a map showing the less-traveled roads and places where you can stop at night and have a shower and a meal or pint of beer. You spend part of the first day on the operator's grounds in Carrigmore, some 12.5 miles (20 kilometers) south of Dublin, to practice caring for the horse. Most are Irish draft horses, patient and strong. A day's journey can be anything from 4 to 12 miles (roughly 7 to 20 kilometers), taking between two and five hours—depending on the weather, terrain, and your route, or whether the fish are biting or how many holes of golf you play. Or you may spot a stately home to visit—such as the 18th-century Palladian-style Powerscourt, one of Ireland's grandest mansions—or gardens to discover, such as the beautiful Mount Usher Gardens on the Killiskey River. The pace is slow, but there's no shortage of things to do.

WHEN TO GO April to October. In June, country roads lead past meadows of wildflowers. A week in September can be pleasant, although the slow lane may be shared with harvesting machinery.

HOW LONG Allow at least a week.

PLANNING First, study Ireland's rich landscape to decide where to go. It doesn't have to be County Wicklow. How about the wilds of Galway, historic County Laois, or the panoramas of County Mayo?

INSIDE INFORMATION Pack mosquito repellent. Plan to walk with the horse when the road is steep. Often you can rent a riding horse as well, allowing you to saddle up and explore away from the caravan.

WEBSITES irishhorsedrawncaravans.com, dochara.com

EUROPE

HIGHLIGHTS

▦ **Village market** stops can be fun. And at sundown, when caravans must be off the road, a **music session** in a pub makes a convivial end to the day. Sweet dreams are assured!

▦ If you go to **Galway**, don't miss the annual summer Arts Festival in Galway city. Horse lovers should try to be there for the late July Galway Races.

▦ For some of Ireland's **best fish and vegetable** shopping, head for Galway's Saturday morning market.

▦ Relax on the **long glorious beaches** of the County Mayo coast, or walk over bridges to the islands sprinkling its shoreline.

Most caravans resemble brightly colored barrels tipped on their side, with space to sleep yet light enough for a horse to pull.

Following the quiet trails of Lubéron Regional Nature Park offers varying degrees of challenge.

| FRANCE |

Cycling Through the Lubéron Mountains

Both a compact range of mountains and a regional park, this area contains some of the most striking natural beauty in all Provence.

A host of glorious towns and villages set within crumbling fortifications dot the hillsides of Lubéron Regional Nature Park. This makes cycling from one place to the next as easy as joining the dots; just follow the extensive network of quiet country roads within the park. If you start at Roussillon, your ride takes you between multicolored cliffs and reddish-hued earthen mounds, characteristic of the ocher deposits mined since Roman times. You head west, taking in the hilltop village of Gordes, perched on the southern edge of the Plateau de Vaucluse with a 12th-century castle. For an easier ride, begin at Cavaillon in the west of the park and follow the 62-mile (100 kilometer) Lubéron en Vélo cycling path east to Forcalquier. It takes you through gems such as Ménerbes, another hilltop village, which has the ruined 13th-century abbey of St. Hilaire. If you have time, return to Cavaillon along the southern section of the cycle path, making a 147-mile (237 kilometer) circuit of the park and passing through Manosque, Lourmarin, and Mérindol.

WHEN TO GO Mid-April to mid-October. The region is never as crowded as the nearby Côte d'Azur, but it's better to go mid-April to June and September to mid-October for great cycling conditions.

HOW LONG A three-night stay in any one central village should allow enough time to explore by bike.

PLANNING The nearest airport is Marseille, and nearest train stations are Aix-en-Provence and Avignon. The nicest villages have small hotels, *gîtes* (cottages for rent by the week), and *chambres d'hôtes* (B&Bs).

INSIDE INFORMATION Even on the quietest roads, stay to the far right; the French are very respectful of cyclists but fast-traveling cars seem to appear without notice. The best roads are often quite narrow.

WEBSITES beyond.fr, velovacations.com, myprovence.fr/en

HIGHLIGHTS

▓ In **Gordes** visit an ancient settlement 2.2 miles (3.5 km) outside the modern village. It consists of rounded drystone structures called *bories*, traditional to Provence, once used as shelters, barns, and homes.

▓ Both **Ménerbes** and **Lourmarin** have been voted among the most beautiful villages in France.

▓ For the ultimate cycling challenge, tackle **Mont Ventoux** to the north of the Lubéron. This 6,273-ft (1,912 m) peak has often been on the Tour de France. Watch out for crosswinds and take change for the cookies at the top — you'll have earned them!

A file of seasoned skaters pace themselves on the marathon route near Dokkum.

THE NETHERLANDS

Friesland's Eleven Cities' Tour

A 124-mile (200 kilometer) route along frozen canals, rivers, and lakes tests the stamina of skaters in the northern Netherlands.

Thousands of Lycra-clad skaters, frost clinging to their eyebrows, elbow past turns and between snowdrifts along the route in the northern province of Friesland. Spectators, often 12 deep, shout, "*Hop! Hop! Hop! Volhouden!*" ("Go! Go! Go! Keep at it!"), as exhausted skaters who have been outside since sunrise near their twilight finish in the Friesian capital of Leeuwarden. This famed ice race—beginning and ending in Leeuwarden—has existed unofficially for centuries, but in 1909 it became a formal event. Since then the Elfstedentocht (Eleven Cities' Tour) has taken place just 15 times, run by an association (Vereniging) of the participating cities which dictates that the ice must be at least 5.9 inches (15 centimeters) thick. There may be only a few days', or even a few hours', notice that it is going to happen. When it does, the Netherlands takes a holiday. Anyone not on the route is glued to the TV. A maximum of 16,000 skaters are allowed to take part, but when the ice thaws anyone can follow the same route in a kayak or along the towpaths on foot, by bike, or even with inline skates.

WHEN TO GO For the ice race, stick close to the Netherlands from December through February. If you plan to follow the route by other means, the best months are July and August; Dutch summers are mild.

HOW LONG You could cycle the route in a day (there's an Elfstedentocht bike race in May), but most organized tours allow a week or longer.

PLANNING Local tour operators can help you choose the best way to navigate the race route in summer. For the ice tour, contact the Vereniging for details of how you can qualify to take part.

INSIDE INFORMATION If you do strap on your inline skates, keep in mind that most Dutch people have been ice- and inline-skating since they were infants – they're fast and strong. Be ready!

WEBSITES fietselfstedentocht.frl, elfstedentocht.frl, cycletours.com

HIGHLIGHTS

■ The **excitement** of the Elfstedentocht is intoxicating. Many Europeans refer to skating as the "Dutch disease." Even royalty takes part; in the 1986 race, Crown Prince Willem-Alexander entered under the "nom de skate" of W. A. Van Buren.

■ You get a special "**passport**" if you complete the route. Even nonskaters get passports, which are stamped 11 times at stops along the route.

■ **Friesland** itself is interesting to visit. It has nearly 200 of the country's 1,200 windmills and its own language, which is closely related to English.

THE NETHERLANDS

Dutch Bulbfields

Cycle around fields of brilliant color, then visit world-famous gardens, where the flower displays are a form of high art.

In spring the famed bulbfields of the province of Zuid-Holland (South Holland) become a blaze of color. This is the heart of the Dutch flower-growing industry, where millions of bulbs are produced each year. They are the essence of the business—the flowers are simpy a by-product. As the growers harvest the bulbs, they dump heaps of blossoms at the roadside. One of the best ways of enjoying the glorious display while still in full bloom is as part of a cycle tour setting out from the seaside resort of Noordwijk and culminating in Keukenhof, the prime showcase for Dutch flower-growing skills. This 79-acre (32 hectare) swath of park and flower gardens was first laid out in the 15th century as the kitchen garden of a powerful local noblewoman, Jacoba van Beieren. Every spring, Holland's top bulb-growers send six million tulips, daffodils, and hyacinths to Keukenhof, creating an astonishing floral extravaganza, where bees and butterflies dance attendance. Each year there is a different set of themes, as Keukenhof puts on arrays of "inspirational gardens" to fire visitors' imaginations with ideas for their own patches of green. Other displays show how the tulip found its way from the steppes of Central Asia via Ottoman palaces to the window boxes of Amsterdam.

WHEN TO GO Late March to mid-June, but the best time is in May, when everything is in full bloom.

HOW LONG The 15.5-mile (25 km) cycle tour is a day trip.

PLANNING The cycle tours start from the VVV Tourist Office in Noordwijk. You go with a guide and start the day off with a breakfast of coffee and pastries in a street café. You can also get to Keukenhof by public transport via the small university city of Leiden; trains run from Amsterdam Centraal Station or Schiphol Airport to Leiden twice hourly, connecting with bus 54 to Keukenhof.

INSIDE INFORMATION On weekends you can buy bargain bulbs from Keukenhof's market stalls – dahlias, lilies, gladioli, begonias, and many more, as well as tulips of every color.

WEBSITES holland.com, hollandrijnland.nl, keukenhof.com

EUROPE

HIGHLIGHTS

▓ The **flower park** at Keukenhof displays more than 50,000 tulips in a dazzling range of color combinations. The giant greenhouse is also a refuge if the weather turns wet and windy. English-speaking guides give free tours.

▓ Keukenhof is one of the few places where you can buy bulbs of the legendary **Black Parrot tulip**. It's really a deep purple – even 400 years of Dutch ingenuity have failed to produce a truly black blossom.

▓ If you go to Leiden, visit Europe's oldest botanical gardens, the **Hortus Botanicus**, founded in 1590. The city has a historic center and a good art gallery, the Lakenhal Museum.

Geometrically straight ranks of red and yellow tulips stretch into the distance, a feast for the eye and the camera.

Top 10 Cycle Routes

Take your pick from these long-distance routes, ranging in challenge from a single day's ride to weeks of grueling effort.

❶ LA ROUTE VERTE, CANADA

The newly completed Route Verte (Green Route) crosses the province of Quebec from east to west, running for more than 2,485 miles (4,000 km) along carefully selected rights-of-way and rural roads. Well signed, it's easy to follow and includes directions to interesting sites. The terrain and vistas vary immensely, from calm stretches along the St. Lawrence River to mountain views in the Laurentides.

PLANNING The government-supported Bienvenue Cyclistes/Welcome Cyclists program makes it easy to find cyclist-friendly accommodation, from campgrounds to hotels. routeverte.com/e

❷ UNDERGROUND RAILROAD BICYCLE ROUTE, U.S.A./CANADA

The Adventure Cycling Association developed this route from Mobile, Alabama, to Owen Sound, Ontario, to honor the bravery of slaves trying to reach freedom and those who helped them. There are five segments, adding up to a total distance of 2,057 miles (3,310 km). Sites along the way highlight the route's history, from former slave markets to museums dedicated to African-American history.

PLANNING In early spring and fall, campsites on the northern section of the route may not be open. adventurecycling.org

❸ RUTA AUSTRAL, CHILE

Mostly surfaced with graded but unpaved gravel, the route runs for more than 810 miles (1,300 km) from Puerto Montt in central Chile, south to Villa O'Higgins in northern Patagonia, with numerous ferryboat transfers along the way. You pass through wild and beautiful landscapes, including Cerro Castillo national parks. Large stretches of forest and huge ferns surround Puyuhuapi Hot Springs, near Queulat.

PLANNING Take everything you need with you, as you pass through several completely isolated areas. gochile.cl/en

❹ MUNDA BIDDI TRAIL, WESTERN AUSTRALIA

In the Noongar Aboriginal language, Munda Biddi means "path through the forest." This cycling trail runs through miles of "jarrah forest"—from the local name for eucalyptus trees. The 206-mile (332 km) section from Mundaring to Collie opened in July 2004, and two extensions will take it to Albany. You may encounter forest natives like western brush wallaby, western gray kangaroos, and brushtail possum.

PLANNING Avoid the heat of the Australian summer, between December and February. mundabiddi.org.au

Near Mai Chau, in Vietnam, cyclists pedal through a colorful patchwork of rice fields nestled between verdant mountains.

⑤ HANOI TO HO CHI MINH CITY, VIETNAM

If bikes and beaches mix well for you, Vietnam combines them on this 746-mile (1,200 km) route between the country's two biggest cities, taking you along vast stretches of sandy coastline. But it's no picnic, as road surfaces vary and there are many natural obstacles like the Hai Van Pass, the historical division point between North and South Vietnam.

PLANNING Cyclists often take a train or fly from Hanoi to Hue, cutting the distance in half. vietnambiketours.com

⑥ GRAN FONDO CAMPAGNOLO, ITALY

This mass-participation ride through the Dolomites around Feltre honors Tulio Campagnolo, who invented the modern gear-shifting system, the derailleur. It takes place each year in mid-June, soon after the mountain roads are cleared of snow. You climb more than 13,780 ft (4,200 m) along the 130-mile (209 km) course, which tops four summits.

PLANNING You'll need a medical certificate to enter. infodolomiti.it

⑦ LUCHON TO BAYONNE, FRANCE

The Tour de France crossed high mountain passes for the first time in 1910. On Stage 10, the most difficult that year, the winner took 14 hours to cycle the 202 miles (325 km) from the mountain spa town of Luchon to the finish at Bayonne, crossing four major passes, all unpaved at the time. Tracing the route is simple—follow the roads that climb the same passes: the Peyresourde, Aspin, Tourmalet, and Aubisque.

PLANNING The passes are closed by snow from late fall through early spring. customgetaways.com, clevacances-65.com

⑧ ROUTE DU COMTE JEAN, BELGIUM/FRANCE

Belgium is known for its Vlaanderen Fietsroute (Flemish Cycle Route) along country roads and paths, many closed to vehicular traffic. The Route du Comte Jean (named for a 14th-century Flemish general) takes in 137 miles (220 km) of the network, from Bruges into northern France. There are no mountains, but coastal winds present a challenge.

PLANNING Pack rain gear no matter what season you go. walloniabelgiumtourism.com

⑨ LAND'S END TO JOHN O'GROATS, BRITAIN

Depending on your route choices, the distance can be 900 miles (1,450 km) or more. Prevailing winds are more likely to be with you going north to south. Even if you take the long way in a relaxed fashion, you should have no problem beating the first official End-to-End record: 65 days, done in 1885 on a high-wheeler.

PLANNING Most cyclists take a week or more using quieter country roads. cyclinguk.org

⑩ CAPE TOWN CYCLE TOUR, SOUTH AFRICA

At 68 miles (109 km), the Cape Argus ride isn't the world's longest open-ride race, but with some 35,000 participants, it may be the biggest. The course does a loop of the Cape Peninsula with constant ups and downs. If you're just happy to finish, you'll enjoy the many coastal sections and the portions through Table Mountain National Park.

PLANNING Register well in advance. capetowncycletour.com

Skiing Mont Blanc's Vallée Blanche

Sheer pistes and extreme conditions present a challenge to seasoned skiers at the highest point in the Alps.

EUROPE

f your nerves aren't tested during the 12,605-foot (3,842 meter) ride on the *téléphérique* (cable car) to Chamonix's granite Aiguille du Midi (Midday Needle), they might be when you see the narrow ridge that greets you as you exit. Before you even start the run, you'll have to negotiate that ridge of snow-covered rock, holding your skis and roped to a guide. The payoff? Once you've strapped on those skis next to the top of Mont Blanc—at 15,750 feet (4,801 meters), the highest mountain in the Alps—you'll take off down the 13.7-mile (22 kilometer) Vallée Blanche (White Valley) ski run. But while its 9,200-foot (2,804 meter) vertical drop might sound intimidating, the Vallée Blanche isn't just for expert-level skiers. With proper equipment and a Chamonix guide, fit intermediate skiers and snowboarders can experience what many call the greatest ski run on the planet. Once past the rocky Glacier du Tacul, the route follows the Mer de Glace, France's largest glacier, truly a sea of swirling, mixed snow and ice. Depending on conditions, you finish either in Chamonix or at the Montenvers railway terminus.

WHEN TO GO February and March offer the best snow, and Mondays offer the shortest lift lines.

HOW LONG If you're a serious skier (and Chamonix is for the serious), you'll want at least a week, maybe two. There are many different mountains, ski runs, and sports options.

PLANNING You can find guides at several places (see websites below). The crucial thing is to book one; no first-timer should ski the Vallée Blanche without a guide.

INSIDE INFORMATION Conditions mean you'll need to pack your gear carefully. Don't forget a whistle and a substantial snack, plus water. The danger from seracs – masses of ice intersected by crevasses – is real. Skiers perish each year when a serac comes crashing down on top of them like a mini-avalanche.

WEBSITES chamonix.com, guides-du-montblanc.com, pistehors.com

HIGHLIGHTS

■ Chamonix is filled with shops and restaurants and has a **lively nightlife** peopled by the very fit – it attracts skiers, not socialites. It was the site of the first Winter Olympics in 1924 and the scene for the final struggle in Mary Shelley's *Frankenstein* (1818).

■ Cold-weather sports sharpen the appetite for regional specialties such as *tartiflette*, a rich concoction of potatoes, white wine, and the local Reblochon cheese.

■ Don't fret if you can't get to France during the ski season. You can **hike** the **Vallée Blanche** in spring and summer. Even better, walking will take you through forests impossible to negotiate on skis.

Skiers prepare to descend the exhilarating Vallée Blanche from the Aiguille du Midi.

The mountainous heart of Romania offers the most splendid, pristine views to the intrepid cyclist.

| ROMANIA |

Crossing Transylvania

Storybook Transylvania—wild forests, howling wolves, and remote medieval castles—really does exist and is waiting to be explored.

Enclosed by the Carpathian Mountains, Transylvania lies in the heart of Romania, and its superb landscape, etched with trails and byways, is ideal for mountain biking. The most popular place for this is in the southeastern Carpathians around the resort town of Sinaia and the city of Brasov. These uplands are areas of unspoiled natural beauty rare in Europe, but at lower altitudes, too, the scenery remains utterly seductive. This is, in part, because the intensive farming practices that have depleted habitats elsewhere in the continent are largely absent here. Taking all this in at a leisurely cycling pace, you can't help but notice how rich your surroundings are—meadows full of wildflowers, an abundance of birds, ancient woodlands, and verdant pastures. Add to this the presence of traditional haystacks and horse-drawn carts, and the effect can easily induce delusions of time travel back to some long-lost Ruritania.

WHEN TO GO From April to October. May and June are especially beautiful.

HOW LONG Most tours last six to eight days.

PLANNING EU membership and the advent of budget flights from London and other western European cities has made Romania easier to visit, and the country's tourist infrastructure is steadily improving. Mountain biking, however, is relatively new, and facilities are not well-developed. Most people go on prebooked specialist tours.

INSIDE INFORMATION If you want to go solo, you can rent mountain bikes and other equipment in Sinaia and Busteni for the Bucegi Massif and the ski resort of Poiana Brasov farther north near Brasov.

WEBSITES adventuretransylvania.com, romaniatravelcentre.com

HIGHLIGHTS

▪ Some of the most beautiful trails lead across the high plateau of the **Bucegi Massif**, covered in ancient beech and pine forests, between Sinaia and the village of Bran, southwest of Brasov. The massif is part of the mountainous barrier that divides Transylvania from the lower-lying lands of Wallachia to the south.

▪ Southwest of Bran, a wonderful descent takes you down from the Fundata Pass through the **Piatra Craiului Mountains**. The village of Fundata is famous locally for its smoked cheese and syrups made from forest fruits.

▪ Nonbiking highlights include **Peles Castle** – a magnificent 19th-century confection, built as a summer palace for the kings of Romania – above Sinaia, Bran Castle of (bogus) Dracula fame, and the picturesque old center of Brasov.

EUROPE

Bird-watching in the Danube Delta

The peace of this watery world makes it a haven for visitors as well as the kaleidoscopic range of birdlife that they come to observe.

Having traversed Europe for some 1,800 miles (2,900 kilometers) from the Black Forest to the Balkans, the Danube River empties into the Black Sea through a vast delta. A sanctuary for more than 300 bird species, this wetland is the world's largest reed bed and one of Europe's last remaining wilderness areas. Most European wading birds and waterfowl—including such exotica as white pelicans, glossy ibis, squacco herons, and spoonbills—can be seen here, along with numerous raptors, iridescent kingfishers, rollers, and bee-eaters. You may also see otters, mink, and jackals. Occasional expanses of open water, such as Lake Fortuna near Crisan, are particularly rewarding for bird-watchers, and there are also areas of meadow, heath, and even some forest, which provide habitats for even more species. This remote, roadless wilderness has a unique end-of-the-world feel, and although it's primarily thought of as a haven for wildlife, it also has a human aspect: these backwaters provided a refuge for Russian Old Believers (the Lipoveni), who fled religious persecution in 18th-century Russia.

WHEN TO GO April–May and September–October are the best times for birds, with migratory species stopping off between Africa and Siberia. May, when all the summer breeding species arrive, is ideal.

HOW LONG Most delta tours last three to five days.

PLANNING You can visit independently – from the city of Tulcea there is river transportation to the main tourist bases of Crisan, Sulina, and Sfântu Gheorghe. Find either a fisherman or a small tour group to reach the bird-watching spots. Best of all, probably, is to join a bird-watching tour.

INSIDE INFORMATION The descendants of Ukrainian fugitives and the Lipoveni have maintained their ancient fishing culture in wooden villages throughout the delta. They are fascinating places to visit.

WEBSITES romaniatravelcentre.com, eco-romania.ro

HIGHLIGHTS

▥ If you have time, **rent a rowboat or canoe** to go exploring. While an outboard motor is the norm, nothing can beat the peace of quietly paddling yourself through some of the delta's labyrinth of remote backwaters.

▥ A **flock of white pelicans** wheeling into the sky on a thermal is one of the delta's more glorious sights.

▥ You can stay with local families in **Crisan** or **Sfântu Gheorghe**. Sfântu Gheorghe is also close to a remote and beautiful **beach**.

▥ The ideal end to a successful day's bird-watching is to dine on **delta carp**, preferably against a vivid sunset and a chorus of marsh frogs.

A Lipovan-Russian fisherman in a traditional wooden boat paddles along a peaceful section of the Danube delta.

Backcountry skiers in Norway experience the ultimate in wonderful isolation and extraordinary skies.

NORWAY

Cross-country Skiing in Lillehammer

Ski the Norwegian way, across sparkling snowscapes where no two tracks are the same, and you get a real sense of journeying.

The snow spreads for miles, studded with birch and pine trees. You ski for hours without seeing a soul, and then you meet a group of red-cheeked adults and children (the smallest pulled along on sleds), who wave as you glide past. Lillehammer in southern Norway is the premier place for cross-country skiing. Located on the northern shore of Lake Mjøsa—just 112 miles (180 kilometers) north of the capital, Oslo—the town is surrounded by mountains, all beckoning the long-distance skier. Many trails lead out from the Birkebeineren Ski Stadium, including one of 3 miles (5 kilometers) that is lit up until 10 each evening. Or you can head up the mountainsides to the east and base yourself in one of the former dairy-farming communities of Nordseter and Sjusjøen, from which 220 miles (350 kilometers) of signposted trails crisscross open countryside, traverse forests, and skirt frozen lakes. Experienced skiers can try the 106-mile (170 kilometer) Troll Trail, from Høvringen to the northwest, through the majestic Rondane National Park to its finish in Lillehammer.

WHEN TO GO Snow is virtually guaranteed in Norway—there are even places where you can cross-country ski during summer—but December to March is best.

HOW LONG Allow two weeks, assuming you're keen on winter sports. There's not much else to do!

PLANNING Lillehammer is easy to reach from Oslo's Gardermoen International Airport. Don't take your own ski equipment; you can rent everything you need in and around Lillehammer.

INSIDE INFORMATION Make sure you stock up on high-energy food and drinks: oranges, juice, chocolate bars, and more. Snacking is essential on the ski trail. Since the top of Hafjell is only about 3,000 ft (910 m) above sea level—much lower than most American ski resorts—altitude sickness is not a worry.

WEBSITES telemarkskico.com, hafjell.no/en, discover-norway.no

HIGHLIGHTS

▦ After hours of skiing through empty countryside, **stops at tiny hamlets** like Pellestova and Hörnsjö for coffee are a treat.

▦ For Norwegians, cross-country skiing is the most popular way to "*går på tur*" ("get outside for a while"), a perfect **family activity**. In most resorts, daycare, babysitters, cribs, and children's ski lessons are all there for the asking.

▦ **Downhill skiing** enthusiasts are catered to as well. There are lifts at Nordseter and Sjusjøen, and the Hafjell Alpine Center is just 9 miles (15 km) north of Lillehammer.

AZORE ISLANDS

Whale-watching in the Azores

*A compact archipelago of tiny islands form a marine paradise
where the great mammals of the sea congregate all year round.*

Cold Atlantic salt spray stings your cheeks as you and your small group bump over wave after wave in your quest to … there! There she blows! *"Baleia a vista! Baleia a vista!"* ("Whale in sight! Whale in sight!") yells the weather-beaten *vigia* (lookout). You're closer to a whale than you could ever have imagined—especially since you're in a simple recreational inflatable boat or on a beautiful catamaran. The waters offshore these nine tiny volcanic islands are a magnet for whales because of the abundant food, and many species can be seen here year-round. The largest and most common are sperm whales, but pilot, blue, fin, humpback, and minke species are also seen. So it is unsurprising that, a quarter century ago, the skipper of your boat might have been captain of a fishing boat, since hunting whales was a major source of income and was only outlawed here in 1987. Now, instead of crews with harpoons at the ready, tourists with cameras scan the water for the trademark Y-shape of a powerful fluke breaking the surface. Many of the whales have been identified by the unique patterning at the end of their tails, and populations and migratory patterns deduced. Don't just take one whale-watching trip—island-hop and experience something different each time. And top off each day back on land with a leisurely dinner of local ingredients and wine, among friendly people.

WHEN TO GO May to September, which also gives the benefit of the balmy summers, when the average temperature is 59–71ºF (15–22ºC). This is also the time for festivals.

HOW LONG If you go just for whale-watching, five days to a week will be sufficient. Spend longer if you can to enjoy these unspoiled and peaceful islands.

PLANNING The Azores are a two-hour flight from Lisbon and a five-hour flight from Boston. Tours tend to visit different locations depending on where the whales are, and each day is spent at sea, until about 4:30–5:30 p.m.

INSIDE INFORMATION You'll want to record what you see, so think carefully about investing in a waterproof camera and/or video equipment.

WEBSITES visitazores.com/en, whalewatchazores.com

HIGHLIGHTS

▦ You may well have the chance to see a 45-ft (14 m) **sperm whale** turning on its side near your boat as it swallows gallons of red krill.

▦ Discover the **differences between the islands**: São Miguel is the largest and most cosmopolitan with a landscape of mountains and lakes; Pico combines exotic vegetation with spectacular rock pools that are a swimmer's dream; while Graciosa, the "white island," offers a pastoral landscape dotted with windmills, hot springs, and a coast prettily decorated with islets.

▦ There are outstanding **dolphin-watching** opportunities. If in a lively mood, dolphins may stay with a boat for some time and leap, feed, and mate while traveling along.

▦ You may also be treated to incidental sightings of other **exciting marine life**, such as the superfast marlin, swordfish, loggerhead turtles, sharks, and seabirds such as Cory's shearwater and roseate tern.

Opposite: The fluke of a sperm whale breaks the surface. The clear waters around the Azores provide ideal conditions for whales … and whale-watching. Above left: Pico's volcano, rising above an unspoiled village on the island's south coast, is Portugal's highest mountain. Above right: Whales are an important part of the islands' heritage.

Riding by camel is the way to experience the ancient mode of transportation of the nomadic Berbers of the Sahara.

MOROCCO

Moroccan Camel Train

Cruising the dunes on the back of a dromedary is both practical and highly romantic, transporting you into an unchanged way of life.

You strike out across the Erg Chebbi in eastern Morocco, golden dunes that seem to stretch forever between the famed Wadi Ziz oasis belt and the Algerian frontier. Following cobalt-clad Tuareg guides, you spend five or six hours a day in the saddle (or walking alongside your beast), traversing the ever shifting sands of a landscape that has existed for thousands of years. Here and there you come across Berber nomad families camped along the edge of the desert, their own camels clustered around palm-shaded wells. At dusk, as the sun sinks over the far-off Atlas Mountains, you pitch camp yourself. A dinner of lamb and couscous is followed by tribal songs around the campfire with your Berber hosts. Afterward, you climb to the top of the nearest dune, fall flat on your back, and listen to the silence beneath the starlit sky.

WHEN TO GO October to May, when temperatures dip low enough to make the desert journey quite comfortable. During midwinter, nights can be chilly.

HOW LONG Three days is about the average amount of time for the camel trek, but you need at least ten days or two weeks to get a real taste of Morocco.

PLANNING International outfitters like Wilderness Travel provide 4x4 transportation from Marrakech or Fez to the dunes, plus camping equipment. All meals are normally included.

INSIDE INFORMATION Sunscreen is a must, even in winter. Those who can't quite get the hang of riding a camel can easily walk the route at around the same speed; some outfitters provide 4x4 vehicles for those who find the dunes daunting.

WEBSITE wildernesstravel.com

HIGHLIGHTS

▓ The **spectacular golden dunes** of Erg Chebbi are among the foremost natural wonders of the entire Sahara and can reach a height of 492 ft (150 m) above the desert floor.

▓ Ancient terminus of the trans-Sahara caravans, **Rissani** is a charming oasis town along the Wadi Ziz that boasts a brooding 17th-century casbah, bustling souk, and some of the best dates you will ever taste.

▓ Savor desert life by drawing water from a nomad well for your own ship of the desert, and wake early to **see the sun rise** over the softly rolling, peaceful landscape.

▓ Two alternative ways to tackle the Moroccan Sahara are **sandboarding** and **dune riding**. The former is a desert version of snowboarding, sailing down the dunes on a single wooden or fiberglass "plank." The latter is another snow-sport conversion: shooting the dunes in a plastic sled or toboggan.

AFRICA

SOUTH AFRICA

Diving With Sharks

This is the closest you'll get to one of the deadliest killers on the blue planet. Enter the ocean if you dare.

Certain things seem intrinsically dangerous, if not foolhardy, and diving with great white sharks is probably one of them. Yet that's exactly what you're doing one bright blue morning in Walker Bay, in a place famously called Shark Alley near the old fishing town of Gansbaai. Your captain has tossed a bucket of chum (ground-up fish) into the water to attract the sharks, and now he assures his passengers one last time that it's quite safe to go down for a closer look—from the safety of a sturdy steel cage tethered to the side of the boat. It takes a while for the first dorsal fin to break the surface, but when it does, your heart rate surges. Moments later you're inside the cage, a snorkel mask over your face and an air hose dangling from your mouth, waterproof camera at the ready. You're shaking, less from fear than excitement. In the murky distance you spot a large shadow. It turns, exposing a huge gray dorsal fin and rows of razor-sharp teeth. Closer and closer it moves, cautious at first, circling around until it has scoped out the situation. Then in a flash it goes in for the "kill," devouring a mouthful of chum in a single gulp. One of the ocean's most efficient killers is so close you could reach out and touch it. But you won't. You want to keep your hand.

WHEN TO GO There are sharks in the water off Cape Town all year, but May–September (winter) is the best time for viewing them. They prefer the colder water and plentiful fish at this time of year.

HOW LONG The trip lasts about half a day.

PLANNING Cage-diving takes place in three locations: False Bay, near Cape Town; Gansbaai, about 68 miles (110 km) southeast of Cape Town; and Mossel Bay, near George. National or local outfitters can arrange trips.

INSIDE INFORMATION Outfitters provide everything you need for diving, including steel cage, wet suit, mask, and air hose. You must have some diving experience and qualifications.

WEBSITES sharkcagediving.co.za, sharkbookings.com

AFRICA

HIGHLIGHTS

▥ Great whites are not the only creatures that inhabit Walker Bay. Whales are also a common sight, especially the **Southern right whales** that migrate this way each year.

▥ The Walker Bay area has various attractions: the resort town of **Hermanus** opposite Gansbaai and local wineries and beaches.

▥ The **Cape of Good Hope** is a nature reserve with wonderful coastal trails and abundant wildlife, such as zebra, ostrich, and baboons.

▥ Visit Cape Town's **Two Oceans Aquarium**, which has a Predator Exhibit with fearsomely large ragged-tooth sharks.

From the safety of your cage, you have nothing to fear from this awesome creature: the great white shark.

Bird-watching in East Africa

On the ground, in the trees, along rivers, and in the sky ... individuals, pairs, and flocks of birds make this a paradise for the ardent ornithologist.

You leave your lodge in the early morning and enter an off-the-beaten-path reserve, such as Kenya's Samburu National Reserve, just as the sun's first rays are beginning to hit the savanna. You head toward the wooded banks of a river—in Samburu's case, the Ewaso Ngiro—and in the few hours it takes you to get there you check off countless African birds on your list, whose names alone evoke their color and variety: crowned plover, crested francolin, red-crested and black-bellied bustard, palm-nut vulture, bateleur, tawny eagle, African mourning dove, Namaqua dove, white-headed mousebird, Fischer's starling, taita fiscal, eastern violet-backed sunbird, and lilac-breasted roller. East Africa, including Kenya and Tanzania, offers some of the best birding opportunities in the world, and for a birder with binoculars poised, it's like being a kid in a candy shop. With more than 1,000 bird species and varying habitats close together, it's possible to see 100 species in a day. Everywhere you travel can guarantee something new for your list. The open plains are home to ground hornbills, secretary birds, ostriches, and different kinds of egrets, bustards, eagles, and vultures, while close to water you'll find stunning flamingos, hammerkops, kingfishers, cranes, African fish eagles, and jacanas. And although it's all about the birding for a birder, the wildlife-watching—including elephants, lions, and water buffalo—is also superb.

WHEN TO GO The birding is good all year round. However, think about going during the fall, when birds are migrating. Visit Ngulia in Kenya's Tsavo West National Park, where the birds literally drop from the sky as they seek a place to rest before continuing their journey south.

HOW LONG Birding safaris can last from a week to a month or more.

PLANNING You must bring a good pair of binoculars and a guide to the birds of East Africa. Ask your doctor about antimalarial medication.

INSIDE INFORMATION Don't forget to start your birding as soon as you step off the plane in Nairobi. You may be able to check pied crow, black kite, and African pied wagtail off your list before you even leave the parking lot.

WEBSITES birdingsafaris.com, natureswonderlandsafaris.com

AFRICA

HIGHLIGHTS

▦ Lake Nakuru in Kenya takes your breath away with the sight of more than a million **pink lesser flamingos** – not to mention giraffe, hyena, and white rhinoceros.

▦ Birding in Serengeti National Park in Tanzania will also bring you into close contact with at least **five species of vultures**, along with zebras and Thomson's gazelles.

▦ You can even watch **wildlife at night**. Many lodges have placed spotlights near water holes so you can see the animals coming to drink after dark.

▦ If you're luxury camping, enjoy the novelty of **formal dining** – white table linen, waiters, and plenty of wine – at the end of the day, even though you're eating in a tent!

Opposite: Crowds of greater and lesser flamingos feed on the edge of an alkaline lake in Kenya, creating a symphony in pink. Above left: Nests of spectacled weaverbirds hang from a tree, silhouetted against the sunset. Above right: A dainty white-fronted bee-eater sings from his perch on a twig.

The sight of a herd of elephants bathing is one of the rewards of a classic African safari.

BOTSWANA

Stalking the "Big Five"

Northern Botswana, where the Chobe basin and the Okavango Delta merge with the Kalahari Desert, is the place for big-game-watching.

More than a hundred elephants surround you in the floodplain of the Chobe River—but they hardly notice you as they munch golden grass, the little ones gingerly stepping between their mothers' legs. This is one of the high points of a safari in which you see every member of the "big five" of African wildlife: lion, leopard, buffalo, rhino, and of course these gray giants. The five species were so-called because they were allegedly the most difficult to hunt. The name persists, although today the shooting is done by cameras rather than with guns. Chobe is where your trip starts, and the safari falls into a dreamy routine—up before dawn to catch the animals in the early morning cool, then back to camp for brunch and a snooze. You are out again in the late afternoon, when leopards and other nocturnal creatures start to emerge. A hearty dinner is followed by tall tales around the campfire. From Chobe you head southwest into the Okavango, where you explore the delta by *mokoro* (dugout canoe), on the lookout for hippo, crocodile, and rare swamp species such as the lechwe antelope. Later you move southeast to Makgadikgadi Pans National Park, where you visit one of the Kalahari pans, dry lakebeds that swarm with creatures after sundown.

WHEN TO GO May to October (winter and spring in the Southern Hemisphere) is the best time to view the big five in this region. The temperatures are cooler, the vegetation is sparser, and the wildlife is concentrated closer to the water.

HOW LONG Allow at least a week, preferably two or more.

PLANNING Licensed tour operators organize ground transportation in 4x4 vehicles, boat travel, lodges and/or tented accommodation, all meals, and English-speaking guides.

INSIDE INFORMATION The Victoria Falls on the border of Zimbabwe and Zambia are only a short distance away from the start of the tour. If possible, try to combine your big-five trip with a visit to them.

WEBSITES botswanatourism.co.bw, theultimatetravelcompany.com

HIGHLIGHTS

■ **Chobe National Park** harbors more elephants than just about any other game park in Africa, along with massive numbers of buffalo, zebra, and antelope. An intermittent waterway cum grassland called the Savuti Channel is one of the park's renowned safari areas.

■ In the dry season, the Linyanti Wildlife Reserve nurtures migratory species, such as elephants and zebras, and their predators: **lions**, **leopards**, and **hyenas**.

■ The **Okavango Delta** is heaven for both bird-watchers and those in search of larger game.

| NAMIBIA |

ATVs in the Namib Dunes

The tall sand peaks of Namibia are a joy to climb in an all-terrain vehicle, while observing strict ecological codes, of course.

Up ahead, at the top of a steep and seemingly perilous peak, a stark line of orange sand contrasts vividly with the bright blue morning sky. The tip of the dune must be the end of the world, you think, a sheer cliff towering above an unimaginable drop. From under your helmet, you peer hesitantly at the guide, so confident astride his ATV (quad bike). You've followed him this far without wiping out, meandering across the gravel plains and weaving over the hills and valleys of the dune field just outside town. But surely he doesn't expect you to go up … that? He smiles. "Accelerate!" he calls, shifting gear and zooming up the dune at top speed. Transfixed, you watch his ATV hang in the air for seconds before vanishing below the horizon. You inhale and follow. At the crest, a downward slope rushes toward you and suddenly you realize you're not falling; you're still seated and careening down the hill. If your breath wasn't already stalled by exhilaration, it would be completely knocked out of you at the sight of the vast Atlantic Ocean, stretching out beyond the rolling fields of sand, nothing but a black ribbon of road along the shore separating desert from water.

WHEN TO GO The coast is cooler than the hot Namibian interior, so visit here any time, including the summer months of November to March. But to enjoy other parts of Namibia as well, visit May–October.

HOW LONG The designated route is about 22 miles (35 km) long. ATV trips, including safety demo and slow puttering to the dunes, last 2.5 hours, but stay in Swakopmund for several days to enjoy all the area has to offer.

PLANNING Travel agents and hotels in Swakopmund book all activities. Only go with a reputable agency that follows the set tracks and adheres to environmental regulations.

INSIDE INFORMATION Don't go out to the dunes on your own, even on foot, as fragile species are easily disturbed. For those less sure of their biking skills, there are semiautomatic ATVs.

WEBSITES namibiatourism.com.na, outback-orange.com/quads.htm

HIGHLIGHTS

▥ Stay in delightful **Swakopmund**, which is home to the most adventure sports in Namibia. Try sandboarding, horse-riding, camel-riding, scenic flights, or skydiving over the desert.

▥ The town's beach is one of the most visited in the country. **Dolphin-viewing cruises** are available nearby and include onboard visits from seals.

▥ Drive north to the inhospitable, bleak, but atmospheric, **Skeleton** Coast to view old shipwrecks through the fog, and enjoy excellent fishing.

▥ Take a safari south to Sesriem, where you can see some of the **tallest dunes** in the world.

A trail of ATVs follows the leader over a softly undulating section of the Namib dunes.

Chapter 8

UP AND AWAY

Certain destinations demand to be seen from on high. A bird's-eye view may be essential for different reasons: to look at inaccessible locations, to experience a landscape to the full, to gain another perspective on famous landmarks, to observe wildlife in close but safe proximity ... There are, surprisingly, many ways to achieve these lofty ambitions. Some of the journeys on the following pages feature short flights by light plane, helicopter, or even hot-air balloon, while others are just a climb via cable car or elevator. Adventurous travelers will savor the chance to skim the Hawaiian island of Kaua'i or to swoop with a skilled pilot over the Alaskan wilderness. Those eager to see rare or shy animals in the wild can take a microlight over the savanna of South Africa's Kruger National Park, spotting elephants, giraffes, white rhinos, and crocodiles. For others fascinated by ancient mysteries, a flight over the Nasca lines of Peru will pique the imagination: why and how did the creators of these 2,500-year-old artworks in the desert etch the huge set of designs that is visible in its entirety only from the air?

A Cessna 185 Skywagon peels through purple skies past the snowcapped mountains of Ruth Gorge, Alaska. Ruth Gorge's enormous peaks make it one of North America's ultimate alpine climbing destinations.

Hoover Dam Air Tour

Leaving Las Vegas never felt so good as you head for a marvel of human ingenuity, a man-made oasis in the orange desert.

The Colorado River winds sinuously through a vermilion landscape so parched it makes you thirsty. Just 35 miles (56 kilometers) southeast of Las Vegas, you've left behind all the glitz and neon and are looking down on one of America's Seven Modern Civil Engineering Wonders: the Hoover Dam. It was constructed from 5 million barrels of cement—which gave rise to the joke that some of it is still drying—by 16,000 workers during the Great Depression. You can try to absorb the vital statistics before your flight, but it's not until you're right above this National Historic Landmark straddling Black Canyon that you feel its enormity. Here the mighty Colorado is held back and stored to give water and electricity to more than a million homes in surrounding states and to irrigate swaths of farmland. The ultramarine depths of Lake Mead, the reservoir that took more than six years to fill after the dam's completion, is today a favored playground of houseboaters, fishermen, and jet skiers. Your flight continues on to the west rim of the Grand Canyon. While the vistas here might not be as majestic as those at the south rim, it's quite something to fly down into or even land in the canyon to witness almost 2 billion years of geological history.

WHEN TO GO Spring and fall. In winter there may be rain, wind, and snow, and summer is scorching. Early morning (5:30–8 a.m.) is best for avoiding the turbulence that occurs when the air warms up later on.

HOW LONG Tours average 2.5–3.5 hours from Las Vegas, depending on the extras you choose.

PLANNING You can take your pick of the packages offered, including champagne picnics in the Grand Canyon and riverside lunches. Several companies offer narrated helicopter flights to Hoover Dam, Lake Mead, and the Grand Canyon.

INSIDE INFORMATION Some helicopters have four seats in a row, so be prepared to position yourself for a window seat.

WEBSITES hooverdamtourcompany.com, scenic.com, paradisefoundtours.com

HIGHLIGHTS

▒ The **proportions of the dam** are immense: 726 ft (221 m) high and 660 ft (200 m) wide at the base, widening to 1,244 ft (379 m) at the top.

▒ When you look down on beautiful **Lake Mead and its beaches,** you see little human dots crisscrossing the glassy water, sailing, cruising, water-skiing, and swimming.

▒ Over 50 ancient **lava flows** mark the volcanic area of Fortification Hill, part of the Lake Mead National Recreation Area, northeast of Hoover Dam.

▒ If you take a sunset tour you will return over the **illuminated Las Vegas Strip** after nightfall, the city's most attractive time.

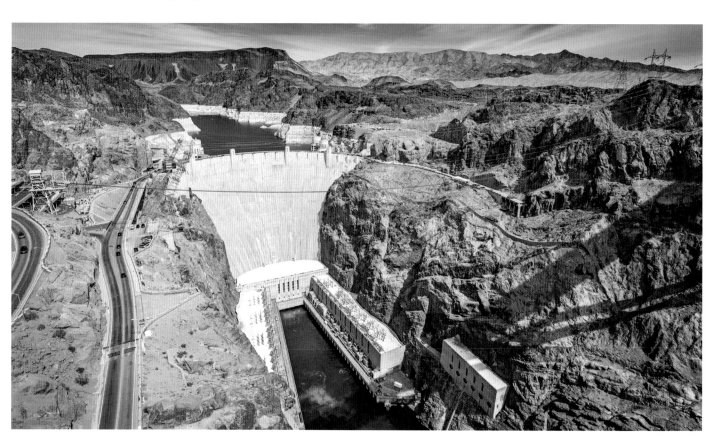

The Hoover Dam straddles the rocky border between Arizona and Nevada. Behind the dam, Lake Mead is held at bay.

Clouds sweep the dramatic peak of Mount McKinley in the half-light.

ALASKA

Bush Plane Adventure

A diminutive aircraft and its superbly skilled pilot takes you to the farthest corners of the Alaskan wilderness.

Taking off from a gravel airstrip, you spot a huge grizzly ambling beside a fast-flowing river. On a windswept hillside just ahead, a female black bear and her cubs browse for berries. Your heart skips a beat as the pilot executes a perfect landing on a grassy shelf atop a 1,000-foot (305 meter) cliff. Scrambling out of the plane, you see a flock of Dall sheep with big curved horns grazing on the steep incline below. Then you're off again, flying through a valley flanked by snow-capped peaks that look close enough to touch. Your pilot maneuvers into a corkscrew dive before another daredevil landing, this time between a pair of gaping crevasses on a glacier. And so it goes on this air safari. One day you're taking off from Anchorage to Denali or Lake Clark wilderness parks for some serious wildlife spotting. The next you're sweeping over Kenai Fjords with its vast glaciers and bays packed with blue icebergs.

WHEN TO GO Alaska's air-safari season runs from late May through mid-September.

HOW LONG There are one-day trips from Anchorage to Denali, Lake Clark, and the Kenai Peninsula. There are also one-day flights around Wrangell-St. Elias from McCarthy, and many opportunities for camping and backpacking. Exploring the far-flung areas of the state requires ten days to two weeks.

PLANNING For fly-in backpacking or camping, even in summer you will need a cold-weather sleeping bag and tent, good hiking boots, and waterproof outer clothing, as well as food and cooking equipment.

INSIDE INFORMATION Avoid the state's notorious bugs by going from early August onward.

WEBSITES nps.gov/dena, ultimathulelodge.com, lakeclarkair.com

HIGHLIGHTS

▥ Lake Clark and Kenai Fjords national parks are known for their scenery and concentrations of wildlife in several ecozones. **Denali National Park**, in the middle of the state, also harbors a diverse range of wildlife and the tallest peak in North America, 20,320-ft (6,194 m) Denali.

▥ Take the chance to visit **ghost towns** and indigenous settlements that cannot be reached by any other means – except by walking for weeks.

▥ America's single largest national park, **Wrangell-St. Elias** lies in Alaska's southeast corner, an expanse of forest, mountain, seacoast, and tundra.

▥ Explore **Cook Inlet** by floatplane – it is home to a resident population of beluga whales.

▥ The **Alaska Aviation Heritage Museum** in Anchorage pays tribute to the state's daring pilots with lively displays and nearly two dozen historic aircraft.

HAWAI'I

Flying High in Paradise

*A helicopter tour brings you up close to the opulent,
sculpted landscape of the Garden Isle of Kaua'i.*

NORTH AMERICA

Few places on Earth can match the impact of Kaua'i's vertical landscapes. The oldest of Hawai'i's islands is still relatively new in geological terms—it is six million years since molten lava petrified to form the fortress-like cliffs that rise 4,000 feet (1,219 meters) above the ocean along the northern Nā Pali Coast. Today, these cliffs and hidden inland valleys form a Garden of Eden enriched with a sense of prehistory. It is little wonder that the island has served as the backdrop for scores of movies from *South Pacific* to *Jurassic Park*. The best way to explore this verdant yet impenetrable landscape is by helicopter. Gliding above the corrugated coast that appears to be carpeted in velvety green, you see white plumes of waterfalls tumbling down hundreds of feet into the waiting shadows of deep, forested valleys. Your heart stops as the land suddenly falls away into the sparkling sea far below. Here and there, the great stone arms of the cliffs shelter lush, flower-filled coves, crescents of fine sand manicured by the waves. Their movement creates a constant swooshing, musical backdrop, at times whipped up into a storm of sound and surf when blustery winds blow. Traditionally in this area, the island chanters walked the smooth boulders at the edge of the sea, intoning their *mele* (chant). If they could be heard above the wind and waves, their training was complete. The spirit of the place is so strong, you long to tell the pilot, "Leave me here. Come back for me in a week, or a month, or whenever."

WHEN TO GO Kaua'i offers plenty of sunshine year-round, but winter (December–March) is officially the wet season. This is also the more expensive high season for tourism. The best weather and greatest bargains are often found in April–May and September–October.

HOW LONG The flight lasts approximately 55 minutes. Allow at least a week to explore the rest of the island at a leisurely pace.

PLANNING Helicopters operate out of the town of Līhu'e. Sunny days make the best flights. If you are visiting outside of high season, watch the weather reports and book your flight on the earliest sunny day after you arrive. Book well in advance for a trip between December and April.

INSIDE INFORMATION The helicopters are temperature-controlled so there is no need for special clothes.

WEBSITES bluehawaiian.com, gohawaii.com

HIGHLIGHTS

▪ Flying into 3,500-ft (1,067 m) deep **Waimea Canyon,** you see weathered and forested landscapes that have been likened to a smaller, greener version of the Grand Canyon.

▪ Spot groups of the **small mountain goats** that make their home along the rocky precipices of the island's rugged interior.

▪ Glide above the sandy expanse of **Kauapea Beach,** commonly known as Secret Beach, to the rocky peninsula that is home to Kīlauea Lighthouse.

▪ After your helicopter tour, hike the Nā Pali landscape via the challenging, and very popular, 11-mile (18 km) **Kalalau Trail** along the north coast. It ascends and descends repeatedly, but rewards you with views of waterfalls, lush valleys, ancient ruins, precipitous cliffs, and finally, beautiful Kalalau Beach itself.

Opposite: Against a backdrop of blue Hawai'ian sea and sky, the sheer, serrated cliffs of Kalalau Valley soar above rain forest graced with giant fern. Above left: The view from the cockpit of a scenic flight. Above right: A helicopter hovers like a dragonfly caught in the net of a misty rainbow over Waimea Canyon.

Floatplane to the Nahanni

Take off from the Mackenzie River at former trading post Fort Simpson, and soar over the sculpted Canadian landscape.

Nahanni National Park Reserve in Canada's remote Northwest Territories became UNESCO's very first World Heritage site in 1978. This is a land of canyons half a mile deep, cut by a surging river and lofty waterfalls, of Canada's largest tufa mounds, and of wilderness where the indigenous Déné people still hunt and gather medicinal plants. Entering the park, your floatplane follows the South Nahanni River through Deadmen Valley, named for prospectors who perished there, and past Pulpit Rock to land on the river just above Virginia Falls, its gushing waters pierced by a huge rock. Here you can stop to hike the river's only portage section and experience the power of the falls from below. Spot foraging black or grizzly bears and moose as you go airborne again alongside Sunblood Mountain, heading upriver to Rabbitkettle, where canoe trips start, and beyond the park boundary to land on Glacier Lake, dominated by the Ragged Range peaks. After another 75-minute hop through the Ram Canyons and over Ram Plateau, the floatplane traverses a cleft in the Nahanni Mountains to land on tranquil Little Doctor Lake. It taxis to a beach in front of rustic Nahanni Mountain Lodge, before the return to base.

WHEN TO GO From the beginning of June through the end of September, after the river ice melts and before the snows and bitter temperatures return.

HOW LONG The tour takes eight hours. A shorter trip, excluding Virginia Falls to Glacier Lake, takes six hours.

PLANNING You can also go on hiking trips along the Nahanni River. You'll need wet-weather gear and sun and mosquito protection. Summer daytime temperatures reach 77ºF (25ºC), sometimes 86ºF (30ºC).

INSIDE INFORMATION Beyond the park's existing boundaries lie the Cirque of the Unclimbables, a cathedral of sheer rock faces in the Ragged Range, and Ram Plateau. You can get a helicopter tour here to explore fossil-filled caves and the Ram Canyons, about 1 mile (1.6 km) deep.

WEBSITES simpsonair.ca, pc.gc.ca, nahanni.com

HIGHLIGHTS

■ **Virginia Falls**, at 295 ft (90 m), is twice the height of Niagara. The floatplane tour allows up to three hours to hike the trails.

■ The Nahanni's **land formations** are the most diverse of any national park in Canada. Look out for Rabbitkettle's tufa mounds – the largest is 89 ft (27 m) high and 243 ft (74 m) across; sand blowouts (sandstone pillars); and limestone karst cliffs riddled with caves, among them Grotte Valerie, with 250,000-year-old stalagmites.

■ **Moose**, and **black** and **grizzly bears** are the most commonly seen of the park's mammal species. Bear mothers will rear up on their hind legs to protect cubs.

The Nahanni's famous Pulpit Rock appears tiny from on high and against the backdrop of the mighty Third Canyon.

A plane begins its descent to land at Vancouver Harbour.

CANADA

Over British Columbia

A tiny seaplane takes you above the dramatic, fjord-riven coast and scattered islands of the Pacific Northwest.

After a short taxi out to a fluorescent buoy in Vancouver Harbour, the spray flies up and you climb quickly, turning above the Lion's Gate Bridge and out over lines of bulk carriers and cruise ships. Sweeping ranges of peaks stretch away to the north. To the west where the Gulf Islands lie, the water is flat and glassy, perfect for wildlife-spotting. Here the plane swoops low between Galiano and Mayne, zigzagging through Active Pass, not far above the ferries that ply this narrow passage. On the way you can see nesting bald eagles, seals, and porpoises in large, gregarious groups; admire the tiny islands that are home to single families living in huge waterside properties; and wave at yachtsmen under their white triangles of sails, brilliant in the sunshine.

WHEN TO GO Late spring through early fall are best, when departures are guaranteed and the weather is more reliable. The winds die down at sunset and the low, warm light adds texture to the views.

HOW LONG You can make 20-minute to two-hour jaunts, including picnic or meal stops; tailor-made trips for as long as you like; or combinations that take in whale-watching boat trips or sportfishing.

PLANNING Book an afternoon flight but check in during the morning. By noon weather conditions for the day are known, and charter flights can be rescheduled for calmer, brighter days if necessary.

INSIDE INFORMATION Out of season, take a scheduled flight to Victoria or Nanaimo, and sit with the pilot; or take the daily "mail run" to remote island harbors, delivering packages and people.

WEBSITES harbourair.com, adventures.ca

HIGHLIGHTS

▓ **The Sunshine Coast** running north of Vancouver to Powell River is patterned with fjords. The trip includes a stop for a meal of Pacific salmon.

▓ At 500 ft (152 m), this is **low-level flying** that takes you below the hilltops and allows you to spot the wildlife of this rich marine ecosystem.

▓ A tour of the **Gulf Islands** from Victoria reveals the delights of coves, where tiny sailboats ride at anchor and houses perch on the water's edge, and offers a great chance of seeing pods of orca, sea lions, and seabirds.

▓ The **final glide** brings a heart-stopping moment, when for the last 50 ft (15 m) the plane does a steep nosedive, as if the pilot is heading straight into the sea.

Overhead views of the island reveal its many splendors, such as this vista of yachts moored at Marigot Bay in the north.

ST. LUCIA

Sky-riding Over St. Lucia

Weave through the ancient rain forest that covers more than one-third of the island, and witness the canopy wildlife at first hand.

The variety of shades and shapes of green is surreal. It's as if you've been living underground all your life and emerge to see that the air itself is green, sprinkled with tiny colorful highlights like the yellow flashes of a passing St. Lucia oriole, or the lavender stars and orange bursts of flowers cascading from branches. Under the tree canopy, the gargling squawk of the vivid St. Lucia parrot competes with the high sweet song of the bananaquit and the piercing whistle of the rufous-throated solitaire. The air is perfumed with the scent of orchids, and jewel-like hummingbirds hover near arrow-sharp heliconia flowers, locally known as Yellow Dancer. How privileged you feel, then, to glide high up through this ebullient nature knowing you are causing no disturbance. At Rain Forest Sky Rides Park up in the mountains, you can fly from tree to tree on the Sky Canopy zip lines or slip through all levels of the forest in an open-sided, nine-person tram—up to 120 feet (37 meters) in the air—and look out for creatures that never descend to the forest floor. Combine pleasure with learning as you listen to a naturalist describing some of the medicinal rain-forest plants—of which there are 105 species—and St. Lucia's equally rich history and culture.

WHEN TO GO High season is mid-December to mid-April. Find bargains June through November, but this is also the season of rainfall and the occasional hurricane.

HOW LONG The rain-forest excursion takes half a day, but a visit to the island requires at least a week.

PLANNING Cameras and binoculars are essential. Trams are wheelchair accessible. Tie back long hair before riding the Sky Canopy zip lines. Immerse yourself in St. Lucian culture in advance by reading Nobel Prize winner Derek Walcott's poems and plays.

INSIDE INFORMATION Take home an eco-friendly memento of the rain forest. Local craft markets sell baskets, woven from climbing palms and dangling roots, and necklaces made from the colored seeds of giant trees in the rain-forest canopy.

WEBSITE rainforestadventure.com

HIGHLIGHTS

▪ **Floating in the air** right above the canopy itself, you see this most beautiful Caribbean island from on high, in all the glory of its mountainous landscape and soft white sandy beaches.

▪ The **sulfur springs** at the world's only "drive-in" volcano near Soufrière, the island's oldest town, lie below the Piton mountains, a majestic backdrop to the area. Nearby are hot and cold waterfalls and mineral baths, which you can sample for their therapeutic properties.

▪ Visit a 250-year-old working **cocoa estate**, where traditional methods of production are used–then try the freshly made chocolate!

NORTH AMERICA

| PERU |

The Nasca Lines

This sophisticated marvel of prehistoric art can be appreciated for its size and completeness only from the sky.

Mystery surrounds the hundreds of animal and geometric figures etched on a high, windless desert plateau in southern Peru. Between 200 B.C. and A.D. 700 these enormous geoglyphs, or earth drawings, were made by the Nasca people, who removed the desert's darker surface pebbles to reveal the lighter subsoil. Archaeologists believe the Nasca made the artworks with the most basic surveying equipment, a point that has been proved by replicating such a method even for the largest figures. More fanciful researchers have claimed that the ancient builders must have been visited by extraterrestrials who aided their work. Others suggest that they may even have had hot-air balloons, enabling them to view their designs from the air—a theory that has also been supported by constructing a viable balloon from prehistoric materials. As you look down from a modern six-seater plane, you can ponder the genesis of the stylized drawings of birds and beasts and the yet more enigmatic triangles, circles, trapezoids, spirals, and myriad long, straight lines, some running for 9 miles (14.5 kilometers). The pilot stands the plane on its wingtips for a better view, and you see the beauty of these images, a testament to the eternal human desire to create.

WHEN TO GO Year-round.

HOW LONG One hour, covering the 135-sq-mile (350 sq km) site.

PLANNING The 300-mile (483 km) drive from Lima to Nasca, for an overnight stay, takes around eight hours. Flying from Lima takes around one hour. Planes leave Nasca every morning for the site.

INSIDE INFORMATION Playa el Chaco, 125 miles (201 km) north of Nasca, is the perfect place to break the long road trip back to Lima. After flying over the lines, you can be drinking a pisco sour by early afternoon as you watch pelicans glide over the Pacific rollers. Next morning, take the boat trip to the Islas Ballestas for an incomparable wildlife spectacle of gannets, cormorants, pelicans, and sea lions.

WEBSITES perufly.com, nascaperu.com/en

HIGHLIGHTS

▥ As you hover over a **landscape of contrasts** you see fertile river valleys, fed by the melting snows of the high Andes, cut green corridors of cotton fields and citrus groves through stretches of desert.

▥ Spot the **animal forms** among the geoglyphs: frog, monkey, spider, whale, lizard, hummingbird, condor, and a 1,000-ft (305 m) long pelican!

▥ The **sense of design** and the sheer scale of individual drawings can only be experienced from an aerial perspective; some of the animal shapes are two football fields in length, yet do not lose in precision.

The condor, one of the imposing animal artworks juxtaposed with geometric patterns made by the Nasca people.

Top 10 Funiculars and Cable Cars

Tiny transparent capsules whisk you up to exceptional places, from the Himalaya to the Australian rain forest via some vibrant cities.

❶ PEAK 2 PEAK, BRITISH COLUMBIA, CANADA

With the longest free-span between ropeway towers in the world, you'll travel the nearly 2 miles (3 km) in just 11 minutes. The 360° views of Canada's Pacific Coast Ranges are stunning; look for a black bear while taking in the Whistler and Blackcomb peaks, coastal rain forest, and glaciers.

PLANNING In spring, summer, and autumn, go hiking on the endless trails; in winter, of course, hit the slopes. whistlerblackcomb.com

❷ ZACATECAS, MEXICO

The *teleférico* (cable car) swings above the mosaic of streets, plazas, rooftops, and domes of this elegant, rose-colored city before ascending Cerro de la Bufa in just a few minutes.

PLANNING Car operates from Cerro del Grillo in the downtown area, daily 10 a.m.–6 p.m., except when too windy. visitmexico.com/en

❸ RIO DE JANEIRO, BRAZIL

The journey first takes you to Urca Hill above Guanabara Bay, then up to the summit of Sugar Loaf Mountain (1,300 ft/ 396 m). In the distance is Rio's famous statue, Christ the Redeemer on Corcovado Mountain, while the city and its beaches fan out below.

PLANNING Car operates daily 8 a.m.–10 p.m., every 30 minutes. Allow two hours for a round-trip. visitbrasil.com/en

❹ MÉRIDA, VENEZUELA

The highest and longest *teleférico* in the world takes an hour to ascend from a plateau in the Andes 10,250 ft (3,125 m) to the top of Pico Espejo. Stop off at four stations on the way if you wish, and at the top admire Pico Bolívar.

PLANNING Cars normally depart 7 a.m.–noon but times can vary. Take warm clothes. You need an extra ticket for the last stage. andesholidays.com

❺ THE PEAK TRAM, HONG KONG, CHINA

This funicular railway rises briskly up Victoria Peak—at a gradient of 4-27 degrees, so that all the buildings seem to be leaning over as you pass by! At the top the city views are spectacular, and you can dine, shop, or walk park trails.

PLANNING The Peak Tram runs daily, every 10–15 minutes, 7 a.m.–midnight. thepeak.com.hk

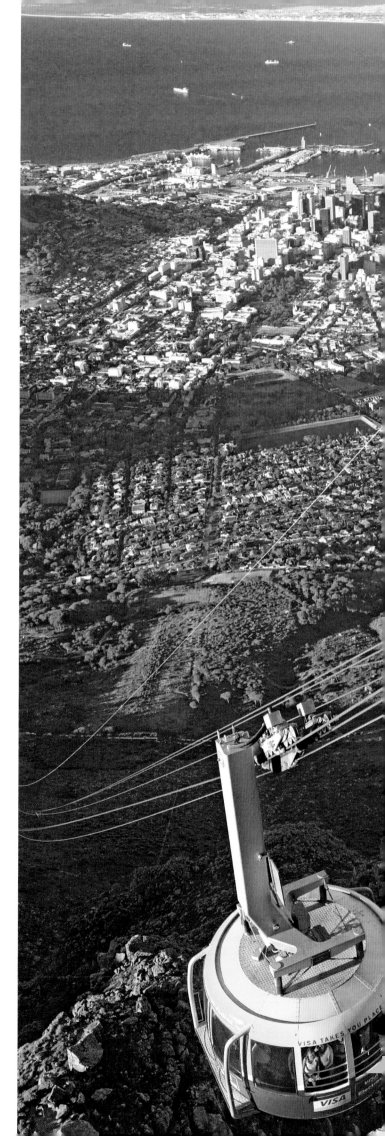

A cable car rides toward Table Mountain; below lies Cape Town with Table Bay in the background.

➏ GENTING SKYWAY, MALAYSIA

The fastest cable cars in the world speed you up the longest cableway in southeast Asia. The journey ends at the Genting Highlands Resort, a cool 6,650 ft (2,027 m) above sea level. There you will find theme parks, shops, hotels, and even a casino.

PLANNING Genting Skyway operates from its lower station at Gohtong Jaya to Highlands Hotel, Sun–Fri 7:30 a.m.–11 p.m. and Sat 7:30 a.m.–midnight. rwgenting.com/attractions/awana-skyway/

➐ PICOS DE EUROPA NATIONAL PARK, SPAIN

These mountains in northern Spain form part of an area of outstanding natural beauty. An excellent entry point is the steep cableway that carries you swiftly above a sunny, wooded valley in the Picos to 6,037 ft (1,840 m). At the top you can walk to the viewpoint of Aliva, where the sight of these mountains may well lure you to further exploration of this spectacular hiking terrain.

PLANNING The lower station of the cableway is next to the parador in Fuente Dé. Open daily; check in advance as times vary according to season. cantur.com

➑ GRINDELWALD-MÄNNLICHEN CABLEWAY, SWITZERLAND

One of the longest cable-car rides in the world links the scenic village of Grindelwald (3,094 ft/943 m) with Männlichen (7,316 ft/2,230 m) in the Swiss Alps, overlooked all the way by such celebrated mountains as the Jungfrau and Eiger. In the space of a comfortable 30 minutes, you can marvel at these rugged peaks and the plunging valleys below, without needing hiking boots or skis! It then takes 15 minutes to walk from the cable car to the summit.

PLANNING Operating times vary according to season. Open daily. Reduced tariffs are available with travel passes and cards. maennlichen.ch/en

➒ TABLE MOUNTAIN CABLEWAY, CAPE TOWN, SOUTH AFRICA

The floor of the cable car rotates 360° to give passengers maximum views on the quick journey to the summit of Table Mountain (3,560 ft/1,085 m). On arrival you can choose from a number of paths for exploring the mountain; take a picnic for a relaxing visit. The atmosphere is often clearest in the early morning or late evening.

PLANNING Directions to the cableway are clearly marked. Operates daily every 10–15 minutes, except when too windy. Check in advance as opening times vary according to season. tablemountain.net

➓ POWELL-HYDE LINE, SAN FRANCISCO, CALIFORNIA

Complete your visit to the city with a trip on the iconic Powell-Hyde Line that trundles upward via the vibrant neighborhood of Russian Hill, before making a steep, lurching descent down San Francisco's famous hills. The Golden Gate Bridge leaps into view and the trip concludes at Fisherman's Wharf.

PLANNING Cable cars operate from the turntable at Powell and Market streets, daily 6:00 a.m.–1:30 a.m. Tickets can be purchased on the car. Start early to avoid crowds. streetcar.org

SEYCHELLES

Island-hopping by Air

Flying between these jewels by helicopter or plane, you see from on high their dense rain forest and matchless shoreline, a taste of what awaits you on the ground.

Along journey from anywhere, the Seychelles lie 1,000 miles (1,600 kilometers) east of Kenya in the South Indian Ocean and offer an abundance of beaches, birds, primeval forests, and seclusion. Flying over them, you see the dramatic differences between the inner, granite islands—the largest and most populated—and the outer, low-lying coral atolls. This way, too, you can easily reach the farthest and quietest spots. On Praslin, take the forest path through fecund, primeval Vallée de Mai, dubbed the Garden of Eden by General Gordon of Khartoum. Here you will find the world's largest seed, that of the coco de mer—the size of a football—and Anse Lazio, considered one of the world's ten most beautiful beaches. That's not to demean those of La Digue, of which Anse Source d'Argent is so photogenic that it often forms the backdrop to movies and commercials. But in the Seychelles you don't just seek out one beach; each is more alluring than the last and invites you to swim, snorkel, gaze at the turquoise water, and revel in the peace. Occasionally, you'll come upon a fisherman knee-deep in the water, pulling in the catch in his net by hand. On the weekend at a tiny hotel in La Digue someone will lead you to the dance floor to show you the *moutia*, once banned by colonial authorities for its erotic movements. When you breakfast outside next day, a bright red Madagascar fody will steal a crumb of your muffin.

WHEN TO GO October through May, avoiding the January–February rainy season.

HOW LONG At least two weeks, depending on how many islands you want to visit. Allow a few days each on Mahé (the largest), Praslin, and La Digue.

PLANNING U.S. visitors, after an all-night flight to Europe, must allow another day's flight from London or Paris to Mahé. From here take flights to the other islands. These can be booked via hotels.

INSIDE INFORMATION Local beer is good, but wine is imported, pricy, and undistinguished. Don't ask for a king-sized bed or a car on La Digue (they have neither), but hotels have bikes for the use of guests and oxcarts to pick up you and your luggage. No matter how used you may be to the currents of the great oceans, never swim when "Danger" signs are posted on beaches.

WEBSITES seychelles.travel, seychelles.org, airseychelles.com

HIGHLIGHTS

▓ Visit **Anse Source d'Argent** an hour before sunset, when the pink granite boulders, white sand, and coconut trees are bathed in a special light.

▓ A must for ornithologists is **Bird Island**, about 125 miles (201 km) from Mahé, where thousands of resident birds are joined May–September by 1,500,000 nesting sooty terns. The air resounds with bird chatter. Cousin Island is another bird sanctuary and an important nesting site for hawksbill turtles.

▓ A former pirate refuge, **Frégate**, the remotest of the granite islands, offers a deluxe eco-hideaway where only 40 guests are taken at a time. Here papaya, coconut, and other indigenous trees make a verdant home for frigate birds (for which the island is named) and turtle doves.

▓ A spectacular array of **endemic species** includes the smallest frog, heaviest tortoise, and only flightless bird of the Indian Ocean. These and other fauna and flora are highly protected, with about half of the Seychelles' landmass being given over to national parks and reserves.

Opposite: The shallow tropical waters of a turquoise lagoon in the Seychelles present a vision of tranquility. Above left: The Seychelles lily is one of the numerous flower species endemic to these islands. Above right: Sculpted granite formations on a palm-fringed beach in La Digue are a characteristic feature of the inner islands.

Angkor Wat, with its five majestic towers and intricate wall carvings, can be seen in its full majesty from the air.

CAMBODIA

Angkor by Helicopter

See the heart of the Khmer empire from on high, then explore its hidden temples—lying like scattered treasure inside the jungle.

As you leave behind the clutter of Phnom Penh and head north for Tonle Sap Lake, the hanging blue mists of the Khmer dawn emerge. They are a wonderful thing, a perfect cool calm before the ferocious heat builds up. From 1,000 feet (305 meters) up, roads are dusty ocher ribbons speckled with a continuous patrol of antlike vehicles. Toylike villages and tiny fishing boats, some a resting place for storks, float in the water of Tonle Sap, the occasional dot denoting a swimmer. Passing over the expanse of the plains, you head for the town of Siem Reap. For hundreds of years, the surrounding jungle held a secret even locals were barely aware of—the ancient site of Angkor. Only from the air can you get a true idea of its sophisticated design. A perfect square delineates the royal capital, Angkor Thom, and an array of wats (temples) with carved facades, sweeping terraces, and lotus domes peek out of the undergrowth. On landing, a perfect stillness descends, broken only by the occasional jungle call, and you wonder how many more temples lie waiting to be discovered.

WHEN TO GO Cambodia has a tropical monsoon climate. Winter (November–March) is the coolest and driest time to visit.

HOW LONG The 188-mile (303 km) journey lasts about two hours. Since you are chartering the flight, you can schedule in as many stops as you like.

PLANNING Visas are issued on entering Cambodia, but check with your embassy before departure.

INSIDE INFORMATION From Siem Reap you can explore the temple complex over a few days, so catch the sunrise at Bayon Wat. The faces carved on the towers come to life in the morning light. For sunset the west-facing Angkor Wat is mandatory, but get there in time to find a quiet spot away from the crowds.

WEBSITES helistarcambodia.com, sacred-destinations.com

HIGHLIGHTS

▥ The largest religious monument in the world, **Angkor Wat**, lies peaceful and resplendent behind its wide moat. An occasional splash of orange against gray stone – a monk shuffling to prayer – emphasizes the temple's overwhelming size.

▥ Be sure to roam **Ta Prohm** on foot. This temple remains exactly as it was found in the 19th century, with massive jungle roots and trees tangled around its stones.

▥ Animal carvings and statues on and around the temples are mirrored in the **jungle wildlife**. Monkeys chatter, elephants call, and parakeets chirp. Tonle Sap supports one of Southeast Asia's largest ecosystems, and many species here are among the most endangered in the world.

AUSTRALIA

Great Australian Pub Crawl

Flit between the water holes of thirst-inducing desert panoramas—the pilot is your designated driver.

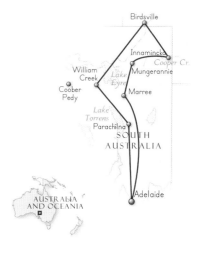

f he's forgotten to phone ahead and warn of his guests' arrival, the pilot will simply dive and buzz an outback pub before landing in a cloud of dust on a nearby strip. If the pub is more than a few paces away, the proprietor drives up to collect the thirsty passengers. The views on the low-level flights out of Adelaide are of a baked landscape laced with dried-out rivers and the occasional small huddle of buildings dwarfed by a magnificent arid emptiness in ocher, red, gray, and pink. Here in South Australia and Queensland the nearest neighbors can be a hundred parched miles away, and the next pub five times farther. Stockmen drive across cattle stations the size of small European countries for a pint and companionship. But the outback is full of surprises, and every remote corner offers something extra. Mungerannie has hot springs, and Innamincka has huge burgers and a desert boating trip. The walls of the rough-and-ready pub at William Creek are festooned with visitors' underwear, while the dignified Marree Hotel has a chef skilled enough to entice people to fly in from Adelaide for dinner. And the feral platter at Parachilna (camel mettwurst, smoked kangaroo, and emu pâté) is not to be missed before a night in the most luxurious accommodation for hundreds of miles.

WHEN TO GO Trips occur year-round on demand. Spring (September–November) sees a sudden brief flowering of the desert if conditions are right, with acacias covered in blossom.

HOW LONG Five days or more, with a mixture of land and air elements as you please.

PLANNING Take plenty of sunscreen, a broad-brimmed hat, a fly net, and a polarizing filter and very large memory card for your camera.

INSIDE INFORMATION Time your trip for the Birdsville Races in September. Dating back to 1882, this is the biggest event in the outback. There's a fair, auctions, a boxing tent, and a lot of drinking. Hundreds of planes fly in to the tiny airstrip, pilots and passengers camping out in the shade of the wings.

WEBSITES vortexair.com.au/index.php/air-tours/outback-pub-crawl, birdsvilleraces.com

HIGHLIGHTS

▧ Visit **Birdsville**, the outback metropolis with a population in nearly three figures. It has a hotel-pub dating from 1882, a dusty cricket oval, and the Working Museum of outback life.

▧ You can boat through the desert from Innamincka on **Cooper Creek**, the banks lined with birdlife.

▧ Discover what a completely subterranean life is like in opal-mining town **Coober Pedy**, with its underground hotel, houses, shops, and churches.

The bar of the Birdsville Hotel in the outback of Queensland is decorated with memorabilia of all sorts – the "visiting cards" of customers past and present.

A six-passenger Skyrail gondola cruises high above the treetop canopy between Kuranda and Cairns.

Skimming Ancient Australian Rain Forest

Swinging above the trees in a gondola, you see incredible sights, from clouds of tiny butterflies to dangling snakes.

Leaving the Kuranda Terminal, the Skyrail Rainforest Cableway glides slowly over the muddy brown Barron River toward the lush canopy of Queensland's tropical rain forest. As you float along just above the treetops, you spot a python, basking languidly in the sun. A flock of chattering rosellas streak by, their red-and-blue plumage a colorful contrast with the leafy green roof below. Then it's time for the first of two stops to view and explore the rain forest at ground level. When you disembark at Barron Falls Station, you might see a pair of iridescent blue Ulysses butterflies dance by as you amble through the misty rain forest to three lookouts for intoxicating views of the gorge and falls. Another gondola takes you to Red Peak Station, where you can follow a guided boardwalk tour through the towering trees, giant ferns, and wild orchids. Bidding your guide "G'day," you hop back on the gondola for the final descent toward Cairns. The forest gives way to vast floodplains and the Coral Sea washes the landscape an azure blue in the distance, a wondrous ending to your aerial voyage.

WHEN TO GO All year. Skyrail operates daily except Christmas Day. Winter (June–September) is drier and cooler; summer (December–March) is wetter, but the rain awakens the forest, enhancing the experience.

HOW LONG Allow 1.5 hours for a one-way trip (4.7 miles/7.6 km), 2.5 hours for a round-trip, including a 30-minute stop at each mid-route station. You can spend more time at these stops if you wish.

PLANNING You can set off from either Kuranda or Cairns, where Skyrail departs from the Caravonica Terminal just outside the town. Make a reservation to eliminate waiting in line on busy days.

INSIDE INFORMATION The forest canopy is thick and dense. If you focus hard, you may see snakes sleeping in the treetops, or birds and butterflies winging by.

WEBSITES skyrail.com.au, tjapukai.com.au

HIGHLIGHTS

■ At the stops you can see **wildlife**, including the chance of an encounter with the endangered southern cassowary, a 6-ft (1.8 m) tall flightless bird, and with the tiny musky rat-kangaroo.

■ In Kuranda you can visit **Australia's largest butterfly sanctuary**; in Birdworld, its largest collection of free-flying birds. In Kuranda Koala Gardens, you can cuddle a koala.

■ At **Tjapukai Aboriginal Cultural Park** in Caravonica, you can learn to play a didgeridoo, sample original bush tucker, and experience the traditions of the Aborigines.

AUSTRALIA AND OCEANIA

AUSTRALIA

Over the Great Barrier Reef

Flightseeing this infinite underwater garden also gives you the
chance to drift among its brilliant, darting fish and sea creatures.

A short run along a palm-fringed airstrip and you are suddenly airborne; almost immediately you're in a shimmering world of blue and white, suspended between land, sea, and sky. Below, the pale turquoise water turns aquamarine, then deepest Prussian blue, and the beauty of the Great Barrier Reef unfolds below you. One of the world's most extensive areas of coral reef runs for more than 1,615 miles (2,600 kilometers) along the coast of Queensland, from the tip of Cape York south to Fraser Island. It encompasses more than 2,900 reefs and hundreds of islands, and its warm, lucid waters act as an aquarium for hundreds of corals and 1,500 species of fish, all part of a dense marine ecosystem. As the plane banks, you can spot manta rays, sea turtles, sharks, and dugong. Here, a boat is moored with divers swimming off a platform at the stern, while a school of dolphins breaches the surface nearby. Foam-crested waves move in toward the "high" islands, the fuzzy green-topped peaks of drowned mountains, while the opalescent coral cays, or "low" islands, fringed by white beaches, seem to float in the water. Submerged coral patterns explode across the seascape until, beyond the farthest reefs, the sea plunges to great depths and acquires a mystery all its own.

WHEN TO GO Fall, winter, and spring (March–November) for safe swimming and diving.

HOW LONG From a 10-minute spin or one- to three-hour flights, to three days, or a week or two.

PLANNING Flights leave from various locations, by light plane, seaplane, or helicopter. Some operators offer flights only, others include visits to beaches, diving, and snorkeling, or provide accommodation, often in major resorts. Make sure your budget allows for transfers between different centers. Some operators charge full price for children over 13 years old, others half price for children up to 16 years old.

INSIDE INFORMATION The coastal strips and mountains behind are almost as spectacular as the reef itself; aerial tours of rain forest, waterfalls, and gorges are well worth taking.

WEBSITES tourismwhitsundays.com.au, queensland.com, www.hamiltonisland.com.au

HIGHLIGHTS

▦ **Heart Reef** is one of nature's icons: a perfectly heart-shaped coral formation that is part of Hardy Reef.

▦ Take in **Hinchinbrook Island**, off Cardwell, one of the largest and most magnificent of the "high" islands.

▦ The Whitsundays reef and Whitehaven scenic flight from Hamilton Island offers a stop at the 4-mile (6.4 km) long **Whitehaven Beach**, a stretch of purest white sand.

▦ From Airlie Beach, gateway to the Whitsundays, fly to **Fantasea Reefworld**, the largest floating facility on the reef, where you can snorkel from semisubmerged platforms to see brilliant reef fish.

A sweep of the Great Barrier Reef reveals its variegated islands and fragmented coral formations.

Top 10 Skywatching Destinations

Star-spangled skies abound in places where light pollution is low. See whole new worlds open up before your eyes in these unique spots.

❶ NATURAL BRIDGES NATIONAL MONUMENT, UTAH

The majestic sandstone arches of this southern Utah park form natural windows to watch the Milky Way and other celestial objects between dusk and dawn. Designated the world's first international dark sky park in 2007, Natural Bridges earned the honor by retrofitting all of its outdoor light fixtures—and being miles away from the nearest city.

PLANNING Natural Bridges runs free ranger-led astronomy programs during the summer months. nps.gov/nabr

❷ ATACAMA DESERT, CHILE

The world's most arid region also boasts incredibly clear night skies. On any given night, the star show is awesome even to the naked eye. But skywatchers can also visit several observatories in the Atacama including the $1.4 billion Atacama Large Millimeter (ALMA), which first became fully operational in 2013, and is the most expensive ground-based telescope of all time.

PLANNING Tierra Atacama Hotel & Spa offers fine dining and massages. nationalgeographiclodges.com/lodges/south-america/tierra-atacama

❸ MAUNA KEA, BIG ISLAND, HAWAI'I

The 4,207-meter (13,802 foot) summit of this ancient volcano, with its cluster of observatories, is only open until 30 minutes after sunset. Farther down the mountain, Onizuka Center for International Astronomy and Visitor Information Station offers nightly stargazing through public telescopes and weekly astronomy lectures, workshops and other programs.

PLANNING Above the visitor center, four-wheel-drive and altitude acclimation is required to reach the summit. ifa.hawaii.edu/mko

❹ STEWART ISLAND, NEW ZEALAND

Floating amid the chilly waters at the bottom end of the South Island, the hilly terrain of Stewart Island offers a chance to view the Aurora Australis (Southern Lights) that form around the South Pole—a sight which the Maori regarded as cosmic flames, either burning in the wake of sky spirits or in the campfires of their ancestors.

PLANNING Stewart Island can be reached via ferry from Bluff or commuter airline from Invercargill on the South Island. stewartisland.co.nz

The Aurora Borealis as seen from Ersfjordbotn, in Norway. This natural phenomenon derives its name from the Roman goddess of dawn (*Aurora*) and the Greek word for northerly wind (*borealis*).

❺ WARRUMBUNGLE NATIONAL PARK, AUSTRALIA

Located in the outback of New South Wales, and crowned down under's premier dark sky preserve in 2016, this park offers great views of the Milky Way—its center passes directly overhead. You might also glimpse nocturnal creatures like the ringtail possum, greater glider, and southern boobook owl.

PLANNING Warrumbungle Observatory, 15 km (9 miles) east of the park, offers 90-minute night sky and telescope viewing sessions. tenbyobservatory.com

❻ MITZPE RAMON, ISRAEL

Cloudless skies and lack of light pollution make the Negev Desert an ideal place for stargazing. The town of Mitzpe Ramon is ground zero for the region's astronomical activities, from Wise Observatory to sleeping under the stars at Bedouin camps in Makhtesh Ramon crater.

PLANNING Astronomy Israel offers naked eye and telescope tours of the night sky around Mitzpe Ramon. astronomyisrael.com

❼ TROMSØ, NORWAY

Located high above the Arctic Circle, Tromsø, the largest city in the north of Norway, lies in the middle of the "aurora oval"—a huge ring above the geomagnetic North Pole—and offers Europe's best chance of viewing the Northern Lights.

PLANNING Given the long days of summer, the best time to view the Aurora Borealis in northern Norway is during the long nights between September and April. visittromso.no/en

❽ IZERA DARK-SKY PARK, POLAND AND CZECHIA

This stargazing reserve in the Carpathian Mountains revolves around the secluded Izera Valley in southwestern Poland, and the Jizerka Valley across the border in Czechia, both created as spaces free from light pollution. Not only was this Europe's earliest dark sky park (2009), but it was also the first transnational reserve dedicated to watching the night sky.

PLANNING Although closer to Wrocław, the park's most convenient gateway is Prague, a two-hour drive to the south. www.izera-darksky.eu/index-en.html

❾ OBSERVATORIO DEL ROQUE DE LOS MUCHACHOS, CANARY ISLANDS, SPAIN

The world's largest optical telescope perches on the summit of Caldera de Taburiente, an 8,000-foot (2,426 m) crater on La Palma Island. The observatory—which specializes in both night and solar astronomy—offers engaging 90-minute public tours any time of year.

PLANNING Astro Camp La Palma arranges daytime observatory and nighttime stargazing tours, and also rents telescopes. lapalmastars.com/en/visits-to-observatory

❿ NAMIBRAND NATURE RESERVE, NAMIBIA

Africa's first international dark sky preserve was founded in 1984 by J. A. Brückner, a German-Namibian businessman. On this land lies one of the naturally darkest yet still accessible places on planet Earth—the Namib Desert—far enough away from the South Atlantic to avoid its notorious fog.

PLANNING The reserve's Beyond Sossusvlei Desert Lodge has a resident astronomer and state-of-the-art observatory for nightly stargazing sessions. www.andbeyond.com

Glaciers by Air

The flight from Mount Cook air base on the South Island opens up an expansive world of ice that is both quiet and enthralling.

Is this a ski trip or an air journey? So you may wonder when you see that the tiny plane you're boarding has a pair of retractable skis. Then again, how else are you going to land on a glacier? As the plane ascends through the Southern Alps, valleys dotted with gravel flats fan out below. Glacial lakes look glassy-smooth, appearing deceptively close. The Great Divide looms, with its summits of 10,000 feet (3,048 meters); jagged ice peaks hang off the mountainsides. The pilot releases the skis, which descend with an impressive thump. Once across the Divide, the plane swoops down toward the glacier and lands smoothly in the snow like a seasoned Olympic champ. You emerge with a collective gasp: you and your fellow passengers are standing alone on the glacier. Surrounding you is a majestic scene of ice, snow, jagged peaks, shimmering sun, and that unfathomably blue New Zealand sky. Ten minutes later, you're airborne again, winging past icefalls and snowy mountains. The rugged west coast and sparkling Tasman Sea come into view on the left; on the right is the vast coastal plain. As you circle more glaciers, the sight has new significance: you have actually set foot on one now, which transforms admiration from afar into the pleasure of familiarity.

WHEN TO GO All year, subject to weather conditions. Flights are cancelled most often during spring rains, but also if comfort or visibility are likely to be affected.

HOW LONG The trip takes one hour, covering 100 miles (160 km).

PLANNING Flights run daily 7:30 a.m.–5.30 p.m., with a 9:30 a.m. start in winter. Dress in layers, since the plane is warm and even the glacier can be surprisingly temperate. Boots are a must, and in winter, a pair of galoshes might be useful as the snow on the glacier can reach knee-deep.

INSIDE INFORMATION For photography, it's best to go in early morning or late afternoon for prime lighting. The day after a big storm you'll probably see the clearest skies.

WEBSITES mtcookskiplanes.com, airsafaris.co.nz

HIGHLIGHTS

■ **The Hochstetter Icefall** is made up of miles of ice crumbling off the mountains, gathering on the Grand Plateau, then cascading down like a frozen waterfall. The only sound is the occasional thunderous wrench of snow and ice on the move.

■ **Landing on the glacier** – which may be the Franz Josef or Tasman – is the prelude to complete silence descending all around you, a sensation to be treasured.

■ Wildlife is rare and not indigenous, so the sight of a **herd of chamois or Himalayan tahr** (a kind of goat) running along the heads of glaciers as they transit from valley to valley makes an uncommon treat.

Tracks in the snow: a light aircraft has made a perfectly smooth landing in the splendid isolation of Franz Josef Glacier.

Green-and-white coral islands, each surrounded by a halo of turquoise, lie scattered around the deep blue Pacific in the area of Fiji.

POLYNESIA

Fly the Coral Route

Combine a seabird's soaring flight with relaxing stopovers
on some of the most idyllic islands of the South Pacific.

From the air the vast ocean appears an infinity of shot silk in blues and greens, interrupted only occasionally by reef-ringed islands or chains of coral atolls. Traveling the legendary Coral Route from Auckland, New Zealand, to Tahiti, French Polynesia, you discover why it was once considered the world's most romantic air adventure. Landing in Nadi, Fiji, you join the legion of snorkelers drifting motionless over the colorful reefs that gave the journey its name. Flying northeast to Apia, Samoa, you are greeted by smiling islanders with garlands of fragrant hibiscus and frangipani. They whisk you away to the legendary Aggie Grey's Hotel, whose founder gave author James Michener the inspiration for the character of Bloody Mary in his *Tales of the South Pacific*. Arriving in Rarotonga, capital of the Cook Islands, you swim in the transparent waters of a lagoon edged by sugar-sand beaches with a backdrop of volcanic mountains. Your final destination is Papeete, Tahiti, the largest of the French Polynesian islands. Tahiti, shaped by Polynesian, European, and Asian influences, works its infectious charm on you, as it always has done on visitors since the days when flying boats ferried the social elite to these remote, storied islands five decades ago.

HIGHLIGHTS

▧ On any of the islands, **sleep above an aquamarine lagoon** in a thatched bungalow perched on stilts.

▧ Discover each island's **character and culture**. On Fiji, join in a kava ceremony, an important social occasion in which you drink the powdered root of the pepper tree; or watch Cook Island dancers in traditional costume perform drum dancing and the hip-swaying *hura*.

▧ Steep yourself in the beauty of the **coral reefs**, by snorkeling, scuba diving, or taking a trip in a glass-bottom boat.

WHEN TO GO Although warm and humid year-round, winter (May–October) is drier and generally more comfortable than the rainy season (November–April), which also has a higher risk of cyclones.

HOW LONG 4,700 miles (7,560 km). Plan on three weeks, staying one week each in Fiji, the Cook Islands, and French Polynesia.

PLANNING Work out your route and plan your reservations well in advance as flights to some islands operate as infrequently as once a week. You will need to book flights on various island airlines as well as Air New Zealand. Some operators organize tailor-made tours for sections of the route.

INSIDE INFORMATION On Fiji, try marinated fish cooked in a *lovo*, or underground oven.

WEBSITES airnewzealand.com, airraro.com, fijiairways.com

Hot-air balloons, often in bright colors, take flight above the idyllic village of Château d'Oex.

Alpine Balloon Festival

Ascend up, up, and away from the everyday by joining this airborne event and hovering above the mountains.

Floating serenely across the sky like so many giant colored lanterns, a drift of hot-air balloons adds touches of brilliance to the Swiss Alps. The valley location of Château d'Oex near Gstaad has ideal air currents and winds for ballooning all year, and it has acquired fame for its International Balloon Festival in winter. This brings together balloonists from all over Europe, who take part in a program offering great visual effects and piloting skills. Entire days are spent sailing above the Alps in formation, or in long-distance races. There are displays of precision flying and parachute jumping, as well as themed competitions. In the Don Quixote Race, each team has to spear ten helium-filled balloons, while in the Hare and Hounds, a "hare" balloon is chased by "hounds" who then drop markers near its landing site. When there are mass takeoffs, the atmosphere buzzes, as round balloons are inflated first, followed by some really imaginative and amusing designs—a tortoise, an elephant, a Scots piper, a rolled-up newspaper, an orange … all adding up to a wonderful festive feeling.

WHEN TO GO Late January for the festival. Summer for longer trips to neighboring countries.

HOW LONG The festival usually takes place over a week. The weekend sees some of its most important and exciting events.

PLANNING You can make your own way by road or rail to the festival site to watch. Alternatively, book a place on a balloon, with gourmet food and wine included, through a travel company.

INSIDE INFORMATION At Château d'Oex visit Espace Ballon to find out more about the history and science of ballooning.

WEBSITES chateau-doex.ch/en/Z4237, buddybombard.com, espace-ballon.ch

HIGHLIGHTS

▥ If you are on a specialist ballooning tour, explore the **snowy wilderness of the Alps** when there are no specific events taking place for a magical experience drifting in a noiseless balloon over the silent peaks.

▥ The accompanying **displays of aerobatics** by hang gliders and paragliders present a stunning sight.

▥ A sense of **international community** is fostered by a real love of this airborne sport, as participants from about 20 countries gather to perform and show their skills.

▥ A **nighttime flight** of illuminated balloons against the starry sky is one of the most magical visions you will see in these mountains. It is staged as a ballet, with music and fireworks to enhance the aesthetic experience.

EUROPE

FRANCE | ITALY | AUSTRIA | SWITZERLAND

Heliskiing the Alps

A high-flying tour brings you the thrill of solo skiing among glamorous peaks smothered in virgin snow.

Staring Alpine peaks in the eye, you look out the helicopter window at the vast expanse of jagged limestone blanketed in white gold. Your pilot sets down on a lonely ridge and you clamber out of the machine, its blades whirring overhead. The chopper lifts off, sending a cloud of snow barreling over you, and the only sound is the familiar click of boots into bindings as you stare at the skier's dream that lies below: acres of untouched snow. An amphitheater of rock and glacier arches skyward as you point your fat skis through a narrow chute. Then gravity takes control and you're practically gliding, your turns leaving behind perfect arcs. Unimpeded by rocks, bumps, trees, or other skiers, you schuss through champagne powder, coming to rest on another ridge. Soon the *thuk-thuk* of the chopper pierces the thin air. The chopper lands with another flurry, and you repeat the process. It's one that not only lets you glide between peaks, but from country to country. Follow breakfast croissants in France with Swiss *rösti* or Italian pasta and wine. At night, tuck away in tiny, family-run hotels on cobblestone streets, emerging once again to leave the crowds behind, take to the rarefied Alpine air, and savor the delight of skiing the pure snow.

WHEN TO GO January to April.

HOW LONG Go for a day or a couple of weeks, according to your time and budget. Operations in Switzerland, Austria, Italy, and France allow you to base yourself at one resort, or make an expedition that crosses borders.

PLANNING Unless you own skis made for backcountry powder, it's best to rent state-of-the-art skis like K2 Pinnacle 95 or Black Crows Corvus – but bring your own boots.

INSIDE INFORMATION Skiing deep, untracked powder requires only intermediate-level experience, but it takes some getting used to. Let the skis do the work and think of gliding on top of the snow.

WEBSITES powderhounds.com/europe/heli-skiing, 9vallees.com

HIGHLIGHTS

▓ Leave your mark on the Alps by **making your own tracks** down the empty expanses of white powder.

▓ You get an amazing overview of the **glorious, pristine scenery** from the chopper and the tops of mountains.

▓ **Crossing borders and cultures** in the same week or even the same day is one of the great advantages of combining flight with skiing.

▓ Visit the hard-to-reach and sometimes **historic places**. For example, you can ski across the Col de Grand St. Bernard, an Alpine route used since the Bronze Age, and have tea with monks at 8,000 ft (2,438 m), at the St. Bernard Hospice.

A lone skier looks toward Mont Blanc from Meribel Valley in France's Haute-Savoie.

| EGYPT |

Nile Balloons

A serene and stately ride over one of the world's great rivers and its legendary sights makes the perfect introduction to an ancient civilization.

Floating above the broad Nile and its desert fringes in the basket of a hot-air balloon is one of the finest experiences Egypt has to offer—even if it does involve a predawn start. To compensate for the early wake-up, a champagne breakfast is served among fields dotted with palm trees while your balloon is readied for takeoff. What happens next depends on the direction of the wind. If an easterly is blowing, you will float first over the rugged hills and royal tombs of the Valley of the Kings and the Valley of the Queens, with an aerial view of the superb Tomb of Hatshepsut. With a west wind, you will drift across an emerald ribbon of fields and over the broad Nile with the huge Karnak temple complex—the largest in the world—spread out below you, while your pilot stays in touch with the "chase vehicle" on the ground by walkie-talkie or mobile phone. Between these exotic, ancient landscapes and monuments, the ride offers glimpses of everyday life in Luxor and the surrounding villages. Gangs of small children yell and wave from fields or flat roofs (where, incongruously, goats and flocks of ducks are kept); white-sailed feluccas ply the river below; and the desert beyond seems to stretch forever until it fades into the hazy horizon. The end of the flight means coming down to Earth with a bump, literally, often in a fallow field where your sudden arrival will attract a welcoming crowd of farmhands.

WHEN TO GO All year, but preferably November–February.

HOW LONG About one hour in the air.

PLANNING The flights take off from Luxor, and operators arrange pickups from hotels. Take a sweater or fleece as the early mornings are chilly. Bring essentials only and leave valuables in the hotel safe – things get lost during bumpy landings.

INSIDE INFORMATION The balloon travels slowly and steadily, and the basket is very stable so there are no problems with "camera shakes" when photographing. Balloons usually stay a few hundred feet up – and not more than 1,000 ft (305 m) at the highest – so conditions are ideal for both looking and taking pictures. Depending on conditions the pilot can "turn" the balloon using "rotation venting" to show off panoramic views.

WEBSITES egypt.travel, luxor-tours.com

AFRICA

HIGHLIGHTS

▥ View the **landscape from above**, as the green ribbon of cultivated land along the Nile winds through the desert, flanked by utterly barren mountains. Vivid lozenge-shaped fields meet clusters of flat-roofed houses the color of the sand. You may well come close enough to hear the muezzin calling the faithful to prayer at the mosque.

▥ North of Luxor lies the ruined but stupendous **temple complex of Karnak**, built over a 1,300-year period. Among its many treasures are the Great Hypostyle Hall and Hatshepsut's pink granite obelisk, at 97 ft (30 m) the second tallest in the world.

▥ Be inspired to visit the **tomb of Nefertari** in the Valley of the Queens. The fragile paintings pay tribute to her beauty and rival in quality those in the Valley of the Kings. They have been carefully restored, and no more than 150 visitors per day may enter the tomb, and then only with masks and shoe pads.

Opposite: At Luxor a magnificent balloon takes off from the desert, steeped in pastel colors by the pearly light of dawn. Above: The trip takes in long, low views of the Valley of the Queens, where the royal wives and children were buried. This is the Tomb of Hatshepsut, one of just a few female pharoahs, who ruled for an extraordinary 15 years.

Top 10 Rooms With a View

Sky-high observation decks and restaurants afford a bird's-eye-view of the world below, as well as a vertigo-induced adrenalin rush.

❶ ONE WORLD OBSERVATORY, FREEDOM TOWER, NEW YORK CITY

Poised at 1,368 feet (417 meters) above Manhattan, the viewing area atop the new Freedom Tower symbolically reaches the same height as the old World Trade Center it replaced. Three sky-high restaurants offer eats and drinks.

PLANNING Among the many ticket choices are family packs, date night and happy hour specials, and priority access. oneworldobservatory.com

❷ SKYDECK CHICAGO, WILLIS TOWER, ILLINOIS

Even Michael Jordan couldn't fly this high—the lofty Skydeck on the 103rd floor of the Willis (Sears) Tower, second tallest building in the U.S. Extending 4.3 feet (1.3 meters) out from the side of the building, glass balconies render a palm-sweating view 1,353 feet (412 meters) straight down to the city streets.

PLANNING On a clear day the view from the Skydeck extends to Wisconsin, Indiana, and even Michigan. theskydeck.com

❸ 360 RESTAURANT, CN TOWER, CANADA

Malpeque oysters, rainbow trout, Quebec pork, and Alberta beef are just a few of the Canadian-flavored dishes offered at the eatery atop the 1,151-foot (351-meter) CN Tower in Toronto. Admission to the tower's viewing gallery and glass floor is complimentary with the purchase of a meal at 360.

PLANNING 360 also boasts a "cellar in the sky" with more than 500 types of wine. cntower.ca/en-ca

❹ TEMBO GALLERIA, TOKYO SKYTREE, JAPAN

The world's tallest tower since its unveiling in 2012, the Skytree rises to a Godzilla-like height of 2,080 feet (634 meters) above Tokyo. The highest public viewing platform, Tembo Galleria, hovers at 1,480 feet (450 meters).

PLANNING After dark the Skytree is illuminated by two different patterns of colored LED lights. tokyo-skytree.jp/en

❺ OZONE SKY BAR, RITZ-CARLTON HOTEL, HONG KONG

The world's highest hotel (1,588 ft/484 m) also features one of the planet's highest drinking spots, the aptly named Ozone Sky Bar on the 118th floor. The Peak, Dragontini, and HK Skyline count among the bar's signature cocktails.

PLANNING Hotel guests can also dive into the world's highest swimming pool. ritzcarlton.com

Every year, more than 1,700 people visit the Willis Tower in Chicago to experience the Skydeck Ledge. Its exhilarating views reach Illinois, Michigan, and even as far as Wisconsin.

6 CÉ LA VI, MARINA BAY SANDS, SINGAPORE

Euro-Asian fusion food and Dom Pérignon play second fiddle to the view of the Singapore skyline from this restaurant on the rooftop SkyPark of the Marina Bay Sands hotel. CLV's club lounge features DJ music and a dance floor. The lofty perch features three other places to eat or drink, as well as a vertigo-inducing observation deck that doubles as the bow of the boat-shaped structure.

PLANNING Check into the hotel to use the incredible rooftop infinity pool. sg.celavi.com

7 AT THE TOP, BURJ KHALIFA, DUBAI, UNITED ARAB EMIRATES

The world's longest elevator ride (in terms of distance) whisks guests to viewing areas on the 124th and 148th floors of the world's tallest freestanding structure at 2,716.5 feet (828 meters). Telescopes on the observation decks are equipped with high-zoom, high-definition cameras for sharper images of the city, desert, and gulf. Tom Cruise did his own stunts on the outside of the 154th floor during the 2011 filming of *Mission: Impossible — Ghost Protocol*.

PLANNING The tower offers great views of the choreographed water show at the adjacent Dubai Fountain. burjkhalifa.ae

8 THE VIEW FROM THE SHARD, LONDON, ENGLAND

Soaring high above London's South Bank, Western Europe's tallest building offers an indoor viewing area on the 69th floor and an open-air terrace on the 72nd floor. The Tower of London, Tower Bridge, and St. Paul's are among the many London landmarks right below The Shard. Interactive telescopes offer insights into London's past, present, and future. Saturday nights, The Shard hosts a "silent disco" with headphones, cocktails, and dreamy evening views.

PLANNING Restrooms also offer panoramic views of the River Thames and central London. theviewfromtheshard.com

9 BAR À CHAMPAGNE, EIFFEL TOWER, FRANCE

With the City of Lights twinkling below, nothing embodies Parisian romance as perfectly as quaffing bubbly at the summit of the Eiffel Tower. Opt for the rosé or a tasty white champagne selection as chosen by celebrity chef Alain Ducasse. On the way to the top, and if you're feeling brave, check out the transparent floor on the tower's recently refurbished level one.

PLANNING Before or after your bubbly, catch a meal at Le Jules Verne restaurant on the second floor. restaurants-toureiffel.com

10 UFO WATCH TASTE GROOVE, SLOVAKIA

Living up to its quirky name, the disk-shaped bar and restaurant atop Bratislava's Nový Most (New Bridge) really does resemble a flying saucer. From high above the Danube river, the breathtaking panoramic views include parts of Slovakia, Austria, and Hungary. The embankment below the tower morphs into a beach during the summer complete with food, drinks, and DJs.

PLANNING UFO restaurant serves Asian and Mediterranean fusion food. facebook.com/UfoBratislava

Victoria Falls by Microlight

Aboard a fragile craft you get a ringside view of the greatest water show on the planet and its magnificent surroundings.

AFRICA

The sound of the engine drowns out the collared sunbirds twittering in the thicket and signals the point of no return. You're strapped into the backseat of a frail-looking microlight and are soon practically clipping the acacia tops that line Maramba Aerodrome. The journey is swift, yet gives you a lift you will remember for life. Within minutes, you are rising over the tree-covered islands that dot the Zambezi River as it approaches Victoria Falls. A rainbow arcs through a veil of mist that shimmers over the largest curtain of water on Earth. Now you are looking straight down at the 354-foot (108 meter) basalt cliff stretching a mile (1.6 kilometers) between Zambia and Zimbabwe. As you soar like the peregrine falcons that nest in the nearby crags, your heart echoes the churning maelstrom below, where the unstoppable wall of water is gathered and squeezed into a narrow crevice at the bottom. The turbulent eddies and whirlpools boil up, then regroup and settle to continue through the Batoka Gorge. You see a tiny figure leap off the side of the gorge, the latest one to try out the newest adventure sport—the "Gorge Swing"—while farther below inflatables and jetboats shoot the rapids. Yet how small humans seem in the face of nature's might.

WHEN TO GO Flights operate throughout the year, except during heavy rainstorms. Early morning and late afternoon flights are less turbulent: 6:30–10:00 a.m. and 3–6 p.m. daily.

HOW LONG The Flight of the Angels trip over Victoria Falls takes 15 minutes, while the Flight of the Angels and Game Viewing is 30-minutes, viewing both the falls and Mosi-oa-Tunya National Park.

PLANNING You can book by phone or Internet, or local operators can arrange a flight.

INSIDE INFORMATION You will be given a jumpsuit and crash helmet to wear. Cameras must be left behind because of the risk of objects – even a stray lens cap – falling into the propeller. A 35mm camera, fixed to the wingtip, is operated remotely by the pilot and provides souvenir photos.

WEBSITES adventure-africa.com, seasonsinafrica.com

HIGHLIGHTS

▪ Flying over Mosi-oa-Tunya National Park on the Zambian bank of the Zambezi allows you to spot **wildlife**: rhinos, hippos, giraffes, eland, and wildebeest.

▪ You will sight some of the 400 or so **bird species** living around the falls: African black swifts and rock martins in the gorge; black herons and little egrets that feed in the shallows; and eagles, augur buzzards, gray-headed parrots, lapwings, and ospreys overhead.

The falls throw up characteristic plumes of smoky mist as the buglike aircraft hovers overhead.

One of Kruger's landmarks, Olifants River, seen here still fresh from summer rains, is a popular watering place all year round.

SOUTH AFRICA

Buzzing Over Kruger National Park

Sweep above the savanna animated by the ever changing movie of African wildlife in all its guises, feeding, resting, hunting, sleeping.

Taking off from a grassy field, your microlight catches an updraft that lifts you high above the veld. It's a magic moment, the sun just rising over Mozambique in the hazy distance, the air surprisingly chilly yet calm as you climb to 1,000 feet (305 meters) above one of Africa's oldest and largest game reserves, home to more than 850 animal species. Now you have the same vantage point as the fork-tailed drongo, Goliath heron, and African fish eagle that patrol the endless plains. Along the banks of a chocolate-colored river you spy a herd of elephants. Your pilot points out crocodiles roused by the shadow of your tiny craft, surprised out of their floating-log posture in the shallows. Banking steeply, you cross a roadless expanse of woodland that can only be explored by air. In every direction you see wildlife: a pair of elegant giraffe munching tender leaves in the canopy of a tall tree; wildebeest and zebra grazing peacefully; a jackal trotting along briskly, in a hurry to get somewhere this morning; and that rarest of rare sights, a white rhino mother and calf relaxing in the lee of a marula tree.

WHEN TO GO Winter (June–October) is best for seeing game because vegetation is thinner and wildlife tends to gather around water sources.

HOW LONG The flights last from 15 minutes to one hour. A week is recommended for ground exploration of the park by self-drive or guided safari tour.

PLANNING Book at lodges or directly with registered operators who offer microlight "flips" over central and southern Kruger. Bring a sweater as it can be cool in the air.

INSIDE INFORMATION Kruger can also be explored by hot-air balloon, helicopter, and small fixed-wing aircraft. You can learn how to pilot a microlight in two- to three-week courses that are run locally by Leading Edge Flight School near Kruger.

WEBSITES southafrica.net/uk/en, timbavati.co.za, lefssa.com

HIGHLIGHTS

▥ The most renowned of Kruger's private reserves, **Sabi Sabi** straddles what is considered the richest game area in South Africa. All of the Big Five – elephant, rhino, leopard, lion, and buffalo – can be seen here.

▥ Timbavati private reserve, once famed for its white lions, is now better known for general game viewing over 160,000 acres (64,750 ha) of **pristine bush** beside central Kruger.

▥ Inside the park, seven **Wilderness Trails** allow you to explore the African bush on foot. Daily guided walks of up to 10 miles (16 km) bring you close to what you have seen by air.

AFRICA

Chapter 9

IN THEIR FOOTSTEPS

The journeys on the following pages bring us to destinations that feed the intellect and spark the imagination. They are the perfect trips for anyone fascinated by history, literature, or music, or with an interest in the visual arts. These transits into vanished or imaginary worlds take many different forms. One epic journey from Europe into the heart of Asia traces Alexander the Great's conquest of the known world; another tracks Mao Zedong and his supporters in the Long March that transformed the history of China. Other routes replicate thrilling voyages of discovery, ranging from Lewis and Clark's crossing of North America to Captain Cook's explorations of Polynesia. For some, the greatest journeys are spiritual as well as spatial, visiting places suffused with the memory of Lord Buddha in India or Jesus in the Holy Land. Others move into geographies of the imagination, encountering Tolstoy's Russia and Jane Austen's England, the Yosemite that inspired the magisterial photographs of Ansel Adams, or shadowing Jack Kerouac's raucous rediscovery of America in the classic 20th-century novel *On the Road*.

A solitary walker seems at one with this mellow scene in fall near Elterwater, in England's Lake District. This area of peaks, forest, and lakes is where the Romantic poet William Wordsworth made his home and found lifelong inspiration.

Cabot Trail

Merchant turned explorer John Cabot landed in Nova Scotia in 1497. The wild beauty he encountered remains unchanged centuries later.

Gulls wheel on the sea breeze. Offshore, humpback whales surface, blow, and feed in the cold, nutrient-rich waters. Cape Breton Island is in northern Nova Scotia, separated from the mainland by the Strait of Canso, and the road around its northern tip was built solely to take you to beauty. Beginning in Baddeck, you drive on a highway that takes you along the island's east coast, tempting your camera with panoramas of mountains rising 2,000 feet (600 meters) from the wave-tossed Gulf of St. Lawrence. The road turns inland through Cape Breton Highlands National Park, where waterfalls cascade into forests and moose graze in bogs. In fall, the rounded hills and deep valleys explode in hues of red, gold, and orange. You reach the west coast, where fishermen tend nets and boats in villages that cling to the steep sides of rocky harbors. Most towns have a proud Scottish heritage, but in Chéticamp a vibrant Acadian culture thrives in shops selling Acadian hooked rugs; in restaurants offering *rappie* (meat and potato) pie; and in the gentle sibilance of the Acadian French spoken by the townspeople.

WHEN TO GO The best time to drive the Cabot Trail is from early September to the first week in October, when the days are long and warm. Fall colors peak in late September. Spring, including June, can be cool and rainy.

HOW LONG Most people arrive in Nova Scotia by car (12 hours from Boston to Halifax) or by ferry from Bar Harbor, Maine, or by flying into Halifax. The drive from Halifax to the Cabot Trail takes two days. Allow another two days for the 185-mile (300 km) loop.

PLANNING Baddeck has excellent restaurants and accommodation. Cape Breton Island's weather can change rapidly, so take warm rainwear. Bring bug spray, good hiking shoes, and binoculars for bird- and whale-watching.

INSIDE INFORMATION The most scenic part of the drive is the 6-mile (10 km) coastal stretch north of Chéticamp, which offers spectacular views.

WEBSITE novascotia.com

HIGHLIGHTS

▦ Take a side tour along the adventurous, unpaved road to Meat Cove, **tracing serpentine curves** along the flanks of the island's northernmost mountains.

▦ The ski lifts at **Ski Cape Smokey**, near Ingonish, take you up 1,000 ft (300 m), with views of Cape Breton Island's mountainous coastline.

▦ In Cape Breton Highlands National Park, have a close (but not too close) encounter with a moose while strolling along the **Bog Trail**.

▦ Enjoy live Celtic music and locally brewed Glenora whiskey at **the legendary Red Shoe Pub** south of the Cabot Trail in Mabou.

A pebble beach is all that lies between you and the vast North Atlantic on the John Cabot Trail, Cape Breton Island.

Once the target of fur trappers, the busy beaver today can swim freely, transporting branches from shore to its watery home.

CANADA

The Hudson's Bay Company Trappers

Discover the world of the early trappers in the remote, sparsely populated wilderness of Canada.

In 1670, two French merchants and several English partners formed the Hudson's Bay Company with the purpose of sourcing beaver fur in Canada and shipping it to Europe. As the numerous surviving forts and trading posts testify, over the next 200 years the Hudson's Bay Company grew as a landowner and trading organization, extending its range and power, and facing fierce and violent competition from French rivals. Start in the beautiful old city of Winnipeg, where the Hudson's Bay Company built a depot, Fort Douglas, in 1812. Many Cree hunters and trappers were employed by the company, and at Norway House, a remote settlement to the north of Lake Winnipeg, you can see what life was like for the aboriginal peoples involved in the fur trade. Norway House was a depot where furs were collected. From here they were transported along the Hayes River to York Factory, the company's most important trading post on Hudson Bay. Farther north, at Churchill, is Prince of Wales Fort on Sloop Cove, which provided a mooring for ships from England. For an insight into the wilderness life of the company men, take a canoe trip along the Hayes River through pristine forest, passing trappers' cabins and the ruins of outposts along the way.

WHEN TO GO Winter in this part of Canada is very cold, with temperatures dropping below −4°F (−20°C), so it is best to undertake this journey in the warmer summer months. Each August, Norway House holds the annual Treaty & York Boat Days festival to celebrate the history of the settlement.

HOW LONG The journey can be done in a few days, incorporating several different sites and museums. Allow extra time for a canoe trip on the Hayes River.

PLANNING The quickest way to travel to the remote sites is by charter flight, and the easiest way is to join a tour group. Norway House can be reached by air or road from Winnipeg. York Factory is accessible by air only from Gillam. Canoe trips on the Hayes River start at either Norway House or York Factory.

INSIDE INFORMATION Be sure to take plenty of insect repellent with you; Canada contains some of the most extensive breeding grounds for mosquitoes in the world.

WEBSITES gov.mb.ca/chc/hrb/prov/p012.html, nhcn.ca, yorkboatdays.ca

HIGHLIGHTS

▓ Visit the Hudson's Bay Company Gallery at the **Manitoba Museum**, and the Hudson's Bay Company Archives, both in Winnipeg.

▓ At Norway House, visit the Archway Warehouse, and take a **ride in a York boat**, one of the large wooden boats that were once used to transport the furs downriver.

Top 10 Explorers' Journeys

"If there is any road not traveled then that is the one I must take," said Edward John Eyre, a view surely echoed by his fellow explorers.

❶ ERIC THE RED, QASSIARSUK, GREENLAND

Exiled from Iceland for murder, Eric the Red sailed west and discovered Greenland in 982 A.D. He returned with 500 settlers to live in Qassiarsuk. There, the chapel Thjodhild and a Norse longhouse have been rebuilt beside beautiful Tunulliarfik fjord (Eriksfjord) on the Great Plain of Greenland.

PLANNING Fly to Narsarsuaq from Copenhagen or Iceland. Then travel to Qassiarsuk by boat or helicopter. visitgreenland.com

❷ HERNÁN CORTÉS, VERACRUZ, MEXICO

Cortés landed here in 1519 at the start of his conquest of Mexico. Today, Veracruz is a busy seaport with a lively cultural life. Stroll along the harbor front Malecón or sit in the Plaza de Armas, where bands play music blending Cuban and Mexican influences. There are good beaches nearby, too.

PLANNING From Mexico City, you can get to Veracruz by air, bus, or train. visitmexico.com/en

❸ CHISTOPHER COLUMBUS, WATLING ISLAND, BAHAMAS

Watling Island could be the island Columbus named San Salvador. Its remoteness has kept it pristine, beautiful, and a wildlife haven. Relax on white sands and swim in crystal waters after you've explored Long Bay and the other three places claimed as the landing site of the *Niña*, *Pinta*, and *Santa Maria*.

PLANNING The Bahamas are easy to reach from Florida; Watling Island is a charter plane or mail boat ride from the main city Freetown. geographia.com/bahamas/bsssin01.htm

❹ FRANCISCO PIZARRO, CUSCO, PERU

The Inca city was sacked by Pizarro in 1533. Today you can experience the grandeur of the baroque church of Santo Domingo. Built on massive granite Inca foundations, it was once the temple of the sun. Then go on to visit Machu Picchu to see what an Inca city would have looked like.

PLANNING You can travel by train from Cusco to Machu Picchu. cuscoperu.com/en, perutourism.com

❺ ISABELLA BIRD, SEOUL, KOREA

The first female member of the British Royal Geographical Society, Bird traveled around Korea in 1897, one of the first Westerners to visit the country. Explore Seoul in her footsteps, visiting the 14th-century Gyeongbok Palace.

PLANNING Weather is extreme, so visit in spring or fall. visitseoul.net

Roped together for security, hikers traverse the Jespersen Glacier at Narsarsuaq, Greenland. They appear like tiny etched figures on the vast undulating blue, gray, and white ice forms.

❻ ABEL TASMAN, TONGA, POLYNESIA

This chain of 156 islands was first explored in 1643 for the Dutch East India Company by Abel Tasman on his way back from Tasmania, Australia, which is named after him. Today you can watch humpback whales at play in an azure blue sea and explore coral reefs in the bright sunhine.

PLANNING The three main islands – Tongatapu, Ha'apai, and Vava'u – can be visited by air. To visit the other islands, you will need to charter a boat. tongaholiday.com

❼ EDWARD JOHN EYRE AND WYLIE, AUSTRALIA

Travel the merciless outback from Streaky Bay to Albany following in the footsteps of Edward John Eyre and Wylie, his Aboriginal companion. They survived in this hot, barren land by drinking the juice of roots and eating their exhausted horses. Today, the monotonous 1,550-mile (2,500 km) Eyre Highway passes through the arid Nullarbor Plain and the Great Australian Bight. Look out for ancient meteorites on the ground: they look like dark rocks against the pale ground.

PLANNING Follow the Eyre Highway along the Nullarbor's southernmost edge. Road hazards include fatigue and kangaroos hopping across the highway at night. Settlements are far apart, gas is expensive, and water supplies are nonexistent. nullarbornet.com.au, atn.com.au

❽ DR. LIVINGSTONE, LAKE TANGANYIKA, TANZANIA

"Dr. Livingstone, I presume?" It is 1871 and the place is Ujiji, near Lake Tanganyika, and Henry Stanley has found the missing explorer David Livingstone. Travel the wild shores of the lake and the untamed lush jungle forests that the two men explored together at Gombe Stream National Park. Take a guided walk deep into the forest to see the chimpanzee colonies made famous by primatologist Jane Goodall.

PLANNING Drink only boiled or bottled water. tanzaniatourism.go.tz/en, janegoodall.org

❾ MARY KINGSLEY, LUANDA, ANGOLA

In the 1890s, Mary Kingsley went to Luanda to live with local people, explore crocodile-infested swamps, meet cannibals, dodge scorpions, and climb Cameroon Mount. Conditions are still difficult following the country's civil war. Take an organized trek through the bush to see elephants and the beauty of Quiçama National Park with its forests, waterfalls, and butterflies. Lying back on Luanda beach and watching the tropical sunset is a must.

PLANNING Travel with an experienced tour company. angola.org

❿ ALFRED RUSSEL WALLACE, BALI AND LOMBOK, INDONESIA

Wallace, a British naturalist, spent nearly ten years, from 1854 to 1862, studying the wildlife of the Malay Archipelago. He noticed that the indigenous animals on the western side of an imaginary line (now known as the Wallace Line) were Asian, while on the eastern side they were Australian, helping to prove Darwin's theory of evolution. Visit the islands of Bali and Lombok, only a short ferry ride apart, and see for yourself.

PLANNING Lombok is more conservative than Bali, so be sensitive to the local traditions in your dress. www.tourismindonesia.com

The sun-washed Sawtooth Mountains cast a giant shadow over the Salmon River, known as "The River of No Return" for its deep, twisting course.

MONTANA | IDAHO

Following Lewis and Clark

The mountainous route taken by the two great trailblazers and their team is less risky but still precipitous and awe-inspiring today.

There's a reason why Lost Trail Pass in southwest Montana has its name. In summer 1805, Meriwether Lewis and William Clark reached the Bitterroot Range on their way to finding a route to the Pacific Ocean. Clark crossed the pass in an attempt to follow the Salmon River, but the way was treacherous, the horses kept falling, and his Shoshone guide lost the trail. Disheartened and out of food, they were forced to eat fish and berries, so they wisely turned back to rejoin Lewis—a difficult enough journey in itself. After regrouping, Lewis and Clark decided to look for a route farther north, eventually crossing the mountains at what is now Lolo Pass. Roads run over the passes these days, but the hillsides of the Bitterroot Range are as steep and wild as they were 200 years ago. Backpackers on a multiday trip can explore the mountains that so impressed the explorers by following a high, remote stretch of the Continental Divide National Scenic Trail south of Lost Trail Pass. The less energetic can explore the region by car following the Lewis & Clark National Historic Trail.

WHEN TO GO As Lewis and Clark knew, the mountains are only passable when they are snow-free— usually late June through September. August is the driest month, with fewer mosquitoes and biting flies.

HOW LONG In addition to hiking time, plan at least three days to see the region's historic sites.

PLANNING The nearest large airport is in Missoula, MT, where you should rent a car. Public transportation in the area is almost nonexistent.

INSIDE INFORMATION The picturesque town of Wisdom, MT, makes a good base for exploring the area by car or on foot and has a great view of the Bitterroot Range to the west.

WEBSITES lewisandclark.org, nps.gov/lecl

HIGHLIGHTS

▓ Visit **Big Hole National Battlefield**, just east of Lost Trail Pass, which commemorates the region's other major historic event, the Battle of the Big Hole between the Nez Perce Indians and the U.S. Army in 1877.

▓ Pause atop the Continental Divide, the **watershed** that separates Atlantic-bound streams and rivers from Pacific-bound waterways.

▓ Catch your breath in Travelers' Rest State Park, the location of a centuries-old **Native American campsite**, used as a rest stop by Lewis and Clark.

▓ The 71-acre (29 ha) **Sacajawea Interpretive Cultural & Educational Center** in Salmon, ID, commemorates the Agai'dika people and the Lewis and Clark expedition.

NORTH AMERICA

MASSACHUSETTS | MAINE |

Thoreau's Wilderness Home

Wander the seashore, forests, and inland waterways of eastern New England, where the presence of the great philosopher lives on.

A gravel footpath winds through the pine and hardwood forest of Walden Pond State Reservation, circling Walden Pond, Henry David Thoreau's home in Concord, Massachusetts. Pausing in the clearing where his cabin once stood, you feel the spirit of this natural philosopher all around you. His writings guide you next to Cape Cod National Seashore, a 40-mile (64 kilometer) oasis of shifting sand dunes and salt marshes. You walk along stretches of buttery yellow sand, the salty air punctuated by the delicate perfume of beach plums and wild roses. Continuing in Thoreau's footsteps, travel north to Greenville in the Maine woods. Launching a canoe on Moosehead Lake, paddle down the Upper West Branch of the Penobscot River to Chesuncook Lake. Your canoe slices through the gently flowing water as a bald eagle watches from a barren treetop. Rounding a bend, you encounter a young bull moose, knee-deep in water. He rips up clumps of reeds and eel grass, rivulets of water dribbling down his massive face. From the porch of Chesuncook Lake House at journey's end, near the site of the cabin where Thoreau stayed, you gaze on 5,267-foot (1,605 meter) Mount Katahdin in the distance. It dares you to climb its craggy slopes, as Thoreau once did.

WHEN TO GO Summer is the most popular time, so visit in late spring or fall to avoid the crowds.

HOW LONG Plan on seven to ten days, including three to five days on the water. The Walden Pond trail is a 35-minute walk.

PLANNING Be prepared for changing weather conditions. Carry insect repellent and proper camping gear for canoeing and plenty of sunblock for when you explore the seashore.

INSIDE INFORMATION Walden Pond State Reservation closes when the lot is full, so call ahead to check on parking availability. Open water swimming is permitted.

WEBSITES nps.gov/caco, maineoutdoors.com/canoeing

HIGHLIGHTS

▥ Although the original is gone, you can visit a full-size, furnished replica of **Thoreau's cabin** at Walden Pond State Reservation.

▥ Cape Cod National Seashore's location on the Atlantic Flyway guarantees sightings of diverse **migratory bird species** in spring and fall. Or you can tour one of the three lighthouses along this section of the cape.

▥ Go for a swim or relax at **Chesuncook Lake House**, a remote wilderness lodge, where solitude and hearty home-cooked meals made of fresh ingredients are de rigueur.

An exact copy of Thoreau's tiny cabin nestles in a woodland clearing near Walden Pond in Concord, Massachusetts.

The sign for B.B. King's Blues Club helps to light up Beale Street in Memphis, Tennessee.

Blues Pilgrimage in Clarksdale

Get with the beat in the birthplace of the blues, home to a community still brimming with musical talent.

Clarksdale in Coahoma County, Mississippi, is an understated town surrounded by farmland that stretches for miles to meet the sky at a flat and hazy horizon. It is not famed for its beauty, but beyond the sun-bleached roads and peeling paint you will find a community steeped in the traditions of blues music. Clarksdale celebrates the history of the blues and its contribution to Western popular music through the Mississippi Blues Trail and the town's museums. The tradition of musical performance also thrives in clubs and at regular festivals in the Mississippi Delta and Tennessee. Walk in the shadow of great musicians who lived or performed around here, such as W. C. Handy and John Lee Hooker, and see their legacy in the artists now playing at venues such as Ground Zero in Blues Alley, part-owned by the actor Morgan Freeman.

WHEN TO GO To get the most out of Clarksdale, time your visit to coincide with the Juke Joint Festival in April or the Sunflower River Blues and Gospel Festival in August.

HOW LONG You could incorporate a visit to Clarksdale into a more extended blues pilgrimage around the Mississippi Delta, taking in Memphis as well, and touring other sites and venues in the area.

PLANNING The nearest airport is Memphis, where you can catch a Delta bus to Clarksdale in the morning. If your flight lands later in the day, consider renting a car and driving the 90-minute route.

INSIDE INFORMATION For a taste of Mississippi dining, try the Bluesberry Cafe, where live music and great regional food go hand in hand.

WEBSITES msbluestrail.org, jukejointfestival.com

HIGHLIGHTS

▥ Stay at the **Riverside Hotel**, which, before it became a hotel in 1944, was the G.T. Thomas Hospital. It was here, in 1937, that Bessie Smith, the highest-paid African-American performer of the 1920s, died after an automobile accident on Highway 61.

▥ Don't miss the **Delta Blues Museum**, which now houses the log cabin of Muddy Waters, moved here from its original site a few miles outside Clarksdale on the Stovall Plantation.

▥ Pay homage at **the crossroads of Highways 49 and 61**, where it is said that Robert Johnson made a pact with the devil, inspiring his song, "Crossroad Blues."

▥ Blues fans with a month to spare can follow Highway 61, the **Blues Highway**, the migratory journey that African Americans made from the south to Chicago, taking their music with them. Stops include New Orleans, Clarksdale, and Memphis.

NORTH AMERICA

On the Road After Kerouac

Cross America from coast to coast, and experience the youthful freedom that blazes through Jack Kerouac's classic Beat novel.

Jack Kerouac moved from city to city at full speed. In this epic journey you visit some of the coolest places in America, the jazz clubs, cafés, and other haunts where Kerouac gleaned inspiration. San Francisco was where the Beat writer felt the most unfettered, and this is where you start. The funky bohemia of North Beach, still a beatnik haven, is a must. Even now, the district swings with the rhythm of the 1950s and is home to great Italian restaurants and The Beat Museum. A short flight takes you to Denver, Colorado, hometown of Kerouac's friend, Neal Cassady, who inspired *On the Road*'s main character, Dean Moriarty. Neon-adorned buildings have thrust the Mile-High City into the future, but flanked by the Rocky Mountains, it still has the beauty that captured Kerouac's heart and delivers a real taste of the Midwest. After a 48-hour train ride past amber waves of grain, the energy of New York is a welcome wake-up. The city's fast-paced rhythms are like Kerouac's quick verse. Grab a hot dog, then hop on the E train to Queens, where Kerouac wrote his first novel, *The Town and the City*, in his parents' home in Ozone Park. The last stop is Lowell, Massachussetts, Kerouac's redbrick hometown and setting for his strange and fantastical novel *Dr. Sax*.

WHEN TO GO Fall, September or October. Arrive in San Francisco early in the week to avoid crowds.

HOW LONG Allow 12 days, which gives you three days in each city.

PLANNING Pack light for easy mobility. Bring *The Portable Jack Kerouac*, an anthology of his writings, and take the CD *Jack Kerouac Reads* On the Road for his take on the jazz joints of San Francisco. Bring a notebook and pen for your own journal writing.

INSIDE INFORMATION Walk around Russian Hill, San Francisco, where Kerouac crashed on friends' couches and floors. He stayed with Cassady in 1951 at 29 Russell Street.

WEBSITES flyfrontier.com, amtrak.com

HIGHLIGHTS

▥ Caffe Trieste on Vallejo Street, North Beach, San Francisco, is great for people-watching. **Poetry and jazz** are featured nightly.

▥ Peruse the Beat literature section at **City Lights bookstore** and feel Kerouac's spirit.

▥ In Denver, **El Chapultepec** has live jazz every night. Kerouac and Neal Cassady drank beers at the booth by the door.

▥ **Glen Patrick's Pub** in Ozone Park, Queens, New York, is located across the street from the house where Kerouac lived with his parents. Order a beer and look out the window.

City Lights, a bookstore in North Beach, San Francisco, remains a haven for lovers of counterculture.

CALIFORNIA

Ansel Adams' Yosemite

Focus on nature in one of North America's great national parks, the photographer's adopted home and object of his lifelong devotion.

It's unlikely that Ansel Adams' parents had any idea of the career they were launching when they gave their 14-year-old son a Kodak No. 1 Box Brownie camera on his first visit to Yosemite Valley. The epic black-and-white images of the American West that Adams went on to capture over a 60-year career were infused with the innate power of these landscapes. They spoke as loudly as he did: Adams was a longtime board member of the Sierra Club—America's oldest and largest environmental organization—and constantly promoted national parks, speaking with more than one American president about the importance of conserving wilderness areas. While living for 30 years in Yosemite Valley, known as the region's "Main Street," Adams trekked among the park's granite peaks, talus slopes, riverbeds, and alpine meadows with his portable darkroom and 100 pounds (45 kilograms) of gear. Follow in his footsteps as you explore the magnificence of places bearing appropriately evocative names like Cathedral Spires and Unicorn Peak. Through the seasons, Adams caught the many moods of El Capitan, the world's largest individual granite rock—twice the size of the Rock of Gibraltar. But Adams would also turn his lens on the fragile details: the flowering dogwood, the single oak, a line of aspen. He died in 1984, aged 82, but his masterfully composed and processed photographs still bear witness to a life devoted to the protection of wild places.

WHEN TO GO Yosemite National Park is open year-round. Crowds and road accessibility are the major seasonal variables. Visit in spring for thunderous waterfalls, summer for warm, dry weather (but lots of crowds), and winter for solitude, but with the risk of restricted road access.

HOW LONG With 230,258 acres (93,182 ha) to explore, you should stay at least one night. A week or longer will let you explore more of Adams' adopted home to your satisfaction.

PLANNING There are many lodging options, from the grand lodge of the Ahwahnee Hotel to backpacking. Aspiring photographers should check out the Yosemite Association's tailored trips and guided tours.

INSIDE INFORMATION The Ansel Adams Gallery provides a handout listing more than ten sites Adams photographed in Yosemite Valley. It'll direct you to more of the scenes you've seen in prints and posters.

WEBSITES anseladams.com, nps.gov/yose/learn/historyculture/ansel-adams.htm

NORTH AMERICA

HIGHLIGHTS

▥ Don't miss the **Ansel Adams Gallery** in Yosemite Valley. It offers workshops and guided hikes, just as Adams did when he and his family lived upstairs. Photographers of all levels can learn composition and technique while following valley trails to some of the spots Adams photographed.

▥ Adams is known for his unpopulated landscapes. But many of his black-and-white photos of visitors playing in the snow are on display at the **Majestic Yosemite Hotel**. This is one of the park's prime places to stay and is named after the original Native American inhabitants. "Yosemite" is the Ahwahnee word for grizzly bear.

▥ The nearby Minarets Wilderness is among the 9 million acres (more than 3.6 million ha) protected by the 1964 Wilderness Act advocated by Adams. It was renamed **Ansel Adams Wilderness** after his death and makes another beautiful trip in his footsteps.

Opposite: The majestic Yosemite Falls are the highest in North America, cascading down from 1,430 ft (436 m). They are at their most impressive in spring when swollen with snowmelt. Above left: A coyote in winter surveys the scene. Above right: Countless wildflowers bejewel the park, such as the wild perennial lupine.

Pablo Neruda at Home

Visiting the three homes of one of Chile's most important writers and political figures is like taking a journey through his mind.

SOUTH AMERICA

Evidence of Neruda's talent came early when he started writing for his local paper at just 13. During his lifetime he became increasingly politicized, and his work reflected his social and political concerns. In 1971, he received the Nobel Prize in Literature. As you tour Neruda's three houses—now museums—you feel his energy, intellect, and passions infusing each one of them. The first stop is La Chascona in Santiago's Bellavista district. This rambling hideaway, which he built for himself and his third wife, Matilde Urratia, is littered with colorful crockery and collections of seashells and butterflies. His bedroom nestles in a tower. Neruda's second—and least-known—retreat is La Sebastiana in the seaport of Valparaíso, 74 miles (119 kilometers) northwest of Santiago. Set in a steep hillside, the town house overlooks the ocean and is full of knickknacks, including nautical paraphernalia, and a stuffed lion. The poet's real home was Isla Negra, sitting on a rocky outcrop 45 minutes south of Valparaíso. Neruda bought it as a stone hut, then added buildings and shaped it to his taste. Ships' figureheads adorn the walls, and Neruda's desk faces the sea.

WHEN TO GO Summer in Chile is from mid-November to mid-February, when temperatures can get very high. The winter months, particularly July and August, are wet and cold.

HOW LONG A trip taking in the three houses can be done in a week. Allow more time if you want to explore the Chilean wine region, the Atacama Desert, or Patagonia in the far south.

PLANNING Rent a car in Santiago. The houses are open Tuesday–Sunday, 10 a.m.–1 p.m. and 3–6 p.m., and are run by the Neruda Foundation, which was established by his late wife Matilde. The roads are good, and you will also be able to explore the coast.

INSIDE INFORMATION Below Isla Negra, along a fence by the sea, you can read messages written by people from all over the world who have been inspired by Neruda's work and his ideas.

WEBSITE fundacionneruda.org

HIGHLIGHTS

▪ At La Chascona you can see the **painting by Diego Rivera** of Neruda's wife Matilde Urratia. In the study is the wooden box where Neruda put the poems that he wrote to her.

▪ There is a **secret passageway** in a dining room cupboard at La Chascona, where the poet claimed he would escape if his guests became too boring.

▪ In an upstairs room at Isla Negra is a **wooden desk carved from a ship's door** that Neruda spotted being washed in on the tide below his house. It was one of his favorite things.

Valparaíso's historic quarter – a UNESCO World Heritage site – is full of reminders of the port's 19th-century heyday as the "jewel of the Pacific."

The writer's room at the Hotel Ambos Mundos in Havana is preserved as he left it, complete with typewriter.

CUBA

Hemingway in Cuba

The much-traveled journalist, writer, and Nobel Laureate found a safe yet stimulating haven on this lovely Caribbean island.

In 1928, Ernest Hemingway arrived in Cuba on a fishing trip from Key West and fell in love with Havana and the Cuban people. A year later, he took up residence in the Hotel Ambos Mundos, in the heart of Old Havana, and this should be your first stop. From the hotel, it is a gentle walk to El Floridita, where he propped up the bar drinking daiquiris. Hemingway indulged his passion for deep-sea fishing from the little village of Cojimar, east of Havana, which provided the setting for *The Old Man and The Sea*. From 1939, Hemingway lived and worked at Finca Vigía, a modest country house set in rambling tropical gardens in San Francisco de Paula near Havana. Looking in through the ample windows, you can see his library (containing 9,000 books), typewriter, and photographs. The bathroom in Finca Vigía has the best view in the house; from the bathroom, Hemingway could see over the harbor to Havana and the sea.

WHEN TO GO The best time to visit is from December to May. The summer months are extremely hot and humid, and October and November are hurricane season.

HOW LONG The trip can be done easily in ten days. But there are fascinating cities and some beautiful Caribbean coastline in the south of the island, which could provide a two- to three-week vacation.

PLANNING Get a visa or "tourist card" in advance; you won't be able to enter without one. Americans are not now permitted to travel to Cuba unless they have a license from the U.S. Department of the Treasury.

INSIDE INFORMATION Another of Hemingway's favorite haunts was La Terraza, in Cojimar, which has a good collection of photographs of him. Eat here and enjoy the view across the harbor.

WEBSITES cuba.com, sc-travel-adventures.co.uk/excursions/cuba/havana/hemingway-in-cuba.htm

HIGHLIGHTS

▥ At Floridita, try the **Papa Hemingway**, the author's favorite cocktail: grapefruit juice, a dash of maraschino, and double rum over crushed ice. You may have to fight for his seat, though.

▥ The **Bodeguita del Medio**, a little bar in Old Havana, is another of the author's drinking holes. Mojitos are the specialty here.

▥ In Cojimar's Plaza Hemingway, don't miss the bust made from the bronze propellers of fishing boats, which stands in a **colonnaded shrine**.

▥ In the garden at Finca Vigía is Hemingway's beloved **40-ft (12 m) boat** *El Pilar*, which he took fishing for marlin in the Gulf Stream.

▥ Stroll along Havana's promenade, the **Malecón**, where tatty colonial mansions look over the Straits of Florida. This was Hemingway's first view of the city when he sailed across from America, and today, as then, it is a lively hangout, with locals drinking rum and fishing from the rocks.

NORTH AMERICA

ECUADOR

A Voyage to the Galápagos

These isolated islands, made famous by British naturalist Charles Darwin, are the home of highly colorful and entertaining creatures.

SOUTH AMERICA

Soft sprays of salt water brush your cheek as your dinghy races from the cruise ship to Isla Santa Fé in the Galápagos Islands. Playful sea lion pups prance around like a marine welcoming committee. As you disembark, you become aware of stark volcanic landscapes filled with forests of prickly cactus plants, soaring tall as trees. Each island harbors different natural treasures, and each day your ship transports you to another island. The journey is like Charles Darwin's 1835 voyage on HMS *Beagle*, which inspired his theory of natural selection. Fearless, fantastic animals appear at every turn. A Galápagos mockingbird pecks at your shoelaces, oblivious to your size. On Española, the pungent scent of musk assails your nostrils as your guide leads you around a harem of female sea lions, jealously guarded by a muscular bull. On Santiago, ancient black lava stones crackle underfoot as you hike to rocks where marine iguanas dive to nibble on green algae, while vibrant orange and red Sally Lightfoot crabs scuttle into crevices. As your cruise continues, blue-footed boobies plunge into the Pacific Ocean to pursue schools of fish, and red-billed tropic birds call out in rapid screeches. Flightless cormorants jackknife into the fertile waters, where sea turtles and manta rays gently glide.

WHEN TO GO Anytime is a good time to visit the Galápagos Islands, but June through November can be a little cooler than other months.

HOW LONG Fly 600 miles (966 km) from mainland Ecuador to Baltra or San Cristóbal in the Galápagos to pick up small ship cruises of four days to two weeks.

PLANNING Bring plenty of sunscreen and a broad-brimmed hat or cap to protect against the strong, equatorial sun, and good hiking shoes.

INSIDE INFORMATION You'll find Internet cafés and shops to buy sunscreen in the town of Puerto Ayora on Santa Cruz island.

WEBSITES www.igtoa.org, galapagos.org

HIGHLIGHTS

▥ "Galápagos" is Spanish for "tortoise," and these amazing islands were named for the giant tortoises that roam free. At the **Charles Darwin Research Station** learn about giant tortoise Lonesome George, the last of his subspecies, who died in 2012.

▥ Love is in the air in the Galápagos. Don't miss the frenetic clicking, rattling, whooping mating dance of the **waved albatross** on Española around April.

▥ Hiking atop the moonlike landscape of Bartolomé's heights, you'll be rewarded with expansive views of **Pinnacle Rock and its beaches**, where Galápagos penguins waddle and hop, and sea lions snooze in the sun.

During the mating season in the Galápagos, the male frigate bird inflates his throat to the proportions of a scarlet balloon to advertise his excellent breeding credentials.

A hawksbill turtle swims over a reef in the cobalt waters of Tahiti, which support a teeming marine life.

| FRENCH POLYNESIA |

Captain Cook's Polynesia

Take a cruise around these magical tropical islands and discover a culture that has captivated visitors for centuries.

When Captain Cook returned from his visit to Polynesia in the 1770s, he became the first of many Europeans to spin tales of the islands' tropical beauty. Begin your own exploration of the islands in Papeete, Tahiti's capital and most populous town. Here you can visit the Pearl Museum and the craft market. As you sail away from Tahiti, the outlines of buildings fade away, and you'll find yourself staring at the island's jutting peaks—a view much like Captain Cook had on his voyages to the region. Huahine and Raiatea are a quiet contrast to bustling Papeete. On Huahine, there is a group of more than 40 sacred sites (*marae*)—the Maeva marae. Although less well known than Tahiti, Raiatea was the most important religious center in old Polynesia and contains its largest, and most important, marae at Taputapuatea. Then you're off to Bora-Bora, where you can dive, sail the lagoon, or visit defensive emplacements from World War II.

WHEN TO GO May, June, September, and October are probably the optimal months, missing the tourist high season (July and August) and the rainier "winter" season (November through April).

HOW LONG A ten-day cruise gives you plenty of time to enjoy days at sea and explore the islands.

PLANNING French Polynesia is an expensive destination and the islands are far-flung across miles of open ocean, so the most comfortable way to see as much as possible is from a cruise ship. If you're flying in from a winter climate, minimize the risk of missed air connections (and a missed cruise) by tacking on a few extra days at the beginning of your trip. Car rentals are available on most islands and easily arranged on the day of arrival.

INSIDE INFORMATION Before returning to Papeete, stop at the island of Moorea, whose volcanic cliffs are among Polynesia's most famous sights. You can see them best on a catamaran ride around the island.

WEBSITES tahiti-tourisme.com, princess.com

| HIGHLIGHTS

▥ The **Gauguin Museum** on the south side of Tahiti traces the artist's Polynesian period.

▥ Divers can explore the **undersea world** and swim with sharks and manta rays. Nondivers can explore via glass-bottomed boats, helmet dives, submarines, or snorkeling trips.

▥ Visit a **pearl farm** on any of the islands to see how the world-famous Tahitian black pearls are cultivated.

▥ The Tiki Village Cultural Center on Moorea offers a **dance and music show** that re-creates old Polynesia.

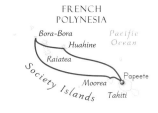

A statue to the people outside the Mao Zedong Mausoleum in Tiananmen Square, Beijing, commemorates those who helped to create the People's Republic in 1949.

Mao's Long March

Visit a major monument of the Long March, set in the mountains of western Sichuan, a region of turbulent rivers, gorges, and glaciers.

In 1935, midway through the 8,000-mile (12,875 kilometer), two-year odyssey that became known as the Long March, 22 men from Mao Zedong's Communist army captured the strategic Luding Bridge over the Dadu River. The growth in "red tourism" in newly affluent China has spurred interest in Luding—the most iconic of the Long March monuments—and although this is a remote location that takes time to reach, it's well worth the effort, not just for the dramatic site itself, but because the scenery is staggeringly beautiful. Begin in Beijing with a visit to the monuments to Mao in Tiananmen Square, and then fly to Chengdu. From here, travel by road to the spectacular Dadu River Valley. At Luding, cross the chain-link bridge over the swirling Dadu River, and visit the monument to the Long Marchers. Beyond Luding, endless ranks of high, wild mountains rise in great waves all the way to Tibet. To the west, just beyond the Tibetan town of Kangding, is the awesome bulk of the Daxue Shan (Great Snowy Mountains). A short distance south of Luding, Hailuogou Glacier surges down from Gongga Shan. There is an amazing giant Buddha at Leshan. The cloud forests and gorges to the north of Chengdu are home to some of China's precious giant panda population.

WHEN TO GO May–September. If you are planning to visit Hailuogou or Kangding, bring warm-weather gear. Lower altitudes are hot and humid from May until September. Waterproof gear is essential as the summer months can bring torrential downpours.

HOW LONG Allow three or four days for a round-trip from Chengdu, the nearest large city. If you want to explore the region more thoroughly, allow at least ten days.

PLANNING Fly from Beijing to Chengdu. Tours of the region can be arranged through tour operators in Chengdu. If you are traveling independently, be prepared for a lot of long, uncomfortable bus journeys. Most organized tours to Luding Bridge include a trip to Hailuogou Glacier or Kangding or both.

INSIDE INFORMATION Chengdu, capital of Sichuan province, is one of China's liveliest cities and probably the best place in the world to sample the famously spicy Sichuanese cuisine.

WEBSITE travelchinaguide.com

HIGHLIGHTS

▦ The **Luding Bridge** is constructed from 13 heavy iron chains, with wooden boards lashed to the chains to form the roadway.

▦ Explore **Kangding**, a lively trading center situated on the edge of the Tibetan plateau. It has a street market, antique market, and the Dorje Drak Monastery.

▦ Marvel at **Hailuogou Glacier** and the views of **Gongga Shan**, at 24,790 ft (7,556 m) the highest peak in China's Sichuan province.

▦ Visit the world-famous **Wolong Panda Reserve**, about 100 miles (160 km) northwest of Chengdu.

NEPAL | INDIA

Road to Enlightenment

Return to the sixth century B.C. to retrace the life of the Buddha, visiting holy places that mark his spiritual journey.

Buddha means "awakened one," and it was by this name that Siddhartha Gautama became known when, after six years of extreme asceticism, he attained enlightenment while meditating under the Bodhi tree (a type of fig tree). The Buddha's spiritual and physical path to this awakening and beyond was preserved by oral tradition for 400 years before being captured in writing, and you can follow his journey today. Begin in the little village of Lumbini, in southern Nepal. Lumbini is Sanskrit for "the lovely," and this sacred location was the Buddha's birthplace. To the east, on the dusty Ganges plain, Kushinagar is the place the Buddha chose for his *parinirvana*, or final exit from Earth. The temple here contains a 20-foot (6 meter) long statue of the Buddha in the recumbent posture, covered in gold leaf. In Sarnath, near Varanasi, visit the deer park where the Buddha delivered his first sermon. Moving east to Bodhgaya, you can see the Bodhi tree said to be a third-generation descendant of the original tree under which the Buddha meditated. End your journey in Patna, one of the oldest places in the world to have been continuously inhabited. The Buddha passed through the city many times, including on his last journey to Kushinagar.

WHEN TO GO October to April is the best. Avoid the monsoon season, which begins in late June–early July and lasts about two months.

HOW LONG 550 miles (885 km) from Lumbini to Patna by road. Allow a minimum of five days.

PLANNING Lumbini can be reached by road from Lucknow or Varanasi.

INSIDE INFORMATION Walk around stupas (large domed shrines) and other sacred objects in a clockwise direction. Patna Museum has a rare collection of antiquities, including stone sculptures of the Buddha and the Holy Relic Casket, containing the Buddha's ashes. Avoid western food as it may not be as fresh as the local cuisine; only eat food that is piping hot.

WEBSITES incredibleindia.org, indianvisaonline.gov.in

HIGHLIGHTS

▓ In Lumbini, visit the **Maya Devi Temple** and the **Ashoka pillar**, which marks the Buddha's birthplace.

▓ Admire the **Mahaparinirvana temple and stupa** in Kushinagar, where the Buddha attained *parinirvana* (died), and the Rambhar Stupa, where he was cremated.

▓ Tour the deer park outside Varanasi, the site of the Buddha's first sermon. Then see Sarnath's Archaeological Museum and take an **early morning boat ride** on the Ganges River.

▓ Sit under the **Bodhi tree** at the Mahabodhi Temple in Bodhgaya, where the Buddha achieved enlightenment.

The Buddha was cremated on a funeral pyre at Rambhar Stupa in 543 B.C.

Tolstoy's writing case and letters are on display at the Tolstoy Museum in Moscow.

Tolstoy's Russia

Make a pilgrimage to the key locations in the life of one of the world's greatest writers and most radical thinkers.

To travel in Count Leo Tolstoy's footsteps, start in St. Petersburg, the old imperial capital, with its opulent palaces, glittering ballrooms, and art collections. This is the world that Tolstoy knew intimately from his youth and that he drew on for novels such as *Anna Karenina*. It is also a symbol of the chasm between the fabulous wealth of the Russian elite and the misery of the poor. Such contrasts came to haunt Tolstoy in later life. Then head to Moscow to see the Tolstoy House Estate Museum, the home where, between 1882 and 1901, he wintered with his wife and family. The highlight of your pilgrimage is a trip to the family estate at Yasnaya Polyana, near Tula, some 125 miles (200 kilometers) south of Moscow. Here, where he was born and raised, Tolstoy wrote his novels, engaged with nature, ran an experimental school, worked alongside peasants, and entertained friends. Here, too, he lies buried in a simple woodland grave.

WHEN TO GO Spring, summer, and fall are best. Winter is possible, but bitterly cold.

HOW LONG Allow at least seven days. Yasnaya Polyana is a day trip from Moscow by rail or bus, but spend a night at the modern Yasnaya Polyana Hotel to see the estate at a more leisurely pace.

PLANNING Check museum opening times locally before setting out; they are often irregular.

INSIDE INFORMATION There are two Tolstoy museums in Moscow: the Tolstoy House Estate Museum (his house) and the more literary Tolstoy Museum, which has manuscripts, first editions, and personal mementos. The latter organizes lectures and themed excursions for private parties and schools.

WEBSITES ypmuseum.ru/en, russianmuseums.info/m299

HIGHLIGHTS

■ The **Tolstoy House Estate Museum** in Moscow still feels like a family home, full of touching mementos and possessions.

■ Tolstoy spent an idyllic childhood at **Yasnaya Polyana**, and it remained his spiritual home. The Tolstoy House Museum has furnished rooms kept much as he and his family left them.

■ Linger in the parkland of Yasnaya Polyana, wandering down the **avenues of linden trees** and enjoying landscapes that remained a lifelong inspiration to Tolstoy.

| CHINA | KYRGYZSTAN | UZBEKISTAN |

The Silk Road

Remote and exotic regions of China and Central Asia unfold before you along an ancient trading route.

The Silk Road, linking China with the Middle East and Europe, was not a single route, but a collection of trails that ran from northwest China to what is now eastern Turkey or western Iran. Travelers were using it from at least the second century B.C. until it was overtaken by maritime trade 1,500 years later. It carried untold riches, and great cities and civilizations prospered along the way. Technological and social changes spread along the route, including gunpowder to the West and Buddhism to China. Modern-day travelers can start from Beijing or Shanghai and visit the eastern, Chinese section with its stunning archeological sites at Xi'an and Dunhuang. Here the section across the Taklimakan desert began. The next major stop was the oasis town of Kashgar, overlooked by the foothills of the Tian Shan range. Kashgar controlled the mountain passes to Central Asia, India, and Persia. Farther west, along one of the busiest sections of the Silk Road, are the two legendary cities of Central Asia—Samarqand and Bukhara. One of the world's oldest inhabited cities, Samarqand rises from the desert, its buildings embellished with ceramic tiles in every shade of blue. Bukhara was once a great center of Islamic learning, and its bazaars were the richest in Central Asia.

WHEN TO GO March–April or September–October are best for avoiding the most extreme temperatures in these mountainous and desertlike regions.

HOW LONG Many companies organize itineraries of up to two weeks along parts of either the Chinese or Central Asian section of the Silk Road. If you have a month to spare, you can travel the route from Beijing or Shanghai to Tashkent in Uzbekistan.

PLANNING The countries of Central Asia have many problems; check official travel advice in advance.

INSIDE INFORMATION *Shadow of the Silk Road* by Colin Thubron is a fascinating account of a 7,000-mile (11,265 km) trip along the Silk Road, essential background reading for would-be travelers.

WEBSITES en.unesco.org/silkroad/about-silk-road, silkroad.co.nz

HIGHLIGHTS

▥ At the **Thousand Buddha Caves** near Dunhuang, you can see superb frescoes and sculptures that were created over a period of 1,000 years.

▥ Don't miss the **terra-cotta warriors of Xi'an**, the fabulous buried army of the first Chinese emperor.

▥ Kashgar has a vibrant Sunday market and notable Islamic sites, including the **Tomb of Abakh Khoja** and **Id Kah Mosque**, China's largest.

▥ Samarqand's **beautiful Islamic architecture** includes the Registan Square, flanked by a trio of Islamic religious colleges, and Tamerlane's tomb. The city has some of the finest examples of Islamic ceramic art.

For local people, the rugged, barren Central Asian sections of the Silk Road are still best tackled with trusty local transportation.

Alexander's Legacy

The conqueror of the ancient world sets the pace on this historic route replete with magnificent archaeological sites.

For more than 2,000 years Alexander the Great has captured the imagination of people around the globe. When barely out of his teens, he invaded Asia with some 45,000 men to conquer the vast Persian Empire. He continued on an epic 22,000-mile (35,400 kilometer) journey, from Troy to Alexandria, Samarqand, and Babylon. By the time he died, aged 32, he had gone beyond the limits of the known world, carving out an empire stretching from Greece to Afghanistan, Israel, and India. Following in his footsteps in Turkey, from Troy to Adana, you savor a magical combination of landscapes, food, and archaeological wonders. At Didyma, between Ephesus and Bodrum, you walk beneath the soaring columns of the Temple of Apollo, where Alexander's victory over the Persians was prophesied. You can still feel the influence of the old gods in the temple's innermost sanctuary, reached along dark vaulted corridors. Gordium was the home of the Gordian Knot—he who untied it would become ruler of Asia. Alexander simply cut the knot with his sword. His great victory over the Persians at Issus in 333 B.C. is now being excavated at Kinet Huyuk, and can be visited by prior arrangement. Then head to the busy city of Adana, your journey's end.

WHEN TO GO Mid–April to early June, or September to October, to avoid the summer heat and crowds.

HOW LONG At least a week to see a few highlights. Two to three weeks will allow you to cover a lot of terrain, visit a great many sites, and appreciate the physical and logistical difficulties faced by Alexander.

PLANNING Many travel companies use Alexander the Great as a headline for tours that have very little to do with him, so scrutinize their itineraries. Independent travelers should buy detailed maps before jetting off. Large-scale maps are often difficult to find in Turkey, especially outside the main cities.

INSIDE INFORMATION In the interior, be wary of Turkey's kangal dogs that protect sheep and goats from wolves and are well-known for their ferocity. Carry a walking stick and some stones for protection.

WEBSITES pothos.org, petersommer.com/tours/alexander-the-great-turkey

HIGHLIGHTS

◾ Istanbul's archaeological museum houses the **Alexander Sarcophagus**. On the sides of the coffin, carved in white marble, Alexander is portrayed at a hunt and rearing up in battle on his stallion Bucephalus.

◾ **Ephesus** has wonderfully preserved villas, baths, a theater for 28,000, and an extraordinary library.

◾ A boat trip takes you to **Phaselis**, where Alexander was crowned with golden wreaths. It lies on Turkey's Lycian shore, northeast of Kas.

◾ **Termessos** stands on a rocky eyrie in the Taurus Mountains northwest of Antalya. It was one of the few cities to resist Alexander and survive.

Just south of Ephesus at Priene, columns of the temple of Athena grace the hillside. It was new in Alexander's time and the citizens allowed him to dedicate it to the goddess.

The monastery of Vlacherna stands on its own islet off the coast of Corfu, which may have been Alcinoös's kingdom of Phaeacia.

TURKEY | GREECE

The Odyssey

Enjoy sun, sea, and places steeped in ancient myths as you sail with Odysseus from Troy to his home on the island of Ithaca.

Odysseus's journey home from the siege of Troy, as recounted in Homer's epic poem, *Odyssey*, is, of course, legend. None of the places where Odysseus lingered can be identified for sure. But we do know where the journey began and ended, and it is entertaining to guess which islands Odysseus may have visited. Cursed by the gods, Odysseus traveled an erratic course homeward from Troy, weaving through the Greek islands. Could the island of the Laestrygonians, giants who hurled huge rocks at passing ships, be the beautiful island of Santoríni, whose volcano may still have been ejecting lava and boulders in Odysseus's time? Persistent local legend claims that the tiny island of Gávdos, off the south coast of Crete, was the island of Circe the sorceress. Perhaps Kíthira, the steep-sided, rocky island between Crete and Cape Tenaron, was the home of the sirens. It lies on Odysseus's route around the southern tip of the Peloponnisos. Corfiots say that the shiplike rock that lies off Corfu harbor is the petrified wreck of Odysseus's ship, so perhaps King Alcinoös's Phaeacia was Corfu. After hearing his tale, Alcinoös gave Odysseus a ship to carry him back to Ithaca.

WHEN TO GO April to October.

HOW LONG Up to three weeks.

PLANNING The only authentic way to follow Homer's *Odyssey* would be to charter a yacht. However, you can reach Troy by bus from Istanbul, then cross by boat from Ayvalik to Lesbos and island-hop to Crete. Boats travel from Chora Sfakion, on the south coast of Crete, to tiny Gávdos. Ferries connect Kastéli on Crete with Kíthira and Gíthio on the southern Greek mainland; from here you can travel by bus to Patras, where there are daily ferries to Ithaca.

INSIDE INFORMATION Corfu, with a perfect natural harbor ringed by pretty old houses and cafés, is a peaceful place to rest for a few days after your travels.

WEBSITES gototurkey.co.uk, visitgreece.gr

HIGHLIGHTS

■ **Ancient tumuli** are Troy's most prominent landmarks. Its location on the Dardanelles strait was the key to its ancient power and wealth.

■ Visit the archaeological museums in Mytilini on the **island of Lesbos**, which Odysseus plundered. In the village of Agiássos, below Mount Olympos, traditional life continues.

■ Eat in one of the superb **fish restaurants** along the waterfront at the unspoiled port of Gíthio, where Helen and Paris embarked for Troy.

■ Relax in Vathí, Ithaca's capital, or try some of the island's **excellent hiking routes**.

Top 10 Film Footsteps

Transitioning from couch potatoes to intrepid travelers, fans of popular movies and television visit some of the greatest locations in the world.

❶ NEW JERSEY: *THE SOPRANOS*

The Garden State is littered with locations where the hit mob show was filmed between 1999 and 2007. Satin Doll nightclub in Lodi doubled as the Bada Bing! Take a drive through the Lincoln tunnel from the show's opening credits, or stop by the real life junkyard in Jersey City which played Barone Sanitation. The famous final scene was shot at Holsten's Brookdale Confectionary in Bloomfield.

PLANNING Several operators offer guided bus tours of Sopranoland including Gray Line. newyorksightseeing.com

❷ GEORGIA: *THE WALKING DEAD*

The zombie outbreak may have started in Atlanta, but small-town Georgia provided most of the gruesome venues for the cult sci-fi series which started in 2010. About an hour south of Atlanta, Senoia was the fictional Woodbury where the wicked Governor reigned supreme. Plenty of other scenes were filmed nearby, in towns like Sharpsburg, Griffin, Newnan, and Grantville.

PLANNING The Woodbury Shoppe in Senoia sells all sorts of TWD products including official gear. woodburyshoppe.com

❸ UTAH: LEGENDARY WESTERNS

The chromatic canyonlands of southern Utah have co-starred in hundreds of movies and TV shows. Monument Valley was the venue for many collaborations between actor John Wayne and director John Ford; classics including *Stagecoach* (1939) and *The Searchers* (1956). Grafton, a ghost town near Zion National Park, was home base for *Butch Cassidy & the Sundance Kid* (1969). Many of the outdoor scenes in HBO's cowboy sci-fi series *Westworld* (2016) were shot in the Castle Valley near Moab.

PLANNING Discover Moab offers a free, downloadable movie locations tour map on its website. discovermoab.com/movie.htm

❹ HAWAI'I: *JURASSIC PARK*

When director Steven Spielberg was searching for a real-life stand-in for the fictional Isla Nublar, he went no further than Kaua'i, the rain forest and waterfall drenched Hawaiian island. Limahuli Garden, Manawaiopuna Falls, the Nā Pali Coast, and Kahili Ranch provided primordial backdrops for the movie's rampaging dinosaurs and their human prey.

PLANNING Island Helicopters offers a *Jurassic*-themed aerial tour that includes landing at the famous falls. islandhelicopters.com

Planted in the 18th century, the spooky white trunks of the Dark Hedges in Stanocum, Northern Ireland, feature in Season Two of *Game of Thrones* when Arya Stark flees along the Kingsroad.

❺ NEW ZEALAND: *LORD OF THE RINGS*

Peter Jackson used his native New Zealand to make the LOTR trilogy, with much of the filming done at outdoor locations on the North Island. Visit Tongariro National Park and Hobbiton, a rural film set near Matamata and the home of Frodo Baggins. Weta Studio in Wellington, which created special effects for the movies, offers daily tours.

PLANNING The New Zealand Tourism website offers a Middle-earth map and information on LOTR tours. newzealand.com/us/home-of-middle-earth

❻ SCOTLAND: *OUTLANDER*

The romantic time travel series that connects medieval and modern-day lovers films at many locations around Scotland including 15th-century Doune Castle, the ancient Rothiemurchus Forest in Cairngorms National Park, and Loch Rannoch in the Highlands.

PLANNING *Ivanhoe* (1952) and *Monty Python & the Holy Grail* (1975) were also filmed at Doune Castle. visitscotland.com

❼ NORTHERN IRELAND: *GAME OF THRONES*

The fictional continent of Westeros in the George R.R. Martin novels and the hit TV show is actually Northern Ireland. From the Dark Hedges and the Caves of Cushendun to the Tollymore Forest and Larrybane Quarry, many of the locations where GOT has filmed sound more like fantasy names than real-life places.

PLANNING Tourism Northern Ireland offers a webpage about guided and self-guided tours of GOT sights around the country. discovernorthernireland.com/gameofthrones

❽ ENGLAND: *DOWNTON ABBEY*

During the drama series that aired in 2010–2015, Highclere Castle in Hampshire doubled as the celebrated manse while Bampton village in the Cotswolds (36 miles/58 km to the north) stood in for Downton village. The abbey railway station is a historic 1882 depot in Horsted Keynes, a stop on the vintage Bluebell Railway Line in West Sussex.

PLANNING Highclere Castle is open to the public for about 70 days each year, mostly during the summer months. highclerecastle.co.uk

❾ TUNISIA: STAR WARS

You don't need the *Millennium Falcon* to reach Tatooine, because the fictional desert planet where so much of Star Wars takes place is actually in the Sahara of southern Tunisia. Due to the super-dry climate, much of the Mos Espa film set survives, as does the Ksar Ouled Soltane granary that doubled as the notorious Slave Quarters in Episode I.

PLANNING Luke Skywalker's subterranean boyhood home is now the modest Hotel Sidi Driss in Matmata. tourismtunisia.com

❿ KENYA: *OUT OF AFRICA* AND *BORN FREE*

On location in Kenya, Meru National Park harbors the rustic camp where George and Joy Adamson raised Elsa the lioness, as well as the big cat's grave. Author Karen Blixen's house is one of Nairobi's major attractions.

PLANNING Much of *Out of Africa* was filmed in the northern sector of the Masai Mara Reserve. magicalkenya.com

A Novelist in Italy

In just a few days—or a lifetime—visit the great cities
of northern Italy that inspired Henry James.

Henry James was fascinated by Old Europe, and Venice, Florence, and Rome in particular feature significantly in his novels. Venice is still steeped in the elegant decadence of which James was both enamored and critical, and which forms the backdrop to his novel *The Aspern Papers*. Moving south to Florence you will be struck by the history of this Renaissance center in its Tuscan landscape of rolling hills. Both are evoked in James's novel *The Portrait of a Lady*. In 1870s Rome, at the end of the Italian Risorgimento, James witnessed great changes as the city became the new capital of Italy. He published vivid descriptions of his time there in the American press, and in 1909 these were published in *Italian Hours*. Wander around Rome's Colosseum and consider what James called its "roughly mountainous quality." Santa Maria Maggiore too will not fail to move. For James, "the place proved so endlessly suggestive that perception became a throbbing confusion of images … . " The sheer size of St. Peter's Basilica will impress perhaps in the way he described: "You think you have taken the whole thing in, but it expands, it rises sublime again, and leaves your measure itself poor."

WHEN TO GO The weather is best in spring and fall. In summer, Venice can be suffocatingly humid, while Florence and Rome get bakingly hot.

HOW LONG Allow at least ten days to give you time to enjoy the best of each city and the countryside in between. Or you could take a leaf out of James's book and take years!

PLANNING You can make the journey by train, bus, or rental car. Book accommodations well in advance, especially in the cities, all three of which attract hordes of tourists throughout the year.

INSIDE INFORMATION If you fly to Venice at the start of the trip, catch an Alilaguna water bus – or a water taxi, if you're feeling rich – from the airport into the city. The 70-minute water-bus journey is a perfect introduction to "La Serenissima" as you approach it across the lagoon, finally arriving in St. Mark's Square.

WEBSITE italia.it

| HIGHLIGHTS

▦ In Venice, **the Grand Canal**, crossed by the Rialto Bridge and overlooked by filigree Renaissance palaces, remains a majestic sight. Here James regularly met with a like-minded group of fellow writers and travelers.

▦ In Florence, the Pitti Palace's **stunning collections**, including paintings by Raphael and Titian, feature in *The Portrait of a Lady*. The works summon a strength of feeling that the heroine, Isabel Archer, is not used to – a common theme in James, which tallies with his own love of Italy.

▦ In Rome, **St. Peter's** left James impressed but not without words. He composed some of his lengthiest articles about it.

A ceiling fresco in the Pitti Palace in Florence encapsulates the lavish conception of this sumptuous Renaissance residence designed by Brunelleschi.

The Pantheon, both church and mausoleum, is one of the best preserved ancient Roman buildings. Here its portico shines in the moonlight.

ITALY

Goethe's Italian Journey

Follow the great poet as far as the southernmost tip of Italy and you will discover some of its finest treasures.

Novelist, poet, dramatist, scientist, theorist, and painter, Johann Wolfgang von Goethe was also chief minister of state for the German Duchy of Weimar. Tired of life as an administrator, he departed abruptly and alone in the middle of the night and made his famous trip to Italy (1786–88). Goethe was both a curious and a conscientious traveler, and he wrote a riveting account of his experiences, *Die italienische Reise* (*Italian Journey*). Today, visitors can trace his journey from Verona and Venice in the north, south to Rome, Naples, and Sicily. He stayed at Torbole on Lake Garda, which he described as "a glorious work of nature at my side." Moving on, he saw yet more to marvel at—"In Rome I have found myself for the first time"—and he made many drawings of statues and ruins. In Naples, then the most vibrant city in Italy, Goethe became friendly with the influential British ambassador, William Hamilton, a vulcan-ologist who took parties up Vesuvius (then very active) and studied its habits. In Sicily, Goethe followed what is now a classic tourist route. In Palermo he carried out significant studies in the Botanical Gardens, a treasure trove of species. He also visited the environs of Palermo and traveled east to Catania and Taormina, stopping at classical temples on the way and taking time out to climb majestic Etna.

WHEN TO GO Spring and fall are best, avoiding the excessive heat of summer in Rome, Naples, and Sicily.

HOW LONG This journey can be made in a week, but you could spend a month or longer.

PLANNING Tickets for trains and buses can be bought at the time of travel. Car rental is best arranged before arriving in Italy. There are many companies offering itinerary-based tours of Italy, though none specific to Goethe. There are comprehensive websites covering Goethe's fascination with Italy.

INSIDE INFORMATION Once you arrive in Italy, pay a visit to local tourist offices to find out more about Goethe associations. They're often a mine of information that you won't find in guidebooks.

WEBSITES italia.it, gocollette.com, romeartlover.it, bestofsicily.com

HIGHLIGHTS

▪ Climb **Vesuvius**, and see why Goethe called it "a peak of hell which towers up in the middle of paradise." He was extremely disappointed to miss a lava flow that happened on the night he left for Sicily.

▪ Lovely **Taormina**, poised above the sea, has an outdoor Greek theater with a backdrop of rolling hills and smoldering Etna. Drive around the pretty villages on Etna's slopes or ascend up to the crater by cable car.

▪ Inland from Palermo, the medieval **cathedral of Monreale** is decorated throughout with world-famous Byzantine mosaics.

A flowery valley in the Cévennes is disturbed by nothing more than a flock of grazing sheep and a solitary walker.

FRANCE

Travels With a Donkey

This challenging walk in the footsteps of one of the world's best-loved writers leads into one of Europe's last wildernesses.

In 1878, the author Robert Louis Stevenson set out on a journey that inspired *Travels with a Donkey in the Cévennes*. This windswept region of granite uplands in the Massif Central's southeast corner is dominated by big skies, where griffon vultures soar, and is even more deserted than in Stevenson's time. Starting in Le Puy, the GR 70 walking trail follows Stevenson and his donkey Modestine from the Auvergne, with its dramatic landscape of volcanic outcrops and basalt plugs, into the Grands Causses, the heart of the Cévennes. It winds through the valleys of the Allier, the Lot, and the Tarn, into wilder, higher country where pine and heather must have reminded Stevenson of his native Scotland. Stone cairns and wooden posts mark the trail across Mont Lozère, through chestnut woods. The trip's highest point is Mont Finiels, at 5,575 feet (1,700 meters), after which the trail descends to the tamer, warmer borders of Provence.

WHEN TO GO April–September.

HOW LONG 160 miles (257 km). It takes about 10–14 days for the complete trail (depending on fitness level).

PLANNING Good hill-walking fitness levels are essential, and map-reading skills are advisable. Campsite, *gîte* (B&B), and hotel accommodation are available at all stages, but advance booking is recommended. Good walking boots, and cold-weather and waterproof clothing are essential – heavy rain, mist, and high winds occur at any time of year. You can also follow the GR 70 by mountain bike – or even donkey!

INSIDE INFORMATION Don't get lost like Stevenson and miss the Lac du Bouchet near St. Nicolas. It's a flooded volcano cone, serene and sheltered by woods.

WEBSITE gr70-stevenson.com/en/index.htm

HIGHLIGHTS

▓ As people have moved out, so **wildlife** has returned to the region. Vultures, mouflons, and beavers have been reintroduced, and otters, black woodpeckers, and horned owls have returned of their own accord.

▓ Before Le Bleymard, you climb the **wooded hill of La Goulet**, which marks the beginning of the Cévennes. Here you will find the tiny source of the Lot, and the views are wonderful.

▓ The pretty village of **Le Pont de Montvert,** 11 miles (18 km) south of Le Bleymard, is the meeting point of three rivers, the Tarn, Rieumalet, and Martinet. Its fine Renaissance houses are set on rocks above the waters.

▓ Before Florac, the **spectacular gorges of the Tarn** demand that you take a day out to explore them.

▓ As you descend toward **Provence**, you can tell from the warm air and appearance of vineyards that you are near your journey's end.

| FRANCE |

Normandy Beaches

More than 70 years later, a visit to the coast where Allied forces began the liberation of France is still a deeply moving experience.

On a summer day, it's impossible to imagine the bloody mayhem that erupted along the tranquil Normandy coast early on June 6, 1944: D-Day. But reminders of Operation Overlord are everywhere, from the crumbling concrete bunkers and gun emplacements of the Third Reich's vaunted Atlantic Wall to the graveyards of so many Allied soldiers. Most of the invasion force—three U.S. divisions, two British, and one Canadian—sailed from Portsmouth in England to land at a chain of beaches, now known as the Côte du Calvados, between Cherbourg and Le Havre. From these beachheads, designated Utah, Omaha, Gold, Juno, and Sword, they were to fight their way inland through Normandy to Paris. The small town of Arromanches, halfway along the Côte du Calvados, saw some of the fiercest fighting and is home to two museums that give insight into the battle. The Arromanches Museum itself stands next to the site of one of the floating Mulberry harbors that were key to the Allied breakout from the beachheads. But to gain a true sense of the meaning of D-Day, visit the U.S. military cemetery at Colleville-sur-Mer. Almost all the soldiers who lie here were young men; very many were teenagers. None of them lived to drink champagne in a free Paris.

WHEN TO GO Any time, but June–September is best.

HOW LONG One day to a week.

PLANNING Several ferries leave daily from Portsmouth to Cherbourg or Le Havre. Plan to sail to one French port and leave from the other. There are all kinds of tours available, for days and half-days, in groups or for individuals in the company of well-informed guides.

INSIDE INFORMATION Two of the stained-glass windows of the church in Sainte-Mère-Église, behind Utah Beach, commemorate the landing of paratrooper John Steele on the church's steeple, a nerve-racking event on which the film *The Longest Day* is based.

WEBSITE en.normandie-tourisme.fr

| HIGHLIGHTS

▌ **Arromanches 360** is a high-tech presentation, using archive film shot by cinematographers who went ashore with the first waves of Allied troops. It takes the visitor a little way into the infantryman's hell of D-Day.

▌ At Ranville the **Pegasus Memorial** commemorates the British 6th Airborne Division, which made a daring predawn assault. The most successful operation on D-Day, it enabled Pegasus Bridge and its sister bridge to be kept open for the Allies and denied access to the Germans.

▌ Visit **Bayeux**, home to the famous Bayeux Tapestry and the first large town to be liberated by the Allies. It survived the war virtually unscathed.

A monument at Utah Beach, accompanied by a French tank, commemorates Free French troops fighting under the command of General Leclerc.

Sit back and relax in one of Grasse's lively squares where perfume scents the air.

FRANCE

Route Napoléon

Follow Napoleon's march into the Alps from the coast of France, and enjoy the spectacular scenery and historic towns along the way.

On March 1, 1815, Napoleon Bonaparte landed at Golfe-Juan on the Mediterranean coast after escaping from exile on the island of Elba. Six days later, after an epic march across southeast France, bypassing Royalist troops, he entered Grenoble. He had set out with 1,200 men; by the end, Bonapartists returning to the imperial colors had swelled their numbers. In 1932, the line of his march was proclaimed the Route Napoléon. You start in Cannes, in 1815 a small port where Napoleon spent the night, and head for Grasse, in the lavender-covered hills that are the home of France's perfume industry. From there, you follow the route Napoleon and his men took over the hills to Castellane, after which they struggled through heavy snow over the 3,755-foot (1,145 meter) Col des Lecques to Barrême. At Sisteron on the Durance River, you see the medieval fortress, which was, surprisingly, undefended, allowing Napoleon to push on to Gap in its glorious Alpine setting. After the Col Bayard and the village of Corps, you arrive in Grenoble, where cheering crowds greeted Napoleon as emperor.

WHEN TO GO Any time of year. For authenticity do it in March, though the mountains of Haute-Provence may still be snowy. The region is most crowded in July and August.

HOW LONG One week on foot. Napoleon covered the 200 miles (322 km) in just six days, pausing only to sleep. You can drive the route in a day, allowing time for stopovers. Driving time is about four hours.

PLANNING The modern N85 highway follows Napoleon's line of march, and the best way to trace his footsteps is by car. You can rent a car in Nice, the nearest airport to the start of the journey. Good stops en route include Castellane and Sisteron. Book accommodation in advance whatever the time of year.

INSIDE INFORMATION Every year over a weekend in March, Napoleon's landing at Golfe-Juan is reenacted in a scenario based on contemporary records. With his generals and soldiers, Napoleon once more sets foot on French soil. There are battle scenes, cavalry displays, exhibitions, and a bivouac on the beach.

WEBSITES myprovence.fr, provenceweb.fr, route-napoleon.com

HIGHLIGHTS

▪ Modern Castellane is the gateway to the spectacular gorges of the **Verdon River** – now a national park. Today you can marvel at Napoleon's ability to inspire his men to follow him in harsh weather through this rugged country.

▪ The highest point is the **Col Bayard**, 4,090 ft (1,247 m), west of Gap, which is covered in magnificent forest.

▪ The historic town of **Grasse** has a dress-circle view of the bay of Cannes. Stop here for the location, the perfume, and the museum dedicated to the artist Jean-Honoré Fragonard.

▪ Explore **Grenoble**, a university town and host to jazz, rock, and theater festivals from March to July.

| SPAIN |

Don Quixote's Spain

Romantic ruins and antique windmills set in an arid landscape await you in La Mancha, the scene of great if misguided knightly exploits.

An elderly minor aristocrat driven by outdated knightly ideals to help the needy and defenseless—this is Don Quixote, the deluded but loveable hero created by Miguel de Cervantes, an adventurer turned writer. Cervantes set his tales of misguided, grandiose quests in his country's most inhospitable landscape: a parched, empty region famously devoid of culture, and even people. It is called La Mancha, from the Arabic *al Manshah*, meaning "dry land." For centuries the region was a buffer zone between Christian Castille and Muslim Andalusia. Don Quixote takes no traceable route, but you can invent your own, starting at beautiful Toledo and finishing at Cuenca. Throughout La Mancha, scattered towns and villages claim a connection to Don Quixote. He tilted at windmills, mistaking them for giants: ranks of such windmills line the dry ridges and flatlands of Consuegra, Campo de Criptana, and Mota del Cuervo. The object of Don Quixote's chivalric passion, the farmgirl Dulcinea, came from El Toboso, west of Mota del Cuervo, where there is a Quixote Museum in a house said to have been hers. But it is the landscape itself that takes center stage. It is best seen at Belmonte, a ruined 15th-century fortress redolent of the world of Don Quixote.

WHEN TO GO To see the landscape at its greenest, dappled with red poppies, go in spring. It can be very cold in winter and very hot in summer.

HOW LONG 125 miles (200 km) from Toledo to Cuenca via Campo de Criptana – perfect for a weekend.

PLANNING Toledo and Cuenca are the most obvious bases. There are two fine parador hotels in the area, both in restored 16th-century convents, to suit the theme: one at Cuenca and the other at Almagro.

INSIDE INFORMATION In 2005, the Ruta de Don Quijote (Don Quixote Route) was created. This is a huge network of roads and paths linking the main towns and villages of La Mancha – best traveled on foot, bicycle, or perhaps even on your own skinny nag, like Don Quixote's Rocinante.

WEBSITES spain.info, donquijote.org

HIGHLIGHTS

▪ Campo de Criptana has ten **windmills**, the largest collection in La Mancha; some of these have been restored to working order and can be visited. They look very pretty in the pink light of the rising or setting sun.

▪ The multiturreted **castle of Belmonte** is one of Spain's finest. Built in 1456, it was restored for Empress Eugénie of France in the 1870s but again fell into disrepair.

▪ La Mancha has its own **Denominación de Origen wine** (produced only in that region using local grape varieties and methods) and is the home of the excellent Manchego, a hard cheese made of ewe's milk.

Windmills and the castle of Consuegra at sunrise sum up the spirit and stark beauty of La Mancha.

SPAIN

Pilgrimage to Santiago

For Christian pilgrims, the road to Santiago de Compostela remains a moving spiritual experience; but even for nonbelievers it is still one of Europe's great journeys.

For almost 1,200 years, the faithful have followed the pilgrimage route to Spain's far west and one of Christendom's holiest shrines, where the relics of the apostle St. James the Great are purportedly interred in the cathedral of Santiago de Compostela. Santiago lies between the Galician seaports of Vigo and A Coruña, close to the most spectacular stretch of coastline in Spain, and of all the pilgrimage routes that converge on it, the best-known is the Camino Francés (French Route), declared a World Heritage site in 1993. The route crosses the Pyrenees by the Roncesvalles Pass—where the legendary Frankish paladin Roland fought his last battle—then heads west, visiting on the way some of the finest examples of medieval religious architecture in Europe. Farther west just beyond Pamplona, the Camino Francés merges with the Camino Aragonés (Aragonese Route) at Puente la Reina, where it crosses a graceful 11th-century bridge. Medieval pilgrims paused at Santo Domingo de la Calzada's hospice, and modern travelers can stay here too—the medieval inn is now a luxury parador. Proceeding westward, the glorious cathedrals of Burgos and León come into view, symbolizing the serenity sought by medieval pilgrims. You come upon relics of a more turbulent past, too, such as the massive Templar castle at Ponferrada. The climax of the journey is, naturally, arrival in the medieval city of Santiago de Compostela.

WHEN TO GO Any time of year, but best in spring and early summer (April–June) or fall (September–October). Winter can be cold and wet and high summer too hot for pleasant walking.

HOW LONG About 150 miles (240 km). It takes about two weeks, walking 6–20 miles (10–30 km) per day.

PLANNING Take good boots and waterproof clothing – it can rain heavily in Galicia at any time of year. There is accommodation of all types at frequent intervals, but booking is advisable as the route has become very popular. Good public transportation (bus and train) is available, and many sections can be done by mountain bike.

INSIDE INFORMATION The Camino Francés is well marked with yellow arrows on walls, trees, and signposts bearing the scallop shell, symbol of St. James the Great and of this pilgrimage route.

WEBSITES spain.info, santiago-compostela.net

HIGHLIGHTS

▓ Catch your breath as you reach the high point of the **Roncesvalles Pass** and begin the descent into Spain.

▓ **Pamplona**, famed for its annual "running of the bulls" during the festival of San Fermín, is the first town on the way. It has a beautiful Gothic cathedral of mellow, ocher-colored stone.

▓ Burgos is the next major town, with a magnificent 13th-century Gothic cathedral. Farther on, visit León Cathedral with its splendid, glowing interior lit by marvelous **stained-glass windows**.

▓ Share **wine and tapas** at an open-air café after a long day's walk.

▓ The first glimpse of Santiago's cathedral spires at the end of the journey brings a real sense of achievement. They dominate the wide square of Praza do Obradoiro at the heart of a **treasury of medieval architecture** that is rivaled by few European cities.

Opposite: The soaring, lavish baroque facade of Santiago's Catedral del Apóstol marks the climax of the pilgrim's journey and gives more than a hint of the glories within. Above: Statues of pilgrims in the city symbolize the spiritual seeking of thousands of believers past and present who have trodden this route.

Tramping After Mark Twain

Follow the route of one of the world's most amusing writers via forests and waterfalls to mountains, glaciers, and ski resorts.

As you stand by the dignified ruins of Heidelberg Castle, looking down on the verdant green valley below, the brown and red roofs of the old town, and the glossy gray-blue of the Neckar River, it is still possible to transport yourself into the past. For here you take on the role of a daring American traveler on the first stop of a tour intended to "improve himself." The intrepid adventurer was that tongue-in-cheek writer of travel fact and fiction, Mark Twain, who in 1878, at the age of 43, set out on his own real-life trip across Europe. His account was to become the subject of his satirical journal, *A Tramp Abroad*. Follow his route as he traveled from southern Germany, through Switzerland, and into Italy. Along the way, you will be delighted as you stroll through the enchanting pine-scented gloom of the Black Forest and discover hidden prizes, such as the waterfall at Triberg, where the water crashes over seven huge granite steps nestling between the trees. As you move on to the chalet-dotted expanse of the Swiss Alps, you might, as Twain did, find that "no sound is quite so inane, and silly, and aggravating as the '*hoo*"hoo' of a cuckoo clock." But you can find distraction by skiing in the shadow of the Matterhorn at the exclusive resort of Zermatt.

WHEN TO GO This journey can be enjoyed at any time of year, but the ski resorts of Switzerland begin to open up in November and are busiest over Christmas and from February to April.

HOW LONG The journey is so versatile that you could spend just a few days in a selection of locations, or dawdle as you desire in between, even extending your travels to Italy as Twain did.

PLANNING If you intend to make this trip into a walking holiday, be sure to take good boots and equipment, and plan carefully what you will need and what you can carry.

INSIDE INFORMATION It may be worth purchasing a Zone C Interrail pass, but it is expensive and does not cover all services, so plan your journey in advance to see whether it would be advantageous.

WEBSITES germany.travel/en/index.html, myswitzerland.com/en-gb, interrail.com

▥ For the authentic Mark Twain experience, take a boat trip along the **Neckar River** – a journey that inspired the voyage of Huckleberry Finn.

▥ Immerse yourself in German history and folklore, and visit some of the castles where Twain once strolled, such as the **four castles of Neckarsteinach** in the Neckar Valley.

▥ Relax like a 19th-century bon vivant with a **soothing thermal bath** at the Roman spa town of Baden-Baden.

▥ If you are averse, as Twain often was, to strenuous walking, then see Switzerland from the comfort of the **Glacier Express** train that runs between Zermatt and St. Moritz.

One of the pleasures of the Swiss leg of this journey is eating outdoors near Zermatt, in view of the Matterhorn.

The view of Windermere from Orrest Head combines the pastoral with the magnificent.

ENGLAND

Wordsworth in the Lakes

This unspoiled area in the north of England helped to nurture the writing of one of the great Romantic poets.

The air smells fresh and sweet as you walk up the garden path of a small lime-washed cottage. Go through a stone porch to enter the houseplace (a northern English term for a parlor). The darkly paneled room is lit by one latticed window, the floor is flagged with slates, and the ceiling crossed by beams. This is Dove Cottage, the first Lake District home of William Wordsworth and his sister Dorothy. The house itself has changed little, but more recent buildings have obscured the view. Then, meadows sloped from their garden to the lake, and they could see Grasmere village on its northern shore sheltered by the great mountain range of Helvellyn. Wordsworth wrote his most memorable poems inspired by the Lake District's magical scenery and the lives of its hardworking people. He chanted the poems aloud as he roamed the fells. Visit nearby Rydal Mount, where Wordsworth spent his later years, dying there in 1850.

WHEN TO GO Spring and fall to avoid the crowds and see the countryside at its best. There are glorious displays of wildflowers in spring and rich colors in fall.

HOW LONG The Lake District is a small, compact area – about 30 miles (48 km) across – but allow plenty of time to walk around and enjoy the scenery.

PLANNING Windermere can be reached easily by bus and train, and there is regular bus service to Grasmere. Accommodation is plentiful, but make reservations in summer. Grasmere and Ambleside are good centers for this journey.

INSIDE INFORMATION The weather on the fells can change suddenly. Take a detailed map, a compass, your mobile phone, and GPS if you have it. Expect wind and rain, so except in heatwave conditions, take waterproof gear and a sustaining snack. Always let someone know your plans before you set out.

WEBSITE wordsworth.org.uk

HIGHLIGHTS

▪ Take a boat to the island in the center of the lake of **Grasmere**, where the Wordsworths liked to picnic. Be sure to buy some gingerbread – made from a highly secret local recipe – at the tiny shop by the churchyard gate.

▪ Enjoy the spectacular **view over Windermere and Rydal Water** from Rydal Mount.

▪ Visit **Hawkshead**, where Wordsworth was educated at the Grammar School. You can still see his name scratched on one of the desks.

▪ Follow in Wordsworth's footsteps to the places where his poems were born. Tramp up the valley beyond Grasmere to **Easedale Tarn**, and then read "My heart leaps up when I behold," which Wordsworth wrote after seeing a rainbow arched above its encircling crags. If you are there in spring, walk along the **shores of Ullswater**, still golden with the breeze-ruffled daffodils he recalls so vividly in his best-known poem.

EUROPE

The Circus in Bath sums up the city's fine looks—light and spacious terraced houses in honey-colored stone.

Jane Austen Tour

An author's home, a gracious Georgian city, and a historic seaside town evoke the world of the most flawless of Regency novelists.

When you stand in the dining parlor of her lovingly restored Hampshire home, Chawton Cottage, you can easily imagine Jane Austen writing in this room. During the eight years she lived here, Jane Austen wrote *Mansfield Park*, *Emma*, and *Persuasion*, and revised *Sense and Sensibility* and *Northanger Abbey*. From Chawton drive to Bath. With its squares, terraces, and crescents, it is the most striking of Georgian cities, and large areas are unchanged since Jane Austen's day. Visit the Pump Room, and take your glass of water from the steaming ornamental fountain. The hot, mineral-rich water tastes and smells terrible but was the reason for Bath's popularity as people came to cure their ailments. Walk up the steep streets to the Upper Rooms, where Jane once danced beneath the chandeliers of the green and gold ballroom. The building, known as the Assembly Rooms, now houses a costume museum, where you can see dresses from the Regency period. Journey south to the small seaside town of Lyme Regis, and walk along The Cobb, a stone wall curving around the harbor. See the flight of stone steps where foolish Louisa Musgrove falls in *Persuasion*. Finish your journey in Winchester, where you will find Jane's grave in the cathedral. The house in which she died is on nearby College Street, marked with a plaque.

WHEN TO GO Chawton Cottage, now called Jane Austen's House Museum, is small and can get very crowded so visit on a weekday in spring or fall. As in Jane's time, Bath is full of life and bustle. On weekends the city is especially busy.

HOW LONG Three days. Allow a day in Chawton and in Lyme Regis, and stay longer in Bath if you can.

PLANNING All the venues are in central southern England, easily reached by car or public transportation.

INSIDE INFORMATION Eat lunch in Bath's Pump Room and you'll feel as though you have gone back in time. For a more modern experience spend a day pampering yourself at the lavishly revamped spa—Thermae Bath Spa—where you can enjoy a range of treatments and bathe in the hot thermal water.

WEBSITES jane-austens-house-museum.org.uk, visitbath.co.uk, fashionmuseum.co.uk

HIGHLIGHTS

▪ Discover the imposing Elizabethan home of Jane's wealthy brother Edward. Also in Chawton, **Chawton House** is now restored and has a library of early English women's writing. Jane worshipped in Chawton's St. Nicholas Church, where her mother and sister are buried.

▪ Enjoy a far-reaching view over the city of Bath from **Beechen Cliff**, where Catherine Morland, the heroine of *Northanger Abbey*, walked with Henry and Eleanor Tilney.

▪ Don't miss the **small cliffside garden** close to The Cobb in Lyme Regis planted in memory of Jane. It is close to the site of the lodging house Wings, where it is believed she stayed. On one of the garden walls there is a stone bust of Jane.

IRELAND

James Joyce's Dublin

*A fictional day-in-the-life created by a groundbreaking
writer in the 1920s still brings visitors to the Irish capital.*

Though born and educated in Dublin, James Joyce spent most of his adult life abroad; even when he was in his twenties he commented that he was "sick of Dublin." He lived in self-imposed exile in Trieste, Zurich, and finally Paris, yet his hometown stands center-stage in his greatest literary works. His books are erudite and vivid, comic and earthy depictions of this most characterful of cities. Joyce's greatest work is *Ulysses*, a landmark in modern literature with its "stream of consciousness" narrative and honest inclusion of all human activity from the cerebral to the sexual. The book still inspires many visits to Dublin. It describes the events of a single day, June 16, 1904, as seen through the eyes of its three principal characters, Stephen Dedalus and Molly and Leopold Bloom, as they journey through various parts of Dublin. The story begins at the Martello Tower at Sandycove on Dublin Bay, takes in the Blooms' home, several pubs, the National Library, a funeral, and much more. Modern-day Joyce fans (many in period costume) celebrate Bloomsday in Dublin each June, retracing the journey and enjoying many of the activities featured in the book.

WHEN TO GO Although there is no official Bloomsday organization, there are more Joyce-related events on and around June 16 than at other times. But Dublin can be enjoyed any time of the year.

HOW LONG The events described in *Ulysses* begin at about 8 a.m. and continue to about 2 a.m. next morning. If you don't want to observe Bloomsday exactly, a visit to Dublin can fill several days.

PLANNING *Ulysses* is a notoriously difficult book to get through. Newcomers to Joyce may find it easier to begin with *Dubliners*, featuring evocative descriptions of many Dublin locations and characters.

INSIDE INFORMATION Be sure to buy a Dublin Pass, which provides entry to visitor attractions and many more of Dublin's top sights, in addition to other benefits.

WEBSITES visitdublin.com, jamesjoyce.ie

EUROPE

HIGHLIGHTS

▓ Leopold Bloom liked a drop of Guinness. The **Guinness Storehouse** is Dublin's number one visitor attraction, or try a pint in the **Temple Bar** area, where many of the best of the city's 1,000 pubs can be found.

▓ The **Davy Byrnes pub** at 21 Duke Street features in both *Dubliners* and *Ulysses*. Have a cheese sandwich and a glass of wine, like Leopold Bloom.

▓ The **James Joyce Centre** has year-round events, tours, and exhibitions, with a special program during the week of Bloomsday. It also organizes regular walks that describe Joyce's relationship with his native city, taking in key literary landmarks.

The superbly elegant Georgian interiors of the Dublin Writers Museum in Parnell Square are a must-see on any literary tour of the city.

Jesus in the Holy Land

Walk the hills and streets where Jesus conducted his ministry, and you sense the deep reverberation of antiquity in these sacred sites.

Of all the places on this journey, Jerusalem and Bethlehem (Bayt Lahm) pack the most emotional punches: leave them until last. Begin with the Church of the Annunciation at Nazareth, where Jesus was raised. Aged about 30, Jesus was baptized by John the Baptist in the Jordan River and began his ministry. Capernaum, on the Sea of Galilee (Lake Tiberias), was the home of Peter and other disciples, and Jesus made his base here. You can see the excavated ruins of the synagogue where he taught. Nearby are the Mount of the Beatitudes, where Jesus is said to have delivered the Sermon on the Mount, and Tabgha, which has a fifth-century church commemorating the miracle of the loaves and fishes. Bethlehem, under the Palestinian Authority, has the Church of the Nativity, built over the grotto where Jesus was born. The Temple Mount in the Old City of Jerusalem was where he confronted the Temple authorities; the flat summit is now occupied by the Dome of the Rock, a shrine for Muslim pilgrims, and the Al-Aqsa Mosque. Overlooking the Old City is the Mount of Olives, site of the Garden of Gethsemane, where Jesus was betrayed and arrested. The place where he was crucified and entombed is now marked by the Church of the Holy Sepulchre.

WHEN TO GO Any time of year is fine. Summer is intensely hot (the hottest month is August); in winter it can snow. At Easter, Jerusalem is full of pilgrims.

HOW LONG Tour groups will cover these sites in about a week to ten days, spending about half the time in Jerusalem and Bethlehem.

PLANNING Border security makes it impossible to move freely around all the sites linked to Jesus' life, or easily between them. Be prepared to alter plans at short notice. That said, a sizeable percentage of tourist visitors to Israel are Christians on pilgrimage, so the route is well trodden.

INSIDE INFORMATION Hitchhiking is a good way to get around in much of Israel: drivers are helpful.

WEBSITES biblewalks.com, jesustrail.com

HIGHLIGHTS

■ Sail across the blue waters of the **Sea of Galilee**, gazing at the landscape of Christ's dynamic ministry and the scene of many of his miracles.

■ The **Church of the Nativity** in Bethlehem is one of the oldest continuously operating churches in the world, administered jointly by the Roman Catholic, Greek Orthodox, and Armenian Apostolic Churches.

■ The Western Wall (or "Wailing Wall") is the last remnant of Herod's great temple in Jerusalem, destroyed by the Romans in 70 A.D. The **Temple Mount** has profound significance for Jews, Christians, and Muslims alike, and the sense of fervor is palpable.

Above Jerusalem's Old City, the site of the Garden of Gethsemane, where Jesus was arrested, has some of the oldest olive trees in the world.

In Gambia the calabash, a pulpy but inedible fruit with a hard shell, is hollowed out and turned into a handheld drum.

HIGHLIGHTS

▥ Gambian drinks tend to be sweet with **herbal aromas**: try *bissap*, *kinkeliba*, or *bouyi*.

▥ The **Roots Homecoming Festival** — a heritage week held in May and June each year — was established to remember enforced enslavement and was inspired by Haley's epic saga. Emphasis is laid on educational, cultural, and traditional activities with workshops on music, dance, and cooking. Visits are arranged to historical sites, museums, and private Gambian homes.

▥ Try the **traditional cuisine** of *domodah* (peanut stew with rice), *plasas* (meat and fish with vegetable leaves), *foufou* (mashed cassava), and *benechin* (fish and rice).

AFRICA

| GAMBIA |

Alex Haley's Roots

A best-selling book led its author across the Atlantic Ocean to trace the origins of his ancestral story in Africa.

Alex Haley, the Pulitzer Prize–winning author of *Roots*, traveled to Gambia only after the book's publication in 1976. He was searching for the birthplace of Kunta Kinte, its pivotal character. The Kinte clan was traced to the village of Juffureh on the northern shore of the Kamby Bolongo (Gambia River), where in the 17th century Kunta Kinte was captured and enslaved while searching for wood to make a drum. Your visit starts at the port in Banjul, Gambia's capital, where you take a boat 15 miles (24 kilometers) upriver to Juffureh. On arrival pay a courtesy call on the chief at the *bantaba* (meeting place). In nearby Aldebra, an old French trading post, the museum hosts a vivid display depicting the slave trade that continued for more than three centuries along the Gambia River. Another short boat ride takes you to James Island, the slave-trading post where Kunta Kinte was herded onto a ship bound for the Americas.

WHEN TO GO December to February, when the weather is dry and warm.

HOW LONG It takes a day to visit Juffureh, but allow several days to explore Gambia.

PLANNING Gambia is a predominantly Islamic society and religious etiquette should be respected. You will need a yellow fever vaccination to enter, and malarial prophylactics are a necessity. Travel up the Gambia River by comfortable cruise ship or pirogue, a narrow wooden boat with outboard engine.

INSIDE INFORMATION Tourism in Juffureh is waning since its peak in the 1970s, allowing a more genuine experience of national life. In Banjul visit the Albert Market. Silver jewelry and batiks are great buys.

WEBSITES rootsgambia.gm, intrepidtravel.com/uk/gambia

Index

Acknowledgments

This book would not have been possible without the hard work of many talented team members at Toucan Books Ltd., and National Geographic Partners. At Toucan, we'd like to thank editorial director Ellen Dupont; senior editor Helen Douglas-Cooper; editors Autumn Green, Andrew Kerr-Jarrett, and Alice Peebles; designer Leah Germann; assistant editors Hannah Bowen, Michael Clark, and Conrad Mason; picture manager Christine Vincent; researchers Tam Church, Kim Tidwell, Sharon Southren, and Mia Stewart-Wilson; proofreaders Marion Dent and René Nel; and indexer Marie Lorimer. At National Geographic, thank you to project editor Allyson Johnson; art director Elisa Gibson; senior photo editor Moira Haney; production design manager Katie Olsen; director, managing editorial Jennifer Thornton; and senior production editor Judith Klein.

PICTURE CREDITS

ABBREVIATIONS:

AL (Alamy), GI (Getty Images), RH (Robert Harding), SS (Shutterstock)

2-3 Louie Psihoyos/Corbis; 4 Richard Du Toit/Minden Pictures/GI; 5 Randall Stewart/SS (1); Chris Mellor/GI (2); Ralph Hopkins//GI; (3) Bryan & Cherry Alexander/Arcticphoto.com (4); John Hay/GI (5); John Hemmingsen/GI (6); Lee Foster/AL (7); 6 Xavier Zimbardo/GI; 8 LOOK Die Bildagentur der Fotografen GmbH/AL; 10 Jean-Pierre Lescourret/GI; 11 Prasit photo/GI; 12-13 Reinhard Schmid/4Corners; 14 Roop_Dey/iStock/GI; 15 Tuul & Bruno Morandi/GI; 16-17 Dallas Stribly/GI; 18 Ann Cecil/GI; 19 Richard Cummins/GI,L; 19 M.Timothy O'Keefe/AL, R; 20 Richard Cummins/GI;21 Orchidpoet/GI; 22 Eliot J. Schechter/Corbis; 23 Paul M.Franklin; 24-25 Krzysztof Dydynski/GI; 26 Richard Cummins/GI; 27 Sylvian Grandadam/RH; 28 Steve Simonsen/GI; 29 Jean-Bernard Carillet/GI,L; 29 Windstar cruises, R; 30 Margie Politzer /GI; 31 Ralph Lee Hopkins/GI; 32 John Borthwick/GI; 33 Lee Foster/AL, L; 33 Leanne Walker/GI, R; 34 Eric L. Wheater/GI; 35 Martin Moos/GI; 36 Jeremy Horner/GI; 37 Preecha Onnu/SS; 38 Craig Pershouse/GI; 39 Lonely Planet Images/GI, L; 39 Paul Beinssen/GI, R; 40 Peter Solness/GI; 41 Becca Posterino; 42 Todd Gipstein/National Geographic Image Collection; 43 Sampo Tours/www.sampotours.com; 44 John Borthwick /GI; 45 Ralph Lee Hopkins/GI, L; 45 Kerry Lorimer/GI, R; 46 Alex Polo/SS; 47 Anders Blomqvist/ GI; 48 Jonathan Smith/GI; 49 Bob Krist/Corbis; 50-51 Charlotte Hindle/GI; 52 David Greedy/ GI; 53 Glenn van der Knijff/ GI; 54-55 Robert Fried/AL; 56 Solange Hando; 57 Dallas Stribley/ GI; 58 Christopher Groenhout/GI; 59 Craig Pershouse/GI, L; 59 Geoge Tsafos/ GI, R; 60 Leamus/GI; 61-62 Ariadne Van Zandbergen/ GI; 63 Karl Lehmann /GI; 64-65 Witold Skrypczak /GI; 66 Izzet Keribar/GI; 67 Peter Ptschelinzew/ GI; 68 Kevin Fleming/Corbis/VCG/GI; 69 Guido Cozzi/Corbis; 70-71 Maurizio Rellini/4Corners; 72 Jeff Greenberg/GI; 73 John Elk/GI; 74 Witold Skrypczak/GI; 75 Ralph Lee Hopkins/ GI; 76 Kraig Lieb/ GI; 77 Ascent/PKS Media Inc./ GI, L; 77 Lawrence Worcester/GI, R; 78 Witold ‑‑‑vpczak/GI; 79 Pung/SS; 80 Chris Barton;

81 James Lyon/GI; 82 Frank Carter /GI; 83 Chris Mellor /GI; 84 Sara-Jane Cleland /GI; 85 Anthony Plummer/GI, L; 85 Lindsay Brown/GI, R; 86 Photo By Martin Cohen Wild About Australia /GI; 87 Holger Leue/GI; 88 John Banagan /GI; 89 Oliver Strewe /GI; 90 Paul Harding /GI; 91 Gareth McCormack /GI; 92 Design Pics Inc./AL; 93 Igor Plotnikov/SS; 94-95 Anthony Ham /GI; 96 David C.Tomlinson /GI; 97 Brent Winebrenner /GI; 98 John Elk III/GI; 99 David C.Tomlinson /GI, L; 99 Ascent/PKS Media Inc./ GI, R; 100 Julian Elliott Photography/ GI; 101 David C.Tomlinson /GI; 102 Chris Mellor/GI; 103 Richard I'Anson/Lonely Planet Images/GI; 104 giraudou laurent/Sygma/GI; 105 Lonely Planet/GI; 106-107 Bob Green Photography; 108 Mark Newman/GI; 109 Mike Danneman; 110-111 Curt Brianchi; 112 John Elk III/GI; 113 Phil Schermeister/GI; 114 Chiva Express; 115 Kenneth Garrett/National Geographic Image Collection; 116-117 Robert Wyatt/AL; 118 kokoroimages.com/GI; 119 Patrick Syder /GI; 120 Bradley Mayhew/GI; 121 PA Photos; 122 Dennis K. Johnson/ GI; 123 Claver Carroll/GI; 124 Richard I'Anson/ GI; 125 Mark Andrew Kirby/ GI; 126 Chris Beall/ GI; 127 Great Southern Railway/www.railaustralia.com.au/Indian_pacific; 128 David Wall Photo/ GI; 129 Jonathan Smith/ GI; 130 Tuul & Bruno Morandi/4Corners; 131 Peter Solness/ GI; 132 canbedone/GI; 133 Anders Blomqvist /GI; 134-135 imageBROKER/AL; 136 Mark Daffey/GI; 137 Dr Shirley Sherwood/Venice Simplon-Orient-Express; 138 David C.Tomlinson/GI; 139 Chris Mellor/ GI, L; 139 Glenn van der Knijff/ GI, R; 140 Jungfraubahnen/www.jungfraubahn.ch; 141 Izzet Keribar/ GI; 142 Ralph Lee Hopkins/ GI; 143 Ariadne Van Zandbergen /GI, L; 143 Mitch Reardon/ GI, R; 144-145 Andrew Bain/GI; 146 AA World Travel Library/AL; 147 Joe Sohm/Visions of America /GI; 148 John Elk III/GI; 149 Mark Newman /GI; 150-151 Grant Dixon /GI; 152 Lorcel/SS; 153 Danita Delmont/AL; 154 Tim Tadder/Corbis; 155 Carol Polich Photo Workshops/ GI, L; 155 John Frisch, R; 156 Brent Winebrenner/GI; 157 Karl Lehmann / GI; 158 Cartagena Connections; 159 Hemis/AL; 160-161 eFesenko/AL; 162 Jeffrey Becom/ GI, L; 163 Judy Bellah /GI, L; 163 Wes Walker /GI, R; 164 Grant Dixon /GI; 165 Chris Barton; 166 Brent Winebrenner /GI; 167 Nick Tapp, L; 167 S.B. Nace/GI, R; 168 Bob Charlton /GI; 169 asavliuk/iStock/GI; 170 Robbie Shone /GI; 171 Peter Solness/ GI, L; 171 Mark Daffey/ GI, R; 172 robertharding/AL; 173 Sara-Jane Cleland/ GI; 174-175 David Muench/Corbis; 176 travelib culture/AL; 177 Andrew Peacock/ GI; 178 Martin Moos/ GI; 179 Christopher Groenhout/ GI; 180 Mark Parkes/ GI; 181 Sally Dillon/ GI; 182-183 Bill Bachman /GI; 184 David Tipling/GI; 185 David Greedy /GI; 186 Chris Mellor /GI; 187 Oliver Strewe/ GI; 188-189 JTB Photos/Photolibrary.com; 190 Witold Skrypczak/GI; 191-192 John Elk III/GI; 193 Roberto Soncin Gerometta /GI, L; 193 Ascent/PKS Media Inc. /GI, R; 194 David C. Tomlinson /GI; 195 Oliver Strewe /GI; 196-197 Alex Hare/GI; 198 Olga Shelego/SS; 199 Juergen Ritterbach/GI; 200 Alma Molemans/Madeira Island Travel/www.madeiratourism.org; 201 GuilhermeSoares/iStock/GI, L; 201 Adina Tovy/GI, R; 202 Travel Library/RH; 203 Richard I'Anson/GI; 204-205 Randall Stewart/SS; 206 Dave G.Houser/Corbis; 207 Layne Kennedy/Corbis; 208 Bill Bachman /GI; 209 Index Stock Imagery/Barry Winiker/GI; 210 Charles Lenars/Corbis; 211 Witold Skrypczak

/GI; 212-213 Markus Lange/robertharding/AL; 214 Reuters/Corbis; 215 Ian Armitage; 216 Patrick Horton/ GI; 217 Oriental Touch/RH; 218 Anders Blomqvist/ GI; 219 Wayne Walton /GI; 220 Eric Crichton/Corbis; 221 David Tipling/GI, L; 221 David Tomlinson/ GI, R; 222 John Arnold Images/Photolibrary.com; 223 Rex Features/SS; 224-225 Mike Powles/GI; 226 Frank Pedrick/Image Works/TopFoto; 227 Lonely Planet/GI; 228 Diana Mayfield/GI; 229 Diana Mayfield/ GI, L; 229 Bildagentur-online/UIG/GI, R; 230 Lonely Planet/GI; 231 Anthony Pidgeon /GI; 232 Lonely Planet /GI; 233 sborisov/iStock/GI; 234-235 Bryan and Cherry Alexander/Arcticphoto.co.uk; 236 agefotostock/SuperStock; 237 Oliver Strewe/GI; 238 George Tsafos/ GI; 239 Hulton/GI; 240 John Elk III/GI; 241 Olivier Cirendini/ GI, L; 241 Wes Walker /GI, R; 242 Anders Blomqvist /GI; 243-244 Richard I'Anson /GI; 245 Richard I'Anson /GI, L; 245 Michael Gebicki /GI, R; 246-247 Oliver Strewe/ GI; 248 Juliet Coombe/ GI; 249 Richard Cummins /GI; 250 Terry Poche/SS; 251 Gary Crabbe/RH; 252-253 L'Atelier de Joël Robuchon; 254 nik wheeler/AL; 255 Brent Winebrenner; 256 Andrew Peacock/GI; 257-258 Richard I'Anson /GI; 259 Juliet Coombe /GI, L; 259 pepsee30/SS, R; 260 Greg Elms /GI; 261 Caroline Parsons; 262 Peter Adams/awl-images.com; 263 Christian Kober/awl-images.com, L; 263 Lucas Vallecillos/RH, R; 264 Dallas Stribley/GI; 265 Robert Harding Productions/RH, L; 265 David Hanson /GI, R; 266 Anders Blomqvist /GI; 267 Rob Blakers/ GI; 268 Maurizio Rellini/4Corners; 269 Margaret River Tourism Association; 270 robertharding/Alamy; 271 Bruichladdich Distillery; 272 Richard Nebesky /GI; 273 Michael Freeman/Corbis; 274 Sandro Vannin/Corbis; 275 Sandro Vannin/Corbis; 276 Mark Bassett/AL; 277 Adam Woolfitt/RH; 278-279 Gary Crabbe/AL; 280 Michael Busselle /RH; 281 Owen Franken/Corbis; 282 John Elk III /GI; 283 Bethune Carmichael /GI; 284 Kevin Levesque /GI; 285 Arkday Mazor/SS; 286 Stefano Politi Markovina /GI; 287 Rui Vale de Sousa/SS; 288 Nico Tondini/RH; 289 Geoffrey Whiting/SS; 290 Michael Aw; 291 Michael Aw /GI, L; 291 Holger Leue /GI, R; 292-293 Blaine Harrington III/AL; 294 Michael Aw /GI; 295 Lee Foster/AL; 296-297 Rick Rudnicki /GI; 298 Bobbie Burns - Taylor Burk/ CMH Heli-Skiing & Summer Adventures; 299 James Fredericks/Catamount Trail Association; 300 John Borthwick/ GI; 301 Richard I'Anson /GI; 302 Miles Haegebaert/AL; 303 John Elk III /GI; 304 Mark Newman /GI; 305 John Elk III /GI; 306 Mark A.Johnson/Corbis; 307 Rossano Boscarino/ Aventuras Tierra Adventro; 308 Ralph Hopkins /GI; 309 Jeff Hunter/GI; 310-311 Maurizio Rellini/SIME/4Corners; 312 Michael Taylor /GI; 313 Tom Boyden /GI; 314 pierivb/GI; 315 Bruno Fert/Corbis; 316 BrasilNut1/GI; 317 Brent Winebrenner/ GI; 318-319 John Hay /GI; 320 maroznc /GI; 321 Andy Rouse/GI; 322 Luca Trovato/GI; 323 Neil Setchfield/GI; 324 Design Pics Inc/AL; 325 Chris Gutowsky; 326 Frans Lemmens/GI; 327 Frans Lemmens/GI; 328-329 Andrew Bain /GI; 330 Christian Kober/GI; 331 Michael Gebicki/ GI; 332 Diana Mayfield/ GI; 333 Kim Hart/RH; 334 Ralph Lee Hopkins/ GI; 335 Wayne Walton/ GI; 336 Sara-Jane Cleland/ GI; 337 Tim Rock/ GI; 338 Chris Weston; 339 Mitch Reardon/GI, L; 339 Ariadne Van Zandbergen/ GI, R; 340 Winfred Wisniewski/GI; 341 Martin Harvey/GI; 342-343 Jeff Schultz / Alaska Stock - Design Pics/SuperStock; 344 canadastock/SS; 345 Ernest Manewal /GI; 346 John Elk III/ GI; 347 Holger

Leue /GI; 348 Peter Ellergard /GI; 349 Brechin Maclean/GI; 350 Michael Lawrence/ GI; 351 Martin Bernetti/AFP/GI; 352-353 Roger de la Harpe/GI; 354-355 Ralph Hopkins/ GI; 356 Juliet Coombe/ GI; 357 Sharon Chapman/GI; 358 Richard I'Anson/ GI; 359 Holger Leue /GI; 360-361 John Hemmingsen/GI; 362 Dennis K. Johnson /GI; 363 David Wall Photo /GI; 364 AGF Srl/AL; 365 Richard Nebesky; 366-367 Juliet Coombe /GI; 368-369 Anadolu Agency/GI; 370 Dana Allen Livingstone's Adventure; 371 Richard I'Anson /GI; 372-373 David C.Tomlinson /GI; 374 Cheryl Forbes /GI; 375 Mark Newman /GI; 376-377 Diane Cook and Len Jenshel/GI; 378 Stephen Saks /GI; 379 Kim Grant /GI; 380 Richard I'Anson /GI; 381 Stefano Politi Markovina /AL; 382 Bill Ross/Corbis; 383 John Mock /GI, L; 383 Lee Foster/AL, R; 384 Chris Barton; 385 Doug McKinlay /GI; 386 Ralph Lee Hopkins/ GI; 387 Michael Aw /GI; 388 Krzysztof Dydynski/GI; 389 Casper1774 Studio/SS; 390 Lonely Planet /GI; 391 Keren Su /GI; 392 Adam Woolfitt/RH; 393 Yvan Travert/Photolibrary.com; 394-395 Peter Zelei Images/GI; 396 Oliver Strewe /GI; 397 Lonely Planet /GI; 398 Jean du Boisberranger/GI; 399 Arterra Picture Library/AL; 400 Peter Horree/AL; 401 Witold Skrypczak /GI; 402 Damien Simonis /GI; 403 Wayne Walton /GI; 404 Glenn van der Knijff /GI; 405 Hugh L.Watts/GI; 406 Glenn Beanland/GI; 407 Bruno Barber/RH; 408 Paul Hellander; 409 Chris Mellor /GI;

COVER PICTURES

Front cover: Neuschwanstein Castle in autumn, near Fussen, Bavaria, Germany (Roberto Moiola/RH)

Back cover: Anse Source D'Argent (La Digue Island), Seychelles (Fingerszz/iStock/GI)

JOURNEYS *of a* LIFETIME

Since 1888, the National Geographic Society has funded more than 13,000 research, exploration, and preservation projects around the world. National Geographic Partners distributes a portion of the funds it receives from your purchase to National Geographic Society to support programs including the conservation of animals and their habitats.

National Geographic Partners
1145 17th Street NW
Washington, DC 20036-4688 USA

Get closer to National Geographic explorers and photographers, and connect with our global community. Join us today at nationalgeographic.com/join

For information about special discounts for bulk purchases, please contact National Geographic Books Special Sales: specialsales@natgeo.com

For rights or permissions inquiries, please contact National Geographic Books Subsidiary Rights: bookrights @natgeo.com

ISBN: 978-1-4262-1973-3

Printed in Hong Kong

18/PPS/1

The information in this book has been carefully checked and to the best of our knowledge is accurate. However, details are subject to change, and the publisher cannot be responsible for such changes, or for errors or omissions. Assessments of sites, hotels, and restaurants are based on the author's subjective opinions, which do not necessarily reflect the publisher's opinion.